Free to Choose?

Thoughts On. . .

Free to Choose?

Book 6 in the "Thoughts On" Series

by David M. Arns

First Edition
Copyright © 2015 David M. Arns.
Eighteenth Printing, March 2023

All rights reserved.
ISBN 978-1-51182-993-9

Copyright © 2015 David M. Arns.

All rights reserved. No part of this publication may be reproduced, distributed, or transmitted in any form or by any means, including photocopying, recording, or other electronic or mechanical methods, without the prior written permission of the author, except in the case of brief quotations embodied in critical reviews and certain other noncommercial uses permitted by copyright law.

Books in the "THOUGHTS ON" Series

All the books below are available both in electronic form and in paperback, and are available from the sources mentioned on the website Bible-Author.DaveArns.com.

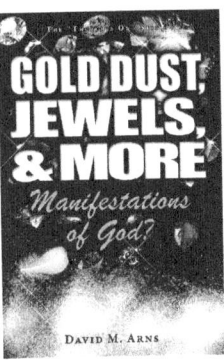

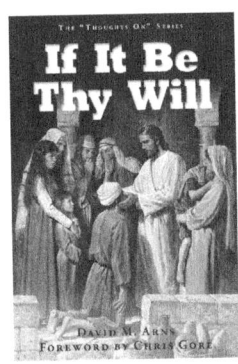

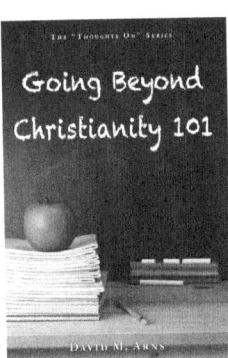

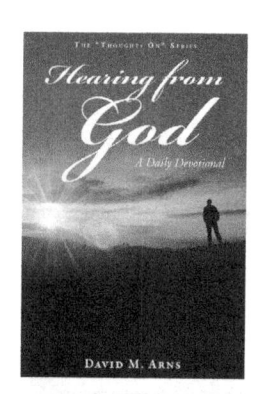

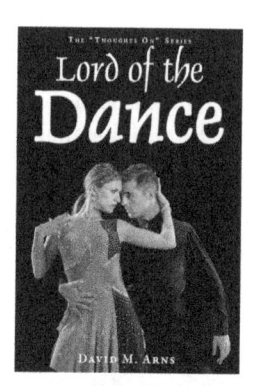

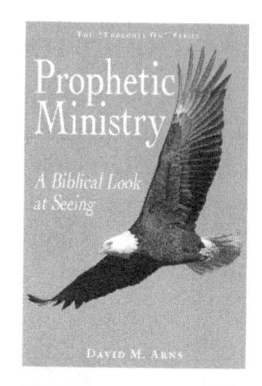

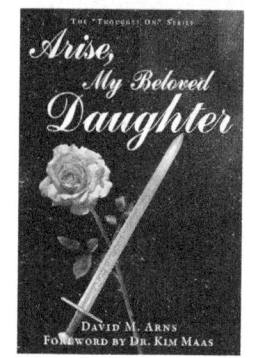

Music in the "WORSHIP ON" Series

All the music below is available both as downloadable electronic files and as physical CDs, and are available from the sources mentioned on the website Music.DaveArns.com.

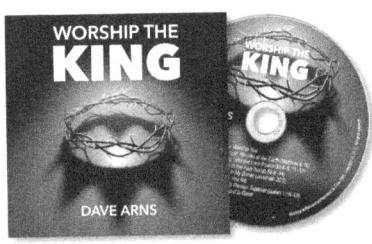

For descriptions and other details of all these books or albums, see the back of this book, or the websites BibleAuthor.DaveArns.com or Music.DaveArns.com, respectively.

Table of Contents

Preface 19
   Typographical Conventions 22
      Scripture References 22

Chapter 1: Free to Choose? 25

Chapter 2: Principles of Reason 29
   The Law of Non-Contradiction 33
      The Constraints on This Law 37
      The Syllogism 38
      Reductio ad Absurdum 39
      The Contrapositive 41
   The Law of Causality 42
   The Basic Reliability of Sense Perception 46
      But Wait a Minute 50
   The Analogical Use of Language 51
      "Wholly Other?" 52
   Logic Gets a Bad Rap 55
   Where Do We Go From Here? 56

Chapter 3: We Have Free Will, and We Can Choose God 59
   Is God Just? 59
   Does God Waste Words? 63
   A Theological Discussion 66
   "Free Will Isn't Even Mentioned in the Bible!" 67
      Enlisting in the Lord's Army 73
   Volunteering Voluntarily 75
      Other Examples of Free Will in the Bible 78
   What Is Love? 80
   God's Sovereignty 84
      Does God Want Everyone to be Saved? 85
      Do All People Get Saved? 90
      The Upshot 93
   Crime and Punishment 93
      When God Takes His Cue From Us 94
         Conditional Blessing 94
         God's Behavior Based on Our Actions 98

Why Was Abraham Chosen? 99
Why Was David Chosen? 100
Righteous Judgment 100
Standing in the Gap 106
Turning Away From, Or Toward, God 107
The Parable of the Unfruitful Fig Tree 108
The Parable of the Talents 109
"Giving Account" 112
The Second Coming of Christ 114
Coming to God 115
God's Behavior Based on Our Attitudes 116
God Acting Because We Asked Him To 119
The Complaint Department 127
Types and Shadows 129
Seeking a Bride for Isaac 129
The Kinsman-Redeemer 132
"A Woman Shall Compass a Man" 133

Chapter 4: The Five Points of Calvinism 137
The Definition of Sovereignty 139
Sovereignty: Infinite Power and Authority 144

Chapter 5: Total Depravity 147
Original Sin 148
Gnosticism 149
Back to Total Depravity 153
Faith vs. Works 154
Old Testament Examples 158
Turning—or Returning—to God 159
Choosing to Receive Jesus 160
Choosing to Believe in Jesus 164
Humbling Ourselves and Submitting to God 166
The Cry of God's Heart 171
Regeneration Precedes Faith? Or Vice Versa? 173
Is Salvation a Gift? 204
A Gift is Something You Receive 207
Ask, Seek, Knock 207
The Disciples' Commission to Preach 208
Receiving or Not 208
Preaching In the Home Town 209
Receiving or Not, Take 2 211

    What Happens When You Receive Christ? 213
    John's Ministry vs. Jesus' Ministry 215
    Jesus' Sermon Before Passover 215
Reconciliation 217
Foot Washing 217
The Result of Repentance 218

Chapter 6: Unconditional Election 223
God is Merciful to How Many? 224
    Men Are Not Cast Off 232
    Jonah's Complaint 234
        God's Plea 234
    The Christmas Story 236
    Burning Down the Samaritans 237
    What Does Paul Say About Mercy? 238
    Being Appointed Unto Wrath 239
But What About His "Chosen People?" 240
God Is Not a Respecter of Persons 242
He That Dwelleth 251
Election 253
Jesus' Yoke 258
Predestination 259
    Pan Am Flight 103 260
    Foreknowledge and Predestination 261
        Does Foreknowledge Imply Predestination? 265
    Secondary Destinations 266
    Does "Ordain" Imply Inevitability? 267
        Our Obedience Is Important 269
    The Lamb's Book of Life 274
    The Nature of God's Foreknowledge 278
"Limited" Omniscience 281
    Jesus Didn't Know Everything 282
    Naming the Animals 285
    God's Response to Antediluvian Sin 285
    Abraham Sacrificing Isaac 286
    Leaving Egypt 287
    Bread from Heaven 288
    Let Me Think About It 289
    Testing the Prophets 289
    Moses' Song 290

Some Enemies Strategically Left in Place. 291
God Breaking His Promise, Take 1 292
Choosing Saul as King 292
The Biggest Blank Check Ever 293
Ahab at Ramoth-Gilead 294
Hezekiah's Judgment. 296
God's Plan to Discover Something 296
Praying that God Forgets 298
Dashing God's Expectations, Part 1. 298
Looking for Someone to Pray 299
Dashing God's Expectations, Part 2. 300
What Hadn't Occurred to God. 302
God Breaking His Promise, Take 2 304
God Promising to Forget. 305
God Being Unsure 305
God "Looking for" Someone. 307
"Destruction! Oh, Never Mind. . ." 308
The Time Has Come 308
Why Do I Live Now? 309
"But Doesn't This Scripture Say. . .?" 311

Chapter 7: Limited Atonement 315
The Impact on Evangelism: The Evangelists 317
Paul's Confirmation 329
The Impact on Evangelism: The Unsaved 332
What's Your Excuse? 332
"The World". 335
Conviction of Sin. 337
The Impact on Holiness 338

Chapter 8: Irresistible Grace 341
Resisting the Holy Spirit 341
Vexing the Holy Spirit. 343
Grieving the Holy Spirit 344
Quenching the Holy Spirit 345
Striving with the Holy Spirit 346
Rahab the Harlot. 347
The Pharisees. 348
The Parable of the Great Supper 349
The Day of Pentecost 350
Wisdom (Holy Spirit) Calling. 351

God Calling. 356
Jesus Calling 360
Stretching Forth the Hands. 361
The Sign of the Prophet Jonah 363
Such a Great Salvation. 364
"Harden Not Your Heart. . ." 365

Chapter 9: Perseverance of the Saints 369
Merely an Appearance? 369
Or Actuality?. 370
Breaking a Relationship. 371
   God Breaking the Relationship. 371
   Satan Snatching Us Away From God. 372
   We Ourselves Terminating the Relationship 373
The Parable of the Sower. 374
Making Certain. 376
For It Is Impossible. 378
Sinning Willfully. 380
Escaping Corruption. . . Temporarily. 380
Being On Guard 384
Forsaking. 385
   God's Promise vs. the People's Behavior. 389
"All That He Has Given Me. . ." 389
Falling From Grace 392
The Lamb's Book of Life, Take 2 396
Ezekiel 33 397
Actual Perseverance of the Saints 398
   The Parable of the Wedding Feast. 401
   The Parable of the Good and Wicked Servants 405
   The Parable of the Ten Virgins 406
   Paul Chimes In 411

Chapter 10: Miscellaneous Topics 413
Hungering for God 413
   Available, But Not to be Taken for Granted 415
When God Does "Bad" Things. 417
   "I, the Lord, Create Evil" 418
   "He Turns Rivers Into a Wilderness". 419
   "God Did Vex Them. . ." 420
   "I Send Pestilence Among My People. . ." 421
   "Evil Came Down from the Lord. . ." 423

Free to Choose?

  "The Evil That I Have Brought. . ." 424
  "I Will Tear and Go Away" 426
  "Desolation Shall Come Upon You Suddenly. . ." 429
  "Hath Not the Lord Done This Evil?" 430
  Calamities from the Most High 431
  The Lord of the Holocaust 432
  And So Forth 434
 "Two-Ditch" Problems 438
 The Problem of Judas Iscariot 442
 None Righteous; No, Not One 454
  Verse 10: None Righteous 454
  The Parable of Grocery Shopping 461
  Back to Romans 3:10 462
  Whom was Paul Quoting? 466
  Verse 11: None Understands 470
  Verse 11: None Seek God 471
 Watchman on the Wall 476
 Ezekiel 18 478
 Romans 9–11 483
  . . .The Purpose of God According to Election. 485
  Pharaoh's Example 486
  The Potter and the Clay 500
  Vessels Unto Honor 505
  . . .Vessels of Wrath Fitted to Destruction. 507
  The Founders of Reformed Theology 510
 "Draw" = "Compel?" 519
 I Have Chosen You. 523
  The "Efficiency" of a Theory 523
  Back to Choosing. 524
 "Altogether Conceived in Sin" 528
 "The Just Shall Live by Faith" 534
 Speaking of Faith. 536

Chapter 11: What Shall We Say, Then? 539
 The Definition of Sovereignty, Take 2 539
 My Surprising Discovery 543

Appendix A: Bible-Study Strategies 545
 Multiple Translations. 545
 Multiple References. 546
 The Preponderance of Scripture 546

The Plain, Surface Meaning. 547
  The Bible Itself Defining Its Terms 547
  Reading in Context 549
  Now, Onward. 550

About the Author 551
  Books in the "Thoughts On" Series. 551
  Music in the "Worship On" Series. 558

Preface

All Scripture references are from the public-domain King James Version (KJV) of the Bible unless otherwise noted. Other versions of the Bible that may be quoted are as follows:

- AMP: Amplified Bible: Copyright © 1954, 1958, 1962, 1964, 1965, and 1987 by the Lockman Foundation, La Habra, CA, 90631. All rights reserved. www.lockman.org.
- AMPC: Amplified Bible, Classic Edition: Copyright © 1954, 1958, 1962, 1964, 1965, 1987 by The Lockman Foundation.
- ASV: American Standard Version of 1901: Public Domain.
- BBE: Bible in Basic English: This text is in the public domain and has no copyright. The Bible In Basic English was printed in 1965 by Cambridge Press in England. Published without any copyright notice and distributed in America, this work fell immediately and irretrievably into the Public Domain in the United States according to the UCC convention of that time.
- BRG: The BRG Bible: Blue Red and Gold Letter Edition™ Copyright © 2012 BRG Bible Ministries. Used by Permission. All rights reserved. BRG Bible is a Registered Trademark in U.S. Patent and Trademark Office #4145648.
- CEB: Common English Bible: All rights reserved.
- CEV: Contemporary English Version: Copyright © 1995 by American Bible Society. All rights reserved.
- CJB: Complete Jewish Bible: Copyright © 1998 by David H. Stern. All rights reserved.
- DARBY: Darby Translation: Public domain. First published in 1890 by John Nelson Darby, an Anglo-Irish Bible teacher associated with the early years of the Plymouth Brethren.
- DLNT: Disciples' Literal New Testament: Disciples' Literal New Testament: Serving Modern Disciples by More Fully Reflecting the Writing Style of the Ancient Disciples, Copyright © 2011 Michael J. Magill. All Rights Reserved. Published by Reyma Publishing (www.ReymaPublishing.com).
- DOUAY: Douay-Rheims Bible, translated from the Latin Vulgate. Rheims New Testament, 1582; Douay Old Testament, 1610.
- EHV: The Evangelical Heritage Version (EHV), New Testament & Psalms ©2017.
- ERV: Easy-to-Read Version: Copyright © 2006 by World Bible Translation Center.
- ESV: The Holy Bible, English Standard Version: Copyright © 2001, 2006, 2011 by Crossway Bibles, a division of Good News Publishers. All rights reserved.
- EXB: The Expanded Bible: Scripture taken from The Expanded Bible. Copyright © 2011 by Thomas Nelson, Inc. Used by permission. All rights reserved.
- GNT: Good News Translation: Copyright © 1992 by American Bible Society. All rights reserved.
- GNV: Geneva Bible: The Geneva Bible (1599), Public Domain.

- GWORD: God's Word Translation: Copyright © 2010 by Baker Publishing Group, © 1995 by God's Words to the Nations. All Rights reserved.
- HCSB: Holman Christian Standard Bible: Copyright © 1999, 2000, 2002, 2003 by Holman Bible Publishers. Holman Christian Standard Bible®, Holman CSB®, and HCSB® are federally registered trademarks of Holman Bible Publishers. Used by permission.
- ICB: International Children's Bible: The Holy Bible, International Children's Bible, Copyright © 2015 Thomas Nelson Inc. All rights reserved.
- ISV: International Standard Version: The Holy Bible: International Standard Version. Release 2.0, Build 2014.07.18. Copyright © 1995–2014 by ISV Foundation. All Rights Reserved Internationally. Used by permission of Davidson Press, LLC.
- JUB: The Jubilee Bible: The Jubilee Bible (from the Scriptures of the Reformation), edited by Russell M. Stendal; Copyright © 2000, 2001, 2010.
- LEB: Lexham English Bible: Scripture quotations marked (LEB) are from the Lexham English Bible. Copyright © 2012 Logos Bible Software. Lexham is a registered trademark of Logos Bible Software.
- MOUNCE: The Mounce Reverse-Interlinear New Testament: Copyright © 2011 by Robert H Mounce and William D Mounce. Used by permission. All rights reserved worldwide.
- MSG: The Message: Scripture taken from The Message. Copyright © 1993, 1994, 1995, 1996, 2000, 2001, 2002. Used by permission of NavPress Publishing Group.
- NABRE: New American Bible, Revised Edition: © 2010, 1991, 1986, 1970 Confraternity of Christian Doctrine, Inc., Washington, DC. All Rights Reserved.
- NASB: New American Standard Bible: Copyright © 1960, 1962, 1963, 1968, 1971, 1972, 1973, 1975, 1977, 1995 by The Lockman Foundation. All rights reserved.
- NCB: New Catholic Bible: Copyright © 2019 by Catholic Book Publishing Corp. All rights reserved.
- NCV: New Century Version: Scripture taken from the New Century Version®. Copyright © 2005 by Thomas Nelson, Inc. Used by permission. All rights reserved.
- NET: New English Translation. The NET Bible®, First Edition (NET); New English Translation, The Translation That Explains Itself™; Copyright © 1996–2005 by Biblical Studies Press, L.L.C. All rights reserved.
- NIRV: New International Readers' Version: Copyright © 1996, 1998 by Biblica.
- NIV: New International Version: Scripture quoted by permission. Quotations designated (NIV) are from The Holy Bible: New International Version (NIV). Copyright © 1973, 1978, 1984 by International Bible Society. Used by permission of Zondervan Publishing House. All rights reserved.
- NKJV: Scripture taken from the New King James Version®. Copyright © 1982 by Thomas Nelson. Used by permission. All rights reserved.

FREE TO CHOOSE?

- NLT: New Living Translation: Holy Bible, New Living Translation, Copyright © 1996, 2004 by Tyndale Charitable Trust. Used by permission of Tyndale House Publishers, Inc., Wheaton Illinois 60189. All rights reserved.
- NLV: New Life Version: Copyright © 1969 Christian Literature International.
- NMB: New Matthew Bible: Copyright © 2016 by Ruth Magnusson (Davis). All rights reserved.
- NOG: Names of God Bible: The Names of God Bible (without notes) © 2011 by Baker Publishing Group. Scripture is taken from God's Word®, © 1995 God's Word to the Nations. Used by permission of Baker Publishing Group.
- NTE: New Testament for Everyone: Scripture quotations from The New Testament for Everyone are copyright © Nicholas Thomas Wright 2011.
- PHILLIPS: J.B. Phillips New Testament: J. B. Phillips, "The New Testament in Modern English," 1962 edition by HarperCollins.
- RSV: Revised Standard Version: Copyright © 1971 by the Division of Christian Education of the National Council of the Churches of Christ in the United States of America
- TEV: Today's English Version: Today's English Version Bible. Copyright © American Bible Society, 1966, 1971, 1976, 1992. Used by permission.
- TLB: The Living Bible: Copyright © 1971 by Tyndale House Foundation. Used by permission of Tyndale House Publishers Inc., Carol Stream, Illinois 60188. All rights reserved.
- TLV: Tree of Life (TLV) Translation of the Bible. Copyright © 2015 by The Messianic Jewish Family Bible Society.
- TPT: The Passion Translation®. Copyright © 2017 by Passion & Fire Ministries, Inc. Used by permission. All rights reserved. thePassionTranslation.com The Passion Translation® is a registered trademark of Passion & Fire Ministries, Inc.
- VOICE: The Voice Bible: The Voice Bible Copyright © 2012 Thomas Nelson, Inc. The Voice™ translation © 2012 Ecclesia Bible Society. All rights reserved.
- WE: Worldwide English: Copyright © 1969, 1971, 1996, 1998 by SOON Educational Publications, Willington, Derby, DE65 6BN, England. Taken from The Jesus Book—The Bible in Worldwide English. Copyright SOON Educational Publications, Derby DE65 6BN, UK. Used by permission.
- WEB: World English Bible: "World English Bible" is a trademark of Rainbow Missions, Inc. Permission is granted to use the name "World English Bible" and its logo only to identify faithful copies of the Public Domain translation of the Holy Bible of that name published by Rainbow Missions, Inc. The World English Bible is not copyrighted.
- WEBSTR: Webster Bible: The Holy Bible, by Noah Webster, L.L.D. (1833). This text is in the public domain and has no copyright.
- WEYMTH: Weymouth New Testament in Modern Speech: Third Edition, 1913. Public Domain—Copy Freely
- WYC: Wycliffe Bible: Wycliffe Bible Copyright © 2001 by Terence P. Noble.
- YLT: Young's Literal Translation of the Holy Bible: This text is in the public domain and has no copyright.

Typographical Conventions

In Scriptural quotes in this book, emphasis (indicated by **boldface** type, and occasionally ***italic* within the boldface**) may be added by the author to draw attention to the portions of the passage that pertain to the topic currently under discussion. This applies throughout, so "emphasis added by author" doesn't need to be stated in every single instance.

In this book, the generic pronouns "he," "him," and "his" are used whenever explicit inclusion of both gender-specific pronouns would result in grammatical cumbersomeness. We know that in Christ, there is no difference between male and female (Galatians 3:28), so the pronouns used in this way should be read as generic, not masculine.

When you see a number prefixed by a "H" or a "G", it represents the word number Hebrew or Greek dictionaries of *Strong's Exhaustive Concordance,* one of the standard tools for Biblical study: *Strong's Hebrew and Chaldee Dictionary of the Old Testament* (Hebrew Strong's) and *Strong's Greek Dictionary of the New Testament* (Greek Strong's), both public domain. So, for example, "G256" indicates that English word being discussed was translated from the word defined in entry 256 in Strong's Greek Dictionary.

In Scripture quotations, the letter case of the English word "Lord" indicates the standard meanings when quoting from the Old Testament. Mixed Case, as in "Lord," indicates the Hebrew name אֲדֹנָי (*Adonay*, H136), while SMALL CAPS, as in "LORD" indicates the Hebrew name יְהוָה (*Yahweh*, H3068), also known as the Tetragrammaton, which literally means "four letters." And finally, when the original Hebrew uses the name יְהוָה אֱלֹהִים (*Yahweh Elohim*, H3068 H430), it is translated and lettercased as "Lord GOD."

Scripture References

This book contains a great number of Scriptural references, and the punctuation used within or between them indicates specific things that are helpful to know, in order to gain the most understanding from the passage.

Here are the various punctuation symbols and what they mean:

- Colon (":"): A colon separates the chapter being specified from the verse being specified, as in "John 3:16" referring to "the book of John, chapter three, verse sixteen." There are two situations in which a colon is not present in a reference:

- When *all* the verses in a particular chapter are being included, as in "I Corinthians 13 is known as 'The Love Chapter.'"
- When the Bible book being referenced has only one chapter, in which case there is no need to specify *which* chapter, as in "But you, dear friends, build yourselves up in your most holy faith and pray in the Holy Spirit (Jude 20)."

- Comma (","): Separates non-contiguous references in a list, or non-contiguous verses in a single chapter, as in "God's glory, which was demonstrated in raising Lazarus from the dead, is mentioned in John 11:4, 40." That is, chapter 11, verses 4 and 40, but not the intervening verses.

- En-dash ("–"): An en-dash indicates a range of chapters or verses, inclusive of both endpoints. For example, "The story of Gideon is found in Judges 6–8" (the book of Judges, starting in chapter 6 and going through chapter 8) or "The story of Jesus healing Bartimaeus of blindness is found in Mark 10:46–52" (the book of Mark, chapter 10, starting in verse 46 and going through verse 52).

- Lowercase letters: These indicate a specific phrase or thought in a particular verse, and it is usually used when the idea under discussion is not the first thing the verse mentions. For example, "Greater is He that is in us than he that is in the world (I John 4:4b)." In this case, the "b" is used to indicate that the given phrase is the *second*, not the first, important point in that verse.

- Lowercase "f": The single lowercase F indicates "and the single verse following," as in "During Jesus' temptation in the wilderness, he hung around with wild animals and angels (Mark 1:12f)." Note that "1:12f" means the same as "1:12–13."

- Lowercase "ff": The two lowercase Fs indicate "and (an unspecified number of) verses following;" for example, "Jesus' command to wait for the power of the Holy Spirit is shown in Acts 1:4ff." Note that "1:4ff" could mean the same as "1:4–5" or "1:4–6" or "1:4–7" or "1:4–8" and so forth, so the end of the passage referenced should be clear from the context. If the ending point is not clear, the en-dash (see above) will be used to avoid confusion.

- Greater-thans and less-thans (">" and "<", respectively): These symbols indicate a reference in the Old Testament being quoted in the New Testament. For example, "Peter quoted Joel in his Pentecost sermon (Acts 2:17<Joel 2:28)." Or, "Joel's prophecy of the outpouring

of the Holy Spirit was fulfilled at Pentecost (Joel 2:28>Acts 2:17)." Which one you use depends on whether the Old Testament passage or the New Testament passage is the main point of the sentence.

- Parallel lines or "pipes" ("||"): These parallel lines indicate parallel verses; i.e., multiple accounts of the same story. For example, "All four gospels quote John the Baptist stating one of Jesus' main purposes on earth, that of baptizing people in the Holy Spirit (Matthew 3:11 || Mark 1:8 || Luke 3:16 || John 1:33)." The parallel lines can also indicate synonymous phrases, as in, "When the 120 disciples in the upper room were 'filled with the Spirit' || 'baptized in the Spirit,' they spoke in tongues."

Chapter 1:

Free to Choose?

One of the most hotly debated concepts in the last 500 years or so has been that of whether people actually have a free will to choose their eternal destiny or not. People debate each other with—shall we say, *religious* fervor—and people on both sides of the debate offer Scriptures to support their viewpoints.

On the one hand, we have people who believe that God offers us a choice to voluntarily repent and turn to Him. Of course, if we have any sense at all, we would choose to serve Him, but God does not force us to make a sensible choice. He loves us and offers a way out of our eternal destiny of much-deserved hell, but will not impose it on us against our will. People who hold this view are traditionally called "Arminians," after Jacobus Arminius, who championed the idea back in the 1500s.

On the other hand, we have people who believe that God is sovereign, and that sovereignty necessarily means that God causes everything that happens; not merely passively *allows* it, but actively *causes* every occurrence, everywhere, throughout eternity. And of course, this would include determining the eternal destination of everyone. A variation on this idea is that we do have free will, but it's a restricted free will that can only choose certain things; specifically, we can choose anything except God, unless He saves us first, enabling us to choose rightly. People who hold a view such as these are traditionally called "Calvinists," after John Calvin, who championed the idea, along with Martin Luther, also back in the 1500s.

So which is right?

Now that's the $64,000 question, isn't it? People have been debating this for hundreds of years, and most of their discussions refer back to, and rely heavily on, other theologians from antiquity for support. What I will attempt to do in this book is to look at the support each view has in the Bible itself, and avoid referring back to non-Biblical sources for support. I may mention and even quote various theologians from time to time, but I won't base any conclusions or try to prove any doctrinal points on their statements—all conclusions and doctrinal points must be supported by the Bible itself, in context, and preferably confirmed in multiple places.

Collectively, the group that adheres to the Calvinist viewpoint refer to themselves as following "Reformed Theology," named after "The Protestant Reformation." This is the name history gives to the movement in the 16th century, in which a grassroots uprising objected to errors they perceived in the Roman Catholic church's doctrine. Note that not all Protestants adhere to what is usually called "Reformed theology," but the ones that do, usually adhere to a particular view of God's sovereignty, and the Five Points of Calvinism that result from it. Much more on this below.

Now, before I go on, I want to make it clear that it is *not* my intention to attack the people who believe the Reformed doctrine (or anyone else, for that matter). They have much in common with every other Christian denomination, as it pertains to the essentials of the faith and to Biblical Christianity in general. I am grateful for the people who adhere to the Reformed theology; they are some of the most godly, humble, sincere, hard-working, giving people I know.

And I know many of them, because I married a Dutch woman with a Christian Reformed upbringing, and am very impressed with their character. So again, in those places where I disagree with doctrinal statements of the Reformed theology, it is a result of a close Scriptural analysis, and is explicitly *not* intended to be an attack on anyone who adheres to it.

A moment ago, I said that there is much that the Reformed theology has in common with virtually all the rest of Christendom: such things include the eternal nature of God, the fact that He is a Spirit, that He is good, that He is holy, all-powerful, immutable, kind, omnipresent, loving, the source of every good gift, and so forth. Those doctrines are not in question; the purpose of this book is to examine those doctrines where the Reformed Theology differs from that of the rest of Christendom. These doctrines are historically—and still—called the Five Points of Calvinism. These will be covered in detail in the introductory chapter The Five Points of Calvinism, and the five chapters following it.

Of course, every Reformed denomination, every Reformed congregation, and every Reformed person adheres to a greater or lesser extent to the actual Five Points of Calvinism and its associated understanding of the sovereignty of God. Some Reformed churches are Reformed almost entirely in name only, and the Five Points are rarely talked about. My wife's childhood church was one such church. They had excellent Biblical instruction and were diligent to live their lives in a very godly way, but after being raised in that environment for eighteen years before moving to a different state to go to college, she wasn't even aware of what some of the Points of Calvinism were.

So again, I am explicitly *not* coming against any denominations, congregations, or people in this book; I am simply analyzing from a Biblical perspective the doctrinal position of the Five Points of Calvinism and the associated understanding of God's sovereignty. If you are interested to hear some of my findings, please continue reading. If you find that I have misinterpreted Scripture or have used faulty logic, please let me know. See "About the Author" for information on contacting me.

We will get into these topics in the following pages. In doing so, we'll repeatedly use the Bible study techniques mentioned in "Appendix A: Bible-Study Strategies;" please refer to that for details.

Free to Choose?

Chapter 2:

Principles of Reason

There exists among theologians a concept known as "systematic theology." This, properly used, does not take a system of thought or a collection of rules and *impose* it onto the Bible. Rather, it looks at the Bible, both as the big picture and as details, and then *observes and describes* the system God employed when writing it.

Systematic theology requires, and rightly assumes, that God's Word is *coherent*. In other words, the Bible, having been written by God, is self-consistent and applies common-sense rules of rationality and logic so as to allow us to understand it. For indeed, without these rules, all science, all theology, all skill, all awareness, all knowledge of *any* kind would be unreliable. If we actually chose to live with disregard for the rules of rationality, we would probably literally be dead in short order. (More on this later.) For now, suffice it to say that we need to understand the rules of rational thought—logic—because God Himself uses them, and it, throughout the Bible, and indeed, throughout the universe.

The Bible uses certain Principles of Reason, also known as Principles of Rationality or Rules of Logic. It doesn't list them or define them, but it uses them everywhere, assumes them to be self-evident, and tacitly acknowledges and endorses them throughout, as we'll see momentarily. And since "it"— the Bible—was inspired by God (II Timothy 3:16 and II Peter 1:21), it is clear that God, too, acknowledges and endorses them; you could say that "He wrote the book on Logic." Indeed, the Rules of Reason/Logic are sometimes stated to be self-evident and, when you get right down to it, they are. If you didn't abide by the Rules of Logic on a day-by-day basis, you would soon be dead, as mentioned above.

Some people have stated that God is above and beyond "mere logic," but that seems to me to be uninformed at best, and blasphemous at worst. Why? Because logic is nothing more than organized, flowing truth, and God *is* truth:

> Deuteronomy 32:4: He is the Rock, his work is perfect: for all his ways are judgment: **a God of truth** and without iniquity, just and right is he.
>
> Psalm 100:5: For the LORD is good; his mercy is everlasting; and **his truth endureth to all generations.**
>
> John 3:33 (AMP): Whoever receives His testimony has set his seal of approval to this: **God is true.** [That man has definitely certified, acknowledged, declared once and for all, and is himself assured that **it is divine truth that God cannot lie**].
>
> John 14:6: Jesus saith unto him, **I am** the way, **the truth,** and the life: no man cometh unto the Father, but by me.
>
> Titus 1:2: In hope of eternal life, which **God, that cannot lie,** promised before the world began. . .
>
> Hebrews 6:18 (ESV): . . .so that by two unchangeable things, in which **it is impossible for God to lie,** we who have fled for refuge might have strong encouragement to hold fast to the hope set before us.
>
> Revelation 15:3: And they sing the song of Moses the servant of God, and the song of the Lamb, saying, Great and marvellous are thy works, Lord God Almighty; **just and true are thy ways,** thou King of saints.

. . .and there are many more, but the above Scriptures should be sufficient to show that God *is* truth, *tells* the truth, and *cannot* lie. And since reason, or logic, is simply one truth flowing into another truth in an organized manner, we can see that God, in addition to being a God of Truth, is also necessarily a God of Reason and Logic. This is absolutely essential, in order for God to avoid confusion in attempting to communicate with us, and we know that "God is not the author of confusion" (I Corinthians 14:33a).

Indeed, in the first chapter of John, we read:

> John 1:1: In the beginning was the Word, and the Word was with God, and the Word was God.

All three occurrences of "Word" in the verse above come from the Greek word λόγος (*logos*, G3056), which is the root of the English word "logic." Strong's Greek Dictionary includes in the definition of *logos* "reasoning (the mental faculty)," "computation," "account," "reason," and "reckon"—all of these are words or phrases that require logic or are intrinsically logical. And because *logos* is where the English word "logic" comes from, it's not at all a stretch to render that verse "In the beginning was the Logic, and the Logic was with God, and the Logic was God."

The Greeks considered the "logos" to be the Organizing Principle behind the universe. Aristotle used the term to refer to "reasoned discourse" or the "argument" in the field of rhetoric. Greek scholars describe *logos* as a logical appeal (which is why the term "logic" was derived from it) and point out that *logos* is typically used to describe facts and figures that support the speaker's point. The word *logos* is credited with appealing to the audience's sense of logic, where logic is defined as "that which is concerned with the thing as-it-is-known."

So when the Greeks considered the "logos" to be the Organizing Principle behind the universe, they were basically correct, as far as they went; they simply didn't know that this Organizing Principle is named Jesus, has a personality, is the uncreated Creator of the universe, and He interacts with it and us, and loves us individually.

Also, consider the following verses:

I Samuel 12:7: Now therefore stand still, **that I** *[Samuel]* **may reason with you** before the LORD of all the righteous acts of the LORD, which he did to you and to your fathers.

Job 13:3: Surely I would speak to the Almighty, and **I** *[Job]* **desire to reason with God.**

Proverbs 26:16: The sluggard is wiser in his own conceit than seven men that can **render a reason.**

Ecclesiastes 7:25: I *[Solomon]* applied mine heart to know, and to search, and to seek out wisdom, and **the reason of things. . .**

Isaiah 1:18: **Come now, and let us reason together, saith the LORD:** though your sins be as scarlet, they shall be as white as snow; though they be red like crimson, they shall be as wool.

(To hear this passage set to music, listen to the song *Let Us Reason Together* on the album *Worship the King* or scan the QR code at right.)

I Peter 3:15: But sanctify the Lord God in your hearts: and **be ready always to give an answer to every man that asketh you a reason** of the hope that is in you with meekness and fear. . .

So there is ample precedent in the Bible for logical, thoughtful reasoning. The quotes above show that there is an intuitive understanding and acknowledgement that logic and reason are appropriate, and that includes the passage from Isaiah, where *God Himself invites us to reason together with Him!* Skeptics have said that in order to become a Christian, you need to turn off your brain. Nothing could be further from the truth; God is not intimidated by logical, rational thought, because He is the Author of it.

So now that we've established a solid Scriptural foundation for the existence and value of logic and reason, what are the official Principles of Reason? The main ones are shown below, and briefly described. There are others as well, which are just as true, but less often encountered, so we will introduce some of those later, as needed.

The main four are these:

1. **The Law of Non-Contradiction:** "No thing can be *A* and *not A* at the same time and in the same relationship/sense/way." In other words, a statement cannot be both true and false at the same time, and in the same way.

2. **The Law of Causality:** "Every effect has a cause." In other words, *someone* or *something* gives rise to every action, phenomenon, object, or condition that exists in the universe. We may not *know* the cause of some particular effect, but we can be confident that there is one.

3. **The Basic Reliability of Sense Perception:** "The sensations we perceive are basically reliable." Of course, there are some things that are too small, too distant, too fast, too slow, and so forth, to perceive, but *basically*, they're reliable.

4. **The Analogical Use of Language:** "We can extrapolate known concepts into unknown areas by using analogies, and we can communicate them via language." In other words, the meaning of words is influenced by the topic currently under discussion.

Let's examine these principles in a bit more detail. But first, a note on terminology: In this book, when I use the words "absurd" or "nonsense," I am not using them as disparaging insults regarding the intelligence of a person who believes whatever topic is currently under discussion. On the contrary, I am using them as the field of logic does, where "nonsense" and "absurdity" indicate a concept that is contrary to rationality and sense—an idea that could not possibly be, because of its intrinsic self-contradiction. But again, no insult is intended.

The Law of Non-Contradiction

"No thing can be *A* and *not A* at the same time and in the same relationship/sense/way." A thing and its opposite must be distinguishable.

> Genesis 2:16–17 (NIV): And the LORD God commanded the man, "**You are free to eat** from any tree in the garden; ¹⁷but **you must not eat** from the tree of the knowledge of good and evil, for when you eat of it you will surely die."

Notice that there is implicit and assumed understanding between the concepts of "*you may* eat of these trees" and "*you may not* eat of that one." If that distinction were not self-evident or already understood, the command would have been meaningless. Not only that, but if the distinction did not exist or were invalid, then eating the forbidden fruit, and *not* eating it, would mean the same thing.

Then in the very next verse, we read:

> Genesis 2:18 (NIV): The LORD God said, "It is not good for the man to be alone. I will make a helper suitable for him."

Note again that God is assuming the existence of, tacitly acknowledging the validity of, and using without apology, the Law of Non-Contradiction when He said, "It is not good for the man to be alone." If the Law of Non-Contradiction did not exist or were invalid, then "It *is not* good" would mean the same as "It *is* good." But there is a definite distinction here, the existence and the validity of which God assumes and tacitly acknowledges.

Very shortly after this:

> Genesis 3:4 (NIV): "You will not surely die," the serpent said to the woman.

Notice how the serpent contradicts God. Above, God said ". . .for when you eat of it *you will surely die.*" So Satan replies, "*You will not surely die.*" There is a distinct, and immensely important difference between "you will surely die" and "you will *not* surely die." Both statements cannot simultaneously be true in the same sense. We saw above that God is a God of truth, and all His ways are true. He is the embodiment of truth, and He cannot lie. So when the serpent says things like this—contradictions of God's statements—who do you think is right. . .?

Free to Choose?

Many other examples that could have been mentioned were omitted from the discussion above, and we haven't even gotten past the Garden of Eden yet! These three are just a tiny fraction of the thousands of examples throughout Scripture, where the Law of Non-Contradiction is assumed and is absolutely *required* in order to understand what God is saying. Were it not for the Law of Non-Contradiction, all communication—indeed, thought itself—would be reduced to meaninglessness, absurdity, nonsense, drivel, gibberish. For example, obedience is different than *dis*obedience, and you can't do both things at the same time and in the same sense. The same goes for righteousness and *un*righteousness, holy and *un*holy behavior, clean and *un*clean things, and so forth.

In fact, God specifically tells the priestly tribe of Levi how to behave, and it's for precisely that reason:

> Leviticus 10:10: . . .and that ye may put **difference between holy and unholy**, and **between unclean and clean**. . .

It was important to God that people were able to perceive and understand the importance of the difference between a thing and its opposite. The Levites were commanded to carry on their service in such a way as to make that difference plain to the people.

The prefix "un" means "not" in word-pairs such as "clean" and "unclean," as does the prefix "dis" in word-pairs like "obedience" and "disobedience." In all such word-pairs, if a concept fits into one of the words, it *cannot* fit into the other word simultaneously and in the same sense; if it did, it would violate the Law of Non-Contradiction.

There are many places where God clearly draws a distinction between "a thing" and "not that thing," as shown in these passages:

> Exodus 12:15, 20 (NIV): Seven days shall you eat **unleavened bread;** even the first day you shall put away yeast out of your houses, for whoever eats **leavened bread** from the first day until the seventh day, that soul shall be cut off from Israel. . . . **You shall eat nothing leavened.** In all your habitations **you shall eat unleavened bread.**

> Leviticus 11:47 (NIV): **You must distinguish between the unclean and the clean,** between living creatures that **may be eaten** and those that **may not be eaten.**

> Leviticus 19:15: Ye shall do no **unrighteousness** in judgment: thou shalt not respect the person of the poor, nor honour the person of the mighty: but in **righteousness** shalt thou judge thy neighbour.

CHAPTER 2: PRINCIPLES OF REASON

- Jeremiah 50:34 (ESV): Their Redeemer is strong; the Lord of hosts is his name. He will surely plead their cause, that he may give **rest** to the earth, but **unrest** to the inhabitants of Babylon.
- Matthew 5:45: That ye may be the children of your Father which is in heaven: for he maketh his sun to rise on the evil and on the good, and sendeth rain on **the just** and on **the unjust.**
- Matthew 23:23: Woe unto you, scribes and Pharisees, hypocrites! for ye pay tithe of mint and anise and cummin, and have omitted the weightier matters of the law, judgment, mercy, and faith: these ought ye to have **done**, and not to leave the other **undone**.
- Romans 1:14: I am debtor both to the Greeks, and to the Barbarians; both to the **wise**, and to the **unwise**.
- Romans 2:25: For circumcision verily profiteth, if thou keep the law: but if thou be a breaker of the law, thy **circumcision** is made **uncircumcision**.
- Romans 5:19: For as by one man's **disobedience** many were made sinners, so by the **obedience** of one shall many be made righteous.
- Titus 2:12: Teaching us that, denying **ungodliness** and worldly lusts, we should live soberly, righteously, and **godly**, in this present world. . .

In *every* case above, the distinction between the thing and its opposite is self-evident, and absolutely required for the statements to be understandable. In fact, without the Law of Non-Contradiction, the Final Judgment of all men would be meaningless, because God couldn't judge people for rejecting Him, because (again, if the Law of Non-Contradiction did not exist) rejecting Him would be the same as *not* rejecting Him. This nonsensical conclusion is the only other option if we do away with the Law of Non-Contradiction, and it should be sufficient evidence for even the hardest of intellectually honest skeptics: God acknowledges and endorses the Law of Non-Contradiction.

When I was in sixth grade, there was a puzzling question that was making the rounds among my classmates. The question was this: "Can God make a rock so big that even He can't lift it?" Note that both potential answers, yes and no, lead to the conclusion that there are some things that God doesn't have enough power to do. When I first heard the question (I still remember the spot on the playground where I was standing when I heard it), my first response was, "Hmm. Interesting question."

Then, as is my wont, I proceeded to dissect the question and boil it down to its simplest form, and after a couple of days I concluded that it simplified down to "Can God do something He can't do?" I saw the inherent contradiction in the question—even though I didn't yet know the word "contradiction"—and I came to the conclusion "If there's *anything* bigger than God, it's the concept of 'not.'"

Looking back on it, that's a pretty heavy thought for a sixth-grader. But it is perfectly accurate (though perhaps not well articulated back then), because God cannot defy his own nature; He cannot be what He is not. The very fact that He is eternal prevents Him from changing: If He changed, He would have to become something *different* than He was before; therefore, He would not be eternal—He would be *becoming* something that He wasn't earlier. And the Bible bears out His unchangeableness—His immutability:

> Psalm 102:25–27 (NIV): In the beginning you laid the foundations of the earth, and the heavens are the work of your hands. ²⁶They will perish, **but you remain;** they will all wear out like a garment. Like clothing you will change them and they will be discarded. ²⁷**But you remain the same,** and your years will never end.

> Malachi 3:6: For I am the LORD, **I change not;** therefore ye sons of Jacob are not consumed.

> Hebrews 1:10–12 (AMP): And [further], You, Lord, did lay the foundation of the earth in the beginning, and the heavens are the works of Your hands. ¹¹They will perish, but **You remain and continue permanently;** they will all grow old and wear out like a garment. ¹²Like a mantle [thrown about one's self] You will roll them up, and they will be changed and replaced by others. But **You remain the same, and Your years will never end nor come to failure.**

> Hebrews 13:8: Jesus Christ **the same yesterday, and to day, and for ever.**

> James 1:17: Every good gift and every perfect gift is from above, and cometh down from the Father of lights, with whom is **no variableness,** neither shadow of turning.

Some people actually deny the Law of Non-Contradiction, at least verbally (and selectively and temporarily). They do not doubt it in their day-to-day life, of course, because that would soon be fatal. For example, entering the highway, a skeptic sees a fast-moving Mack truck headed for him, and says, "There's a Mack truck headed for me. Which means that there is *not* a Mack truck headed for me. Which means it's safe to go." Splat.

Even God must abide by the Law of Non-Contradiction. At this, someone might ask, "Why would God have to obey *any* law?" Let's look at the Scriptures:

II Timothy 2:13: If we believe not, yet he *[Jesus]* abideth faithful: **he cannot deny himself.**

CEB: . . .he can't be anything else than what he is.

CEV: . . .Christ cannot deny who he is.

ERV: . . .he cannot be false to himself.

EXB: . . .he must be true to who he is.

ISV: That's who he is, he cannot change!

PHILLIPS: . . .He cannot deny his own nature.

NLV: . . .He cannot go against what He is.

WE: . . .he cannot say he is not what he is.

The answer to the question "Why would God have to obey *any* law?" becomes apparent when we realize the fact that He is eternal. Since He is eternal, He cannot change—because if He *did* change, He would become something new, which would mean He would not be eternal. The new attribute would have a starting point, and one of the characteristics of "eternal" is "without a starting point." Also involved in answering the question is the definition of Truth, which Jesus is: "**I am** the way, **the truth,** and the life. . ." (John 14:6). If He is eternal, and He is also Truth, He could never lie, because it would defy His very nature.

The Constraints on This Law

Note that there are two constraints contained in the definition of the Law of Non-Contradiction: "at the same time" and "in the same relationship/sense/way." These two constraints are necessary for the Law to reflect how reality works.

For example, my son Matthew was conceived in January of 1981 and born that October. So if, in 1980, I had said "I do not have a son," and then in 1982 "I do have a son," would I have contradicted myself? No, because those are two different points in time, and both statements would have been true *when I made them.* But if I were to refer to a *single* point in time and then make both statements about it, I would have contradicted myself because of their simultaneity. Hence, the need for the phrase "at the same time" in the Law of Non-Contradiction.

Similarly for the other constraint: if I say "I am both a father and a son," would that be possible? Of course. My father's name was Don and, as mentioned, my son's name is Matthew. I can be a father to Matthew and a son to Don at the same time. Why is that possible? Because of the definitions of "father" and "son," and because I am talking about *two different relationships*. However, if I had said, "I am Matthew's father and Matthew's son," that would be a contradiction, because of the definitions of "father" and "son," and because I am talking about only the *same* relationship.

Another way to use the second constraint in the Law of Non-Contradiction is this: Suppose my son Matthew got saved and started serving the Lord before I did, and because of his testimony and evangelistic efforts, he leads me to Christ and I get saved. Then, I could truthfully say "I am Matthew's father and Matthew's son" if, by that, I meant that "I am Matthew's *biological* father and Matthew's *spiritual* son." This uses the second constraint of the Law of Non-Contradiction as "in the same sense." Even though it was the same relationship, it was a different *sense* of fatherhood and sonship. Hence the need for the second constraint in the Law of Non-Contradiction.

The Syllogism

One of the most common ways that logic "flows"—one truth progressing into another truth in an organized manner—is the *syllogism*. The word comes from Greek *syn* ("with") and *logizesthai* ("to calculate"), and the root word of *logizesthai* is—you guessed it—*logos*.

So basically, a syllogism is a way of "calculating" with logic. The form is two statements ("premises" or "propositions") and a conclusion: if the premises are true and related properly, we are logically compelled to acknowledge that the conclusion must also be true. Perhaps the most famous example of a syllogism is this:

- Premise 1: All men are mortal.
- Premise 2: Socrates is a man.
- Conclusion: Socrates is mortal.

Note that if the premises are true and are related in this way, the conclusion *has* to be true also. In the context of this book, here is another syllogism:

- Premise 1: Salvation is by faith.
- Premise 2: Salvation is not by works.
- Conclusion: Having faith is not a work.

For much Scriptural support for the premises and conclusion in this syllogism, refer to the section "Faith vs. Works," below.

A few paragraphs above, I stated that "if the premises are true *and are related in this way,* the conclusion has to be true also." That is correct, but I want to point out *why* they have to be related "in that way." Consider the following:

- Premise 1: All men are mortal.
- Premise 2: My cat has gray fur.
- Conclusion: Swimming is impossible in July.

The first two premises are indeed true, so does that mean that the conclusion must be true? Obviously not. Why? Because the two premises are not related; men being mortal is completely unrelated to whether or not my cat has gray fur. And therefore, even though the conclusion *may accidentally* be true, it is completely unreliable (as illustrated above) because the premises were unrelated.

Reductio ad Absurdum

There is an extremely useful method of logical thought called *reductio ad absurdum* (Latin for "reducing it to an absurdity" or "reduction to the absurd"), and it makes use of the Law of Non-Contradiction. It works like this: A true-or-false assertion is presented, the truth of which we desire to ascertain; and, if one of the potential answers leads to absurd conclusions (for example, that true and false are equivalent), the other potential answer must, in fact, be correct.

For example, let's state our assertion as "The verse that says 'There is none righteous; no, not one' applies to all people, everywhere, under all circumstances, throughout history." That statement is very black-and-white; it is either true or it is not.

But how can we determine whether the assertion is true or not? Here's where *reductio ad absurdum* comes in: we'll assume for the moment, for the sake of the discussion, that we know the answer—we'll say it's true—and then see what logical implications result from that assumption. If the assumed answer, true, leads to ridiculous conclusions, we can confidently state that the initial assumption was wrong, and the other answer, false, must be correct.

So in our case, we'll assume for the moment that it is indeed true that "The verse that says 'There is none righteous; no, not one' applies to all people, everywhere, under all circumstances, throughout history." Now let's examine the logical implications of that statement. If this assertion is true, then:

- Luke must have been mistaken when he said Zacharias and Elisabeth were righteous:

    Luke 1:5–6: There was in the days of Herod, the king of Judaea, a certain priest named **Zacharias**, of the course of Abia: and his wife was of the daughters of Aaron, and her name was **Elisabeth**. ⁶And **they were both righteous** before God, walking in all the commandments and ordinances of the Lord blameless.

- The writer of Hebrews must have been mistaken when he said Abel was righteous:

    Hebrews 11:4: By faith Abel offered unto God a more excellent sacrifice than Cain, by which he obtained witness that **he was righteous**, God testifying of his gifts: and by it he being dead yet speaketh.

- Peter must have been mistaken when he said Lot was righteous:

    II Peter 2:7–8: And delivered just **Lot**, vexed with the filthy conversation of the wicked: (For **that righteous man** dwelling among them, in seeing and hearing, vexed **his righteous soul** from day to day with their unlawful deeds). . .

- God must have been mistaken when he said Noah was righteous:

    Genesis 7:1: And the LORD said unto **Noah**, Come thou and all thy house into the ark; for **thee have I seen righteous** before me in this generation.

I don't think I need to go any further. We have clearly been compelled into absurd conclusions—Luke is wrong, Hebrews is wrong, Peter is wrong, and even God is wrong—*if* we assume that our initial assertion ("The verse that says 'There is none righteous; no, not one' applies to all people, everywhere, under all circumstances, throughout history.") is true. Therefore we are logically obligated to conclude that the initial assertion is indeed false. More specifically, one or more of the four **universal inclusives,** or **universal affirmatives** (*all* people, *every*where, under *all* circumstances, *throughout* history) should not be universal, but should have some conditions or limitations applied.

This topic is covered in much more detail in the section "None Righteous; No, Not One;" see that section for a more in-depth examination of this concept.

The Contrapositive

The *contrapositive* is just a fancy word for a particular way of applying the Law of Non-Contradiction. Its definition is "the inference drawn from a logical proposition by negating its terms and reversing their order." Huh? Let's look at an example; it's a lot easier to understand by example than by definition.

Suppose I make a true statement about animals; for example, "All cats are mammals." Its contrapositive, which would necessarily also have to be true, would be "If it's not a mammal, it's not a cat." How do we know that the contrapositive is true? Because of the first statement: if it *were* a cat, it *would* be a mammal.

Let's look at a Scriptural example of the contrapositive:

Hebrews 11:6 (NIV): And **without faith it is impossible to please God,** because anyone who comes to him must believe that he exists and that he rewards those who earnestly seek him.

The equivalent meaning of the highlighted phrase could be expressed: "If you don't have faith, you will not please God." The contrapositive, formed by negating the terms and reversing their order, would be: "If you *do* please God, you *do* have faith." (You probably have other attributes pleasing to God as well, but if you please God, you must at least have faith.)

Let's look at another one:

I John 4:7–8 (NKJV): Beloved, let us love one another, for love is of God; and **everyone who loves is born of God and knows God.** ⁸**He who does not love does not know God,** for God is love.

The first highlighted phrase above says "If you love, you are born of God and know God." The contrapositive, formed by negating the terms and reversing their order, would be: "If you are not born of God and don't know God, you do not love." The second highlighted phrase says "If you do not love, you do not know God." The contrapositive would be, "If you *do* know God, you *do* love."

So, vv. 7–8 basically say "If you love, you know God, and if you don't love, you don't know God." The respective contrapositives are: "If you don't know God, you don't love, and if you do know God, you do love." This is perfectly clear and valid, because God and love are inseparable: you can't really love without knowing God, and you can't really know God without loving.

The Law of Causality

The Law of Causality states: "Every effect has a cause." Note that it does *not* say "Every*thing* has a cause." This common, but dangerously wrong misstatement of the Law of Causality is very serious, because the difference between the actual Law of Causality and the common misstatement of it has an enormous impact on what we conclude about God. Let me explain.

The Law of Causality, as it is properly articulated—"every effect has a cause"—allows God to be eternal, which He is. This is because of the definitions of the words "cause" and "effect." In the philosophical arena, a cause is defined as "that which produces an effect," and an effect is defined as "that which is produced by a cause." So we can see that the Law of Causality is simply a special case of the Law of Non-Contradiction: the Law of Causality *must* be true, because it is true *by definition* of its component words. In other words, it is "formally true."

Compare the above to the common but mistaken version of the Law of Causality—"Everything must have a cause"—and note what the logical results would have to be. If it's true that *everything* must have a cause, then *God Himself* would have to have a cause. Then, whatever caused God would have to have a cause. And then, whatever caused God's cause would have to have its own cause, and so on into the past, *ad infinitum*.

This may seem like a trivial distinction, but it is not. The British philosopher Bertrand Russell (1872–1970) thought the Law of Causality said "Everything must have a cause" and reasoned correctly (from this fallacious premise) that God must have a cause, and on and on, as just described. This conclusion caused him to reject Christianity, reject Jesus, reject redemption, reject forgiveness of his sins, and all the rest, as he described in his book *Why I Am Not a Christian*.

Russell apparently didn't have any godly friends who could speak into his life, or if he did, they apparently didn't know enough about logic to show him the error of his premise. Hopefully, he cried out to God for mercy before he died. This kind of situation makes it all the more important to take I Peter 3:15 to heart: ". . .be ready always to give an answer to every man that asketh you a reason of the hope that is in you. . ." The consequences if we cannot answer people's questions can be dire indeed.

It's obvious that anything that brings you to the conclusion that "something caused God" must be wrong, for God *cannot* have a cause; He is the Uncaused Cause of everything else. And that is not merely the "Christian party line"—on the contrary, that is the conclusion to which you are logically *compelled* when you try to explain the universe, assuming you don't violate the Laws of Reason and Rationality in the process. In other words, *logic and reason demand* that there must be an eternal, self-existent, uncaused, transcendent God out there, Who created everything else.

Now of course, just because logic and rationality demand it, doesn't mean that you have to believe it; it simply means that you retreat into the illogical and irrational in order to avoid acknowledging the logical and rational conclusion that Someone has to be behind everything in the universe.

One more thing: the Law of Causality says only that every effect *has* a cause; it says nothing about whether we actually *know* what that cause is. In many cases, things happen and we don't know the cause of them. But the fact that we don't *know* the cause doesn't mean that there *isn't* one. The Scottish philosopher David Hume (1711–1776) wrote extensively on causality (among other things), and some people consider him to have "abolished" causality. He did nothing of the sort; he simply stated that we don't necessarily *know* the cause for a particular effect. He did *not* say that there wasn't one.

So does the Bible support the Law of Causality? It most certainly does. Like the Law of Non-Contradiction, the Bible doesn't label it as such, but it uses it and assumes its validity hundreds, perhaps thousands of times over.

There are three uses of the word "cause" in the Bible:

- The first is similar in meaning to the modern word "case" (as in "legal case") where it refers to a matter that must be decided by a court or arbiter, as in:

    Proverbs 22:22–23: Rob not the poor, because he is poor: neither oppress the afflicted in the gate: [23]For the LORD will plead their **cause,** and spoil the soul of those that spoiled them.

- The second use of the word "cause" in the Bible means "good, justifiable, valid reason", as in:

    Proverbs 3:30: Strive not with a man **without cause,** if he have done thee no harm.

    TEV: Don't argue with others **for no reason** when they have never done you any harm.

The above two usages of "cause" are not relevant to the Law of Causality, so I do not address them here. But the third usage does indeed include the concept of a cause producing an effect, and since that is the concept under discussion, those are the Scriptures I include here. There are hundreds throughout the Bible; here are just a few of the more obvious ones.

At the beginning of the Noah's flood, why did the rain start falling? For no reason? No, it was because God caused it:

> Genesis 7:4: For yet seven days, and **I will cause it to rain** upon the earth forty days and forty nights; and every living substance that I have made will I destroy from off the face of the earth.

Joseph was very fruitful and prosperous when he was in Egypt; was there a reason that this happened? Of course there was: the Law of Causality requires it. And in this case we know what the cause of his fruitfulness was:

> Genesis 41:52: And the name of the second [son] called he Ephraim: For **God hath caused me to be fruitful** in the land of my affliction.

When Joseph wanted to reveal to his brothers just who he was, there were other people in the room as well. He knew that they would stay there unless something caused them to leave. So:

> Genesis 45:1: Then Joseph could not refrain himself before all them that stood by him; and he cried, **Cause every man to go out from me.** And there stood no man with him, while Joseph made himself known unto his brethren.

When God was talking to Moses out of the burning bush, right after Moses had complained that he wasn't a good speaker, God asked him a very significant question:

> Exodus 4:11a: And the LORD said unto him, Who hath made man's mouth? or who maketh the dumb, or deaf, or the seeing, or the blind?

The obvious implication is that someone had to make these things. If they existed, and were not eternal, *there had to be a cause.* And then God answers His own question:

Exodus 4:11b: Have not I the LORD?

The Bible says that God raises up rulers and He brings them down (Nehemiah 13:26, Daniel 2:21, 4:32, 5:21, John 19:11, etc.) So why did God raise up Pharaoh to be king of Egypt, when surely He knew that Pharaoh would defy Him over and over again? Because, as I've said for decades, "When you decide to reject the Right Answer, it doesn't much matter which *wrong* answer you choose." I had been saying this statement for decades before I discovered that William Law, and eighteenth-century Anglican priest, had said the same thing: "If you have not chosen the Kingdom of God first, it will in the end make no difference what you have chosen instead."

God knew what kind of person Pharaoh was, and although God didn't *force* Pharaoh to reject Him, God apparently knew he would, so therefore God arranged the situation so that His promise to Abraham in Genesis 12:3 would be fulfilled, and God's Name would be exalted:

> Exodus 9:13–16: And the LORD said unto Moses, Rise up early in the morning, and stand before Pharaoh, and say unto him, Thus saith the LORD God of the Hebrews, Let my people go, that they may serve me. [14]For I will at this time send all my plagues upon thine heart. . . [16]And in very deed **for this cause have I raised thee up**, for to shew in thee my power; and that my name may be declared throughout all the earth.

As an aside, notice that this Scripture says God raised up Pharaoh in order to show Himself strong, but it does *not* say that He raised up Pharaoh in order to show Himself strong *through Egypt's destruction*. Whether Egypt was destroyed or not depended on whether Pharaoh cooperated with God or not. [Author's note: One of those choices is much wiser than the other.] See "Pharaoh's Example" for a much more thorough treatment of this topic.

One of the plainest of Scriptures dealing with Causality is in Proverbs, where it says that curses only come when there is an actual cause; they don't just randomly pop up for no reason. Again, if a curse comes, we may not *know* what the cause is, but there definitely is one, so we should find out what it is and close that door.

> Proverbs 26:2: As the bird by wandering, as the swallow by flying, so **the curse causeless shall not come.**
>
> ASV: As the sparrow in her wandering, as the swallow in her flying, So **the curse that is causeless alighteth not.**
>
> JUB: As the sparrow in its wandering, as the swallow in its flight, so **the curse causeless shall never come.**
>
> NET: Like a fluttering bird or like a flying swallow, so **a curse without cause does not come to rest.**
>
> VOICE: Like a bird that flits and flutters or a swallow in mid-flight, so **a curse that lacks cause will never come to light.**
>
> WYC: . . .(Like a bird flying over to high places, and like a sparrow going into uncertainty; so **cursing brought forth without a reasonable cause, shall simply go over someone, and not touch them.**)

God tells Ezekiel about some of the judgments He is going to send upon Israel and ends His statements with:

> Ezekiel 14:23 (NLT): When you meet them and see their behavior, you will understand that **these things are not being done to Israel without cause.** I, the Sovereign LORD, have spoken!

When Nicodemus came to talk to Jesus, he and the other Pharisees acknowledged there had to be a cause for Jesus' miracle-working power. That cause was simply that God was with Him:

> John 3:1–2: There was a man of the Pharisees, named Nicodemus, a ruler of the Jews: ²The same came to Jesus by night, and said unto him, Rabbi, **we know that thou art a teacher come from God: for no man can do these miracles that thou doest, except God be with him.**

> 3:2, EXB: Teacher [Rabbi], we know you are a teacher sent from God, **because** no one can do the miracles [signs] you do unless God is with him.

Later on, the writer of Hebrews says:

> Hebrews 3:4 (NASB): For **every house is built by someone**, but the builder of all things is God.

This verse is talking specifically about how Jesus (the builder) created us (His house), but notice the general principle of which that is a specific example. The specific example here is "Every house is built by someone." What does that mean, in the general sense? It means *everything that is not eternal has a cause.* Every building has a builder. Every creation has a creator. Every sculpture has a sculptor. Every painting has a painter. Every garden has gardener. This is not rocket science: everything that is not eternal—which includes everything in the physical universe, plus angels, demons, and so forth—was created. Therefore, the effect (everything in the universe) was produced (created) by the Cause (God). In other words, the Builder, or Creator, of all things is God.

The Basic Reliability of Sense Perception

The only "gateways" there are from the external world to the mind and consciousness are our physical senses. (Of course, in that statement, we are excluding for the moment God's ability to reveal things directly to our spirits.) There are certain things we can deduce entirely within our minds and with no sensory input from without: that we exist, that we are finite, that we must have been created, that the Creator is not us, that the Creator must be eternal and transcendent, etc. Yes, you can actually, and *reliably*, deduce all those things with absolutely no awareness of the outside world.

But we cannot deduce things like: the grass is green, that other people exist, that the earth revolves around the sun, that the Redeemer's name is Jesus, etc. For a knowledge of those kinds of things, we must get input from the external world through our senses.

Of course, our senses are not infallible: there are things that are too small, too distant, too fast, too obscured, too quiet, too high-pitched, too distorted, too hidden, and so forth, for us to perceive with our senses. The fact that our senses are not infinite in their abilities is not a problem, but we must be able to rely on our senses at least at a basic level, or we could not survive.

Here are some examples:

- You're driving down the street and a small child runs out in front of your car, and you slam on the brakes. Why did you slam on the brakes? To avoid running over the child. Why did you think a child was there? *Because you saw him.*

- You're sitting on the sofa reading the newspaper, and you hear a long honk, a screech of tires, and a loud crash. You run to the door, cell phone already in hand and starting to dial 911 before you even look outside. Why are you considering calling 911? Because of the car accident. But why did you think there was a car accident? *Because you heard it.*

- You're hurrying to get ready for work one morning, because you're running a little behind schedule, so you pop a couple pieces of bread in the toaster, and then run back to the bedroom to make the bed. Then you stop in front of the bathroom mirror to adjust your hair, and suddenly the aroma of smoldering charcoal wafts into the room. Exasperated, you run back to the kitchen and take two slabs of carbon out of the smoking toaster. Why did you run out to the kitchen so fast? Because the toast was burning. Why did you think the toast was burning? *Because you smelled it.*

- Your eight-year-old daughter wants to do something special for your birthday, so she decides to bake you some cookies all by herself. You give her the recipe, set the oven temperature, and go into the other room to read a book. Later, she comes in with a plate of warm cookies, just out of the oven. You thank her, take a bite, and almost gag. She sees your facial expression and says, "What's wrong, Mommy?" You struggle to swallow, and then ask, "Did you follow the recipe?"

"Yes, and I used the right amounts and everything!" Then you ask, "Where did you get the sugar? Was it in a dark blue, round cardboard container labeled 'Morton'?" Wide-eyed, she nods. Why did you think she used salt instead of sugar? *Because you tasted it.*

- You run a bath after a hard day's work, setting the faucets to the positions you always do. When the tub is sufficiently full, you step in, and immediately snatch your foot out with a gasp, watching a whole crop of goose bumps form all over your body. You turn on the hot-water tap full blast, and it still comes out cold. You shake your head and mutter, "The pilot light on the water heater went out again." Why did you think that? Because the water that was supposed to be hot was cold. How did you know? *Because you felt it.*

In all of the examples above, you wouldn't question what you sensed; you would assume—and rightly so—that what you sensed communicated the real state of affairs. For example, when the child runs out in front of your moving car, you wouldn't think, "Hmm. I'm perceiving a child running out in front of my car. But it could be a deception; maybe my eyes are playing tricks on me. Or maybe my eyes are working fine, but my mind is just hallucinating the image of a child. Maybe. . ." Thud.

Of course not. In all the scenarios above, if you don't assume at least a basic reliability of sense perception, it will soon be fatal to you or to someone else, as alluded to in the previous, somewhat grisly paragraph.

And as you might expect by now, the Bible too, silently assumes, tacitly acknowledges, and unobtrusively endorses the basic reliability of sense perception. Shortly after Adam and Eve had sinned, God was looking for them. How did they know that He was there, and that He was looking for them? They *heard* Him:

> Genesis 3:8–10: And **they heard the voice of the LORD God** walking in the garden in the cool of the day: and Adam and his wife hid themselves from the presence of the LORD God amongst the trees of the garden. ⁹And **the LORD God called unto Adam,** and said unto him, Where art thou? ¹⁰And he said, **I heard thy voice** in the garden, and I was afraid, because I was naked; and I hid myself.

In the following verse, God tells the Israelites to teach their children and grandchildren about all the wonderful deeds He had done. And note that God considers the fact that they had *seen* these deeds to be sufficient proof that they had indeed happened, the deeds were true, they were factual, they were beyond question:

> Deuteronomy 4:9: Only take heed to thyself, and keep thy soul diligently, lest thou forget the things **which thine eyes have seen,** and lest they depart from thy heart all the days of thy life: but teach them thy sons, and thy sons' sons. . .

In the verse below, Moses is talking to the children of Israel and recounting the story of their wanderings in the wilderness, and of all the signs and wonders God performed in caring for them, providing for them, and protecting them. Note what Moses says here: basically, "You *know* what I'm saying is true: *you saw it with your own eyes.*"

> Deuteronomy 10:21: He is thy praise, and he is thy God, that hath done for thee these great and terrible things, **which thine eyes have seen.**

The Queen of Sheba had heard stories about the wisdom of Solomon. They were enough to pique her curiosity, but not enough to convince her, because the stories were *so* amazing. So she went to visit him herself:

> II Chronicles 9:1–6 (TEV): The queen of Sheba heard of King Solomon's fame, and she traveled to Jerusalem to test him with difficult questions. She brought with her a large group of attendants, as well as camels loaded with spices, jewels, and a large amount of gold. When she and Solomon met, she asked him all the questions that she could think of. ²He answered them all; there was nothing too difficult for him to explain. ³The queen of Sheba heard Solomon's wisdom and saw the palace he had built. ⁴She saw the food that was served at his table, the living quarters for his officials, the organization of his palace staff and the uniforms they wore, the clothing of the servants who waited on him at feasts, and the sacrifices he offered in the Temple. It left her breathless and amazed. ⁵She said to the king, "What I heard in my own country about you and your wisdom is true! **⁶I did not believe what they told me until I came and saw for myself.** I had not heard of even half your wisdom. You are even wiser than people say."

Again, the Queen of Sheba had an intuitive and correct realization that she could check the reliability of the stories about Solomon and his kingdom if she saw them herself.

The Apostle John, in his first epistle, describes Jesus as the Word of Life, the Son of God, and the source of eternal life. How did he and the other disciples know this teaching was true? Because they *saw* Him heal the sick, they *heard* Him speak and the storm stopped; the Redeemer was a real flesh-and-blood person that they could *touch and feel:*

> I John 1:1–3 (NIV): That which was from the beginning, which **we have heard,** which **we have seen with our eyes,** which **we have looked at** and **our hands have touched**—this we proclaim concerning the Word of life. ²The life appeared; **we have seen it** and testify to it, and we proclaim to you the eternal life, which was with the Father and has appeared to us. ³We proclaim to you what **we have seen and heard,** so that you also may have fellowship with us. And our fellowship is with the Father and with his Son, Jesus Christ.

But Wait a Minute. . .

At this point, the more astute readers may have asked the question, "But if sense perception is so important and reliable, doesn't that negate the need for faith?" As the Queen of Sheba stated above, "I did not believe what they told me until I came and saw for myself." Basically, "Seeing is believing." Doesn't that concept conflict with statements like the following?

> Hebrews 11:1, 6 (NIV): Now **faith is being sure** of what we hope for and certain **of what we do not see.** . . . . ⁶And **without faith it is impossible to please God,** because anyone who comes to him must believe that he exists and that he rewards those who earnestly seek him.

That is a good question, and the answer is No, it does not. Here's why.

As mentioned above, we need to acknowledge the reality of the *basic* reliability of sense perception. But—also as mentioned above—some potentially perceptible stimuli are too quiet, too dim, too small, too distant, so forth. Add to that the potential for misunderstanding some sensory input; the classic example is Plato's bent oar: When you look at an oar on dry land, it may look straight. But submerge half its length in water, and it looks bent because of the refraction of light through water. So no one is denying that our senses can be fooled at times.

Plus, the physical senses pertain almost exclusively to the *physical* world; the exceptions being where the intensity of activity in the spiritual world is great enough that it "leaks" into the physical world, and can be perceived with the physical senses, as in these examples:

- Moses' face glowing with the glory of God after spending almost six weeks in His presence (Exodus 34:29–35).
- The pillar of cloud by day and the pillar of fire by night, leading the Israelites through the wilderness (Exodus 13:21–22).

- Ornan and David both see the angel of judgment the Lord sent because David had commanded a census of Israel (I Chronicles 21:20, 30).
- The cloud of glory that filled Solomon's Temple so thickly the priests couldn't even stand up (II Chronicles 5:14).
- At Jesus' baptism, the heavens opened, the Holy Spirit, in the form of a dove, descended, and the Father spoke (Matthew 3:16–17).
- Shortly before His crucifixion, Jesus prayed, and God answered audibly. Bystanders heard God's voice, but thought it was thunder, while others thought it was an angel (John 12:29–30).
- When Jesus temporarily blinded Saul of Tarsus and spoke to him, all his companions heard Jesus' voice, but did not see anyone (Acts 9:7).

And there are other Scriptural examples also, where spiritual intensity leaks into the physical realm sufficiently to be perceived by the physical senses. Most of the time, though, when people see things in the spiritual realm, it's because God opens their eyes to see the spiritual realm, rather than the spiritual realm leaking into the physical.

The fact that our physical senses relatively rarely see into the spiritual realm doesn't prohibit the existence, or minimize the importance, of the spiritual world: God, heaven, angels, living creatures, seraphim, and so forth, as well as the destructive elements: Satan, demons, and hell. The physical world, and the physical senses with which we perceive it, are not evil—God created them—but we must not lose sight of the existence and superiority of the spiritual world. That is God's domain (John 4:24), and it is that realm about which we are required to have faith first, *before* seeing the manifestation (Hebrews 11:1, 8–10).

The Analogical Use of Language

The "analogical use of language" sounds very grandiose and technical, but it is not; that is a fancy name for something people do every day in normal speech without even realizing it. Basically, it means that the definition of some words adjusts in proportion to the topic under discussion. Here's an example.

What does the word "good" mean? If you're talking about a dog, a "good dog" is one who doesn't chew your belongings to pieces, doesn't bite people, and is housebroken. If you're talking about a man, a "good man" is one who, for example, serves God to the best of his ability, is faithful to his wife, loving to his kids, is an upstanding citizen in the community, and so forth. And if you're talking about God, "good" takes on even more noble meanings: benevolent, providential, loving, wise, just, holy, and so forth.

Each kind of being mentioned above is "good" in its own domain, but because the kind of being under discussion varies, so does the meaning of the word "good." It varies in a proportional, or an *analogous,* manner. Using the wrong sense for the being under discussion could be insulting or just plain humorous; for example, saying that your neighbor Bob is a good man because he doesn't chew your belongings to pieces, he doesn't bite people, and is housebroken. (Hopefully Bob has a sense of humor if you tell him that.)

So "analogous" or "analogical" means comparable in certain respects, and the analogy is usually used in a way that clarifies the nature of one of the things being compared. In other words, the known is extrapolated into the unknown.

We are familiar with "good dogs" and "good men," so if we extrapolate the concept of "good" as far as we can imagine, we are just about to nudge the first atom in the process of scratching the surface of how good God is. The same process applies to the words "holy," "loving," "faithful," "true," and a host of other words that describe God's character and essence.

"Wholly Other?"

I have heard God described as "wholly other" than us. This concept means, in other words, that He is "completely different" than us, "entirely disparate" from us, or "utterly unlike" us. Is this concept accurate? I think not, because of what this phrase means, as contrasted with what the Bible says.

Think about what the phrase "wholly other" and its synonymous phrases mean. If God actually were *wholly* other, that means that would be *no* commonality between us at all. Which means there would be no way to communicate with God, or for Him to communicate with us. After all, if He were *wholly* other, we would have no language in common, no words in common, no gestures in common, no symbols in common, no concepts in common, no emotions in common, no *essence* in common. "Wholly other" technically means "so unlike that there is no basis for comparison."

A moment's reflection should bring to mind many Scriptures that invalidates the "wholly other" idea; below are just a few.

God can't be "wholly other" than us because we have the same image and the same likeness as Him:

> Genesis 1:26–27: And God said, Let us make **man in our image, after our likeness.** . . . ²⁷So **God created man in his own image, in the image of God created he him;** male and female created he them.
>
> v. 26a, NLT: Then God said, "**Let us make human beings** in our image, **to be like us.**"

As you can see, when God created us in His "likeness," that is the same as saying that He created us to be "like" Him. Already, in the very first chapter of Genesis, the idea of God being wholly other than us is blown out of the water, because to be "wholly other" is to be "utterly unlike." But He created us to be like Him!

Continuing on: Jesus can't be "wholly other" than us because we can do the same miracles He did:

> John 14:12 (TEV): I am telling you the truth: **those who believe in me will do what I do**—yes, they will do even greater things, because I am going to the Father.

Jesus can't be "wholly other" than us because we received the same words from God that He did. And the fact that we can "accept" them and "know with certainty" what they mean shows that we understand the same kinds of words, the same kinds of symbols (think about the parables), and the same kinds of concepts:

> John 17:8 (NIV): For **I gave them the words you gave me** and they accepted them. They knew with certainty that I came from you, and they believed that you sent me.

Jesus can't be "wholly other" than us because we are both of another world:

> John 17:14, 16 (NIV): I have given them your word and the world has hated them, for **they are not of the world any more than I am of the world.** . . . ¹⁶**They are not of the world, even as I am not of it.**

Jesus can't be "wholly other" than us because we have the same assignment while on this earth:

> John 17:18 (NIV): **As you sent me into the world, I have sent them into the world.**
>
> John 20:21 (WEB): Jesus therefore said to them again, "Peace be to you. **As the Father has sent me, even so I send you.**"

Jesus can't be "wholly other" than us because we have both been sanctified:

> John 17:19 (NIV): For them **I sanctify myself, that they too may be truly sanctified.**

Jesus can't be "wholly other" than us because we can experience oneness with each other in the same way that God the Father and Jesus the Son experience oneness:

> John 17:20–21 (NIV): My prayer is not for them alone. I pray also for those who will believe in me through their message, [21]that **all of them may be one, Father, just as you are in me and I am in you.** May they also be in us so that the world may believe that you have sent me.

Jesus can't be "wholly other" than us because we have been given the same glory, and here too is a restatement of the Oneness similarity noted above:

> John 17:22 (NIV): **I have given them the glory that you gave me,** that **they may be one as we are one.** . .

Jesus can't be "wholly other" than us because we have the same Father. And, the same God:

> John 20:17: Jesus saith unto her, Touch me not; for I am not yet ascended to my Father: but go to my brethren, and say unto them, I ascend unto **my Father, and your Father;** and to **my God, and your God.**

The Lord can't be "wholly other" than us because we have the same Spirit:

> I Corinthians 6:17: But he that is joined unto the Lord is **one spirit.**

Jesus can't be "wholly other" than us because we are commanded to have the same behavior as Him:

> I Peter 1:15 (NIV): But just as **he who called you is holy, so be holy** in all you do. . .

. . .and the list goes on and on. So it is clear that the Bible completely demolishes the "wholly other" concept.

Now in all fairness, the proponents of the "wholly other" concept of God probably *are* promoting a valid concept, but using the phrase "wholly other" to label it or describe it is *severely* misleading and is a gross misuse of the meanings of the words.

When I have heard people use the phrase "wholly other," the context of their words—the gist of their statements—is usually that God is infinitely beyond us in some attribute or another. And that is true: we are to be good, but

God is infinitely more good; we are to be merciful, but God is infinitely more merciful; we are to be holy, but God is infinitely more holy; we are to be loving, but God is infinitely more loving; we are to be truthful, but God is infinitely more truthful; we are to be faithful, but God is infinitely more faithful. . . This list, too, goes on for a long time.

This latter concept—God's unimaginably limitless essence and blessings—is described well by Paul:

> Ephesians 3:20–21 (AMP): Now to Him Who, by (in consequence of) the [action of His] power that is at work within us, is able to [carry out His purpose and] **do superabundantly, far over and above all that we [dare] ask or think [infinitely beyond our highest prayers, desires, thoughts, hopes, or dreams]**— ²¹To Him be glory in the church and in Christ Jesus throughout all generations forever and ever. Amen (so be it).

But to think that the phrase "wholly other" describes God's infinitude and eternality is a corruption of the word meanings; and especially so, since we saw the multitudes of Scriptures above that show just a few of the many things we have in common with God. He is indeed infinite in every good attribute. But He is certainly *not* "wholly other." And for that very reason, the analogical use of language can be used to impart understanding about God, and Jesus did just that in every parable He told.

Logic Gets a Bad Rap

Many people seem to think that Logic and God are opposed to each other; that they are on opposite sides. You hear this in sermons, in section headings of books, and even in book titles. But Logic and God are not on opposing sides; far from it. As noted above, logic is nothing more than organized truth, and Jesus said He *is* truth.

Oftentimes, the problems that people describe as being the fault of logic are best described by the acronym "GIGO," which stands for "Garbage In, Garbage Out." This acronym comes from the early days of computer science when it became common knowledge that a computer program can be perfectly accurate and correct, and still turn out wrong answers because the information that was fed into it was wrong.

That is invariably the case when people blame logic for wrong actions, or consider it to be incompatible with God. The problem is that the logic, which may have been perfectly valid, was given incomplete, biased, or downright wrong information to work with. For example, in one book I'm currently reading is a section heading called "Faith Versus Logic." In this section are numerous examples where someone came to wrong conclusions, or did foolish or sinful actions "because they used logic." But upon a moment's reflection, we see that logic wasn't the problem at all. The problem was that the person failed to take God into account, and was making his decisions entirely on human abilities, human resources, and human knowledge. *Of course* you'll arrive at ridiculous conclusions if you leave God out of the picture; the logic was perfectly valid, but the input was foolish, incomplete, and/or wrong, because God's input was not considered. So naturally you'd come to unreliable conclusions.

Another example of this is James Dobson's book *When God Doesn't Make Sense.* The implication from the book title is that sometimes God doesn't make sense; that is, sometimes God is illogical, or sometimes God even makes mistakes. Now of course, that was not what Dobson meant by that title. We all know what he meant: he was discussing how to respond when God doesn't make sense *to us,* because our perception of a person or a situation is biased, incomplete, and/or entirely mistaken. But it would have been rather cumbersome to entitle the book *When God Doesn't Make Sense To Us Because Our Perception of a Person or Situation is Biased, Incomplete, and/or Entirely Mistaken.*

So again, we need to realize that God is not opposed to logic; it is part of His very nature. We simply need to put God's point of view, His character, His goodness, His power, and His will into the picture, and then we will see that logic is perfectly reliable when it has the right information to work with.

So how do we put "God's point of view" and the rest of the items just mentioned into the picture, in the context of determining how to live the Christian life? Simply get our information—our doctrinal source material—from the Bible, as opposed to people's opinions, rumors, popular media, and so forth. Any information we receive from sermons we hear or books we read should be well-substantiated by Scriptures taken in context. And it is *our* responsibility to examine it Scripturally and make a sound determination (John 7:24 [AMP], Acts 17:11, I Thessalonians 5:21).

Where Do We Go From Here?

Now that we've seen the most basic laws of logic—the most foundational principles for all rational thought—let's use them to learn from the Bible. Since God presumes them, acknowledges them, tacitly endorses them, and uses them throughout His Word, we can see they are valid, and they are essential tools for understanding what He says to us.

In the context of this book, we'll use the Principles of Reason to analyze the validity of the main points of Reformed theology: the Five Points of Calvinism, as well as the doctrine of Original Sin and the Reformed understanding of the sovereignty of God. So, fasten your seat belt and put your thinking cap on. . .

Chapter 3:

We Have Free Will, and We *Can* Choose God

The first concept I'll discuss in detail is that of free will, and whether or not the Bible supports the notion. In my studies, I have concluded that the Bible does indeed support the notion of free will, in the sense of "every human has the ability to accept or reject God's offer of redemption without someone else deciding for him." Thoughtfully and prayerfully read the following chapters, check the Bible references, and come to a cumulative conclusion on the matter. In other words, don't base your entire conclusion on just a single, or a few, Scriptures, since there are *many* that address this topic. Rather, after reading *all* the Scriptural passages referenced in this book, decide for yourself what is the overall leaning of the Bible on this topic.

Is God Just?

The very question posed in the section heading above is sure to ruffle some feathers. "*Of course* God is just!" some will say, "Just look at the Bible!"

And they're correct, of course, as is confirmed by Scriptures such as these:

Deuteronomy 32:4: He is the Rock, his work is perfect: for all his ways are judgment: a God of truth and without iniquity, **just and right is he.**

Isaiah 45:21: Tell ye, and bring them near; yea, let them take counsel together: who hath declared this from ancient time? who hath told it

FREE TO CHOOSE?

from that time? have not I the LORD? and there is no God else beside me; **a just God** and a Saviour; there is none beside me.

Zephaniah 3:5: **The just LORD is in the midst** thereof; he will not do iniquity: every morning doth he bring his judgment to light, he faileth not; but the unjust knoweth no shame.

Zechariah 9:9: Rejoice greatly, O daughter of Zion; shout, O daughter of Jerusalem: behold, **thy King cometh unto thee: he is just,** and having salvation; lowly, and riding upon an ass, and upon a colt the foal of an ass.

Acts 3:14: But ye denied the **Holy One and the Just,** and desired a murderer to be granted unto you. . .

Revelation 15:3: And they sing the song of Moses the servant of God, and the song of the Lamb, saying, Great and marvellous are thy works, Lord God Almighty; **just and true are thy ways,** thou King of saints.

Okay, so without a doubt, God is just. Now hold that thought, and let's look at another Scriptural truth. In many places, God commands us (as in "all people") to obey Him:

Deuteronomy 13:4: Ye shall walk after the LORD your God, and fear him, and keep his commandments, and **obey his voice**, and ye shall serve him, and cleave unto him.

Deuteronomy 30:8–14 (NIV): **You will again obey the Lord and follow *all* his commands** I am giving you today. ⁹Then the Lord your God will make you most prosperous in all the work of your hands and in the fruit of your womb, the young of your livestock and the crops of your land. The Lord will again delight in you and make you prosperous, just as he delighted in your fathers, ¹⁰**if you obey the Lord your God and keep his commands and decrees** that are written in this Book of the Law and turn to the Lord your God with all your heart and with all your soul. ¹¹Now **what I am commanding you today is not too difficult for you or beyond your reach.** ¹²It is not up in heaven, so that you have to ask, "Who will ascend into heaven to get it and proclaim it to us so we may obey it?" ¹³Nor is it beyond the sea, so that you have to ask, "Who will cross the sea to get it and proclaim it to us so we may obey it?" ¹⁴No, **the word is very near you; it is in your mouth and in your heart so you may obey it.**

Jeremiah 7:23: But this thing commanded I them, saying, **Obey my voice**, and I will be your God, and ye shall be my people: and walk ye in all the ways that I have commanded you, that it may be well unto you.

Chapter 3: We Have a Free Will, and We Can Choose God

Jeremiah 11:4: Which I commanded your fathers in the day that I brought them forth out of the land of Egypt, from the iron furnace, saying, **Obey my voice**, and do them, according to all which I command you: so shall ye be my people, and I will be your God. . .

Jeremiah 38:20b: **Obey, I beseech thee, the voice of the Lord**, which I speak unto thee: so it shall be well unto thee, and thy soul shall live.

John 14:15: If ye love me, **keep my commandments.**

John 14:21: He that **hath my commandments, and keepeth them,** he it is that loveth me: and he that loveth me shall be loved of my Father, and I will love him, and will manifest myself to him.

John 14:23: Jesus answered and said unto him, **If a man love me, he will keep my words:** and my Father will love him, and we will come unto him, and make our abode with him.

John 15:14: Ye are my friends, **if ye do whatsoever I command you.**

Acts 17:30–31: And the times of this ignorance God winked at; but now **commandeth all men every where to repent:** [31]Because he hath appointed a day, in the which he will judge the world in righteousness by that man whom he hath ordained; whereof he hath given assurance unto all men, in that he hath raised him from the dead. . .

I Corinthians 7:19: Circumcision is nothing, and uncircumcision is nothing, but **the keeping of the commandments** of God.

I John 5:2–3: By this we know that we love the children of God, when we love God, and **keep his commandments.** [3]For this is the love of God, that **we keep his commandments:** and his commandments are not grievous.

And here is where God's justice becomes relevant to our discussion. We've seen that God commands us to obey Him. *Would God be just if He commanded us to do something that we actually couldn't do?* Especially if the results of unrepentant disobedience is eternal suffering; how could God be just if we were doomed to suffer for disobeying commands we are actually incapable of obeying?

Let me give you an example. When our son Matthew was born, suppose I waited until he was a whole week old, and then told him to go mow the lawn. Would he do it? No. Why? Because he was being rebellious? Of course not; a one-week-old baby doesn't have the understanding to know what a lawn is and what mowing entails, but even more importantly, he doesn't have the physical ability—size, balance, strength, etc.—to push a lawn mower around.

Now here's the crux of the matter: Would I, as a father, have been acting justly to punish Matthew for not mowing the lawn? After all, I clearly told him to, and he didn't do it. That's disobedience, right? Punishment is in order, right? Obviously not, and I would *not* have been acting justly to punish him for not doing what he had no ability to do. If I were a loving father, I would not command him to do something he actually had no ability to do. And if I were a loving father, I *certainly* wouldn't punish him for not doing what he had no ability to do.

But is that even appropriate? To think God should act a certain way just because I do? In certain cases, yes. When Jesus was talking about how a good father behaves, he said:

> Matthew 7:9–12 (NIV) Which of you, if his son asks for bread, will give him a stone? [10]Or if he asks for a fish, will give him a snake? [11]If you, then, though you are evil, know how to give good gifts to your children, **how much more will your Father in heaven give good gifts to those who ask him!** [12]So in everything, do to others what you would have them do to you, for this sums up the Law and the Prophets.

So Jesus basically said, "If you earthly fathers know how to be nice to your kids, don't you think God knows even better how to be nice to you?" And notice that God's "knowing better" did not change the goodness of the human fathers' gifts to their kids (which Jesus acknowledges) into badness when God gives things to His kids.

I find it fascinating that Jesus concludes this section of "If you, being evil... *how much more*" with "do to others what you would have them do to you." Does God obey that Golden Rule? Of course. Would *you* like to be punished for not doing something you had no ability to do?

In the same way I wouldn't be just in commanding one-week-old Matthew to mow the lawn, God wouldn't be just if He commanded us to do something we actually couldn't do, and *especially* so if we ended up suffering for it. Therefore, we must conclude that we indeed *can* choose to obey Him when he commands us to do something. And this is confirmed in Deuteronomy 30, quoted above, where God bluntly states that obeying *all* His commands is "not too difficult for you or beyond your reach."

Here, the astute reader will think of Jesus' commands to His disciples (and therefore by extension, all of us) to "Heal the sick, cleanse the lepers, raise the dead, cast out devils" (Matthew 10:8). We in ourselves can't possibly do that

(John 15:5); does that fact indicate that God is unjust? Good question, but the answer is no, and the difference between this situation and the one above is that we have the ability to choose to obey Him, and when we submit to Him and obey Him in things He has commanded, He Himself supplies the raw power needed. In modern times, this is often expressed as, "We provide the *availability*, and God provides the *ability*." That is, we choose to obey Him, but He makes it happen.

Paul reinforces this in his second letter to the Corinthians:

II Corinthians 3:5 (CEV): We don't have the right to claim that we have done anything on our own. **God gives us what it takes to do all that we do.**

II Corinthians 4:7 (ERV): We have this treasure from God, but we are only like clay jars that hold the treasure. This is to show that **the amazing power we have is from God, not from us.**

So we see that if we *can't* choose to obey Him—because He has already chosen for us—but we still suffer the consequences of disobedience, that particular combination of circumstances is what would (if God actually behaved that way) show Him to be unjust. But since He is *not* unjust, we can confidently conclude that we must be able to choose to obey Him. And the obvious best response to the realization that we *can* choose to obey Him, is to actually do so. Failure to do so would be the worst possible choice a human being could make.

Does God Waste Words?

A topic that is related to, but not identical with the previous one, is whether God "wastes" words. Saying it another way, does God say words that are deceptive, misleading, or even meaningless? I think most Christians would say that He does not; especially the first two, because of Titus 1:2, mentioned earlier.

But how about the third one? Might God ever say something that is meaningless, pointless, vanity? I don't think so, but let's look at some Scriptures that will help us decide:

Deuteronomy 11:26–28: Behold, I set before you this day a blessing and a curse; ²⁷**A blessing, if ye obey** the commandments of the LORD your God, which I command you this day: ²⁸And **a curse, if ye will not obey** the commandments of the LORD your God, but turn aside out of the way which I command you this day, to go after other gods, which ye have not known.

Deuteronomy 28:1–3, 15–16: And it shall come to pass, **if thou shalt hearken diligently unto the voice of the Lord thy God**, to observe and to do all his commandments which I command thee this day, that the Lord thy God will set thee on high above all nations of the earth: ²And **all these blessings shall come on thee, and overtake thee**, if thou shalt hearken unto the voice of the Lord thy God. ³Blessed shalt thou be in the city, and blessed shalt thou be in the field. . . ¹⁵But it shall come to pass, **if thou wilt not hearken unto the voice of the Lord thy God**, to observe to do all his commandments and his statutes which I command thee this day; that **all these curses shall come upon thee, and overtake thee:** ¹⁶Cursed shalt thou be in the city, and cursed shalt thou be in the field. . .

Deuteronomy 30:19 (TEV): **I am now giving you the choice** between life and death, between God's blessing and God's curse, and **I call heaven and earth to witness the choice you make. Choose life.**

Joshua 24:15 (NIV): But if serving the Lord seems undesirable to you, then **choose for yourselves this day whom you will serve**, whether the gods your forefathers served beyond the River, or the gods of the Amorites, in whose land you are living. **But as for me and my household, we will serve the Lord.** . .

I Samuel 12:14–15: **If ye will fear the Lord, and serve him, and obey his voice**, and not rebel against the commandment of the Lord, **then shall both ye and also the king that reigneth over you continue following the Lord your God:** ¹⁵But **if ye will not obey the voice of the Lord**, but rebel against the commandment of the Lord, **then shall the hand of the Lord be against you**, as it was against your fathers.

I Kings 18:21a (NIV): Elijah went before the people and said, "How long will you waver between two opinions? **If the Lord is God, follow him; but if Baal is God, follow him.**"

Proverbs 1:28–32a: Then shall they call upon me, but I [Wisdom] will not answer; they shall seek me early, but they shall not find me: ²⁹For that **they hated knowledge, and did not choose the fear of the Lord:** ³⁰They would none of my counsel: they despised all my reproof. ³¹Therefore shall they eat of the fruit of **their own way**, and be filled with **their own devices.** ³²For the turning away of the simple shall slay them. . .

Proverbs 3:31: Envy thou not the oppressor, and **choose none of his ways.**

Isaiah 56:4–5 (NIV): For this is what the LORD says: "To the eunuchs who keep my Sabbaths, **who choose what pleases me and hold fast to my covenant**— [5]to them I will give within my temple and its walls a memorial and a name better than sons and daughters; I will give them an everlasting name that will not be cut off."

Isaiah 65:12 (NIV): I will destine you for the sword, and you will all bend down for the slaughter; for I called but you did not answer, I spoke but you did not listen. You did evil in my sight and **chose what displeases me**.

Isaiah 66:4 (NIV): . . .so I [God] also will choose harsh treatment for them and will bring upon them what they dread. For when I called, no one answered, when I spoke, no one listened. **They did evil in my sight and chose what displeases me.**

Jeremiah 21:8 (TEV): Then the Lord told me to say to the people, "Listen! **I, the Lord, am giving you a choice between the way that leads to life and the way that leads to death.**"

Hebrews 11:24–26 (NIV): By faith Moses, when he had grown up, refused to be known as the son of Pharaoh's daughter. [25]**He chose to be mistreated along with the people of God rather than to enjoy the pleasures of sin for a short time.** [26]He regarded disgrace for the sake of Christ as of greater value than the treasures of Egypt, because he was looking ahead to his reward.

In several of the passages above, God gives, along with the command, a warning to motivate us to obey Him. After all, nobody *wants* curses, sickness, failure, poverty, sorrow, and such in their lives, so God's warnings are to keep us away from that—or *that* away from *us*. And here's my point: these commands that God gives us are completely pointless if we don't have the ability to choose our response to His commands. Why bother giving a warning if it can't be heeded?

And in addition to being pointless, meaningless, and vanity, it is certainly misleading as well. Since we know God is not those things (see Scriptures above), we are compelled to conclude that we *do*, in fact, have the ability to choose our response to Him. There will be consequences either way—desirable if we choose to follow Him, and undesirable if we choose to rebel against Him, but nonetheless we can choose either way.

Not only that, but in Deuteronomy 30:19, Joshua 24:15, I Kings 18:21, and Proverbs 3:31, all quoted above, God *commands* us to choose. If we still claim that we do not have the free will to choose, we revert to the situation described in the previous section: God is unjust because He commands us to do something we cannot actually do.

Here is another way of looking at this concept. As we saw in the Scriptures above as well as the one below, many of God's blessings are contingent upon our obedience:

> Exodus 19:5–6: Now therefore, **if** ye will obey my voice indeed, **and** keep my covenant, **then** ye shall be a peculiar treasure unto me above all people: for all the earth is mine: And ye shall be unto me a kingdom of priests, and an holy nation. These are the words which thou shalt speak unto the children of Israel.

Note the logical progression here; it's almost algorithmic in its logical presentation. Converting into a computer pseudo-code is easy:

```
IF (YeWillObey AND KeepMyCovenant) THEN {
   Ye =   PeculiarTreasure + KingdomOfPriests +
          HolyNation;
}
```

Here's the point: Why would God say "*If* you do this" then certain things will happen, if we have no choice in the matter? That would be very misleading of Him to do that. And keep in mind that God is referring here to selecting one of only two alternatives: serving Him or not.

A Theological Discussion

In this chapter, which discusses whether or not we actually have a free will, let's do a little thought experiment. Consider this scenario: Two people are discussing theology, and one says, "Free will does not exist." If that is indeed true, he had no choice but to say that because he couldn't choose, in himself, to do so—God irresistibly caused him to make that statement.

But then his friend says, "Free will does indeed exist." If free will did not, in fact, exist, then this second speaker too would have had no choice but to say what he said—God would have irresistibly caused him to make that statement. Which means that God would have caused him to say something He knew to be untrue; that is, to speak a lie.

But lying is a sin, as plainly shown by the Scriptures below, and a plethora of others:

> Exodus 16:20 (TLB): You must not lie.
>
> CEV: Do not tell lies about others.
>
> Psalm 5:6a (AMPC): You will destroy those who speak lies. . .

CEV: You destroy every liar. . .

Proverbs 6:16–19 (NASB): There are six things which the Lord hates, Yes, seven which are an abomination to Him: ¹⁷Haughty eyes, **a lying tongue,** and hands that shed innocent blood, ¹⁸a heart that devises wicked plans, feet that run rapidly to evil, ¹⁹**a false witness who utters lies,** and one who spreads strife among brothers.

So lying is clearly a sin. Which means that if free will does not exist, but someone says it does exist (like I am saying now), God is irresistibly causing me to sin. But we know that God does not *cause* us to sin; in fact, He doesn't even *tempt* us to sin:

James 1:13 (NASB): Let no one say when he is tempted, "I am being tempted by God"; for God cannot be tempted by evil, and **He Himself does not tempt anyone.**

Are we willing to claim that God causes people to sin? Since I am claiming in this book that free will *does* exist, if you believe otherwise, you are unavoidably driven to the conclusion that God is causing me to make false statements; that He is causing me to lie about Him, and I cannot do otherwise. If it's all the same to you, I would rather not make such a claim.

Here is a perfect example of *reductio ad absurdum:* Free will *must* exist, because if it doesn't, logic inexorably compels us to an absurd conclusion: that God causes some people to sin.

"Free Will Isn't Even Mentioned in the Bible!"

If you listen to some Bible teachers of the Reformed persuasion, they will often say (I have heard it) that free will doesn't exist, and the support offered is (and I quote): "Free will isn't even mentioned anywhere in the Bible!" Is that a true statement? Let's see.

It's true that the verbatim phrase "free will" doesn't appear *in the King James Version,* but then neither do the particular words and phrases "rapture," "Trinity," "good Samaritan," "Second Coming," "sovereignty," "selflessness," "prodigal son," "incarnation," and a host of others that are obviously Biblical concepts, but are just not expressed *in those particular words.* But let's look again at the claim that "free will" is not found in the King James Version of the Bible.

As any frequent reader of the KJV will have noticed, language changes over time, and it has been more than four centuries since the KJV was printed

Free to Choose?

in 1611—plenty of time for significant linguistic change to occur. For example, "today" used to be spelled differently:

> Hebrews 5:5: So also Christ glorified not himself to be made an high priest; but he that said unto him, Thou art my Son, **to day** have I begotten thee.

Not only that, but "tomorrow" used to be spelled differently:

> I Corinthians 15:32: If after the manner of men I have fought with beasts at Ephesus, what advantageth it me, if the dead rise not? let us eat and drink; for **to morrow** we die.

Not only that, but "forever" used to be spelled differently:

> Genesis 13:15: For all the land which thou seest, to thee will I give it, and to thy seed **for ever.**

Not only that, but "everywhere" used to be spelled differently:

> Acts 17:30: And the times of this ignorance God winked at; but now commandeth all men **every where** to repent. . .

Not only that, but "everything" used to be spelled differently:

> Ecclesiastes 3:11: He hath made **every thing** beautiful in his time: also he hath set the world in their heart, so that no man can find out the work that God maketh from the beginning to the end.

Not only that, but "anything" used to be spelled differently:

> Jeremiah 42:21: And now I have this day declared it to you; but ye have not obeyed the voice of the LORD your God, nor **any thing** for the which he hath sent me unto you.

Not only that, but "nowhere" used to be spelled differently:

> I Samuel 10:14: And Saul's uncle said unto him and to his servant, Whither went ye? And he said, To seek the asses: and when we saw that they were **no where**, we came to Samuel.

Not only that, but "meanwhile" used to be spelled differently:

> John 4:31: In the **mean while** his disciples prayed him, saying, Master, eat.

The list could go on, but you get the point. And then there are the obvious changes since the KJV was printed: "thou" is now "you" (as is "ye" and "thee"), "thy" is now "your," "thine" is now "yours," "whither" is now "where," "hither" is now "here," "thither" is now "there," and so forth.

So we can see that one common linguistic change over the centuries is for letters to change, and for spaces to be removed from common phrases, coalescing them into single words. But another linguistic change is to *add* spaces to certain compound words, breaking them into the multi-word phrases from which they were originally formed.

It just so happens that "free will" is one of those, especially when being used as an adjective:

Leviticus 22:18: Speak unto Aaron, and to his sons, and unto all the children of Israel, and say unto them, Whatsoever he be of the house of Israel, or of the strangers in Israel, that will offer his oblation for all his vows, and for all his **freewill** offerings, which they will offer unto the Lord for a burnt offering. . .

Leviticus 22:21: And whosoever offereth a sacrifice of peace offerings unto the Lord to accomplish his vow, or a **freewill** offering in beeves or sheep, it shall be perfect to be accepted; there shall be no blemish therein.

Leviticus 22:23: Either a bullock or a lamb that hath any thing superfluous or lacking in his parts, that mayest thou offer for a **freewill** offering; but for a vow it shall not be accepted.

Leviticus 23:38: Beside the sabbaths of the Lord, and beside your gifts, and beside all your vows, and beside all your **freewill** offerings, which ye give unto the Lord.

Numbers 15:3: And will make an offering by fire unto the Lord, a burnt offering, or a sacrifice in performing a vow, or in a **freewill** offering, or in your solemn feasts, to make a sweet savour unto the Lord, of the herd, or of the flock. . .

Numbers 29:39: These things ye shall do unto the Lord in your set feasts, beside your vows, and your **freewill** offerings, for your burnt offerings, and for your meat offerings, and for your drink offerings, and for your peace offerings.

Deuteronomy 12:6: And thither ye shall bring your burnt offerings, and your sacrifices, and your tithes, and heave offerings of your hand, and your vows, and your **freewill** offerings, and the firstlings of your herds and of your flocks. . .

Deuteronomy 12:17: Thou mayest not eat within thy gates the tithe of thy corn, or of thy wine, or of thy oil, or the firstlings of thy herds or of thy flock, nor any of thy vows which thou vowest, nor thy **freewill** offerings, or heave offering of thine hand. . .

Deuteronomy 16:10: And thou shalt keep the feast of weeks unto the LORD thy God with a tribute of a **freewill** offering of thine hand, which thou shalt give unto the LORD thy God, according as the LORD thy God hath blessed thee. . .

Deuteronomy 23:23: That which is gone out of thy lips thou shalt keep and perform; even a **freewill** offering, according as thou hast vowed unto the LORD thy God, which thou hast promised with thy mouth.

II Chronicles 31:14: And Kore the son of Imnah the Levite, the porter toward the east, was over the **freewill** offerings of God, to distribute the oblations of the LORD, and the most holy things.

Ezra 1:4: And whosoever remaineth in any place where he sojourneth, let the men of his place help him with silver, and with gold, and with goods, and with beasts, beside the **freewill** offering for the house of God that is in Jerusalem.

Ezra 3:5: And afterward offered the continual burnt offering, both of the new moons, and of all the set feasts of the LORD that were consecrated, and of every one that **willingly** offered a **freewill** offering unto the LORD.

Ezra 7:13: I make a decree, that all they of the people of Israel, and of his priests and Levites, in my realm, which are minded of their own **freewill** to go up to Jerusalem, go with thee.

Ezra 7:16: And all the silver and gold that thou canst find in all the province of Babylon, with the **freewill** offering of the people, and of the priests, offering **willingly** for the house of their God which is in Jerusalem. . .

Ezra 8:28: And I said unto them, Ye are holy unto the LORD; the vessels are holy also; and the silver and the gold are a **freewill** offering unto the LORD God of your fathers.

Psalm 119:108: Accept, I beseech thee, the **freewill** offerings of my mouth, O LORD, and teach me thy judgments.

Hmm. So much for "free will" not being in the KJV. It isn't, except for the 17 cases just listed. Unless, of course, "freewill" means something different than "free will." But no, that won't even work, because in Ezra 3:5 and 7:16 above, the Bible defines what "freewill" means: It means "willingly," as in "to choose by one's own will; voluntarily."

"But wait," someone might say. "Those Scriptures refer only to sacrifices and offerings made to the Lord. How do you know it also applies to how we get saved?" That is true (except for Ezra 7:13, which refers to choosing to obey God or not). But that is a good question. The answer lies in Paul's letter to the Romans:

> Romans 12:1 (NIV): Therefore, I urge you, brothers, in view of God's mercy, to **offer your bodies as living sacrifices**, holy and pleasing to God—this is your spiritual act of worship.

This verse shows that getting saved, or submitting ourselves to God *is* an offering—*we* offer everything our bodies do (which necessarily includes the thoughts and motivations behind making our bodies do those things) to God. If our own choice, or free will, had nothing to do with it, Paul's exhortation would be pointless.

And likewise, getting saved, or submitting ourselves to God *is* a sacrifice—*we* must be willing to get out of the "driver's seat" of our lives, so to speak, and whenever our wills differ from God's, we must be willing to choose His will, as Jesus did:

> Luke 22:42: Saying, Father, if thou be willing, remove this cup from me: nevertheless **not my will, but thine, be done**.

So even if we restrict the application of "freewill" to offerings and sacrifices, the two Scriptures above show that our response to God—serving Him or not—is indeed in both of those categories.

So it is clear that the statement "free will is not mentioned in the Bible" is patently false, even if we are limiting ourselves to just the KJV. But what about other phrases that mean the same thing? If we could find some, it would show that free will, as a *concept*, is Scriptural, even if, for whatever reason, someone might be gun-shy about using the verbatim *phrase* "free will." One way to find such examples would be to search for verses containing "free will" in other, non-KJV versions of the Bible, and then look at those same verses in the KJV to see what some of the other ways of expressing the concept are.

> Deuteronomy 18:6 (NET): Suppose a Levite comes **by his own free will** from one of your villages, from any part of Israel where he is living, to the place the LORD chooses. . .
>
> > KJV: And if a Levite come from any of thy gates out of all Israel, where he sojourned, and come **with all the desire of his mind** unto the place which the LORD shall choose. . .

Ezra 7:13 (WEBSTR): I make a decree, that all they of the people of Israel, and of his priests and Levites, in my realm, who are **disposed of their own free will** to go to Jerusalem, go with thee.

KJV: I make a decree, that all they of the people of Israel, and of his priests and Levites, in my realm, which are **minded of their own freewill** to go up to Jerusalem, go with thee.

Psalm 54:6 (WEB): With a **free will** offering, I will sacrifice to you. I will give thanks to your name, Yahweh, for it is good.

KJV: I will **freely** sacrifice unto thee: I will praise thy name, O LORD; for it is good.

Amos 4:5 (WEB): "Offer a sacrifice of thanksgiving of that which is leavened, And proclaim **free will** offerings and brag about them: For this pleases you, you children of Israel," says the Lord Yahweh.

KJV: And offer a sacrifice of thanksgiving with leaven, and proclaim and publish the **free** offerings: for this liketh you, O ye children of Israel, saith the Lord GOD.

John 10:18 (GWORD): No one takes my life from me. I give my life **of my own free will**. I have the authority to give my life, and I have the authority to take my life back again. This is what my Father ordered me to do.

KJV: No man taketh it from me, but I lay it down **of myself**. I have power to lay it down, and I have power to take it again. This commandment have I received of my Father.

II Corinthians 8:3 (GWORD): I assure you that **by their own free will** they have given all they could, even more than they could afford.

KJV: For to their power, I bear record, yea, and beyond their power **they were willing of themselves**. . .

II Corinthians 8:17 (GWORD): He accepted my request and eagerly went to visit you **by his own free will**.

KJV: For indeed he accepted the exhortation; but being more forward, **of his own accord** he went unto you.

Philemon 14 (ASV): but without thy mind I would do nothing; that thy goodness should not be as of necessity, but **of free will**.

> KJV: But without thy mind would I do nothing; that thy benefit should not be as it were of necessity, but **willingly.**

> James 1:18 (AMP): And it was **of His own [free] will** that He gave us birth [as sons] by [His] Word of Truth, so that we should be a kind of firstfruits of His creatures [a sample of what He created to be consecrated to Himself].

> KJV: **Of his own will** begat he us with the word of truth, that we should be a kind of firstfruits of his creatures.

And there are numerous other similar Scriptures omitted for the sake of brevity. So it is evident that there are *many* different phrases in the KJV—and other versions as well—that refer to someone using his free will, though the concept may be expressed in different words. And of course, all these Scriptures would be very troubling if we were determined to maintain that the Bible doesn't mention or acknowledge free will.

We can see, from looking at the same verses in other translations, these different KJV ways of expressing the "free will" concept: "with all the desire of [one's] mind," "freely," "free," "willingly," "of [one's] own will," "of [one's] self," "willing of [one's] self," and "of [one's] own accord." All these were found quite easily from looking up "free will" in just a few of the other translations, and then checking the same Scriptures in the KJV. And there are dozens of translations I didn't even check because the proof was already overwhelming.

So the claim "Free will is not mentioned in the Bible" is patently, glaringly, obviously, plainly, unquestionably, and undeniably *false*. One could just as reliably claim "There are no fish in the oceans." These two claims are *so* easy to disprove, it's astonishing that anyone would even make them. And as far as I know, no one *has* made the second claim. . .

Enlisting in the Lord's Army

As students of the Bible know, God is often called the "Lord of hosts." What does that mean? What is a "host," in that context? It simply means an army: God is the Commander-in-Chief of the armies of heaven. If that seems insufficiently pacifistic for someone's view of God, let's look at some Scriptures.

> Exodus 15:3: **The Lord is a man of war:** the Lord is his name.

> I Samuel 17:45 (NASB): Then David said to the Philistine, "You come to me with a sword, a spear, and a javelin, but I come to you in the

name of **the Lord of hosts,** the God of the armies of Israel, whom you have taunted."

II Samuel 6:18 (BBE): And after David had made the burned offerings and the peace-offerings, he gave the people a blessing in the name of **the Lord of armies.**

Psalm 24:10 (GWORD): Who, then, is this king of glory? **The Lord of Armies** is the king of glory! Selah.

NLT: Who is the King of glory? **The Lord of Heaven's Armies**— he is the King of glory. Interlude

Psalm 84:1 (NLT): How lovely is your dwelling place, O **Lord of Heaven's Armies.**

The KJV word "host" comes from the Hebrew word צָבָא (*tsaba*, H6635), whose definitions include "a mass of persons, especially organized for war (an army); by implication, a campaign, literally or figuratively—army, battle, company, host, service, soldiers, waiting upon, war(-fare)." Sounds rather military.

Notice in the passages above, that God is the Lord of both earthly armies and heavenly armies: for example, the "armies of Israel" in I Samuel 17:45, and "Heaven's Armies" in the noted Psalms. How does one become a member of God's earthly army? He volunteers:

Psalm 110:1–3 (AMP): The Lord (God) says to my Lord (the Messiah), Sit at My right hand, until I make Your adversaries Your footstool. ²The Lord will send forth from Zion the scepter of Your strength; rule, then, in the midst of Your foes. ³**Your people will offer themselves willingly** in the day of Your power, in the beauty of holiness and in holy array out of the womb of the morning; to You [will spring forth] Your young men, who are as the dew.

v. 3a, CJB: On the day your forces mobilize, **your people willingly offer themselves**. . .

ERV: **Your people will gladly join you** when you gather your army together.

ESV: **Your people will offer themselves freely** on the day of your power. . .

GWORD: **Your people will volunteer** when you call up your army.

GNT: On the day you fight your enemies, **your people will volunteer.**

HCSB: **Your people will volunteer** on Your day of battle.

ISV: **Your soldiers are willing volunteers** on your day of battle. . .

NASB: **Your people will volunteer freely** in the day of Your power. . .

NIV: **Your troops will be willing** on your day of battle.

VOICE: **Your people will come as volunteers** that day. . .

If I'm not mistaken, this sounds suspiciously like God's people will come as volunteers, freely and willingly. It sounds like people are joining of their own free will. . .

Volunteering Voluntarily

Several of the translations above used the word "volunteer." What does that word mean? The New Oxford American Dictionary defines it as "a person who *freely offers* to take part in an enterprise or undertake a task." To "freely offer" sure sounds like making a free-will choice to do something. The definition of "voluntary," another form of the word, supports that interpretation: "done, given, or acting *of one's own free will.*"

Well, isn't that interesting! If "volunteer" and "voluntary" indicate acting on one's free will, might there be any Bible verses that use either of these words? Let's see:

Exodus 36:2 (NET): Moses summoned Bezalel and Oholiab and every skilled person in whom the LORD had put skill—**everyone whose heart stirred him to volunteer to do the work.**

Exodus 35:29 (MSG): Every man and woman in Israel whose heart moved them freely to bring something for the work that GOD through Moses had commanded them to make, brought it, **a voluntary offering for GOD.**

Leviticus 1:3: If his offering be a burnt sacrifice of the herd, let him offer a male without blemish: he shall offer it **of his own voluntary will** at the door of the tabernacle of the congregation before the LORD.

Leviticus 7:16: But if the sacrifice of his offering be a vow, or **a voluntary offering,** it shall be eaten the same day that he offereth his sacrifice: and on the morrow also the remainder of it shall be eaten. . .

Leviticus 22:21 (CEV): When you offer a sacrifice to ask my blessing, there must be nothing wrong with the animal. This is true, whether the sacrifice is part of a promise or **something you do voluntarily.**

Numbers 15:3 (NLT): . . .you will offer special gifts as a pleasing aroma to the LORD. These gifts may take the form of a burnt offering, a sacrifice to fulfill a vow, **a voluntary offering,** or an offering at any of your annual festivals, and they may be taken from your herds of cattle or your flocks of sheep and goats.

Deuteronomy 23:23 (AMP): The vow which has passed your lips you shall be watchful to perform, **a voluntary offering** which you have made to the LORD your God, which you have promised with your mouth.

Judges 5:2, 9 (CEV): We praise you, LORD! **Our soldiers volunteered, ready to follow you.** ⁹I praise you, LORD, and I am grateful for **those leaders and soldiers who volunteered.**

II Kings 12:4 (AMP): And Joash said to the priests, All the current money brought into the house of the LORD to provide the dedicated things, also the money [which the priests by command have] assessed on all those bound by vows, also all the money that **it comes into any man's heart voluntarily to bring** into the house of the LORD. . .

I Chronicles 12:38 (CEV): **All of these soldiers voluntarily came** to Hebron because they wanted David to become king of Israel. In fact, everyone in Israel wanted the same thing.

I Chronicles 28:21 (TLB): And these various groups of priests and Levites will serve in the Temple. **Others with skills of every kind will volunteer,** and the army and the entire nation are at your command.

I Chronicles 29:5 (CSB): . . .the gold for the gold work and the silver for the silver, for all the work to be done by the craftsmen. Now **who will volunteer to consecrate himself to the LORD today?**

I Chronicles 29:17 (AMP): I know also, my God, that You try the heart and delight in uprightness. In the uprightness of my heart I have freely offered all these things. And now I have seen with joy Your people who are present here **offer voluntarily and freely to You.**

II Chronicles 17:16 (CEV): Amasiah son of Zichri, who **had volunteered to serve the LORD,** was third in command, with two hundred thousand soldiers under him.

II Chronicles 35:8 (NIV): His *[Josiah's]* officials also **contributed voluntarily** to the people and the priests and Levites. Hilkiah, Zechariah and Jehiel, the administrators of God's temple, gave the priests twenty-six hundred Passover offerings and three hundred cattle.

Ezra 3:5 (TLB): They also offered the special sacrifices required for the Sabbaths, the new moon celebrations, and the other regular annual feasts of the LORD. **Voluntary offerings of the people** were also sacrificed.

Nehemiah 7:70 (MSG): Some of the heads of families made **voluntary offerings** for the work. The governor made a gift to the treasury of 1,000 drachmas of gold (about nineteen pounds), 50 bowls, and 530 garments for the priests.

Psalm 54:6 (NLT): I will sacrifice **a voluntary offering** to you; I will praise your name, O LORD, for it is good.

Psalm 68:31 (NET): They come with red cloth from Egypt. **Ethiopia voluntarily offers tribute to God.**

Ezekiel 46:12: Now when the prince shall prepare **a voluntary burnt offering or peace offerings voluntarily** unto the LORD, one shall then open him the gate that looketh toward the east, and he shall prepare his burnt offering and his peace offerings, as he did on the sabbath day: then he shall go forth; and after his going forth one shall shut the gate.

I Corinthians 9:19 (MSG): Even though I am free of the demands and expectations of everyone, **I have voluntarily become a servant** to any and all in order to reach a wide range of people. . .

II Corinthians 8:3 (AMP): For, as I can bear witness, [they gave] according to their ability, yes, and beyond their ability; and [**they did it**] **voluntarily. . .**

Philemon 14 (AMP): But it has been my wish to do nothing about it without first consulting you and getting your consent, in order that your benevolence might not seem to be the result of compulsion or of pressure but might **be voluntary** [**on your part**].

I Peter 5:2 (WEB): Shepherd the flock of God which is among you, exercising the oversight, not under compulsion, but **voluntarily,** not for dishonest gain, but willingly. . .

My goodness! People volunteering all over the Bible! Old Testament and New, in the Law, Wisdom, Prophets, and Epistles, from numerous Bible translations! A whole new crop of people, of their own free will, volunteering to do a variety of things in the service of God. And isn't it strange that all these translation teams, from all these translations, over so many years, conspired together to make us believe that the Reformed doctrines aren't true?

Other Examples of Free Will in the Bible

There are many other places where the Bible casually refers to the will of humans, with a pretty strong implication that it is something they can freely use: either wisely, to their benefit, or foolishly, to their destruction. Several such passages follow (some of which you've seen earlier).

Exodus 35:21–22 (AMP): And they came, **each one whose heart stirred him up and whose spirit made him willing,** and brought the LORD's offering to be used for the [new] Tent of Meeting, for all its service, and the holy garments. ²²They came, both men and women, **all who were willinghearted,** and brought brooches, earrings or nose rings, signet rings, and armlets or necklaces, all jewels of gold, everyone bringing an offering of gold to the LORD.

Exodus 36:2–3 (AMP): And Moses called Bezalel and Aholiab and every able and wisehearted man in whose mind the LORD had put wisdom and ability, **everyone whose heart stirred him up** to come to do the work; ³And they received from Moses all the **freewill offerings** which the Israelites had brought for doing the work of the sanctuary, to prepare it for service. And they continued to bring him **freewill offerings** every morning.

Psalm 81:11–12 (NET): But my people did not obey me; Israel did not submit to me. ¹²**I gave them over to their stubborn desires; they did what seemed right to them.**

Jeremiah 5:23 (AMP): But **these people have hearts that draw back from God and wills that rebel against Him;** they have revolted and quit His service and have gone away [into idolatry].

Matthew 16:24–25: Then said Jesus unto his disciples, **If any man will come after me,** let him deny himself, and take up his cross, and follow me. ²⁵For whosoever **will** save his life shall lose it: and whosoever **will** lose his life for my sake shall find it.

ASV: . . .**If any man would** come after me. . . ²⁵For **whosoever would** save his life shall lose it. . .

AMP: . . .**If anyone desires** to be My disciple. . . ²⁵For **whoever is bent on** saving his [temporal] life. . .

CEB: . . .**All who want to** come after me. . . ²⁵**All who want to** save their lives will lose them.

Matthew 20:26–27 (AMP): Not so shall it be among you; but **whoever wishes** to be great among you must be your servant, [27]And whoever desires to be first among you must be your slave. . .

Matthew 20:32: And Jesus stood still, and called them, and said, **What will ye** that I shall do unto you?

AMP: And Jesus stopped and called them, and asked, **What do you want** Me to do for you?

Matthew 21:28–31 (NIV): "What do you think? There was a man who had two sons. He went to the first and said, 'Son, go and work today in the vineyard.' [29]'I will not,' he answered, but later **he changed his mind** and went. [30]Then the father went to the other son and said the same thing. He answered, '**I will, sir**,' but he did not go. [31]Which of the two did what his father wanted?" "The first," they answered. Jesus said to them, "I tell you the truth, the tax collectors and the prostitutes are entering the kingdom of God ahead of you."

Matthew 26:41 (NASB): "Keep watching and praying, that you may not enter into temptation; **the spirit is willing**, but the flesh is weak."

John 5:35 (NIV): John was a lamp that burned and gave light, and **you chose for a time** to enjoy his light.

John 7:17 (NIV): **If anyone chooses to do God's will**, he will find out whether my teaching comes from God or whether I speak on my own.

II Corinthians 8:3–4 (TEV): I can assure you that they gave as much as they could, and even more than they could. **Of their own free will** [4]they begged us and pleaded for the privilege of having a part in helping God's people in Judea.

II Corinthians 8:11–12 (NIV): Now finish the work, so that **your eager willingness** to do it may be matched by your completion of it, according to your means. [12]For **if the willingness is there**, the gift is acceptable according to what one has, not according to what he does not have.

James 4:4 (NIV): You adulterous people, don't you know that friendship with the world is hatred toward God? **Anyone who chooses to be a friend of the world** becomes an enemy of God.

I Peter 4:3 (NIV): For you have spent enough time in the past doing **what pagans choose to do**—living in debauchery, lust, drunkenness, orgies, carousing and detestable idolatry.

Revelation 22:17: And the Spirit and the bride say, Come. And let him that heareth say, Come. And let him that is athirst come. And **whosoever will, let him take the water of life freely.**

AMP: The [Holy] Spirit and the bride (the church, the true Christians) say, Come! And let him who is listening say, Come! And let everyone come who is thirsty [who is painfully conscious of his need of those things by which the soul is refreshed, supported, and strengthened]; and **whoever [earnestly] desires to do it, let him come, take, appropriate, and drink the water of Life without cost.**

NIV: The Spirit and the bride say, "Come!" And let him who hears say, "Come!" Whoever is thirsty, let him come; and **whoever wishes, let him take the free gift of the water of life.**

GWORD: The Spirit and the bride say, "Come!" Let those who hear this say, "Come!" Let those who are thirsty come! **Let those who want the water of life take it as a gift.**

So after reading all the above Scriptures, can anyone seriously maintain the claim that the Bible doesn't mention free will? Yet I have heard that claim plainly stated by one of the most prominent teachers of Reformed theology of today—one with *decades* of seminary teaching experience. That is absolutely mind-boggling.

What Is Love?

That is a profound question. We know that God is love, and God has many wonderful attributes that show His love. We also know that I Corinthians 13, a.k.a. the "Love Chapter," has a detailed listing of what love does and does not do. But there are other attributes of love that I Corinthians 13 does not specifically mention, but which God acknowledges. It is one of those we will explore here.

As an aside, another question that is very troubling for some people is "The Question of Evil." In a nutshell, this question asks "If God is good, why does He allow evil in this world?" A variation on this theme, with a bit more detail, is "Because evil is in the world, how could God be both good and all-powerful? If He *can* stop evil, but chooses not to, He is not good. If He *wants* to stop evil, He must not be all-powerful, because evil is still here."[1]

---

[1] Even the acknowledgement of the existence of evil presupposes an objective standard of good, from which evil departs. This objective standard of good must come from an awareness of God, because if we simply evolved (assuming the laws of math and physics could be suspended long enough for it to happen), there would be no objective standard of good, because

The quick answer to The Question of Evil is, "It ain't over yet." He both chooses to, and is entirely capable of stopping evil (Revelation 21:3–4); we just haven't gotten there yet. Indeed, *we* are the ones He left in charge, and with the power and authorization to destroy the works of the enemy (Matthew 10:1–8, 28:18–20, Luke 9:1–6, Acts 1:8, etc.). So we can't blame God for the sad condition of the earth.

But both of the above forms of the question betray a lack of Scriptural understanding. The answer to The Question of Evil is: "Because He wants a loving relationship with us." At this point, some readers will get quizzical (or even sarcastic) expressions on their faces and say, "God wants us to love Him, so He made evil?" Not exactly. Let me explain.

When God put Adam and Eve in the Garden of Eden, He told them not to eat of one particular tree:

> Genesis 2:16–17 (NIV): And the LORD God commanded the man, "You are free to eat from any tree in the garden; ¹⁷but **you must not eat from the tree of the knowledge of good and evil**, for when you eat of it you will surely die."

Note what God did, in giving them a command: *He gave them the choice of whether to obey it or not.* Obviously, Adam and Eve were not *forced* to obey God, because they disobeyed Him. And there was nothing magical about the Tree of the Knowledge of Good and Evil; the command could just as easily have been "Don't swim in that stream" or "Don't dig a hole more than one foot deep" or "Don't arrange rocks into a triangle" or "Don't ride a horse backwards" or anything else. The important point is that He gave them a choice: they could obey Him or not.

Why is that important? Because in order for love to be real, *it must be voluntary.* Of course, God could have made us to be robots that would mindlessly parrot, "I love You, God. I love You, God. I love You, God. I love You, God." for eternity. But it's obvious that would not be fulfilling nor rewarding nor satisfying—it would be no more emotionally satisfying than saying "I love you" into a voice recorder and setting it for continuous playback.

No, in order for our love for God to be real, it has to be voluntary. Which means that *it has to be possible to reject Him*. C.S. Lewis puts it this way: "There is no use saying you choose to lie down when it has become impossible to

---

we'd all be random, meaningless, biological accidents. Therefore, everybody's opinion of good and evil—assuming we even had one—would simply be an opinion that is no better than anyone else's. See Book 14: *Oh, Evolve! (Good Luck With That. . .)* for much discussion on how the theory of evolution ignores or defies numerous observable, repeatable, and testable laws of probability and physics.

stand up." That concept is valid in *any* context. In our context, it becomes "It's meaningless to say we love God if it is not possible to do anything else." Which means that, if that possibility actually exists, some people *will* reject Him. And right there is where evil comes from: people rejecting God and what He has to offer, and choosing to run their own lives without regard to what He thinks.

Remember what Hebrews 11 says about the nature of God?

> Hebrews 11:6: But without faith it is impossible to please him: for he that cometh to God must believe that he is, and that **he is a rewarder** of them that diligently seek him.

So God is a rewarder of those who diligently seek Him. Did you catch that? He is a *rewarder*. It is in His nature to reward His children, as it is in the nature of any good father to do when his children do well. But a reward is meaningless if there is no choice about how to respond in a situation for which being rewarded is a possibility.

The very fact that He "rewards" us for diligently seeking Him shows us that it is not inevitable that we diligently seek Him; that is, there must be an option to seek Him or not—we must have a free choice, or else any "reward" is meaningless. That would be like rewarding a hammer, with which you just pounded a nail, for pounding the nail. How did the hammer earn the reward for good behavior, since it had no choice in the matter? It didn't, and therefore the reward means nothing. Personally, I don't want to be the one telling God that His rewards are meaningless. Note that while salvation is based on grace (Ephesians 2:8–9), rewards are based on works (Matthew 16:27).

This freedom of choice inherent in genuine love is absolutely necessary in order for two Scriptural concepts to be valid at the same time. Those two concepts are the idea that some people will indeed suffer torment for eternity (as we'll see in the section "Do All People Get Saved?", below), and the idea of "every knee shall bow and every tongue will confess that Jesus Christ is Lord" (Romans 14:11, Philippians 2:10).

But here's an even more fundamental question: *Who put the Tree of the Knowledge of Good and Evil in the garden in the first place?* Obviously, God did. But why? If He hadn't done that, Adam and Eve wouldn't have sinned, and all the resulting corruption, heartache, sin, sickness, and death could have been avoided. So why in the world did God do that?

It was clearly very important to Him that man have a free choice, and therefore, that man could actually have a true loving (i.e., voluntary) relationship with Him. God knew that if disobedience is impossible, obedience is meaningless, and if rejecting Him is impossible, accepting Him is meaningless.

Notice what God says about the state of things *before* Adam and Eve sinned, but the Tree of the Knowledge of Good and Evil was already in the Garden:

> Genesis 1:31a: And God saw **every thing** that he had made, and, behold, **it was very good.**

I think it's very significant that, in describing a situation in which man would have the choice of obeying God or not, He described it as "very good."

We now realize that answering the question of "What is love?" with the very true (but clearly non-comprehensive) answer of "It must be voluntary," we have also answered The Question of Evil: Evil exists as a necessary alternative resulting from rejecting Good. Again, rejecting and disobeying God *must* be an actual option, or else accepting and obeying Him are meaningless.

Not only that, but in answering The Question of Evil, we see that our love for God, and the resulting desire to be with Him, be like Him, obey Him, and be pleasing to Him, must also be voluntary. In other words, we must be able to choose to love God or not:

> Mark 12:28–30 (NIV): One of the teachers of the law came and heard them debating. Noticing that Jesus had given them a good answer, he asked him, "Of all the commandments, which is the most important?" [29]"**The most important one**," answered Jesus, "**is this:** 'Hear, O Israel, the Lord our God, the Lord is one. [30]**Love the Lord your God** with all your heart and with all your soul and with all your mind and with all your strength.'"

If we are actually not able to *choose* to love God of our own free will, then the "love" we have for Him is meaningless; we are reduced to automatons, mindlessly doing whatever our programmed instructions call for us to do. And if that is actually the case—that we do *not* have a free will with which to choose our response to God—then we have reduced what Jesus said was the "most important commandment" to meaninglessness. And if it's all the same to you, I'd rather not be the one who tells Jesus that He got things wrong about what's important.

One more thing: Couldn't God *force* us to love Him? And wouldn't that have avoided The Question of Evil altogether? Well, think about it. If an action is forced, it is involuntary; i.e., not voluntary. What is it called when someone attempts to "force love" on someone? Or *from* someone? It is called *rape*. And that is not the way God operates.

God's Sovereignty

Is God sovereign? I think most Christians would say Yes. But people vary greatly on what sovereignty implies. What does sovereignty mean, technically? It means "having ultimate or supreme power and authority." Does God have that? Yes; when it comes to sheer quantity of power and authority, God has it all:

Genesis 18:14a: **Is any thing too hard for the LORD?**

Job 42:2 (TEV): I know, LORD, that **you are all-powerful; that you can do everything you want.**

Psalm 115:3 (NASB): But our God is in the heavens; **He does whatever He pleases.**

Psalm 135:6 (ESV): **Whatever the LORD pleases, he does,** in heaven and on earth, in the seas and all deeps.

Jeremiah 32:17: Ah Lord GOD! behold, thou hast made the heaven and the earth by thy great power and stretched out arm, and **there is nothing too hard for thee. . .**

Jeremiah 32:27: Behold, I am the LORD, the God of all flesh: **is there any thing too hard for me?**

Daniel 4:35 (NLT): All the people of the earth are nothing compared to him. **He does as he pleases among the angels of heaven and among the people of the earth. No one can stop him** or say to him, 'What do you mean by doing these things?'

Matthew 19:26: But Jesus beheld them, and said unto them, With men this is impossible; but **with God all things are possible.**

Matthew 28:18: And Jesus came and spake unto them, saying, **All power is given unto me** in heaven and in earth.

AMP: Jesus approached and, breaking the silence, said to them, **All authority (all power of rule) in heaven and on earth has been given to Me.**

Mark 14:36 (NIV): "Abba, Father," he said, **"everything is possible for you.** Take this cup from me. Yet not what I will, but what you will."

Luke 1:37: For **with God nothing shall be impossible.**

Revelation 19:6: And I heard as it were the voice of a great multitude, and as the voice of many waters, and as the voice of mighty thunderings, saying, Alleluia: for **the Lord God omnipotent reigneth**.

But, as I said above, the implications of sovereignty are disagreed upon by Christians (for more discussion on the topic of God's sovereignty, see "The Definition of Sovereignty," below). One opinion is that sovereignty means that He makes *all* decisions and actively causes *all* events, including whether we love and serve God or not. Another opinion states that since God is indeed sovereign, He can do anything, including the creation of beings with actual free will. Clearly, these two opinions are mutually exclusive: if the first opinion is true, the second cannot be, and if the second opinion is true, the first cannot be. We saw in the "Principles of Reason" chapter that the Law of Non-Contradiction states that a thing and its opposite cannot be the same. In this situation, "We have a free will" and "We do *not* have a free will" are clearly saying opposite things, and therefore cannot both be true. So let's dig into the Scriptures and see what we find.

Does God Want Everyone to be Saved?

This is a very good question, and God answers it with undeniable certainty:

Ecclesiastes 12:13 (NASB): The conclusion, when all has been heard, is: fear God and keep His commandments, because **this applies to *every* person.**[2]

Isaiah 45:22 (NIV): **Turn to me and be saved, *all* you ends of the earth;** for I am God, and there is no other.

Isaiah 55:3 (AMP): **Incline your ear [submit and consent to the divine will] and come to Me; hear,** and your soul will revive; and I will make an everlasting covenant or league with you, even the sure mercy (kindness, goodwill, and compassion) promised to David.

Jeremiah 29:11–13 (NIV): "For I know the plans I have for you," declares the LORD, "**plans to prosper you and not to harm you, plans to give you hope and a future.** ¹²Then you will call upon me and come and

---

[2] As you remember, Solomon, the wisest man who ever lived, was greatly blessed by God with wisdom and many other blessings (I Kings 3:10–14). After Solomon's idol-worshipping binge (described in I Kings 11:4–8), he returned to serving the Lord, as this passage shows, and his writings once again reflected God's heart. For further study on the implications of "fearing God," see the section entitled "The Fear of the Lord" in Book 7: *Be Filled with the Spirit*.

pray to me, and I will listen to you. ¹³You will seek me and find me when you seek me with all your heart."

Ezekiel 18:23 (TEV): "Do you think I enjoy seeing evil people die?" asks the Sovereign LORD. "No, **I would rather see them repent and live.**"

Ezekiel 18:32 (NIV): For **I take no pleasure in the death of *anyone*,** declares the Sovereign LORD. **Repent and live!**

Ezekiel 33:11 (NLT): As surely as I live, says the Sovereign LORD, I take no pleasure in the death of wicked people. **I only want them to turn from their wicked ways so they can live.** Turn! Turn from your wickedness, O people of Israel! Why should you die?

Ezekiel 34:16 (AMP): **I will seek that which was lost and bring back that which has strayed,** and I will bandage the hurt and the crippled and will strengthen the weak and the sick, but I will destroy the fat and the strong [who have become hardhearted and perverse]; I will feed them with judgment and punishment.

Joel 2:32 (NIV): And **everyone** who calls on the name of the LORD will be saved; for on Mount Zion and in Jerusalem there will be deliverance, as the LORD has said, among the survivors whom the LORD calls.

Matthew 18:11 (WEB): For **the Son of Man came to save that which was lost.**

Matthew 18:14 (NIV): In the same way **your Father in heaven is not willing that *any* of these little ones should be lost.**

Luke 3:6 (AMP): And **all mankind** shall see (behold and understand and at last acknowledge) the salvation of God (the deliverance from eternal death decreed by God).

Luke 15:4–7 (NIV): Suppose one of you has a hundred sheep and loses one of them. **Does he not** leave the ninety-nine in the open country and **go after the lost sheep until he finds it?** ⁵And when he finds it, he joyfully puts it on his shoulders ⁶and goes home. Then he calls his friends and neighbors together and says, '**Rejoice with me; I have found my lost sheep.**' ⁷I tell you that in the same way **there will be more rejoicing in heaven over one sinner who repents** than over ninety-nine righteous persons who do not need to repent.

Luke 9:56a: For **the Son of man is not come to destroy men's lives, but to save them.**

Luke 19:10 (NASB): "For the Son of Man has come to seek and **to save that which was lost.**"

CHAPTER 3: WE HAVE A FREE WILL, AND WE CAN CHOOSE GOD

John 1:7–9 (BBE): He [John the Baptist] came for witness, to give witness about the light [Jesus], **so that *all* men might have faith through him.** ⁸He himself was not the light: he was sent to give witness about the light. ⁹**The true light, which gives light to *every* man,** was then coming into the world.

John 3:16–18 (WEB): For God so loved the world, that he gave his one and only Son, that *whoever* **believes in him should not perish, but have eternal life.** ¹⁷For God didn't send his Son into the world to judge the world, but **that the *world* should be saved through him.**

John 10:9: I am the door: by me **if *any man* enter in, he shall be saved,** and shall go in and out, and find pasture.

John 12:32 (GWORD): When I have been lifted up from the earth, **I will draw *all* people toward me.**

John 12:47: And if any man hear my words, and believe not, I judge him not: for **I came not to judge the world, but to save the *world*.**

Acts 2:21: And it shall come to pass, that *whosoever* **shall call on the name of the Lord shall be saved.**

Acts 17:30 (GWORD): God overlooked the times when people didn't know any better. But **now he commands *everyone everywhere* to turn to him and change the way they think and act.**

Romans 5:10 (AMP): For if **while we were enemies we were reconciled to God through the death of His Son,** it is much more [certain], **now that we are reconciled,** that we shall be saved (daily delivered from sin's dominion) through His [resurrection] life.

II Corinthians 5:14–15 (GWORD): Clearly, Christ's love guides us. **We are convinced of the fact that one man has died for *all people*.** Therefore, all people have died. ¹⁵**He died for *all people*** so that those who live should no longer live for themselves but for the man who died and was brought back to life for them.

Romans 5:18 (AMP): Well then, as one man's trespass [one man's false step and falling away led] to condemnation for all men, so one Man's act of righteousness [leads] to **acquittal and right standing with God and life for *all men*.**

II Corinthians 5:19 (AMP): It was God [personally present] in Christ, **reconciling and restoring the *world* to favor with Himself, not counting up and holding against [men] their trespasses [but cancelling

87

them], and committing to us the message of reconciliation (of the restoration to favor).

Colossians 1:19–23 (NIV): For God was pleased to have all his fullness dwell in him, ²⁰and through him **to reconcile to himself *all* things**, whether things on earth or things in heaven, by making peace through his blood, shed on the cross. ²¹Once you were alienated from God and were enemies in your minds because of your evil behavior. ²²But **now he has reconciled you** by Christ's physical body through death **to present you holy in his sight, without blemish and free from accusation—** ²³*if* **you continue in your faith**, established and firm, not moved from the hope held out in the gospel. This is the gospel that you heard and that has been proclaimed to every creature under heaven, and of which I, Paul, have become a servant.

I Thessalonians 5:9–10 (NIV): For **God did not appoint us to suffer wrath but to receive salvation** through our Lord Jesus Christ. ¹⁰**He died for us so that,** whether we are awake or asleep, **we may live together with him.**

I Timothy 1:15 (AMP): The saying is sure and true and worthy of full and universal acceptance, that **Christ Jesus (the Messiah) came into the world to save sinners**, of whom I am foremost.

I Timothy 2:3–4: *[Pray,]* For this is good and acceptable in the sight of God our Saviour; **Who will have *all* men to be saved**, and to come unto the knowledge of the truth.

AMP: . . .**Who wishes *all* men to be saved** and [increasingly] to perceive and recognize and discern and know precisely and correctly the [divine] Truth.

ASV: . . .who would have *all* men to be saved, and come to the knowledge of the truth.

BBE: . . .Whose desire is that *all* men may have salvation and come to the knowledge of what is true.

DARBY: . . .who desires that *all* men should be saved and come to [the] knowledge of [the] truth.

GWORD: **He wants *all* people to be saved** and to learn the truth.

HCSB: . . .who wants *everyone* to be saved and to come to the knowledge of the truth.

NIV: . . .who wants *all* men to be saved and to come to a knowledge of the truth.

CHAPTER 3: WE HAVE A FREE WILL, AND WE CAN CHOOSE GOD

TEV: . . . .who wants *everyone* to be saved and to come to know the truth.

WEB: . . . .who desires *all* people to be saved and come to full knowledge of the truth.

YLT: . . . .who doth will *all* men to be saved, and to come to the full knowledge of the truth. . .

I Timothy 2:5–6 (AMP): For there [is only] one God, and [only] one Mediator between God and men, **the Man Christ Jesus,** ⁶**Who gave Himself as a ransom for** *all* **[people,** a fact that was] attested to at the right and proper time.

Titus 2:11 (DARBY): For the grace of God which carries with it **salvation for** *all* **men** has appeared. . .

Hebrews 2:9: But we see Jesus, who was made a little lower than the angels for the suffering of death, crowned with glory and honour; that he by the grace of God **should taste death for** *every* **man.**

II Peter 3:9: The Lord is not slack concerning his promise, as some men count slackness; but is longsuffering to us-ward, **not willing that** *any* **should perish, but that** *all* **should come to repentance.**

BBE: The Lord is not slow in keeping his word, as he seems to some, but he is waiting in mercy for you, **not desiring the destruction of** *any,* **but that** *all* **may be turned from their evil ways.**

NET: The Lord is not slow concerning his promise, as some regard slowness, but is being patient toward you, because **he does not wish for** *any* **to perish but for** *all* **to come to repentance.**

CJB: The Lord is not slow in keeping his promise, as some people think of slowness; on the contrary, he is patient with you; for **it is not his purpose that** *anyone* **should be destroyed, but that** *everyone* **should turn from his sins.**

CEV: The Lord isn't slow about keeping his promises, as some people think he is. In fact, God is patient, because **he wants** *everyone* **to turn from sin and** *no one* **to be lost.**

ERV: The Lord is not being slow in doing what he promised—the way some people understand slowness. But God is being patient with you. **He doesn't want** *anyone* **to be lost. He wants** *everyone* **to change their ways and stop sinning.**

GNT: The Lord is not slow to do what he has promised, as some think. Instead, he is patient with you, because **he does not want *anyone* to be destroyed, but wants *all* to turn away from their sins.**

MSG: God isn't late with his promise as some measure lateness. He is restraining himself on account of you, holding back the End because **he doesn't want *anyone* lost. He's giving *everyone* space and time to change.**

NLT: The Lord isn't really being slow about his promise, as some people think. No, he is being patient for your sake. **He does not want *anyone* to be destroyed, but wants *everyone* to repent.**

VOICE: Now the Lord is not slow about enacting His promise—slow is how some people want to characterize it—no, He is not slow but patient and merciful to you, **not wanting *anyone* to be destroyed, but wanting *everyone* to turn away from following his own path and to turn toward God's.**

WE: God will do what he promised. He is not slow though, as some people think he is. But he is waiting a long time for you. **He does not want *anyone* to die, but he wants *all* people to stop their wrong ways.**

I John 2:1–2 (NIV): My dear children, I write this to you so that you will not sin. But if anybody does sin, we have one who speaks to the Father in our defense—Jesus Christ, the Righteous One. ²He is the atoning sacrifice for our sins, and **not only for ours but also for the sins of the *whole world*.**

So, out of the mouth of two or three (or thirty-four) witnesses shall every word be established: if you're lost—if you are a sinner—He came to save you. Period. The thirty-four Scriptures above prove beyond a shadow of a doubt that God wants *all* people to be saved; that is His goal, His intent, His desire. Okay now, hold that thought, and let's look at another set of Scriptures.

Do All People Get Saved?

Another truth upon which the Bible is unambiguous is the fact that not everybody gets saved, and therefore, not everybody goes to heaven. Let's look at some Scriptures that show this:

Isaiah 66:24: And they shall go forth, and look upon the carcases of the **men that have transgressed against me: for their worm shall not die, neither shall their fire be quenched;** and they shall be an abhorring unto all flesh.

Daniel 12:2: And many of them that sleep in the dust of the earth shall awake, some to everlasting life, and **some to shame and everlasting contempt.**

Matthew 3:11–12 (NIV): "I baptize you with water for repentance. But after me will come one who is more powerful than I, whose sandals I am not fit to carry. He will baptize you with the Holy Spirit and with fire. [12]His winnowing fork is in his hand, and he will clear his threshing floor, gathering his wheat into the barn and **burning up the chaff with unquenchable fire.**"

Matthew 18:8: Wherefore if thy hand or thy foot offend thee, cut them off, and cast them from thee: it is better for thee to enter into life halt or maimed, rather than having two hands or two feet **to be cast into everlasting fire.**

Matthew 25:41 (ESV): "Then he will say to those on his left, '**Depart from me, you cursed, into the eternal fire prepared for the devil and his angels.**'"

Matthew 25:46 (ESV): "And **these will go away into eternal punishment,** but the righteous into eternal life."

Mark 3:29: But he that shall blaspheme against the Holy Ghost hath never forgiveness, but **is in danger of eternal damnation.** . . .

Mark 9:43–48: And if thy hand offend thee, cut it off: it is better for thee to enter into life maimed, than having two hands **to go into hell, into the fire that never shall be quenched:** [44]**Where their worm dieth not, and the fire is not quenched.** [45]And if thy foot offend thee, cut it off: it is better for thee to enter halt into life, than having two feet **to be cast into hell, into the fire that never shall be quenched:** [46]**Where their worm dieth not, and the fire is not quenched.** [47]And if thine eye offend thee, pluck it out: it is better for thee to enter into the kingdom of God with one eye, than having two eyes **to be cast into hell fire:** [48]**Where their worm dieth not, and the fire is not quenched.**

Luke 3:16–17 (NIV): John answered them all, "I baptize you with water. But one more powerful than I will come, the thongs of whose sandals I am not worthy to untie. He will baptize you with the Holy Spirit and with fire. [17]His winnowing fork is in his hand to clear his threshing floor and to gather the wheat into his barn, but **he will burn up the chaff with unquenchable fire.**"

Luke 16:22–24 (AMP): The time came when the beggar died and the angels carried him to Abraham's side. The rich man also died and was buried. ²³**In hell, where he was in torment,** he looked up and saw Abraham far away, with Lazarus by his side. ²⁴So he called to him, 'Father Abraham, have pity on me and send Lazarus to dip the tip of his finger in water and cool my tongue, because **I am in agony in this fire.**'

John 5:28–29: Marvel not at this: for the hour is coming, in the which all that are in the graves shall hear his voice, ²⁹And shall come forth; they that have done good, unto the resurrection of life; and **they that have done evil, unto the resurrection of damnation.**

Romans 2:6–8 (ESV): He will render to each one according to his works: ⁷to those who by patience in well-doing seek for glory and honor and immortality, he will give eternal life; ⁸but for **those who are self-seeking and do not obey the truth, but obey unrighteousness, there will be wrath and fury.**

II Thessalonians 1:7–9: And to you who are troubled rest with us, when the Lord Jesus shall be revealed from heaven with his mighty angels, ⁸In flaming fire taking vengeance on **them that know not God, and that obey not the gospel of our Lord Jesus Christ:** ⁹**Who shall be punished with everlasting destruction** from the presence of the Lord, and from the glory of his power. . .

Jude 7 (ESV): Just as Sodom and Gomorrah and the surrounding cities, which likewise **indulged in sexual immorality and pursued unnatural desire, serve as an example by undergoing a punishment of eternal fire.**

Revelation 14:11: And **the smoke of their torment ascendeth up for ever and ever: and they have no rest day nor night,** who worship the beast and his image, and whosoever receiveth the mark of his name.

Revelation 20:10: And the devil that deceived them was cast into the lake of fire and brimstone, where **the beast and the false prophet are, and shall be tormented day and night for ever and ever.**

Revelation 20:15 (ESV): And **if anyone's name was not found written in the book of life, he was thrown into the lake of fire.**

Revelation 21:8 (ESV): But as for the cowardly, the faithless, the detestable, as for murderers, the sexually immoral, sorcerers, idolaters, and all liars, **their portion will be in the lake that burns with fire and sulfur, which is the second death.**

That is a pretty sobering set of Scriptures. But we can clearly see that not everybody is ultimately saved; some people end up in hell, suffering for eternity.

The Upshot

But here's where these Scriptures drive us to a conclusion:

1. God *desires* all people to be saved (clearly proven by the first group of Scriptures above).
2. But not everyone *is* ultimately saved (clearly proven by the second group of Scriptures above).
3. Therefore, if our choice is not a factor in this situation, *God cannot be all-powerful* because someone or something is overriding Him and preventing His will from coming to pass.
4. Since there is nothing and no one more powerful than God, we are compelled through resistless logic, that *our choice must be a factor in our salvation.* There is no alternative.

So here we have yet another Scriptural proof that we must have a free will. The logical implications, if we *don't* have a free will, quickly become ludicrous.

Crime and Punishment

Let's consider law enforcement for a moment. Suppose a crime has been committed; someone has been murdered. Upon investigation, the detective finds that the victim was bludgeoned to death with a baseball bat—security-camera footage shows the perpetrator, the victim, the witnesses, the weapon, and the act itself—it's an open-and-shut case. The media gets a copy of the footage and broadcasts it, and the public is outraged at such a callous act of cruelty. So the judge and jury, after just a short time of deliberation, reach a unanimous verdict: justice will be served by imprisoning the baseball bat for 50 years.

To those who were intently reading the previous paragraph, my apologies for the letdown in the final sentence. You were probably either annoyed at the foolishness of the fictitious judge and jury, or perhaps you laughed out loud by the ridiculousness of the whole scenario. But *why* is it so obvious that the judge and jury were foolish, or that the whole situation was ridiculous?

A moment's reflection makes it clear that to imprison a baseball bat for murder, even if it was demonstrably the weapon used in the murder, is foolish and ridiculous because *the baseball bat did not choose to commit the crime.* The bat could not choose to be involved in the crime, nor could it choose to *not* be involved—a baseball bat does not have the ability to choose; it has no free will. It was merely a tool in the hands of the perpetrator of the crime, and therefore punishing the baseball bat, when it had no choice in the matter, is ludicrous.

And it would be just as ludicrous to honor and give a commendation to a different baseball bat, which happened to be leaning against a wall during the murder, because it was *not* involved with the crime.

No doubt, you see where this is going.

When God Takes His Cue From Us

Let's take a look at another set of Scriptures. I haven't mentioned most of these passages earlier in the book, but I may have mentioned some that were similar. But let's think about them in this crime-and-punishment context.

Conditional Blessing

The collection of Scriptures below all have one thing in common: they show the conditional nature of God's blessings: basically, you'll be blessed if you obey Him, and you won't if you don't. As you're reading, observe that many, if not all, of these verses would be completely meaningless if it were not within our power to choose to obey Him or not.

> Genesis 18:26 (NKJV): So the Lord said, "**If** I find in Sodom fifty righteous within the city, **then** I will spare all the place for their sakes."
>
> Exodus 19:5 (NASB): Now then, **if** you will indeed obey My voice and keep My covenant, **then** you shall be My own possession among all the peoples, for all the earth is Mine. . .
>
> Numbers 14:8 (AMP): **If** the Lord delights in us, **then** He will bring us into this land and give it to us, a land flowing with milk and honey.
>
> Deuteronomy 8:19–20 (NIV): **If** you ever forget the LORD your God and follow other gods and worship and bow down to them, I testify against you today that you will surely be destroyed. [20]Like the nations the LORD destroyed before you, so you will be destroyed for not obeying the LORD your God.
>
> Deuteronomy 28:1–2 (NIV): **If** you fully obey the LORD your God and carefully follow all his commands I give you today, the LORD your God will set you high above all the nations on earth. [2]All these blessings will come upon you and accompany you **if** you obey the LORD your God. . .

Deuteronomy 28:9: The L`ORD` shall establish thee an holy people unto himself, as he hath sworn unto thee, **if** thou shalt keep the commandments of the L`ORD` thy God, and walk in his ways.

Deuteronomy 28:15 (NIV): However, **if** you do not obey the L`ORD` your God and do not carefully follow all his commands and decrees I am giving you today, all these curses will come upon you and overtake you. . .

Joshua 24:20 (NASB): **If** you forsake the L`ORD` and serve foreign gods, **then** He will turn and do you harm and consume you after He has done good to you.

I Chronicles 28:9 (NASB): As for you, my son Solomon, know the God of your father, and serve Him with a whole heart and a willing mind; for the L`ORD` searches all hearts, and understands every intent of the thoughts. **If** you seek Him, He will let you find Him; but **if** you forsake Him, He will reject you forever.

II Chronicles 7:14 (NIV): . . .**if** my people, who are called by my name, will humble themselves and pray and seek my face and turn from their wicked ways, then will I hear from heaven and will forgive their sin and will heal their land.

II Chronicles 7:17–20 (ESV): And as for you, **if** you will walk before me as David your father walked, doing according to all that I have commanded you and keeping my statutes and my rules, [18]**then** I will establish your royal throne, as I covenanted with David your father, saying, 'You shall not lack a man to rule Israel.' [19]But **if** you turn aside and forsake my statutes and my commandments that I have set before you, and go and serve other gods and worship them, [20]**then** I will pluck you up from my land that I have given you, and this house that I have consecrated for my name, I will cast out of my sight, and I will make it a proverb and a byword among all peoples.

II Chronicles 15:1–2 (NIV): The Spirit of God came upon Azariah son of Oded. [2]He went out to meet Asa and said to him, "Listen to me, Asa and all Judah and Benjamin. The L`ORD` is with you **when** you are with him. **If** you seek him, he will be found by you, but **if** you forsake him, he will forsake you."

II Chronicles 30:9: For **if** ye turn again unto the L`ORD`, your brethren and your children shall find compassion before them that lead them captive, so that they shall come again into this land: for the L`ORD` your God is gracious and merciful, and will not turn away his face from you, **if** ye return unto him.

Psalm 7:12 (AMP): **If** a man does not turn and repent, [God] will whet His sword; He has strung and bent His [huge] bow and made it ready [by treading it with His foot].

Psalm 81:10–16 (NIV): I am the LORD your God, who brought you up out of Egypt. Open wide your mouth and I will fill it. [11]"But my people would not listen to me; Israel would not submit to me. [12]So I gave them over to their stubborn hearts to follow their own devices. [13]**If** my people would but listen to me, **if** Israel would follow my ways, [14]how quickly would I subdue their enemies and turn my hand against their foes! [15]Those who hate the LORD would cringe before him, and their punishment would last forever. [16]But you would be fed with the finest of wheat; with honey from the rock I would satisfy you."

Isaiah 1:19–20: **If** ye be willing and obedient, ye shall eat the good of the land: [20]But **if** ye refuse and rebel, ye shall be devoured with the sword: for the mouth of the Lord hath spoken it.

(To hear this passage set to music, listen to the song *Let Us Reason Together* on the album *Worship the King* or scan the QR code at right.)

Isaiah 7:9 (GWORD): The capital of Ephraim is Samaria, and the leader of Samaria is Remaliah's son. **If** you don't remain faithful, you won't remain standing.

John 6:51 (NIV): I am the living bread that came down from heaven. **If** anyone eats of this bread, he will live forever. This bread is my flesh, which I will give for the life of the world.

John 8:24 (GWORD): For this reason I told you that you'll die because of your sins. **If** you don't believe that I am the one, you'll die because of your sins.

John 8:31–32 (NIV): To the Jews who had believed him, Jesus said, "**If** you hold to my teaching, you are really my disciples. [32]**Then** you will know the truth, and the truth will set you free."

John 8:51 (MSG): I say this with absolute confidence. **If** you practice what I'm telling you, you'll never have to look death in the face.

John 13:17 (NASB): **If** you know these things, you are blessed **if** you do them.

Chapter 3: We Have a Free Will, and We Can Choose God

John 15:5, 10, 14 (NIV): I am the vine; you are the branches. **If** a man remains in me and I in him, he will bear much fruit; apart from me you can do nothing. ¹⁰**If** you obey my commands, you will remain in my love, just as I have obeyed my Father's commands and remain in his love. ¹⁴You are my friends **if** you do what I command.

Romans 8:11 (NKJV): But **if** the Spirit of Him who raised Jesus from the dead dwells in you, He who raised Christ from the dead will also give life to your mortal bodies through His Spirit who dwells in you.

Romans 8:13 (NIV): For **if** you live according to the sinful nature, you will die; but **if** by the Spirit you put to death the misdeeds of the body, you will live. . .

Romans 10:9 (ESV): . . .because, **if** you confess with your mouth that Jesus is Lord and believe in your heart that God raised him from the dead, you will be saved.

I Corinthians 3:14 (NIV): **If** what he has built survives, he will receive his reward.

Galatians 3:29 (GWORD): **If** you belong to Christ, then you are Abraham's descendants and heirs, as God promised.

Hebrews 3:14 (BBE): For **if** we keep the substance of the faith which we had at the start, even till the end, we have a part with Christ. . .

Revelation 3:20 (NLT): Look! I stand at the door and knock. **If** you hear my voice and open the door, I will come in, and we will share a meal together as friends.

Note that the Scriptures above were from the Old Testament and the New Testament, and were from books of the Law, History, Wisdom, Prophets, Gospels, Epistles, and Revelation. And notice the conspicuous use of the word "if" in every passage above! There are other words and phrases that communicate a similar idea of "on the condition that," "in the event that," or "provided that." In other words, God's actions toward us are largely (but not *completely*, of course) influenced by our actions toward Him.

And again, many similar Scriptures were left out for the sake of brevity. But notice: in *every one* of the passages above, God states the blessed consequences of obeying Him, and the severe consequences of disobeying Him. But if we, like the baseball bat described above, have no choice when it comes to our actions, then our being punished for disobedience, when there is no other option, is just as silly as the hypothetical judge sentencing the baseball

God's Behavior Based on Our Actions

One of the most well documented principles in the Bible is that of God judging people according to their actions; according to whether they obey or disobey His commands. When Abraham was talking to God shortly before God was to pour out judgment on Sodom and Gomorrah for their sin, Abraham was alarmed at the prospect of people *not* involved in sodomy being judged along with the people who *were* involved in sodomy. It was obviously unfair (i.e., exhibiting favoritism or partiality) to judge people innocent of that sin the same way as those guilty of that sin.

Abraham thought that surely there were *some* uncorrupted people in those cities, so he said to God:

> Genesis 18:25 (NIV): Far be it from you to do such a thing—to kill the righteous with the wicked, treating the righteous and the wicked alike. Far be it from you! **Will not the Judge of all the earth do right?**

It was so repugnant to Abraham—the prospect of judging people in a way that was *unrelated* to their behavior—that he stood up to God. Abraham interceded for the people: "What if there are 50 righteous people in Sodom; will you still destroy it?" And look at God's answer, and the subsequent conversation:

> Genesis 18:26–32 (NIV): The LORD said, "**If I find fifty righteous people in the city of Sodom, I will spare the whole place** for their sake." [27]Then Abraham spoke up again: "Now that I have been so bold as to speak to the Lord, though I am nothing but dust and ashes, [28]what if the number of the righteous is five less than fifty? Will you destroy the whole city because of five people?" "**If I find forty-five there,**" he said, "**I will not destroy it.**" [29]Once again he spoke to him, "What if only forty are found there?" He said, "**For the sake of forty, I will not do it.**" [30]Then he said, "May the Lord not be angry, but let me speak. What if only thirty can be found there?" He answered, "**I will not do it if I find thirty there.**" [31]Abraham said, "Now that I have been so bold as to speak to the Lord, what if only twenty can be found there?" He said, "**For the sake of twenty, I will not destroy it.**" [32]Then he said, "May the Lord not be angry, but let me speak just once more. What if only ten can be found there?" He answered, "**For the sake of ten, I will not destroy it.**"

As mentioned, Abraham was horrified at the idea of punishing the righteous along with the sinners. But notice that *God agreed with him.* Also notice the extent of God's mercy: He said He would spare *all* the sinful people of Sodom for the sake of only 50 righteous people! But what is that, percentage-wise? Some archeological estimates range as high as 200,000 people in this plain that contained Sodom and Gomorrah. And, a cemetery was discovered nearby, and there are an estimated 1.5 *million* bodies in this one cemetery! So the population was quite large.

But still, with all those people, not even 50 righteous could be found. Not even 45, or 40, or 30, or 20, or even ten, in such a large city! No wonder God said:

> Genesis 18:20–21 (AMP): And the Lord said, Because **the shriek [of the sins] of Sodom and Gomorrah is great** and **their sin is exceedingly grievous,** ²¹I will go down now and see whether they have done altogether [as vilely and wickedly] as is the cry of it which has come to Me; and if not, I will know.

Apparently, there was only one righteous person in the whole city—Lot himself:

> II Peter 2:6–9 (NIV): If he condemned the cities of Sodom and Gomorrah by burning them to ashes, and made them an example of what is going to happen to the ungodly; ⁷and if he rescued **Lot, a righteous man,** who was distressed by the filthy lives of lawless men ⁸(for **that righteous man,** living among them day after day, **was tormented in his righteous soul by the lawless deeds he saw and heard**)— ⁹if this is so, then the Lord knows how to rescue godly men from trials and to hold the unrighteous for the day of judgment, while continuing their punishment.

It behooves us to pay attention to what Abraham said to God in v. 25: "Will not the Judge of all the earth do right?" The strong implication is that it would be *wrong* to judge people in a way that was not related to their actions. And, as pointed out above, God agreed.

Why Was Abraham Chosen?

Was Abraham the father of the Jewish nation? Of course; every student of the Bible knows that (or will soon)—see Matthew 3:8–9, John 8:53–56, etc., for confirmation. But here's a harder question to answer: *Why* was Abraham chosen to be the father of the Jewish nation?

FREE TO CHOOSE?

The answer is simply because he obeyed God. Abraham's obedience was the cause, and God's blessing—specifically, his being selected to father the Jewish nation—was the effect.

> Genesis 22:17–18 (NIV): I will surely bless you and make your descendants as numerous as the stars in the sky and as the sand on the seashore. Your descendants will take possession of the cities of their enemies, ¹⁸and through your offspring all nations on earth will be blessed, **because you have obeyed me.**

And just in case the above Scripture isn't quite plain enough, God says the same thing about Abraham to his son. The following passage is God talking to Isaac, Abraham's son, through whom God would fulfill His promise to Abraham, to make him the father of the Jewish nation:

> Genesis 26:4–5 (NIV): I will make your descendants as numerous as the stars in the sky and will give them all these lands, and through your offspring all nations on earth will be blessed, ⁵**because Abraham obeyed me and kept my requirements, my commands, my decrees and my laws.**

Another undeniable example of God doing something *because*, or *as a result of*, what a human does.

Why Was David Chosen?

In the passage below, God unequivocally says that there is a reason He chose David to be King of Israel. And He tells us what that reason was:

> I Kings 11:34: Howbeit I will not take the whole kingdom out of his *[Solomon's]* hand: but I will make him prince all the days of his life for David my servant's sake, whom **I chose, because he kept my commandments and my statutes...**

Note the order of causation: David was *already* keeping God's commandments and statutes, and it was *because* of that fact that God chose him to be King of Israel.

Righteous Judgment

As we saw above, when Abraham expressed revulsion at the idea that people would be judged in a way unrelated to their behavior, he strongly implies that it would be wrong, and then we saw that God agreed. Below, we see judgment that *does* correspond to people's behavior, so according to Abraham, it is just. And since God is doing it, that confirms our conclusion. In the following passages, God is pronouncing judgment on people, because they have rejected and spurned His love and protection.

Let's look at Deuteronomy first:

> Deuteronomy 7:9–10 (ESV): Know therefore that the LORD your God is God, the faithful God who **keeps covenant and steadfast love with those who love him** and keep his commandments, to a thousand generations, [10]and **repays to their face those who hate him, by destroying them.** He will not be slack with one who hates him. He will repay him to his face.

Now take a look at this prophetic message given to Eli the priest, who didn't think diligence in serving God was all that important:

> I Samuel 2:30 (NASB): "Therefore the LORD God of Israel declares, 'I did indeed say that your house and the house of your father should walk before Me forever'; but now the Lord declares, 'Far be it from Me—**for those who honor Me I will honor, and those who despise Me will be lightly esteemed.**'"

Here's what David said:

> II Samuel 22:21, 25 (AMP): **The LORD rewarded me according to my uprightness** with Him; **He compensated and benefited me according to the cleanness of my hands.** [25]Therefore **the LORD has recompensed me according to my righteousness, according to my cleanness in His [holy] sight.** *[See also Psalm 18:20, 24]*

When Solomon was praying during the dedication of the Temple, he stated:

> II Chronicles 6:23 (ESV): . . .then hear from heaven and act and judge your servants, **repaying the guilty by bringing his conduct on his own head, and vindicating the righteous by rewarding him according to his righteousness.**

Later on, Solomon said this:

> Proverbs 11:24–25 (NLT): **Give freely and become more wealthy; be stingy and lose everything.** [25]**The generous will prosper; those who refresh others will themselves be refreshed.**

Let's look at Isaiah next:

> Isaiah 59:18a (NIV): **According to what they have done, so will he repay wrath to his enemies and retribution to his foes.** . .

Free to Choose?

> Isaiah 64:5 (NIV): **You come to the help of those who gladly do right, who remember your ways. But when we continued to sin against them, you were angry.** How then can we be saved?

Then Jeremiah says the same thing:

> Jeremiah 17:10 (NIV): "I the LORD search the heart and examine the mind, **to reward a man according to his conduct, according to what his deeds deserve.**"

> Jeremiah 25:14 (BBE): For a number of nations and great kings will make servants of them, even of them: and **I will give them the reward of their acts, even the reward of the work of their hands.**

> Jeremiah 32:19 (MSG): *[You, God, are]* determined in purpose and relentless in following through, **you see everything that men and women do and respond appropriately to the way they live, to the things they do.**

Later, Ezekiel says the same thing:

> Ezekiel 7:3–4, 8–9 (NIV): The end is now upon you and I will unleash my anger against you. **I will judge you according to your conduct and repay you for all your detestable practices.** ⁴I will not look on you with pity or spare you; **I will surely repay you for your conduct and the detestable practices among you.** Then you will know that I am the Lord. ⁸I am about to pour out my wrath on you and spend my anger against you; **I will judge you according to your conduct and repay you for all your detestable practices.** ⁹I will not look on you with pity or spare you; **I will repay you in accordance with your conduct and the detestable practices among you.** Then you will know that it is I the Lord who strikes the blow.

How can one possibly misinterpret that? Then a few chapters later, God is telling Ezekiel that a certain proverb that was apparently making the rounds in Israel—one that claimed that sons would be punished for their fathers' sins—was wrong:

> Ezekiel 18:3–4 (NIV): As surely as I live, declares the Sovereign LORD, you will no longer quote this proverb in Israel. ⁴For every living soul belongs to me, the father as well as the son—both alike belong to me. **The soul who sins is the one who will die.**

Chapter 3: We Have a Free Will, and We Can Choose God

Some time later, when the Babylonians attacked Jerusalem, because the Israelites had abandoned God yet again, God tells Ezekiel:

> Ezekiel 24:14 (NIV): "'I the LORD have spoken. The time has come for me to act. I will not hold back; I will not have pity, nor will I relent. **You will be judged according to your conduct and your actions,** declares the Sovereign LORD.'"

Hosea adds this:

> Hosea 4:6 (NLT): My people are being destroyed because they don't know me. **Since you priests refuse to know me, I refuse to recognize you as my priests. Since you have forgotten the laws of your God, I will forget to bless your children.**

This is *really* difficult to misinterpret: God is clearly behaving toward us like we have behaved toward Him. (For more discussion on God forgetting things, or choosing to not know things, see "Limited Omniscience" in the Unconditional Election chapter.) But then Malachi chimes in as well:

> Malachi 2:2 (NIV): "**If you do not listen, and if you do not set your heart to honor my name,**" says the Lord Almighty, "**I will send a curse upon you,** and I will curse your blessings. Yes, **I have already cursed them, because you have not set your heart to honor me.**"

What will be the outcome of Judgment Day? Basically, God will give to us, starting at that moment, what we have been giving to Him during our lives. So again, His behavior towards us is determined by our prior behavior towards Him:

> Matthew 16:27: For the Son of man shall come in the glory of his Father with his angels; and then **he shall reward every man according to his works.**

In the Sermon on the Mount and other sermons, Jesus includes the following, which are completely unambiguous and definitive statements that show beyond doubt that how we act toward God determines how He acts toward us, and even more so:

> Matthew 6:14–15 (NASB): For **if you forgive men** for their transgressions, **your heavenly Father will also forgive you.** ¹⁵But **if you do not forgive men, then your Father will not forgive your transgressions.**

> Matthew 10:32–33: Whosoever therefore shall **confess** me before men, him will I **confess** also before my Father which is in heaven. ³³But

103

whosoever shall **deny** me before men, him will I also **deny** before my Father which is in heaven.

Matthew 18:33–35 (NIV): 'Shouldn't you have had mercy on your fellow servant just as I had on you?' ³⁴In anger his master turned him over to the jailers to be tortured, until he should pay back all he owed. ³⁵**This is how my heavenly Father will treat each of you unless you forgive your brother from your heart.**

Mark 11:25–26 (NASB): Whenever you stand praying, **forgive, if you have anything against anyone, so that your Father who is in heaven will also forgive you** your transgressions. ²⁶But **if you do not forgive, neither will your Father who is in heaven forgive your transgressions.**

Luke 6:37–38 (NIV): **Do not judge, and you will not be judged. Do not condemn, and you will not be condemned. Forgive, and you will be forgiven.** ³⁸**Give, and it will be given to you.** A good measure, pressed down, shaken together and running over, will be poured into your lap. For **with the measure you use, it will be measured to you.**

John 5:29: And shall come forth; **they that have done good, unto the resurrection of life;** and **they that have done evil, unto the resurrection of damnation.**

And the apostle Paul is in agreement concerning the principle that God treats us according to how we treat Him:

Romans 11:22 (NLT): Notice how God is both kind and severe. He is severe toward those who disobeyed, but **kind to you if you continue to trust in his kindness. But if you stop trusting, you also will be cut off.**

II Corinthians 9:6 (ASV): The point is this: **whoever sows sparingly will also reap sparingly, and whoever sows bountifully will also reap bountifully.**

II Thessalonians 1:6 (GWORD): Certainly, **it is right for God to give suffering to those who cause you to suffer.**

Peter makes an interesting statement in his first epistle:

I Peter 1:17 (NIV): Since you call on a **Father who judges each man's work impartially,** live your lives as strangers here in reverent fear.

Why should we live our lives here on earth in reverent fear? Because *God judges each man's work impartially,* and not according to a predetermined decision unrelated to our thoughts, desires, behavior, and choices.

James also confirms that God pays back to people what they have been putting out:

> James 2:13 (NIV): . . .because **judgment without mercy will be shown to anyone who has not been merciful.** Mercy triumphs over judgment!

In Revelation, John writes the following:

> Revelation 20:12–13 (AMP): I [also] saw the dead, great and small; they stood before the throne, and books were opened. Then another book was opened, which is [the Book] of Life. And **the dead were judged (sentenced) by what they had done** [their whole way of feeling and acting, their aims and endeavors] in accordance with what was recorded in the books. ¹³And the sea delivered up the dead who were in it, death and Hades (the state of death or disembodied existence) surrendered the dead in them, and all were tried and **their cases determined by what they had done** [according to their motives, aims, and works]. . .

And a couple chapters later, continues with this:

> Revelation 22:12 (AMP): Behold, I am coming soon, and I shall bring My **wages and rewards** with Me, **to repay and render to each one just what his own actions and his own work merit.**

And especially this:

> Galatians 6:7–8: Be not deceived; God is not mocked: for **whatsoever a man soweth, that shall he also reap.** ⁸For **he that soweth to his flesh shall of the flesh reap corruption; but he that soweth to the Spirit shall of the Spirit reap life everlasting.**

This whole concept of reaping what you sow would have to be thrown out if the Reformed doctrines of Unconditional Election and Limited Atonement (discussed in later chapters) were true. And the concepts of sowing and reaping are foundational to all of Christianity; they are cornerstones of the heart—the essence—of God's Word. Remember what Jesus said to the disciples when they asked Him to explain the Parable of the Sower? He makes a stunning statement:

> Mark 4:13 (NIV): Then Jesus said to them, "Don't you understand this parable? **How then will you understand any parable?**"

In other words, if we don't understand the concept of sowing and reaping, we will completely misunderstand almost all of what Jesus spoke. And since the Reformed doctrines of Unconditional Election and Limited Atonement completely contradict the concept of reaping what you sow—those doctrines claim that you reap either eternal life or eternal death, completely unrelated to what you have sown—we are forced to choose between Jesus' words, which say one thing, and the Reformed doctrines, which say the opposite. This is no small matter.

In the light of these Scriptures, it is exceedingly difficult to maintain the position that God determines the eternal home of people in a way that is *unrelated* to their behavior on earth. No, these verses clearly, unquestionably, and repeatedly indicate that in order for God's judgment to be righteous, He must judge people according to their actions, choices, and motives.

Whether God accepts us or not depends on our own actions; specifically, whether we trust in Him (believe in Him, rely on Him, receive Him as Lord, etc.):

> Acts 10:35 (AMP): But in every nation **he who venerates and has a reverential fear for God, treating Him with worshipful obedience and living uprightly, is acceptable to Him** and sure of being received and welcomed [by Him].

> Hebrews 5:9: And being made perfect, he became the author of **eternal salvation unto all them that obey him. . .**

Note that venerating God and obeying Him with upright living is the *cause*, and being accepted, received, and welcomed by Him unto eternal salvation is the *effect*.

Standing in the Gap

Remember in the book of Ezekiel when God was searching for an intercessor—someone to "stand in the gap" for His people? Let's read it:

> Ezekiel 22:30–31 (AMP): And I sought a man among them **who should build up the wall and stand in the gap before Me for the land, that I should not destroy it,** but I found none. ³¹Therefore have I poured out My indignation upon them; I have consumed them with the fire of My wrath; **their own way have I repaid [by bringing it] upon their own heads,** says the Lord God.

Note that in this passage, there are two examples of God following our lead, or taking His cue from us:

- First, Israel sinned and therefore God was going to punish them: they rejected Him, so He rejected them. God wouldn't have rejected Israel had not they rejected Him first.

- Second, God was looking for an intercessor to pray for them, and could find none, so there was nothing to hold back His chastisement. God would have held back the well-deserved punishment upon Israel, had anyone in Israel had the spiritual maturity to pray and repent on behalf of the nation.

Turning Away From, Or Toward, God

When God promises to never leave us or forsake us, there is an implicit condition: that *we* don't leave or forsake *Him*. Why do I say that? Because of the following:

> Deuteronomy 31:6, 8 (NKJV): Be strong and of good courage, do not fear nor be afraid of them; for the Lord your God, He is the One who goes with you. **He will not leave you nor forsake you.** . . . ⁸And the Lord, He is the One who goes before you. He will be with you, **He will not leave you nor forsake you**; do not fear nor be dismayed.

That sounds pretty open-and-shut, doesn't it? God will not leave us or forsake us under any circumstances. Well, you could get that idea unless you read it in context. Just a few verses later, God says this:

> Deuteronomy 31:16–17 (NKJV): And the Lord said to Moses: "Behold, you will rest with your fathers; and this people will rise and play the harlot with the gods of the foreigners of the land, where they go to be among them, and **they will forsake Me** and break My covenant which I have made with them. ¹⁷**Then** My anger shall be aroused against them in that day, and **I will forsake them,** and I will hide My face from them, and they shall be devoured. And many evils and troubles shall befall them, so that they will say in that day, 'Have not these evils come upon us because our God is not among us?'"

So here is God, plainly saying He will forsake us, only a few verses after saying He will never forsake us. What changed? In the second case, *the people had forsaken Him first.* Clearly, the promise God gives in vv. 6 and 8—that He will never leave us forsake us—is ironclad *unless we forsake Him*. If we do forsake God, He is under no obligation to keep His end of the covenant, and He is free to forsake us.

And check out what David said to Solomon:

> I Chronicles 28:9 (NLT): And Solomon, my son, learn to know the God of your ancestors intimately. Worship and serve him with your whole heart and a willing mind. For the Lord sees every heart and knows

every plan and thought. If you seek him, you will find him. But **if you forsake him, he will reject you forever.**

. . .and what the prophet Azariah said to King Asa of Judah:

II Chronicles 15:2 (NKJV): And he *[Azariah]* went out to meet Asa, and said to him: "Hear me, Asa, and all Judah and Benjamin. The Lord is with you while you are with Him. If you seek Him, He will be found by you; but **if you forsake Him, He will forsake you.**"

So again, here we have God forsaking (rejecting, casting off, leaving, turning away from, turning his back on, abandoning) people who forsake Him first. In cases where people do forsake God, He often keeps His end of the covenant anyway because of His love, but He is under no *obligation* to do so, because we have broken the covenant. It is a serious thing indeed to reject God.

So here is another case of God following our lead: if we forsake Him, He forsakes us, or at least, is perfectly justified in doing so. But the flip side is true as well—praise God!—as we can see not only from the penultimate conditionals in the two passages above, but also this:

Malachi 3:7 (HCSB): "Since the days of your fathers, you have turned from My statutes; you have not kept them. **Return to Me, and I will return to you,**" says the Lord of Hosts. But you ask: "How can we return?"

Note the wording: "Return to Me, and I will return to you." Pretty hard to misunderstand. So even in our connection with God, He will honor our choice of whether or not we want to have a relationship with Him.

The Parable of the Unfruitful Fig Tree

In the parable of the Unfruitful Fig Tree, note the very profound meaning:

Luke 13:6–9 (NIV): Then he told this parable: "A man had a fig tree, planted in his vineyard, and he went to look for fruit on it, but did not find any. [7]So he said to the man who took care of the vineyard, '**For three years now I've been coming to look for fruit on this fig tree and haven't found any. Cut it down! Why should it use up the soil?**' [8]'Sir,' the man replied, 'leave it alone for one more year, and I'll dig around it and fertilize it. [9]**If it bears fruit next year, fine! If not, then cut it down.**'"

Here are some of the things we can learn from the parable above:
- The man planted a fig tree with the intent, goal, and expectation that it would bear fruit. Side note: We are to bear fruit, but we are not to *try* to bear fruit. We are supposed to abide in the Vine (see John 15:4), and when we do that, the bearing of fruit is an automatic side effect—an automatic by-product.
- The fig tree was given plenty of time and opportunity to bear fruit.
- When, contrary to the planter's intentions and expectations, it *didn't* bear fruit, judgment was pronounced. We see from this that the fig tree's sole purpose was to bear fruit, and if it failed at that, there was no more reason to keep it.
- Intercession on behalf of the unfruitful fig tree delayed the judgment, buying it more time and opportunities to bear fruit. Note that extra effort was expended on behalf of the fig tree, in the hope it would finally bear fruit.
- Although judgment was delayed, it was not going to be completely cancelled in the event that the fig tree still didn't bear fruit, even after all the additional time, opportunities, and encouragement.

The message meshes perfectly with Jesus' teaching on the Vine and Branches:

> John 15:1–2 (NIV): I am the true vine, and my Father is the gardener. ²**He cuts off every branch in me that bears no fruit,** while every branch that does bear fruit he prunes so that it will be even more fruitful.

So here is yet another example of God's behavior toward us reflecting how we have behaved toward Him. See also the Scriptures in the section "Forsaking," below, for other examples of God acting toward us as we have acted toward Him.

The Parable of the Talents

In the following parable, notice that there is a king and a number of servants:

> Luke 19:12–27 (NIV) He said: "A man of noble birth went to a distant country to have himself appointed king and then to return. ¹³So he called ten of his servants and gave them ten minas. **'Put this money to work,'** he said, **'until I come back.'"**

Important point: *all* of the servants heard the king's command and knew what was expected of them. There were ten servants altogether, but only three are described in detail below. To continue:

> ¹⁴"But his subjects hated him and sent a delegation after him to say, 'We don't want this man to be our king.' ¹⁵He was made king, however, and returned home. Then he sent for the servants to whom he had given the money, in order to find out what they had gained with it. ¹⁶The first one came and said, 'Sir, your mina has earned ten more.' ¹⁷'Well done, my good servant!' his master replied. **'Because you have been trustworthy in a very small matter, take charge of ten cities.'** ¹⁸The second came and said, 'Sir, your mina has earned five more.' ¹⁹His master answered, 'You take charge of five cities.'"

Another important aside: Two of the servants obeyed the king, and because they obeyed, *even though they had different levels of success,* they were both rewarded. Both these servants took what their king gave them, *made more with it,* and were considered "good and faithful servants" and were rewarded. This idea of "taking what God gave us and making more with it" is confirmed by Jesus in a different conversation He had:

> Luke 17:9–10 (AMP): Is he grateful and does he praise the servant because he did what he was ordered to do? ¹⁰Even so on your part, when you have done everything that was assigned and commanded you, say, **We are unworthy servants [possessing no merit, for we have not gone beyond our obligation]; we have [merely] done what was our duty to do.**

Notice the phrasing: Jesus is commanding us to consider ourselves "unworthy" servants when "we have not gone beyond our obligation" and have "merely done what was our duty" to do. Jesus likes initiative in us; He would much rather have us attempt to obey Him—*even if we fail*—than to be too afraid to even try.

As Hugh Halter says in his book *The Tangible Kingdom,* "spiritual fervor in the wrong direction is still better than spiritual apathy in the right direction." Jesus said basically the same thing to the church in Laodicea:

> Revelation 3:15–16: I know thy works, that thou art neither cold nor hot: I would thou wert cold or hot. ¹⁶So then **because thou art lukewarm, and neither cold nor hot, I will spue thee out of my mouth.**
>
> (To hear this passage set to music, listen to the song *The Lukewarm Blues* on the album *Dry Bones to Living Stones* or scan the QR code at right.)

16, CJB: So, **because you are lukewarm, neither cold nor hot,** I will vomit you out of my mouth!

EXB: But because you are **lukewarm—neither hot, nor cold—**I am ready to spit [vomit] you out of my mouth.

MSG: You're not cold, you're not hot—**far better to be either cold or hot! You're stale. You're stagnant.** You make me want to vomit.

MOUNCE: So because you are **lukewarm, neither hot nor cold,** I am about to vomit you out of my mouth!

WEB: So, because you are **lukewarm, and neither hot nor cold,** I will vomit you out of my mouth.

WYC: . . .but for thou art **lukewarm, and neither cold, neither hot,** I shall begin to cast thee out of my mouth. [but for thou art lukewarm, and neither cold, nor hot, I shall begin for to vomit thee out of my mouth.]

Note that the thing that was most disgusting to Jesus—the most "vomitogenic," if you will—was not that people were cold; it was that they were lukewarm, stale, stagnant, apathetic.

But how can we possibly take what God has given us and make more with it? Because God is creative, and He made us in His image. So we too are creative. At least, we are creative if we want to be good and faithful servants. When the king said, "Put this money to work," his understanding of that apparently meant to "take what I've given you and make more with it," because that is what he rewarded his servants for.

But let's continue with the parable:

[20]"Then another servant came and said, 'Sir, here is your mina; I have kept it laid away in a piece of cloth. [21]I was afraid of you, because you are a hard man. You take out what you did not put in and reap what you did not sow.' [22]His master replied, 'I will judge you by your own words, you wicked servant! You knew, did you, that I am a hard man, taking out what I did not put in, and reaping what I did not sow? [23]Why then didn't you put my money on deposit, so that when I came back, I could have collected it with interest?'"

Interesting. The servant who gave back to the king *only* what the king had given to him, was considered a "wicked" (or "worthless" in NASB and others, or "bad" in TEV and others, or "evil" in DLNT and others; you get the message) servant.

Free to Choose?

Then, here's the remainder of the story:

> ²⁴"Then he said to those standing by, 'Take his mina away from him and give it to the one who has ten minas.' ²⁵'Sir,' they said, 'he already has ten!' ²⁶**He replied, 'I tell you that to everyone who has, more will be given, but as for the one who has nothing, even what he has will be taken away.'"**

And just as an aside, note the closing verse this parable:

> ²⁷But those enemies of mine **who did not want me to be king over them**—bring them here and kill them in front of me.

Note that it was the *people's* decision to accept the Lord as their ruler or not. Also note that rejecting the Lord as one's ruler results in death. And this death is not a spiteful, hateful execution; it is the inevitable result of rejecting God, the *only* source of life. Had these servants been faithful to obey their Lord, as the other servants had, they too would have been blessed.

The take-away lesson from this parable is that he who is faithful in little will be given much. So here again is a very clear example of God's actions toward us being determined by our actions toward him.

Jesus also said it this way:

John 15:4a (NLT): Remain in me, and I will remain in you.

So Jesus remains in us if, and only if, we remain in Him. And then in Romans, Paul reinforces the idea that God acts toward us like we act toward Him, and it works the same whether we are God's chosen people or not:

> Romans 2:9–11 (NIV): There will be **trouble and distress for every human being who does evil:** first for the Jew, then for the Gentile; ¹⁰but **glory, honor and peace for everyone who does good:** first for the Jew, then for the Gentile. ¹¹For God does not show favoritism.

Notice that the doing evil occurs *before* the trouble and distress happens, and the doing good occurs *before* the glory, honor, and peace happens.

"Giving Account"

What does it mean to "give account" to someone? Said another way, what does it mean to "be accountable" to someone? Basically it means that someone is expected or required to explain and justify his decisions and/or actions. Are there cases of this in the Bible? Specifically, are people accountable to God for their actions and attitudes? Let's investigate.

Actually, the concept of "giving account" to God, or "being accountable" to God is a common theme, both in the Old Testament and the New Testament. Looking at the following verses in other translations reveals synonymous words and phrases that mean the same as "giving account" or "being accountable" to God:

Exodus 32:34 (HCSB): Now go, lead the people to the place I told you about; see, My angel will go before you. But **on the day I settle accounts, I will hold them accountable** for their sin.

Deuteronomy 18:19 (NIV): If anyone does not listen to my words that the prophet speaks in my name, **I myself will call him to account.**

Deuteronomy 23:21 (NET): When you make a vow to the Lord your God you must not delay in fulfilling it, for otherwise **he will surely hold you accountable as a sinner.**

Ecclesiastes 11:9 (NLT): Young people, it's wonderful to be young! Enjoy every minute of it. Do everything you want to do; take it all in. But remember that **you must give an account to God for everything you do.**

Ezekiel 7:3 (NET): The end is now upon you, and I will release my anger against you; I will judge you according to your behavior, **I will hold you accountable** for all your abominable practices.

Matthew 12:36 (BBE): And I say to you that in the day when they are judged, **men will have to give an account** of every foolish word they have said.

John 9:41 (MSG): Jesus said, "If you were really blind, you would be blameless, but since you claim to see everything so well, **you're accountable for every fault and failure.**"

Romans 3:19 (NASB): Now we know that whatever the Law says, it speaks to those who are under the Law, that every mouth may be closed, and **all the world may become accountable to God. . .**

Romans 14:12 (NIV): So then, **each of us will give an account of himself to God.**

Hebrews 4:13 (NLT): Nothing in all creation is hidden from **God.** Everything is naked and exposed before his eyes, and **he is the one to whom we are accountable.**

Hebrews 13:17 (TEV): Obey your leaders and follow their orders. They watch over your souls without resting, since **they must give to God an account** of their service. If you obey them, they will do their work gladly; if not, they will do it with sadness, and that would be of no help to you.

I Peter 4:4–5 (GWORD): Unbelievers insult you now because they are surprised that you no longer join them in the same excesses of wild living. ⁵They **will give an account** to the one who is ready to judge the living and the dead.

So these passages, and others that were omitted, reinforce the idea that we all will give an account to God for our attitudes and actions. In order for this concept to make any sense at all in the context of a just God, it is absolutely imperative that we have a free will with which to choose to obey or disobey God. If the Reformed idea of God's sovereignty were correct, in which our obedience to God is *God's* choice instead of ours, we would have nothing of which to give an account, since we would have had no alternative but to act as we did. Thus, if the Reformed idea of God's sovereignty is valid, all of the above passages would be meaningless and highly misleading.

The Second Coming of Christ

One of the most amazing examples of God taking His cue from us is in the timing of the Second Coming of Jesus. Read what Peter says:

II Peter 3:12 (CEB): . . .waiting for and **hastening the coming day of God**. Because of that day, the heavens will be destroyed by fire and the elements will melt away in the flames.

Really? *We* can actually cause the Day of God—the Second Coming—to occur sooner? That is astonishing! At least, it's astonishing if that is an accurate translation. Let's look at some other translations and see if they concur.

It turns out many English translations actually use the word "hasten" in this verse. The verb "hasten," when used with an object, means "to accelerate, to make to go faster, to hurry." But many other synonymous words and phrases were used by other translation teams; here is the first half of that verse in various translations:

CJB: . . .as you wait for the Day of God and **work to hasten its coming.**

CEV: You should look forward to the day when God judges everyone, and **you should try to make it come soon.**

GNT: . . .as you wait for the Day of God and **do your best to make it come soon.** . .

TLB: You should look forward to that day and **hurry it along.** . .

NIV: . . .as you look forward to the day of God and **speed its coming.**

NLV: You should look for the day of God to come. **You should do what you can to make it come soon.**

NLT: . . .looking forward to the day of God and **hurrying it along.**

NTE: . . .as you look for God's day to appear, and **indeed hurry it on its way. . .**

TPT: . . .while we anticipate and **help to speed up the coming of the day of God. . .**

WE: You should look for the day of God and **do everything you can to make it come quickly.**

WYC: . . .abiding and **hieing into the coming of the day of our Lord Jesus Christ. . .**

Sounds like a lot more than just "looking forward to it," doesn't it? (By the way, the word "hieing" used in the Wycliffe translation is an archaic verb that means "to hurry, hasten, or speed.") But here's the point of this section: if God responds to humans in the timing of something as enormous as the Second Coming of Christ, it seems silly to think He wouldn't respond to humans in much smaller and less significant ways.

Coming to God

There are a couple verses in Hebrews that are quite intriguing, if you think about their implications, as they pertain to the Reformed doctrines. Here they are:

Hebrews 5:9 (CEB): After he *[Jesus]* had been made perfect, he became the source of **eternal salvation for everyone who obeys him.**

ERV: This made him the perfect high priest, who provides the way for **everyone who obeys him to be saved** forever.

Hebrews 7:25 (NASB): Therefore He *[Jesus]* is able also to **save forever those who draw near** to God through Him, since He always lives to make intercession for them.

HCSB: Therefore, He is always able to **save those who come to God** through Him, since He always lives to intercede for them.

So who is Jesus able to save? *Those who obey Him, and those who come to God through Him.* But these two groups of people are actually the same group because (as we saw in great detail earlier, in "Does God Want Everyone to be Saved?") if we obey Him, we will come to Him for salvation. How do we know this? Because in many passages, God commands *all* people to come to Him for salvation. Coming to God—also known as "receiving" Him, "accepting" Him, or "believing in" Him—is a matter of our choice. God made a way for all mankind to be redeemed (covered in the aforementioned section) but the benefits of salvation only kick in if we submit ourselves to God.

God's Behavior Based on Our Attitudes

Not only does God act toward us in a way that is consistent with our actions toward Him, but can also see our hearts; He knows our thoughts. Which means that we can't fool Him by acting nice and still having a bad attitude; He will see right through our attempted deception, and won't be fooled for a second. This means that even when we do a "good" thing, if we do it with a lousy attitude, it won't be beneficial. God will still respond to us according to our attitudes.

This tendency to "act" nicely but have lousy attitudes and motives has been with us for millennia:

> Isaiah 29:13 (NASB): Then the Lord said, "Because this people draw near with their words and **honor Me with their lip service, but they remove their hearts far from Me,** and their reverence for Me consists of tradition learned by rote. [14]Therefore behold, I will once again deal marvelously with this people, wondrously marvelous; And the wisdom of their wise men shall perish, and the discernment of their discerning men shall be concealed."

One of the clearest examples of this comes from the prophet Amos, where God is reprimanding Israel because they had wrong attitudes. They were doing the right "things," but they were hypocrites—their attitudes were repugnant to God:

> Amos 5:21–23 (NIV): **I hate, I despise** your religious feasts; **I cannot stand** your assemblies. [22]Even though you bring me burnt offerings and grain offerings, **I will not accept them.** Though you bring choice fellowship offerings, **I will have no regard for them.** [23]Away with the noise of your songs! **I will not listen** to the music of your harps.

And Jesus dealt with the same thing in His day:

> Mark 7:6–9 (NIV): He replied, "Isaiah was right when he prophesied about you hypocrites; as it is written: 'These people **honor me with their lips, but their hearts are far from me.** [7]They worship me in vain; their teachings are but rules taught by men.' [8]You have let go of the commands of God and are holding on to the traditions of men." [9]And he said to them: "You have a fine way of **setting aside the commands of God in order to observe your own traditions!**"

Chapter 3: We Have a Free Will, and We Can Choose God

So it's clear that when we try to do "good" things with bad motives or attitudes, we're not fooling God, and He will deal with us appropriately.

As you're probably aware, King Saul tried to kill David on many occasions, and though David had multiple opportunities to retaliate and kill Saul, he wouldn't do it. David didn't take vengeance himself, because He knew that wasn't his job. Finally, Saul and the rest of David's enemies die in battle, and David writes a song of thanks to the Lord, which later becomes Psalm 18. In it, he says:

> II Samuel 22:26–27 (NIV): **To the faithful** you show yourself faithful, **to the blameless** you show yourself blameless, ²⁷**to the pure** you show yourself pure, but **to the crooked** you show yourself shrewd.

That's pretty amazing: this Scripture unmistakeably shows that God behaves toward us *in the same way,* good or bad, that we are behaving toward Him.

When King Asa of Judah, needing help in a military campaign, sought the help of the king of Syria instead of the help of God, the seer Hanani reprimands him. Among other things, Hanani says:

> II Chronicles 16:9a: For the eyes of the LORD run to and fro throughout the whole earth, to shew himself strong **in the behalf of them whose heart is perfect toward him.**

Note that the people's hearts were *already* "perfect toward him" and that is what caused Him to show Himself strong on their behalf.

Here is a portion of Psalm 18 (mentioned above), which David wrote after God delivered him from his enemies. You may be wondering, since I already quoted this idea from II Samuel 22, why do I quote it from Psalms as well? A better question might be, why did God include it in the Bible twice? Could it be that He *really* wanted us to understand the concept?

> Psalm 18:25–26: **With the merciful** thou wilt shew thyself merciful; **with an upright man** thou wilt shew thyself upright; ²⁶**With the pure** thou wilt shew thyself pure; and **with the froward** thou wilt shew thyself froward.

The word "froward" is somewhat uncommon these days; what does it mean? Think of the phrase "to and fro"—it means to alternate or oscillate between moving in one direction (or toward something) and then moving in the opposite direction (or away from that thing). When we act "toward" God, we act in a way that brings us nearer to Him; when we act "froward" God, we act in a way that moves us farther from Him. In modern times, the word "un-

FREE TO CHOOSE?

toward" is more common than "froward," but it means the same thing, since "to" and "fro" are opposites, and "un" negates the word following it; e.g., "righteous" vs. "unrighteous."

And of course, another way to find out what "froward" means is to look at the above Scripture in other translations to see its synonyms:

> Psalm 18:26b (AMP): . . .with the **perverse** You will show Yourself contrary.
>
> CEV: . . .you treat the **unfaithful** as their deeds deserve.
>
> ERV: . . .you outsmart the **wicked**, no matter how clever they are.
>
> ESV: . . .with the **crooked** you make yourself seem tortuous.
>
> EXB: . . .you are [show yourself] against [hostile/shrewd/cunning/perverse to] those who are bad [**perverse; devious; crooked**].
>
> GNT: . . .hostile to those who are **wicked**.
>
> HCSB: . . .with the **crooked** You prove Yourself shrewd.
>
> ISV: . . .to the **morally corrupt**, you appear to be perverse.
>
> JUB: . . .with the **perverse** thou wilt show thyself adversary.
>
> TLB: You give. . . pain to **those who leave your paths**.
>
> NCV: . . .you are against those who are **bad**.
>
> NLV: With the **sinful** You show Yourself to be against them.
>
> VOICE: . . .with the **twisted**, You make Yourself contrary.
>
> YLT: . . .with the **perverse** showest Thyself a wrestler. . .

Wow. Those Scriptures are certainly enlightening, as well as indisputable: God definitely behaves toward us in the same way as we act toward Him. And He acts that way toward us not coincidentally, nor accidentally, nor randomly, but *because* we act that way toward Him.

In Psalm 119, Scripture offers another place where God's behavior toward us depends on our behavior toward Him.

> Psalm 119:132 (TEV): Turn to me and have mercy on me **as you do on all those who love you.**

In Lamentations, Jeremiah says a comparable thing:

> Lamentations 3:25: The Lord is good unto them that **wait for him**, to the soul that **seeketh him**.

Note that the waiting for, and seeking of God is the *cause* of the Lord being good to people. In other words, this verse says that God is good to people who wait for Him and seek Him, *because* they wait for Him and seek Him.

Then Zechariah shows how God responds to our repentance:

Zechariah 1:3 (NASB): "Therefore say to them, 'Thus says the Lord of hosts, **"Return to Me,"** declares the Lord of hosts, **"that I may return to you,"** says the Lord of hosts.'"

James, in his epistle to all of Israel, exhorts them:

James 4:8a: **Draw nigh to God, and he will draw nigh to you.**

The order of causation—which thing was the cause and which thing was the effect—is clear: The cause is our drawing nigh to God, and the effect is that He draws nigh to us.

God Acting Because We Asked Him To

In the Scriptures below, circumstances are changed because people pray. Here is another place where Scripture refutes the Reformed idea of predestination. Now be assured that I am *not* saying that "Scripture refutes predestination"—it certainly does not—but Scripture does refute the *Reformed* interpretation of predestination: the idea of predestination that claims that all our thoughts, actions, decisions, and so forth are fated, set in stone, inevitable, unchangeable. We'll see more on this distinction in the "Predestination" section below.

For example, the Israelites were delivered from bondage in Egypt. Why? Because they prayed, and God answered their prayers:

Exodus 3:7–8a (NIV): The LORD said, "I have indeed seen the misery of my people in Egypt. **I have heard them crying out** because of their slave drivers, and I am concerned about their suffering. [8]**So I have come down to rescue them** from the hand of the Egyptians and to bring them up out of that land into a good and spacious land, a land flowing with milk and honey. . ."

In Numbers 13–14, when the twelve spies went into the land of Canaan to check out the land, ten of the spies came back with fearful reports; only Joshua and Caleb came back with faithful reports. But the influence of the fearful spies poisoned the minds of the Israelites, and they complained about Moses and Aaron and wanted to elect a new leader to take them back to Egypt.

When Joshua and Caleb tried to tell the Israelites that God could easily give them the victory, the Israelites wanted to stone them. God was angered, and was ready to wipe out the whole nation, and Moses interceded, asking God to forgive them:

> Numbers 14:20: And the LORD said, I have pardoned **according to thy word**...

After Moses and Joshua died, and the children of Israel abandoned God and started serving idols, things went poorly for them (surprise, surprise). Israel was conquered by Chushanrishathaim, king of Mesopotamia, and were in bondage to him for eight years:

> Judges 3:9: And **when the children of Israel cried unto the LORD, the LORD raised up a deliverer to the children of Israel, who delivered them,** even Othniel the son of Kenaz, Caleb's younger brother.

When David and his men were returning home to Ziklag, they discovered that the Amalekites had attacked, captured their wives and families, stolen all their valuables, and burned the city. After the initial shock of the discovery had passed, David prayed for guidance:

> I Samuel 30:8 (TEV): David asked the LORD, "Shall I go after those raiders? And will I catch them?" He answered, "Go after them; you will catch them and rescue the captives."

The widow of Zarapheth supported the ministry of Elijah the prophet, and gave him room and board, and the Lord miraculously caused her food to never run out. Eventually, her only son fell ill and died and, distraught, she begged Elijah for help:

> I Kings 17:21–22 (NIV): Then he stretched himself out on the boy three times and cried to the LORD, "O LORD my God, let this boy's life return to him!" ²²**The LORD heard Elijah's cry, and the boy's life returned to him, and he lived.**

In Psalm 2, God commands us to ask Him, and He will give us, well, basically, the world:

> Psalm 2:8 (CEB): **Just ask me, and I will make the nations your possession;** the far corners of the earth will be your property.
>
> CEV: **Ask me for the nations**, and every nation on earth will belong to you.

Chapter 3: We Have a Free Will, and We Can Choose God

The psalmist praises the greatness of the Lord, and says:

Psalm 99:6: Moses and Aaron among his priests, and Samuel among them that call upon his name; **they called upon the Lord, and he answered them.**

Moses is the reason that the Israelites are still around—God would have destroyed them had Moses not interceded for them:

Psalm 106:23 (AMP): Therefore He said **He would destroy them. [And He would have done so] had not Moses, His chosen one, stepped into the breach** before Him to turn away His threatening wrath.

Intercession on behalf of others is so important to God that he searches for them, so that they will pray and cry out for him to bless. Mercy triumphs over judgment (James 2:13), but if no one is willing to obey God and intercede, judgment is the only remaining option:

Ezekiel 22:29–31 (NIV): The people of the land practice extortion and commit robbery; they oppress the poor and needy and mistreat the alien, denying them justice. ³⁰"**I looked for a man among them who would build up the wall and stand before me in the gap on behalf of the land so I would not have to destroy it,** but I found none. ³¹So I will pour out my wrath on them and consume them with my fiery anger, bringing down on their own heads all they have done, declares the Sovereign Lord."

Jesus, in the Sermon on the Mount, tells all His listeners:

Matthew 7:7–11 (NIV): **Ask and it will be given to you;** seek and you will find; knock and the door will be opened to you. ⁸For **everyone who asks receives;** he who seeks finds; and to him who knocks, the door will be opened. ⁹Which of you, if his son asks for bread, will give him a stone? ¹⁰Or if he asks for a fish, will give him a snake? ¹¹If you, then, though you are evil, know how to give **good gifts** to your children, how much more will your Father in heaven **give good gifts to those who ask him!**

Not everybody receives, but those who ask, do. (More on this passage later, in the section "Ask, Seek, Knock.")

In the book of Acts, the early church was being persecuted by the Jewish religious leaders, and imprisoned them and threatened them with worse, the apostles went back to their friends and prayed:

> Acts 4:29–31 (NIV): "Now, Lord, consider their threats and **enable your servants to speak your word with great boldness.** ³⁰Stretch out your hand to heal and perform miraculous signs and wonders through the name of your holy servant Jesus." ³¹After they prayed, the place where they were meeting was shaken. And they were all filled with the Holy Spirit and **spoke the word of God boldly.**

In Joppa, there was a godly woman named Tabitha. She fell ill and died and was prepared for burial, but some friends of hers sent for Peter, who was in a neighboring town about ten miles away. Peter came in response to their plea, and went to see the body. . .

> Acts 9:40: But **Peter** put them all forth, and kneeled down, and **prayed;** and turning him to the body said, Tabitha, arise. And **she opened her eyes: and** when she saw Peter, she **sat up.**

Later on, Peter was jailed again, and put in maximum security:

> Acts 12:5–12 (TEV): So Peter was kept in jail, but **the people of the church were praying earnestly to God for him.** ⁶The night before Herod was going to bring him out to the people, Peter was sleeping between two guards. He was tied with two chains, and there were guards on duty at the prison gate.

Looks pretty hopeless for Peter, no?

> ⁷Suddenly an angel of the Lord stood there, and a light shone in the cell. The angel shook Peter by the shoulder, woke him up, and said, "Hurry! Get up!" At once the chains fell off Peter's hands. ⁸Then the angel said, "Tighten your belt and put on your sandals." Peter did so, and the angel said, "Put your cloak around you and come with me." ⁹Peter followed him out of the prison, not knowing, however, if what the angel was doing was real; he thought he was seeing a vision. ¹⁰They passed by the first guard station and then the second, and came at last to the iron gate that opens into the city. The gate opened for them by itself, and they went out. They walked down a street, and suddenly the angel left Peter. ¹¹Then Peter realized what had happened to him, and said, **"Now I know that it is really true! The Lord sent his angel to rescue me from Herod's power and from everything the Jewish people expected to happen."**

The same concept—God taking His cue from us, and choosing His actions based on our actions, specifically, our prayers—also applies in our receiving of spiritual gifts:

> I Corinthians 12:11 (NIV): All these *[spiritual gifts]* are the work of one and the same Spirit, and **he gives them to each one, just as he determines.**

So if the Holy Spirit "determines" who gets what spiritual gifts, do we have any say in the matter? Actually, yes:

> I Corinthians 12:31a (NIV): But **eagerly desire the greater gifts.**

> I Corinthians 14:1 (NIV): Follow the way of love and **eagerly desire spiritual gifts, especially the gift of prophecy.**

> I Corinthians 14:12 (NIV): So it is with you. Since you are eager to have spiritual gifts, **try to excel in gifts that build up the church.**

> I Corinthians 14:13 (NIV): For this reason anyone who speaks in a tongue should **pray that he may interpret** what he says.

> I Corinthians 14:31 (NIV): For **you can all prophesy** in turn so that everyone may be instructed and encouraged.

> I Corinthians 14:32 (NIV): **The spirits of prophets are subject to the control of prophets.**

> I Corinthians 14:39 (NIV): Therefore, my brothers, **be eager to prophesy,** and do not forbid speaking in tongues.

Think about what Paul says here: if the Holy Spirit did things irresistibly, or if God determines which spiritual gifts we get without regard to our actions, desires, or choices, the list of Scriptures above would be pointless or downright erroneous. So just as we've seen in other areas, the Holy Spirit gives spiritual gifts to each one, just as He determines (I Corinthians 12:11, shown above), but it becomes obvious if we continue reading, that *what He "determines" is greatly influenced by what we desire, and what we pray for.* If that were not the case:

- It would be pointless for Paul to instruct us to "eagerly desire" the greater gifts (12:31).
- It would be pointless for Paul to instruct us to "eagerly desire. . . especially the gift of prophecy" (14:1).
- It would be fruitless for us to try to "excel" in *any* kind of gifts, let alone those that build up the church (14:12).

- It would be completely ineffectual for any speaker in tongues to pray to interpret his message (14:13).
- It would be false for Paul to say "you can all prophesy" because we have no say in the matter (14:31).
- It would be in error to say that "the spirits of prophets are subject to the control of prophets" (14:32).
- It would be pointless for Paul to encourage us to "be eager to prophesy" (14:39).

So unless we are willing to say that the seven statements above are true, which would mean that all seven of Paul's corresponding statements are either false or pointless, we must conclude that what the Holy Spirit "determines" in giving us spiritual gifts is greatly influenced by what we seek and pursue in prayer. In other words, here's another case of God's actions being influenced by our actions; God taking His cue from us. For much more detail on the spiritual gifts, see Book 7: *Be Filled with the Spirit.*

James, the half-brother of Jesus, writes this:

> James 5:16: Confess your faults one to another, and pray one for another, that ye may be healed. **The effectual fervent prayer of a righteous man availeth much.**

We've seen examples from both the Old Testament and the New, that's God's behavior and actions can be strongly influenced by people. But let's go back to the Old Testament one more time while we're on this subject, to see what may be the most astonishing example of God being moved by the actions of a human. Remember when Moses was up on Mount Sinai in the glory of God, and the Israelites below built and worshiped the golden calf? Here's how God responded to them:

> Exodus 32:9–10 (NIV): "I have seen these people," the Lord said to Moses, "and they are a stiff-necked people. [10]**Now leave me alone so that my anger may burn against them and that I may destroy them.** Then I will make you into a great nation."

Wow! Here's God saying to Moses, "Go away. I'm going to burn down the whole nation." Now, there's no question that they deserved it, and their destruction would have been entirely justified. But notice how Moses responds—he *disobeyed* God's command to "go away," and instead, interceded for Israel:

> Exodus 32:11 (NIV): **But Moses sought the favor of the Lord his God.**
> "O Lord," he said, "why should your anger burn against your people,

CHAPTER 3: WE HAVE A FREE WILL, AND WE CAN CHOOSE GOD

whom you brought out of Egypt with great power and a mighty hand?"

Note that Moses sought the favor of God *for Israel*, not for himself, in spite of the fact that God had already told Moses He would make him into a great nation. Moses selflessly interceded for Israel, his own potential gain notwithstanding, and continued in this vein for a couple more verses, pointing out to God that His reputation would be tarnished, and also reminding Him of His covenant with Abraham, Isaac, and Jacob. How did God respond to Moses' intercession?

> Exodus 32:14 (NIV): Then **the Lord relented** and did not bring on his people the disaster he had threatened.

How on earth did Moses have the boldness and the audacity to *disobey* a direct command of God, and instead, *intercede* for these rebellious, stiff-necked people, that God would avert their well-deserved judgment? Because Moses knew what God was like, and how He operated:

> Psalm 103:7 (NIV): **He made known his ways to Moses,** his deeds to the people of Israel. . .

In the Scripture above, where God said He showed His *deeds* to the children of Israel, it does not mean that He failed to also show them His ways. As we'll see in the following Scripture, they *should* have known God's ways, but because they hardened their hearts, they did not learn God's ways, and He was grieved with them as a result:

> Psalm 95:10–11 (NIV): For forty years I was angry with that generation; I said, **"They are a people whose hearts go astray, and they have not known my ways."** ¹¹So I declared on oath in my anger, "They shall never enter my rest."

See also Hebrews 3:10–11. But what are God's ways? That's too big of a question to answer; the ways of God are at least numerous, and probably infinite in number. So what are God's ways, *as they pertain to the current topic?*

> I Chronicles 16:34: O give thanks unto the Lord; for **he is good; for his mercy endureth for ever.**

Comparable statements about the Lord's goodness and mercy are reiterated in II Chronicles 5:13, 7:2, Ezra 3:11, Psalm 86:5, 100:5, 106:1, 107:1, 109:21, 118:29, 136:1, Jeremiah 33:11, and many other places.

How much clearer could it be that God's actions are *strongly* influenced by ours? We've seen case after case where God answers prayer—that is, His actions of answering occur as a result of our actions of asking, and He is always motivated by love and mercy.

And, as you are no doubt aware, there are hundreds of other examples of answered prayer that I could have included above, but the ones above suffice to get the point across. The point being this: because people prayed, things changed. God answered prayer, and there is every indication from the passages above that God answered *because they asked.* Which means that the things they were praying for were not Calvinistically predestined to happen (more about this in subsequent chapters), but they happened because people, moved by their own free will, petitioned God, and He, responding to their faith, answered them.

So we can see that God answers prayers *because* people prayed and asked Him to intervene in their situation. And the reverse is also true:

> James 4:2 (TEV): You want things, but you cannot have them, so you are ready to kill; you strongly desire things, but you cannot get them, so you quarrel and fight. **You do not have what you want *because* you do not ask God for it.**

Also notice that *every one* of the Scriptures in this section, as well as the two prior sections, shows God's behavior being influenced by *our* behavior. It takes one of three forms: "If you do this, I will do that" (action oriented), "If you're like this, I'll be like that" (attitude oriented), or "If you ask, I will answer" (intercession oriented). In these three ways, it's easy to see that God often mirrors our actions and attitudes. And in all three cases, the evidence refutes the idea of God having already decided every last detail in the universe from eternity past.

Again, *all* the above Scriptures have God's attitudes and actions toward us being determined, or at least *heavily* influenced, by our attitudes and actions toward Him. Why would all the above Scriptures show God responding to *us*, if we have no choice but to do as our programmed instructions dictate? That would make all of our existence seem like a pointless puppet show.

Even if we adopt the less strict version of the no-free-will idea—the one that says we actually *do* have free will, except for in the matter of salvation, where it really matters—the Scriptures above militate against even that moderated form of the doctrine. Because, if you notice, almost all the Scriptures above are talking about the situation that *does* really matter: our choosing to serve God or not.

The Complaint Department

God takes His cues from us in another area as well: He *really* doesn't like it when we grumble, murmur, and complain.

> Numbers 17:10: And the Lord said unto Moses, Bring Aaron's rod again before the testimony, to be kept for a token against the rebels; and thou shalt quite **take away their murmurings from me, that they die not.**

> CEB: Then the Lord said to Moses, "Return Aaron's staff in front of the chest containing the covenant to serve as a sign to the rebels **so that their complaints against me end and they don't die.**"

> CEV: But the Lord told Moses, "Put Aaron's stick back! Let it stay near the sacred chest as a warning to anyone who might think about rebelling. **If these people don't stop their grumbling about me, I will wipe them out.**"

> GNT: The Lord said to Moses, "Put Aaron's stick back in front of the Covenant Box. It is to be kept as a warning to the rebel Israelites that **they will die unless their complaining stops.**"

Would God really do that? Would he actually destroy people because they complained? Actually, yes, and He had already done it:

> Numbers 11:1: And **when the people complained, it displeased the Lord:** and the Lord heard it; and **his anger was kindled; and the fire of the Lord burnt among them, and consumed them** that were in the uttermost parts of the camp.

This event was later described in the Psalms:

> Psalm 106:21–25 (NIV): They **forgot** the God who saved them, who had done great things in Egypt, ²²miracles in the land of Ham and awesome deeds by the Red Sea. ²³So he said he would destroy them—had not Moses, his chosen one, stood in the breach before him to keep his wrath from destroying them. ²⁴Then they **despised** the pleasant land; they **did not believe** his promise. ²⁵**They grumbled in their tents and did not obey the Lord.**

Wow. What's the big deal about complaining? Actually, plenty:

- When we complain, we are not being thankful, which is how we are to approach God (Psalm 100:4).
- When we complain, we are revealing that we believe the enemy's strength to be greater than God's (Numbers 13:1–14:4).

FREE TO CHOOSE?

- When we complain, we are lacking faith (Psalm 106:24), without which it is impossible to please God (Hebrews 11:6).
- When we complain, we are being disobedient to God (Psalm 106:25).

. . .and so forth. But not only that, but when we complain, *we provoke God to give us the very things we are complaining about:*

Numbers 14:26–30: And the Lord spake unto Moses and unto Aaron, saying, ²⁷How long shall I bear with this evil congregation, which **murmur** against me? I have heard the **murmurings** of the children of Israel, which they **murmur** against me. ²⁸Say unto them, **As truly as I live, saith the Lord, as ye have spoken in mine ears, so will I do to you:** ²⁹Your carcases shall fall in this wilderness; and all that were numbered of you, according to your whole number, from twenty years old and upward, which have **murmured** against me, ³⁰Doubtless ye shall not come into the land, concerning which I sware to make you dwell therein, save Caleb the son of Jephunneh, and Joshua the son of Nun.

v. 28, CEV: . . .to give this message to the people of Israel: You sinful people have complained against me too many times! **Now I swear by my own life that I will give you exactly what you wanted.**

ERV: So tell them, 'The Lord says that **he will surely do all those things to you that you complained about.** This is what will happen to you. . .'

EXB: So tell them, 'This is what the Lord says [the utterance/decree of the Lord]. I heard what you said, and **as surely as I live, I will do those very things to you. . .'**

GWORD: So tell them, 'As I live, declares the Lord, I solemnly swear **I will do everything to you that you said I would do.'**

HCSB: "Tell them: As surely as I live," this is the Lord's declaration, "**I will do to you exactly as I heard you say.**"

NIV: So tell them, 'As surely as I live, declares the Lord, **I will do to you the very thing I heard you say. . .'**

Here is another blatant example of God taking His cue from us, and behaving toward us in the same way we have acted toward Him—indeed, *giving us the very things we complain about.* It kinda makes you want to think twice before saying things like the following, when things don't go your way:

- "That's just my luck!"
- "Wouldn't you know it!"

CHAPTER 3: WE HAVE A FREE WILL, AND WE CAN CHOOSE GOD

- "Well, that's just typical!"
- "You have the flu? Great. Now I'm gonna get it too."
- "This *always* happens to me!"
- "We have the lousiest president in the world!"
- "My grandfather and father both died of cancer, so I probably will too."

Maybe it's true, what the following verse says, in more ways than one:

Proverbs 18:21 (AMP): **Death and life are in the power of the tongue, and they who indulge in it shall eat the fruit of it [for death or life].**

CEV: **Words can bring death or life!** Talk too much, and you will eat everything you say.

ERV: **The tongue can speak words that bring life or death.** Those who love to talk must be ready to accept what it brings.

GNT: **What you say can preserve life or destroy it;** so you must accept the consequences of your words.

Types and Shadows

The Old Testament contains many "types and shadows" of things to be revealed later, in the New Testament. What are types and shadows, in this context? They could be described as "situational prophecies" in which a situation, story, feast, or whatever in the Old Testament symbolizes in multiple ways some truths that would be more fully revealed in the New.

Perhaps the most obvious one of these is that of the Passover Lamb, described in Exodus, and which in many ways foreshadowed Jesus' death on the cross. Of course, the Old Testament contains many other types and shadows; will look at a few of them here.

Seeking a Bride for Isaac

Genesis 24 tells the story of Abraham sending the chief steward of his house, his eldest servant Eliezer, to seek a bride for his son Isaac. Abraham is a type of God, Isaac is a type of Jesus, and Eliezer is a type of the Holy Spirit, and this will become clear as we read the story. Let's look at the high points of this narrative:

Genesis 24:2–4 (NIV): He *[Abraham]* said to the chief servant in his household, the one in charge of all that he had, "Put your hand under my thigh. ³I want you to swear by the Lord, the God of heaven and the God of earth, that you will not get a wife for my son from the daughters of the Canaanites, among whom I am living, ⁴but will go to my country and my own relatives and **get a wife for my son Isaac."**

The "chief servant" referred to in v. 2 is Eliezer. Although he is not referred to by name in this passage, he is named in an earlier passage:

Genesis 15:2 (NLT): But Abram replied, "O Sovereign Lord, what good are all your blessings when I don't even have a son? Since you've given me no children, **Eliezer** of Damascus, a servant in my household, will inherit all my wealth."

The phrase "put your hand under my thigh" is a way of swearing a solemn vow. For millennia, oaths have been solemnified and made even more binding by swearing on—putting your hand on—something sacred; for example, "swearing on the Bible." Back in Abraham's days, before there was a Bible, the most sacred thing Abraham had was his covenant with God, symbolized by circumcision and which included the promise that Abraham's offspring would be innumerable. Abraham's "seed" here implies "sperm" and the resulting descendents, and this carries forward into the New Testament as well, where the English word "seed" is translated from the Greek word σπέρμα (*sperma*, G4690).

Of course, seed/sperm are created in the testicles, and there has been a long-standing association between solemn oaths and testicles ever since, likely because of the sacredness of Abraham's covenant with God. Consulting a dictionary for the etymologies of the words "testify," "testimony," "testament," "testate," and so forth, will reveal that all these words are related to "testis" or "testicle."

So "thigh" is not the best translation here; a better translation is "genitals," as in Abraham saying to Eliezer "put your hand on my genitals." Whether the emphasis was on the penis, because of the circumcision that represented the covenant, or the testicles, because they were the source of the seed required for his offspring, is unclear. With apparently little concern for the sensitivities and approval of modern American churchgoers, reproduction and the reproductive organs seem to be quite important to God. So in short, Abraham was making the most solemn oath possible with his servant Eliezer.

CHAPTER 3: WE HAVE A FREE WILL, AND WE *CAN* CHOOSE GOD

But why are the reproductive organs so important to God? Probably because reproduction is the vehicle through which the Redeemer entered the world:

> Genesis 3:15 (NIV): And I *[God]* will put enmity between you and the woman, and **between your offspring and hers; he will crush your head,** and you will strike his heel.

> Luke 1:30–31, 34–35 (NASB): The angel said to her, "Do not be afraid, Mary; for you have found favor with God. ³¹And behold, **you will conceive in your womb and bear a son,** and you shall name Him Jesus." ³⁴Mary said to the angel, **"How can this be, since I am a virgin?"** ³⁵The angel answered and said to her, **"The Holy Spirit will come upon you, and the power of the Most High will overshadow you;** and for that reason the holy Child shall be called the Son of God."

Another interesting point is that the name "Eliezer" means "God's helper." Jesus described the Holy Spirit as a "Comforter," which comes from the Greek word παράκλητος (*parakletos*, G3875), whose definition is "one called to assist another" or "one who pleads the cause of another" (Mounce Greek Dictionary). Romans 8:26 also describes the Spirit helping us; in that case, helping us to pray when we don't know *how* to pray.

So in the solemn oath, Abraham charges Eliezer to go seek a bride for Isaac. Notice that Isaac did not go and forcibly *take* a bride, but Eliezer was to go *seek* for a willing one. The story continues:

> Genesis 24:5–5 (NIV): The servant asked him, **"What if the woman is unwilling** to come back with me to this land? Shall I then take your son back to the country you came from?" ⁶**"Make sure that you do not take my son back there,"** Abraham said.

Note that Eliezer realized that there was a chance that the woman would be unwilling to be Isaac's bride. Who does Isaac's bride represent? Since Isaac represents Christ, His bride represents the bride of Christ; i.e., the Church. People must be willing to become part of the bride of Christ. Jesus came to earth as a servant and died on the cross to open the way back to God, and that was once and for all (Hebrews 10:10); He will never need to do that again. Hence, Abraham's statement "Make sure that you do not take my son back there."

Abraham continues:

> Genesis 24:7–8 (NIV): "The Lord, the God of heaven, who brought me out of my father's household and my native land and who spoke to me

131

and promised me on oath, saying, 'To your offspring I will give this land'—he will send his angel before you so that you can get a wife for my son from there. **⁸If the woman is unwilling to come back with you, then you will be released from this oath of mine.** Only do not take my son back there."

Abraham acknowledges the possibility that the woman might be unwilling to come back with Eliezer to become Isaac's bride. He also reiterates the command about not taking his son "back there." Later, we see that the bride is offered many precious gifts, and that is not insignificant. There are many other parallels between the story of Abraham seeking a bride for Isaac, and the story of redemption, which we will omit here for the sake of brevity. But the important thing, as it relates to the topic of this book, has already been stated: There was the possibility that Isaac's *potential* bride might be unwilling to become his *actual* bride.

Also note that Eliezer (who represents the Holy Spirit) was *released* from the assignment if the woman was unwilling to come voluntarily. In other words, Eliezer was not obligated to forcibly take a woman to become Isaac's wife. Similarly, the Holy Spirit does not act in "irresistible mode" when wooing people to Jesus; if we are unwilling, He is released from His task. Because of His love, the Holy Spirit is often persistent, but He will not save us against our wills.

This idea of the woman *choosing* whether or not to go and become Isaac's bride is reinforced yet again a little later in the chapter:

Genesis 24:57–58 (NIV): Then they said, **"Let's call the girl and ask her** about it." ⁵⁸So they called Rebekah and asked her, **"Will you go** with this man?" **"I will go,"** she said.

The Kinsman-Redeemer

The story of Ruth is another highly symbolic narrative that foreshadows the story of redemption. The setup for the story is as follows: Elimilech and his wife Naomi and their two sons Mahlon and Kilion lived in Bethlehem. Because of a famine in Judah (where Bethlehem was), they moved to Moab, and while they were there, the two boys married Moabite women, Ruth and Orpah. Through some unfortunate—and unspecified—circumstances, Elimilech died, and then more than ten years after moving to Moab, Mahlon and Kilion died as well.

Soon, Naomi hears that the famine in Judah has ended, and decides to go back home. So the three ladies pack up and start the journey to Judah.

But almost as soon as they're on the road, Naomi has second thoughts about taking her daughters-in-law with her, since they wouldn't know anyone in Judah, and their marriage prospects would be dim. After a tearful farewell, Orpah returns to her homeland, but Ruth faithfully stays with Naomi.

To make a short summary of the story, Boaz was a relative—a *kinsman*—of Elimilech, Naomi's dead husband, so after Ruth has gleaned grain for several days from Boaz's fields, Naomi counsels Ruth to put on her best clothes, go to the meal that Boaz and his workers would eat after winnowing the barley that evening, and take note of where Boaz lay down for the night. When he was asleep, she quietly slipped under the blanket at his feet.

Later on, Boaz awakens with a start, astonished to find a woman at his feet. He asks her who she is, and she identifies herself, and then asks him to "spread the corner of his garment over her;" that is, take her to be his wife, since he was her kinsman-redeemer.

After taking care of some legalities, Boaz does just that: he buys all the property of Elimilech and his sons, and takes Ruth to be his wife. Boaz and Ruth have a son, Obed, who became the father of Jesse, who became the father of David. As in, *King* David, ancestor of Jesus.

Again, this story pertains to the topic of this book because *Ruth* approached, and basically proposed to, *Boaz,* the Kinsman-Redeemer. Not the other way around.

"A Woman Shall Compass a Man"

Jeremiah 31 contains much about how God feels about His people:

- He favors them and gives them rest (v. 2),
- He loves them everlastingly (v. 3),
- He draws them with lovingkindness (v. 3),
- He builds them up (v. 4),
- He gathers them (v. 8),
- He watches over them (v. 10),
- He ransoms and redeems them (v. 11),
- He gives them comfort and joy (v. 13),
- He satisfies them and fills them with bounty (v. 14),

...and more. That is quite an amazing influx of blessing. Why did it happen? Because, after God disciplines them for their sin, they repent and turn back to God. As always, God's discipline is redemptive, not punitive:

Jeremiah 31:18–22 (AMP): I have surely heard Ephraim [Israel] moaning thus: **You have chastised me,** and I was chastised, like a bullock unac-

FREE TO CHOOSE?

customed to the yoke; bring me back, **that I may be restored,** for You are the Lord my God.

There it is: God chastised them that they may be restored. Continuing on:

> ¹⁹**Surely after I [Ephraim] was turned [from You], I repented; and after I was instructed, I penitently smote my thigh.** I was ashamed, yes, even confounded, because I bore the disgrace of my youth [as a nation]. ²⁰Is Ephraim My dear son? Is he a darling child and beloved? For as often as I speak against him, I do [earnestly] remember him still. Therefore My affection is stirred and My heart yearns for him; I will surely have mercy, pity, and loving-kindness for him, says the Lord. ²¹Set up for yourselves highway markers [back to Canaan], make for yourselves guideposts; turn your thoughts and attention to the way by which you went [into exile]. Retrace your steps, O Virgin Israel, return to these your cities. ²²How long will you waver and hesitate [to return], O you backsliding daughter? **For the Lord has created a new thing in the land [of Israel]: a female shall compass (woo, win, and protect) a man.**

So here are God's people *finally* responding to His love and choosing to pursue Him like they should have done all along. In fact, He *helps* them to passionately seek Him; if we are at all willing, He will meet us much more than halfway.

But look at v. 22: what does it mean when it says she "woos" Him? A one-sided romance is not fulfilling for either party. We know that God loves us—there are multitudes of Scriptures confirming that—but when we romance Him in return, when we speak to Him in *His* love languages, we open the door to receiving the blessings that God has intended for us all along, and our receiving also gives Him pleasure (Luke 12:32). God's love for us is no longer unrequited, so the windows of blessing are opened wide.

So what does that Scripture mean when it says she "wins" Him? Basically, it means that we won't let anything else get between us and our Lord. In other words, it is simple obedience to Exodus 20:3 ("You shall have no other gods before me") and I Corinthians 9:24b ("Run in such a way that you may win"), while doing everything possible to avoid being like the church in Ephesus, which had lost its first love (Revelation 2:1–5).

The Jeremiah passage above also says that she "protects" God, and. . . now, wait a minute: how could she *protect* God? God doesn't need protection from anybody. True: with *all* power and *all* authority, no one could ever hope to threaten God in any way. Then what does this mean?

In the same way that God is jealous over us when we do not seek Him first (Exodus 34:14), people who are passionately in love with God are jealous when other people don't love Him first. For example, Elijah:

> I Kings 19:9–10 (AMP): There he came to a cave and lodged in it; and behold, the word of the Lord came to him, and He said to him, What are you doing here, Elijah? [10]He replied, **I have been very jealous for the Lord God of hosts;** for the Israelites have forsaken Your covenant, thrown down Your altars, and killed Your prophets with the sword. And I, I only, am left; and they seek my life, to take it away.

And David:

> Psalm 69:9 (AMP): For zeal for Your house has eaten me up, and **the reproaches and insults of those who reproach and insult You have fallen upon me.**

And Paul, in a couple places:

> Acts 17:16 (NASB): Now while Paul was waiting for them *[Silas and Timothy]* at Athens, **his spirit was being provoked within him as he was beholding the city full of idols.**

> II Corinthians 11:2 (NASB): For **I am jealous for you with a godly jealousy;** for I betrothed you to one husband, that to Christ I might present you as a pure virgin.

So of course, God doesn't need "protection" from any human—that's utterly laughable when comparing our strength to His—however, God is very pleased when we are so passionately in love with Him that our protective instincts are stirred up when His Name is mocked or His commands are spurned. Of course He can take care of Himself: as we've already seen in earlier pages, and will see even more in subseqent pages, people will be judged justly and fairly, according to their own actions.

So in this passage from Jeremiah, we see that is it is the *woman* who is pursuing the *man*. And of course, as noted above, this symbolizes people pursuing Him. People who pursue God become God's people. Did we initiate the whole process? No, we love Him because He first loved us (I John 4:19). But just because God loves everybody and offers salvation and unimaginable blessings to everybody, doesn't mean that everybody necessarily responds to that love in a rational manner. *But we can.*

These three passages—Abraham seeking a bride for Isaac, Ruth pursuing Boaz, and the woman compassing the man—which all foreshadow the process of redemption, illustrate a very important point: it's the *woman* who chooses whether or not she wants to become her Suitor's bride; *she* decides whether or not she wants to reciprocate His advances. And just in case someone is thinking that the above three passages apply only to Israel, we must remember this:

Galatians 3:7 (NLT): The real children of Abraham, then, are **those who put their faith in God.**

Remember when Paul talked about offering ourselves as living sacrifices to God?

Romans 12:1 (NIV): Therefore, I urge you, brothers, in view of God's mercy, **to offer your bodies as living sacrifices,** holy and pleasing to God—this is your spiritual act of worship.

When offering ourselves as living sacrifices to Him, we should be like the Israelites in this passage:

Exodus 35:21–22 (AMP): And they came, **each one whose heart stirred him up and whose spirit made him willing,** and brought the Lord's offering to be used for the [new] Tent of Meeting, for all its service, and the holy garments. ²²They came, both men and women, **all who were willinghearted,** and brought brooches, earrings or nose rings, signet rings, and armlets or necklaces, all jewels of gold, everyone bringing an offering of gold to the Lord.

Stir up your heart! Let your spirit make you willing! When you offer yourself unreservedly to God, you'll be glad you did.

Chapter 4:

The Five Points of Calvinism

In this chapter and the following five, we'll discuss what is usually referred to as Reformed Theology, or Calvinist Theology, and examine the relevant Scriptures. Historically, there are five main ideas to the Calvinist doctrines, and they are summarized in, and usually referred to as, the "Five Points of Calvinism."

The five points, often remembered by use of the mnemonic acrostic "TULIP," are shown in the table below, along with a *very* abbreviated description, according to Reformed theology:

T: Total Depravity
 (People can't choose to serve God. . .)

U: Unconditional Election
 (. . .so God chooses for us; some for heaven, some for hell)

L: Limited Atonement
 (Jesus' blood was not intended to redeem everybody)

I: Irresistible Grace
 (Those whom God wants to save, can't refuse)

P: Perseverance of the Saints
 (Once saved, always saved)

We'll cover these topics in detail in the following five chapters. These next five chapters are labelled with the names of the Five Points of Calvinism, but bear in mind that all these concepts are interrelated, and a Scripture that applies to one of the Five Points will likely also apply to others. Therefore, I encourage you to read *all* the chapters—all five major points of TULIP—and *then* analyze to see whether my points are valid and if the Scripture passages were interpreted correctly.

But before we launch into the Five Points of Calvinism themselves, we'll need to address the question of God's sovereignty. Now please note that I am not questioning *whether* God is sovereign; the Bible clearly says He is. But I am questioning one particular definition of sovereignty—that definition adhered to by Reformed theology, and which militates against our having a free will—and seeing if the Bible supports that definition of sovereignty, or if there is a different (and perhaps better) one.

When discussing whether we, as human beings, are able to choose whether or not we want to serve God, the topic of "free will" arises, and for good reason; it is inseparably connected to the topic at hand. Again, proponents of one side of the discussion state that we have a free will and can choose to love and serve God or not; proponents of the other side state that because God is sovereign, He makes *all* decisions and actively causes *all* events, including whether we love and serve God or not. Or at the very least, He chooses whether we serve Him or not, and we are not involved in the decision in any way.

So obviously, one of the first things we need to do in analyzing the Five Points of Calvinism is to determine whether true "free will" is a Biblical concept, since Calvinism—Reformed theology—is so heavily dependent on whether or not it actually exists. And we have done so in the previous chapter, in quite a bit of detail.

But doesn't the concept of free will run head-on into God's sovereignty? Wouldn't the existence of one preclude the possibility of the other? The Bible supports God's sovereignty in many Scriptures:

Psalm 115:3 (AMP): But our God is in heaven; **He does whatever He pleases.**

Psalm 135:6 (NASB): **Whatever the LORD pleases, He does,** in heaven and in earth, in the seas and in all deeps.

Isaiah 14:24, 27 (NIV): The Lord Almighty has sworn, "Surely, **as I have planned, so it will be, and as I have purposed, so it will stand.** [27]For the Lord Almighty has purposed, and who can thwart him? **His hand is stretched out, and who can turn it back?**"

Isaiah 46:10–11 (NASB): Declaring the end from the beginning and from ancient times things which have not been done, Saying, '**My purpose** will be established, and I will accomplish all My good pleasure. . .' ¹¹Calling a bird of prey from the beast, The man of My purpose from a far country. Truly I have spoken; truly **I will bring it to pass. I have planned it, surely I will do it.**

Daniel 4:34–35 (NIV): At the end of that time, I, Nebuchadnezzar, raised my eyes toward heaven, and my sanity was restored. Then I praised the Most High; I honored and glorified him who lives forever. His dominion is an eternal dominion; his kingdom endures from generation to generation. ³⁵All the peoples of the earth are regarded as nothing. **He does as he pleases with the powers of heaven and the peoples of the earth. No one can hold back his hand or say to him: "What have you done?"**

Isaiah 55:11 (TEV): So also will be the word that I speak—**it will not fail to do what I plan for it; it will do everything I send it to do.**

So there's no doubt that God can and will do everything He wants to do; the Scriptures above show that beyond doubt. But the interpretation and application of the Scriptures above, though they are completely true in what they say, can be skewed by our making unwarranted or inaccurate assumptions on what God "wants" to do. This book will look into that very question in great depth in the following pages.

Few Christians would be willing to give up the idea of a sovereign God, and as the Scriptures above show, there is no reason to do so. So how then can free will and a sovereign God co-exist? How can you have both of these two options simultaneously, since they are mutually exclusive? (At least, allegedly so.) Well, as it turns out, they are mutually exclusive *only* if we assume that the Reformed idea of sovereignty is actually correct. But there may be an even better idea of sovereignty, and one that squares with the whole of Scripture much more compatibly than does the Reformed version.

The Definition of Sovereignty

In a discussion such as this, proponents of the no-free-will concept often defend it by saying "God is Sovereign." And included in that definition of sovereignty is the idea that God makes *all* decisions and actively causes *all* events, or at least the decision of whether we love and serve God or not.

Is that a Scriptural definition? As we'll see in most of the rest of this book, sovereignty (supreme power and authority) need not—in fact, *cannot*—include the idea of making all decisions for everyone everywhere, given the way the Scriptures read. But just in case there's still a question in anyone's mind, let's look at a bit more of the logical fallout of such an idea. Again, let me hasten to say that I am *not* saying that God is not sovereign; I am merely maintaining that the nature of God's sovereignty is not exactly like Reformed doctrine says it is.

If God makes *all* decisions and actively causes *all* events, then:

- God's will is always done, and therefore every "choice" that anyone ever seems to have made, was actually chosen by God. This means, if sin exists at all, that God would be the only sinner, since God is the only one making choices.
- Or, God's will is always done, and therefore disobedience is impossible, since everything done is according to God's will. This means that there is no sin.

Again, we are compelled by logical necessity to arrive at one of these two conclusions, if indeed, God is the only one with the ability to choose. Either God is the only sinner, or there is no sin. Both are logical conclusions if God's will is always done and nothing happens outside of His will. The only difference between them is whether you want to allow the existence of sin.

Even a pittance of Scriptural knowledge will show that both of these two conclusions are wrong in a most severe way. Since both conclusions are absurd, but the logic and reasoning are valid, we must conclude that the original premise—that God is the only one who can make choices—must be in error. And therefore, we too must be able to choose.

Here's a bit more clarification on the second bullet item above, which hypothesizes that "God's will is always done," and therefore unavoidably, disobedience is impossible. If He gives us a command and then *causes* us to disobey it—as those who reject the notion of free will tell us—He is a house divided against itself, and therefore His Kingdom will fall (Matthew 12:25 || Luke 11:17). So again, is it even *possible* to disobey God if the Reformed theology is correct? If there is a command that we are "supposed to" obey but God causes us to disobey it, we are doing what God intended for us to do: i.e., disobey the command. In other words, we obeyed Him by disobeying Him. By its intrinsic and inescapable self-contradiction, this hypothesis is patently absurd.

Clearly, the above scenario is logically self-contradictory. It's like the sentence "This statement is false." If the statement is actually true, then we can be confident that it is false, as it clearly states. But at the same time, if the statement is false in its assertion about its falsity, then it must be true. Therefore the statement must be true and false at the same time and in the same sense—a thing and its opposite are identical.

Once again, this is a logical self-contradiction, violating the most fundamental law of all rational thought. Therefore, the statement that leads to such a contradiction cannot be rational, but must be nonsense/absurdity. Thus, in this context, we are driven to the conclusion that God does not—*cannot*—cause us to disobey; any disobedience must be the cause the result of our free will. Otherwise, the idea immediately leads to the self-contradiction described above.

Note that the above conclusion is based on the idea that God can choose things too. But can He? If He is eternal, and His will is perfect, can He actually "choose" anything? Or is His will "rigid," so to speak, so that anything He would "choose" that hadn't already been decided in eternity past would indicate that He had made a mistake? These are good questions, and it just so happens that the Bible addresses them.

As we can see from the following Scriptures, God can and indeed *does* choose things. He chose the tribe of Levi to be the priests of Israel:

> Deuteronomy 21:5 (NIV): The priests, the sons of Levi, shall step forward, for **the LORD your God has chosen them** to minister and to pronounce blessings in the name of the LORD and to decide all cases of dispute and assault.

Toward the end of David's life, he called together all his governmental officials, tribal leaders, stewards, military brass, and warriors, and said:

> I Chronicles 28:5–7 (NIV): Of all my sons—and the LORD has given me many—**he has chosen my son Solomon** to sit on the throne of the kingdom of the LORD over Israel. ⁶He said to me: 'Solomon your son is the one who will build my house and my courts, for **I have chosen him to be my son,** and I will be his father. ⁷I will establish his kingdom forever if he is unswerving in carrying out my commands and laws, as is being done at this time.'

After Solomon built the Temple, God said that He would live there:

> II Chronicles 7:12, 16 (NIV): . . .the LORD appeared to him at night and said: "I have heard your prayer and **have chosen this place** for myself as a temple for sacrifices. ¹⁶**I have chosen and consecrated this temple** so that my Name may be there forever. My eyes and my heart will always be there."

Solomon started out well: he built the temple, his own house, and was known far and wide for his wisdom and wealth that God had given him. But after Solomon started out so well, after a while, and "swerved" from carrying out God's commands and influenced by the idolatry of some of his wives, Solomon turned away from God.

As a result, God told him that He would take the kingdom away from him, but not quite yet:

> I Kings 11:11–13 (NIV): So the LORD said to Solomon, "Since this is your attitude and you have not kept my covenant and my decrees, which I commanded you, I will most certainly tear the kingdom away from you and give it to one of your subordinates. ¹²Nevertheless, for the sake of David your father, I will not do it during your lifetime. I will tear it out of the hand of your son. ¹³Yet I will not tear the whole kingdom from him, but will give him one tribe for the sake of David my servant and for the sake of **Jerusalem, which I have chosen**."

Then in the book of Isaiah, he prophesies to the whole nation of Israel:

> Isaiah 41:8–10 (NIV): "But you, **O Israel, my servant, Jacob, whom I have chosen**, you descendants of Abraham my friend, ⁹I took you from the ends of the earth, from its farthest corners I called you. I said, 'You are my servant'; **I have chosen you and have not rejected you.** ¹⁰You are my witnesses," declares the LORD, "and my servant **whom I have chosen**, so that you may know and believe me and understand that I am he. Before me no god was formed, nor will there be one after me."

And later, Isaiah says this:

> Isaiah 58:5–8 (NIV): **Is this the kind of fast I have chosen**, only a day for a man to humble himself? Is it only for bowing one's head like a reed and for lying on sackcloth and ashes? Is that what you call a fast, a day acceptable to the LORD? ⁶**Is not this the kind of fasting I have chosen**: to loose the chains of injustice and untie the cords of the yoke, to set the oppressed free and break every yoke? ⁷Is it not to share your food with the hungry and to provide the poor wanderer with shelter— when you see the naked, to clothe him, and not to turn away from your own flesh and blood? ⁸Then your light will break forth like the dawn, and your healing will quickly appear; then your righteousness will go before you, and the glory of the LORD will be your rear guard.

(To hear this passage set to music, listen to the song *This Is the Fast* on the album *Worship the King* or scan the QR code at right.)

So I think that pretty well answers the questions about whether God can choose: In the passages above, He chose a tribe, an individual, a building, a city, a whole nation, and a lifestyle. And Jesus chose things too, as we'll see later. But here is where that fact becomes significant to our discussion: since God can choose things, and we're made in His image and in His likeness, *we* must also be able to choose things:

Genesis 1:26–27 (NIV): Then God said, "Let us make man **in our image, in our likeness,** and let them rule over the fish of the sea and the birds of the air, over the livestock, over all the earth, and over all the creatures that move along the ground." ²⁷So God created man **in his own image, in the image of God** he created him; male and female he created them.

And if we are able to choose, and we choose to reject God's offer to save us from the well-deserved consequences of our sin, then the Scriptures about eternal torment are shown to be just. If we reject the *only* source of life, what else is there but death? If we reject the *only* source of love, what else is there but hatred and cruelty? If we reject the *only* source of joy, what else is there but sorrow? If we reject the *only* source of hope, what else is there but despair? If we reject the *only* source of peace, what else is there but turmoil? So it behooves us to consider seriously what our choice will be when it comes to serving God or not.

And indeed, God tells us to do just that:

Deuteronomy 30:19 (CEB): I call heaven and earth as my witnesses against you right now: I have set life and death, blessing and curse before you. **Now choose life—so that you and your descendants will live. . .**

Joshua 24:15 (MSG): **"If you decide that it's a bad thing to worship God, then choose a god you'd rather serve**—and do it today. Choose one of the gods your ancestors worshiped from the country beyond The River, or one of the gods of the Amorites, on whose land you're now living. As for me and my family, we'll worship God."

Psalm 25:9 (GWORD): Who, then, is this person that fears the Lord? He is the one whom the Lord will teach **which path to choose.**

NLT: Who are those who fear the Lord? He will show them the path **they should choose.**

RSV: Who is the man that fears the Lord? Him will he instruct in **the way that he should choose.**

Even in those translations that translate this verse using the singular "he" as opposed to the plural "they," the singular pronouns are being used representatively, and the understood plural is justified by the context, as we can see from reading vv. 13 and 14. But notice the point here: God teaches us the way we should choose, but *it is still up to us to actually do the choosing.*

Sovereignty: Infinite Power and Authority

Probably few Christians would argue with a definition of sovereignty that defined it to be "infinite power and authority." But in theology, there are different "sizes" of infinity, just like in mathematics, where there are some infinite numbers that are larger than others. For example, the number of integers is infinite, and is usually called $\aleph_0$, where the symbol before the subscripted zero is *aleph,* the first letter of the Hebrew alphabet. But the number of "real numbers" (decimal fractions) is a larger infinite number, and is usually called $\aleph_1$. Still larger infinite numbers are designated $\aleph_2$, $\aleph_3$, and so on.

The emphasis and the scope of this book is not to discuss higher mathematics, but in my opinion, the different sizes of infinity illustrate something about God's sovereignty. Let me explain.

Adherents to Reformed theology state that God is sovereign, and there is no argument about that. But as mentioned, the *nature* of that sovereignty is a subject of impassioned debate. The first definition we'll consider is the belief that God deliberately causes *everything* to happen, down to the movement of the smallest atomic particle—and down to the selection *for* us of every supposed "choice" we think we're making. This seems to be a good definition of sovereignty. (Except for the multitudes of Scriptures that militate against it.)

A second, and better definition of sovereignty, in my opinion, is where God's overarching will is accomplished, *in spite of* the free-will choices of billions of people. The ability for a human to make an *actual* free-will choice (as opposed to doing something that he only *thinks* is a free-will choice but was in actuality a result of the irresistible causation of the Holy Spirit), does not in any way detract from God's sovereignty. God getting His to-do list done, in spite of actual free-will choices of humans, seems to me to be even more impressive, more grand, more magnificent, *more sovereign,* than simply "making everything happen."

Of course, there are some things decided in eternity past that God would make *sure* they occurred. The Atonement is a good example: no devil in hell, and no human opposition could in the slightest way prevent that event from happening.

For example, in Peter's Pentecost sermon, he says:

Acts 2:22–24: Ye men of Israel, hear these words; Jesus of Nazareth, a man approved of God among you by miracles and wonders and signs, which God did by him in the midst of you, as ye yourselves also know: [23]**Him, being delivered by the determinate counsel** and foreknowledge of God, ye have taken, and by wicked hands have crucified and slain: [24]Whom God hath raised up, having loosed the pains of death: because it was not possible that he should be holden of it.

v. 23, AMP: This Jesus, when delivered up **according to the definite and fixed purpose and settled plan** and foreknowledge of God, you crucified and put out of the way [killing Him] by the hands of lawless and wicked men.

NIV: This man was handed over to you **by God's set purpose** and foreknowledge; and you, with the help of wicked men, put him to death by nailing him to the cross.

TEV: **In accordance with his own plan God had already decided** that Jesus would be handed over to you; and you killed him by letting sinful men crucify him.

But if we allow that God could be capable enough and sovereign enough to make beings that actually did have a free will, He could still get His must-do items accomplished while still allowing man to choose to serve Him or not.

As you'll see in the following sections, there are *far* fewer contradictions with Scripture if we define sovereignty this way, where God creates free-will beings, but *still* accomplishes every task He wants to accomplish. As you're reading the rest of this book, think back often on these two definitions of sovereignty and see how many Scriptural difficulties go away when the second definition is used.

Chapter 5:

Total Depravity

The first of the five points of Calvinism, Total Depravity, is often misunderstood because of applying the word "total" in a way that the Reformed theologians did not intend. Specifically, it does not state that everyone is so completely depraved that it would be impossible for their spirits, minds, habits, attitudes, and actions to be worse in any way.

On the contrary, Total Depravity, as the Reformed theologians intended it, is that *every part* of human nature is depraved. As it pertains to this book, the "every part" includes the part of our will that would allow us to recognize God's goodness and accept His gift to us—the gift of salvation.

The Westminster Confession of Faith (the 17th-century British statement of Reformation Theology) describes Total Depravity in this way:

> Man, by his fall into a state of sin, hath wholly lost all ability of will to any spiritual good accompanying salvation, so as a natural man, being altogether averse from that good, and dead in sin, *is not able by his own strength* to convert himself or *to prepare himself thereunto."* (emphasis added)

In other words we, in our unredeemed state, can't even accept, or receive, or choose, God's offer of redemption, or even repent of our sins.

Free to Choose?

The quote above was based on Calvin's position on whether we have a free will. He said:

> If we mean by 'free will' that fallen man has the ability to choose what he wants, then of course, fallen man has free will. If we mean by that term that man, in his fallen state, has the moral power and the ability to choose righteousness, then 'free will' is far too grandiose a term to apply to fallen man.

So in a nutshell, Calvin said yes, we have a free will, just not in the one area that counts.

Some contemporary Reformed theologians take the absence of free will even farther than that; they say that we don't have a free will even about choices *unrelated* to salvation. Their support for that belief is that if we had *any* ability to choose *anything*, then God would not be sovereign, or that salvation would have to be by works (more on this in the next section). Some have observed that there are modern Reformed theologians that are more Calvinistic than Calvin, and this appears to be true.

In an effort to reduce confusion about its name, Total Depravity is sometimes called "total inability" or "radical corruption," where "radical" harks back to its Latin etymology of "radix," or "root"; i.e., we are corrupted to the root.

Because the main emphasis of Total Depravity is our alleged inability to even ask God to save us or accept His unspeakable gift, that will be the concept we concentrate on, and analyze the most intensely, in this chapter.

Original Sin

The concept of Total Depravity—indeed, the "need" for it—is based on another concept called Original Sin. Martin Luther, as well as John Calvin, depended heavily on the validity of this doctrine for the development of the doctrines now summarized in the Five Points of Calvinism, but where did it come from? Luther and Calvin did not invent this doctrine of Original Sin; they borrowed heavily from the teachings of Augustine, who promoted it strongly.

Augustine (354–430AD) was extremely intelligent and without doubt a powerful man of God, and his teachings have been helpful to generations of Christians. However, before Augustine became a Christian, he was a Manichaean—a member of a Gnostic sect called Manichaeism—and was heavily influenced by Manichaeism in his early years.[3] Many modern theolo-

---

[3] TeSelle, Eugene (1970). *Augustine the Theologian*. London. pp. 347–349. ISBN 0-223-97728-4. March 2002 edition: ISBN 1-57910-918-7.

gians concede that some of the concepts from the Gnostic religions can be found in Augustine's Christian writing.

Note that although Augustine had distinct Gnostic leanings in his beliefs in total depravity and its results, he was very familiar with the miraculous workings of the Holy Spirit. See the section "Augustine's Inadvertent Influence" in Book 7: *Be Filled With the Spirit* for details.

Gnosticism

The particular flavor of Gnosticism known as Manichaeism, of which Augustine was a part, was founded by the third-century Iranian soothsayer Mani, although Gnosticism itself was around much earlier than that. Gnosticism was present as an acknowledged heresy even when Jesus and the original twelve disciples walked the earth. In fact, there are many passages of Scripture that seem to be specifically and pointedly refuting Gnosticism. We'll look at some of those in a moment.

Of course, any religion has a great number of individual doctrines, but two of the main ones of Gnosticism—and the two that are most relevant to the subject of this book—are these:

- Gnosticism derives its name from the Greek word γινώσκω (*ginosko*, G1097), whose definition includes "allow, be aware (of), feel, (have) know(-ledge), perceive." In general, it means "to know." Of course, there is nothing inherently wrong with knowing things—Proverbs 1:7 tells us that "The fear of the LORD is the beginning of knowledge"—but *the Gnostics overemphasized head knowledge* at the expense of experiencing God. In essence, knowledge *became* their god; in other words, the Gnostics' version of salvation came about not through a personal relationship with the Son of God, but by learning some "secret knowledge."

- Gnosticism included a dualistic approach to reality; specifically, the spiritual world was all good, and the physical world was all evil. So strongly did the Gnostics believe this that they could not conceive of the possibility that *anything* in the physical world could be validly considered "good." This is completely refuted by Genesis 1:31, where God saw everything He had made (i.e., the physical universe), and "behold, **it was very good**."

It is this second doctrine that pertains most closely to the topic at hand. As mentioned, Gnosticism existed as a cult in Jesus' day, and the Gnostic take on Jesus essentially was: "Since we know that nothing in the physical world could actually be good, but rather is completely evil, Jesus couldn't *really* have been born as a physical human being; He must only have *seemed* to be physical in nature." This was already an error springing up even in the first century, and many Scriptures pointedly emphasize that, yes, Jesus actually *did* come in the flesh; He didn't merely "seem to" have come in the flesh:

John 1:14: And **the Word was made flesh,** and dwelt among us, (and we beheld his glory, the glory as of the only begotten of the Father,) full of grace and truth.

John 6:51: I am the living bread which came down from heaven: if any man eat of this bread, he shall live for ever: and **the bread that I will give is my flesh,** which I will give for the life of the world.

Acts 2:31: He seeing this before spake of the resurrection of Christ, that his soul was not left in hell, **neither his flesh did see corruption.**

II Corinthians 5:16: Wherefore henceforth know we no man after the flesh: yea, though **we have known Christ after the flesh,** yet now henceforth know we him no more.

Ephesians 2:13–15 (NIV): But now in **Christ Jesus** you who once were far away have been brought near through the blood of Christ. ¹⁴For he himself is our peace, who has made the two one and has destroyed the barrier, the dividing wall of hostility, ¹⁵by abolishing **in his flesh** the law with its commandments and regulations. His purpose was to create in himself one new man out of the two, thus making peace. . .

Ephesians 5:30: For we are members of his body, **of his flesh,** and of his bones.

Colossians 1:21–22 (AMP): And although you at one time were estranged and alienated from Him and were of hostile attitude of mind in your wicked activities, ²²Yet now has [Christ, the Messiah] reconciled [you to God] **in the body of His flesh** through death, in order to present you holy and faultless and irreproachable in His [the Father's] presence.

I Timothy 3:16: And without controversy great is the mystery of godliness: **God was manifest in the flesh,** justified in the Spirit, seen of angels, preached unto the Gentiles, believed on in the world, received up into glory.

Hebrews 10:19–20 (NASB): Since therefore, brethren, we have confidence to enter the holy place by the blood of Jesus, ²⁰by a new and living way which He inaugurated for us through the veil, that is, **His flesh. . .**

I Peter 3:18 (TEV): For **Christ died** for sins once and for all, a good man on behalf of sinners, in order to lead you to God. **He was put to death physically,** but made alive spiritually. . .

I Peter 4:1 (NASB): Therefore, since **Christ has suffered in the flesh,** arm yourselves also with the same purpose, because he who has suffered in the flesh has ceased from sin. . .

So we see that each of these Biblical writers (read "God") considers the fact that Jesus did indeed come *in the flesh* to be of great importance. But perhaps the clearest Scriptures that address and refute this dualistic Gnostic idea are these, from John's epistles:

I John 4:1–3 (AMP): Beloved, do not put faith in every spirit, but prove (test) the spirits to discover whether they proceed from God; for many false prophets have gone forth into the world. ²By this you may know (perceive and recognize) the Spirit of God: **every spirit which acknowledges and confesses [the fact] that Jesus Christ (the Messiah) [actually] has become man and has come in the flesh is of God** [has God for its source]; ³And **every spirit which does not acknowledge and confess that Jesus Christ has come in the flesh [but would annul, destroy, sever, disunite Him] is not of God** [does not proceed from Him]. This [nonconfession] is the [spirit] of the antichrist, [of] which you heard that it was coming, and now it is already in the world.

II John 7 (NIV): Many **deceivers, who do not acknowledge Jesus Christ as coming in the flesh,** have gone out into the world. Any such person is the deceiver and the antichrist.

So what *is* the doctrine of Original Sin? Here's where the above discussion becomes relevant to the overall topic of this book. Some people think Original Sin is just the *first* sin—Eve (or both Adam and Eve) eating the forbidden fruit. But because Augustine had so much experience with Gnosticism in general and Manichaeism in particular, he was steeped in the idea that "everything physical is evil" (already refuted by Genesis 1:31 above).

A natural conclusion—a perfectly reasonable and logical result of Augustine's fallacious premise—is that man, being physical in nature, could not have any good in him. Wrapped in Biblical terminology, Augustine considered Adam and Eve's sin to be *so bad* that all of mankind not only inherited sin and death from them, but also an *inability* to serve God or turn to Him for help. This Gnostic-influenced conclusion would necessarily include the idea that a physical human being was incapable of choosing to start obeying God (repent), and incapable of choosing to receive Jesus' offer of forgiveness of sins (accepting salvation).

Now if we assume that the concept of Original Sin (which was based on the Gnostic-influenced dualistic view of reality) is a valid concept, look at the logical fallout:

- If Original Sin is true, then we are completely incapable of choosing anything good (because we are merely physical beings). Hence, this conclusion became the Reformed doctrine of Total Depravity.
- If Total Depravity is true and we can't choose anything good, God will have to choose for us. Hence, this necessitates the Reformed doctrine of Unconditional Election, where God causes salvation for people with no input from their wills (if they have wills at all).
- If Unconditional Election is true and God must *cause* (not just *offer*) our salvation, then the Scriptures that show that not everyone is ultimately saved must have meant that God wanted it that way. Hence, this necessitates the Reformed doctrine of Limited Atonement.
- If Unconditional Election is true and people's salvation experiences are *only* a matter of God's choosing, plus Total Depravity, where we are unable to choose anything good, that must mean that when God chooses people to be saved, we would refuse if we could (because we allegedly can't choose anything good), so God has to override our wills. Hence, this necessitates the Reformed doctrine of Irresistible Grace.
- If Irresistible Grace is true, then that means that once God chooses a person for salvation, that condition of being saved is unchangeable, since God doesn't make mistakes, and we are not involved. Hence, this necessitates the Reformed doctrine of the Perseverance of the Saints.

Wow. This is quite enlightening. *All* the Reformed doctrines logically and reasonably depend on the concept of Original Sin, which demonstrably is a direct result of a Gnostic doctrine. This, in my opinion, casts significant suspicion on the validity of the Reformed doctrines.

Now of course, you may not be swayed by my opinion, *nor should you be.* My opinion is irrelevant when it comes to what you believe; a Christian's final doctrinal authority should be the Bible. So what I ask is that you carefully read, in context, the Scriptures mentioned on the following pages, along with the ones already mentioned on the preceding pages, and come to your own conclusion on whether or not the Reformed doctrines have solid Scriptural support. Then put into effect in your own life what you have discovered in the pages of the Bible.

Back to Total Depravity

As noted above, Total Depravity states that people are, by their very nature, incapable of loving God. In other words, because of that depraved nature, we serve our own interests exclusively, and we *always* reject the rule of God, because we're unable to accept it. So *every* person, by his own nature, is morally unable to choose to follow God and thus be saved, because he is unwilling to do so, and cannot become willing by himself. Again, the term "total" in this context refers to sin affecting every part of a person, not that every person is as evil as he could possibly be.

In discussing this concept of Total Depravity, Reformed theologians consider, and bluntly state, that if one were able to say "yes" to the offer of salvation that Jesus makes to us, that that acceptance would prove the salvation to be a "salvation by works," because the recipient did something to accept the gift. That seems to me to be quite a stretch. But of course, what "seems to me" is irrelevant, as I mentioned above; we need some solid Scriptural evidence in support of any statement in order to sensibly rely on it. So, let's investigate it further.

Let me illustrate what I mean, by moving this situation into a medical context. Suppose a man has some serious disease that will prove fatal if left untreated. Since he lives alone and doesn't get out much, the disease progresses seriously: his kidneys shutting down, lesions all over his skin, tachycardia, feverish but still clammy, no appetite, coughing up blood, and so forth. A visiting friend is horrified by his condition, and rushes him to the hospital, where a physician examines him.

After the examination, the physician says, "I know what the problem is, and I can still treat it, even though you've let it go for so long. May I treat it?" The man nods weakly, the physician replies, "Will do," and gets to work.

After a while the man wakes up and notices that he's hungry, which he realizes is a good sign. He also notices he has to go to the bathroom, which indicates his kidneys are working again. His skin is clearing up and scabs are falling off, and as he feels his forehead, he realizes that his skin is no longer clammy and his fever is gone. In fact, the disease completely gone, and his body is regaining health and strength. He is thrilled, and when the physician checks up on him, he repeatedly expresses his heartfelt thanks.

Now here's the point: How did the patient "heal" himself? What "works" did he do to cause his own healing? In my estimation, he did none at all. He was completely unable to heal himself, but he *could* give the doctor permission to do so. What can a doctor do if a patient refuses treatment? The physician's hands are tied, and even though he can protest, try to intimidate, and make all sorts of grave prognoses about the patient and his condition, he cannot *treat* the patient if he refuses to give his permission.

How this relates to Total Depravity is just this: A person can be completely unable to save himself, while still retaining the ability to *ask* the Physician to save him and *receive* the gift of salvation. The patient doesn't have to do anything but give permission to let Jesus do what only Jesus can do: save him. I conclude that the patient choosing to grant permission to the physician does not qualify as a "work."

I came to this conclusion by reading a host of Scriptures that show either of two things: 1) People choosing to accept or reject God, and 2) God commanding people to choose. Because God commanded them to do it, and they did it, we can be confident that it is possible. A plethora of Scriptures and their implications were discussed in the chapter We Have a Free Will, and We *Can* Choose God; refer back to that chapter for details.

However, even though the parable above is illustrative, that doesn't make it so. Are there Scriptures that back up the idea of faith not being considered a "work?"

Faith vs. Works

It all seems to boil down to whether or not "asking God to save you," "believing God will save you," or "accepting His gift of salvation," can be rightly described as a "work." If so, then the doctrine of Total Depravity is correct, and all of the other tenets of Reformed theology become necessary. But again, does the Bible indicate whether believing in Him is to be considered a work? If not, Total Depravity collapses, and the need for the remaining points of Calvinism collapses with it.

> Romans 10:9: That **if thou shalt confess with thy mouth the Lord Jesus, and shalt believe in thine heart that God hath raised him from the dead, thou shalt be saved.**
>
> AMP: **Because if you** acknowledge and confess with your lips that Jesus is Lord and **in your heart believe (adhere to, trust in, and rely on the truth) that God raised Him from the dead, you will be saved.**

CEV: So **you will be saved, if you honestly say, "Jesus is Lord," and if you believe with all your heart that God raised him from death.**

NIRV: Say with your mouth, "Jesus is Lord." **Believe in your heart that God raised him from the dead.** *Then* **you will be saved.**

NLV: If you say with your mouth that Jesus is Lord, and **believe in your heart that God raised Him from the dead, you will be saved from the punishment of sin.**

MSG: Say the welcoming word to God—"Jesus is my Master"—embracing, body and soul, God's work of doing in us what he did in raising Jesus from the dead. That's it. **You're not "doing" anything; you're simply calling out to God, trusting him to do it for you. That's salvation.**

What can we understand from the previous Scripture? Several things:

- Faith is a required condition for salvation, *not* the other way around. "If this, then that." Read it again to confirm.
- Since faith is a required condition for salvation, it cannot be considered a work.

So I claim that faith cannot be considered a work. But why do I say that? How can we know that?

Romans 4:5 (NIV): However, to the man who **does not work but trusts God** who justifies the wicked, his faith is credited as righteousness.

Ephesians 2:8: For by grace are ye **saved through faith**; and that not of yourselves: it is the gift of God: ⁹**Not of works**, lest any man should boast.

These verses say that salvation is not of works. But they also say that salvation *is* by trusting, or through faith. But what does "*through* faith" mean? It means *by means of the vehicle of* (or *through the agency of*) faith. If salvation *is* through faith but it is *not* of works, then faith cannot be rightly considered a work. Remember the syllogism in the Principles of Reason chapter? It went like this:

- Premise 1: Salvation is by faith.
- Premise 2: Salvation is not by works.
- Conclusion: Having faith is not a work.

But there is a potential problem here: How do we know that "through" (as in "you are saved *through* faith") is synonymous with "by means of the ve-

Free to Choose?

hicle of," as stated above? If that is true, there should be some Biblical confirmation of it. And there is. In the other translations of that verse below, I've highlighted the other ways "through" has been translated into English:

> Ephesians 2:8 (CEV): You are saved by God's grace **because of** your faith. This salvation is God's gift. It's not something you possessed.
>
> CEV: You were saved **by** faith in God, who treats us much better than we deserve. This is God's gift to you, and not anything you have done on your own.
>
> MSG: Saving is all his idea, and all his work. **All we do is** trust him enough to **let him do it.** It's God's gift from start to finish!
>
> NIRV: God's grace has saved you **because of** your faith in Christ. Your salvation doesn't come from anything you do. It is God's gift.
>
> NLT: God saved you by his grace **when** you believed. And you can't take credit for this; it is a gift from God.
>
> WE: You have been saved by God's love and kindness **because** you believed. It was not because of anything you did, but it was a gift from God.

Remember Abraham, the father of our faith? What does God say about him? Did he believe because he had been counted righteous? Or was he counted as righteous because he believed? Let's see:

> Romans 4:2–5 (NLT): If his *[Abraham's]* good deeds had made him acceptable to God, he would have had something to boast about. But that was not God's way. ³For the Scriptures tell us, "Abraham believed God, and **God counted him as righteous *because* of his faith.**" ⁴When people work, their wages are not a gift, but something they have earned. ⁵But **people are counted as righteous, not because of their work, but because of their faith in God** who forgives sinners.

Note that what it says about Abraham applies to all people.

So it is clear that faith is the vehicle—the *means by which*—salvation is obtained. Faith in Christ's atoning work is the *cause* of salvation, as shown in the Scriptures above, and there is no doubt whatsoever about the direction of causality. And since we've already seen that salvation is not by works, we can safely conclude that believing in Christ unto salvation is *not* a work. Therefore, the whole foundation for Total Depravity is shown to be faulty, and it suddenly evaporates. And with it, the rest of the Five Points of Calvinism.

CHAPTER 5: TOTAL DEPRAVITY

The astute reader would now say, "Ah, but in John's gospel, Jesus said that believing *is* a work. How do you deal with that?" Good question; let's look at that passage:

> John 6:28–29: Then said they unto him, What shall we do, that we might work the works of God? ²⁹Jesus answered and said unto them, **This is the work of God, that ye believe on him whom he hath sent.**

Wow. This does indeed sound like Jesus is saying that believing is a work. But doesn't that contradict Ephesians 2:8–9, which clearly says that having faith (believing) is *not* a work? Let's look at the passage in John again.

If you read this passage in context, you'll see that it is one in which Jesus refers to Himself as the "bread of life." The people had been looking for Jesus, and they had just found Him. He stated that they were looking for Him not for spiritual reasons but because He had just given them a good meal (in the Feeding of the Five Thousand).

Jesus tells them not to labor—or work—exclusively for regular food, but for the food He would give them, that would result in eternal salvation. They replied, "How do we work the works of God?" And that's where Jesus says, "This is the work of God: to believe on the One He sent." Then Jesus goes on to say that He was the bread from heaven, and that He was the bread of life.

Reading this passage in context makes it clear that Jesus was not talking about believing being a "work of the law" where people had to "earn" their way into God's good favor and thus obtain salvation. If people had to do any works to "earn" salvation, that would be salvation by works, clearly. But Jesus had already said that He would *give* them the bread of life that results in salvation. Thus, it was a *gift*, and not *wages*.

This was just as it was during the Feeding of the Five Thousand: no one forced them to eat, and no one demanded payment for the physical bread that Jesus was providing. It was there, it was available, and for no cost, but they had to actually receive what was being offered to them, in order for their hunger to be satisfied.

So it is significant to note that *something was required of the people*. Not to "earn" the salvation which comes through the bread of life, but simply to appropriate—to *take advantage of*—the salvation which comes through the Bread of Life that was being freely offered to them.

And what was that requirement? To believe in Him. It was something they needed to do, but it was not a "work of the Law" that would get them into God's favor. They already *had* God's favor, which is why He was freely offering them Jesus, the Bread of Life. All they needed to do was to receive Him.

So the "work" that Jesus said they should do was simply to receive Him, because salvation is received by believing in (cleaving to, trusting in, relying on, having faith in) Jesus. This understanding is made clearer by reading the verse in other translations:

> AMP: Jesus replied, **This is the work (service) that God asks of you: that you believe** in the One Whom He has sent [that you cleave to, trust, rely on, and have faith in His Messenger].
>
> CEB: Jesus replied, "**This is what God requires, that you believe** in him whom God sent."
>
> CEV: Jesus answered, "**God wants you to have faith** in the one he sent."
>
> NET: Jesus replied, "**This is the deed God requires—to believe** in the one whom he sent."
>
> NLT: Jesus told them, "**This is the only work God wants from you: Believe** in the one he has sent."
>
> TEV: Jesus answered, "**What God wants you to do is to believe** in the one he sent."
>
> WEYMTH: "This," replied Jesus, "**is above all the thing that God requires—that you should be believers** in Him whom He has sent."

So it is clear that the kind of "work" God requires is not a legalistic "performance" to earn one's way into God's favor, but rather that He freely gives salvation to anyone and everyone who will receive it.

Old Testament Examples

People have been choosing, *for themselves,* whether or not to serve and obey God ever since Adam and Eve in the Garden of Eden and God's conversation with Cain, where He urged Cain to master the sin that was crouching at the door (Genesis 4:7, NIV). Here are just some examples:

> Joshua 24:22 (NASB): And Joshua said to the people, "You are witnesses against yourselves that **you have chosen for yourselves the LORD, to serve Him.**" And they said, "We are witnesses."

By the way, if you are familiar with the Reformed doctrines summarized in the Five Points of Calvinism, you may notice that several of them (besides just Total Depravity) are discredited by many of the Scriptures in the following few sections. I will defer detailed discussion of these until later chapters, but

I encourage you to carefully read these Scriptures, and ponder how many of them would have to be considered either wrong, or at least pointless, if the Reformed doctrines were actually true.

> Psalm 119:30 (NIV): **I have chosen the way of truth;** I have set my heart on your laws.
>
> Psalm 119:173 (NASB): Let Thy hand be ready to help me, for **I have chosen Thy precepts.**
>
> Isaiah 56:4–5 (AMP): For thus says the Lord: To the eunuchs **who keep My Sabbaths and choose the things which please Me** and hold firmly My covenant— ⁵To them I will give in My house and within My walls a memorial and a name better [and more enduring] than sons and daughters; I will give them an everlasting name that will not be cut off.
>
> Isaiah 65:12 (AMP): I will destine you [says the Lord] for the sword, and you shall all bow down to the slaughter, because when I called, you did not answer; **when I spoke, you did not listen or obey.** But you did what was evil in My eyes, and **you chose that in which I did not delight.**
>
> Isaiah 66:3b (NIV): **They have chosen their own ways,** and their souls delight in their abominations. . .

It's interesting to note that in all the cases shown above, it was the *human* making the decision on whether or not to serve God. Some chose to serve Him; others did not. But *in every case,* the human chose, and note that in most of the cases above, they chose God. This clearly refutes Total Depravity, which says that humans *can't* choose God. And, incidentally, Isaiah 65:12 also refutes Irresistible Grace, but we'll see much more detail on that later.

Turning—or *Returning*—to God

Since Total Depravity alleges that people do not have the ability to turn to God, it raises a curious question: What do we do with all the Scriptures that encourage or command us to turn (or *return*) to God?

For example, take a look at these passages:

> Deuteronomy 4:29–30 (CEV): In all of your troubles, you may finally decide that you want to worship only the LORD. And **if you turn back to him and obey him completely, he will again be your God.**
>
> 1 Samuel 7:3 (NASB): Then Samuel spoke to all the house of Israel, saying, "**If you return to the LORD with all your heart,** remove the foreign gods and the Ashtaroth from among you and direct your hearts to the

LORD and serve Him alone; and He will deliver you from the hand of the Philistines."

Jeremiah 4:1 (GWORD): **The LORD declares, "If you come back, Israel, if you come back to me,** if you take your disgusting idols out of my sight and you don't wander away from me, ²if you take the oath, "As the LORD lives. . ." in an honest, fair, and right way, then the nations will be blessed, and they will be honored by me."

Hosea 12:6 (AMP): Therefore **return to your God!** Hold fast to love and mercy, to righteousness and justice, and wait [expectantly] for your God continually!

Joel 2:12–13 (NKJV): **"Now, therefore,"** says the LORD, **"Turn to Me with all your heart,** with fasting, with weeping, and with mourning. ¹³So rend your heart, and not your garments; **return to the LORD your God,** for He is gracious and merciful, slow to anger, and of great kindness; and He relents from doing harm."

And there are many more. So if it is impossible for a person to choose to turn to God, as Total Depravity claims, why does God tell us to do it? Why have a Scripture—which quotes God—that tells us to turn to God, if it is not doable? And then in Joel 2:13 above, it says we are to *return* to God. You can't "return" to God if you have never been *with* God in the first place; you can only return to God if you were with Him, and then left Him, and then repented of forsaking Him. (This idea of forsaking God also refutes the Reformed doctrine of the Perseverance of the Saints, but we will talk about this in great detail in a later chapter.)

If you think about it, giving a command to do something when compliance with the command-giver's will is impossible (for example, "I command you to stop the earth from spinning!"), or when compliance is compelled or unavoidable (for example, "I command you to continue being a human being!"), is completely pointless. If obedience is impossible, the command is unnecessary and also unjust, and if obedience is compelled or unavoidable, the command is likewise unnecessary and also redundant. This directly leads us to the conclusion that either 1) God put a lot of unnecessary and meaningless filler in the Bible, or 2) we can indeed choose—with actual free will—to turn to God, or *re*turn to Him.

Choosing to Receive Jesus

Okay, we saw Old Testament examples of people choosing to serve God, but did that happen in the New Testament? In modern-day terminology, is it possible to "receive" Jesus into our hearts and lives, as so many evangelists think? Or to "accept" Him? Even though Total Depravity says it's impossible for us to do so? Is there a Biblical answer to such questions? (I mean, besides all the Scriptures quoted earlier.) Yes, there is. Look at these passages:

> Matthew 18:5 (AMP): And whoever receives and accepts and welcomes one little child like this for My sake and in My name **receives and accepts and welcomes Me.**
>
> Mark 9:37 (AMP): Whoever in My name and for My sake accepts and receives and welcomes one such child also **accepts and receives and welcomes Me; and whoever so receives Me receives not only Me but Him Who sent Me.**
>
> Mark 10:15 (NASB): Truly I say to you, **whoever does not receive the kingdom of God like a child shall not enter it at all.**
>
> John 1:12 (NIV): Yet **to all who received him,** to those who believed in his name, **he gave the right to become children of God. . .**
>
> John 5:43 (AMP): I have come in My Father's name and with His power, and **you do not receive Me [your hearts are not open to Me, you give Me no welcome];** but if another comes in his own name and his own power and with no other authority but himself, you will receive him and give him your approval.
>
> John 12:48 (AMP): **Anyone who rejects Me** and persistently sets Me at naught, **refusing to accept My teachings,** has his judge [however]; for the [very] message that I have spoken will itself judge and convict him at the last day.
>
> John 13:20: Verily, verily, I say unto you, He that receiveth whomsoever I send **receiveth me; and he that receiveth me receiveth him that sent me.**
>
> John 20:22: And when he had said this, he breathed on them, and saith unto them, **Receive ye the Holy Ghost. . .**
>
> Acts 8:14–17 (NIV): When the apostles in Jerusalem heard that **Samaria had accepted the word of God,** they sent Peter and John to them. [15]When they arrived, **they prayed for them that they might receive the Holy Spirit,** [16]because the Holy Spirit had not yet come upon any of them; they had simply been baptized into the name of the Lord Jesus. [17]Then Peter and John placed their hands on them, and **they received the Holy Spirit.**

Acts 10:43: To him give all the prophets witness, that **through his name whosoever believeth in him shall receive remission of sins.**

Acts 10:47 (TEV): **These people have received the Holy Spirit,** just as we also did. Can anyone, then, stop them from being baptized with water?

Acts 11:1 (AMP): Now the apostles (special messengers) and the brethren who were throughout Judea heard [with astonishment] that the **Gentiles (heathen) also had received and accepted and welcomed the Word of God** [the doctrine concerning the attainment through Christ of salvation in the kingdom of God].

Acts 19:2–6 (NIV): While Apollos was at Corinth, Paul took the road through the interior and arrived at Ephesus. There he found some disciples ²and asked them, "**Did you receive the Holy Spirit when you believed?**" They answered, "No, we have not even heard that there is a Holy Spirit." ³So Paul asked, "Then what baptism did you receive?" "John's baptism," they replied. ⁴Paul said, "John's baptism was a baptism of repentance. He told the people to believe in the one coming after him, that is, in Jesus." ⁵On hearing this, they were baptized into the name of the Lord Jesus. ⁶When Paul placed his hands on them, the **Holy Spirit came on them, and they spoke in tongues and prophesied.**

Acts 26:17–18 (NASB): *[I, Jesus, am]* delivering you *[Paul]* from the Jewish people and from the Gentiles, to whom I am sending you, ¹⁸to open their eyes **so that they may turn from darkness to light and from the dominion of Satan to God, in order that they may receive forgiveness of sins** and an inheritance among those who have been sanctified by faith in Me.

Romans 5:17 (TEV): It is true that through the sin of one man death began to rule because of that one man. But how much greater is the result of what was done by the one man, Jesus Christ! **All who receive God's abundant grace and are freely put right with him** will rule in life through Christ.

Romans 8:15 (NIV): For you did not receive a spirit that makes you a slave again to fear, but **you received the Spirit of sonship.** And by him we cry, "Abba, Father."

I Corinthians 2:12 (GWORD): Now, we didn't receive the spirit that belongs to the world. Instead, **we received the Spirit who comes from God** so that we could know the things which God has freely given us.

I Corinthians 15:1 (NIV): Now, brothers, I want to remind you of **the gospel I preached to you, which you received** and on which you have taken your stand.

Galatians 1:9: As we said before, so say I now again, If any man preach any other **gospel** unto you than **that ye have received**, let him be accursed.

Galatians 3:2 (AMP): Let me ask you this one question: **Did you receive the [Holy] Spirit** as the result of obeying the Law and doing its works, or was it **by hearing [the message of the Gospel] and believing [it]?** [Was it from observing a law of rituals or from a message of faith?]

Galatians 3:14 (NIV): He redeemed us in order that the blessing given to Abraham might come to the Gentiles through Christ Jesus, so that **by faith we might receive the promise of the Spirit.**

Colossians 2:6–7 (NIV): So then, just as **you received Christ Jesus as Lord,** continue to live in him, ⁷rooted and built up in him, strengthened in the faith as you were taught, and overflowing with thankfulness.

I Thessalonians 1:6 (TEV): You imitated us and the Lord; and even though you suffered much, **you received the message** with the joy that comes from the Holy Spirit.

I Thessalonians 2:13 (NASB): And for this reason we also constantly thank God that when **you received from us the word of God's message, you accepted it not as the word of men, but for what it really is, the word of God,** which also performs its work in you who believe.

James 1:21 (AMP): So **get rid of all uncleanness** and the rampant outgrowth of wickedness, and in a humble (gentle, modest) spirit **receive and welcome the Word** which implanted and rooted [in your hearts] contains the power to save your souls.

I Peter 1:9 (AMP): [At the same time] **you receive the result (outcome, consummation) of your faith, the salvation of your souls.**

So in the collection of Scriptures above, we see people receiving Jesus, receiving the Father, receiving the Holy Spirit, receiving the gospel, receiving the Kingdom of God, and receiving the Word (which is either Jesus Himself, as in John 1:14, or the Holy Spirit, as in John 6:63).

Let's look at something else Paul wrote, where he says the same thing in different words:

> II Corinthians 5:19–20 (NKJV): . . .God was in Christ **reconciling the world to Himself,** not imputing their trespasses to them, and has committed to us the word of reconciliation. ²⁰Now then, we are ambassadors for Christ, as though God were pleading through us: we implore you on Christ's behalf, **be reconciled to God.**

So from God's point of view, He has done everything necessary to provide salvation. He has reconciled everyone in the world to Him by not imputing our sins against us (v. 19). He has forgiven us, and has removed the barrier between Himself and us—He made peace with us (Colossians 1:20–23). He did everything necessary for us to be able to come into His presence. Now, using our sacred gift of free will, the ball is in our court, to accept His gift or not. This is why Paul urges us to be reconciled to Him (v. 20)—this two-party covenant requires the participation of both parties.

Now that's curious, isn't it? If Total Depravity were true, they *couldn't* choose to receive Christ, which is why, supposedly, Unconditional Election (where God "receives Himself into our lives for us") is necessary. But if Unconditional Election were true, people's "reception" of Christ (or absence thereof) would already have been settled from eternity past, so what's the point of exhorting them to do it? This doesn't bode well for Total Depravity.

Choosing to Believe in Jesus

Did Jesus address whether or not *we* could choose whether or not to believe in Him? Did He ever exhort people to believe in Him? Or *not* to believe in Him under certain conditions? Or what results from believing in Him? Actually, yes.

> John 3:36 (NIV): Whoever **believes in the Son has eternal life,** but whoever **rejects the Son will not see life,** for God's wrath remains on him.

It's very significant that "believing" and "rejecting" result in opposite results. From this we can see that the opposite of rejecting—i.e., accepting—must, at least in the context of salvation, be synonymous with believing. And we can likewise deduce that the opposite of believing—i.e., disbelieving—must be synonymous with rejecting.

> Mark 16:16 (NIV): Whoever believes and is baptized will be saved, but **whoever does not believe will be condemned.**

John 3:18 (GWORD): **Those who believe in him won't be condemned.** But those who don't believe are **already condemned because they don't believe** in God's only Son.

John 5:24 (GWORD): I can guarantee this truth: **Those who listen to what I say and believe in the one who sent me will have eternal life.** They won't be judged because they have already passed from death to life.

John 6:29 (NASB): Jesus answered and said to them, "This is the work of God, that you **believe in Him whom He has sent.**"

John 6:35 (NIV): Then Jesus declared, "I am the bread of life. He who comes to me will never go hungry, and **he who believes in me will never be thirsty.**"

John 6:40 (AMP): For this is My Father's will and His purpose, that **everyone who sees the Son and believes in and cleaves to and trusts in and relies on Him should have eternal life,** and I will raise him up [from the dead] at the last day.

John 7:38 (NIV): **Whoever believes in me,** as the Scripture has said, **streams of living water will flow from within him.**

John 10:37–38 (NIV): **Do not believe me** unless I do what my Father does. ³⁸But if I do it, even though you do not believe me, **believe the miracles,** that you may know and understand that the Father is in me, and I in the Father.

John 11:25–26 (GWORD): Jesus said to her, "I am the one who brings people back to life, and I am life itself. **Those who believe in me will live** even if they die. ²⁶**Everyone who lives and believes in me will never die.** Do you believe that?"

John 12:46 (NASB): I have come as light into the world, that **everyone who believes in Me may not remain in darkness.**

John 14:1 (AMP): Do not let your hearts be troubled (distressed, agitated). You believe in and adhere to and trust in and rely on God; believe in and adhere to and trust in and rely also on Me.

John 14:11–12 (NIV): **Believe me** when I say that I am in the Father and the Father is in me; **or at least believe** on the evidence of the miracles themselves. ¹²I tell you the truth, **anyone who has faith in me will do what I have been doing. He will do even greater things than these,** because I am going to the Father.

John 17:20 (NIV): My prayer is not for them alone. I pray also for **those who will believe in me through their message.** . .

Acts 16:31 (NASB): They said, "**Believe in the Lord Jesus, and you will be saved,** you and your household."

Now this, too, is curious, isn't it? If Total Depravity were true, they *couldn't* choose to believe, and they couldn't believe at all, unless their "election" had already happened. But if Unconditional Election were true, their belief (or absence thereof) would already be settled from eternity past, so what's the point of telling them to do it or to *not* do it? Even more importantly, if their election had already happened, all the above exhortations would be completely pointless. This *really* doesn't bode well for Total Depravity.

Most of Christendom would agree that "believing in Jesus" and "having faith in Jesus" would be synonymous phrases. If you are one of those people who agrees with that statement, then a whole raft of other Scriptures come to bear. For example, in his letter to the Ephesians, Paul prays:

Ephesians 3:17a: That **Christ may dwell in your hearts** *by* **faith**. . .

AMP: May **Christ** *through* **your faith** [actually] **dwell** (settle down, abide, make His permanent home) **in your hearts**. . .

CEV: that **Christ will live in your hearts** *because of* **your faith**. . .

MSG: that **Christ will live in you** *as you open the door* and invite him in. . .

NIRV: Then **Christ will live in your hearts** *because you believe* in him. . .

NLT: Then **Christ will make his home in your hearts** *as you trust* in him. . .

And so on. See the section "Regeneration Precedes Faith? Or Vice Versa?" below for much more detail.

Humbling Ourselves and Submitting to God

Do we have the ability to humble *ourselves* before God? Or submit *ourselves* to Him? These are two more questions the Biblical answers to which are very troublesome for the Reformed doctrines. And to both of those questions, God thinks the answer is yes, as shown in the Scripture below, where God is talking to Solomon:

II Chronicles 7:14: If my people, which are called by my name, shall **humble themselves,** and pray, and seek my face, and turn from their wicked ways; then will I hear from heaven, and will forgive their sin, and will heal their land.

In this chapter about Total Depravity, we definitely need to look at a passage written by the third apostle James.

The third apostle James—after James the brother of John and son of Zebedee (Matthew 10:2), and James the son of Alphaeus (Matthew 10:3)—was James the half-brother of Jesus (same mother, different fathers). This James grew up in the same family as Jesus, and lived with Him day in and day out for the better part of thirty years, before Jesus' public ministry began. I think it is safe to say that James picked up a few points about how to live in a godly and responsible way as he was growing up, and in his apostolic ministry (Galatians 1:19), this wisdom powerfully comes out.

Here is the passage:

James 4:6–10 (NIV): But he gives us more grace. That is why Scripture says: "God opposes the proud but **gives grace to the humble.**" ⁷**Submit yourselves, then, to God.** Resist the devil, and he will flee from you. ⁸**Come near to God and he will come near to you. Wash your hands, you sinners, and purify your hearts, you double-minded.** ⁹Grieve, mourn and wail. Change your laughter to mourning and your joy to gloom. ¹⁰**Humble yourselves before the Lord,** and he will lift you up.

So how would the Reformed doctrine of Total Depravity respond to the various statements in the above passage?

- Verse 7a: "You can't submit *yourself* to God! Since you're totally depraved, you don't have the capacity to choose anything good, like submitting yourself to God!"

- Verse 7b: "You can't resist the devil either! Since you're totally depraved, you can't choose anything good, like resisting the father of lies!"

- Verse 8a: "You can't come near to God, for the same reason as before! You would have to be able to make good choices in order to do that!"

- Verse 8b: "You can't do the action that 'wash your hands' metaphorically represents, and you certainly can't purify your hearts! Did I mention that you are totally depraved?"

- Verse 9: "The grieving, mourning and wailing referred to in this verse clearly indicates remorse and repentance. But you can't do that because you're totally depraved!"

- Verse 10: "You can't humble yourself before the Lord, because you can't make a good choices, being totally depraved and all!"

Wow. *Six times* in only four verses, the Bible commands us to do something that Total Depravity says is not possible. It appears that we will have to choose which doctrines we will believe: the Bible, which says to do these things, or the Reformed doctrines, which say it's impossible to do these things.

This passage from James is particularly hard-hitting and conclusive in its disagreement with the Reformed doctrines. Let's take a closer look:

- In v. 6, note that the people who God is giving grace to are *already* humble, and that is why He is giving them grace. Of course, God has given everyone grace enough to repent, but the people who actually *do* repent (humbling themselves before God) get more grace, as the first part of this verse says. This overturns Total Depravity.
- In v, 7, James exhorts his listeners to submit themselves to God. Clearly, then, it must be possible to do so. This, too, overturns Total Depravity.
- In v. 8, we are commanded to draw near to God, and *then as a result,* He will draw near to us. Reread all the examples of this in the section "When God Takes His Cue from Us" for confirmation. James quickly follows up with exhorting sinners to "wash their hands" and "purify their hearts." This, again, overturns Total Depravity.
- Finally, in v. 10, James again exhorts us to humble *ourselves.* This, yet again, overturns Total Depravity.

Here are some more passages that confirm the concept even further:

Exodus 10:3 (AMP): So Moses and Aaron went to Pharaoh, and said to him, Thus says the Lord, the God of the Hebrews, How long will you refuse to **humble yourself** before Me? Let My people go, that they may serve Me.

I Kings 21:29 (NASB): "Do you see how **Ahab has humbled himself** before Me? Because **he has humbled himself** before Me, I will not bring the evil in his days, but I will bring the evil upon his house in his son's days."

II Kings 22:19 (NIV): Because your heart was responsive and you *[Josiah]* **humbled yourself** before the Lord when you heard what I have spoken against this place and its people, that they would become accursed and laid waste, and because you tore your robes and wept in my presence, I have heard you, declares the Lord.

II Chronicles 12:6–7 (GWORD): Then **the commanders of Israel and the king** *[Rehoboam]* **humbled themselves.** "The Lord is right!" they said. ⁷When the Lord saw that **they had humbled themselves,** he spoke his word to Shemaiah: **"They have humbled themselves.** I will not destroy them. In a little while I will give them an escape. I will not use Shishak to pour my anger on Jerusalem."

II Chronicles 12:12 (NLT): Because **Rehoboam humbled himself,** the Lord's anger was turned away, and he did not destroy him completely. There were still some good things in the land of Judah.

II Chronicles 30:11 (AMP): Yet, **a few of Asher, Manasseh, and Zebulun humbled themselves** and came to Jerusalem.

II Chronicles 32:26 (NASB): However, **Hezekiah humbled the pride of his heart, both he and the inhabitants of Jerusalem,** so that the wrath of the Lord did not come on them in the days of Hezekiah.

II Chronicles 33:12 (NIV): In his distress **he** *[Manasseh]* sought the favor of the Lord his God and **humbled himself greatly** before the God of his fathers.

II Chronicles 34:27 (NIV): Because your heart *[Josiah]* was responsive and **you humbled yourself before God** when you heard what he spoke against this place and its people, and because **you humbled yourself before me** and tore your robes and wept in my presence, I have heard you, declares the Lord.

Ezra 8:21 (CEV): Beside the Ahava River, I asked the people to go without eating and to pray. **We humbled ourselves** and asked God to bring us and our children safely to Jerusalem with all of our possessions.

Psalm 35:13 (NKJV): But as for me *[David]*, when they were sick, my clothing was sackcloth; **I humbled myself** with fasting; and my prayer would return to my own heart.

Proverbs 6:1–3 (AMP): My son, if you have become security for your neighbor, if you have given your pledge for a stranger or another, ²You are snared with the words of your lips, you are caught by the speech of your mouth. ³Do this now [at once and earnestly], my son, and deliver yourself when you have put yourself into the power of your neighbor; go, bestir and **humble yourself,** and beg your neighbor [to pay his debt and thereby release you].

Daniel 10:12 (NLT): Then he *[the angel]* said, "Don't be afraid, Daniel. Since the first day you began to pray for understanding and **to humble**

yourself before your God, your request has been heard in heaven. I have come in answer to your prayer."

Micah 6:8 (AMP): He has showed you, O man, what is good. And what does the Lord require of you but to do justly, and to love kindness and mercy, and **to humble yourself** and walk humbly with your God?

Matthew 18:4 (AMP): **Whoever will humble himself** therefore and become like this little child [trusting, lowly, loving, forgiving] is greatest in the kingdom of heaven.

Matthew 23:12 (NIV): For whoever exalts himself will be humbled, and **whoever humbles himself** will be exalted.

Luke 14:11 (NIV): For everyone who exalts himself will be humbled, and **he who humbles himself** will be exalted.

Luke 18:14 (GWORD): "I can guarantee that this tax collector went home with God's approval, but the Pharisee didn't. Everyone who honors himself will be humbled, but **the person who humbles himself will be honored.**"

II Corinthians 11:7 (NLT): Was I *[Paul]* wrong when **I humbled myself** and honored you by preaching God's Good News to you without expecting anything in return?

James 4:10 (WEB): **Humble yourselves** in the sight of the Lord, and he will exalt you.

I Peter 5:6 (NIV): **Humble yourselves, therefore, under God's mighty hand,** that he may lift you up in due time.

So above we see even more Scriptures that refute the Reformed doctrine of Total Depravity, which says that humans cannot choose to turn to God, we cannot humble ourselves, we cannot submit ourselves to God, we cannot repent, nor can we receive or accept what He has to offer. This is because, allegedly, if *we* did any of those things, that would constitute a "work," and since salvation by works is not valid, we *can't* repent, or humble ourselves, so God has to do it for us. But we saw, via the syllogism in the section "Faith Vs. Works," that believing, or repenting, or humbling oneself, cannot Scripturally be called a "work."

The Cry of God's Heart

There is a fascinating passage in Deuteronomy, where God reveals His heart for people:

> Deuteronomy 5:29: **O that there were such an heart in them,** that they would fear me, and keep all my commandments always, that it might be well with them, and with their children for ever!
>
> BBE: **If only they had such a heart in them at all times,** so that they might go in fear of me and keep my orders and that it might be well for them and for their children for ever!
>
> GWORD: **If only they would fear me and obey all my commandments** as long as they live! Then things would go well for them and their children forever.
>
> HCSB: **If only they had such a heart to fear Me and keep all My commands always,** so that they and their children will prosper forever.
>
> NET: **If only it would really be their desire to fear me and obey all my commandments** in the future, so that it may go well with them and their descendants forever.
>
> NIV: **Oh, that their hearts would be inclined to fear me and keep all my commands always,** so that it might go well with them and their children forever!
>
> TEV: **If only they would always feel this way! If only they would always honor me and obey all my commands,** so that everything would go well with them and their descendants forever.

Now, seriously: if God chose all our decisions for us, and we didn't have free will, and everything we think and say and do was "fated" for us to think and say and do, why would God cry out, "*If only* they would honor and obey Me, that everything would go well with them!"? That question is just as valid even if you adhere to the less extreme version of the no-free-will doctrine—where we lack free will only in the area of choosing to serve God or not—because this Scripture manifestly discusses the question of our serving Him or not. It's the whole point of the verse.

And notice that the reason He wants us to obey Him is so that "everything would go well" with us. Why? Because He loves us.

Free to Choose?

In his prophetic message from God, the psalmist Asaph echoes Deuteronomy, when he says:

Psalm 81:13–16 (NASB): "**Oh that My people would listen to Me, that Israel would walk in My ways!** ¹⁴I would quickly subdue their enemies and turn My hand against their adversaries. ¹⁵Those who hate the Lord would pretend obedience to Him, and their time of punishment would be forever. ¹⁶But I would feed you with the finest of the wheat, and with honey from the rock I would satisfy you."

And then Isaiah reiterates the cry of God's heart again:

Isaiah 48:17–18: This is what the Lord says— your Redeemer, the Holy One of Israel: "I am the Lord your God, who teaches you what is good for you and leads you along the paths you should follow. ¹⁸**Oh, that you had listened to my commands!** Then you would have had peace flowing like a gentle river and righteousness rolling over you like waves in the sea."

And then, in case we still haven't understood, God repeats it again. Ezekiel, too, reveals the heart of God when he says:

Ezekiel 33:11 (TEV): Tell them that as surely as I, the Sovereign LORD, am the living God, I do not enjoy seeing sinners die. **I would rather see them stop sinning and live. Israel, stop the evil you are doing.** Why do you want to die?

Jesus expressed the same grief over the people of Jerusalem when they rejected His Person and His message:

Matthew 23:37 (NIV): O Jerusalem, Jerusalem, you who kill the prophets and stone those sent to you, **how often I have longed to gather your children together,** as a hen gathers her chicks under her wings, **but you were not willing.**

Note that this heartcry of Jesus above, and the heartcry of God before that, make absolutely no sense *if* the doctrine of Total Depravity were true: *of course* they were not willing to be gathered to Him, because He hadn't chosen them as some of the elect and thus caused them to *be* willing.

And then there's this statement from Paul:

II Corinthians 12:21 (NIV): I am afraid that when I come again my God will humble me before you, and **I will be grieved over many who have sinned earlier and have not repented** of the impurity, sexual sin and debauchery in which they have indulged.

Now think about it: if people couldn't repent voluntarily, and those who are unrepentant are in that condition because God deliberately caused them to be in that condition, why would Paul grieve over them? He would be grieving because people are in the condition that God intentionally put them in!

Obviously, this doesn't make sense, especially if you believe that the Holy Spirit inspired Paul to make this statement. In that case, you are forced to conclude that the Holy Spirit inspired Paul to say that he was grieved the people were in the condition God intentionally put them in! Clearly, Paul did not buy into the theory that people cannot choose to repent, and apparently neither did the Holy Spirit.

To see a *great* deal of detail on the concept of repentance, what it is, and whether God expects us to do it, see Book 2: *Is It Possible to Stop Sinning?*

So in the above passages, we see that the Law, the Psalms, the Prophets, the Gospels, and the Epistles all agree that God wants us to repent of sin so He can bless us. Do you think it might be true? Even though Total Depravity says we *can't* repent?

Regeneration Precedes Faith? Or Vice Versa?

Reformed doctrine includes the idea that "Regeneration precedes Faith." This means, in a nutshell, that one implication of the Total Depravity doctrine is that we cannot respond to God in any way; the effects of the Fall of Man were so severe that we are unable to ask God to help us, or even receive help that He offers, without Him "accepting for us." Therefore, God has to save us *before* we could have the faith or motivation to believe in Him. Does this square with Scripture?

Now notice that the word "precedes" doesn't necessarily imply "before" in a temporal sense. It may *also* be that, but the Reformed doctrine understands "precedes" in a logical sense, rather than a temporal sense. So one *causes* the other, instead of one merely happening *prior to* the other.

In order to investigate that question of "which precedes which," I followed this procedure:

1. I looked up all the Scriptures I could find that contained a faith-related word (faith, believe, trust, etc.) and also contained a regeneration-related word (save, salvation, justified, etc.).
2. Of those Scriptures discovered in Step 1, I selected the ones that indicated a *causal* relationship; that is, where the presence of one of them resulted in the presence of the other.

3. Of those Scriptures remaining in Step 2—those containing a causal relationship between the two concepts—I examined *which way* the causation operated: did A cause B, or did B cause A?

4. Finally, I listed the verses in two forms: first, as they actually appear in the Bible (Column 1 in the tables below), and second, with the sense of the causation reversed, just for the sake of comparison (Column 2 in the tables below).

I was interested to find that in *every one* of the Scriptures that mentioned both a faith-related word and a salvation-related word, and indicated a causal relationship, *faith was the cause and salvation was the effect.* I didn't find a single exception. If you, the reader, know of any unambiguous exceptions to this finding, please let me know (see the "About the Author" section at the end of this book for how to contact the author).

So, read the Scriptures below, as well as their "modified" versions, and then you decide for yourself whether you think "faith precedes regeneration" or "regeneration precedes faith." (Note: the skull-and-crossbones symbols in the second-column table headings below are to remind the reader that my modified versions of these verses are *not* quotes from the Bible, even though they may superficially, and temporarily, sound like it.)

✝ **Faith Precedes Regeneration** (Actual Scripture Quote)	☠ **Regeneration Precedes Faith** (Warning: Not Real Scripture)
Genesis 15:6: And he *[Abram]* believed in the LORD; and **he counted it to him for righteousness.**	And God made Abram righteous, and then Abram believed in the LORD; **he counted it to him for faith.**
GWORD: Then Abram believed the LORD, and **that faith was regarded as the basis of Abram's approval** by the LORD.	Then Abram was given approval by the LORD, and **that approval was regarded as the basis of Abram's faith** in the LORD.
TEV: Abram put his trust in the LORD, and **because of this** the LORD was pleased with him and accepted him.	The LORD was pleased with Abram and accepted him, and **because of this**, he put his trust in the LORD.
ERV: Abram **believed the LORD, and because of this faith** the LORD accepted him as one who has done what is right.	The LORD accepted Abram as one who would later do what is right, and **because of this acceptance** he believed the LORD.
EXB: Abram believed [put his trust/faith in] the LORD. And **the LORD accepted Abram's faith, and that faith made him right with God.** . .	The LORD accepted Abram and made him right with God, and **that acceptance made Abram believe** [put his trust/faith in] the LORD.
GNT: Abram put his trust in the LORD, and **because of this** the LORD was pleased with him and accepted him.	The LORD was pleased with Abram and accepted him, and **because of this**, he put his trust in the LORD.

Right off the bat, we see Abram, the "father of the faith" (Galatians 3:7), being made righteous *because of his faith,* not the other way around.

✝ Faith Precedes Regeneration (Actual Scripture Quote)	☠ Regeneration Precedes Faith (Warning: Not Real Scripture)
Psalm 17:7: Shew thy marvellous lovingkindness, O thou that **savest by thy right hand them which put their trust in thee** from those that rise up against them.	Shew thy marvellous lovingkindness, O thou that **givest trust** to them **whom thou hast saved** by thy right hand from those that rise up against them.
CEV: Show your wonderful love. Your mighty arm **protects those who run to you** for safety from their enemies.	Show your wonderful love. You **cause to run to you** for safety **those whom your mighty arm has protected** from their enemies.
ERV: Show your amazing kindness and **rescue those who depend on you.** Use your great power and protect them from their enemies.	Show your amazing kindness and **cause to depend on you those whom you have rescued.** Use your great power and protect them from their enemies.

He saves *those who trust in Him,* not the other way around.

✝ Faith Precedes Regeneration (Actual Scripture Quote)	☠ Regeneration Precedes Faith (Warning: Not Real Scripture)
Psalm 37:40: And the LORD shall help them, and deliver them: **he shall deliver them from the wicked, and save them, because they trust in him.**	And the LORD shall help them, deliver them: **he shall cause to trust in him those whom he has delivered** from the wicked, because he has saved them.
CEB: The LORD will help them and rescue them—rescue them from the wicked—and **he will save them because they have taken refuge in him.**	The LORD will help them and rescue them—rescue them from the wicked—and **they will take refuge in him because he has saved them.**
ERV: The LORD helps good people and rescues them. **They depend on him, so he rescues them** from the wicked.	The LORD helps good people and rescues them. **He rescues them** from the wicked, **so they depend on him.**

God delivers people *because* they trust in Him, not vice versa.

Free to Choose?

✝ **Faith Precedes Regeneration** (Actual Scripture Quote)	☠ **Regeneration Precedes Faith** (Warning: Not Real Scripture)
Psalm 86:2: Preserve my soul; for I am holy: O thou my God, save thy servant that trusteth in thee.	Make me holy, for thou hast preserved me: O thou my God, cause to trust in thee thy servant that you have saved.
AMP: Preserve my life, for I am godly and dedicated; O my God, save Your servant, for I trust in You [leaning and believing on You, committing all and confidently looking to You, without fear or doubt].	Make me godly and dedicated, for you have preserved my life; O my God, cause to trust in You [to lean and believe on You, commit all and confidently look to You, without fear or doubt], for Your servant has been saved.
NIRV: Keep my life safe, because I am faithful to you. Save me, because I trust in you. You are my God.	Make me faithful to you, because you have kept my life safe. Make me trust in you, because I am saved. You are my God.

He keeps our lives safe *because* we trust in Him, not the other way around.

✝ Faith Precedes Regeneration (Actual Scripture Quote)	☠ Regeneration Precedes Faith (Warning: Not Real Scripture)
Mark 16:16: He that believeth and is baptized shall be saved; but he that believeth not shall be damned.	He that is saved shall believe and be baptized; but he that be damned shall believe not.
AMP: He who believes [who adheres to and trusts in and relies on the Gospel and Him Whom it sets forth] and is baptized will be saved [from the penalty of eternal death]; but he who does not believe [who does not adhere to and trust in and rely on the Gospel and Him Whom it sets forth] will be condemned.	He who is saved [from the penalty of eternal death] shall believe [adhere to and trust in and rely on the Gospel and Him Whom it sets forth] and shall be baptized; but he who is condemned shall not believe [shall not adhere to and trust in and rely on the Gospel and Him Whom it sets forth].

He that believes shall be saved, not the other way around.

✝ Faith Precedes Regeneration (Actual Scripture Quote)	☠ Regeneration Precedes Faith (Warning: Not Real Scripture)
Luke 7:50: And he said to the woman, **Thy faith hath saved thee**; go in peace.	And he said to the woman, **Thy salvation hath given you faith**; go in peace.
CEV: But Jesus told the woman, "**Because of your faith, you are now saved.** May God give you peace!"	But Jesus told the woman, "**Because you are saved, you now have faith.** May God give you peace!"
WE: Jesus said to the woman, '**You are saved because you believed.** Go in peace.'	Jesus said to the woman, '**You believe because you are saved.** Go in peace.'

Her faith saved her; not "her salvation gave her faith."

FREE TO CHOOSE?

✝ **Faith Precedes Regeneration** (Actual Scripture Quote)	☠ **Regeneration Precedes Faith** (Warning: Not Real Scripture)
Luke 8:12: Those by the way side are they that hear; then cometh the devil, and taketh away the word out of their hearts, **lest they should believe and be saved.**	Those by the way side are they that hear; then cometh the devil, and taketh away the word out of their hearts, **lest they should be saved and start believing.**
EXB: The seed that fell beside the road [along the footpath] is like the people who hear God's teaching, but [then] the devil comes and takes it away from them [their hearts] so **they cannot believe it and be saved.**	The seed that fell beside the road [along the footpath] is like the people who hear God's teaching, but [then] the devil comes and takes it away from them [their hearts] so **they cannot be saved and thus believe it.**
NIRV: The seed on the path stands for God's message in the hearts of those who hear. But then the devil comes. He takes away the message from their hearts. **He does it so they won't believe. Then they can't be saved.**	The seed on the path stands for God's message in the hearts of those who hear. But then the devil comes. He takes away the message from their hearts. **He does it so they won't be saved. Then they can't believe.**

The devil took the word out of their hearts to prevent them from believing, and thus to prevent them from getting saved (in that order). Another interesting thought: If the person in the Scriptures in the first column above had been unchangeably predestined to be saved, how could the devil take the word out of his heart?

✝ Faith Precedes Regeneration (Actual Scripture Quote)	☠ Regeneration Precedes Faith (Warning: Not Real Scripture)
Luke 18:42: And Jesus said unto him, Receive thy sight: **thy faith hath saved thee.**	And Jesus said unto him, Receive thy sight: **thy salvation hath given thee faith.**
CEV: Jesus replied, "Look and you will see! **Your eyes are healed because of your faith.**"	Jesus replied, "Look and you will see! **You have faith because of the healing of your eyes.**"
NCV: Jesus said to him, "Then see. **You are healed because you believed.**"	Jesus said to him, "Then see. **You believe because you are healed.**"

Granted, this Scripture refers to "saved" in the sense of physical healing, but there are many passages where physical healing and spiritual healing are closely associated. For much more detail, see the section "Forgiveness and Healing Together" in Book 5: *If It Be Thy Will.*

FREE TO CHOOSE?

✝ **Faith Precedes Regeneration** (Actual Scripture Quote)	☠ **Regeneration Precedes Faith** (Warning: Not Real Scripture)
Acts 13:39: And by him **all that believe are justified from all things**, from which ye could not be justified by the law of Moses.	And by him **all that have been justified** from all things from which ye could not be justified by the law of Moses, **believe**.
AMP: And that through Him **everyone who believes** [who acknowledges Jesus as his Savior and devotes himself to Him] **is absolved (cleared and freed) from every charge** from which he could not be justified and freed by the Law of Moses and given right standing with God.	And that through Him **everyone who has been absolved (cleared and freed) from every charge** from which he could not be justified and freed by the Law of Moses and given right standing with God, **believes** [acknowledges Jesus as his Savior and devotes himself to Him].
CEB: . . .through Jesus **everyone who believes is put in right relationship with God**.	. . .through Jesus **everyone who has been put in right relationship with God believes**.
DARBY: . . .and from all things from which ye could not be justified in the law of Moses, in him **every one that believes is justified**.	. . .in him **every one that is justified** from all things from which ye could not be justified in the law of Moses, **believes**.
ERV: The Law of Moses could not free you from your sins. But **you can be made right with God if you believe in Jesus**.	The Law of Moses could not free you from your sins. But **you can believe in Jesus if you have been made right with God**.
HCSB: . . .and **everyone who believes in Him is justified** from everything that you could not be justified from through the law of Moses.	. . .and **everyone who has been justified** from everything that you could not be justified from through the law of Moses, **believes in Him**.

Those who believe are justified, not the other way around.

✝ **Faith Precedes Regeneration** (Actual Scripture Quote)	☠ **Regeneration Precedes Faith** (Warning: Not Real Scripture)
Acts 16:31: And they said, **Believe on the Lord Jesus Christ, and thou shalt be saved, and thy house.**	And they said, **If you have been chosen to be saved, thou and thy house shalt believe on the Lord Jesus Christ.**
AMP: And they answered, **Believe in the Lord Jesus Christ [give yourself up to Him, take yourself out of your own keeping and entrust yourself into His keeping] and you will be saved, [and this applies both to] you and your household as well.**	And they answered, **If you have been chosen to be saved, you will be able to believe in the Lord Jesus Christ** [give yourself up to Him, take yourself out of your own keeping and entrust yourself into His keeping], [and this applies both to] you and your household as well.
PHILLIPS: And they replied, "**Believe in the Lord Jesus and then you will be saved,** you and your household."	And they replied, "**If you have been chosen to be saved, then you will be able to believe in the Lord Jesus,** you and your household."

Believe, and you will be saved; not the other way around.

✝ **Faith Precedes Regeneration** (Actual Scripture Quote)	☠ **Regeneration Precedes Faith** (Warning: Not Real Scripture)
Romans 1:16: For I am not ashamed of the gospel of Christ: for **it is the power of God unto salvation to every one that believeth**; to the Jew first, and also to the Greek.	For I am not ashamed of the gospel of Christ: for **it is the power of God unto belief to every one that has been elected to be saved**; to the Jew first, and also to the Greek.
CJB: For I am not ashamed of the Good News, since it is **God's powerful means of bringing salvation to everyone who keeps on trusting**, to the Jew especially, but equally to the Gentile.	For I am not ashamed of the Good News, since it is **God's powerful means of bringing trust to everyone who keeps on being saved**, to the Jew especially, but equally to the Gentile.
NLV: I am not ashamed of the Good News. It is the power of God. It is the way **He saves men from the punishment of their sins if they put their trust in Him**. It is for the Jew first and for all other people also.	I am not ashamed of the Good News. It is the power of God. It is the way **He enables men to put their trust in Him if they have been elected to be saved from the punishment of their sins**. It is for the Jew first and for all other people also.

Salvation to every one who believes, not the other way around.

Chapter 5: Total Depravity

✝ **Faith Precedes Regeneration** (Actual Scripture Quote)	☠ **Regeneration Precedes Faith** (Warning: Not Real Scripture)
Romans 1:17 For therein is the righteousness of God revealed from faith to faith: as it is written, **The just shall live by faith.**	For therein is the righteousness of God revealed from faith to faith: as it is written, **Those with faith shall live by their justice.**
CEV: The good news tells how God accepts everyone who has faith, but only those who have faith. It is just as the Scriptures say, "**The people God accepts because of their faith will live.**"	The good news tells how God accepts everyone who has faith, but only those who have faith. It is just as the Scriptures say, "**The people God chose to live will have faith because of it.**"
ERV: The Good News shows how God makes people right with himself. **God's way of making people right begins and ends with faith.** As the Scriptures say, "**The one who is right with God by faith will live forever.**"	The Good News shows how God makes people right with himself. **God's way of making people right begins and ends with His electing us, discounting faith.** As the Scriptures say, "**The one who is right with God by having been chosen to live forever will have faith.**"
PHILLIPS: I see in it **God's plan for imparting righteousness to men, a process begun and continued by their faith.** For, as the scripture says: 'The just shall live by faith'.	I see in it **God's plan for imparting righteousness to men, a process begun and continued at his discretion.** For, as the scripture says: 'The faithful shall live by their justice'.

God accepts people because of their faith, not the other way around.

✝ **Faith Precedes Regeneration** (Actual Scripture Quote)	☠ **Regeneration Precedes Faith** (Warning: Not Real Scripture)
Romans 3:22: Even **the righteousness of God which is by faith of Jesus Christ unto all and upon all them that believe:** for there is no difference. . .	Even the faith of Jesus Christ unto all and upon all them, **which is by having been given the righteousness of God:** for there is no difference. . .
AMP: Namely, **the righteousness of God which comes by believing** with personal trust and confident reliance on Jesus Christ (the Messiah). [And it is meant] for all who believe. For there is no distinction. . .	Namely, **the believing** with personal trust and confident reliance on Jesus Christ (the Messiah) **which comes by having been given the righteousness of God.** [And it is meant] for all who have been made righteous. For there is no distinction. . .
CEV: God treats everyone alike. **He accepts people only because they have faith in Jesus Christ.**	God treats everyone alike. **He gives people faith in Jesus Christ only because they have been accepted.**
GNT: God **puts people right through their faith in Jesus Christ. God does this to all who believe in Christ,** because there is no difference at all. . .	God **gives people faith in Jesus Christ through their having been put right.** God does this to all who have been put right, because there is no difference at all. . .
TLB: Now **God says he will accept and acquit us—declare us "not guilty"—if we trust Jesus Christ** to take away our sins. And we all can be saved in this same way, by coming to Christ, no matter who we are or what we have been like.	Now **God says he will enable us to trust Jesus Christ** to take away our sins **if we have been accepted and acquitted—declared to be "not guilty."** And we all can have faith in this same way, by having been accepted, no matter who we are or what we have been like.

(Table continues on next page. . .)

(Table continued from previous page. . .)

✝ **Faith Precedes Regeneration** (Actual Scripture Quote)	☠ **Regeneration Precedes Faith** (Warning: Not Real Scripture)
NIRV: We are made right with God by putting our faith in Jesus Christ. This happens to all who believe. It is no different for the Jews than for the Gentiles.	We are able to put our faith in Jesus Christ by having been made right with God. This happens to all who have been made right with God. It is no different for the Jews than for the Gentiles.
WE: God puts people right with himself when they believe in Jesus Christ. He does this for all who believe. They are all alike.	God enables people to believe in Jesus Christ when they have been put right with himself. He does this for all who have been put right. They are all alike.

God accepts people because of their faith, not the other way around.

✝ Faith Precedes Regeneration (Actual Scripture Quote)	☠ Regeneration Precedes Faith (Warning: Not Real Scripture)
Romans 3:26: To declare, I say, at this time his righteousness: that he might be just, and **the justifier of him which believeth in Jesus.**	To declare, I say, at this time his righteousness: that he might be just, and **the giver of belief in Jesus to him which has been justified.**
AMP: It was to demonstrate and prove at the present time (in the now season) that He Himself is righteous and that **He justifies and accepts as righteous him who has [true] faith in Jesus.**	It was to demonstrate and prove at the present time (in the now season) that He Himself is righteous and that **He gives [true] faith in Jesus to him who has been justified and accepted as righteous.**
ERV: And in our own time he still does what is right. God worked all this out in a way that allows him to judge people fairly and still **make right any person who has faith in Jesus.**	And in our own time he still does what is right. God worked all this out in a way that allows him to judge people fairly and still **give faith in Jesus to any person who has been made right.**
GWORD: He waited so that he could display his approval at the present time. This shows that he is a God of justice, a **God who approves of people who believe in Jesus.**	He waited so that he could display his approval at the present time. This shows that he is a God of justice, a **God who enables to believe in Jesus those people he approves of.**
NIV: . . .he did it to demonstrate his righteousness at the present time, so as to be just and the one **who justifies those who have faith in Jesus.**	. . .he did it to demonstrate his righteousness at the present time, so as to be just and the one **who gives faith in Jesus to those who have been justified.**

(Table continues on next page. . .)

(Table continued from previous page. . .)

✝ **Faith Precedes Regeneration** (Actual Scripture Quote)	☠ **Regeneration Precedes Faith** (Warning: Not Real Scripture)
NLV: But now God proves that He is right in saving men from sin. He shows that He is the One Who has no sin. **God makes anyone right with Himself who puts his trust in Jesus.**	But now God proves that He is right in saving men from sin. He shows that He is the One Who has no sin. **God allows to put trust in Jesus anyone He has made right with Himself.**
NLT: . . .for he was looking ahead and including them in what he would do in this present time. God did this to demonstrate his righteousness, for he himself is fair and just, and **he declares sinners to be right in his sight when they believe in Jesus.**	. . .for he was looking ahead and including them in what he would do in this present time. God did this to demonstrate his righteousness, for he himself is fair and just, and **he declares sinners to be believing in Jesus when they are right in his sight.**

God justifies him who has faith, not the other way around.

189

✝ **Faith Precedes Regeneration** (Actual Scripture Quote)	☠ **Regeneration Precedes Faith** (Warning: Not Real Scripture)
Romans 10:9: That **if thou shalt confess with thy mouth the Lord Jesus, and shalt believe in thine heart that God hath raised him from the dead, thou shalt be saved.**	That **if thou hast been elected to be saved, thou shalt be enabled to confess with thy mouth the Lord Jesus, and believe in thine heart that God hath raised him from the dead.**
CEV: **So you will be saved, if you honestly say, "Jesus is Lord," and if you believe with all your heart that God raised him from death.**	So you will be able to honestly say, "Jesus is Lord," and believe with all your heart that God raised him from death, if you've been elected to be saved.
MSG: Say the welcoming word to God—"Jesus is my Master"—embracing, body and soul, God's work of doing in us what he did in raising Jesus from the dead. That's it. **You're not "doing" anything; you're simply calling out to God, trusting him to do it for you.** That's salvation.	It is not possible to say the welcoming word to God—"Jesus is my Master"—embracing, body and soul, God's work of doing in us what he did in raising Jesus from the dead, unless you've been chosen. That's it. You can't "do" anything; you can't even call out to God, or trust him to do it for you, unless you're already one of the elect. That's salvation.

If you believe, you will be saved, not the other way around.

I apologize in advance for the large number of translations used in the following table; I used them because the direction of causality is *so* obvious I didn't want it to go by unnoticed. The words indicating causality are italicized within the bold text.

✝ Faith Precedes Regeneration (Actual Scripture Quote)	☠ Regeneration Precedes Faith (Warning: Not Real Scripture)
Romans 10:10: For **with the heart man believeth *unto* righteousness; and with the mouth confession is made unto salvation.**	For **righteousness is imparted to man *unto* believing with the heart; and salvation is imparted to man unto confession with the mouth.**
AMP: For **with the heart a person believes (adheres to, trusts in, and relies on Christ) *and so* is justified (declared righteous, acceptable to God), and with the mouth he confesses (declares openly and speaks out freely his faith) and confirms [his] salvation.**	For **justification (being declared righteous, acceptable to God) occurs, *and so* with the heart a person believes (adheres to, trusts in, and relies on Christ), and [his] salvation having been confirmed, he confesses (declares openly and speaks out freely his faith) with the mouth.**
CEB: **Trusting with the heart *leads to* righteousness, and confessing with the mouth leads to salvation.**	**Righteousness *leads to* trusting with the heart, and salvation leads to confessing with the mouth.**
CEV: **God will accept you and save you, *if* you truly believe this and tell it to others.**	**You will truly believe this and tell it to others, *if* God has accepted you and saved you.**
DLNT: For **it is believed with the heart *resulting in* righteousness, and it is confessed with the mouth resulting in salvation.**	For **righteousness is granted, *resulting in* believing with the heart, and salvation is granted, resulting in confession with the mouth.**
GWORD: ***By* believing you receive God's approval, and by declaring your faith you are saved.**	***By* receiving God's approval you can believe, and by being saved you can declare your faith.**

(Table continues on next page. . .)

(Table continued from previous page. . .)

✝ **Faith Precedes Regeneration** (Actual Scripture Quote)	☠ **Regeneration Precedes Faith** (Warning: Not Real Scripture)
HCSB: One believes with the heart, *resulting in* righteousness, and one confesses with the mouth, resulting in salvation.	Righteousness happens, *resulting in* one believing with the heart, and salvation happens, resulting in one confessing with the mouth.
PHILLIPS: For **it is believing in the heart** *that makes* **a man righteous before God,** and it is stating his belief by his own mouth that confirms his salvation.	For **it is a man's being righteous before God** *that makes* **him believe in the heart,** and it is his salvation that confirms the statement of his belief by his own mouth.
NOG: *By* **believing you receive God's approval**, and by declaring your faith you are saved.	*By* receiving God's approval you believe, and by being saved you declare your faith.
NCV: **We believe with our hearts,** *and so* **we are made right with God.** And we declare with our mouths that we believe, and so we are saved.	We are made right with God, *and so* we believe with our hearts. And we are saved, and so we declare with our mouths that we believe.
NET: For **with the heart one believes** *and thus* **has righteousness** and with the mouth one confesses and thus has salvation.	For one has righteousness *and thus* with the heart believes and one has salvation and thus with the mouth confesses.
VOICE: **Belief begins in the heart** *and leads to* **a life that's right with God;** confession departs from our lips and brings eternal salvation.	A life that's right with God *and leads to* belief in the heart; eternal salvation brings confession departing from our lips.

Belief results in righteousness, not the other way around.

✝ **Faith Precedes Regeneration** (Actual Scripture Quote)	☠ **Regeneration Precedes Faith** (Warning: Not Real Scripture)
I Corinthians 1:21: For after that in the wisdom of God the world by wisdom knew not God, it pleased God by the foolishness of preaching **to save them that believe.**	For after that in the wisdom of God the world by wisdom knew not God, it pleased God by the foolishness of preaching **to make them believe that are saved.**
CJB: For God's wisdom ordained that the world, using its own wisdom, would not come to know him. Therefore God decided to use the "nonsense" of what we proclaim as his means of **saving those who come to trust in it.**	For God's wisdom ordained that the world, using its own wisdom, would not come to know him. Therefore God decided to use the "nonsense" of what we proclaim as his means of **permitting to come to trust in it those who are saved.**
CEB: God was wise and decided not to let the people of this world use their wisdom to learn about him. Instead, **God chose to save only those who believe the foolish message we preach.**	God was wise and decided not to let the people of this world use their wisdom to learn about him. Instead, **God chose to allow to believe the foolish message we preach only those who are saved.**

It pleased God to save them who believe, not the other way around.

✝ Faith Precedes Regeneration (Actual Scripture Quote)	☠ Regeneration Precedes Faith (Warning: Not Real Scripture)
Ephesians 2:8: For by grace **are ye saved through faith;** and that not of yourselves: it is the gift of God. . .	For by grace are ye given faith through salvation; and that not of yourselves: it is the gift of God. . .
ERV: I mean that **you have been saved by grace because you believed.** You did not save yourselves; it was a gift from God.	I mean that **you believed because you have been saved by grace.** You did not save yourselves; it was a gift from God.
NLT: **God saved you by his grace when you believed.** And you can't take credit for this; it is a gift from God.	**You believed when God saved you by his grace.** And you can't take credit for this; it is a gift from God.
WE: **You have been saved by God's love and kindness because you believed.** It was not because of anything you did, but it was a gift from God.	You believed because you have been saved by God's love and kindness. It was not because of anything you did, but it was a gift from God.

We are saved through faith, not the other way around.

✝ Faith Precedes Regeneration (Actual Scripture Quote)	☠ Regeneration Precedes Faith (Warning: Not Real Scripture)
II Thessalonians 2:13: But we are bound to give thanks alway to God for you, brethren beloved of the Lord, because God hath from the beginning chosen you to **salvation through sanctification of the Spirit and belief of the truth**. . .	But we are bound to give thanks alway to God for you, brethren beloved of the Lord, because God hath from the beginning chosen you to **sanctification of the Spirit and belief of the truth through salvation**. . .
CEB: But we always must thank God for you, brothers and sisters who are loved by God. This is because he chose you from the beginning to be the first crop of the harvest. This brought **salvation, through your dedication to God by the Spirit and through your belief in the truth.**	But we always must thank God for you, brothers and sisters who are loved by God. This is because he chose you from the beginning to be the first crop of the harvest. This brought **your dedication to God by the Spirit and your belief in the truth, through your salvation.**
ERV: Brothers and sisters, you are people the Lord loves. And we always thank God for you. That's what we should do, because God chose you to be some of the first people to be saved. **You are saved by the Spirit making you holy and by your faith in the truth.**	Brothers and sisters, you are people the Lord loves. And we always thank God for you. That's what we should do, because God chose you to be some of the first people to be saved. **The Spirit making you holy and your having faith in the truth come by virtue of your salvation.**

We are saved by our faith in the truth, not the other way around.

✝ **Faith Precedes Regeneration** (Actual Scripture Quote)	☠ **Regeneration Precedes Faith** (Warning: Not Real Scripture)
II Timothy 3:15: And that from a child thou hast known the holy scriptures, which are able to make thee wise unto **salvation through faith which is in Christ Jesus.**	And that from a child thou hast known the holy scriptures, which are able to make thee wise unto **faith which is in Christ Jesus through salvation.**
CEV: Since childhood, you have known the Holy Scriptures that are able to make you wise enough to **have faith in Christ Jesus and be saved.**	Since childhood, you have known the Holy Scriptures that are able to make you wise enough to **be saved and have faith in Christ Jesus.**
ERV: You have known the Holy Scriptures since you were a child. These Scriptures are able to make you wise. And that wisdom leads to **salvation through faith in Christ Jesus.**	You have known the Holy Scriptures since you were a child. These Scriptures are able to make you wise. And that wisdom leads to **faith in Christ Jesus through salvation.**

Salvation is through faith, not the other way around.

✝ **Faith Precedes Regeneration** (Actual Scripture Quote)	☠ **Regeneration Precedes Faith** (Warning: Not Real Scripture)
Hebrews 10:39: But we are not of them who draw back unto perdition; but of them that **believe to the saving of the soul**.	But we are not of them who draw back unto perdition; but of them whose souls are saved to belief.
CEB: But we aren't the sort of people who timidly draw back and end up being destroyed. We're the sort of people who **have faith so that our whole beings are preserved**.	But we aren't the sort of people who timidly draw back and end up being destroyed. We're the sort of people whose whole beings are preserved so that we have faith.
CEV: We are not like those people who turn back and get destroyed. **We will keep on having faith until we are saved.**	We are not like those people who turn back and get destroyed. We will keep on being saved until we have faith.
PHILLIPS: Surely we are not going to be men who cower back and are lost, but **men who maintain their faith until the salvation of their souls is complete!**	Surely we are not going to be men who cower back and are lost, but men who maintain the complete salvation of their souls until they have faith!
TLB: But we have never turned our backs on God and sealed our fate. No, **our faith in him assures our souls' salvation.**	But we have never turned our backs on God and sealed our fate. No, **our souls' salvation assures our faith in him.**
NLT: But we are not like those who turn away from God to their own destruction. **We are the faithful ones, whose souls will be saved.**	But we are not like those who turn away from God to their own destruction. **We are ones whose souls are saved, who will get faith.**

We believe to the saving of our soul, not the other way around.

FREE TO CHOOSE?

✝ Faith Precedes Regeneration (Actual Scripture Quote)	☠ Regeneration Precedes Faith (Warning: Not Real Scripture)
Hebrews 11:7: By faith Noah, being warned of God of things not seen as yet, moved with fear, prepared an ark to the saving of his house; by the which he condemned the world, and became heir of the **righteousness which is by faith.**	By righteousness Noah, being warned of God of things not seen as yet, moved with fear, prepared an ark to the saving of his house; by the which he condemned the world, and became heir of the **faith which is by** righteousness.
CJB: By trusting, Noach, after receiving divine warning about things as yet unseen, was filled with holy fear and built an ark to save his household. Through this trusting, he put the world under condemnation and **received the righteousness that comes from trusting.**	By trusting, Noach, after receiving divine warning about things as yet unseen, was filled with holy fear and built an ark to save his household. Through this trusting, he put the world under condemnation and **received the trusting that comes from righteousness.**
PHILLIPS: It was through faith that Noah, on receiving God's warning of impending disaster, reverently constructed an ark to save his household. This action of faith condemned the unbelief of the rest of the world, and won for Noah the **righteousness before God which follows such a faith.**	It was through faith that Noah, on receiving God's warning of impending disaster, reverently constructed an ark to save his household. This action of faith condemned the unbelief of the rest of the world, and **won for Noah the faith before God which follows such a righteousness.**

(Table continues on next page. . .)

(Table continued from previous page...)

✝ **Faith Precedes Regeneration** (Actual Scripture Quote)	☠ **Regeneration Precedes Faith** (Warning: Not Real Scripture)
TLB: Noah was another who trusted God. When he heard God's warning about the future, Noah believed him even though there was then no sign of a flood, and wasting no time, he built the ark and saved his family. Noah's belief in God was in direct contrast to the sin and disbelief of the rest of the world—which refused to obey—and **because of his faith he became one of those whom God has accepted.**	Noah was another who trusted God. When he heard God's warning about the future, Noah believed him even though there was then no sign of a flood, and wasting no time, he built the ark and saved his family. Noah's belief in God was in direct contrast to the sin and disbelief of the rest of the world—which refused to obey—and **because he was one of those whom God had accepted he obtained faith.**

Righteousness comes from trusting, not the other way around.

FREE TO CHOOSE?

✝ **Faith Precedes Regeneration** (Actual Scripture Quote)	☠ **Regeneration Precedes Faith** (Warning: Not Real Scripture)
I Peter 1:9: Receiving **the end of your faith**, even the salvation of your souls.	Receiving **the end of the salvation of your souls**, even your faith.
AMP: [At the same time] you receive **the result (outcome, consummation) of your faith**, the salvation of your souls.	[At the same time] you receive **the result (outcome, consummation) of the salvation of your souls**, your faith.
CEB: You are receiving **the goal of your faith**: your salvation.	You are receiving the **goal of your salvation**: your faith.
CJB: And you are receiving **what your trust is aiming at**, namely, your deliverance.	And you are receiving **what your deliverance is aiming at**, namely, your trust.
CEV: **You are to be saved.** That's why you have faith.	**You are to have faith.** That's why you were saved.
ERV: Your faith has a goal, and you are reaching that goal—**your salvation**.	Your salvation has a goal, and you are reaching that goal—**your faith**.
GNT: . . .because you are receiving **the salvation of your souls, which is the purpose of your faith** in him.	. . .because you are receiving **your faith in him, which is the purpose of the salvation of your souls**.
PHILLIPS: . . .and all the time you are receiving **the result of your faith in him—the salvation of your own souls**.	. . .and all the time you are receiving **the result of the salvation of your own souls—your faith in him**.
TLB: And your further **reward for trusting him will be the salvation of your souls**.	And your further **reward for having had your souls saved will be trusting in him**.
NIV: . . .for you are receiving **the end result of your faith, the salvation of your souls**.	. . .for you are receiving the **end result of the salvation of your souls, your faith**.

Salvation is the result of our faith, not the other way around.

Now for you readers who dearly love the Bible and "tremble at His Word," you may have been offended or even angered by my audacity to rewrite Scriptures, like I did in the second column of the tables above. I know exactly what you are feeling, and those are my sentiments exactly. Even though it is a good illustration, and profoundly enlightening, it was an extremely distasteful exercise. *But that's my point.*

Just look at the sentence structure in many of the verses above: "God does this (or this will happen) to people who do that." It's obvious from reading how the sentences are written that the "this" is done *because* of the "that," even when they don't use the word "because." But in many cases the verses *do* use the word "because," which completely removes any question about the direction of causality. For example, in Psalm 37:40, it says that God will "save them, *because* they trust in him." Or Luke 7:50 (WE): "You are saved *because* you believed." Or Romans 1:17 (CEV): "The people God accepts *because* of their faith will live." Or Ephesians 2:8 (ERV): ". . .you have been saved by grace *because* you believed." Or Hebrews 11:7 (TLB): "*because* of his faith he became one of those whom God has accepted." Et cetera.

And just as significantly, look at the other parts of speech used by the various translations to indicate the direction of causality:

- We believe "unto" righteousness.
- We believe "and so" are saved.
- Our trust "leads to" righteousness.
- We are accepted "if" we believe.
- Our belief "results in" righteousness.
- "By" believing we are accepted by God.
- Believing "makes" a man righteous.
- We believe "and thus" have righteousness.
- We are saved "through" faith.
- We believe "to the" saving of our souls.
- Righteousness is "by" faith.
- Righteousness "comes from" trusting.
- Righteousness "follows" faith.
- Salvation is the "end of" our faith.
- Salvation is the "result of" our faith.
- Salvation is the "outcome" of our faith.
- Salvation is the "consummation" of our faith.
- Salvation is the "goal" of our faith.
- Deliverance is what our trust is "aiming at."
- Salvation is "why" we are to have faith.

- Salvation is the "purpose" of our faith.
- Salvation is the "reward" of our faith.
- Salvation is the "end result" of our faith.

And as usual, for the sake of brevity, I have omitted other supporting Scriptures and translations from the tables above. (Seriously: I left out a lot.) But I think I have made my point: Scripture does *not* support—*at all*—the idea of "regeneration precedes faith."

If one insists on adhering to the "regeneration precedes faith" idea, *all* the Scriptures in the first column of the tables above must be ignored or misinterpreted (or rewritten, as shown in the second column of the tables above). *That* should make us tremble.

Remember where Isaiah told people how to get saved? They were supposed to copy how someone else had done it:

Isaiah 51:1 (CEV): **If you want to do right and obey the Lord, follow Abraham's example.** He was the rock from which you were chipped.

EXB: The Lord says, "Listen to me, those of you who try to live right [pursue righteousness] and follow [seek] the Lord. **Look at [or to] the rock from which you were cut;** look at [or to] the stone quarry from which you were dug [**referring to their ancestors Abraham and Sarah; see v. 2**]."

TPT: "Listen to me, **you who chase after righteousness, you who passionately pursue the Lord. Look back to Abraham,** the rock from which you were cut, to Sarah, the quarry from which you were dug, and remember what I did for them."

So what did Abraham do? Why is he the example we should follow? Simply because he believed God, and that faith was accounted to him for righteousness:

Genesis 15:6 (AMP): And **he [Abram] believed in** (trusted in, relied on, remained steadfast to) the Lord, **and He counted it to him as righteousness** (right standing with God).

Romans 4:3 (NLT): For the Scriptures tell us, "**Abraham believed God, and God counted him as righteous because of his faith.**"

Romans 4:9 (CEV): Are these blessings meant for circumcised people or for those who are not circumcised? Well, the Scriptures say **that God accepted Abraham because Abraham had faith in him.**

Romans 4:21–22 (GWORD): . . .and *[Abraham]* was absolutely confident that God would do what he promised. ²²That is why **Abraham's faith was regarded as the basis of his approval by God.**

Galatians 3:6 (TEV): Consider the experience of Abraham; as the scripture says, **"He believed God, and because of his faith God accepted him as righteous."**

James 2:23 (NLT): And so it happened just as the Scriptures say: **"Abraham believed God, and God counted him as righteous because of his faith."** He was even called the friend of God.

So, Isaiah was saying to his readers: "If you want to be righteous, do what Abraham did." In Abraham's life, faith in God came first, and then righteousness was imputed as a result—read the above verses again to confirm—and *that's* why Abraham is the model to be copied. More on this topic later. . .

Talk about the *preponderance* of Scripture! And I didn't even mention:

Isaiah 55:7 (CSB): Let the wicked one abandon his way and the sinful one his thoughts; **let him return to the Lord,** *so* **he may have compassion on him,** and to our God, for he will freely forgive.

> ESV: . . .let the wicked forsake his way, and the unrighteous man his thoughts; **let him return to the Lord,** *that* **he may have compassion on him, and to our God, for he will abundantly pardon.**
>
> CEB: Let the wicked abandon their ways and the sinful their schemes. **Let them return to the Lord** *so that* **he may have mercy on them,** to our God, because he is generous with forgiveness.
>
> ERV: Evil people should stop living evil lives. They should stop thinking bad thoughts. **They should come to the Lord again,** *and* **he will comfort them.** They should come to our God because he will freely forgive them.

Luke 24:47 (AMP): And that **repentance [with a view to and as the condition of] forgiveness of sins** should be preached in His name to all nations, beginning from Jerusalem.

John 20:31 (NET): But these are recorded so that you may believe that Jesus is the Christ, the Son of God, and that **by believing you may have life in his name.**

Acts 2:21 (AMP): And it shall be that **whoever shall call** upon the name of the Lord [invoking, adoring, and worshiping the Lord—Christ] **shall be saved.**

II Corinthians 7:10 (NIV): Godly sorrow brings **repentance that leads to salvation** and leaves no regret, but worldly sorrow brings death.

Galatians 2:16 (NASB): . . .nevertheless knowing that a man is not justified by the works of the Law but through faith in Christ Jesus, even **we have believed in Christ Jesus, so that we may be justified** by faith in Christ and not by the works of the Law; since by the works of the Law no flesh will be justified.

I Peter 1:9 (AMP): [At the same time] you receive **the result (outcome, consummation) of your faith, the salvation of your souls.**

CEB: You are receiving **the goal of your faith: your salvation.**

GNT: . . .because you are receiving **the salvation of your souls, which is the purpose of your faith in him.**

TLB: And your further **reward for trusting him will be the salvation of your souls.**

NIV: . . .for you are receiving **the end result of your faith, the salvation of your souls.**

Enough said?

Is Salvation a Gift?

One facet of the Reformed-theology concept of Total Depravity is this: If we could do *anything* to cause salvation to have any effect in our lives, that would prove that it is a salvation by works. Now, we already saw in the sections above that that argument—the one that says faith itself is a work—collapses catastrophically when faced with the mountains of relevant Scripture. So now let's analyze whether "receiving" or "accepting" God's gift of salvation yields comparable results or not.

First of all, is it appropriate to consider salvation itself to be a gift? We need to answer this question first, before it would make sense to consider whether we can "receive" or "accept" it as a gift.

When Jesus was talking to the Samaritan Woman at the Well, He says this:

John 4:10 (AMP): Jesus answered her, If you had only known and had recognized **God's gift** and Who this is that is saying to you, Give Me a drink, you would have asked Him [instead] and He would have given you living water.

Was Jesus talking about Himself being the gift, or was the gift the living water He offered? The living water clearly refers to salvation, as is confirmed a few verses later when He describes it as "a spring of water welling up (flowing, bubbling) [continually] within him unto (into, for) eternal life." And, of course, Jesus is the source of that salvation. So in the context of this question, either way—whether Jesus is the Gift because He brings salvation, or His salvation itself is the Gift—*either way*, it portrays the salvation as a Gift.

In the book of Romans, Paul is describing the work of Christ, and says:

Romans 5:15–17 (NASB): But the **free gift** is not like the transgression. For if by the transgression of the one the many died, much more did the grace of God and **the gift** by the grace of the one Man, Jesus Christ, abound to the many. [16]And **the gift** is not like that which came through the one who sinned; for on the one hand the judgment arose from one transgression resulting in condemnation, but on the other hand **the free gift** arose from many transgressions resulting in justification. [17]For if by the transgression of the one, death reigned through the one, much more those who receive the abundance of grace and of the **gift of righteousness** will reign in life through the One, Jesus Christ.

Here too, salvation is referred to as a "gift." And we know that the gift being referred to is salvation because this passage is contrasting the first Adam, who brought sin, with the second Adam, Jesus, Who brought salvation. And the fact that the gift is free. And the fact that the gift results in justification. And the fact that the gift also results in righteousness. And the fact that it came through Jesus Christ. So, clearly, the gift Paul refers to here is the salvation that comes only through Jesus Christ.

As an aside, v. 18 mentions in passing that salvation is made available to *all* men, not just some men, as the doctrines of Unconditional Election and Limited Atonement would have us believe:

Romans 5:18: Therefore as by the offence of one judgment came upon all men to condemnation; even so by the righteousness of one **the free gift came upon** *all men* unto justification of life.

AMP: Well then, as one man's trespass [one man's false step and falling away led] to condemnation for all men, so one Man's act of righteousness [leads] to **acquittal and right standing with God and life for** *all men.*

NIV: Consequently, just as the result of one trespass was condemnation for all men, so also the result of one act of righteousness was **justification that brings life for** *all men.*

> TEV: So then, as the one sin condemned all people, in the same way the one righteous act sets *all people* free and gives them life.

But more on Unconditional Election and Limited Atonement later.

In the next chapter, Paul reconfirms that salvation is a gift:

> Romans 6:23 (NASB): For the wages of sin is death, but **the free gift of God is eternal life in Christ Jesus our Lord.**

Note that wages are what you *earn*, but a gift is something you can freely *receive* if someone offers it to you. The very fact that it is a gift, and not wages, shows that you didn't *earn* it or *work for* it.

When Paul writes to the church in Corinth, he again refers to God's Gift, and the context identifies it as salvation:

> II Corinthians 9:13–15 (AMP): Because at [your] standing of the test of this ministry, they will glorify God for **your loyalty and obedience to the Gospel of Christ** which you confess, as well as for your generous-hearted liberality to them and to all [the other needy ones]. [14]And they yearn for you while they pray for you, because of the surpassing measure of God's grace (His favor and mercy and spiritual blessing which is shown forth) in you. [15]Now thanks be to God for **His Gift,** [precious] beyond telling [**His indescribable, inexpressible, free Gift**]!

And again, this time to the church in Ephesus:

> Ephesians 2:8–9: For **by grace are ye saved through faith;** and that not of yourselves: **it is the gift of God:** [9]**Not of works,** lest any man should boast.

This passage not only points out that salvation is a Gift, but also that being able to be saved by faith is not by works. Thus, as discussed in the "Faith vs. Works" section above, believing unto salvation cannot validly be considered a "work."

The writer of Hebrews concurs:

> Hebrews 6:4: For it is impossible for those who were once enlightened, and have tasted of the heavenly **gift,** and were made partakers of the Holy Ghost. . .

This passage (discussed in much more detail in For It Is Impossible. . ., below) also calls salvation a Gift.

By now, it should be clear that the Bible does indeed consider salvation to be a gift—and an amazingly enormous and important gift, at that. The obvious human implication is that a gift, when offered, needs to be received, or accepted, and if it is not, the gift does the intended recipient no good. But just because that's the *human* implication certainly doesn't necessarily make it so in the Kingdom of God. So let's look into the Scriptures and see if this seemingly reasonable inference actually has Scriptural support.

A Gift is Something You Receive

Now that we've seen that Scripture does indeed consider salvation to be a gift, let's see if there is any indication that we as humans should, or even *can,* "accept" or "receive" this Gift. If so, it would deal a severely damaging blow to the idea of Unconditional Election, which says that since we *can't* accept Christ (because of Total Depravity), He decides for us whether we will ultimately be saved or not.

Ask, Seek, Knock

In Jesus' Sermon on the Mount, He says:

Matthew 7:7–11 (NIV): **Ask and it will be given to you;** seek and you will find; knock and the door will be opened to you. ⁸For **everyone who asks receives;** he who seeks finds; and to him who knocks, the door will be opened. ⁹Which of you, if his son asks for bread, will give him a stone? ¹⁰Or if he asks for a fish, will give him a snake? ¹¹If you, then, though you are evil, know how to give **good gifts** to your children, how much more will your Father in heaven **give good gifts to those who ask him!**

Note the progression here. Jesus unambiguously commands His listeners to "Ask!" Why should they? Because as a result of their asking, He said "it will be given to you." He continues, "Everyone who asks receives." Jesus then compares earthly fathers to the heavenly Father, and says, "If *you* know how to give good gifts to your kids, *how much more* will your heavenly Father give good gifts to those who ask Him!" (And remember that salvation is a Gift—the best possible gift.)

Note the strong emphasis on receiving: Who receives from God? Those who ask. And we know that they are willing to receive because of the very fact that they asked Him in the first place.

The Disciples' Commission to Preach

A few chapters later, Jesus commissions the disciples to go preach the message of the Kingdom; i.e., the Gospel. He says:

> Matthew 10:7–8: And as ye go, preach, saying, The **kingdom of heaven is at hand.** ⁸Heal the sick, cleanse the lepers, raise the dead, cast out devils: **freely ye have received, freely give.**

Jesus said that the disciples had received something. What had they received? The message of the Kingdom—"repent and believe" (see Mark 1:15), which results in salvation—that was the message they were supposed to go preach, and to do the signs and wonders to prove its validity. And notice *how* they received. In some contexts, the word "receive" doesn't imply a willing and eager reception of something; for example, a soldier in battle might "receive" a bullet wound. But obviously, that is not something that would be lovingly offered to him as a gift, nor would he eagerly and willingly accept it.

No, that is not the usage of "receive" here, when Jesus describes how the disciples received the message and power of the Kingdom. On the contrary, He says, "*freely* you have received." It was offered freely (without charge), and they accepted it freely (they weren't coerced or forced into accepting the message for themselves or preaching it to others). And therefore, they should do the same when they preached the message: offer it freely and without charge. And people will either accept the message or not, of their own free will.

Receiving or Not

But wait a minute: is that last statement justified? Do people actually need to "receive" the gospel to benefit from it? It seems so; look at Jesus' words just a few verses later:

> Matthew 10:12–15 (NASB): And as you enter the house, give it your greeting. ¹³And if the house is worthy, let your greeting of peace come upon it; but if it is not worthy, let your greeting of peace return to you. ¹⁴And **whoever does not receive you, nor heed your words,** as you go out of that house or that city, shake off the dust of your feet. ¹⁵Truly I say to you, it will be more tolerable for the land of Sodom and Gomorrah in the day of judgment, than for that city.

Notice that some people do not *receive* the gospel when it is offered to them, and there will be severe judgment because of that. Why judgment? Because God angrily and vengefully pushes the "Smite" button to teach those no-good reprobates a lesson? Of course not; God is a loving Father—remember the parables of the Prodigal Son and the Lost Sheep. But Jesus is the *only* way to salvation (John 14:6), and if people reject Him, there is no "Plan B." Or, as I phrased it earlier, "If you reject the Right Answer, it doesn't much matter which wrong answer you choose." And when people do reject (i.e., refuse to receive) God's love, it grieves Him deeply. Remember The Cry of God's Heart, above?

And again, just a few verses later, Jesus reiterates the concept of receiving Him or not. He casually talks about it as if it were self-evident that some people would receive Him and others would not.

> Matthew 10:32–34 (TEV): **Those who declare publicly** that they belong to me, **I will do the same** for them before my Father in heaven. [33]But those who **reject** me publicly, I will **reject** before my Father in heaven.

> Matthew 10:40 (NASB): **He who receives you receives Me, and he who receives Me receives Him who sent Me.**

> Matthew 11:14 (TEV): . . .and **if you are willing to believe** their message, John is Elijah, whose coming was predicted.

Note in the second verse above that Jesus is not talking about being personally "received" into someone's home in a hospitality context, because He wasn't even going to be there Himself; He was sending the *disciples* out to preach. No, He was talking about people receiving His message of the Gospel; i.e., salvation.

Preaching In the Home Town

In Luke, there is the story of how Jesus went back to Nazareth, His home town, to preach. What did the people do? Did they accept Him and His message? No, they rejected Him, and they rejected His message. How did Jesus respond to that rejection?

> Luke 4:24: And he said, Verily I say unto you, No prophet is **accepted** in his own country.

The implication is that prophets *are* accepted in other places more often than in their own home towns. So did these people in Jesus' home town politely and courteously "agree to disagree" with Jesus when they didn't accept Him? No, not by a long shot: they rejected Him *violently*. They were enraged, drove Jesus out of town, and would have killed Him by throwing Him off a cliff, except for an apparently miraculous, but not clearly described, deliverance where He "passing through the midst of them, went His way" (Luke 4:29–30).

Did Jesus gain super strength at that moment, like a Samson on steroids (Judges 16:3, 9, 12, 14)? Did he gain a super speed, so he could run faster

FREE TO CHOOSE?

than a galloping horse, like Elijah (I Kings 18:46), and simply run away from his assailants? Did He become invisible, so as to prevent people from seeing Him (Luke 24:31)? Did He blind their eyes like the angel did to protect Lot in Sodom (Genesis 19:11)? Was He suddenly enveloped in so much glory that everyone fell under the power (Matthew 17:5–6, John 18:6)? Did God supernaturally transport Jesus away like He did Philip (Acts 8:39)?

We don't know. All of the above examples are possibilities, and the Biblical references show that God has done all of them. But since the Bible doesn't specify precisely what happened in this particular case, we can only speculate as to the exact mechanism God used to allow Jesus to "pass through the midst" of an enraged crowd that was highly motivated to assassinate Him at that very moment.

A similar thing happened in John 8:59: The Jews were infuriated that Jesus would have the gall to claim that He was the Son of God, and they, with murderous fury, picked up stones to stone Him. What did Jesus do?

> John 8:59: Then took they up stones to cast at him: but **Jesus hid himself, and went out of the temple, going through the midst of them, and so passed by.**

When Jesus "hid Himself," do you think He scampered away in a panic to hide himself behind a wall, fearing for His life and cowering in terror at the big bad Jews? Hardly. Jesus, who perfectly understood God's perfect love, never succumbed to fear (I John 4:18), because fear is simply the result of believing that a problem is bigger than God's ability to handle it. And Jesus knew better than anyone else on earth how big and powerful God is. So what does it mean that Jesus "hid Himself" or, as some other translations render it, "concealed Himself?"

The Phillips translation renders it much more clearly:

> John 8:59 (PHILLIPS): At this, they picked up stones to hurl at him, but **Jesus disappeared and made his way out of the Temple.**

It was simply not yet Jesus' time to die, so God miraculously delivered Him, in a way not completely specified, from the hands of the outraged Jews. But the main point of this section is that Jesus was preaching the Gospel to them—He was teaching in the synagogue, revealing that He was the Messiah—and *the Jews rejected Him.* That is, they chose not to receive Him.

Receiving or Not, Take 2

Luke's account of Jesus' instructions to the disciples as He commissioned them to preach the Gospel of the Kingdom is even more clear than Matthew's account above.

> Luke 10:5–12 (AMP): Whatever house you enter, first say, Peace be to this household! [Freedom from all the distresses that result from sin be with this family]. ⁶And if anyone [worthy] of peace and blessedness is there, the peace and blessedness you wish shall come upon him; but if not, it shall come back to you. ⁷And stay on in the same house, eating and drinking what they provide, for the laborer is worthy of his wages. Do not keep moving from house to house. ⁸Whenever you go into a town and **they receive and accept and welcome you,** eat what is set before you; ⁹And **heal the sick** in it and say to them, **The kingdom of God has come close to you.** ¹⁰But whenever you go into a town **and they do not receive and accept and welcome you,** go out into its streets and say, ¹¹Even the dust of your town that clings to our feet we are wiping off against you; yet know and understand this: the kingdom of God has come near you. ¹²I tell you, it shall be more tolerable in that day for Sodom than for that town.

And if that weren't clear enough by itself, to indicate that it is possible to accept Jesus and it is likewise possible to reject Him, a few verses later, He goes on to say:

> Luke 10:16: He that heareth you heareth me; and he that despiseth you despiseth me; and he that despiseth me despiseth him that sent me.
>
> AMP: He who hears and heeds you [disciples] hears and heeds Me; and he who slights and rejects you slights and rejects Me; and he who slights and rejects Me slights and rejects Him who sent Me.
>
> CEV: My followers, whoever listens to you is listening to me. Anyone who says "No" to you is saying "No" to me. And anyone who says "No" to me is really saying "No" to the one who sent me.
>
> NLT: Then he said to the disciples, "Anyone who accepts your message is also accepting me. And anyone who rejects you is rejecting me. And anyone who rejects me is rejecting God, who sent me."

Jesus matter-of-factly refers to some people accepting the bearers of the Gospel (and therefore Him and therefore God), and then, just as matter-of-factly refers to some other people rejecting the bearers of the Gospel (and therefore Him and therefore God). So obviously, both options are possible.

The fact that the Kingdom of God came to these people and they rejected it—they did not "receive and accept and welcome" the disciples and their message—makes it seem pretty clear to me that it is possible to reject what God offers. And the previous group, who *did* receive and accept and welcome it, makes it pretty clear that it is also possible to receive it.

Let's take a look at what Paul said to the church in Thessalonica, in reference to the end-times man of evil, empowered by Satan, that would come on the scene:

> II Thessalonians 2:10: And with all deceivableness of unrighteousness in them that perish; **because they *received not* the love of the truth, *that* they might be saved.**
>
> AMP: And by unlimited seduction to evil and with all wicked deception for those who are perishing (going to perdition) **because they *did not welcome* the Truth but refused to love it *that* they might be saved.**
>
> CEB: It will happen with every sort of wicked deception of those who are heading toward destruction because *they have refused* **to love the truth *that would allow them* to be saved.**
>
> CJB: He will enable him to deceive, in all kinds of wicked ways, those who are headed for destruction because *they would not receive* **the love of the truth that *could have saved* them.**
>
> ERV: The Man of Evil will use every kind of evil to fool those who are lost. **They are lost *because* they refused to *love the truth and be saved.***
>
> EXB: He will use every kind of evil to trick [or wicked deception against/toward] those who are lost [perishing; heading toward destruction], *because they refused* **to love the *truth that would save them.***
>
> HCSB: . . .and with every unrighteous deception among those who are perishing. **They perish because *they did not accept* the love of the truth *in order to be saved.***
>
> TLB: He will completely fool those who are on their way to hell because they have said no to the Truth; **they have *refused to believe it* and love it *and let it save them.* . . .**

James concurs in the idea of how we have to respond to what God makes available. Even though God makes His blessings available to everyone, they do us no good unless we receive those blessings. Here is how James says it:

> James 2:5 (NKJV): Listen, my beloved brethren: Has God not chosen the poor of this world to be rich in faith and heirs of **the kingdom which He promised to those who love Him?**
>
> MSG: Listen, dear friends. Isn't it clear by now that God operates quite differently? He chose the world's down-and-out as the kingdom's first citizens, with full rights and privileges. **This kingdom is promised to anyone who loves God.**

Although God loves everyone, not everyone loves God in return. But anyone *can* love God if he chooses to. Those who love God, by choosing to do so, are receiving those gifts that He has offered to all of mankind.

There are two very important truths we can realize from reading the verses above:

- It is possible to refuse the invitation of God, the atonement offered by Jesus through His blood, and the moving of the Holy Spirit (much more on this in the chapter on Irresistible Grace). We know it must be possible, because this verse says people will do it. The height of foolishness, clearly, but possible nonetheless. Note the wording: these people who will be lost "receive not," they "did not welcome," they "refused," they "would not receive," they "did not accept" the love of the Truth. They are being lost *because* they refused to accept the Truth. What, or *Who*, is the Truth?

  > John 14:6a Jesus saith unto him, **I am** the way, **the truth,** and the life. . .

- *Believing* the Truth (i.e., Jesus) results in salvation. Again, pay close attention to the words used here: this verse talks about "receiving," "welcoming," and "accepting" the love of the Truth "*that they might* be saved," "*that would allow them* to be saved," "*that could have* saved them," and "that *would* save them." Rather unambiguous.

The above passage is a perfect segue into the next section, which reconfirms the same thing.

What Happens When You Receive Christ?

In the gospel of John, chapter 1, the Beloved Disciple says this:

> John 1:11–12: He came unto his own, and **his own received him not.** ¹²But **as many as received him, to them gave he power to become the sons of God, even to them that believe on his name.** . .

FREE TO CHOOSE?

Wow. Right here in a single short passage, the Bible describes some people who do *not* receive Christ, and other people who *do* receive Christ. This immediately dispels any question of whether people can actually "receive" Him or not. And just as important is the *result* of receiving Christ: What does v. 12 say, above? ". . .as many as received him, to them gave he power to become the sons of God, even to them that believe on his name." Note the causation, and its direction: the cause is "believing," and the effect is "becoming a son of God." *Not* the other way around.

Let's look at v. 12 in some other translations, just for confirmation:

John 1:12 (AMP): But **to as many as did receive and welcome Him,** He gave the authority (power, privilege, right) to become the children of God, **that is, to those who believe in (adhere to, trust in, and rely on) His name**. . .

CEB: **But those who did welcome him, those who believed in his name,** he authorized to become God's children. . .

CJB: But **to as many as did receive him, to those who put their trust in his person and power,** he gave the right to become children of God. . .

CEV: Yet **some people accepted him and put their faith in him.** So he gave them the right to be the children of God.

DLNT: But **all who did receive Him,** He gave them—**the ones believing in His name**—the right to become children of God. . .

ERV: But **some people did accept him. They believed in him,** and he gave them the right to become children of God.

ESV: But to **all who did receive him, who believed in his name,** he gave the right to become children of God. . .

. . .and so forth; you get the point. This tells us two very important things: first, that receiving Christ results in that receiving person becoming a child of God. Second, "receiving" Christ is synonymous with "believing on His Name." And "believing on" His Name is more than just an intellectual assent that He exists and that He is God (even the demons do that; see James 2:19). As shown in the Amplified Bible, "believing on His Name" means to "adhere to, trust in, and rely on" Christ for salvation.

So "believing on" Jesus means to "adhere to, trust in, and rely on" Him for one's salvation, and that is synonymous with "receiving" Him. The result of this action is that the person becomes a child of God; i.e., he is saved.

Since the passage above equated "receiving" Christ with "believing in" Him, suddenly a great number of other Scriptures become relevant, about "believing unto salvation." Review the section "Faith vs. Works" above, for conclusive evidence that having faith to be saved cannot rightly be considered a "work." Then because of this passage in John 1 that equates "receiving" Christ with "believing on" Him, we can confidently conclude that "receiving" Christ cannot rightly be considered a "work" either.

John's Ministry vs. Jesus' Ministry

John the Baptist was questioned by the Jews regarding Jesus' ministry versus his own, and in reply, John said:

> John 3:32–33 (NASB): What He has seen and heard, of that He bears witness; and no man **receives His witness.** ³³**He who has received His witness** has set his seal to this, that God is true.

> AMP: It is to what He has [actually] seen and heard that He bears testimony, and yet no one **accepts His testimony** [no one **receives His evidence as true**]. ³³Whoever **receives His testimony** has set his seal of approval to this: God is true. [That man has definitely certified, acknowledged, declared once and for all, and is himself assured that it is divine truth that God cannot lie].

Here, yet again, we have a single short passage that mentions both possibilities: of receiving or accepting the Gospel, and *not* receiving or accepting the Gospel. And, like the previous passage from John 1, this one also equates "receiving" with "believing." It's easier to follow in the AMP, so I'll quote from v. 33 here: "Whoever receives His testimony" (that's Jesus' testimony, the Gospel, the message of the Kingdom), has "definitely certified, acknowledged, declared" and is "assured" that it is divine truth.

That's just a fancy way of saying "he believes it" or "has faith in it." This belief or faith or trust or assurance, as shown in the John 1 passage above (plus the entire content of the "Faith vs. Works" section above), results in the person receiving salvation. Again, faith precedes regeneration.

Jesus' Sermon Before Passover

In the passage below, Jesus had just finished talking to Jewish religious leaders who believed in Him, but because of possible retribution from the Pharisees, didn't want anybody to know they believed in Him. "They loved the praise of men more than the praise of God" (John 12:43). Right after that:

> John 12:44–48 (NIV): Then Jesus cried out, "**When a man believes** in me, he does not believe in me only, but in the one who sent me. ⁴⁵When he looks at me, he sees the one who sent me. ⁴⁶I have come into the world as a light, so that **no one who believes in me should stay in darkness**. ⁴⁷As for the person who hears my words but does not keep them, I do not judge him. For I did not come to judge the world, **but to save it.** ⁴⁸There is a judge for **the one who rejects me and does not accept my words**; that very word which I spoke will condemn him at the last day."

Yet another passage just pregnant with profound meaning. Look at some of the nuggets contained here:

- It is possible to believe in Jesus (v. 44).
- When someone believes in Jesus, he does not stay in darkness (v. 45); in other words, believing results in salvation. This shows the direction of causality: *The one who believes comes out of darkness,* and not *the one who has been brought out of darkness believes.* This verse refutes the Reformed doctrine of Total Depravity, which says that man cannot even believe or accept Jesus by his own will. It also refutes the Reformed doctrine of Unconditional Election, which says that people are saved by God's choice in eternity past, not by the person's choice to believe in Jesus in the here and now.
- Jesus' purpose for coming into the world was to save it, not to judge it (v. 47). What is "the world" here? *All mankind.* He didn't come to save only a certain subset of mankind that had been selected in eternity past; he came to save *the world* (see also John 3:16–17 and the section "The World," below). This verse refutes the Reformed doctrines of Unconditional Election and Limited Atonement.
- It is possible to reject Jesus (v. 48). This verse refutes the Reformed doctrine of Irresistible Grace.
- Rejecting Jesus is synonymous with not accepting His words (v. 48).

So we have seen that it is possible to respond to Jesus' gift of salvation by accepting it. The Scriptures above do serious damage to several of the Reformed doctrines, especially that of Total Depravity.

Reconciliation

Look at this short passage Paul wrote in his second letter to the Corinthians:

> II Corinthians 5:18–20 (GWORD): God has done all this. **He has restored our relationship with him** through Christ, and has given us this ministry of restoring relationships. ¹⁹In other words, **God was using Christ to restore his relationship with humanity.** He didn't hold people's faults against them, and he has given us this message of restored relationships to tell others. ²⁰Therefore, we are Christ's representatives, and through us God is calling you. **We beg you on behalf of Christ to become reunited with God.**

In vv. 18 and 19, Paul points out that God has restored His relationship with humanity. In other words, all that needs to be done on His end has been done. However, as v. 20 says, we need to respond to the offer; we need to receive the Gift. Again, this two-party covenant requires the cooperation and engagement of both parties in order to cause it to take effect.

So here, Paul is begging the Corinthians to do something that Total Depravity says is impossible. What do we make of that?

Foot Washing

What does "washing someone's feet" symbolize? I think most Christians would agree that it symbolizes several things, including our need to have humility, and our responsibility to serve one another regardless of our "status" in life. But one other thing that comes out of the story is that washing someone's feet represents forgiveness:

> John 13:3–11 (BBE): **Jesus, being conscious that the Father had put everything into his hands**, and that he came from God and was going to God, ⁴Got up from table, put off his robe and took a cloth and put it round him. ⁵Then he put water into a basin and was washing the feet of the disciples and drying them with the cloth which was round him.

That's pretty profound already: Jesus, knowing that He was the absolute Supreme Lord of the Universe, stoops to serve others in a very unglamorous way. But let's continue:

> ⁶So he came to Simon Peter. Peter said, Lord, are my feet to be washed by you? ⁷And Jesus, answering, said to him, What I do is not clear to you now, but it will be clear to you in time to come. ⁸Peter said, I will

never let my feet be washed by you, never. Jesus said in answer, **If I do not make you clean you have no part with me.** ⁹Simon Peter said to him, Lord, not my feet only, but my hands and my head. ¹⁰Jesus said to him, **He who is bathed has need only to have his feet washed and then he is clean all over: and you, my disciples, are clean,** but not all of you. ¹¹(He had knowledge who was false to him; that is why he said, You are not all clean.)

So was my statement above true? That washing someone's feet symbolizes forgiveness? It certainly sounds like it, because of Jesus' statement in v. 8 above: "If I do not make you clean you have no part with me." Having "no part" with Jesus is clearly a salvation issue, which is why Peter immediately backpedaled and asked Jesus to wash him all over.

But here is the point: notice that Jesus was willing to submit to Peter's decision, to allow Him to wash Peter's feet or not. Jesus clearly was willing to and desired to wash Peter's feet, and it symbolized something that was spiritually necessary, as shown in v. 8 above. But when Peter initially refused, Jesus did not force it upon him; He simply explained the consequences of such a decision. Once Peter heard that, he immediately changed his mind. He made a very sensible decision: he "received" what Jesus offered. Nonetheless, it was Peter's decision—*his choice*—whether or not to allow Jesus to wash his feet. We can do the same with Jesus' offer of forgiveness: we can accept it or reject it, and there will be consequences either way. Very good consequences in the former case, and very bad consequences in the latter case.

Jesus reinforces this whole concept yet again just a few verses later:

John 13:20 (BBE): Truly I say to you, **He who takes to his heart anyone whom I send, takes me to his heart; and he who so takes me, takes him who sent me.**

The action of "taking" is an action we do as receivers, not an action that Jesus does as the Giver. And notice that Jesus is stating it is *people* who are taking to heart those whom Jesus sends, and therefore taking to heart Jesus Himself, and therefore taking to heart the Father.

The Result of Repentance

Repentance is a change of one's mind, and when applied toward a life of sin against (or indifference to) God, repentance results in a change of behavior from disobedience to obedience—from rejecting God to accepting Him. This is covered in great deal in Book 2: *Is It Possible to Stop Sinning?*, so refer to that book for in-depth study of repentance and related concepts.

As shown above, repentance is essentially what the Reformed doctrine of Total Depravity claims that people are incapable of doing, even though we are commanded to do so in numerous places in the Bible. But let's look at one particular Scripture that shows the results of repenting from sin (which, again, we are commanded to do):

> Acts 3:19: Repent ye therefore, and be converted, **that** your sins may be blotted out, when the times of refreshing shall come from the presence of the Lord. . .
>
> AMP: So repent [change your inner self—your old way of thinking, regret past sins] and return [to God—seek His purpose for your life], **so that** your sins may be wiped away [blotted out, completely erased], so that times of refreshing may come from the presence of the Lord [restoring you like a cool wind on a hot day];
>
> CEV: So turn to God! Give up your sins, **and** you will be forgiven.
>
> ERV: So you must change your hearts and lives. Come back to God, **and** he will forgive your sins.
>
> GWORD: So change the way you think and act, and turn to God **to have** your sins removed.
>
> TLB: Now change your mind and attitude to God and turn to him **so he can** cleanse away your sins and send you wonderful times of refreshment from the presence of the Lord. . .
>
> MSG: Now it's time to change your ways! Turn to face God **so he can** wipe away your sins, pour out showers of blessing to refresh you. . .
>
> MOUNCE: Repent therefore, and turn again, **for** the blotting out of your sins. . .
>
> NIRV: So turn away from your sins. Turn to God. **Then** your sins will be wiped away.
>
> VOICE: So now you need to rethink everything and turn to God **so** your sins will be forgiven and a new day can dawn. . .
>
> WE: Stop doing wrong things. Turn to God again. **Then** the wrong things you have done will be wiped away altogether.

Clearly, from the Scripture above, in all those translations, when people turn to God, then, *as a result,* their sins are forgiven. Repentance is the cause, and forgiveness is the effect—*not* the other way around. This is unmistakable due to the words used: "repent *that* your sins may be blotted out," "repent *so that* your sins may be wiped away," "turn to God *and* you will be forgiven," "change the way you think and act *to have* your sins removed," "turn to face God *so he can* wipe away your sins," "repent *for* the blotting out of your sins," "turn to God, *then* your sins will be wiped away," and so forth.

And this concept is consistent across both the Old Testament and New Testament. Isaiah says the same thing in his book:

> Isaiah 59:20 (NKJV): **"The Redeemer will come** to Zion, and **to those who turn from transgression** in Jacob," says the Lord.

> TEV: The Lord says to his people, "**I will come** to Jerusalem to defend you and **to save all of you that turn from your sins."**

Fascinating: Note that *the Redeemer comes to those who turn from transgression,* or *to save those who turn from their sins;* this is the repentance referred to above.

The direction of causality is indisputable: the forgiveness of sins is a *result* of our repentance. Jeremiah concurs:

> Jeremiah 4:14 (EHV): Jerusalem, **wash the evil from your heart *so that you will be saved.*** How long will your wicked thoughts live inside you?

> MSG: **Scrub the evil from your lives** *so you'll be fit* for salvation. How much longer will you harbor devious and malignant designs within you?

> RSV: O Jerusalem, **wash your heart from wickedness,** *that you may be* **saved.** How long shall your evil thoughts lodge within you?

Notice the direction of causality. And then, in the next chapter Jeremiah says:

> Jeremiah 5:3 (AMP): O Lord, do not your eyes look on the truth? [They have meant to please You outwardly, but You look on their hearts.] You have stricken them, but they have not grieved; You have consumed them, but **they have refused to take correction or instruction.** They have made their faces harder than a rock, **they have refused to repent and return to You.**

Note that the people "refused" to repent. To "refuse" something is to use the power of free will to choose to abstain from something, and here, they were abstaining from repentance. It is completely nonsensical to use the word "refuse" to describe a person in a context where said person has no choice in a matter.

Later on in Jeremiah, God confirms the same concept, that His forgiveness is contingent on our repentance. Or, more precisely, *our ability to derive benefit* from His forgiveness is contingent on our repentance:

> Jeremiah 36:3 (AMP): **It may be that** the house of Judah will hear all the evil which I purpose to do to them, so that **each one may** *turn from* **his evil way**, *that I may forgive* their iniquity and their sin.
>
> MSG: **Maybe the community of Judah** will finally get it, finally understand the catastrophe that I'm planning for them, *turn back from* **their bad lives, and** *let me forgive* their perversity and sin.
>
> NET: **Perhaps** when the people of Judah hear about all the disaster I intend to bring on them, **they will all** *stop doing* **the evil things they have been doing.** *If they do, I will forgive* their sins and the wicked things they have done.
>
> NLT: **Perhaps the people of Judah will** *repent* when they hear again all the terrible things I have planned for them. *Then I will be able to forgive* their sins and wrongdoings.

Though offered to everyone, without exception, forgiveness is predicated upon our repentance: our choice to believe in, trust in, and rely on God's mercy, and the resulting change in our behavior. And repentance is something that the Reformed doctrine of Total Depravity says is impossible—*that* should make us think. Now let's look at the next Point of Calvinism.

Chapter 6:

Unconditional Election

The Reformed concept of Unconditional Election is also called "sovereign election" or "predestination," and this doctrine states that God has chosen in eternity past those people whom He will bring to Himself, and which ones He will not. His choice is not based on any merit, virtue, or faith exhibited by those chosen people; on the contrary, His choice is unconditionally grounded in His choice to grant mercy alone to those elected to be saved.

In a nutshell, God has chosen from eternity to extend mercy to those He has chosen and to withhold mercy from those He has not chosen. Those chosen receive salvation through Christ alone. Those not chosen receive the just wrath that is warranted for their sins against God.

Is the above description just? In other words, would God be just if He did what is described in the previous paragraph? Actually, yes. He is not *obligated* to provide salvation for anybody, and to do so for even one person is merciful. Those He didn't choose for salvation will suffer everlasting punishment, and justly so, for we have all sinned, and we deserve it. So the situation as described in the previous paragraph is plausible and God would be just to do so.

However—and this is an enormous monkey wrench for the concept described in the paragraph above—the scenario in the paragraph above is *not* reasonable because of many other things that God has shown us in His Word. Said another way: If all God had told us was that contained in the first paragraph of this chapter, He would be perfectly just to do Unconditional Election

Free to Choose?

in the manner described by Reformed theology. But the problem is that *He's told us a lot of other stuff* that must be ignored or changed if we want to preserve the Reformed concept of Unconditional Election. Let's look into some of those things.

The first thing is that Unconditional Election is diametrically opposed to the concept of us choosing whom we will serve, which God *commands* us to do in several places in the Bible; refer back to the chapter We Have a Free Will, and We *Can* Choose God for details.

God is Merciful to How Many?

In addition to the above we have to consider what God told Moses, when Moses was in the glory cloud of God's presence on Mount Sinai the *second* time (the first time was for almost six weeks, and this second time it would again be almost six weeks):

> Exodus 34:6–7: And the LORD passed by before him, and proclaimed, The LORD, The LORD God, **merciful** and gracious, longsuffering, and abundant in goodness and truth, ⁷**Keeping mercy for thousands,** forgiving iniquity and transgression and sin, and that will **by no means clear the guilty;** visiting the iniquity of the fathers upon the children, and upon the children's children, unto the third and to the fourth generation.

Interesting that God describes Himself as One Who will *by no means* clear the guilty. But Unconditional Election, along with Total Depravity, has God clearing the guilty, *without* them repenting, because they are allegedly unable to respond to God (repent) before He does the redeeming work in their hearts. Hence, the whole "regeneration precedes faith" idea.

It's also interesting that God describes Himself as "merciful" and He keeps "mercy for thousands." Does this literally mean there is a specific number of thousands of people that He will be merciful to, and once the quota is filled, He stops being merciful? Of course not. When the Bible says "a thousand" or gives some other large number in reference to spiritual things, it means an infinite number.

For example, consider this Scripture:

> I Chronicles 16:15 (NASB): Remember His covenant forever, **the word which He commanded to a thousand generations. . .**

But, boy, if you're in the 1001st generation or later, you're out of luck—no point in remembering it, since it doesn't apply to you anyway. Now consider this one:

> Psalm 50:10 (NIV): for every animal of the forest is mine, and **the cattle on a thousand hills.**

So does this mean that if there were a thousand *and one* hills, all of which had cattle on them, there would be one hill whose cattle God *wouldn't* own? Or how about this one:

> Psalm 84:10a (NIV): Better is one day in your courts than **a thousand elsewhere.** . .

Does this mean a thousand *and one* days elsewhere could be just a smidge better than one day in God's courts? Or how about this one:

> Psalm 90:4 (NIV): For **a thousand years in your sight** are like a day that has just gone by, or like a watch in the night.

Does this imply that a thousand *and one* years could seem like "a really long time" in God's sight?

> Psalm 68:17a (AMP): **The chariots of God are twenty thousand,** even thousands upon thousands.

Does this mean that they ran out of raw material on the assembly line before they could finish the 20,001st chariot?

> Song 5:10 (NLT): *Young Woman* My lover is dark and dazzling, **better than ten thousand others!**

Does this mean that the Shulamite's lover, Solomon, could have finished in second place, had there been a contest between 10,001 hunks?

Obviously, for all the above questions, of course not. And multiples of 1000 are not the only numbers that imply infinity. For example, when Peter asked Jesus about forgiveness:

> Matthew 18:21–22: Then came Peter to him, and said, Lord, how oft shall my brother sin against me, and I forgive him? till seven times? ²²Jesus saith unto him, I say not unto thee, Until seven times: but, **Until seventy times seven.**

Now did Jesus really mean by that we can keep tabs on every time we've forgiven someone, and once we reach 490, we're off the hook and don't have to forgive anymore? No, that's obviously silly; the point is that we should *al-*

ways be ready and willing to forgive. "Coincidentally," that is how love is described:

> I Corinthians 13:5 (CEV): Love isn't selfish or quick tempered. **It doesn't keep a record of wrongs that others do.**

So it's safe to understand God, when He was talking to Moses, as saying, "I am merciful to everybody, not just certain people."

But how does that square with other Scriptures that say God is merciful to only, or at least *especially*, those who serve Him and not to evildoers since, according to Total Depravity, *everybody* is an evildoer and *can't* serve Him until He has already cleared the guilty and extended mercy? Such as:

> Psalm 25:10: All the paths of the LORD are **mercy and truth unto such as keep his covenant and his testimonies.**

> Psalm 59:5: Thou therefore, O LORD God of hosts, the God of Israel, awake to visit all the heathen: **be not merciful to any wicked transgressors.** Selah.

> Psalms 73:1 (NIV): Surely **God is good** to Israel, **to those who are pure in heart.**

> Psalm 86:5: For thou, Lord, art good, and ready to forgive; and **plenteous in mercy unto all them that call upon thee.**

The answer is simply that *anybody* can become a follower of Christ. The apparent bias God has toward His people over the unsaved completely evaporates when we realize that *anyone* can become one of "His people."

But someone might say, upon reading Psalm 86:5 above, "Yes, He is ready to forgive those *who call upon God*, but the only ones who can call upon Him are those He's elected." Does this hold water? Actually no, because God commands everyone to call to Him:

> Psalm 50:15 (NASB): **Call upon Me in the day of trouble;** I shall rescue you, and you will honor Me.

Is a sinner on his way to hell in trouble? Definitely yes. So this rescue—this forgiveness, this salvation—applies to him. Therefore, those on their way to hell are commanded to call upon God, and He says that He is merciful to those who call upon Him. Again, this encompasses every person on the planet (and off, if you happen to be an astronaut).

Note that the Jews, who can symbolize Christians (Galatians 3:7), are the ones who are especially near to God's heart, because He chose them to spread the Gospel to everyone else. But the Gentiles, who can symbolize the unsaved

(Isaiah 61:6), are still loved by God. Note that these two groups are mentioned in this one passage:

> Ephesians 2:11–19 (NLT): Don't forget that you **Gentiles** used to be outsiders. You were called "uncircumcised heathens" by the **Jews,** who were proud of their circumcision, even though it affected only their bodies and not their hearts. ¹²In those days you were living **apart from Christ.** You were excluded from citizenship among the people of Israel, and you did not know the covenant promises God had made to them. You lived in this world without God and without hope. ¹³But now you have been united with Christ Jesus. **Once you were far away from God, but now you have been brought near to him** through the blood of Christ. ¹⁴For Christ himself has brought peace to us. **He united Jews and Gentiles** into one people when, in his own body on the cross, he broke down the wall of hostility that separated us. ¹⁵He did this by ending the system of law with its commandments and regulations. He made peace between Jews and Gentiles by creating in himself one new people from the two groups. ¹⁶Together as one body, Christ reconciled both groups to God by means of his death on the cross, and our hostility toward each other was put to death. ¹⁷He brought this Good News of **peace to you Gentiles who were far away from him, and peace to the Jews who were near.** ¹⁸Now all of us can come to the Father through the same Holy Spirit because of what Christ has done for us. ¹⁹So now you Gentiles are no longer strangers and foreigners. You are citizens along with all of God's holy people. You are members of God's family.

Note that the Good News of peace applies to those who are near and those who are far: the ones already know about it, and the ones who don't. The ones who love Him, and the ones who don't. That about covers all of mankind, doesn't it? King David seems to think so:

> Psalm 145:9: **The LORD is good to** *all:* and **his tender mercies are over** *all* **his works.**
>
> NIV: **The Lord is good to** *all;* he has **compassion on** *all* he has made.
>
> MSG: **God is good to one and** *all;* everything he does is suffused with grace.
>
> VOICE: But **the Eternal's goodness** is not exclusive—it **is offered freely to** *all.* **His mercy extends to** *all* **His creation.**

This verse, by itself, completely overturns Unconditional Election and Limited Atonement. And how about this one, from the prophet Joel, who prophesied about the outpouring of the Holy Spirit at Pentecost:

> Joel 2:13 (NASB): And rend your heart and not your garments. Now return to the LORD your God, for He is gracious and compassionate, slow to anger, abounding in lovingkindness and **relenting of evil.**
>
> AMP: Rend your hearts and not your garments and return to the LORD, your God, for He is gracious and merciful, slow to anger, and abounding in loving-kindness; and **He revokes His sentence of evil [when His conditions are met].**
>
> GWORD: Tear your hearts, not your clothes. Return to the LORD your God. He is merciful and compassionate, patient, and **always ready to forgive and to change his plans about disaster.**
>
> MSG: Change your life, not just your clothes. Come back to God, your God. And here's why: God is kind and merciful. He takes a deep breath, puts up with a lot, this most patient God, extravagant in love, **always ready to cancel catastrophe.**
>
> NLT: Don't tear your clothing in your grief, but tear your hearts instead. Return to the LORD your God, for he is merciful and compassionate, slow to get angry and filled with unfailing love. **He is eager to relent and not punish.**

Notice how the above verse would have to be taken if there were such a thing as "unelect" people, in the sense of the Reformed doctrine of Unconditional Election, where the unelect are sent to hell without any other option. God would be saying to the unelect, "I *won't* relent of evil in your case. I *won't* revoke my sentence of evil, regardless of what conditions you meet. I'm *not* ready to cancel catastrophe, I *am* eager to punish, and I'm *not* ready to forgive and change my plans about disaster." As we can see from reading the Bible, God is not like that.

In fact, God's aversion for pouring out judgment, unless absolutely necessary, is exactly what Jonah complained about. After Jonah finally got to Nineveh and announced God's impending judgment, the people honestly repented, in hopes that God would have mercy. Sure enough, God saw their repentance and cancelled the destruction.

But Jonah was upset because his prophecy—which was inspired by God—didn't come true, so he thought that would make him look bad:

> Jonah 4:2 (NASB): He prayed to the LORD and said, "Please LORD, was not this what I said while I was still in my own country? Therefore in order to forestall this I fled to Tarshish, for I knew that You are a gracious and compassionate God, slow to anger and abundant in lovingkindness, and **one who relents concerning calamity.**"
>
> AMP: He prayed to the LORD and said, "O LORD, is this not what I said when I was still in my own country? That is why I ran to Tarshish, because I knew that You are a gracious and compassionate God, slow to anger and great in lovingkindness, **and [when sinners turn to You] You revoke the [sentence of] disaster [against them].**"
>
> GWORD: So he prayed to the LORD, "LORD, isn't this what I said would happen when I was still in my own country? That's why I tried to run to Tarshish in the first place. I knew that you are a merciful and compassionate God, patient, and **always ready to forgive and to reconsider your threats of destruction.**"
>
> MSG: He yelled at GOD, "GOD! I knew it—when I was back home, I knew this was going to happen! That's why I ran off to Tarshish! I knew you were sheer grace and mercy, not easily angered, rich in love, and **ready at the drop of a hat to turn your plans of punishment into a program of forgiveness!**"
>
> NLT: So he complained to the LORD about it: "Didn't I say before I left home that you would do this, LORD? That is why I ran away to Tarshish! I knew that you are a merciful and compassionate God, slow to get angry and filled with unfailing love. **You are eager to turn back from destroying people.**"

So God's change of heart upon seeing the Ninevites' repentance, rather than making Jonah look bad, made God look good. It is undeniably true that God is gracious, compassionate, and great in lovingkindness, and when people repent of their sin, He jumps at the chance of aborting judgment, *even if He's already announced it* (Jeremiah 18:7–8). Here again, Unconditional Election would have God sending some people (the "unelect") to hell with no recourse. Of course they deserve hell—just like the elect—but as the passage above shows, the heaven-or-hell decision is predicated on our decision whether or not to repent, not on God's decision in eternity past. Remember, He is not willing that *any* should perish, but that *all* should come to repentance (II Peter

3:9). So Jonah 4:2, like Joel 2:13, decisively overturns Unconditional Election.

Oh, and by the way, the fact that God's judgment was averted *because of* the repentance of the Ninevites, that verse also (again) overturns Total Depravity.

And here's another verse that addresses God's mercy:

> Deuteronomy 4:31 (NIV): For the LORD your God is a merciful God; he will not abandon or destroy you or forget the covenant with your forefathers, which he confirmed to them by oath.

Now how would you have to read the above verse if you filtered it through the lens of the Reformed doctrines? If you happened to be one of the unelect, it would turn out to mean something like the following:

> For the LORD your God (well, at least the *elect's* God) is a merciful God (except in your case, because He didn't elect you); he will not abandon or destroy you (except after you die and are sent to eternal abandonment and destruction because He chose to do that to you) or forget the covenant with your forefathers (except in your case because it doesn't apply to unelect people like you), which he confirmed to them by oath (but not to you because—did I mention?—you're one of the unelect).

Now if you inwardly grimaced at the results of applying the concepts of Reformed theology to the passage above, you would surely shudder in abject horror at the thought of re-interpreting *the whole Bible* through such lenses. But that's my point: when you consistently add the TULIP principles to the Bible, you come out with a grievously distorted view of God and His goodness. And if you *don't* apply them consistently, you are being intellectually dishonest.

But there's more:

> Psalm 118:1–4, 29 (CEV): Tell the LORD how thankful you are, because **he is kind and *always* merciful.** ²Let Israel shout, **"God is *always* merciful!"** ³Let the family of Aaron the priest shout, **"God is *always* merciful!"** ⁴Let every true worshiper of the LORD shout, **"God is *always* merciful!"** ²⁹Tell the LORD how thankful you are, because **he is kind and *always* merciful.**

If we didn't know better, it almost sounds, from reading the above Scriptures, like God is always merciful. But we *do* know better, because of the doctrine of Limited Atonement, which says that God can be unmerciful in this case because He created the unelect for the express purpose of burning in hell forever, so He doesn't give them the ability to repent, Acts 17:30 notwithstanding. Right?

I'm being facetious, of course. Psalm 145:9, above, says *what* God is merciful to: *all of His creation*. And Psalm 118:1–4, 29, also above, says *when* he is merciful: *always* (or as other translations render it, "forever"). So if God is always merciful to all His creation, that kinda blows the theory of an "unelect" group of humanity out of the water, doesn't it?

Then God speaks through Isaiah:

Isaiah 55:7–9 (NIV): Let the **wicked** forsake his way and the **evil man** his thoughts. Let him turn to the LORD, and **he will have mercy on him,** and to our God, for **he will freely pardon.** ⁸"For my thoughts are not your thoughts, neither are your ways my ways," declares the LORD. ⁹"As the heavens are higher than the earth, so are **my ways higher than your ways and my thoughts than your thoughts."**

v. 7b, AMP: . . .He will abundantly pardon.

CEB: . . .he is generous with forgiveness.

CJB: . . .he will freely forgive.

DOUAY: . . .he is bountiful to forgive.

GNV: . . .he is very ready to forgive.

GNT: . . .he is merciful and quick to forgive.

MSG: . . .our God, who is lavish with forgiveness.

NLV: . . .He will for sure forgive all his sins.

VOICE: Our God's forgiveness is inexhaustible.

Here again is a single, short passage that overturns Unconditional Election. Note that this exhortation and promise is directed at "wicked" and "evil" people; those who are no longer wicked and evil have repented, God has already had mercy on, and has pardoned—that is *why* they are no longer wicked and evil. Reformed theology would call these people the "elect." But notice that God is calling the *wicked and evil* people (the unelect), promising them that He will have mercy on them and pardon them if they turn away from their wickedness.

That pretty well covers it: God has already pardoned some people, and He is inviting the rest. The fact that He is inviting the rest discredits Unconditional Election and Limited Atonement, which say that God doesn't want to redeem some people. And since God is calling people to forsake their wicked ways and evil thoughts (i.e., to repent), that discredits Total Depravity, which says we are unable to do that.

One more thing: Notice that God's attitude toward the wicked and evil people is not "You low-down scum o' the earth. . ." but rather, "Repent! I long to forgive you!" Notice the sequence: v. 7 specifies that repentance (forsaking evil ways and thoughts and turning to the Lord) precedes the activation, in that person's life, of the abundant pardon that God offers. It is not insignificant how God describes His desire to "have mercy on" and "pardon" people: His ways are "higher than our ways," and His thoughts are "higher than our thoughts." If we want to increase our wisdom, we need to start thinking like God does.

And here's one more, for good measure:

Luke 6:35 (CEB): Instead, love your enemies, do good, and lend expecting nothing in return. If you do, you will have a great reward. You will be acting the way children of the Most High act, for **he is kind to ungrateful and wicked people.**

So God is kind to "wicked people." Who would the wicked people be, according to Reformed theology? It would have to be the unelect, right? But if people were unchangeably destined to hell, regardless of their actions, attitudes, and choices, that would certainly not be "kind."

And if people are *not* wicked, that would have be because God elected them, right? So this passage is definitely talking about the unelect, and the only way God could be kind to people who are wicked is if those people are wicked by their own choice. The reason is what was stated above: if they are wicked because God doomed them to be that way, that is certainly not kindness.

But wait: couldn't some of the wicked be people who are ultimately elect, but God just hasn't saved them yet? No. Jesus' words above do not say or imply that the Most High is kind to "some" wicked people, or those who are only "temporarily" wicked. The very strong implication from Jesus' words is that God is kind to *all* the wicked. And, as pointed out above, this absolutely requires that they are wicked of their own free will.

Men Are Not Cast Off

In Lamentations, Jeremiah writes the following:

Lamentations 3:31–33 (NIV): **For men are not cast off by the Lord forever.** [32]Though he brings grief, he will show compassion, so great is his unfailing love. ³³**For he does not willingly bring affliction or grief to the children of men.**

This short three-verse passage contains *two* verses that each refute the doctrine of Unconditional Election. Unconditional Election says, in effect, "God *does* cast off many men forever" (namely, the "unelect"). It also says that God willingly condemns many (again, the unelect) to an eternity of torment in hell, which sounds pretty much like affliction and grief to me. . .

Let's examine verse 33 a little more closely, especially the part about God bringing affliction or grief to people:

Lamentations 3:33 (AMPC): For He does not willingly and from His heart afflict or grieve the children of men.

CSB: For he does not enjoy bringing affliction or suffering on mankind.

CEB: He definitely doesn't enjoy affliction, making humans suffer.

CJB: For he does not arbitrarily torment or punish human beings.

ERV: He does not enjoy causing people pain. He does not like to make anyone unhappy.

TLB: For he does not enjoy afflicting men and causing sorrow.

MSG: He takes no pleasure in making life hard, in throwing roadblocks in the way. . .

But throughout the Bible, there are examples of God causing unpleasant circumstances for people. If God doesn't enjoy or take pleasure in causing afflictions or grief, why does He do it? Because He sees the big picture, whereas we usually do not.

The book of Hebrews explains it clearly:

Hebrews 12:10–11 (ESV): For they *[our earthly fathers]* disciplined us for a short time as it seemed best to them, but he *[God]* disciplines us **for our good, that we may share his holiness.** ¹¹For the moment all **discipline** seems painful rather than pleasant, but later it **yields the peaceful fruit of righteousness** to those who have been trained by it.

This redemptive quality of God's judgments and punishments is not only a New Testament concept; we will see this same redemptive essence in numerous places in the Old Testament as we continue through this book. But note that this grief-causing and affliction God causes is during people's life on earth, precisely to steer them *away* from an eternity without Him. So we can see that Jeremiah was indeed correct: men are *not* cast off by the Lord forever, as

Unconditional Election claims about the unelect. Rather, God makes every effort to persuade people to submit themselves to Him while there is still time, so they won't, by their own choice, cast *themselves* out of His presence forever.

Jonah's Complaint

Students of the Bible are familiar with Jonah, who ran away toward Spain when God called him to preach to Nineveh (in modern-day Iraq). Involuntarily hitching a ride in the nearest big fish, he eventually got to Nineveh, and all 120,000 inhabitants of Nineveh repented, and God spared them from being judged.

But Jonah complained! With all those people getting saved, what was there to complain about? Apparently, his own reputation as a prophet, because after the 40-day time limit had passed, and Nineveh was *not* burned down, here's what happened:

> Jonah 4:1–2 (MSG): Jonah was furious. He lost his temper. ²He yelled at God, "God! I knew it—when I was back home, I knew this was going to happen! That's why I ran off to Tarshish! **I knew you were sheer grace and mercy, not easily angered, rich in love, and ready at the drop of a hat to turn your plans of punishment into a program of forgiveness!**"

So, if God is "sheer grace and mercy, not easily angered, rich in love, and ready at the drop of a hat to turn His plans of punishment into a program of forgiveness" (and He is), how in the world does that square with the Reformed doctrine of Limited Atonement, in which God condemns a large fraction of humanity to eternal torment in hell, regardless of their attitudes, actions, or choices? It doesn't.

God's Plea

This passage was mentioned briefly in a previous chapter, but only as an example illustrating a point. Let's look into it a bit more deeply.

Why does God do anything? Is He obligated to? No, there is no one above Him to whom He would be obliged to do anything. He does things because He is *pleased* to do them; He *wants* to do them (Psalm 115:3, 135:6, Luke 12:32, etc.). And *especially* so if He didn't take human desires, actions, choices, or attitudes into account.

So let's see what He likes to do, or what He doesn't like to do:

> Ezekiel 18:23, 29–32 (CEV): **I, the Lord God, don't like to see wicked people die. I enjoy seeing them turn from their sins and live.** . . .
> ²⁹But you still say that I am unfair. You are the ones who have done

wrong and are unfair! ³⁰**I will judge each of you** *for what you've done.* **So stop sinning, or else you will certainly be punished.** ³¹Give up your evil ways and start thinking pure thoughts. And be faithful to me! Do you really want to be put to death for your sins? ³²**I, the Lord God, don't want to see that happen to anyone. So stop sinning and live!**

Some points of note:

- v. 23: God *doesn't* like to see wicked people die. This overturns Unconditional Election and Limited Atonement, because if they were true, wicked people—the unelect—who have no choice but to be that way, are punished for being that way. Since no one can make God do anything, He would have sent the unelect to hell because it pleased Him to do so, which contradicts v. 23.

- v. 23: God *does* like to see wicked people turn from their sins and live. This overturns Total Depravity, which says wicked people cannot turn from their sins.

- v. 30: God judges people *for what they've done.* This overturns Unconditional Election and Limited Atonement, which says the unelect are doomed because of God's decision in eternity past, not because of their actions.

- v. 30: God tells wicked people to *stop sinning.* This overturns Total Depravity, which says that people cannot choose anything good, such as stopping sinning.

- v. 31: God tells wicked people to give up their evil ways, think pure thoughts, and be faithful to Him. All three of these commands overturn Total Depravity, which says that people cannot choose anything good, such as these three things.

- v. 31: God asks people *if they want something*—that is, asking them to choose. This requires that people have a free will with which to choose. This overturns Unconditional Election, which says people can't choose.

- v. 31: God again says that people die *because of their sins,* not because of a decision God made before they were born.

- v. 32: God does *not* want to see *anyone* die for their sins. This would certainly include the unelect, so this overturns Limited Atonement, which says God doesn't want some people to be saved.

- v. 32: God tells wicked people to *stop sinning.* This again overturns Total Depravity, which says that people cannot do that.

Not bad for one little passage, eh? But especially relevant to this context are the two unmistakable statements that say God does not want to see wicked people die in their sins. These statements contradict the whole basis of Calvinism.

The Christmas Story

Remember the Christmas story? It's that section from the gospel of Luke that is read by millions of people worldwide every Christmas season. One important part of that story is when the angels appeared to the shepherds and made their announcement:

> Luke 2:8–11: And there were in the same country shepherds abiding in the field, keeping watch over their flock by night. [9]And, lo, the angel of the Lord came upon them, and the glory of the Lord shone round about them: and they were sore afraid. [10]And the angel said unto them, Fear not: for, behold, I bring you **good tidings of great joy, which shall be to all people.** [11]For unto you is born this day in the city of David **a Saviour, which is Christ the Lord.**

Think about it: why in the world would a message of the Savior be "good tidings of great joy to *all people*" if a large fraction of people were unavoidably doomed to spend an eternity in the tormenting fires of hell, as Unconditional Election postulates? It certainly wouldn't be good news to the unfortunate souls of the "unelect." No, the only way that news about the Savior could be good news to *all* people is if it *applied* to all people—if it were offered to *everyone* equally, and not just certain privileged ones.

Then, after telling the shepherds where to find the Christ child, this happens:

> Luke 2:13–14: And suddenly there was with the angel a multitude of the heavenly host praising God, and saying, [14]Glory to God in the highest, and on earth peace, **good will toward men.**

Notice that the heavenly host was not saying, "good will toward *some* men," or "good will toward *certain* men," or "good will toward just the *elect* men." No, as we saw in v. 10, this announcement was good news to *all* people. This unquestionably requires that the "good will" be to that same audience: *all* people. If God had created some people to be unavoidably tormented in hell forever, that doesn't sound much like "good will" toward men, does it?

Burning Down the Samaritans

Remember when Jesus and the disciples tried to go through the Samaritan village, and the Samaritans wouldn't let them?

> Luke 9:52–56 (AMP): And He sent messengers before Him; and they reached and entered a Samaritan village to make [things] ready for Him; ⁵³But [the people] would not welcome or receive or accept Him, because His face was [set as if He was] going to Jerusalem. ⁵⁴And when His disciples James and John observed this, they said, Lord, **do You wish us to command fire to come down from heaven and consume them,** even as Elijah did? ⁵⁵But He turned and rebuked and severely censured them. He said, You do not know of what sort of spirit you are, ⁵⁶For **the Son of Man did not come to destroy men's lives, but to save them** [from the penalty of eternal death]. And they journeyed on to another village.

I think it's very revealing what Jesus said here. After the Samaritans refused to accept Him (or "receive" Him or "welcome" Him), James and John want to burn them down, and ask Jesus' permission to do so. Jesus' response? First, He rebuked them for suggesting such a thing (v. 55). What does "rebuke" mean in this verse? Other translations render it "severely censured" (AMP, shown above), "spoke sternly" (CEB), "criticized" (ERV), "scolded" (EXB), "reproved" (PHILLIPS), "spoke sharp words" (NLV), and so forth.

So what they suggested must have been pretty repugnant to Jesus for Him to respond like this. But in that same verse, there's more. After the rebuke (or perhaps as part of it), Jesus says:

> AMP: You do not know of what sort of spirit you are. . .

> EXB: You don't know what kind of spirit you belong to.

> NASB: You do not know what kind of spirit you are of. . .

> NLV: You do not know what kind of spirit you have.

> WE: You do not think about what kind of spirit you are showing.

Wow. This is a pretty serious statement: Jesus basically says that their suggestion to destroy the people by fire was demonic in origin. (This situation is similar to when Peter suggested to Jesus in Mark 8:33 that He wouldn't have to die, and Jesus' response was, "Get behind Me, Satan!")

Then in v. 56, Jesus explains *why* the disciples' suggestion was so repugnant to Him: because it was diametrically opposed to the will of God:

> Luke 9:56a: For the Son of man is not come to destroy men's lives, but to save them.
>
> DOUAY: The Son of man came not to destroy souls, but to save.
>
> JUB: For the Son of man is not come to lose men's souls, but to save them.
>
> NCV: The Son of Man did not come to destroy the souls of people but to save them.
>
> VOICE: The Son of Man didn't come to ruin the lives of people, but He came to liberate them.
>
> WE: The Son of Man did not come to kill people, but to save them.

So in this verse, Jesus plainly states what He did *not* come to accomplish (destroy people's lives), and then what He *did* come to accomplish (save people's lives).

But isn't it interesting that the doctrine of Unconditional Election portrays God as deliberately deciding to destroy the lives and souls of a huge number of people (the unelect) with fire? That Unconditional Election puts forth the same idea that Jesus rebuked the disciples for suggesting? That Unconditional Election offers the same concept that Jesus strongly implied was demonic in origin? That Unconditional Election tenders the same proposal that Jesus said was completely opposite of His purpose? Interesting, isn't it?

What Does Paul Say About Mercy?

In Romans 11, Paul states very clearly *how many* people God has mercy on:

> Romans 11:32: For God hath concluded them all in unbelief, **that he might have mercy upon *all*.**
>
> CEV: All people have disobeyed God, and that's why he treats them as prisoners. But he does this, **so that he can have mercy on *all* of them.**
>
> ERV: All people have refused to obey God. And he has put them all together as people who don't obey him **so that he can show mercy to *everyone*.**
>
> EXB: God has given [imprisoned] all people over to their stubborn ways [to/in disobedience] **so that he can show mercy to *all*.**

GWORD: God has placed all people into the prison of their own disobedience **so that he could be merciful to** *all* **people.**

ICB: All people have refused to obey God. God has given them all over to their stubborn ways, **so that God can show mercy to** *all.*

NOG: God has placed all people into the prison of their own disobedience **so that he could be merciful to** *all* **people.**

This verse too, all by itself, completely discredits Unconditional Election and Limited Atonement. It very clearly states that God took this action *so that* (for the explicit, intended purpose such that) He could extend mercy to *all* people; not just the subset of people that Reformed doctrine states.

Being Appointed Unto Wrath

Paul makes another statement to the Thessalonians, along the same lines:

I Thessalonians 5:9: For **God hath not appointed us to wrath, but to obtain salvation** by our Lord Jesus Christ. . .

This verse too seems to overturn the doctrine of Unconditional Election; at least the part of the doctrine that talks about God choosing some people to be unelect, thereby preventing them from obtaining salvation and thus appointing them to wrath. But just to make sure we're understanding it correctly, let's read this verse from some other translations:

I Thessalonians 5:9 (AMP): For **God has not destined us to [incur His] wrath [that is, He did not select us to condemn us], but to obtain salvation** through our Lord Jesus Christ. . .

CEB: **God didn't intend for us to suffer his wrath but rather to possess salvation** through our Lord Jesus Christ.

CJB: For **God has not intended that we should experience his fury, but that we should gain deliverance** through our Lord Yeshua the Messiah. . .

CEV: **God doesn't intend to punish us, but wants us to be saved** by our Lord Jesus Christ.

ERV: **God did not choose us to suffer his anger. God chose us to have salvation** through our Lord Jesus Christ.

ISV: For **God has not destined us to receive wrath but to obtain salvation** through our Lord Jesus, the Messiah. . .

PHILLIPS: For **God did not choose us to condemn us, but that we might secure his salvation** through Jesus Christ our Lord.

NIV: For **God did not appoint us to suffer wrath but to receive salvation** through our Lord Jesus Christ.

NLV: **God planned to save us from the punishment of sin** through our Lord Jesus Christ. **He did not plan for us to suffer from His anger.**

Seems rather open-and-shut, doesn't it? How could we *mis*understand the message that God wants us to be saved? But then someone might say, "Sure, God planned salvation for *us*, but not for *them*. If you read the context, there is a clear distinction being made between 'us' and 'them.'"

Is that a valid argument? I don't think so, and here is why. Although Paul does state that believers are children of light and unbelievers are children of darkness, we cannot infer that that situation was God's *intent*. Indeed, we would have to ignore, remove, or rewrite hundreds of other Scriptures, were we to interpret this one as indicating that God's original intention was to create some people for the express purpose of burning in hell.

And just think of the violence that the concept of an "unelect" does to God's oft-repeated statement that He is not a respecter of persons! See the section "God is Not a Respecter of Persons," below, for a great deal of Scriptural support.

But What About His "Chosen People?"

Again, the Scriptures above were listed in order to answer the question, "how do the Scriptures that say God is merciful to *all*, square with other Scriptures that say God is merciful to *only those who serve Him* and not to evildoers?"

As stated earlier, the answer is simply that God has offered mercy to all people in an Atonement that is meant for all people, but whether we actually *get* extraordinary mercy depends on whether or not we choose to submit ourselves to Him; whether or not we choose to "adhere to, trust in, and rely on" Him for salvation. This is because, as we saw in the section "Crime and Punishment," God responds to us largely according to how we behave toward Him:

Psalm 62:12: Also unto thee, O Lord, belongeth mercy: for **thou renderest to every man according to his work.**

A perfect example of this concept is from Hebrews, where it refers back to the children of Israel wandering in the wilderness. They had the gospel (the good news that God will forgive your sins if you repent and trust Him to forgive you) preached to them like we have, and the result is one of only two possibilities: for those who believe, salvation, and for those who didn't believe, death.

Note the highlighted text below:

Hebrews 3:17–4:2 (NIV): And with whom was he angry for forty years? Was it not with those who sinned, whose bodies fell in the desert? ¹⁸And to whom did God swear that they would never enter his rest if not to those who disobeyed? ¹⁹So we see that **they were not able to enter, because of their unbelief.** ⁴:¹Therefore, since the promise of entering his rest still stands, let us be careful that none of you be found to have fallen short of it. ²For we also have had the gospel preached to us, just as they did; but **the message they heard was of no value to them, because those who heard did not combine it with faith.**

Make specific note in the passage above that:

- The ones who are never able to enter into God's rest are those who disobey Him.
- The ones who were not able to enter were those who didn't believe the message of the gospel.
- The message of the gospel did not profit the unbelievers, because they didn't mix it—combine it, unite it—with faith. The cause was: their absence of faith; the effect was: the gospel was not profitable to them.

So we can see that God extends mercy, salvation, forgiveness, to all, but it doesn't benefit us and open the floodgates of blessing unless and until we receive it by faith. But if we harden our hearts, as the Hebrews did in the wilderness, we miss out, as the Word says:

Psalm 95:8–10 (NIV): **Do not harden your hearts** as you did at Meribah, as you did that day at Massah in the desert, ⁹where your fathers tested and tried me, though they had seen what I did. ¹⁰For forty years I was angry with that generation; I said, "**They are a people whose hearts go astray,** and they have not known my ways."

Hebrews 3:8 (AMP): **Do not harden your hearts,** as [happened] in the rebellion [of Israel] and their provocation and embitterment [of Me] in the day of testing in the wilderness. . .

Hebrews 3:15 (NIV): As has just been said: "Today, if you hear his voice, **do not harden your hearts** as you did in the rebellion."

Hebrews 4:7 (NASB): He again fixes a certain day, "Today," saying through David after so long a time just as has been said before, "Today if you hear His voice, **do not harden your hearts.**"

Apparently, this is an important point, and He wants us to understand that we are not to harden our hearts. And the very fact that He is exhorting us to *not* harden our hearts and disbelieve/reject Him, clearly shows that it is *our* decision whether or not we believe and accept Him.

What did Jesus indicate about how people start following Him?

Luke 9:23a: And he *[Jesus]* said to them all, If any man **will** come after me. . .

AMP: . . .If any person **wills to** come after me. . .

MSG: . . .Anyone who **intends to** come with me. . .

NASB: . . .If anyone **wishes to** come after Me. . .

NIV: . . .Whoever **wants to** be my disciple. . .

NKJV: . . .If anyone **desires to** come after Me. . .

NMB: . . .if any person **would** come after me. . .

Regardless of the translation, these are clearly all choices of the free will.

God Is Not a Respecter of Persons

As we've seen, the Reformed doctrines of Unconditional Election and Limited Atonement portray God as choosing some people to be blessed in heaven forever, while leaving others to suffer eternal torment in hell, with *no* regard for their attitudes, actions, choices, or desires. One of the most obvious things about those doctrines is that in order for God to do that, He would have to show favoritism, to play favorites, to show partiality, be a respecter of persons.

But what *is* favoritism, anyway? What does it mean to have "respect of persons?" It is showing favor to one person over another person, treating people unfairly, or giving one person an advantage you don't give to another, being prejudiced, and so forth. (If you disagree with some of these definitions of "respect of persons," keep reading.)

Respect of persons, as in, God saying to some unfortunate soul, "You are no better or worse than the next guy, but I've decided to let him into heaven, while you burn in hell forever." Stating it that way may be more blunt than some are comfortable with, but that is essentially what must happen if God actually chooses our eternal destination for us, regardless of our attitudes, actions, choices, or desires.

Does that mean that God fundamentally loves some people more than others? If not—and most Christians would agree that God loves everyone the same—then it becomes even worse: "I really love you as much as I love the next guy, but I'll send you to hell anyway." That is favoritism—and hypocrisy—on steroids. God doesn't send people to hell; hell wasn't even built for us, but for the devil and his angels (Matthew 25:41). People go there only if they insist upon it, because God freely offers to everyone a way out, and *urges* us to take advantage of it (I Thessalonians 5:9–10). That "way out"— that means of avoiding an eternity of torment in hell—is available simply for the asking: salvation through faith in Jesus.

Now please note that in the above paragraph I am *not* accusing God of favoritism and hypocrisy, and it is precisely for that reason that I cannot accept a doctrine that portrays Him as such. And the Bible has quite a bit to say about favoritism.

> Exodus 23:3 (HCSB): **Do not show favoritism** to a poor person in his lawsuit.
>
> > GNT: **Do not show partiality** to a poor person at his trial.
>
> Leviticus 19:15 (NIV): Do not pervert justice; **do not show partiality to the poor or favoritism** to the great, **but judge your neighbor fairly.**
>
> > CEB: You must not act unjustly in a legal case. **Do not show favoritism to the poor or deference to the great;** you must judge your fellow Israelites **fairly.**
> >
> > CEV: **Be fair,** no matter who is on trial—**don't favor** either the poor or the rich.

From this verse, we see that showing partiality or favoring one person over another is forbidden, and their opposite—being fair—is important to God.

> Deuteronomy 10:17 (GWORD): The LORD your God is God of gods and Lord of lords, the great, powerful, and awe-inspiring God. **He never plays favorites** and never takes a bribe.
>
> > CEV: The LORD your God is more powerful than all other gods and lords, and his tremendous power is to be feared. **His decisions are always fair,** and you cannot bribe him to change his mind.
> >
> > ERV: The LORD is your God. He is the God of gods and the Lord of lords. He is the great God. He is the amazing and powerful fighter.

To him everyone is the same. He does not accept money to change his mind.

Again, we see that fairness is more than merely "important" to God; it is integral to His nature.

Proverbs 24:23b: **It is not good to have respect of persons** in judgment.

NLT: **It is wrong to show favoritism when passing judgment.**

LEB: **Partiality in judgment is not good.**

NOG: **Showing partiality as a judge is not good.**

NET: **To show partiality in judgment is terrible. . .**

Note that it says here that it is wrong to show favoritism when passing judgment. *Which means that God wouldn't do it,* because we know that God cannot even be *tempted* to sin (James 1:13), let alone actually commit one. And *that* means that the Reformed doctrine of Unconditional Election (as well as Limited Atonement) is incompatible with yet another set of Scriptures.

Malachi 2:9 (NLT): "So I have made you despised and humiliated in the eyes of all the people. For **you have not obeyed me but have shown favoritism** in the way you carry out my instructions."

AMP: Therefore have I also made you despised and abased before all the people, inasmuch as **you have not kept My ways but have shown favoritism** to persons in your administration of the law [of God].

CEV: So I caused everyone to hate and despise you, because **you disobeyed me and failed to treat all people alike.**

GNT: So I, in turn, will make the people of Israel despise you because **you do not obey my will,** and when you teach my people, **you do not treat everyone alike.**

God says here that if we show favoritism, we are not keeping His ways. This clearly shows that His way is to *not* show favoritism; it *is* His way to treat all people alike. Does an unchangeable sentence of an eternity of punishment and torment for only *some* people (regardless of whether or not we all deserve it), as Reformed Theology defines Unconditional Election, sound like God "treating everybody alike?"

Take a look at this: even the *Pharisees*—not known for their spiritual insight—knew Jesus was not a respecter of persons:

> Matthew 22:16b (NLT): "Teacher," they said, "we know how honest you are. You teach the way of God truthfully. **You are impartial and don't play favorites.**"
>
>> ERV: They said, "Teacher, we know you are an honest man. We know you teach the truth about God's way. You are not afraid of what others think about you. **All people are the same to you.**"
>>
>> NASB: "Teacher, we know that You are truthful and teach the way of God in truth, and defer to no one; for **You are not partial to any.**"

These Pharisees saw that Jesus was impartial and didn't play favorites. And since Jesus is "the radiance of God's glory and the *exact representation* of his being" (Hebrews 1:3, NIV), God the Father must also be impartial and not play favorites.

> Mark 12:14a (NLT): "Teacher," they said, "we know how honest you are. **You are impartial and don't play favorites.** You teach the way of God truthfully."

Ditto.

> Luke 20:21 (GWORD): They asked him, "Teacher, we know that you're right in what you say and teach. Besides, **you don't play favorites. Rather, you teach the way of God truthfully.**"
>
>> CEB: They asked him, "Teacher, we know that you are correct in what you say and teach. **You don't show favoritism but teach God's way as it really is.**"
>>
>> ESV: So they asked him, "Teacher, we know that you speak and teach rightly, and **show no partiality, but truly teach the way of God.**"

Isn't it interesting that these people understood that "playing favorites" and "teaching the way of God truthfully" were mutually exclusive concepts? Fascinating.

> Acts 10:34 (GWORD): Then Peter said, "Now I understand that **God doesn't play favorites.**"
>
>> HCSB: Then Peter began to speak: "Now I really understand that **God doesn't show favoritism. . .**"
>>
>> NET: Then Peter started speaking: "I now truly understand that **God does not show favoritism** in dealing with people. . ."

CEB: Peter said, "I really am learning that **God doesn't show partiality to one group of people over another.**"

DARBY: And Peter opening his mouth said, Of a truth I perceive that **God is no respecter of persons. . .**

GNT: Peter began to speak: "I now realize that it is true that **God treats everyone on the same basis.**"

CEV: Peter then said: Now I am certain that **God treats all people alike.**

Does an unchangeable, predetermined sentence of an eternity in hell for only *some* people, as Reformed Theology defines Unconditional Election, sound like God "treating everyone on the same basis" or God "treating everybody alike?"

Paul weighs in with the same sentiments in his letter to the church in Rome:

Romans 2:11: For **there is no respect of persons with God.**

GWORD: **God does not play favorites.**

HCSB: **There is no favoritism with God.**

TLB: For **God treats everyone the same.**

NLT: For **God does not show favoritism.**

ERV: **God judges everyone the same. It doesn't matter who they are.**

EXB: **For God judges all people in the same way** [there is no partiality with God].

GNT: For **God judges everyone by the same standard.**

PHILLIPS: For **there is no preferential treatment with God.**

NIRV: **God treats everyone the same.**

NLV: **God does not show favor to one man more than to another.**

And again I ask, if God "judges everyone by the same standard," "treats everyone the same," "is always fair," and "does not show favor to one man more than to another," *how in the world* could that be reconciled with the Reformed doctrine of Unconditional Election? They can't be. They are diametrically opposed; they are mutually exclusive concepts.

Paul continues in that vein in his epistle to the church in Galatia:

Galatians 2:6 (GWORD): Those who were recognized as important people didn't add a single thing to my message. (What sort of people they were makes no difference to me, since **God doesn't play favorites.**)

NLT: And the leaders of the church had nothing to add to what I was preaching. (By the way, their reputation as great leaders made no difference to me, for **God has no favorites.**)

HCSB: Now from those recognized as important (what they really were makes no difference to me; **God does not show favoritism,**)—they added nothing to me.

NET: But from those who were influential (whatever they were makes no difference to me; **God shows no favoritism between people**)—those influential leaders added nothing to my message.

. . .and in Ephesus:

Ephesians 6:9: And, ye masters, do the same things unto them, forbearing threatening: knowing that your Master also is in heaven; **neither is there respect of persons with him.**

GWORD: Masters, treat your slaves with respect. Don't threaten a slave. You know that there is **one master in heaven** who has authority over both of you, and **he doesn't play favorites.**

NLT: Masters, treat your slaves in the same way. Don't threaten them; remember, **you both have the same Master in heaven, and he has no favorites.**

HCSB: And masters, treat your slaves the same way, without threatening them, because you know that both their Master and yours is in heaven, and **there is no favoritism with Him.**

ERV: Masters, in the same way, be good to your slaves. Don't say things to scare them. You know that the one who is your Master and their Master is in heaven, and **he treats everyone the same.**

EXB: Masters, treat your slaves the same way. Do not threaten them. Remember that the One who is your Master and their Master is in heaven, and he **treats everyone alike [has no favorites; shows no favoritism].**

NCV: Masters, in the same way, be good to your slaves. Do not threaten them. Remember that the One who is your Master and their Master is in heaven, and **he treats everyone alike.**

> NIRV: Masters, treat your slaves in the same way. When you warn them, don't be too hard on them. You know that the God who is their Master and yours is in heaven. And **he treats everyone the same.**

Another very blunt, completely unmistakeable statement that God treats everyone alike.

And then, to the church in Colosse:

> Colossians 3:25: But he that doeth wrong shall receive for the wrong which he hath done: and **there is no respect of persons.**
>
> GWORD: The person who does wrong will be paid back for the wrong he has done. **God does not play favorites.**
>
> NLT: But if you do what is wrong, you will be paid back for the wrong you have done. For **God has no favorites.**
>
> HCSB: For the wrongdoer will be paid back for whatever wrong he has done, and **there is no favoritism.**
>
> NCV: But remember that anyone who does wrong will be punished for that wrong, and **the Lord treats everyone the same.**
>
> NIRV: Anyone who does wrong will be paid back for what they do. **God treats everyone the same.**
>
> WE: The person who does wrong will be punished for the wrong he has done. **God does not love one person more than another.**

Here again we have God stating that people will be judged *for what they have done,* not for some decision made for them in eternity past. And then, almost in passing, Paul states the profound principle that explains *why* it is appropriate for God to judge people according to their own actions: He deals with everybody on the same, level playing field.

Then, in his first letter to Timothy, Paul reiterates:

> I Timothy 5:21 (GWORD): I solemnly call on you in the sight of God, Christ Jesus, and the chosen angels to **be impartial** when you follow what I've told you. **Never play favorites.**
>
> HCSB: I solemnly charge you before God and Christ Jesus and the elect angels to observe these things **without prejudice, doing nothing out of favoritism.**

NET: Before God and Christ Jesus and the elect angels, I solemnly charge you to carry out these commands **without prejudice or favoritism of any kind.**

NLT: I solemnly command you in the presence of God and Christ Jesus and the highest angels to **obey these instructions without taking sides or showing favoritism to anyone.**

NIV: I charge you, in the sight of God and Christ Jesus and the elect angels, to **keep these instructions without partiality,** and to **do nothing out of favoritism.**

ERV: Before God and Jesus Christ and the chosen angels, I tell you to make these judgments without any prejudice. **Treat every person the same.**

ISV: With God as my witness, as well as the Messiah Jesus and the chosen angels, I solemnly call on you to carry out these instructions **without prejudice, doing nothing on the basis of partiality.**

TLB: I solemnly command you in the presence of God and the Lord Jesus Christ of the holy angels to do this whether the pastor is a special friend of yours or not. **All must be treated exactly the same.**

NIRV: I command you to follow these instructions. I command you in the sight of God and Christ Jesus and the chosen angels. **Treat everyone the same. Don't favor one person over another.**

WE: I say this before God and Christ Jesus and the chosen angels of God. Do these things in an honest way. **Do not treat one person better than another person.**

Above, we see Paul telling Timothy, in his instruction to Timothy on how to be a godly man and leader in the church, to treat everyone in a fair, unprejudiced, impartial manner.

My goodness. Are we seeing a pattern here?

Then James adds his two bits:

James 2:1 (HCSB): My brothers, **do not show favoritism** as you hold on to the faith in our glorious Lord Jesus Christ.

NASB: My brethren, **do not hold your faith** in our glorious Lord Jesus Christ **with an attitude of personal favoritism.**

NIV: My brothers, as believers in our glorious Lord Jesus Christ, **don't show favoritism.**

FREE TO CHOOSE?

The above Scripture says we are not to show favoritism, and then a few verses later, James below tells us *why* we are not to show favoritism:

> James 2:9 (HCSB): But **if you show favoritism, you commit sin** and are convicted by the law as transgressors.
>
> CEV: But **if you treat some people better than others, you have done wrong,** and the Scriptures teach that **you have sinned.**
>
> ESV: But **if you show partiality, you are committing sin** and are convicted by the law as transgressors.
>
> GWORD: **If you favor one person over another, you're sinning,** and this law convicts you of being disobedient.
>
> NET: But **if you show prejudice, you are committing sin** and are convicted by the law as violators.
>
> NIRV: But **you sin if you don't treat everyone the same.** The law judges you because you have broken it.
>
> NIV: But **if you show favoritism, you sin** and are convicted by the law as lawbreakers.
>
> NLT: But **if you favor some people over others, you are committing a sin.** You are guilty of breaking the law.

Here we see very plainly why God doesn't show favoritism: if He did, He would be sinning. It's not like "Favoritism is a sin unless God does it." No, favoritism is a sin. Period. But He cannot sin, therefore He must treat everyone the same, and therefore Unconditional Election—which portrays God treating the elect and the unelect *very* differently—cannot be a valid doctrine.

Just a little later, James talks about godly wisdom: "the wisdom from above:"

> James 3:17 (HCSB): But **the wisdom from above is** first pure, then peace-loving, gentle, compliant, full of mercy and good fruits, **without favoritism** and hypocrisy.
>
> NLT: But **the wisdom from above** is first of all pure. It is also peace loving, gentle at all times, and willing to yield to others. It is full of mercy and good deeds. It **shows no favoritism** and is always sincere.

The verse above says that the "wisdom from above" does not show favoritism. Isn't God likely to follow the wisdom from above, since He is the source of it?

Then Peter, in his first epistle, reiterates what he said in Acts 10 (above):

I Peter 1:17 (GWORD): So if you call God your Father, live your time as temporary residents on earth in fear. He is the God who judges all people by what they have done, and **he doesn't play favorites.**

NLT: And remember that the heavenly Father to whom you pray **has no favorites.** He will judge or reward you according to what you do. So you must live in reverent fear of him during your time as "foreigners in the land."

Now there is another interesting verse: not only does it reinforce the idea that God doesn't play favorites, but it also says He judges all people not by some decision made for them in eternity past, but *by what they have done.* Wow. That almost sounds like—dare I say it?—*free will.*

Okay, that's probably enough to get a feel for what God thinks on the subject. From the above Scriptures, we can plainly see these things:

- "Showing partiality," "being a respecter of persons," "playing favorites," "being prejudiced," "being unfair," "showing favoritism," "showing deference," and "favoring," are all synonymous phrases.

- "Being fair," "treating everyone the same," "treating everyone alike," and "treating everyone on the same basis" are synonymous phrases.

- God treats everyone the same in judgment, does not show partiality, does not show preferential treatment of any, and does not show favor to one man more than another.

- *We* are not to show favoritism to the rich, the poor, our friends, our relatives, our employees, our employers, or *anyone else.*

- It is a sin to show favoritism. Obviously, this is why God doesn't do it, and neither should we.

So, either the Reformed doctrine of Unconditional Election is true, or the Scriptures above are true. But they say opposite things, so according to the Law of Non-Contradiction (*the* most fundamental law of rational thought), if one is true, the other cannot be. It's up to you to choose which one you'll believe.

He That Dwelleth. . .

Psalm 91—the famous "He that dwelleth in the secret place" passage—contains several shifts in point of view. That is, there are several changes in who is speaking and who/what is being spoken about. These changes are present, but are not announced or labeled, so you can miss a lot of the impact if you don't notice who is talking and what he's talking about.

Let's look at the relevant information for each verse:

Verses	Speaking	Spoken To	Spoken About
1	Psalmist	Reader	Reader
2	Psalmist	Reader/God	God/Psalmist
3–4	Psalmist	Reader	God/Reader
5–7	Psalmist	Reader	Reader/Threats
8	Psalmist	Reader	Reader/Evildoers
9	Psalmist	Reader	Reader/God/Psalmist
10	Psalmist	Reader	Reader/Threats
11	Psalmist	Reader	God/Angels/Reader
12	Psalmist	Reader	Angels/Reader/Threats
13	Psalmist	Reader	Reader/Threats
14–16	God	Reader	Protected one/God

Keeping in mind what is being said, and who is saying it, here are two more indicators that we ourselves do indeed choose whether to serve God or not, and that our salvation is not the result of an unchangeable decision by God made on our behalf in eternity past and unrelated to our choices, preferences, decisions, and actions. Let's look at the first one:

Psalm 91:9 (AMP): Because *you* have made the Lord your refuge, and the Most High your dwelling place, ¹⁰There shall no evil befall you, nor any plague or calamity come near your tent.

Note in v. 9 that it says "...*you* have made the Lord your dwelling place," not "the Lord has made Himself your dwelling place." The speaker is clearly addressing the reader of the psalm and is saying to the reader that he, the reader, is the one responsible for making the Lord his dwelling place (or "habitation," as other translations render it). Some Bible translations express the thought conditionally, as in, "*If* you make the Lord your habitation..." but whether it is expressed declaratively or conditionally, it still clearly indicates that it is *we* who make the Lord our habitation. *We* choose.

This idea is reinforced in v. 14, and this time it is *God* speaking; not "merely" the psalmist:

> Psalm 91:14 (AMP): Because *he* **has set his love upon Me,** therefore will I deliver him; I will set him on high, because he knows and understands My name [has a personal knowledge of My mercy, love, and kindness—trusts and relies on Me, knowing I will never forsake him, no, never].

Reading this verse in context, we can clearly see that the speaker is God; indeed, many translations explicitly insert a clarifying phrase to the effect of "God said." The one God is speaking to is the reader, and the one He is speaking about is the person He is promising to protect. And notice what God says about this one being protected: ". . .*he* has set his love upon me." Not "*I* have set his love upon me."

Did you catch those? In v. 9, the Psalmist says that the *reader* made the Lord his refuge, and then in v. 14, God Himself says that the *protected one*—the human whom God is promising to protect—set his love on the Lord. But according to Total Depravity, a human does not have the capacity to make decisions like making the Lord his refuge, or setting his love on the Lord. And therefore, according to Unconditional Election, that's God's job. But both of these doctrines are overturned by this psalm.

Election

Part of the doctrine of Unconditional Election is, unsurprisingly, the concept of "election." What is election, according to Reformed theology? It is the process of God choosing which people are to be saved to spend eternity in heaven and spared from hell, and which people, by *not* having been chosen for the first group, are relegated to suffering torment in hell forever. Similarly, the word "elect" (in Reformed theology) means "those who have been chosen by God to be saved and spared from hell."

What does the Bible say about the "elect?" Let's look at some Scriptures:

> Matthew 24:22 (NASB): And unless those days had been cut short, no life would have been saved; but for the sake of the **elect** those days shall be cut short.

> Matthew 24:31 (NIV): And he will send his angels with a loud trumpet call, and they will gather his **elect** from the four winds, from one end of the heavens to the other.

> Romans 11:5: Even so then at this present time also there is a remnant according to the **election** of grace.

And there are many more verses that refer to the "elect." That's not a problem—it is obviously a Scriptural word—but the problem arises when we apply a different *meaning* to the word than that which the Biblical authors (read: "God") intended. The problem that arises here, as mentioned in "The Bible Itself Defining Its Terms," is simply: How do we know what the correct meanings of Biblical words are? The approach we'll use in this case—to help us understand what the Bible means by "elect"—is to see how the Bible uses the word.

Will such an approach help us determine what the meaning of the word "elect" is? Or at least what it *isn't*? Actually, yes. Look at the Scripture below:

> I Timothy 5:21 (NIV): I charge you, in the sight of God and Christ Jesus and the **elect angels**, to keep these instructions without partiality, and to do nothing out of favoritism.

Elect *angels*? Did God, in eternity past, choose some of the angels to be "saved," serve Him and be blessed forever, while others were fated and doomed to become puffed up in pride, rebel against Him, get cast out of heaven, become demons, and endure an eternity of suffering in hell? If so, then because the angels weren't tempted by a fallen and deceptive third party (like Adam and Eve were), God *causing* them to become prideful and rebel would kinda make God the author of sin, wouldn't it? This already throws a serious monkey wrench into the Reformed idea of election having been done in eternity past.

Or how about this one:

> I Peter 5:13 (CEB): The **fellow-elect church** in Babylon greets you, and so does my son Mark.

Here is a *whole church* that is "elect." Not merely the individuals in the church, but the church itself.

Let's look at another couple of passages. The first is a Messianic prophecy in Isaiah, and the second is from one of Peter's epistles:

> Isaiah 42:1 (AMP): Behold My Servant, Whom I uphold, My **elect** in Whom My soul delights! I have put My Spirit upon Him; He will bring forth justice and right and reveal truth to the nations.

> I Peter 2:4–6: To whom coming, as unto a living stone, disallowed indeed of men, but **chosen** of God, and precious, ⁵Ye also, as lively stones, are built up a spiritual house, an holy priesthood, to offer up spiritual sacrifices, acceptable to God by **Jesus Christ**. ⁶Wherefore also it is contained in the scripture, Behold, **I lay in Sion a chief corner stone, elect, precious**: and he that believeth on him shall not be confounded.

Wait, *what?* Jesus *Himself* is "elect?" If this is true (and it is), then the Reformed understanding of "elect" being defined as "those to whom God has chosen to grant mercy, and bring to Himself, effecting salvation in them" is in big trouble. Obviously, "elect" means "chosen," but it doesn't look like it could possibly mean "chosen" in the way that Reformed theology says it does.

How about this one:

> Isaiah 45:4: For Jacob my servant's sake, and **Israel mine elect**, I have even called thee by thy name: I have surnamed thee, though thou hast not known me.

Here's a whole *nation* being called the "elect" of God. So from the fact that angels, Jesus Himself, and whole nations can be "elect" of God, we are driven to conclude that in order to determine the accurate meaning of "elect," we must gather it from the actual context of the passage. Reading it in context. Now *there's* a thought.

The word "elect" clearly means "chosen," but God can choose people (or angels or churches or Jesus or whole nations) for any number of reasons. Assuming by default that it means "chosen to be saved from hell without regard to our attitudes, actions, or choices" in the Reformed theological sense would be unwarranted and unreliable, and that interpretation is *especially* suspect since there are so many Scriptures that militate against the whole concept.

Here are a couple other enlightening verses on this subject:

> Matthew 20:16: So the last shall be first, and the first last: **for many be called, but few chosen.**

> Matthew 22:14: For **many are called**, but **few are chosen.**

The word "chosen" in the verses above come from the Greek word ἐκλεκτός (*eklektos*, G1588), which is the same Greek word usually translated as "elect." Keeping that in mind, the verses above state that "Many are called, but few are elect." If, as the Reformed doctrine of Unconditional Election states, God elected people in eternity past, and in a way that was unrelated to their behavior or choices, *why would He call them?* It would be pointless for God to "call" people if there was no possibility of them responding, since they hadn't already been included as part of the "elect" (the only ones who *can* respond, according to the Reformed doctrine of Total Depravity, and even then only *after* they have been saved).

No, it seems that the only way to interpret the Scriptures above in a way that squares with the rest of Scripture is to take it as saying, "God calls everyone, but since only few respond to his call, only few are elected/chosen to participate in His plan." In other words, *we* decide if we're elect or not. We become the chosen of God—His special people—when we choose to believe in Him and accept what He did for us. And of course, we must also remain faithful to Him, so we don't end up like the unfruitful seeds in the Parable of the Sower.

One example of this concept is in the group of the original twelve apostles:

> Matthew 10:1: And when **he had called unto him his twelve disciples,** he gave them power against unclean spirits, to cast them out, and to heal all manner of sickness and all manner of disease.

> John 13:18 (ESV): I speak not of you all: **I know whom I have chosen:** *[Judas Iscariot being the lone exception]* but that the scripture may be fulfilled, He that eateth bread with me hath lifted up his heel against me.

Why did Jesus "call" all twelve of his disciples, but at the Last Supper, only consider eleven of them to be "chosen?" Simply because when God calls us, *we* have the responsibility to respond affirmatively. If we don't, we fall into the "few are chosen" category—*not* a good place in which to be.

Those three concepts—God's calling us, our responding to His call, and our faithfulness to Him over the long haul—are beautifully portrayed in Revelation, where the angel is explaining to John the meaning of one part of his vision:

> Revelation 17:12–14 (NIV): "The ten horns you saw are ten kings who have not yet received a kingdom, but who for one hour will receive authority as kings along with the beast. ^{13}They have one purpose and will give their power and authority to the beast. ^{14}They will make war against the Lamb, but the Lamb will overcome them because he is Lord of lords and King of kings—and **with him will be his called, chosen and faithful followers."**

Make a note of who is with Jesus here: those who are His called, *and* chosen, *and* faithful followers. As in the two verses from Matthew, above, the word "chosen" in Revelation 17:14 was translated from the Greek word ἐκλεκτός (*eklektos,* G1588), which is usually translated as "elect," as discussed earlier. Many were called, but these people, because they answered His call, were chosen ("elected") to participate in His plan, and they were also faithful to Him.

This is why Peter said what he did:

II Peter 1:10: Wherefore the rather, brethren, **give diligence to make your calling and election sure:** for if ye do these things, ye shall never fall. . .

> AMP: Therefore, believers, **be all the more diligent to make certain about His calling and choosing you** [be sure that your behavior reflects and confirms your relationship with God]; for by doing these things [actively developing these virtues], you will never stumble [in your spiritual growth and will live a life that leads others away from sin];
>
> CEB: Therefore, brothers and sisters, **be eager to confirm your call and election.** Do this and you will never ever be lost.
>
> CJB: Therefore, brothers, **try even harder to make your being called and chosen a certainty.** For if you keep doing this, you will never stumble.

If our election—our being chosen by God for salvation—was a done deal, completely detached from our attitudes, choices, and behavior, why would it be necessary to make our election *sure* or *certain* or *confirmed*? If the Reformed definition of "election" is accurate, not only would such confirmation be unnecessary, but it would be completely impossible.

And then, just in case it wasn't already clear to us, Peter follows with:

II Peter 1:11 (HCSB): **For in this way,** entry into the eternal kingdom of our Lord and Savior Jesus Christ will be richly supplied to you.

See also the section "Perseverance of the Saints" below for the importance of being faithful.

So it's clear from the above Scriptures that whether one ends up in heaven or hell for eternity is not determined by your "election" status—whether you were "unconditionally elected" or not—which allegedly happened in eternity past with no regard to our desires, actions, or choices. What sends a person to hell, according to Unconditional Election, is simply a matter of not having been in the group called the "elect." But is that really what determines whether someone ends up in hell or not?

Let's take a look at something Jesus taught. In this passage, notice what Jesus said about what causes people to perish. He had just been asked if, because some Galileans were mercilessly killed, that proved they were greater sinners than other people. Jesus replied:

> Luke 13:3: I tell you, Nay: but, **except ye repent, ye shall all likewise perish.**
>
> AMP: I tell you, No; but **unless you repent (change your mind for the better and heartily amend your ways, with abhorrence of your past sins), you will all likewise perish and be lost eternally.**
>
> CEV: Not at all! But **you can be sure that if you don't turn back to God, every one of you will also be killed.**
>
> GWORD: No! I can guarantee that they weren't. But **if you don't turn to God and change the way you think and act, then you, too, will all die.**
>
> NLT: Not at all! And **you will perish, too, unless you repent of your sins and turn to God.**

Note that Jesus is extremely unambiguous about what causes people to perish eternally—about what sends people to hell: the absence of repentance, not an ironclad decision God made for us before the world began.

But just in case there is still any confusion, Jesus gives another example of people who died because a wall collapsed on them. After reaffirming that they did not die because their "sinfulness score" was excessively high, He says:

> Luke 13:5: I tell you, Nay: but, **except ye repent, ye shall all likewise perish.**

Virtually identical wording to His previous statement. Maybe Jesus was trying to make a point. . .

Jesus' Yoke

Matthew's gospel tells us about Jesus and His yoke:

> Matthew 11:28–30 (NIV): **Come to me, all you who are weary and burdened,** and I will give you rest. ²⁹**Take my yoke upon you** and learn from me, for I am gentle and humble in heart, and you will find rest for your souls. ³⁰For my yoke is easy and my burden is light.

Several fascinating points here:

- Jesus says "Come to me," and He is addressing his invitation to those who are "weary and burdened." We know that this means the people who have not yet come to Him: if they *had* come to Him already, they would no longer be weary, because He would have given them rest. In other words, He is telling people to repent and turn to God: something that Total Depravity says is impossible.

- Jesus is clearly indicating that He wants *all* people to be saved, because He is specifically inviting the weary ones. Those who are no longer weary have come to Him already, which is why they are no longer weary. The ones who have come to Jesus (the rested), plus the ones who have not yet come to Jesus (the weary), equals *all people.* So, Jesus is teaching something that Unconditional Election and Limited Atonement say is not the case.

- Jesus says "take my yoke upon you." Clearly, He is inviting *us* to choose *Him*, and He abides by our decisions. Unconditional Election states the opposite: that *God* chooses some people to be saved, and He also chooses some people to be tormented forever in hell, irrespective of the people's actions, desires, choices, or attitudes.

Paul describes the same event to the Corinthian church:

I Corinthians 6:17 (NASB): But **the one who joins himself to the Lord** is one spirit with Him.

Note that Paul describes joining *ourselves* to the Lord; not the Lord joining us to Him regardless of our desires or choices. Like Jesus, Paul is clearly showing that we *voluntarily* take Jesus' yoke upon ourselves—we *voluntarily* join ourselves to the Lord, thus becoming one spirit with Him.

Predestination

As mentioned above, another word closely associated with "election" is "predestination." The Bible does indeed use the word "predestinated," but again, the big question is: Does it mean what Reformed doctrine says it does? We've already seen that the Reformed definition of "elect" is in trouble, because the Bible says that some angels are elect, as well as Jesus Himself, as well as the whole nation of Israel. Could it be that the Reformed definition of predestination is also skewed? Let's examine this.

Think grammatically about what the word "predestination" means. "Pre" means "beforehand," and "destination" means "where you are planning on going, or where you are intended to go." The big question here is this: Can anything interfere with you getting to your destination? In other words, does *every* person fulfill his destiny?

Free to Choose?

According to Reformed theology, *nothing* can interfere with us getting to our destination, and *everybody* fulfills his destiny, even if that is burning in hell forever. Thus predestination, according to Reformed doctrine, is basically the same as fate: unavoidable, unchangeable, inevitable, set in stone, beyond our control or influence, certain, doomed, bound, guaranteed. Is that a Scripturally sound definition?

Pan Am Flight 103

Here is an illustration: Have you ever heard of Pan American Airways Flight 103? It was a regularly scheduled transatlantic flight from Frankfurt, Germany to Detroit, Michigan with connections in London's Heathrow airport and New York City's JFK airport. So, not counting the stopovers, the source of the flight was Frankfurt and the destination was Detroit. However, on December 21st, 1988, a terrorist bomb that had been smuggled on board exploded, destroying the plane and killing all 243 passengers and 16 crew members. In addition, debris from the plane fell on the little town of Lockerbie, Scotland, killing 11 more people on the ground.

So here's where the story becomes relevant: What was the destination of Flight 103? They were *destined* for Detroit. And when did the pilots, air-traffic controllers, and/or airline execs decide that they should head for Detroit? After they were in the air? Of course not; Flight 103 was *pre-destined* to go to Detroit. That was the intent, that was the goal, that was the expectation, and that destination was decided long before the plane took off. However, something happened that derailed the original, intended destination: the terrorist bomb.

Could it be that a similar situation exists with the Biblical concept of predestination? Could it be that we're all predestined to go to heaven, but that something—our unrepentant rejection of God—could derail that original intention? Interesting thought, but is there Scriptural support for it?

We'll investigate that question in the following sections, but just for clarification, the phrase "the *Reformed* idea of predestination," or "the *Calvinistic* idea of predestination" would refer to the idea of blessing or cursing being fated, certain, bound, guaranteed, and inevitable, because of God's unchangeable decisions made in eternity past. And the phrase (for lack of a better term) "the *Arminian* idea of predestination" would refer to the idea of things being created with the intent, goal, and encouragement of blessing, but our unrepentant rebellion against God can derail the blessing and change it to cursing.

Foreknowledge and Predestination

Another concept that is often put together with predestination is that of foreknowledge; i.e., "to know something beforehand." It comes from the Greek word προγινώσκω (*proginosko*, G4267), whose definition is "to know beforehand, i.e., foresee: — foreknow." This word comes from προ (*pro*, G4253), which means "before, in front of, prior," as the prefix indicating the timeframe, and then the same word we saw in the Gnosticism section, γινώσκω (*ginosko*, G1097), whose definition includes "allow, be aware (of), feel, (have) know(-ledge), perceive," and as we saw in the chapter on Total Depravity, is the word from which we get the words "Gnosticism" (which was a heretical cult back in Jesus' day, as well as nowadays) and "Gnostic" (which is a member of this cult).

The above excursion into the Greek is enlightening, but actually not necessary to realize the import of the following verse:

Romans 8:29: For **whom he did foreknow, he also did predestinate** to be conformed to the image of his Son, that he might be the firstborn among many brethren.

This phrase about God "foreknowing" us could be interpreted three different ways:

1. Those of whom God was aware before they were created;
2. Those whom God knew would voluntarily choose Him;
3. Those whom God would choose to be elect/saved in the Calvinistic sense, and therefore would be His children.

All too often, we assume interpretation #3 above, as if that interpretation is a foregone conclusion. But actually, the text itself doesn't support that interpretation; we have to *impose* it on the text. And once we do, of course it "supports" the Calvinistic interpretation. In other words, we can prove it's true if we first assume it's true.

Let's look at the verse in another translation:

AMP: For those whom He foreknew [**of whom He was aware** and loved beforehand], He also destined from the beginning [foreordaining them] to be molded into the image of His Son [and share inwardly His likeness], that He might become the firstborn among many brethren.

The question that immediately rises is this: "Of all the people God created, of how many of them was He aware?" Clearly, all of them. He was aware of us and loved us before He created us, regardless of whether we would ultimately choose to serve Him or not. So this supports interpretation #1 above.

Now let's look at another translation:

> BBE: Because **those of whom he had knowledge** before they came into existence, were marked out by him to be made like his Son, so that he might be the first among a band of brothers. . .

Again, this is referring to the people that God had knowledge of before they came into existence. How many is that? Clearly, all of us.

But could this verse be referring to those whom God was aware would ultimately choose to serve Him? Yes, unless this is one of those topics in which God chooses to limit His omniscience (which He apparently does surprisingly often; see the "Limited Omniscience" section for more detail on this topic).

> NLV: **God knew from the beginning who would put their trust in Him.** So He chose them and made them to be like His Son. Christ was first and all those who belong to God are His brothers.

> TLB: For from the very beginning God decided that **those who came to him—and all along he knew who would**—should become like his Son, so that his Son would be the First, with many brothers.

Interpretation #2 is supported by these translations, as you can see. But even in this case, the verses show people voluntarily "putting their trust in Him" and "coming to Him," not God irresistibly capturing people. And, based on the people's actions, God's actions followed suit. Again, based on so many Scriptures we've already seen, and more to come, Interpretation #3 above requires us to impose a presupposition on the text in order to make it support Unconditional Election.

Now let's analyze what it says in more detail: "whom he did foreknow, he also did predestinate to be conformed to the image of his Son." That means that *every* person God foreknew, He predestinated to be part of the elect. Which means *every* person is part of the elect. This is indisputable, if being conformed to the image of God's Son means the same as being part of the elect. Of course, the Reformed doctrine of Limited Atonement objects strenuously to the conclusion that *all* people are elect.

However, what's the alternative? If all people are not elect, in the Reformed sense, that means that God didn't foreknow them. And let's consider the definition of *ginosko*. It *can* indicate an intimate, personal, loving knowledge like the Hebrew word *yada*, as in when Adam "knew" Eve and she bore a son; it does, for example, in Matthew 1:25, where Joseph did not "know" Mary until after Jesus was born. But the definition doesn't *necessarily* imply that. In fact, almost every other usage of a form of *ginosko* in the New Testament implies simply an intellectual knowledge—a mere recognition, realization, or awareness.

So in the lion's share of the cases, *ginosko* carries little if any of the intimacy of *yada;* again, it just means to be aware of, to have knowledge of, or perceive. But if this is the case (and it certainly seems to be), the question arises: Could God have created the "unelect" without being aware of that fact? Or without being aware of them as creations? Of course, the Reformed understanding of God's sovereignty objects strenuously to this conclusion also.

Let's look at the above Scripture again, but this time out of the Amplified version:

> Romans 8:29 (AMP): For **those whom He foreknew** [of whom He was aware and loved beforehand], **He also destined from the beginning** [foreordaining them] **to be molded into the image of His Son** [and **share inwardly His likeness**], that He might become the firstborn among many brethren.

So again I ask: Of all the people that God created, what percentage of them was He aware of? Clearly, *all of them*. And of all the people that God created, what percentage of them did He love? Again, *all of them*. Therefore, He destined them—He foreordained them—to be molded into the image of His Son and share His inward likeness. How could anyone be molded into the image of Jesus and be inwardly like Him without being saved? Sounds to me like God wants everyone to be saved...

The Reformed doctrines, therefore, simply because of this one verse, are between the proverbial rock and the hard place. The verse says that *everyone* He foreknew, He also predestined to conform to the image of Jesus. So either everyone was predestined to inevitably be saved, or God created the "unelect" without realizing it. Reformed theology disallows both of these options, although logic dictates that one or the other must be true.

The resolution to this "problem" is something else that Reformed theology objects to: that to be "predestined" is not to be inevitably, certainly, unchangeably fated, but rather that when God made us, His *goal* and *intention* was that we would all be conformed to the image of His Son, as discussed above in the section about Pan Am Flight 103 being destined for Detroit. But, of course, our own rebellion can be the terrorist bomb and can derail His intended blessings for us. Therefore, *our* participation in the two-party Covenant is required: we need to obey Him when He says "Seek My face" (Psalm 27:8).

The Amplified translation of Romans 8:29 shown above is easier to understand than the KJV, but the Message translation makes it clearer yet:

> Romans 8:29 (MSG): God knew what he was doing from the very beginning. **He decided from the outset to shape the lives of those who love him along the same lines as the life of his Son.** The Son stands first in the line of humanity he restored. **We see the original and intended shape of our lives there in him.**

Note how predestination is explained in the verse above: God does not unchangeably decide that certain people (the "elect") will be saved, and other people (the "unelect") will be doomed. Rather, God *did* unchangeably decide that whoever freely chose Him will be saved, and whoever freely rejected Him will be doomed. There is a world of difference. . .

We can see from the above Scriptures that salvation—being one of God's people—is a two-party covenant that both parties must voluntarily enter into, and the actions of one party can (and usually does) greatly influence the actions of the other party.

This is illustrated in the Old Testament by God's covenant with Solomon, where God says to Solomon in his dream:

> II Chronicles 7:14 (CEV): **If my own people will** humbly pray and turn back to me and stop sinning, **then I will** answer them from heaven. I will forgive them and make their land fertile once again.

Every covenant between God and man includes certain conditions that must be met by the participants in order to ratify, validate, or put into effect, that covenant. But the thing that is most germane to our current context is not those conditions, but the clear indication that both parties must voluntarily choose to engage in that covenant.

Stripping out the conditions from the above verse—which are hugely important but can distract us from noticing the point I'm trying to make right here—what remains is this: "if my people will. . . then I will. . ."

Note again that God's actions are dependant on our actions. So yes, two-party covenants require participation by both parties. And notice also that it must be voluntary participation: if one party were overpowered or coerced by the other, it would no longer be a two-party covenant; it would be a conquest.

Does Foreknowledge Imply Predestination?

Here's another question that is very relevant to the topic of this book. Some people say that since God foreknows things, that very foreknowledge unavoidably *causes* the thing that was foreknown. In other words, God can't foreknow something without it coming to pass.

However, that belief is not Scriptural. God *can* foreknow something without that foreknowledge forcing the event to come to pass, as we'll see in the following passage in I Samuel. In this story, David and his men are in a town called Keilah, and Saul wants to go there and capture him:

> I Samuel 23:7–13 (NIV): Saul was told that David had gone to Keilah, and he said, "God has handed him over to me, for David has imprisoned himself by entering a town with gates and bars." ⁸And Saul called up all his forces for battle, to go down to Keilah to besiege David and his men. ⁹When David learned that Saul was plotting against him, he said to Abiathar the priest, "Bring the ephod." ¹⁰David said, "O LORD, God of Israel, your servant has heard definitely that Saul plans to come to Keilah and destroy the town on account of me. ¹¹Will the citizens of Keilah surrender me to him? **Will Saul come down, as your servant has heard?** O LORD, God of Israel, tell your servant." **And the LORD said, "He will."** ¹²Again **David asked, "Will the citizens of Keilah surrender me and my men to Saul?" And the LORD said, "They will."** ¹³**So David** and his men, about six hundred in number, **left Keilah** and kept moving from place to place. When **Saul** was told that David had escaped from Keilah, he **did not go there.**

Did you see that? When David asked God if Saul would come to Keilah, the LORD said, "He will." *But Saul didn't.* And when David asked God if the men of Keilah would turn him over to Saul, the LORD said, "They will." *But they didn't.* What is going on? Was God wrong? Is God a false prophet? Of course not.

Given the situation as it was when David asked his questions, the LORD's foreknowledge and the resulting answers were completely correct and accurate. So why didn't things turn out the way God said they would? *Because David used his free will to choose to leave Keilah.* Therefore, the situation changed, and the answers that were applicable to the situation *before* David left were no longer applicable to the situation *after* David left. But God's answers were not wrong when He gave them, because He was answering based on the current circumstances.

Note that this series of events could not have happened if free will had not been a real thing. The fact that these events *did* happen forces us to acknowledge that free will is a reality.

And notice the domino effect: Because David chose to leave Keilah, Saul did not go there (but he would have otherwise). And because Saul did not go there, the men of Keilah did not turn David over to him (which they would have otherwise). This realization that God's foreknowledge does *not* imply predestination (in the Calvinistic sense of fated inevitability) has enormous implications for those who are considering the Reformed doctrines.

Secondary Destinations

We saw above that it sure looks like God predestined everyone to be conformed to the image of His Son. But obviously, that destination can be aborted by our rebellion to God, our refusal to repent of our sins and thereby take advantage of the forgiveness He offers us.

But if someone does indeed abort his predestined port of call by rebelling against God until physical death, he must end up *somewhere*. And as we saw in "Do All People Get Saved?" above, he ends up getting his heart's desire: existence without God, otherwise known as hell. After all, there are only two options. But our choices affect our lives both on earth *before* physical death, as well as our lives in eternity *after* physical death:

> Isaiah 65:12 (AMP): **I will destine you** [says the LORD] **for the sword,** and you shall all bow down to the slaughter, **because when I called, you did not answer; when I spoke, you did not listen or obey.** But you did what was evil in My eyes, and **you chose that in which I did not delight.**
>
> MSG: Well, you asked for it. Fate it will be: **your destiny, Death.** For **when I invited you, you ignored me; when I spoke to you, you brushed me off.** You did the very things I exposed as evil; **you chose what I hate.**
>
> NIV: **I will destine you for the sword,** and you will all bend down for the slaughter; for **I called but you did not answer, I spoke but you did not listen.** You did evil in my sight and **chose what displeases me.**
>
> TLB: . . .therefore **I will "destine" you to the sword,** and your "fate" shall be a dark one; for **when I called, you didn't answer; when I spoke, you wouldn't listen.** You deliberately sinned before my very eyes, **choosing to do what you know I despise.**

Note that God's people were not originally destined for judgment, but they became destined for judgment *only after they rebelled against God.* He called but they did not answer; He spoke but they did not listen. They intentionally elected to do evil (knowing good and well that it was evil) rather than what God had called them to do. And as a result of that, their destiny changed from blessing to judgment. *Their destiny was determined by how they responded to God's invitation.* They were pre-destined for blessing, but their rebellion against God changed their destiny and destination. Let us resolve to not follow in their footsteps.

Does "Ordain" Imply Inevitability?

According to Reformed theology, if something was "ordained" by God, it carries the same weight and implications as predestination does: inevitability, certainty, fatedness. Is that reasonable, Scripturally speaking? Let's investigate.

For example:

Romans 9:23: And that he might make known the riches of his glory on the vessels of mercy, which he had **afore prepared** unto glory. . .

Ignoring for the moment that the context of Romans 9–11 is how God has not rejected the Jews, this verse is often used in support of Reformed theology, as in, "God prepares, or ordains, certain vessels unto glory. Those are the elect." The Greek word translated "prepared" in the KJV is προετοιμάζω (*proetoimazo*, G4309), and it can indeed be translated "ordained." Its definition in Strong's Concordance includes "to fit up in advance," "ordain before," and "prepare before." It sounds like pretty solid evidence for predestination.

At least, until we see this verse:

Ephesians 2:10: For we are his workmanship, created in Christ Jesus unto good works, which God hath **before ordained** that we should walk in them.

Here, using the same Greek word, God ordains that we walk in the good works that He has ordained for us to walk in. Now here is the problem: If *proetoimazo* indeed implies inevitability, certainty, and fatedness, that means that every Christian who has ever lived has obeyed God in *every* good work laid out for him to do, and that there was no other possibility, since God had ordained them.

Does anyone really want to claim that such a statement is true? Can anyone say, with a straight face, that he has *never* missed *any* good work that God wanted him to do? I'm not talking only about deliberate disobedience here (i.e., sin), but also honest-hearted mistakes, brought about by immaturity, the learning process, lack of knowledge, hesitation, and the like.

Since no one can truthfully claim to have never missed even *one* of the works that God has ordained for him, we can plainly see that just because something was ordained by God *does not* guarantee its completion, when people are involved. Again, this is not because God lacks the raw power to enforce it, but because He wants a loving, intimate relationship with us, and such a relationship, by its very nature, *must be voluntary*.

So we are driven to acknowledge that God simply having *ordained* these works for us to accomplish, does *not* guarantee their being done. Why? Because our obedience is another essential ingredient. If God ordains some good work for me to do, but I choose not to obey Him, the work doesn't get done. At least, it doesn't get done *by me;* God may then ordain someone else, more obedient than I, to do it if I disobey. But if I disobey, it is to my own detriment.

God foreordains some *events* in a cast-in-concrete way; for example, Christ's atoning work on the cross was one of God's must-do items. But He did not foreordain *which* humans were to be involved with Jesus' earthly ministry or *how* they were to be involved; that depended on who was willing to follow Him. This idea also shows up in the book of Esther, where Mordecai tells his cousin, Queen Esther, the following:

> Esther 4:14 (WEB): For **if you altogether hold your peace at this time, then will relief and deliverance arise to the Jews from another place,** but you and your father's house will perish: and who knows whether you haven't come to the kingdom for such a time as this?

Note that although God chose to use Queen Esther to deliver the Jews from the evil machinations of Haman, it's not like the whole plan of Redemption would have fallen apart, had Esther refused to participate. God is infinitely resourceful, and though He wants to bless us by using us for His purposes, if we refuse, His ultimate goals will not be derailed. The preservation of the Jews was on God's must-do list, and Esther was invited to participate. But was she *forced* to participate? No; she (wisely) chose to cooperate with God's plan.

Another example of God predestining events, but not the particular people involved, comes from Jesus' disciples. On the one hand, Jesus says:

> Luke 22:22 (WEYMTH): For indeed the Son of Man goes on His way—His pre-destined way; yet **alas for that man who is betraying Him!**

But Jesus also says, to *all twelve* of the disciples:

> Luke 22:28–30 (WEYMTH): You however have remained with me amid my trials; ²⁹and **I covenant to give you,** as my Father has covenanted to give me, **a Kingdom—** ³⁰**so that you shall eat and drink at my table in my Kingdom, and sit on thrones as judges over the twelve tribes of Israel.**

Note that Judas' turning against Jesus, failure to repent, and subsequent eternal damnation was *not* cast in concrete; if it had been, Jesus' offer to Judas (to receive a kingdom, eat and drink at the Lord's table, sit on a throne, and judge one of the tribes of Israel) would have been fraudulent. If Judas was doomed to perdition since eternity past, Jesus' covenant offer to him would have been a lie. For much more thorough coverage of this topic, see "The Problem of Judas Iscariot," below.

Our Obedience Is Important

Continuing the previous thought—that of our choosing to obey God being really important—let's look at some Scriptures that back up that claim. This is sometimes necessary, when people believe either of the two following ideas:

- God's will cannot be thwarted, because it is impossible to disobey Him.
- Obeying God is just legalism left over from the Old Testament, which we are no longer under.

The first idea above, that of it allegedly being impossible to disobey God, has been so completely overthrown by the hundreds of Scriptures earlier in this book, and even more hereafter, that there is no need to cover it again here. But the second idea, that obeying God is no longer necessary because "we're under grace now," is actually believed by some modern-day Christians. So let's deal with that belief by seeing what the Bible says on the topic.

First, let's look at the parable of building your house on the sand vs. the rock (Matthew 7:21–27 and Luke 6:46–49):

> Matthew 7:21, 24–27 (NIV): "Not everyone who says to me, 'Lord, Lord,' will enter the kingdom of heaven, but **only he who *does* the will of my Father** who is in heaven. ²⁴Therefore everyone who hears these words of mine **and puts them into practice** is like a wise man who built his house on the rock. ²⁵The rain came down, the streams rose, and the winds blew and beat against that house; yet **it did not fall,** because it had its foundation on the rock. ²⁶But everyone who hears these words

of mine **and does not put them into practice** is like a foolish man who built his house on sand. ²⁷The rain came down, the streams rose, and the winds blew and beat against that house, and **it fell with a great crash.**"

(To hear this passage set to music, listen to the song *Hear and Do* on the album *I Have Not Forgotten You* or scan the QR code at right.)

So Jesus likens the ones who build their houses on the sand to those who hear but *do not do* what He says. Conversely, the ones who build their houses on the rock (the better alternative) are the ones who hear His sayings *and do them*. That parable in itself should be enough to convince us that obedience to God is still important, even though we're under grace.

Second, and especially noteworthy, is how Jesus introduces the parable in Luke's account:

Luke 6:46 (NIV): Why do you call me, 'Lord, Lord,' **and do not do what I say?**

The message here is clearly that He is not your Lord if you disobey Him. Is He blunt, or is He blunt?

Third, note what Jesus said during the Last Supper, about our obeying His commandments:

John 13:17 (AMP): If you know these things, **blessed and happy and to be envied are you if you practice them** [if you act accordingly and really do them].

But there are some people who, when they encounter commands from Jesus (as in the three passages above) that they aren't really excited about obeying, dismiss them by saying things like, "Oh, we don't have to obey that statement. That was technically the *Old* Testament, because Jesus hadn't been crucified and resurrected yet." (Yes, I have heard that one too.) As if Jesus' commands can be casually disregarded with impunity!

Remember what Jesus said to the rich young ruler?

Matthew 19:16–23 (NLT): Someone came to Jesus with this question: "Teacher, what good deed must I do to have eternal life?" ¹⁷"Why ask me about what is good?" Jesus replied. "There is only One who is good. But to answer your question—**if you want to receive eternal life, keep the commandments.**"

Did Jesus really say that? That sounds like salvation by works, doesn't it? Not really. "Faith" implies "faithfulness"—hearing God and obeying Him (Exodus 19:5–6, Jeremiah 7:23, 11:4, Micah 6:8, etc.)—and faith without works is dead (James 2:20). Continuing on:

> [18]"Which ones?" the man asked. And Jesus replied: "'You must not murder. You must not commit adultery. You must not steal. You must not testify falsely. [19]Honor your father and mother. Love your neighbor as yourself.'" [20]"I've obeyed all these commandments," the young man replied. "What else must I do?" [21]Jesus told him, "If you want to be perfect, go and sell all your possessions and give the money to the poor, and you will have treasure in heaven. Then come, follow me." [22]But when the young man heard this, he went away sad, for he had many possessions. [23]Then Jesus said to his disciples, "I tell you the truth, it is very hard for a rich person to enter the Kingdom of Heaven."

So here, Jesus delivers the punchline. He saw that the man worshipped his possessions, so here He points that out. Have you ever wondered why Jesus listed the Commandments in the order He did? Why didn't He list the First Commandment first? (The First Commandment is "You shall have no other gods before me.")

So again, why didn't Jesus list the First Commandment first? Because it drove the point home much more forcefully by saying it last. When Jesus told him to sell all he had and give the money to the poor, He pointed out in no uncertain terms that the man did indeed have another god ahead of YHWH: his possessions.

But back to the main point: Keeping the commandments is supremely important, and keeping the commandments includes loving God first and foremost. If you love God, you already believe He is real, and if you love Him, *of course* you'll obey Him. So in that sense, yes, it is salvation by works (John 6:28–29, James 2:21–22).

Many people comfort themselves with the following verse (and very rightly so):

> John 15:15 (NASB): No longer do I call you slaves, for the slave does not know what his master is doing; but **I have called you friends, for all things that I have heard from My Father I have made known to you.**

But we must beware of thinking that it's not a problem to disobey God simply because "we are his friends." As a case in point, do you know what the verse is right before the one quoted above? In other words, Jesus' statement made immediately prior to v. 15 above? It is this:

John 15:14 (NASB): You are My friends **if you do what I command you.**

In order to get an accurate understanding of what Jesus was saying, these two verses must be read and considered *together*, not separately.

What does the Bible—*after* the Resurrection—have to say on this topic?

I Timothy 6:3–4a (GWORD): **Whoever** teaches false doctrine and **doesn't agree with the accurate words of our Lord Jesus Christ** and godly teachings ⁴is a conceited person. He shows that he **doesn't understand anything.**

MSG: **If you have leaders** there who teach otherwise, **who refuse the solid words of our Master Jesus** and this godly instruction, ⁴**tag them for what they are: ignorant windbags** who infect the air with germs of envy, controversy, bad-mouthing. . .

II John 9 (NASB): **Anyone who** goes too far and **does not abide in the teaching of Christ,** *does not have God;* the one who abides in the teaching, he has both the Father and the Son.

AMP: **Anyone who** runs on ahead [of God] and **does not abide in the doctrine of Christ** [who is not content with what He taught] *does not have God;* but he who continues to live in the doctrine (teaching) of Christ [does have God], he has both the Father and the Son.

Those passages speak for themselves.

Fourth, Jesus' half-brother James adds:

James 1:22–25 (NLT): But **don't just listen to God's word. You must do what it says.** Otherwise, you are only fooling yourselves. ²³**For if you listen to the word and don't obey,** it is like glancing at your face in a mirror. ²⁴You see yourself, walk away, and forget what you look like. ²⁵But if you look carefully into the perfect law that sets you free, and **if you do what it says** and don't forget what you heard, **then God will bless you for doing it.**

But there are people (I have heard some of them) who will need more proof than that. So, here is more:

Matthew 6:9–10 (NKJV): In this manner, therefore, **pray:** Our Father in heaven, hallowed be Your name. ¹⁰Your kingdom come. **Your will be done on earth as it is in heaven.**

Luke 11:27–28 (NIV): As Jesus was saying these things, a woman in the crowd called out, "Blessed is the mother who gave you birth and nursed you." ²⁸He replied, **"Blessed rather are those who hear the word of God and obey it."**

John 8:51: Verily, verily, I say unto you, If a man **keep my saying,** he shall never see death.

John 15:10: If ye **keep my commandments,** ye shall abide in my love; even as I have kept my Father's commandments, and abide in his love.

Acts 10:35: But in every nation he that feareth him, and **worketh righteousness,** is accepted with him.

I Corinthians 7:19: Circumcision is nothing, and uncircumcision is nothing, but **the keeping of the commandments** of God.

> AMP: For circumcision is nothing and counts for nothing, neither does uncircumcision, but **[what counts is] keeping the commandments** of God.
>
> BBE: Circumcision is nothing, and its opposite is nothing, but **only doing the orders of God is of value.**
>
> NIV: Circumcision is nothing and uncircumcision is nothing. **Keeping God's commands is what counts.**
>
> TEV: For whether or not a man is circumcised means nothing; **what matters is to obey God's commandments.**

Ephesians 4:27 (CEB): **Don't provide an opportunity for the devil.**

Ephesians 6:13 (NET): For this reason, take up the full armor of God **so that you may be able to stand your ground** on the evil day, and having done everything, **to stand.**

James 4:7 (WEB): Be subject therefore to God. But **resist the devil, and he will flee from you.**

I Peter 5:8 (TEV): **Be alert, be on watch!** Your enemy, the Devil, roams around like a roaring lion, **looking for someone to devour.**

I John 3:8 (NIV): He who does what is sinful is of the devil, because **the devil has been sinning from the beginning.** The reason the Son of God appeared was to destroy the devil's work.

I John 5:2–3: By this we know that we love the children of God, when we love God, and **keep his commandments.** ³For this is the love of God, that **we keep his commandments:** and his commandments are not grievous.

BBE: In this way, we are certain that we have love for the children of God, when we have love for God and **keep his laws**. ³For **loving God is keeping his laws:** and his laws are not hard.

The passages above show us two things. First, that it is important to obey God, even in the New Testament; obedience is not simply leftover legalism from the Old Testament. And second, that we have a choice of whether or not to obey God, and there will be consequences either way—desirable or undesirable, depending on what we choose.

So we can plainly see that our obedience to God's commands is also an essential ingredient to our walking in the good works, and they don't get done simply because God "ordained" them. And because that same word προετοιμάζω (*proetoimazo*, G4309) is used to describe how God "prepared" or "ordained" people to glory, we can likewise conclude that we need to cooperate with Him—receive what He's offering and obey Him—in order for it to do us any good. For us to pick and choose when we want the word to mean "inevitable" and when we *don't* want it to mean "inevitable" is disingenuous, to say the least. We need to adjust our thinking to what the Bible says, not vice versa.

The Lamb's Book of Life

A concept that is mentioned several times throughout Scripture is that of the Lamb's Book of Life, sometimes called the Book of the Living. In a nutshell, it is a book that contains the names of everyone who will spend eternity in heaven, as these Scriptures show:

Daniel 12:1 (NIV): At that time Michael, the great prince who protects your people, will arise. There will be a time of distress such as has not happened from the beginning of nations until then. But at that time **your people—everyone whose name is found written in the book—** will be delivered.

Malachi 3:16 (AMP): Then those who feared the Lord talked often one to another; and the Lord listened and heard it, and **a book of remembrance was written before Him of those who reverenced and worshipfully feared the Lord** and who thought on His name.

Luke 10:20 (PHILLIPS): Yet it is not your power over evil spirits which should give such joy, but the fact that **your names are written in Heaven.**

Philippians 4:3 (NLT): And I ask you, my true partner, to help these two women, for they worked hard with me in telling others the Good News.

They worked along with Clement and the rest of my co-workers, **whose names are written in the Book of Life.**

Hebrews 12:23 (TEV): You have come to the joyful gathering of God's first-born, **whose names are written in heaven.** You have come to God, who is the judge of all people, and to the spirits of good people made perfect.

Revelation 13:8 (AMP): And all the inhabitants of the earth will fall down in adoration and pay him homage, everyone whose name has not been **recorded in the Book of Life** of the Lamb that was slain [in sacrifice] from the foundation of the world.[4]

Revelation 20:12 (GWORD): I saw the dead, both important and unimportant people, standing in front of the throne. Books were opened, including **the Book of Life.** The dead were judged on the basis of what they had done, as recorded in the books.

Revelation 20:15 (NIV): If anyone's name was not found written in **the book of life,** he was thrown into the lake of fire.

Revelation 21:27 (NASB): . . .and nothing unclean and no one who practices abomination and lying, shall ever come into it [the city of God, the New Jerusalem], but only those whose names are written in the **Lamb's book of life.**

But one very interesting thing on this topic is that in several places, the Bible talks about some people's names being *removed* from the Book of Life. Let's look at what the Bible says about it:

Exodus 32:32–33 (AMP): Yet now, if You will forgive their sin—and if not, **blot me, I pray You, out of Your book** which You have written! ³³But the Lord said to Moses, **Whoever has sinned against Me, I will blot him [not you] out of My book.**

Psalm 69:28: **Let them be blotted out of the book of the living;** and with the just let them not be written.

Revelation 3:5: He that overcometh, the same shall be clothed in white raiment; and **I will not blot out his name out of the book of life,** but I will confess his name before my Father, and before his angels.

---

[4] By the way, the phrase "from the foundation of the world" modifies "the Lamb who was slain" in the Greek; it does *not* modify "names written in the book of life," as the NASB and some other translations render it. The rendering in the NASB is a huge change in meaning from the original Greek, and such an unjustified change has been described as "a deliberate alteration of the translated text to match a prior theological position." See *Spiritual Restoration, Volume 1,* by Skip Moen, Ph.D., p. 82, for more details.

Revelation 22:19: And if any man shall take away from the words of the book of this prophecy, **God shall take away his part out of the book of life,** and out of the holy city, and from the things which are written in this book.

Here's the point: If God had unalterably chosen every person's eternal landing point in eternity past, *why are some people removed from the Lamb's Book of Life?* After all, they couldn't be removed unless they were in there to begin with. Could it be that God *predestined* everyone to go to heaven—that was his *intention*—and only if we reject and rebel against God without ultimately repenting before we die, are we blotted out? Such unrepentant rebellion against God would act like the terrorist bomb that prevented Flight 103 from reaching its intended destination of Detroit—the unrepentant rebellion would prevent us from reaching our intended destination of heaven.

Is such a scenario reasonable, Scripturally speaking? Actually, it fits God's character much better than does Unconditional Election. Here's why I say that: One of God's most notable attributes is that He is a loving God; anyone who puts any credibility at all in the Bible would acknowledge that this is indisputable. Here is just a smattering of passages that clearly show this:

John 3:16: For **God so loved the world,** that he gave his only begotten Son, that whosoever believeth in him should not perish, but have everlasting life.

Romans 5:8 (NIV): But **God demonstrates his own love for us** in this: While we were still sinners, Christ died for us.

Romans 8:38–39 (NIV): For I am convinced that neither death nor life, neither angels nor demons, neither the present nor the future, nor any powers, ³⁹neither height nor depth, nor anything else in all creation, will be able to separate us from **the love of God** that is in Christ Jesus our Lord.

II Corinthians 13:11: Finally, brethren, farewell. Be perfect, be of good comfort, be of one mind, live in peace; and **the God of love** and peace shall be with you.

Galatians 2:20: I am crucified with Christ: nevertheless I live; yet not I, but Christ liveth in me: and the life which I now live in the flesh I live by the faith of **the Son of God, who loved me,** and gave himself for me.

Ephesians 2:4–5 (NASB): But God, being rich in mercy, because of **His great love with which He loved us,** ⁵even when we were dead in our transgressions, made us alive together with Christ (by grace you have been saved)...

Ephesians 3:19 (NLT): May you experience the **love of Christ,** though it is too great to understand fully. Then you will be made complete with all the fullness of life and power that comes from God.

I John 4:8 (NIV): Whoever does not love does not know God, because **God is love.**

So now let's look at a part of the Love Chapter, I Corinthians 13, because of its detailed descriptions of how Love behaves:

I Corinthians 13:7 (AMP): Love bears up under anything and everything that comes, **is ever ready to believe the best of every person,** its hopes are fadeless under all circumstances, and it endures everything [without weakening].

> TLB: If you love someone, you will be loyal to him no matter what the cost. **You will always believe in him, always expect the best of him,** and always stand your ground in defending him.

> MSG: Puts up with anything, trusts God always, **always looks for the best,** never looks back, but keeps going to the end.

> NLT: Love never gives up, **never loses faith, is always hopeful,** and endures through every circumstance.

So if Love—the word that best describes God's nature and essence—is "ever ready to believe the best of every person," doesn't it make sense that He would initially plan for us to end up in a good place, rather than a place of torment?

Then, if God is love (and He is), and love believes the best about everyone (and it does), it sounds like God's initial intention for everyone would be for them to choose wisely and therefore end up in heaven with Him. And that is what it sounds like David is saying here:

Psalm 139:16 (AMP): Your eyes saw my unformed substance, and **in Your book all the days [of my life] were written before ever they took shape, when as yet there was none of them.**

> NIV: ...your eyes saw my unformed body. **All the days ordained for me were written in your book before one of them came to be.**

> NLT: You saw me before I was born. **Every day of my life was recorded in your book. Every moment was laid out before a single day had passed.**

Notice that David was written in God's book before he was even born! And remember, God is not a respecter of persons. That sure makes it sound like it is God's intent that *everyone* end up in heaven with Him, and only unrepentant rebellion will derail that plan for any given person, and cause God to blot his name out of the Book of Life.

That sounds good, but is it compatible with the idea of God being absolutely omniscient—of Him knowing every single thing that could ever be known? This is an excellent point because, as we saw earlier in this chapter, a concept that is often associated with predestination is that of *foreknowledge,* which is omniscience (infinite awareness) of things in the future. Let's look into that in a little more detail here. It's very reasonable to associate these two concepts, because of Scriptures like these:

> Romans 8:29: For **whom he did foreknow, he also did predestinate** to be conformed to the image of his Son, that he might be the firstborn among many brethren.
>
> I Peter 1:2: **Elect according to the foreknowledge** of God the Father, through sanctification of the Spirit, unto obedience and sprinkling of the blood of Jesus Christ: Grace unto you, and peace, be multiplied.

So what exactly is the nature of God's foreknowledge? We know it exists; those Scriptures shown above prove it. But they don't give a detailed description of what foreknowledge means, and there are different schools of thought on that topic. Because of Romans 8:29 (shown above), one idea that seems like an attempt to blend Reformed theology with the concept of free will, states that "God knew who would ultimately choose to believe in Him, and so he predestined only them to heaven." Almost as if, "Why waste the time and effort preparing a place for someone if you know he'll never show up?"

The Nature of God's Foreknowledge

The above question—about the nature of God's foreknowledge—arises sometimes because of Scriptures that could be interpreted to support Calvinism. They *could* be. The problem with such interpretations is, of course, that there are *hundreds* of other Scriptures (many of which we've already seen) that would have to be swept under the rug, because they unambiguously discredit one or more of the Reformed doctrines.

One example of such a Scripture that *could* be interpreted to support the Reformed doctrines is this one:

> I Peter 2:8 (NKJV): . . .and "a stone of stumbling and a rock of offense." **They stumble, being disobedient to the word, to which they also were appointed.**

"See?" someone might say, "it says right there they were *appointed* to be disobedient to the word and stumble! That means that they were *predestined* to! They were chosen to be unelect!" And this passage could indeed sound like it supports the Calvinistic idea of "elect" and "unelect." Then, upon further reflection, we realize that there are multiple things that the phrase "to which they were appointed" might refer, and which one we choose completely changes the meaning of the sentence.

So, as usual, let's look at some other translations of the Bible and see if they clarify the meaning of the sentence, or at least open our eyes to alternative interpretations:

> AMP: And, a Stone that will cause stumbling and a Rock that will give [men] offense; **they stumble because they disobey** and disbelieve [God's] Word, as **those [who reject Him] were destined (appointed) to do.**

Well, that makes a lot more sense, Scripturally speaking: Those who willfully reject God and disobey His Word are destined to stumble and fall because of that freewill rejection and disobedience. The law of sowing and reaping is plainly evident, because sure enough, rejecting the One who is able to *keep* them from stumbling (Jude 24), guarantees that they will stumble. And fall. Hard.

Let's look at another one:

> CSB: . . .and a stone to stumble over, and a rock to trip over. **They stumble because they disobey the word;** they were destined for this.

Same as before: those who disobey God's word are destined to stumble. *But they don't have to disobey God in the first place.* Let's look at a few more:

> ERV: For them he is also "a stone that makes people stumble, a rock that makes people fall." **People stumble because they don't obey** what God says. **This is what God planned to happen** *to those people.*

> EHV: . . .and, a stone over which they stumble and a rock over which they fall. **Because they continue to disobey the word, they stumble** over it. And **that is the** *consequence* **appointed** *for them.*

ICB: To people who do not believe, he is "a stone that causes people to stumble. It is a rock that makes them fall." *Isaiah 8:14* **They stumble because they do not obey what God says. This is what God planned to happen** *to them.*

PHILLIPS: And he is, to them, 'a stone of stumbling and a rock of offence'. Yes, **they stumble at the Word of God for in their hearts they are unwilling to obey it—which makes stumbling a foregone conclusion.**

LEB: . . .and "A stone of stumbling and a rock of offense," who stumble **because they disobey the word to which also they were consigned.**

TLB: And the Scriptures also say, "He is the Stone that some will stumble over, and the Rock that will make them fall." **They will stumble because they will not listen to God's Word nor obey it, and** *so this punishment must follow*—that they will fall.

MOUNCE: . . .and, "a stone that makes people stumble and a rock that makes them fall." **They stumble, as they were destined to do,** *since they do not obey* **the word.**

NLV: The Holy Writings say, also, "Christ is the Stone that some men will trip over and the Rock over which they will fall." **When they do not obey the Word of God, they trip over it. This is what happens** *to such men.*

So we can see that there are *three* different things that the phrase "to which they were appointed" could refer to:

- The people were appointed/predestined to disobey and stumble. This is the interpretation that is understood by adherents to the Reformed doctrines.

- The people who, by their free will, disobeyed God were appointed/predestined to reap the consequences: to stumble and fall. This is simply one example of the law of sowing and reaping (Galatians 6:7–8).

- The people were appointed/predestined to hear and obey God's Word (Jeremiah 7:23, Micah 6:8), but because they disobeyed, their disobedience was like the terrorist bomb on Flight 103, and they not only lost the predestined blessing, but they also unavoidably stumbled and fell (Jude 24).

So we can see that not only are other interpretations of I Peter 2:8 possible, but they are actually supported by numerous translation teams. Not only that, but non-Calvinistic interpretations, which include actual free will, are far more compatible with the rest of Scripture.

But that brings up yet another point: Is free will even *possible* if God knows the outcome from the beginning? Some people say that if He knows what "we" will choose, it's not really free choice, because it's already settled. Other people say that just because God *knows* what we will choose, that doesn't inherently *cause* us to choose that. Here again is a causality question: does A cause B, or does B cause A?

But is that even the right question? We could debate forever, but does the Bible address the nature of God's foreknowledge? Does it make statements from which we can reliably *infer* facts about God's foreknowledge? For example, we could go a long way toward answering the question in the previous paragraph if we could answer whether God does indeed know the future. Now at this point, some Christians will scoff and say, "Well, *of course* He knows the future! Any bonehead knows that!" And other Christians will say, "Do you have a Scripture for that?" So let's find out what the Bible has to say about the subject.

"Limited" Omniscience

It is likely that some of you readers of this book, when seeing the heading above, snorted with disdain at the absurdity of it. After all, since "omniscience" means "unlimited knowledge," "*limited* omniscience" would have to mean "limited unlimited knowledge," which is intrinsically self-contradictory. And that is true. So now that I have your attention, let me explain what I mean.

Few would dispute that God *could* know absolutely everything if He chose to: "For with God nothing shall be impossible" (Matthew 19:26, Genesis 18:14, Job 42:2, Jeremiah 32:17, 27, Matthew 28:18, Mark 14:36, Luke 1:37). But here's where the question pertains to the topic at hand: Could God, if He chose to, selectively *not* be aware of certain things? In other words, could he voluntarily limit His awareness in some areas? Of course: "For with God nothing shall be impossible" (Matthew 19:26, Genesis 18:14, Job 42:2, Jeremiah 32:17, 27, Matthew 28:18, Mark 14:36, Luke 1:37).

The answer to the question posed in the previous section—If God *knows* beforehand what our "free" choice will be, do we truly have a free choice?—is involved with the seemingly contradictory concept of limited omniscience.

Let's delve into the Word and see if there is any evidence for or against God voluntarily choosing to *not* know certain things.

Jesus Didn't Know Everything

We *do* know that it is possible for God to limit Himself; he did that in the incarnation, when Jesus became a man. Jesus wasn't *only* a man, of course—He was still no less a part of the Godhead than before the incarnation—but He limited Himself to a life where He had no access to the advantages of His "God-ness;" He lived simply as a man empowered by the Holy Spirit in the same way we can be.

> Philippians 2:5–8: Let this mind be in you, which was also in Christ Jesus: [6]Who, being in the form of God, **thought it not robbery to be equal with God:** [7]But **made himself of no reputation,** and took upon him the form of a servant, and was made in the likeness of men: [8]And being found in fashion as a man, **he humbled himself,** and became obedient unto death, even the death of the cross.

> AMP: Let this same attitude and purpose and [humble] mind be in you which was in Christ Jesus: [Let Him be your example in humility:] [6]Who, although **being essentially one with God and in the form of God** [possessing the fullness of the attributes which make God God], **did not think this equality with God was a thing to be eagerly grasped or retained,** [7]But **stripped Himself** [of all privileges and rightful dignity], so as to assume the guise of a servant (slave), in that He became like men and was born a human being. [8]And after He had appeared in human form, **He abased and humbled Himself [still further]** and carried His obedience to the extreme of death, even the death of the cross!

> BBE: Let this mind be in you which was in Christ Jesus, [6]To whom, **though himself in the form of God, it did not seem that to take for oneself was to be like God;** [7]But **he made himself as nothing,** taking the form of a servant, being made like men; [8]And being seen in form as a man, **he took the lowest place,** and let himself be put to death, even the death of the cross.

> GWORD: Have the same attitude that Christ Jesus had. [6]**Although he was in the form of God and equal with God, he did not take advantage of this equality.** [7]Instead, **he emptied himself** by taking on the form of a servant, by becoming like other humans, by having a human appearance. [8]**He humbled himself** by becoming obedient to the point of death, death on a cross.

ISV: Have the same attitude among yourselves that was also in the Messiah Jesus: [6]**In God's own form existed he, and shared with God equality, deemed nothing needed grasping.** [7]Instead, **poured out in emptiness**, a servant's form did he possess, a mortal man becoming. In human form he chose to be, [8]and lived in all humility, death on a cross obeying.

NLT: You must have the same attitude that Christ Jesus had. [6]**Though he was God, he did not think of equality with God as something to cling to.** [7]Instead, **he gave up his divine privileges;** he took the humble position of a slave and was born as a human being. When he appeared in human form, [8]he humbled himself in obedience to God and died a criminal's death on a cross.

TEV: The attitude you should have is the one that Christ Jesus had: [6]**He always had the nature of God, but he did not think that by force he should try to remain equal with God.** [7]**Instead of this, of his own free will he gave up all he had,** and took the nature of a servant. He became like a human being and appeared in human likeness. [8]He was humble and walked the path of obedience all the way to death— his death on the cross.

TLB: Your attitude should be the kind that was shown us by Jesus Christ, [6]who, **though he was God, did not demand and cling to his rights as God,** [7]but **laid aside his mighty power and glory**, taking the disguise of a slave and becoming like men. [8]And **he humbled himself even further,** going so far as actually to die a criminal's death on a cross.

WEYMTH: Let the same disposition be in you which was in Christ Jesus. [6]**Although from the beginning He had the nature of God He did not reckon His equality with God a treasure to be tightly grasped.** [7]Nay, **He stripped Himself of His glory**, and took on Him the nature of a bondservant by becoming a man like other men. [8]And being recognized as truly human, **He humbled Himself** and even stooped to die; yes, to die on a cross.

So we see from the Scriptures above that God the Son voluntarily set aside His power and abilities as God: He "emptied Himself," "humbled Himself," "stripped Himself of all privileges and rightful dignity," "gave up His divine privileges," "made Himself as nothing," "of His own free will He gave up all He had," "stripped Himself of His glory," "poured Himself out in emptiness," "laid aside His mighty power and glory," and "made Himself nothing." And this is confirmed in the Scriptures by the facts that Jesus got hungry (Luke 4:2), He thirsted (John 19:28), He got tired (Luke 8:23), He didn't know everything (Mark 13:32), He suffered pain (Luke 24:22), He was subject to injury (Matthew 27:26), and He was subject to death (Luke 23:46).

Did you notice that in the previous list, one of the manifestations of Jesus' "emptying Himself" was that He didn't know everything? He was talking about when the end of the age should come, and He said "No one knows about that day or hour, not even the angels in heaven, *nor the Son,* but only the Father." So it's very plausible that God could voluntarily choose to not know some things; after all, He's done it before.

This same fact of Jesus setting aside His omniscience while he was on earth is the reason He could be surprised at things. For example, when the Roman centurion came to Jesus on behalf of his sick servant, He was amazed at how much faith the centurion had:

> Matthew 8:10: When Jesus heard it, **he marvelled,** and said to them that followed, Verily I say unto you, I have not found so great faith, no, not in Israel.

> Luke 7:9: When Jesus heard these things, **he marvelled** at him, and turned him about, and said unto the people that followed him, I say unto you, I have not found so great faith, no, not in Israel.

In other translations, the Greek word θαυμάζω (*thaumazo,* G2296), translated "marvelled" in both verses above, was rendered in other translations of the Bible as "amazed," "impressed," "surprised," "wondered," "astonished," "taken aback," and "stunned." This pertains to our current discussion because if Jesus had been exercising absolute omniscience, why would He—or *how could* He—have been surprised, astonished, and stunned?

He was likewise pretty floored by the *unbelief* of other people:

> Mark 6:6: And he [Jesus] **marvelled** because of their unbelief. And he went round about the villages, teaching.

In the Greek, this is the same word *thaumazo* as above, and other English translations render it as "appalled," "amazed," "surprised," "wondered," "astonished," and "could hardly accept the fact." Again, such a response in Jesus would not, and *could* not have happened, had He been omnisciently aware since the beginning of eternity that they would react like this.

At this point, someone might say, "But that was *Jesus* who set aside his omniscience, not the Father!" Does that mean, then, that Jesus can do things that the Father can't? I think most Christians would not want to make that claim, nor should we, because the Father is greater than Jesus (John 14:28). So is there any evidence in the Bible for the idea that God might choose to not know certain things? Let's look.

Naming the Animals

Remember when God brought all the animals to Adam so he could name them? Let's note the exact wording here:

> Genesis 2:19 (AMP): So the Lord God formed out of the ground every animal of the field and every bird of the air, and brought them to Adam **to see what he would call them;** and whatever the man called a living creature, that was its name.

> ESV: Now out of the ground the Lord God had formed every beast of the field and every bird of the heavens and brought them to the man **to see what he would call them.** And whatever the man called every living creature, that was its name.

> NIV: Now the Lord God had formed out of the ground all the wild animals and all the birds in the sky. He brought them to the man **to see what he would name them;** and whatever the man called each living creature, that was its name.

> YLT: And Jehovah God formeth from the ground every beast of the field, and every fowl of the heavens, and bringeth in unto the man, **to see what he doth call it;** and whatever the man calleth a living creature, that [is] its name.

Note the bold phrase in the translations above; the various translations (and numerous others) are remarkably consistent in their wording of this phrase. If God were operating with absolute omniscience, why would He bring the animals to Adam "to see" what he would call them? With absolute omniscience, God would have known since eternity past what Adam would name the animals.

God's Response to Antediluvian Sin

Read these Scriptures, contemplate the questions that they raise, and decide for yourself:

> Genesis 6:6: And **it repented the Lord** that he had made man on the earth, and **it grieved him** at his heart.

> > CEB: **The Lord regretted** making human beings on the earth, and **he was heartbroken.**

> ERV: **The Lord was sorry** that he had made people on the earth. **It made him very sad in his heart.**
>
> EXB: **He was sorry** [regretted] he had made human beings on the earth, and **his heart was filled with pain.**
>
> NIV: **The Lord regretted** that he had made human beings on the earth, and **his heart was deeply troubled.**
>
> VOICE: At that point **God's heart broke**, and **He regretted having ever made man** in the first place.

The obvious question the above Scripture raises is this: If God knew for certain, from all eternity, that man would sin in the ways he did, why did God regret the decision to create man? Why was He sorry, heartbroken, and sad? It's not like their behavior was unexpected. Or was it?

If the Reformed doctrine of Total Depravity were true, humans would have been unable to behave otherwise unless God directly intervened. So again, why was He sorry, heartbroken, and sad that they were behaving poorly when He, by not "electing" them, was the One *preventing* them from behaving otherwise?

Abraham Sacrificing Isaac

Change of scene: Remember when God commanded Abraham to sacrifice his son Isaac? Isaac was the son of promise, the son of Abraham and Sarah in their old age. Abraham had already heard God say that through their son Isaac would come a nation of God's chosen people, so Abraham figured that if he had to sacrifice Isaac, God would raise him from the dead (Hebrews 11:17–19). So Abraham obeys, up to the point that he was about to plunge the knife into Isaac, when God stops him:

> Genesis 22:12 (AMP): And He said, Do not lay your hand on the lad or do anything to him; for **now I know** that you fear and revere God, since you have not held back from Me or begrudged giving Me your son, your only son.

Here it is again: God says, "*now* I know that you fear and revere God." The obvious question is, didn't God know before that? If He had chosen to exercise absolute omniscience, of course He would have. But this sounds like He had chosen to "discover" whether Abraham would be obedient or not.

I have heard Bible teachings where the teacher stated, "When God said, 'Now I know,' what He *really* meant was 'Now *you* know. . .'" That sounds pretty desperate—as if God got his pronouns mixed up? But if we allow the possibility that God can choose to *not* know certain things, as He did when Jesus walked the earth, it's perfectly reasonable.

Leaving Egypt

After the Exodus from Egypt, God led the Israelites *around* the land of the Philistines; not *through* it. Why?

> Exodus 13:17: And it came to pass, when Pharaoh had let the people go, that God led them not through the way of the land of the Philistines, although that was near; for God said, **Lest peradventure** the people repent when they see war, and they return to Egypt. . .
>
> CJB: After Pharaoh had let the people go, God did not guide them to the highway that goes through the land of the P'lishtim, because it was close by—God thought that **the people**, upon seeing war, **might change their minds** and return to Egypt.
>
> CEV: After the king had finally let the people go, the Lord did not lead them through Philistine territory, though that was the shortest way. God had said, "**If** they are attacked, **they may decide** to return to Egypt."
>
> NABRE: Now, when Pharaoh let the people go, God did not lead them by way of the Philistines' land, though this was the nearest; for God said: **If** the people see that they have to fight, **they might change their minds** and return to Egypt.
>
> NIRV: Pharaoh let the people go. The shortest road from Goshen to Canaan went through the Philistine country. But God didn't lead them that way. God said, "**If** they have to go into battle, **they might** change their minds. **They might** return to Egypt."
>
> WEB: When Pharaoh had let the people go, God didn't lead them by the way of the land of the Philistines, although that was near; for God said, "Lest **perhaps** the people change their minds when they see war, and they return to Egypt. . ."

Now that's strange. God avoids leading the Israelites through the land of the Philistines because "if" they have to fight, they "*may* change their minds and return to Egypt." *If* they have to fight? Didn't God know whether they would have to fight or not? And what does "peradventure" mean, in the KJV? It means "maybe," "possibly," or "perhaps." Why would God say "maybe" they'll go back to Egypt? Why would God say "they may," "they might," and "perhaps?" Didn't He know? Of course He *could* have known, but this might be one of those cases where He chose to not know something. Mightn't it?

287

Bread from Heaven

When God gave manna to the children of Israel when they were in the wilderness, he had them gather just a certain amount every day: not hoarding it, as if they couldn't quite trust God to take care of them tomorrow. Why did He do that daily rationing?

He did it, apparently, to "discover" something:

> Exodus 16:4 (ASV): Then said Jehovah unto Moses, Behold, I will rain bread from heaven for you; and the people shall go out and gather a day's portion every day, **that I may prove them**, whether they will walk in my law, or not.
>
> AMP: Then the Lord said to Moses, "Behold, I will cause bread to rain from heaven for you; the people shall go out and gather a day's portion every day, so **that I may test them [to determine] whether or not** they will walk [obediently] in My instruction (law)."
>
> CEV: The Lord said to Moses, "I will send bread down from heaven like rain. Each day the people can go out and gather only enough for that day. **That's how I will see** if they obey me."
>
> EXB: Then the Lord said to Moses, "I will cause food [bread] to fall like rain from the sky [heaven] for all of you. Every day the people must go out and gather what they need for that day. **I want to see if** the people will do what I teach them [**test them to see if** they will walk in my law/instruction or not]."
>
> GNT: The Lord said to Moses, "Now I am going to cause food to rain down from the sky for all of you. The people must go out every day and gather enough for that day. In this way **I can test them to find out** if they will follow my instructions."
>
> NCV: Then the Lord said to Moses, "I will cause food to fall like rain from the sky for all of you. Every day the people must go out and gather what they need for that day. **I want to see if** the people will do what I teach them."

If God was using absolute omniscience, why would He test the Israelites and specifically state that He's doing it to "see," to "find out," to "determine" whether or not they will obey Him? He would have known since eternity past exactly how they would behave.

Let Me Think About It

While Moses was up on Mount Sinai getting the Ten Commandments, the people were down below, worshipping their brand-new golden calf. Needless to say, God was rather irritated by this, and basically told Israel, "Fine. You go up to the promised land yourselves. I'll send an angel along, but I'm staying here so I don't smoke you" (Exodus 33:1–3).

At this point, they knew they were in trouble, so they settled down quickly. Then God says something interesting in v. 5:

> Exodus 33:5: For the Lord had said unto Moses, Say unto the children of Israel, Ye are a stiffnecked people: I will come up into the midst of thee in a moment, and consume thee: therefore now put off thy ornaments from thee, **that I may know what to do unto thee.**
>
> MSG: God said to Moses, "Tell the Israelites, 'You're one hard-headed people. I couldn't stand being with you for even a moment—I'd destroy you. So take off all your jewelry **until I figure out what to do with you.**'"
>
> NABRE: The Lord spoke to Moses: Speak to the Israelites: You are a stiff-necked people. Were I to go up in your company even for a moment, I would destroy you. Now off with your ornaments! **Let me think what to do with you.**
>
> NLT: For the Lord had told Moses to tell them, "You are a stubborn and rebellious people. If I were to travel with you for even a moment, I would destroy you. Remove your jewelry and fine clothes **while I decide what to do with you.**"
>
> TLV: Adonai said to Moses, "Say to Bnei-Yisrael, 'You are a stiff-necked people. If I were going up among you for one moment, I would consume you. Take off your ornaments, **so that I may consider what to do to you.**'"

Curiouser and curiouser: Why would God say that He needed to "figure out" or "think" or "decide" or "consider" what to do with the nation of Israel, if He were always in absolute-omniscience mode? He would have had His plan of action determined from eternity past.

Testing the Prophets

Let's look at this next passage for something comparable:

> Deuteronomy 13:1–3: If there arise among you a prophet, or a dreamer of dreams, and giveth thee a sign or a wonder, ²And the sign or the

wonder come to pass, whereof he spake unto thee, saying, Let us go after other gods, which thou hast not known, and let us serve them; ³Thou shalt not hearken unto the words of that prophet, or that dreamer of dreams: for **the Lord your God proveth you, to know whether** ye love the Lord your God with all your heart and with all your soul.

3b, AMP: For **the Lord your God is testing you to know whether** you love the Lord your God with all your [mind and] heart and with your entire being.

CEV: The **Lord your God will be watching to find out whether** or not you love him with all your heart and soul.

ERV: . . .because **the Lord your God is testing you. He wants to know if** you love him with all your heart and all your soul.

GNT: The **Lord your God is using them to test you, to see if** you love the Lord with all your heart.

So why would God do this, for the explicit purpose to "know," to "find out," or to "see if" the people loved Him, if He were exercising absolute omniscience?

Moses' Song

Later in Deuteronomy, Moses is talking to the people of Israel—or rather, teaching them a song that describes God's dealings with them—and he states:

Deuteronomy 32:20: And he *[God]* said, I will hide my face from them, **I will see what their end shall be:** for they are a very froward generation, children in whom is no faith.

CEB: He said: I will hide my face from them—**I will see what becomes of them**—because they are a confused generation; they are children lacking loyalty.

CEV: and said, "You are unfaithful and can't be trusted. So I won't answer your prayers; **I'll just watch and see what happens to you."**

EXB: He said, "**I will** turn away [my face away] from them and **see what will happen to them** [their end will be]. They are evil people [a perverted generation], unfaithful [untrustworthy] children."

GWORD: He said, "**I will** turn away from them and **find out what will happen to them.** They are devious people, children who can't be trusted."

ISV: So he said: "Let me hide my face from them. **I will observe what their end will be,** because they are a perverted generation, children within whom there is no loyalty."

How odd. God says He will turn His face away from Israel and then He will "see" what becomes of them; or He will "find out" what will happen, or He will "observe" what their end will be. Notice that He doesn't say, "*you* will see" or even "*we* will see," but He says "*I* will see" what happens. Curious.

Some Enemies Strategically Left in Place

Later on, after Israel arrives in the Promised Land, God left some of their enemies in the land. Why did He do that?

Judges 3:4: And they were to prove Israel by them, **to know whether they would hearken** unto the commandments of the LORD, which he commanded their fathers by the hand of Moses.

CEB: They were to be the test for Israel, **to find out whether they would obey** the Lord's commands, which he had made to their ancestors through Moses.

EXB: Those nations were in the land to test the Israelites—**to see if they would obey** the commands the Lord had given to their ancestors by [the hand of] Moses.

HCSB: The LORD left them to test Israel, **to determine if they would keep the Lord's commands** He had given their fathers through Moses.

ISV: They remained there to test Israel, **to reveal if they would obey** the commands of the Lord that he issued to their ancestors through Moses.

NET: They were left to test Israel, **so the LORD would know** if his people would obey the commands he gave their ancestors through Moses.

Again, this seems a little odd: God did something "to know whether" the Israelites would obey or not? Didn't He know? Why would God set up circumstances to "find out," "to see," "to determine" how somebody would respond? Why would God need to set up circumstances in such a way so that He "would know" whether people would obey or not? That seems a little strange, if He had chosen to exercise absolute omniscience, as the Reformed definition of sovereignty requires.

God Breaking His Promise, Take 1

During the time of the Judges of Israel, the Levitical priesthood had sunk into great wickedness rather than serving God, as they had been charged to do. One prominent example of this is Eli.

Eli was the priest of Israel, and his sons Hophni and Phinehas, were exceptionally wicked: They didn't know or care about the Lord (I Samuel 2:12), they took—by force, if necessary—the sacrifices that people brought to sacrifice to the Lord, so they could eat it themselves (2:16), they had sex with the women who served at the entrance of the Tabernacle (2:22), and more. So their sin was "very great" (2:17), and Eli knew what they were doing (2:22). Although Eli verbally reprimanded them (2:23–24), He actually preferred to please them more than he wanted to please God, and he himself profited from their wickedness (2:29).

Because Eli's sin was so grievous, in not stopping his sons from their wickedness even though he knew about it (3:13), God judged him severely, but justly. And here's the point of including this passage in this section of the book:

> I Samuel 2:30 (NIV): Therefore the Lord, the God of Israel, declares: '**I promised** that your house and your father's house would minister before me forever.' **But now the Lord declares: 'Far be it from me!** Those who honor me I will honor, but those who despise me will be disdained.'

Wow! God promised something and then reversed His promise because of the sin of the people to whom the promise was made. If God had been exercising absolute omniscience all along, He would have known these people would sin in this way, which means His original promise would have been made with full knowledge that He would later annul His promise. But that would be a lie, and God cannot lie (John 3:33, Titus 1:2, Hebrews 6:18). There seems to be no other alternative, than to concede that God sometimes chooses not to know some things that we perceive to be "in the future."

Choosing Saul as King

After the era of the Judges of Israel, God raised up Samuel as a prophet and told him to anoint Saul to be the king of Israel. He did so, but later, Saul got into a bad habit of disobeying God over and over, until God finally said, in effect, "Fine. I'll take the kingdom away from you and give it to someone else." Here's how God broke the news to Samuel:

> I Samuel 15:11: **It repenteth me** that I have set up Saul to be king: for he is turned back from following me, and hath not performed my commandments. And it grieved Samuel; and he cried unto the LORD all night.
>
> AMP: **I regret** making Saul king, for he has turned back from following Me and has not performed My commands. And Samuel was grieved and angry [with Saul], and he cried to the Lord all night.
>
> CEV: "Saul has stopped obeying me, and **I'm sorry** that I made him king." Samuel was angry, and he cried out in prayer to the LORD all night.
>
> NIRV: "**I am very sad** I have made Saul king. He has turned away from me. He has not done what I directed him to do." When Samuel heard that, he was angry. He cried out to the LORD during that whole night.

Same thing as when God regretted creating man: If God knew all along that Saul would behave like this, why did set him up as king in the first place? Why would God repent, regret, be sorry and sad for His actions, if He had planned them since eternity past, and knew exactly how Saul would behave? If God knew all along that Saul would act this way, and even prevented him from acting otherwise by not including him in the "elect," but still regretted the decision to make him king, wouldn't that imply that God made a mistake?

The Biggest Blank Check Ever

Fast-forward past Saul and David, to David's son, King Solomon. Remember when God appeared to Solomon in the dream and asked him what he wanted? Let's look at that passage:

> I Kings 3:5–14 (NIV): At Gibeon the Lord appeared to Solomon during the night in a dream, and God said, "Ask for whatever you want me to give you."

Wow! Talk about a blank check!

> [6]Solomon answered, "You have shown great kindness to your servant, my father David, because he was faithful to you and righteous and upright in heart. You have continued this great kindness to him and have given him a son to sit on his throne this very day. [7]Now, O Lord my

God, you have made your servant king in place of my father David. But I am only a little child and do not know how to carry out my duties. ⁸Your servant is here among the people you have chosen, a great people, too numerous to count or number. ⁹So give your servant a discerning heart to govern your people and to distinguish between right and wrong. For who is able to govern this great people of yours?" ¹⁰**The Lord was pleased that Solomon had asked for this.** ¹¹So God said to him, "Since you have asked for this and not for long life or wealth for yourself, nor have asked for the death of your enemies but for discernment in administering justice, ¹²I will do what you have asked. I will give you a wise and discerning heart, so that there will never have been anyone like you, nor will there ever be. ¹³Moreover, I will give you what you have not asked for—both riches and honor—so that in your lifetime you will have no equal among kings. ¹⁴And if you walk in my ways and obey my statutes and commands as David your father did, I will give you a long life."

Let's look in more detail at God's response to Solomon's request:

I Kings 3:10: And the speech **pleased** the Lord, that Solomon had asked this thing.

ERV: The Lord was **happy** that Solomon asked for wisdom.

MSG: God, the Master, was **delighted** with Solomon's response.

WYC: Therefore the word **pleased** before the Lord, that Solomon had asked (for) such a thing.

Here's the point: If God had known since eternity past what Solomon would request, why did God feel pleasure when he actually asked it? Why was God "happy" or "delighted" with Solomon's request? Being "pleased" or "delighted" as a result of some event are responses of *discovery*, which, obviously, God could not do if He were exercising absolute omniscience.

Ahab at Ramoth-Gilead

Here is a fascinating story: Ahab was one of the most evil kings Israel ever had, and after he and his wife Jezebel had caused unimaginable sin and corruption in Israel, it was time for him to reap what he had sown—it was time for him to die.

Now of course, God could have accomplished this in myriad ways: stop his heart, have him fall down the stairs and break his neck, give him a stroke, have him choke on a chicken bone—any number of things. But God's preferred way was to have him die in battle at a place called Ramoth-gilead. But here's the fascinating part: *God asked the angels for advice on how it should happen.*

Here's how it went down: Ahab, the evil king of Israel, and Jehoshaphat, the godly king of Judah, were considering going to battle at Ramoth-gilead to take that area back from the king who had captured it, and they were consulting the prophets for guidance. Ahab had many false prophets at his disposal, whom he liked to consult because they told him what he wanted to hear, and there was also one prophet of God named Micaiah. Ahab kept him in prison because he didn't like the things that Micaiah said to him (Ahab being an evil king and all).

Micaiah had a vision of the courtroom of heaven, where God had gathered the angels together to get their ideas on how they could get Ahab to Ramoth-gilead so he could die in battle. As he was telling Ahab and Jehoshaphat what he saw, he said this:

> I Kings 22:19–23 (NIV): Micaiah continued, "Therefore hear the word of the LORD: I saw the LORD sitting on his throne with all the host of heaven standing around him on his right and on his left. [20]And the LORD said, 'Who will entice Ahab into attacking Ramoth Gilead and going to his death there?' One suggested this, and another that."

What? Why was *God* asking anyone's advice? He knows everything, doesn't He? Let's continue reading:

> [21]"Finally, a spirit came forward, stood before the LORD and said, 'I will entice him.' [22]'By what means?' the LORD asked. 'I will go out and be a lying spirit in the mouths of all his prophets,' he said. 'You will succeed in enticing him,' said the LORD. 'Go and do it.' [23]So now the LORD has put a lying spirit in the mouths of all these prophets of yours. The LORD has decreed disaster for you."

So again, why would God ask *anyone* for advice? Could it be that He sometimes voluntarily restricts His omniscience so He can experience the pleasure of real conversation with His creations, rather than the boredom of watching them run through their scripted lines, which He has memorized down to the minutest detail?

Hezekiah's Judgment

And then look at this passage, where Isaiah is prophesying to Hezekiah:

> II Kings 20:1–5 (NASB): In those days Hezekiah became mortally ill. And Isaiah the prophet the son of Amoz came to him and said to him, "Thus says the LORD, 'Set your house in order, for **you shall die and not live.**'"

So "thus says the LORD." And Isaiah is a pretty reliable prophet. But to continue:

> ²Then he turned his face to the wall, and prayed to the LORD, saying, ³"Remember now, O LORD, I beseech Thee, how I have walked before Thee in truth and with a whole heart, and have done what is good in Thy sight." And Hezekiah wept bitterly. ⁴And it came about before Isaiah had gone out of the middle court, that the word of the LORD came to him, saying, ⁵"Return and say to Hezekiah the leader of My people, 'Thus says the LORD, the God of your father David, "I have heard your prayer, I have seen your tears; behold, **I will heal you**. On the third day you shall go up to the house of the LORD."'"

So why did God say to Hezekiah, "You're going to die," and then, only moments later, after Hezekiah prayed, did God say, "I will heal you," if He knew all along how Hezekiah would respond? If He knew that Hezekiah would repent, His first statement—"You're going to die"—would have been a lie; God would have said Hezekiah was soon going to die when He knew good and well that he wouldn't. But God cannot lie (John 3:33, Titus 1:2, Hebrews 6:18), so what gives? Could it be that God might choose to restrict His omniscience on some subjects or in certain situations?

God's Plan to Discover Something

Hezekiah the king, just described, went through the same cycle that we often go through:

1. God blesses us.
2. We get prideful.
3. God humbles us.
4. We repent.
5. (Go to Step 1)

Step 2 and 3 were described above. It was during Steps 3 and 4 of the above sequence that the following passage of Scripture takes place. God had humbled Hezekiah by telling him he was going to die, he repented, and God healed him; this was discussed in the previous section.

But God also did something much more amazing than the upcoming supernatural healing: God gave Hezekiah a miraculous sign to confirm that He was going to heal him. The miraculous sign was that the shadow on the sundial *backed up* 10°; i.e., God reversed the rotation of the earth, so that day was 40 minutes longer than usual. Hezekiah's miraculous healing, as well as the fact that the sun backed up 10° because of Isaiah's prayer, were known far and wide, so Babylon sent some representatives to find out more about it:

> II Chronicles 32:31 (CEB): . . .even in the matter of the ambassadors sent from Babylonian officials to find out about the miraculous sign that occurred in the land, when God had abandoned him **in order to test him and to discover what was in his heart.**
>
> CEV: Even when the leaders of Babylonia sent messengers to ask Hezekiah about the sign God had given him, God let Hezekiah give his own answer **to test him and to see if he would remain faithful.**
>
> ESV: And so in the matter of the envoys of the princes of Babylon, who had been sent to him to inquire about the sign that had been done in the land, God left him to himself, **in order to test him and to know all that was in his heart.**
>
> GWORD: When the leaders of Babylon sent ambassadors to ask him about the miraculous sign that had happened in the land, God left him. God did this **to test him, to find out everything that was in Hezekiah's heart.**
>
> TLB: However, when ambassadors arrived from Babylon to find out about the miracle of his being healed, God left him to himself in order **to test him and to see what he was really like.**

How very strange. God steps back from Hezekiah in order to "discover" what was in his heart; to "see if" he would remain faithful. If God were exercising absolute omniscience, why would He need to do anything to "know," or to "find out" what was in somebody's heart, or to "see what he was really like?" He would have known with complete certainty. Indeed, if the Reformed doctrines were true, God would have been the *direct cause* of the condition of Hezekiah's heart, and therefore He would have known exactly what that condition was. It sure sounds like God had chosen to restrict His omniscience to some extent.

Praying that God Forgets

Below is a prayer, inspired by the Holy Spirit, in which David prays that the Lord would forget something. If this were impossible, why would God include it in the Bible?

> Psalm 25:7: **Remember not the sins of my youth, nor my transgressions:** according to thy mercy remember thou me for thy goodness' sake, O LORD.

Here's another example, this one written by Asaph:

> Psalm 79:8: O **remember not against us former iniquities:** let thy tender mercies speedily prevent us: for we are brought very low.

Apparently, God was in favor of what David and Asaph said above, because He said He would do it:

> Isaiah 43:25: **I, even I,** am he that blotteth out thy transgressions for mine own sake, and **will not remember thy sins.**

So here we see God plainly stating that He will voluntarily choose to limit His omniscience by not remembering certain things we perceive to be "in the past." Fascinating.

Dashing God's Expectations, Part 1

Is it possible for God to expect one thing, but have results turn out differently than He expected? Yes, if God exercises limited omniscience:

> Isaiah 5:7 (CSB): For the vineyard of the Lord of Armies is the house of Israel, and the men of Judah, the plant he delighted in. **He expected justice but saw injustice; he expected righteousness but heard cries of despair.**
>
> CEV: I am the Lord All-Powerful! Israel is the vineyard, and Judah is the garden I tended with care. **I had hoped for honesty and for justice, but dishonesty and cries for mercy were all I found.**
>
> ESV: For the vineyard of the Lord of hosts is the house of Israel, and the men of Judah are his pleasant planting; and **he looked for justice, but behold, bloodshed; for righteousness, but behold, an outcry!**
>
> GNT: Israel is the vineyard of the Lord Almighty; the people of Judah are the vines he planted. **He expected them to do what was good, but instead they committed murder. He expected them to do what was right, but their victims cried out for justice.**

NASB: For the vineyard of the Lord of armies is the house of Israel, And the people of Judah are His delightful plant. So **He waited for justice, but behold, there was bloodshed; For righteousness, but behold, a cry for help.**

How could God expect a particular thing, and have the outcome differ from what He expected? If God chooses to not know certain things—as so many passages we've seen do—this is not at all difficult to understand.

Looking for Someone to Pray

Remember in Isaiah where God was seeking an intercessor to pray for Israel, and He couldn't find even *one*? He had seen gross iniquity and rebellion among the people, and His Justice demanded that they be punished. However, since "mercy triumphs over judgment" (see James 2:13), He would prefer to pardon them and forgive their sins. But since God chooses to move through people (see whole Bible), He requires someone to pray and intercede for mercy for these sinners. Let's pick up the narrative:

Isaiah 59:16: And he *[God]* saw that there was no man, and **wondered that there was no intercessor:** therefore his arm brought salvation unto him; and his righteousness, it sustained him.

AMP: He saw that there was no man, and was **amazed** that there was no one to intercede [on behalf of truth and right]; therefore His own arm brought salvation to Him, And His own righteousness sustained Him.

CEB: Seeing that there was no one, and **astonished** that no one would intervene, God's arm brought victory, upheld by righteousness. . .

ERV: He did not see anyone speak up for the people. He was **shocked** to see that no one stood up for them. So with his own power he saved them. His desire to do what is right gave him strength.

GWORD: He sees that there's no one to help. He's **astounded** that there's no one to intercede. So with his own power he wins a victory. His righteousness supports him.

ICB: He could not find anyone to help the people. He was **surprised** that there was no one to help. So the Lord used his own power to save the people. His own goodness gave him strength.

ISV: He saw that there was no one, and was **appalled** that there was no one to intervene; so his own arm brought him victory, and his righteous acts upheld him.

> MSG: He **couldn't believe** what he saw: not a soul around to correct this awful situation. So he did it himself, took on the work of Salvation, fueled by his own Righteousness.

Look at those words! When God "wondered" that there was no intercessor, what does that mean? In the other translations we see that God Himself was "amazed," "astonished," "shocked," "astounded," "surprised," and "appalled," at what he saw. The idea that there was *nobody* to be found who would be willing to intercede for the people was so horrifying that He "couldn't believe" it.

So again the question comes up: If God were exercising absolute omniscience, why would He be amazed, astonished, and astounded at the realization? And *how* could He ever be *surprised* by anything? If He were exercising absolute omniscience, He couldn't; that is clear from the very definitions of the words. But if He had chosen to limit His omniscience in certain ways, it's very plausible.

Dashing God's Expectations, Part 2

Like in Isaiah 5:7 we saw above, God tells Jeremiah a similar thing. In the passage below, God is describing to Jeremiah how He had courted and wooed His people in an attempt to draw them back to Him. How did they respond?

> Jeremiah 3:7 (ASV): And **I said** after she had done all these things, **She will return unto me; but she returned not:** and her treacherous sister Judah saw it.
>
> CEB: **I thought** that after she had done all this **she would return to me, but she didn't.** Her disloyal sister Judah saw this.
>
> CEV: I knew that the kingdom of Israel had been unfaithful and committed many sins, yet **I still hoped she might come back to me. But she didn't. . .** Her sister, the kingdom of Judah, saw what happened. . .
>
> EHV: **I told myself** that after she did all this, **she would return to me, but she did not return,** and her treacherous sister Judah saw it.
>
> ERV: **I said to myself, 'Israel will come back to me** after she has finished doing these evil things.' **But she did not come back to me.** And Israel's unfaithful sister, Judah, saw what she did.

> MSG: **I assumed** that after she had gotten it out of her system, **she'd come back, but she didn't.** Her flighty sister, Judah, saw what she did.
>
> NCB: But **I truly believed that** after she had done all this, **she would return to me. However, she did not return**, and her faithless sister Judah saw this.

Amazing! God says, "She *[Israel]* will return to me," *but she didn't.* If God were exercising absolute omniscience, why would He say such a thing, knowing it was false? How could God "think" Israel would come back—how could He "hope," "tell Himself," "say to Himself," "assume," or "believe" Israel would come back—and then have His expectations dashed, if He were exercising absolute omniscience?

Then a few verses later, God says a similar thing:

> Jeremiah 3:19b–20 (AMP): **I thought you would call Me My Father and would not turn away from following Me.** ²⁰ Surely, as a wife treacherously and faithlessly departs from her husband, **so have you dealt treacherously and faithlessly with Me**, O house of Israel, says the Lord.
>
> MSG: "And **I imagined that you would say, 'Dear father!' and would never again go off and leave me. But no luck.** Like a false-hearted woman walking out on her husband, **you, the whole family of Israel, have proven false to me.**" God's Decree.
>
> NLV: "And **I said, 'You will call Me, "My Father," and not turn away from following Me.'** ²⁰For sure, as a woman is not faithful and leaves her husband, so **you have not been faithful to Me**, O people of Israel," says the Lord.

Again, this is pretty amazing, that God would say something, think something, or imagine something would happen, and not have it turn out that way. Unless, of course, He chose for whatever reason to restrict His omniscience on some subjects.

But it happened yet again:

> Zephaniah 3:7: I said, Surely thou wilt fear me, thou wilt receive instruction; so their dwelling should not be cut off, howsoever I punished them: **but they rose early, and corrupted all their doings.**
>
> NIV: **I said to the city, 'Surely you will fear me and accept correction!'** Then her dwelling would not be cut off, nor all my punishments

come upon her. **But they were still eager to act corruptly in all they did.**

NLT: **I thought, 'Surely they will have reverence for me now! Surely they will listen to my warnings.** Then I won't need to strike again, destroying their homes.' **But no, they get up early to continue their evil deeds.**

All of these passages are completely nonsensical if we assume that God operates in absolute omniscience at all times. But if we are willing to concede that He could choose to limit His awareness of certain things (as we will soon see Him plainly promising to do), they make perfect sense.

What Hadn't Occurred to God

In Jeremiah 7, God is talking about the intensity of the evil that the children of Israel had committed: they had gone so low as to burn their own children as sacrifices to the idol Tophet:

Jeremiah 7:31: And they have built the high places of Tophet, which is in the valley of the son of Hinnom, to burn their sons and their daughters in the fire; which I commanded them not, **neither came it into my heart.**

AMP: . . .which I did not command, **nor did it come into My mind or heart.**

CEB: . . .although I never commanded such a thing, **nor did it ever cross my mind.**

CJB: . . .something I never ordered; **in fact, such a thing never even entered my mind!**

ERV: . . .This is something I never commanded. **Something like this never even entered my mind!**

GWORD: . . .I did not ask for this. **It never entered my mind.**

TLB: . . .a deed so horrible I've never even thought of it, let alone commanded it to be done.

This is quite sobering: *people* thinking about things and acting out behaviors that were *so* evil, even *God* hadn't thought about them. Granted, these were exceedingly repugnant sins, which are diametrically opposed to all that God is, but it still indicates that God can choose to not know certain things.

In Jeremiah 19, God is again talking to Jeremiah about the sins of Israel, and he says a similar thing about another idol they were worshipping—Baal, in this case—and again, even to the extent of child sacrifice:

> Jeremiah 19:5: They have built also the high places of Baal, to burn their sons with fire for burnt offerings unto Baal, which I commanded not, nor spake it, **neither came it into my mind.** . .
>
> AMP: . . .which I commanded not nor spoke of it, **nor did it come into My mind and heart—**
>
> CEB: . . .although I never commanded or ordered such a thing, **nor did it ever cross my mind.**
>
> CJB: . . .something I never ordered or said; **it never even entered my mind.**
>
> DOUAY: . . .which I did not command, nor speak of, **neither did it once come into my mind.**
>
> ERV: . . . I did not ask them to offer their sons as sacrifices. **I never even thought of such a thing.**
>
> ICB: . . . I did not speak about it or tell them to do that. **I never even thought of such a thing.**
>
> TLB: . . .a thing I never commanded them **nor even thought of!**
>
> VOICE: . . . I never taught them to do such unspeakable evil. **It never even crossed My mind.**

Wow. God said it again: it had never even *occurred* to Him that people would act this horribly.

But wait; there's more. In Jeremiah 32, God is again talking to Jeremiah about Israel's idol worship (including Molech, this time), and yet again to the extent that they were sacrificing their own children:

> Jeremiah 32:35: And they built the high places of Baal, which are in the valley of the son of Hinnom, to cause their sons and their daughters to pass through the fire unto Molech; which I commanded them not, **neither came it into my mind, that they should do this abomination,** to cause Judah to sin.
>
> AMP: . . .which I did not command them, **nor did it come into My mind or heart that they should do this abomination,** to cause Judah to sin.

CEB: . . .though I never commanded them—**nor did it even cross my mind**—**that they should do such detestable things**, leading Judah to sin.

ERV: I never commanded them to do such a terrible thing. **I never even thought the people of Judah would do such a terrible thing.**

EXB: . . . But I never commanded them to do such a hateful thing [abomination]. **It never entered my mind [heart] that they would do such a thing** and cause Judah to sin [7:30–34; 19:1–6].

These last three passages, in all these translations (and there are more), state that the behavior of the Israelites was so corrupt that such behavior had not even *occurred* to God. That is an amazing statement! If you research this topic further, you'll notice that some translations imply that the idea of *commanding* the Israelites to do such behavior, as opposed to simply contemplating it, had not even occurred to God. But *either way*, it shows that God, at least in some cases, chooses not to exercise absolute omniscience, because either way, *something* had not occurred to Him.

God Breaking His Promise, Take 2

Another example of God being under no obligation to fulfill His part of a covenant with Israel, because Israel had failed to fulfill their end first, is shown here:

Jeremiah 17:4 (NIV): **Through your own fault you will lose** the inheritance I gave you. I will enslave you to your enemies **in a land you do not know**, for you have kindled my anger, and it will burn forever.

The above is significant in the context of limited omniscience for two reasons. First, Israel lost the land that was theirs, and second, they were enslaved in a foreign country.

Why is this significant? Because of this:

Jeremiah 25:5 (NIV): They *[the prophets]* said, "Turn now, each of you, from your evil ways and your evil practices, and you can stay in the land the Lord gave to you and your fathers for ever and ever."

Do you see the connection? God gave the land to the nation of Israel "for ever and ever." But they *didn't* have it forever; Israel was conquered and hauled away as slaves to Assyria, Babylon, and elsewhere. Did God fall down on the job? No; He told them in great detail what would happen if they rebelled against the covenant He gave through Moses (Deuteronomy 28:15–68).

Here is why this passage is in the limited omniscience section: If God had known through absolute omniscience that Israel would rebel against Him and lose the land by conquest and be hauled away as slaves, and He still told them He gave them the land "for ever and ever," He would have been knowingly misrepresenting His intentions, because He incited the other countries to come and conquer Israel. Therefore, that "for ever and ever" part would have been a lie, but since God can't lie, it seems to imply that God was choosing to not know some things about Israel's future behavior.

God Promising to Forget

Later in Jeremiah, just like the quote from Isaiah a few pages ago, God says that He will choose to not know some things anymore, that He used to know—i.e., limit His omniscience:

> Jeremiah 31:34: And they shall teach no more every man his neighbour, and every man his brother, saying, Know the LORD: for they shall all know me, from the least of them unto the greatest of them, saith the LORD: for I will forgive their iniquity, and **I will remember their sin no more.**
>
> AMP: **I will [seriously] remember their sin no more.**
>
> CEV: . . .I will forgive their sins and **forget the evil things they have done.**
>
> LEB: I will forgive their iniquity and **their sin I will no longer remember.**
>
> TLB: . . .**I will forgive and forget their sins.**
>
> MSG: . . .**I'll forget they ever sinned!**
>
> VOICE: . . .**I will never call to mind** or mention **their sins again.**

Some will say of the above Scripture (as well as Isaiah 43:25, above, and Hebrews 8:12 and 10:17) that it means God, even though He technically "remembers" our sins in His mind, He will no longer hold them against us on our "rap sheet," so to speak. And that is certainly plausible in this case, but it doesn't address the other passages that strongly imply, and even plainly articulate, that God may choose to restrict His awareness of different things.

God Being Unsure

Still later in Jeremiah, in at least two places, God says that some things "may" happen, as if He doesn't know for sure. Did He voluntarily choose not to know some things?

Jeremiah 26:3 (NKJV): **Perhaps** everyone will listen and turn from his evil way, that I may relent concerning the calamity which I purpose to bring on them because of the evil of their doings.

AMP: **It may be** that they will listen. . .

CJB: **Maybe** they will listen. . .

DARBY: **Peradventure** they will hearken. . .

DOUAY: **If so be** they will hearken. . .

MSG: **Just maybe** they'll listen. . .

Jeremiah 36:3: **It may be** that the house of Judah will hear all the evil which I purpose to do unto them; that they may return every man from his evil way; that I may forgive their iniquity and their sin.

CEB: **Perhaps** when the people of Judah hear about every disaster I intend to bring upon them, they will turn from their evil ways, and I will forgive their wrongdoing and sins.

CEV: . . .**Maybe** they will stop sinning when they hear what terrible things I plan for them. And if they turn to me, I will forgive them.

DOUAY: **If so be**, when the house of Juda shall hear all the evils that I purpose to do unto them, that they may return every man from his wicked way: and I will forgive their iniquity, and their sin.

ESV: **It may be** that the house of Judah will hear all the disaster that I intend to do to them, so that every one may turn from his evil way, and that I may forgive their iniquity and their sin.

JUB: If **peradventure** the house of Judah will hear all the evil which I purpose to do unto them; that they may turn each one from his evil way; and I will forgive their iniquity and their sin.

Again, why would God say "perhaps," "maybe," "peradventure," and so forth, if He knew exactly how they would respond? (And, by the way, did you notice in both of the above passages that repentance occurs *before* forgiveness? This too overturns Total Depravity, and therefore makes the rest of the Five Points moot as well.)

And Jeremiah is not the only one to whom God expressed potentiality, but not surety, of people's future actions:

Ezekiel 12:3: Therefore, thou son of man, prepare thee stuff for removing, and remove by day in their sight; and thou shalt remove from thy place to another place in their sight: **it may be** they will consider, though they be a rebellious house.

CEB: But you, human one, prepare a backpack for going into exile. In the daytime while they watch, go into exile; while they watch, go out from your place to another. Even though they are a household of rebels, **perhaps** they will understand.

CEV: So before it gets dark, here is what I want you to do. Pack a few things as though you were going to be taken away as a prisoner. Then go outside where everyone can see you and walk around from place to place. **Maybe** as they watch, they will realize what rebels they are.

GNV: Therefore thou son of man, prepare thy stuff to go into captivity, and go forth by day in their sight: and thou shalt pass from thy place to another place in their sight, **if it be possible that they may** consider it: for they are a rebellious house.

Same question.

God "Looking for" Someone

Ezekiel echoes the cry of God's heart in Isaiah 59, which we saw above, where God was looking for an intercessor: someone to "stand in the gap" on behalf of the people who have been rebelling against Him. As before, judgment was demanded, but God's mercy wanted to find expression, so He was looking for someone to pray for them so He could answer the intercessor's prayer for the people who would otherwise have to be punished for their sin.

Ezekiel 22:30: And **I sought for a man** among them, that should make up the hedge, and stand in the gap before me for the land, that I should not destroy it: but I found none.

AMP: **I searched for a man** among them who would build up the wall and stand in the gap before Me for [the sake of] the land, that I would not destroy it, but I found no one [not even one].

CEB: **I looked for anyone** to repair the wall and stand in the gap for me on behalf of the land, so I wouldn't have to destroy it. But I couldn't find anyone.

TLB: **I looked in vain for anyone** who would build again the wall of righteousness that guards the land, who could stand in the gap and defend you from my just attacks, but I found not one.

Curious wording here: God "sought," "searched for," and "looked for" someone to intercede for the people. If He had been exercising absolute omniscience, He would have known going into it that there wasn't one, and would have judged them right away. But still, this choice of words could be just one way for God to express His desire that *someone* would pray. That, in itself, is convicting enough, don't you think?

"Destruction! Oh, Never Mind. . ."

And this one, from Jonah, is especially puzzling if we assume absolute omniscience in all cases:

> Jonah 3:4–5, 10 (NASB): Then Jonah began to go through the city one day's walk; and he cried out and said, "Yet forty days and **Nineveh will be overthrown**." ⁵Then the people of Nineveh believed in God; and they called a fast and put on sackcloth from the greatest to the least of them. . . . ¹⁰When God saw their deeds, that they turned from their wicked way, then **God relented concerning the calamity** which He had declared He would bring upon them. And **He did not do it.**

Think of the implications here. Notice that the warning was not "Yet forty days and Nineveh will be overthrown, *unless you repent.*" It was simply, "Yet forty days and Nineveh will be overthrown." Period. *But it was not overthrown in forty days.* So if God was exercising absolute omniscience, He would have known everything, including how people will respond to Him. Therefore, He would have known that they would repent, and that He would cancel the destruction. Which means, he told Jonah to say something that He knew good and well was not true. That's called a lie.

But God cannot lie, so again, what gives? Could it be that God voluntarily chooses to not know certain things, like how people will respond to Him? Hmm.

And this is not the only place in the Bible where God changes His mind—even to the point of aborting judgments that have already been announced—based on how people respond to Him. It sounds like God was serious when He said that "mercy triumphs over judgment" (James 2:13, NIV). Read the section "The Potter and the Clay" for details.

The Time Has Come

Remember the story about Jesus and the disciples being invited to the wedding in Cana, where He turned the water into wine? Up to this point, He had been preaching and baptizing people—well, actually, His disciples did the baptizing (John 4:1–2). But Jesus hadn't done any miracles yet, because it wasn't yet time for Him to be openly revealed as the Messiah.

When they ran out of wine, His mother asked Jesus to do something about it:

> John 2:4 (ESV): And Jesus said to her, "Woman, what does this have to do with me? **My hour has not yet come.**"

Whereupon Mary says to the servants, "Whatever He says to you, do it." And suddenly, it *was* time; Jesus' hour *had* come. Now this may not seem like a case of limited omniscience, because Jesus had already "emptied Himself," so He had already clearly given up the advantages of omniscience during His earthly ministry. At least it *seems* like it's not a case of limited omniscience, until you read these verses:

> John 8:28 So Jesus said, "When you lift up the Son of Man, then you will know that I am He, and **I do nothing on My own initiative, but I speak these things as the Father taught Me.**"

> John 12:49 (NASB): "For I did not speak on My own initiative, but **the Father Himself who sent Me has given Me a commandment as to what to say and what to speak.** ⁵⁰I know that His commandment is eternal life; therefore **the things I speak, I speak just as the Father has told Me.**"

You may have heard that Jesus only did what He saw the Father doing, and that is true (John 5:19–20, 30, 36, 8:29, 38, 14:10-11, 31), but the two passages above show that *Jesus also only spoke what He heard the Father say.* This is significant because that means when Jesus said "It's not yet my time," He was saying what He heard the Father say. But just seconds later, apparently in response to Mary's faith, it *was* Jesus' time, He told the servants to fill the waterpots, and then draw some out for the head steward to taste. But again, He was saying what the Father had told him to say!

He had turned the water into wine and, as v. 11 says, He "revealed His glory." Why did the Father tell Jesus it was *not* His time, but then only seconds later, tell Him is *was* His time? Was it just that much of a coincidence that Mary asked Jesus to do something only a few seconds before "His time" arrived? Or could it have been that God was exercising limited omniscience as to how much faith Mary would exhibit in her response to the wine shortage?

Why Do I Live *Now?*

Have you ever wondered why you were born in the particular time in history that you were born? Or why you live where you do? The Bible makes it

Free to Choose?

sound like God put you where he did, and *when* He did, to give you the best chance of finding Jesus as your Savior. Look at this passage:

> Acts 17:26–27: And [God] hath made of one blood all nations of men for to dwell on all the face of the earth, and hath determined the times before appointed, and the bounds of their habitation; ²⁷That they should seek the Lord, **if haply they might feel after him, and find him,** though he be not far from every one of us:
>
> AMP: And He made from one [common origin, one source, one blood] all nations of men to settle on the face of the earth, having definitely determined [their] allotted periods of time and the fixed boundaries of their habitation (their settlements, lands, and abodes), ²⁷So that they should seek God, **in the hope that they might feel after Him and find Him,** although He is not far from each one of us.
>
> BBE: And he has made of one blood all the nations of men living on all the face of the earth, ordering their times and the limits of their lands, ²⁷**So that they might make search for God, in order, if possible, to get knowledge of him** and make discovery of him, though he is not far from every one of us. . .
>
> NASB: . . .and He made from one, every nation of mankind to live on all the face of the earth, having determined their appointed times, and the boundaries of their habitation, ²⁷that they should seek God, **if perhaps they might grope for Him and find Him,** though He is not far from each one of us. . .
>
> v. 27, ERV: God wanted people to look for him, and **perhaps in searching all around for him, they would find him.** But he is not far from any of us.
>
> PHILLIPS: . . .so that they might search for God, **in the hope that they might feel for him and find him**—yes, even though he is not far from any one of us.
>
> WYC: . . .**to seek God, if peradventure they feel him, either find,** though he be not far from each of you.

Read again the words the Bible uses: "haply," "in the hope that," "they *might* feel after Him," "perhaps," "they might make search," "if possible," and "peradventure." Now don't worry, I'm not going to start a new denomination called "The Church of the Limited Omniscience" or anything. But I think it's worth noting that all these Scriptures cast suspicion on the Reformed theory of God's sovereignty (where God knows, or at least *chooses* to know, absolutely everything) and/or they are incompatible with the Reformed doctrine of Unconditional Election (where God irrevocably chooses in eternity past who will serve Him).

But if the above Scriptures are saying what it looks like they're saying, it should be a relief to those who feel that if God foreknows every choice we're going to make, that fact somehow negates our freedom in making those choices.

"But Doesn't This Scripture Say. . .?"

When researching the topic of limited omniscience, I came across this Scripture:

> Acts 15:18: Known unto God are all his works from the beginning of the world.

This Scripture could be considered quite a blow to the whole idea of limited omniscience that the other passages implied, and I was wondering if I would have to abandon the idea. Then I read the above passage in some other translations, and it came across completely differently:

> ASV: Saith the Lord, who maketh these things known from of old.
>
> AMP: Says the Lord, Who has been making these things known from long ago.
>
> CEB: known from earliest times.
>
> CJB: says Adonai, who is doing these things.' All this has been known for ages.
>
> CEV: I promised it long ago."
>
> ERV: 'All this has been known from the beginning of time.'
>
> GWORD: He is the one who will do these things that have always been known!'
>
> NCV: And these things have been known for a long time.'
>
> NLV: God has made all His works known from the beginning of time.'
>
> VOICE: who has been revealing these things since ancient times.

In short, relatively few translations actually imply that God knew all of his works since eternity past, as the King James implies. (Of course, neither do they imply that He didn't; they simply don't address that idea at all.) Far more common are translations that say something to the effect of "God has been telling us this all along." So it looks like that Scripture can't be used to support the Calvinistic understanding of the omniscience after all.

But before we go on, let's read the above Scripture in its context; that is always a good idea. When we read a few verses around this one, we discover that the apostle James (this was Jesus' half-brother, not the son of Zebedee; this one was a different apostle James) is talking with the other apostles about the ministry of Paul and Barnabas to the Gentiles.

Even though Peter had already seen Cornelius and his household get saved, baptized in the Holy Spirit, and speak in tongues, it was still an enormous paradigm shift for most Jews that Gentiles were actually acceptable to God. So when Paul and Barnabas had had such tremendous success evangelizing the Gentiles, it was still hard for some to believe. That's what the current discussion was about, and was the conversation from which the above verse was taken.

> Acts 15:13–19 (NIV): When they finished, James spoke up: "Brothers, listen to me. [14]Simon has described to us how God at first showed his concern by taking from the Gentiles a people for himself. [15]The words of the prophets are in agreement with this, as it is written: [16]'After this I will return and rebuild David's fallen tent. Its ruins I will rebuild, and I will restore it, [17]**that the remnant of men may seek the Lord**, and all the Gentiles who bear my name, says the Lord, who does these things' [18]that have been known for ages. [19]It is my judgment, therefore, that we should not make it difficult for the Gentiles who are turning to God."

When reading the above passage, vv. 16–17 jumped out at me: God would rebuild David's tent, or tabernacle, "that the remnant of men may seek the Lord." What does "the remnant of men" mean? Let's read it in other translations and see if they shed any light on what is meant here:

> v. 17, AMP: So that **the rest of mankind** may seek the Lord. . .

> CEB: so that **the rest of humanity** will seek the Lord. . .

> ERV: Then **the rest of the world** will look for the Lord God. . .

> GNT: And **so all the rest of the human race** will come to me. . .

> ISV: so that **the rest of the people** may search for the Lord. . .

> NIRV: Then **everyone else** can look to the Lord.

So just reading the context of a verse that could, if read from certain translations, be interpreted to support the Reformed understanding of God's omniscience and foreknowledge, we find a statement that refutes the Reformed doctrine of Limited Atonement, which says that salvation is only for some people. But at this point, someone might say, "But after the phrases you quoted above, there are other phrases that allow for people to not get saved!"

Such phrases would be "upon whom My name is called" (KJV), "who belong to me" (CEB), "who are my people too" (ERV), "who are called by my name" (ERV), and so forth. And that could indeed be a valid objection if it didn't fly in the face of the fact that God is not a respecter of persons. And if there were no difference between a person *actually* getting saved, and the person *being able to* get saved.

Once we start thinking about what the Five Points of Calvinism actually mean, it becomes harder and harder to read the Bible for any length of time at all without finding passages that refute one or more of the Five Points.

Chapter 7:

Limited Atonement

The Reformed doctrine of Limited Atonement, which is sometimes called "particular redemption" or "definite atonement," says that Jesus' substitutionary atonement was not limited in its *power* to accomplish its purpose, but it was limited in the *subset* of humanity for which it was done. In other words, according to Reformed theology, only the sins of the elect—those chosen in eternity past to be saved—were atoned for by Jesus' death.

For the other group, the unelect, Jesus' blood didn't even *attempt* to atone for *their* sins, because if it had attempted, it surely would have succeeded. And since it's very clear Scripturally that not everyone makes it to heaven, the only option that Reformed doctrines allow is that God didn't *want* them to go to heaven.

This idea that the Atonement is limited, in the sense that it is intended for some but not all, some Calvinists have summarized as "The atonement is *sufficient* for all and *efficient* for the elect." Reformed theology affirms that the blood of Christ would have been powerful enough to pay for the sins of every single human being *if* it were God's intention to save every single human being. But Reformed doctrine claims that was *not* God's intention.

So again, what Scriptural support is there that God's desire and intention was *not* to save everybody? (The doctrine of Limited Atonement is heavily interdependent on Total Depravity and Unconditional Election, so in this chapter, I will also mention those other two doctrines when appropriate.)

We covered this in great detail in the section "Does God Want Everyone to be Saved?" Rather than list all those Scriptures again here, refer back to that section to refresh your memory on the details before continuing with those below.

Okay, now that you're back from reviewing the Scriptures in the section "Does God Want Everyone to be Saved?", it should be painfully clear already that, yes, God wants everyone to be saved. But wait; there's more. Let's look at some other Scriptures that confirm that idea yet again:

> Matthew 18:12–14 (NIV): What do you think? If a man owns a hundred sheep, and one of them wanders away, will he not leave the ninety-nine on the hills and go to look for the one that wandered off? ¹³And if he finds it, I tell you the truth, he is happier about that one sheep than about the ninety-nine that did not wander off. ¹⁴In the same way **your Father in heaven is not willing that any of these little ones should be lost.**

In Luke's account, he ends this parable with:

> Luke 15:7 (AMP): Thus, I tell you, there will be more joy in heaven over one [especially] wicked person who **repents (changes his mind,** abhorring his errors and misdeeds, and **determines to enter)** upon a better course of life) than over ninety-nine righteous persons who have no need of repentance.

Who are the "sheep" Jesus is referring to here? Just the twelve disciples? Just those who lived around Galilee? Just Jews? Just those in the first century? Of course not:

> Psalm 130:7: Let Israel hope in the Lord: for with the Lord there is mercy, and **with him is *plenteous* redemption.**
>
> CEV: Israel, trust the Lord **He is *always* merciful,** and he has the power to save you.
>
> GWORD: O Israel, put your hope in the Lord, because with the Lord there is mercy and **with him there is *unlimited* forgiveness.**
>
> TEV: Israel, trust in the Lord, because his love is constant and **he is *always* willing to save.**
>
> Isaiah 53:6: *All* we like sheep have gone astray; we have turned every one to his own way; and **the Lord hath laid on him *[Jesus]* the iniquity of us *all*.**

> Mark 16:15 (AMP): And He said to them, Go into **all the world** and preach and publish openly the good news (the Gospel) **to** *every creature* **[of the whole human race]**.
>
> John 6:33: For the bread of God is he which cometh down from heaven, and **giveth life unto the** *world.*
>
> I Corinthians 15:22 (NIV): For as in Adam all die, so **in Christ** *all* **will be made alive.**
>
> Colossians 1:28–29 (ESV): Him [Christ] we proclaim, **warning** *everyone* **and teaching** *everyone* with all wisdom, **that we may present** *everyone* **mature in Christ.** ²⁹For this I toil, struggling with **all his energy that he powerfully works within me.**
>
> I Timothy 4:10 (BBE): And this is the purpose of all our work and our fighting, because our hope is in **the living God, who is the Saviour of** *all* **men, and specially of those who have faith.**

Hmm. It's beginning to sound like maybe God wants all people to be saved. . .

The Impact on Evangelism: The Evangelists

The pair of concepts—Unconditional Election and Limited Atonement—reinforce each other in the ideas that only some will be saved, the selection has already been irrevocably made, and our actions, attitudes, desires, and choices are not a factor in any way. What impact must that have on evangelism?

According to Reformed theology, there are only two options for each person—you've been chosen to be saved, or you've been chosen to burn, and *nothing* we can do will influence the outcome. So why preach? Why evangelize? If the person we're talking to has been selected for salvation, he'll get to heaven whether we evangelize or not. If the person we're talking to has been selected for damnation, he *won't* get to heaven whether we evangelize or not. So what's the point?

One Reformed evangelist, when asked this very question, replied, "Well, *I* don't know which ones have been predestined to be saved. Do *you?*" While that would certainly be true, if Unconditional Election and Limited Atonement were valid concepts, it still wouldn't have changed the fact that none of his evangelistic efforts would have had the slightest effect on people's eternal landing-place.

317

Does it sound like a loving or wise Father God to tell us to engage in an activity (evangelism in this case) that *could never have any spiritual fruit?* Especially when we're commanded to bear fruit? (See John 15:8, 16.) Evangelism—if Unconditional Election and Limited Atonement were true—could *never* bear fruit, because the decision was made for people before they were born. But God does indeed tell us to evangelize; let's look at some of the examples:

> Ephesians 4:11–13: And he [Jesus] gave some, **apostles; and some, prophets; and some, evangelists; and some, pastors and teachers;** ¹²For the perfecting of the saints, for the work of the ministry, for the edifying of the body of Christ: ¹³Till we all come in the unity of the faith, and of the knowledge of the Son of God, unto a perfect man, unto the measure of the stature of the fulness of Christ. . .

In the above list of people-gifts that Jesus gave to the church, He includes evangelists right alongside apostles, prophets, pastors, and teachers. So the only possible conclusion, if Reformed doctrine is true, is that if you feel called to be an evangelist, you must resign yourself to the fact that nothing you do in fulfilling your calling could possibly have any beneficial effect on anyone. After all, the decision was made long ago, right? And irrevocably so, right? And so the whole concept of evangelism is "vanity of vanities," right?

I think it's very likely that you recoiled inwardly to those statements I made in the previous paragraph. If you did, or merely realized that my statements in the previous paragraph were wrong, I suspect it's because you *know* evangelism is not pointless. But if evangelism can be beneficial to people, it must be able to influence their decision (there's that pesky free will again) in favor of submitting themselves to Christ and trusting Him for their salvation.

Jesus called John the Baptist the greatest Old Testament man who ever lived:

> Matthew 11:11 (AMP): Truly I tell you, among those born of women **there has not risen anyone greater than John the Baptist;** yet he who is least in the kingdom of heaven is greater than he.

What was John's purpose on earth? How did he "prepare the way of the Lord?" For one thing, John—as well as Jesus, as well as the twelve disciples, as well as the seventy-two—preached that people should repent; i.e., stop sinning and turn to God (for much detail on this, see Book 2: *Is It Possible to Stop Sinning?*):

> Matthew 3:1–2 (NIV): In those days John the Baptist came, preaching in the Desert of Judea ²and saying, "**Repent**, for the kingdom of heaven is near."

The obvious problem here is that, if Unconditional Election and Limited Atonement are true, all John's preaching of repentance would have been pointless. But we know it *wasn't* pointless, because of what the angel told Zacharias before John was born:

> Luke 1:16 (NASB): "And **he will turn back many of the sons of Israel to the Lord their God**."

The apostle John seemed to believe the same thing:

> John 1:6–7 (NIV): There came **a man** who was sent from God; **his name was John.** ⁷He came as a witness to testify concerning that light, so that **through him all men might believe.**

Wait a minute: *John* turned people back to God? Didn't he know that was impossible? At least, assuming Unconditional Election and Limited Atonement are true, and it's looking less and less like they could be.

And the Apostle John didn't think this idea of turning people to God was the job of *only* John the Baptist, because he reports that Samaritans believed in Jesus because of the report of the woman at the well:

> John 4:39 (NIV): **Many of the Samaritans from that town believed in him *because of* the woman's testimony,** "He told me everything I ever did."

The apostle John was in good company, because apparently Jesus also believed that people could be persuaded to turn to Him because of the testimony of other people:

> John 17:20 (NASB): I do not ask on behalf of these alone, but for **those also who believe in Me through their word. . .**

Hmm. Jesus seems to think that His *disciples* will also be able to turn people toward God, but He must not have been aware of Unconditional Election. Let's look at some more evangelism-related Scriptures:

> I Corinthians 7:16 (NLT): Don't you wives realize that **your husbands might be saved because of you?** And don't you husbands realize that **your wives might be saved because of you?**

What? A person can be influenced toward salvation by a spouse? Yes. Although the above passage certainly does not guarantee that a spouse will be saved, *it shows that it is possible.*

II Timothy 4:5b: . . .**do the work of an evangelist,** make full proof of thy ministry.

Surely we don't think that Paul is exhorting Timothy to spend large amounts of time and effort on an exercise in futility, do we?

This next Scripture we saw above, but let's get into a bit more detail:

Colossians 1:28–29 (ESV): Him [Christ] we proclaim, **warning** *everyone* **and** *teaching* **everyone** with all wisdom, **that we may present** *everyone* **mature in Christ.** ²⁹For this I toil, struggling **with all his energy that he powerfully works within me.**

Paul and Timothy, the writers of Colossians, are saying that they proclaim, warn, and teach people so that they can present everyone mature in Christ. Wait: so *they* can? Yes, that's what it says; read it again. But if Unconditional Election and Limited Atonement are true, all their work was for nothing—fruitless and pointless. Not only that, but God's energy that He worked within Paul was also expended for nothing, because (according to Unconditional Election and Limited Atonement) all salvation decisions had already been made, even before the world began.

This next Scripture we saw above, but let's get into a bit more detail:

Colossians 1:28–29 (ESV): Him [Christ] we proclaim, **warning** *everyone* **and teaching** *everyone* with all wisdom, **that we may present** *everyone* **mature in Christ.** ²⁹For this I toil, struggling with **all his energy that he powerfully works within me.**

Paul and Timothy, the writers of Colossians, are saying that they proclaim, warn, and teach people so that they can present everyone mature in Christ. Wait: so *they* can? Yes, that's what it says; read it again. But if Unconditional Election and Limited Atonement are true, all their work was for nothing—fruitless and pointless. Not only that, but God's energy that He worked within Paul was also expended for nothing, because (according to Unconditional Election and Limited Atonement) all salvation decisions had already been made, even before the world began.

Why do preachers preach? (The Christian ones, I'm talking about.) If they have good motivations, it would be to communicate the Gospel to people who hadn't heard it (or hadn't yet responded) in hopes that they would be convicted of their sins, realize their need of a Redeemer, and therefore trust

God for salvation. John the Baptist did it a lot; Jesus did it a lot, the apostles did it a lot, the body of Christ in general did it—and still does it—a lot.

But if Total Depravity is true, nobody could be affected or influenced by their preaching. If Unconditional Election is true, the decision would already have been made, so preaching (at least, the evangelistic aspects thereof) is a completely ineffectual exercise. If Limited Atonement is true, then Jesus' blood didn't cover your sins anyway if you're one of the unelect, so it's hopeless; you're doomed.

Let's take a look at one of Solomon's nuggets of wisdom:

Proverbs 11:30: The fruit of the righteous is a tree of life; and **he that winneth souls is wise.**

This one simple verse contains (at least) three very important truths. First, *some people are righteous* (see "None Righteous; No, Not One" for a discussion of how this is commonly misunderstood). Secondly, *the righteous do bear fruit.* In the Bible, the metaphor of people bearing fruit refers to spiritual reproduction—winning people for Christ and discipling them; see John 15:1–8.

This verse in Proverbs refers to that same idea: righteous people bear fruit in the form of other righteous people; their fruit is spiritual life being made manifest in others. But if Unconditional Election is true, the first part of Proverbs 11:30 would be false because the fruit is already been borne (by God) in eternity past; it wouldn't be a fruit of the righteous person, but of God, when He made His selections.

The second part of this verse in Proverbs is, "he that wins souls is wise." But if Limited Atonement is true, "he that wins souls is nonexistent," because God will already have chosen, from eternity past, all winnable souls, and guaranteed their salvation by virtue of being part of the elect. So "winning souls," in the sense of evangelism or preaching or witnessing with the goal of influencing people's decisions toward God, would be impossible, and attempting to do so would be nothing but futility.

But perhaps I misinterpreted Proverbs 11:30 above. It would help establish the validity of my interpretation if we could find another Scripture that talks about one person influencing another to repent and choose to serve God. Are there any?

Glad you asked.

Jeremiah 23:22 (NIV): But if they *[the false prophets]* had stood in my council, **they** would have proclaimed my words to my people and would have turned them from their evil ways and from their evil deeds.

In this verse, in which God states the purpose of prophetic ministry, He plainly shows that the job of the *prophets* is to turn people from their sin! The whole purpose of prophetic ministry, according to God in the verse shown above, is to turn people away from their sin, and toward God. If people can't have any effect on other people's eternal destination, as the Reformed doctrine of Unconditional Election states, the whole prophetic calling is pointless, and we'll need to throw out the majority of our Bibles as being of no value. This verse, all by itself, refutes Unconditional Election—no other verses are needed. But many more equally conclusive passages exist.

> Daniel 12:3 (NIV): Those who are wise will shine like the brightness of the heavens, and **those who lead many to righteousness, like the stars for ever and ever.**

This verse clearly describes the rewards that will be given to people who influence other people to righteousness, which Unconditional Election and Limited Atonement say cannot happen. "But," someone might say, "that is an Old Testament Scripture, and we're not under the Old Testament anymore." (Regardless of the fact that Daniel is prophesying about the end times, which seems rather a New Testament topic to me. . .) But it's a good question: *are* there any New Testament Scriptures that show someone, or *command* someone, to influence others toward the Kingdom?

It just so happens that there are. And not just a few:

> Acts 13:43: Now when the congregation was broken up, many of the Jews and religious proselytes followed **Paul and Barnabas: who, speaking to them, persuaded them to continue in the grace of God.**

Wait: *Paul and Barnabas* persuaded them? That shouldn't be possible if Unconditional Election is true.

The next week, Paul and Barnabas were again talking to the rabble-rousing Jews in Antioch, they said:

> Acts 13:46–47 (NIV): Then Paul and Barnabas answered them boldly: "We had to speak the word of God to you first. Since you reject it and do not consider yourselves worthy of eternal life, we now turn to the Gentiles. [47]For this is what the Lord has commanded us: 'I have made you a light for the Gentiles, **that you may bring salvation to the ends of the earth.**'"

Now of course, if humans cannot influence other humans to turn to God, as Unconditional Election claims, what the Lord commanded Paul and Barnabas to do was ineffectual and pointless. But let's look at some more verses:

> Acts 14:1 (NASB): In Iconium **they** *[Paul and Barnabas]* entered the synagogue of the Jews together, and **spoke in such a manner that a large number of people believed,** both of Jews and of Greeks.

Even though the Bible says here that the people believed because of the way the Paul and Barnabas spoke, we know that couldn't really be the case, because such decisions are made in eternity past by God Himself, right?

> Acts 18:4: And **he** *[Paul]* reasoned in the synagogue every sabbath, and **persuaded the Jews and the Greeks.**

Same comment: Paul couldn't have persuaded Jews or Greeks or anyone else, because of Unconditional Election and Limited Atonement, right?

> Acts 18:28: For **he** *[Apollos]* **mightily convinced the Jews,** and that publickly, shewing by the scriptures that Jesus was Christ.

Nope, not possible that Apollos convinced them; that's God's job, according to Unconditional Election and Limited Atonement.

> Acts 19:8 (ESV): And **he** *[Paul]* entered the synagogue and for three months **spoke boldly, reasoning and persuading them about the kingdom of God.**

There goes Luke again, claiming things that Calvinism clearly says are impossible. . .

> Acts 26:17–18 (NIV): I will rescue you from your own people and from the Gentiles. **I am sending you to them** [18]**to open their eyes and turn them from darkness to light, and from the power of Satan to God, so that they may receive forgiveness of sins** and a place among those who are sanctified by faith in me.

Notice that Jesus assigns Paul three tasks—to minister to the Gentiles in three ways:

- To open their eyes,
- To turn them from darkness to light, and
- To turn them from the power of Satan to God.

What??? *Paul* will do those things? Surely Paul couldn't open anyone's spiritual eyes, or turn them from darkness to light, or from the power of Satan to God so they could receive forgiveness! Paul couldn't possibly do these things—Unconditional Election and Limited Atonement tell us so! Didn't Jesus realize that? Didn't Jesus remember that He and the rest of the Godhead, several eternities ago, had already decided on all of the "turning people from darkness to light" that would ever be done?

As we've seen, if Unconditional Election—God having made unchangeable heaven-or-hell selections for everyone in eternity past—is true, people could not in any way influence other people toward or away from salvation. But Jesus acknowledges that people will believe *because of the words of others* (i.e., not because of God's decision in eternity past):

> John 17:20: Neither pray I for these alone, but for **them also which shall believe on me through their word. . .**

Whew! So we are safe in pursuing evangelism.

> Acts 28:23 (WEB): When they had appointed him *[Paul]* a day, many people came to him at his lodging. **He explained to them**, testifying about the Kingdom of God, and **persuading them concerning Jesus**, both from the law of Moses and from the prophets, from morning until evening.

As we saw above, Unconditional Election and Limited Atonement tell us Paul couldn't possibly persuade anyone. So Luke must have been wrong here too, attributing to Paul things that Paul had no possibility of actually doing.

Well, how about Paul himself? Surely *he* understood Unconditional Election and Limited Atonement, didn't he? Most Calvinistic doctrines are supported (at least allegedly so) by Paul's epistles, so surely he wouldn't talk about people influencing others toward salvation.

Oh, wouldn't he?

> I Corinthians 3:5–9 (NIV): What, after all, is Apollos? And what is Paul? Only servants, through whom you came to believe—as the Lord has assigned to each his task. ⁶I planted the seed, Apollos watered it, but God made it grow. ⁷So neither he who plants nor he who waters is anything, but only God, who makes things grow. ⁸The man who plants and the man who waters have one purpose, and each will be rewarded according to his own labor. ⁹For we are God's fellow workers; you are God's field, God's building.

Let's think about what Paul and Sosthenes (the human authors of this epistle, I Corinthians 1:1–2) actually say here:

- v. 5: Paul says that he and Apollos were servants of God *through whom the Corinthians came to believe* in Christ! And the Lord *assigned* them to their tasks? That is not consistent with the Calvinistic doctrine of the "elect" being elected by God. The Corinthians got saved because of Paul and Apollos doing their assigned tasks! Remarkable!
- v. 6: Paul planted the seed, and Apollos watered it. What is the seed? According to Biblical symbology, the seed is the Word of God, which, when planted into a human soul and cultivated, bear fruit of salvation (Luke 8:11–15). Of course God made it grow, but *He did so only after Paul planted it and Apollos watered it.* Apparently, they did something helpful.
- v 7: This verse, removed from its context, *could* be interpreted to imply that human involvement is not necessary for evangelism. Let's not remove it from its context.
- v. 8: People who plant or water the seed of God's Word—that is, those who engage in evangelism—*have a purpose* in doing so. If Unconditional Election and Limited Atonement were real, there would be no purpose in evangelism, since it could not possibly have any effect on the unelect. So why would God reward Paul and Apollos for their labor, since it would have been irrelevant?
- v. 9: We are God's "fellow workers," His co-laborers, as in, we work with Him and He works with us (Mark 16:20, Acts 14:3, I Corinthians 1:9, II Corinthians 6:1, Hebrews 2:2–4). "Co-laboring with God" is an irrational concept if we actually contribute nothing.

It's amazing how many Biblical passages descend into absurdity or futility when we attempt to interpret them within the framework of the TULIP doctrines.

II Corinthians 5:11: Knowing therefore the terror of the Lord, **we persuade men**; but we are made manifest unto God; and I trust also are made manifest in your consciences.

Paul himself must have been mistaken here, because he contradicted Unconditional Election and Limited Atonement: people can't persuade other people to turn to God; that's God's choice in eternity past, and we haven't the slightest influence on people's decisions, do we?

Later, Paul tells the church at Colosse:

Colossians 1:28 (NASB): We proclaim Him, admonishing every man and teaching every man with all wisdom, so that **we may present every man complete in Christ.**

Let's look at some of the parts of speech in the previous sentence. There is one subject, and four verbs: *we* proclaim, *we* admonish, *we* teach, and *we* present every man perfect in Christ. But *we* couldn't possibly present anyone perfect in Christ because, according to Unconditional Election, all those decisions were made by God in eternity past, and are now set in concrete. Right?

I Timothy 4:16 (NIV): Watch your life and doctrine closely. Persevere in them, because **if you do, you will save both yourself and your hearers.**

Whoa! Didn't Paul realize that what he told Timothy to do would be impossible, because of the Reformed doctrine of Unconditional Election and Limited Atonement? No, apparently he didn't.

Here's another one:

James 5:20: . . .**he which converteth the sinner** from the error of his way **shall save a soul from death,** and shall hide a multitude of sins.

> AMP: . . .**whoever turns a sinner from his evil course will save [that one's] soul from death** and will cover a multitude of sins [procure the pardon of the many sins committed by the convert].

> GWORD: Realize that **whoever brings a sinner back from the error of his ways will save him from death,** and many sins will be forgiven.

> TLB: . . .**that person who brings him back to God will have saved a wandering soul from death,** bringing about the forgiveness of his many sins.

> NCV: . . .remember this: **Anyone who brings a sinner back from the wrong way will save that sinner's soul from death** and will cause many sins to be forgiven.

So who is the "sinner" here? If you take "sinner" to mean a person who has never known Christ, this verse describes a *person* influencing him to repent, which discredits Unconditional Election (because it's the *person* doing the influencing) as well as Total Depravity (because repenting is choosing to change our ways for the better, which is something we're allegedly unable to do).

However, if you take "sinner" to mean someone who *was* a Christian and fell away (which is more reasonable, when read in context), that's a problem for the Reformed doctrines too. This person fell away from Christ to the point that he would have gone to hell, had he died before being "brought back" into the fold—notice that his *soul* was being saved "from death." And that, of course, discredits Irresistible Grace and Perseverance of the Saints. So either way you interpret this verse, it refutes *something* in the Reformed doctrines.

Now take a look at this one:

Revelation 22:16–17 (CEB): "I, Jesus, have sent my angel to bear witness to all of you about these things for the churches. I'm the root and descendant of David, the bright morning star. ¹⁷**The Spirit and the bride say, 'Come!' Let the one who hears say, 'Come!'** And let the one who is thirsty come! Let the one who wishes receive life-giving water as a gift."

v. 17, AMP: **The [Holy] Spirit and the bride (the church, the true Christians) say, Come! And let him who is listening say, Come!** And let everyone come who is thirsty [who is painfully conscious of his need of those things by which the soul is refreshed, supported, and strengthened]; and whoever [earnestly] desires to do it, let him come, take, appropriate, and drink the water of Life without cost.

The Reformed doctrines would not have a problem with the Spirit saying "Come," but they might with the *bride* saying it, because the bride of Christ is people, as shown in the AMP, above. And surely, people can't have any effect on other people coming to God—the Reformed doctrines tell us so.

Be aware that the above passage is one of those non-chronological sections in the book of Revelation. Jesus' revelation to John about the future events starts in Chapter 4, where He says, "Come up here, and I will show you what must take place in the future" (4:1b, AMP), and continues through chapter 21, where He talks about the new heaven and the new earth. Then the vision of the future ends, and chapter 22 is back to John's life on the island of Patmos, as Jesus gives him some closing remarks.

Even though John was still seeing heaven in chapter 22, the vision of the future had ended. It is clear that the temporal context of chapter 22 had returned to John's first-century existence because of many things Jesus said to him, which would make no sense if they were said *after* the new heaven and new earth were in place.

Free to Choose?

Things like:

- "Behold, I am coming soon!" (v. 7, 12, NIV). Christ's second coming had not yet happened.

- "Blessed is he who keeps the words of the prophecy in this book." (v. 7, NIV). The option of choosing to keep (or "heed") the words of the prophecy was still available.

- ". . .the time when things are brought to a crisis and the period of their fulfillment is near" (v. 10, AMP). Once the new heaven and new earth appear, the time for fulfillment of things would be already past.

- "Let the evildoer still do evil, and the filthy still be filthy, and the righteous still do right, and the holy still be holy." (v. 10, ESV). Once the new heaven and new earth appear, there won't be any more evildoers or filthy people.

. . .and there are more, but the above should suffice to confirm that the temporal context of Revelation 22 is still the first century. And therefore, statements made in chapter 22 are still relevant to the question of whether the Reformed doctrines are accurate representations of Scriptural truths. So now let's return to v. 17:

> Revelation 22:17 (CEB): "**The Spirit and the bride say, 'Come!' Let the one who hears say, 'Come!'** And let the one who is thirsty come! Let the one who wishes receive life-giving water as a gift."

When Jesus says that the *bride* is issuing an invitation for people to come into the Kingdom of God, as well as when He says that *those who hear* issue the same invitation, He is describing people influencing other people to come to Jesus, which the Reformed doctrine of Unconditional Election says is impossible. According to that doctrine, all such decisions were made by God in eternity past, and nothing humans do could ever alter the outcome. But this passage seems to refute such an idea.

Note too that Jesus is inviting anyone who "wishes"—or, as other translations render it, anyone who "wills," "desires," "wants to," "craves," or "is willing"—to partake of the water of life, to do so. These words are clearly indicating an act of free will, to receive the gift of life. This statement overturns another of the Reformed doctrines: that of Total Depravity, in which, we are supposedly unable to choose to serve God, because our wills are so totally depraved.

I could go on, but I think I've made my point: people can indeed influence other people either toward or against the Gospel. Therefore, unchangeable decisions in this regard are *not* made for us by God with utter disregard to our choices, decisions, and actions. It's not looking good for Limited Atonement, *or* Unconditional Election, *or* Total Depravity. . .

Paul's Confirmation

As alluded to in the previous section, the Apostle Paul apparently didn't know about the doctrines of Total Depravity, Unconditional Election, and Limited Atonement, because he spent countless hours, and engaged in grueling work for many years, to accomplish something that—if these doctrines are actually true—was a complete waste of effort.

> I Corinthians 9:19–23: For though I be free from all men, yet have I made myself servant unto all, **that I might gain the more.** ²⁰And unto the Jews I became as a Jew, **that I might gain the Jews;** to them that are under the law, as under the law, **that I might gain them that are under the law;** ²¹To them that are without law, as without law, (being not without law to God, but under the law to Christ,) **that I might gain them that are without law.** ²²To the weak became I as weak, **that I might gain the weak:** I am made all things to all men, **that I might by all means save some.** ²³And this I do for the gospel's sake, that I might be partaker thereof with you.

Look at that! he did all these things *for the purpose* of persuading people to choose to submit themselves to God, to become Christians, to "get saved." Where the KJV says "gain the more," other translations say it in different phraseology, but the meaning is the same:

> AMP: . . .**gain** the more [for Christ].
>
> CEB: . . .to **recruit** more of them.
>
> CJB: . . .in order to **win** as many people as possible.
>
> ERV: I do this to help **save** as many people as I can.
>
> EXB: I make myself a slave to all people to **win** as many as I can.
>
> MSG: . . .I have voluntarily become a servant to any and all in order to **reach** a wide range of people: religious, nonreligious, meticulous moralists, loose-living immoralists, the defeated, the demoralized—whoever.
>
> NIRV: I do it to **win** as many as I can to Christ.
>
> NLV: I do this so I might **lead** more people to Christ.

NLT: . . .I have become a slave to all people to **bring** many to Christ.

VOICE: I have become a slave by my own free will to everyone in hopes that I would **gather** more believers.

WE: I have done this so that I might **win** more people to Christ.

So Paul used all that time and energy to "win" people to Christ, to "lead" them to Christ, to "bring" them to Christ, to "reach" them, to "recruit" them, to "gather" them, to "save" them. Why spend all that time and effort on such a fruitless endeavor? Didn't Paul know about Total Depravity, Unconditional Election, and Limited Atonement? Didn't he realize that salvation was limited to only some people and not the rest? Didn't he realize that the salvation decisions had already all been made before the creation of the world? Didn't Paul realize that nothing he could do, and nothing his listeners could do, could affect their ultimate destination in any way? Didn't he *know* his efforts were a colossal waste of time and effort? Apparently not. This should tell us something, shouldn't it?

Paul continues in that vein in the next chapter:

I Corinthians 10:33 (AMP): Just as I myself strive to please [to accommodate myself to the opinions, desires, and interests of others, adapting myself to] all men in everything I do, not aiming at or considering my own profit and advantage, but that of the many **in order that they may be saved.**

Here again, Paul is adjusting his behavior around other people for the explicitly stated purpose "that they may be saved." But if Unconditional Election and Limited Atonement are true and everyone's salvation status was decided before they were born, all such behavior by Paul was the epitome of futility, fruitlessness, and vanity.

Paul says a comparable thing to the Ephesians:

Ephesians 3:8–9 (NKJV): To me, who am less than the least of all the saints, this grace was given, that I should preach among the Gentiles the unsearchable riches of Christ, ⁹and **to make all see what is the fellowship of the mystery,** which from the beginning of the ages has been hidden in God who created all things through Jesus Christ;

What? Paul was called to make all men see the gospel? Surely that's just a translation error, right? Other translations don't imply that Paul could actually influence people toward God, do they?

> Ephesians 3:9 (AMPC): Also **to enlighten all men and make plain to them what is the plan** [regarding the Gentiles and providing for the salvation of all men] of the mystery kept hidden through the ages and concealed until now in [the mind of] God Who created all things by Christ Jesus.
>
> CEV: **God,** who created everything, **wanted me to help everyone understand** the mysterious plan that had always been hidden in his mind.
>
> GNV: And **to make clear unto all men** what the fellowship of the mystery is, which from the beginning of the world hath been hid in God, who hath created all things by Jesus Christ. . .
>
> GNT: . . .and of **making all people see** how God's secret plan is to be put into effect. God, who is the Creator of all things, kept his secret hidden through all the past ages. . .
>
> MSG: This is my life work: **helping people understand and respond to** this Message.
>
> NIV: . . .and **to make plain to everyone** the administration of this mystery, which for ages past was kept hidden in God, who created all things.
>
> NLV: I was **to make all men understand the meaning** of this secret. God kept this secret to Himself from the beginning of the world. And He is the One Who made all things.
>
> NTE: **My job is to make clear to everyone** just what the secret plan is, the purpose that's been hidden from the very beginning of the world in God who created all things.

The Reformed doctrines of Unconditional Election (which states that God has unchangeably chosen who will respond to the Gospel and who will not) and Limited Atonement (which states that God doesn't want all people to be saved) would seriously take issue with Paul's statement that *he*—Paul himself—was to "enlighten," "make clear" and "plain," "make all people see" and "understand" the mystery of the Gospel. *All* people! *Everyone!* Why, that implies that God wants everyone to be saved! (II Peter 3:9) And that people can influence others toward God! Indeed it does.

Apparently Paul thought he was accomplishing something with all his preaching, encouraging, healing, delivering, teaching, and so forth. And either he actually *was* accomplishing something, *or* the doctrines of Total Depravity, Unconditional Election, and Limited Atonement are true. But they are mutually exclusive concepts, so they cannot both be true at the same time. Which conclusion do you think is more reliable?

Jude also weighs in on the subject:

> Jude 22–23 (NIV): Be merciful to those who doubt; [23]**snatch others from the fire and save them;** to others show mercy, mixed with fear—hating even the clothing stained by corrupted flesh.

Obviously, this command is completely useless and pointless, not to mention being impossible to obey, if Unconditional Election and Limited Atonement are valid concepts.

The Impact on Evangelism: The Unsaved

Not only are the concepts of Total Depravity, Unconditional Election, and Limited Atonement de-motivating for evangelists—because their efforts couldn't possibly make a difference—but it has the same effect on the unsaved.

Imagine a sinner hearing about Christ, but also mixed in with the message of Christ are the doctrines of Total Depravity, Unconditional Election, and Limited Atonement. These doctrines effectively communicate, "If you've been chosen, you'll be saved, and if you haven't, you won't. Period." Since that is the message—albeit stated rather bluntly—why should the sinner change his ways? Why should the sinner repent? (Oh yes, I forgot: he can't.) His eternal landing-place is already decided, so why should he give up the fun of sin? Total Depravity says that he *can't* repent unless God has already chosen him, so why do anything?

What's *Your* Excuse?

In the first chapter of Romans, Paul states that God has shown enough of Himself to every man who has ever lived, that they could repent and turn to Him, should they so choose:

> Romans 1:18–25 (NIV): The wrath of God is being revealed from heaven against all the godlessness and wickedness of **men who suppress the truth** by their wickedness, [19]since **what may be known about God is plain to them, because God has made it plain to them.** [20]For since the creation of the world **God's invisible qualities—his eternal power and divine nature—have been clearly seen, being understood** from what has been made, so that **men are without excuse.** [21]For although **they knew God,** they neither glorified him as God nor gave thanks to him, but their thinking **became** futile and their foolish hearts **were** darkened. [22]Although they claimed to be wise, they **became** fools [23]and

exchanged the glory of the immortal God for images made to look like mortal man and birds and animals and reptiles. [24]**Therefore God gave them over** in the sinful desires of their hearts to sexual impurity for the degrading of their bodies with one another. [25]They **exchanged** the truth of God for a lie, and worshiped and served created things rather than the Creator—who is forever praised. Amen.

This passage is just loaded with deep and profound content. Basically it's saying that God has given *all* men enough revelation of Himself that they could choose to follow Him, or they could choose not to:

- In v. 18, Paul refers to people who "suppress" the truth by their wickedness. They know that it's the truth, and yet they suppress it anyway. Why do I say that they know it's the truth? Because the very next phrase (in v. 19) says, "what may be known about God is plain to them, because God has made it plain to them." That's pretty blunt: they know it because God showed them.

- Then, as if to reinforce the idea that God has made the truth plain to them already, Paul goes on, in v. 20, saying that "God's invisible qualities—his eternal power and divine nature—have been clearly seen." So, God made it plain to them, and His power and divinity have been clearly seen.

- Then, as if to reinforce the idea of "made plain" and "clearly seen," Paul points out that these things *were understood* by those to whom it was made plain, and those who had clearly seen (v. 20). It's not that they "didn't get it;" *they understood.*

- And what is the result of God's clear and effective communication of His attributes on these wicked people under discussion? Because they knew, and they *still* rejected Him and rebelled against Him, "they are without excuse." Why is it important to point out that people who suppress the truth, even though they plainly, clearly saw it and understood it, are "without excuse?" For one thing, it shows that Total Depravity, Unconditional Election, and Limited Atonement are not valid; if these doctrines *were* true, the wicked would have a *perfect* excuse for their wickedness: "I rejected God because it was impossible for me to do otherwise." But God is just and justified in pouring out His wrath against the wicked *because they knew better*—vv. 19–20 just said that in three different ways—but they rejected Him anyway, *by their own free choice.*

333

- Then v. 21 gets even more disturbing: not only did these wicked people know *about* God, but *they knew God*. Did they know Him to the point of salvation and then rebel? Perhaps. But they at least knew Him to the point of understanding His eternality, His deity, His power, and so forth. So they knew Him, but did not glorify Him or thank Him.

- The result of their rejection? Their thinking *became* futile. It wasn't futile all along; it *became* futile. This is another perfect example of what I mentioned earlier: "When you decide to reject the Right Answer, it doesn't much matter which wrong answer you choose." These people knew God and understood His attributes (read the passage again to confirm those statements), but they rejected Him anyway, and *that's* when their thinking became futile and their foolish hearts were darkened.

- Reiterating the results of their rejection of God, Paul goes on in v. 22: they *became* fools. Again, they weren't fools to begin with, but when they rejected God after knowing Him and His attributes, they *became* fools.

- These wicked people, who suppress truth, also did something else, as shown in v. 23: they *exchanged* the glory of the immortal God for images of creatures. The point? They couldn't exchange God's glory for something else, unless they had God's glory to begin with. You can't trade away something you don't have.

- *Therefore*—and that's a connecting word that indicates causality—God gave them over to corrupt thinking (v. 24). Here again is God acting toward us in kind, and in response to, how we act toward Him (for many more examples and Scriptures on this concept, see "When God Takes His Cue From Us," above).

- Then, just for good measure, Paul says it yet again in v. 25: they had the truth of God to begin with, but they traded it away in exchange for a lie.

So the point of this subsection being placed in the section entitled "The Impact on Evangelism: The Unsaved" is simply this: the doctrines of Total Depravity, Unconditional Election, and Limited Atonement give the unsaved the *perfect* excuse—an *ironclad* excuse—for rejecting God. These doctrines claim that we *can't* respond positively to Him. How much better excuse could there *be* for not responding positively to Him? But as Romans 1 shows, this reasoning does not fly.

"The World"

Just in case the multitude of Scriptures in the section "Does God Want Everyone to be Saved?" is insufficient to convince us, there are certainly more. It appears that God *really* wants us to understand that He loves *everyone* and desires *all* people to be saved, not only from the Scriptures above, but those in this section as well.

In the New Testament, the word "world" can mean several things;

> Matthew 13:49: So shall it be at the end of the **world**: the angels shall come forth, and sever the wicked from among the just. . .
>
> > NIV: This is how it will be at the end of the **age**. The angels will come and separate the wicked from the righteous. . .

In this case, "world" was translated from the Greek word αἰών (*aion*, G165), which technically means a long duration of time—an *age*, as the NIV translates it. This word is where we get the English word "eon." But this is not the concept I'll be talking about in this section, so I will not address Scriptures that use the word "world" if it was translated from αἰών.

Another meaning of the word "world" in the New Testament connotes the idea of location, specifically, on this planet where humans live:

> John 8:23 (NIV): But he continued, "You are from below; I am from above. You are of this **world**; I am not of this **world**."
>
> John 16:28: I came forth from the Father, and am come into the **world**: again, I leave the **world**, and go to the Father.

Clearly, the scriptures above, as well as others with a similar context, are referring to location. In this case, the word "world" comes from the Greek word κόσμος (*kosmos*, G2889). This is the correct word we're looking for, but not with this particular nuance of meaning.

Another meaning that the Greek word *kosmos* has is when it refers to the *people* of the planet; i.e., all mankind. When Scripture uses *kosmos* in this sense, the verses also contain the idea or context of a *relationship*. This is the meaning of *kosmos* we will investigate here.

> John 1:9: That was the true Light, **which lighteth every man that cometh into the *world*.**
>
> John 1:29 (NIV): The next day John saw Jesus coming toward him and said, "Look, the **Lamb of God, who takes away the sin of the *world*!**"

John 3:16–17 (NIV): For **God so loved the *world*** that he gave his one and only Son, that whoever believes in him shall not perish but have eternal life. ¹⁷For **God did not send his Son into the world to condemn the *world*, but to save the *world* through him.**

John 4:42: . . .and they were saying to the woman, "It is no longer because of what you said that we believe, for we have heard for ourselves and know that **this One is indeed the Savior of the *world*.**"

John 6:33: For the bread of God is he which cometh down from heaven, and **giveth life unto the *world*.**

John 6:51 (AMP): I [Myself] am this Living Bread that came down from heaven. If anyone eats of this Bread, he will live forever; and also **the Bread that I shall give for the life of the *world* is My flesh** (body).

John 8:12: Then spake Jesus again unto them, saying, **I am the light of the *world*:** he that followeth me shall not walk in darkness, but shall have the light of life.

John 12:47: And if any man hear my words, and believe not, I judge him not: for **I came not to judge the *world*, but to save the *world*.**

John 17:21: That they all may be one; as thou, Father, art in me, and I in thee, that they also may be one in us: **that the *world* may believe** that thou hast sent me.

Romans 11:15 (NIV): For if their rejection is **the reconciliation of the *world*,** what will their acceptance be but life from the dead?

II Corinthians 5:19 (NASB): . . .namely, that **God was in Christ reconciling the *world* to Himself,** not counting their trespasses against them, and He has committed to us the word of reconciliation.

I Timothy 1:15: This is a faithful saying, and worthy of all acceptation, that **Christ Jesus came into the *world* to save sinners**; of whom I am chief.

I John 2:2 (AMP): And He [that same Jesus Himself] is the propitiation (the atoning sacrifice) for our sins, and **not for ours alone but also for [the sins of] the whole *world*.**

I John 4:14 (NASB): And we have beheld and bear witness that **the Father has sent the Son to be the Savior of the *world*.**

Now in some cases above, it's not clear whether the word "world" (*kosmos*) should be interpreted "*all* mankind" or merely "*unsaved* mankind." But in the context of the point I'm making, it doesn't matter: the point is supported by the Scriptures above whether you interpret "world" as "all mankind" or just "unsaved mankind."

And, technically, two of the Scriptures above use *kosmos* in the sense of *location* instead of *mankind* (John 1:9 and I Timothy 1:15), but the remainder of the text in those verses clearly shows that the relationship between us and God is the subject, so I've included those two verses in the above list.

But just look at the list of things the Bible says about why Jesus came and what He did:

- Jesus lights *every man that comes into the world.*
- The Lamb of God *takes away the sin of the world.*
- God so loved the world that He sent His Son to *save the world.*
- Jesus is called *"the Savior of the world."*
- Jesus *gives life unto the world.*
- Jesus sacrificed Himself *for the life of the world.*
- Jesus is *the light of the world.*
- Jesus came *not to judge the world, but to save the world.*
- Jesus came *that the world may believe.*
- The Jews' rejection of Jesus resulted in *the reconciliation of the world.*
- Christ *reconciled the world to Himself.*
- Christ Jesus *came into the world to save sinners.*
- Jesus is the propitiation *for the sins of the whole world.*
- The Father *sent the Son to be the Savior of the world.*

Now, seriously: *how in the world* could anyone read the Scriptures above and still maintain that God offers salvation to only *some* of mankind? Again, you'll come to the same conclusion whether you interpret "world" in the above verses to mean "all mankind" or just "sinful mankind." The Scriptures above are yet another deathblow to the Reformed doctrines of Unconditional Election and Limited Atonement, which say that God offers salvation only to a subset of humanity.

Conviction of Sin

If the Reformed doctrines are correct, for what purpose does the Holy Spirit convict people of their sins? Does not the Holy Spirit convict people of their sins *in order to persuade them* to discontinue their way of life, repent of their sins and turn to God for forgiveness?

> John 16:7–11 (NIV): But I tell you the truth: It is for your good that I am going away. Unless I go away, the Counselor will not come to you; but if I go, I will send him to you. ⁸When he comes, **he will convict the world of guilt in regard to sin** and righteousness and judgment:

> ⁹**in regard to sin, because men do not believe in me;** ¹⁰in regard to righteousness, because I am going to the Father, where you can see me no longer; ¹¹and in regard to judgment, because the prince of this world now stands condemned.

And notice in the Scripture above that the Holy Spirit convicts "the world" of their sin; He is reaching out to *everyone,* not just the elect, as Unconditional Election and Limited Atonement claim. That fact, combined with the Scriptures listed in Do All People Get Saved?, shows that it is possible to resist the Holy Spirit, which confutes the doctrine of the Irresistible Grace.

The Impact on Holiness

Here's another aspect of the whole Reformed predestination idea that has a significant impact on people's attitudes and actions. A person, in trying to decide whether he should do a good thing or an evil thing, might be influenced by Total Depravity, Unconditional Election, and Limited Atonement to reason as follows: "If I'm part of the elect, that can't change, so why should I resist this temptation? After all, it will be fun, and I'll still get to heaven. And if I'm *not* part of the elect, that can't change either, so again, why should I resist this temptation? After all, it will be fun, and I'll still end up in hell, so why bother with doing good?"

This is very realistic thinking for the world out there. And it's flawless logic. The reason we come to absurd conclusions, even though the logic is sound, is because we started with erroneous premises (Total Depravity, Unconditional Election, and Limited Atonement). So what does the Bible have to say about personal holiness?

> Romans 6:6–7, 22 (NIV): For we know that our old self was crucified with him so that the body of sin might be done away with, that **we should no longer be slaves to sin—** ⁷because anyone who has died has been freed from sin. ²²But **now that you have been set free from sin** and have become slaves to God, **the benefit you reap leads to holiness,** and the result is eternal life.

> I Corinthians 5:7–8 (NIV): Get rid of the old yeast that you may be a new batch without yeast—as you really are. For Christ, our Passover lamb, has been sacrificed. ⁸Therefore let us keep the Festival, **not with the old yeast, the yeast of malice and wickedness, but with bread without yeast, the bread of sincerity and truth.**

> Ephesians 4:22–24 (NIV): You were taught, with regard to your former way of life, to **put off your old self,** which is being corrupted by its de-

ceitful desires; ²³to be made new in the attitude of your minds; ²⁴and to **put on the new self, created to be like God in true righteousness and holiness.**

Ephesians 5:27 (AMP): That He might present the church to Himself in glorious splendor, **without spot or wrinkle or any such things [that she might be holy and faultless].**

Colossians 1:22 (TEV): But now, by means of the physical death of his Son, God has made you his friends, **in order to bring you, holy, pure, and faultless,** into his presence.

Colossians 3:9–10 (TEV): Do not lie to one another, for **you have put off the old self** with its habits ¹⁰and **have put on the new self.** This is the new being which God, its Creator, is constantly renewing in his own image, in order to bring you to a full knowledge of himself.

I Thessalonians 4:7 (TEV): God did not call us to live in immorality, **but in holiness.**

I Peter 1:15–16 (AMP): But as the One Who called you is holy, **you yourselves also be holy in all your conduct** and manner of living. ¹⁶For it is written, **You shall be holy,** for I am holy.

II Peter 3:11 (NIV): Since everything will be destroyed in this way, what kind of people ought you to be? **You ought to live holy and godly lives. . .**

And there are dozens, scores, perhaps *hundreds* of other Scriptures that address our personal holiness. (For much more detail, see Book 2: *Is It Possible to Stop Sinning?*) But doesn't it seem strange that the Bible is so diligent about commanding, encouraging, and exhorting us to stop living with our old, sinful habits, and to change them to new, holy habits, if it has no bearing or effect on our eternal landing-place? Because if the Reformed doctrines of Total Depravity, Unconditional Election, and Limited Atonement are true, our own personal habits and behavior don't make the slightest difference in our eternal home. So why bother?

But the Bible clearly indicates that personal holiness is of paramount importance. But why *is* holiness important? Simply this:

Hebrews 12:14: **Follow** peace with all men, and **holiness,** *without which no man shall see the Lord. . .*

That's rather sobering. Especially when side by side with doctrines that are *demotivating* in the area of increasing our own personal holiness.

Chapter 8:

Irresistible Grace

The Reformed doctrine of Irresistible Grace, sometimes also called "efficacious grace," asserts that the saving grace of God is effectually applied to those whom He has determined to save (i.e., the elect; those predestined to be saved) and overcomes their resistance to obeying the call of the gospel, bringing them to a saving faith (again, this presumes the validity of the doctrine of Total Depravity). This means that when God sovereignly chooses to save someone, that person will certainly (unavoidably, inevitably, inescapably, ineluctably) be saved.

Resisting the Holy Spirit

The doctrine of Irresistible Grace states that this purposeful influence of God's Holy Spirit "cannot be resisted," but that the Holy Spirit, "graciously causes the elect sinner to cooperate, to believe, to repent, to come freely and willingly to Christ."

But think about that statement for a moment: the Holy Spirit "cannot be resisted," and He "causes" the sinner to "come freely and willingly" to Christ. Do you see the self-contradiction? The Spirit "irresistibly causes" people to come "freely and willingly." The problem, of course, is that if the Holy Spirit *irresistibly causes* someone to get saved, it was not freely and willingly, even if the human believes it was. They are completely opposite, and mutually exclusive, concepts.

Free to Choose?

The doctrine of Irresistible Grace reminds me of a book I read many years ago, in which one of the characters was a political leader, backed up by the military. When he heard that the populace expressed—shall we say, "dissatisfaction"—with his laws and leadership style, he pounded his fist on the table and shouted to his generals, "We *will* have voluntary compliance!" In the book, the obvious self-contradiction was humorous; in the Reformed doctrine of Irresistible Grace, trying to believe such a self-contradiction could have eternal consequences for one's soul.

So again, let's look into the Bible and examine some Scriptures that relate to this concept. Here is an excerpt from Stephen's sermon to the elders, scribes, hired rabble-rousers, and others who would soon stone him to death. Stephen said:

> Acts 7:51: Ye stiffnecked and uncircumcised in heart and ears, **ye do always resist the Holy Ghost: as your fathers did, so do ye.**
>
> HCSB: You stiff-necked people with uncircumcised hearts and ears! **You are always resisting the Holy Spirit; as your ancestors did, so do you.**
>
> NLT: You stubborn people! You are heathen at heart and deaf to the truth. **Must you forever resist the Holy Spirit? That's what your ancestors did, and so do you!**
>
> AMP: You stubborn and stiff-necked people, still heathen and uncircumcised in heart and ears, **you are always actively resisting the Holy Spirit. As your forefathers [were], so you [are and so you do]!**

Wow. Right off the bat, the doctrine of Irresistible Grace—that idea that the Holy Spirit moves on people in an irresistible way—is overthrown, because the Bible talks right here about people resisting the Holy Spirit. God's *chosen* people, no less. And not just as an occasional aberration, but for many generations, and habitually. Very important detail: Note that these people are not resisting the Holy Spirit because they are the non-elect (in the Unconditional Election sense); the Holy Spirit is *trying* to doing something with them, *but they refused.*

The Bible is clear that when God speak through someone prophetically, it is the Spirit Who gives the words being spoken (Numbers 11:25–29, I Samuel 10:6, 10, 19:20, 23, Nehemiah 9:30, Joel 2:28, Zechariah 7:12, Acts 2:17–18, I Corinthians 12:9–10, Ephesians 3:5). So when God calls people to repent, it is the Holy Spirit issuing the call.

Is it possible to refuse to heed the Spirit's invitation? Oh, yes:

Jeremiah 7:13 (NET): You also have done all these things, says the Lord, and I have spoken to you over and over again. But you have not listened! **You have refused to respond when I called you to repent!**

The point here is not that the Holy Spirit lacks the raw power to do anything He wants to do, but rather, He loves us and wants us to love Him back. And as pointed out earlier, love *must* be voluntary, or it is not love; attempting to "force love" immediately degenerates it into rape.

Notice also that Acts 7:51 above describes people who resist the Holy Spirit as being "stiff-necked." What does that mean? Why were those words chosen? When someone approaches someone else, bowing is a common gesture of respect (as to a friend), submission (as to a superior), or worship (as to God). What does bowing entail? Tipping your head forward, which requires bending the neck. Maybe also the waist and the knees, but at least the neck. When one is being stiff-necked, he is defiantly communicating "I will *not*. . ." Does the other person *force* the stiff-necked person to bow? Usually not, especially if he loves the stiff-necked person. But the message has been communicated nonetheless.

Vexing the Holy Spirit

Stephen was not just getting agitated here; he was quoting from Isaiah, where God said a similar thing to the children of Israel of that day:

Isaiah 63:9–10: In all their affliction he was afflicted, and the angel of his presence saved them: in his love and in his pity he redeemed them; and he bare them, and carried them all the days of old. [10]**But they rebelled, and vexed his holy Spirit:** therefore he was turned to be their enemy, and he fought against them.

Not a good choice the Israelites made here. Look at how God acted toward them:

- When they hurt, God hurt (was compassionate).
- God protected (saved) them from their enemies.
- God redeemed them. Why? Because He loved and pitied them.
- God supported them and supplied their needs continuously.

That sounds really cool. But how did the Israelites respond?

- They rebelled against Him.
- They vexed the Holy Spirit.

And what were the results?

- God *became* their enemy. (He wasn't, originally.)
- God fought against them.

So again, we have another Scripture that shows God reaching out and being loving to people, and they rebelled against Him and vexed His Spirit. Then, and *only* then, did God reject them and fight against them. In the pattern that we've seen repeatedly now, God takes His cue on how to act toward us by how we act toward Him.

In addition, this Old Testament passage is another deathblow to the Reformed idea that the Holy Spirit operates like a spiritual bulldozer, overcoming anything that tries to resist. It is obvious, from reading these Scriptures that talk about people resisting the Holy Spirit, that He doesn't operate in "irresistible mode." It *is* possible to resist the Holy Spirit. It's just stupid.

Proponents of Reformed theology may take exception to the image I've painted above, that of the Holy Spirit being a "bulldozer." They will say that His Spirit enables us to desire Him in the first place, and that is true. But as we saw above, He does that in a way that doesn't show favoritism, or unfairly give an advantage to one that He doesn't give to another (see "God is Not a Respecter of Persons" for Scriptural support for this statement). In other words, He wants *all* people to be saved (see "Does God Want Everyone to be Saved?" for Scriptural support for this statement). But obviously, not everyone *is* saved (see "Do All People Get Saved?" for Scriptural support for this statement). So unless someone is overriding God, we must be able to resist the Holy Spirit. Terminally foolish, without question. But possible.

Grieving the Holy Spirit

Let's look at some other instances of resisting the Holy Spirit, though expressed in different words.

Ephesians 4:30a: And **grieve** not the holy Spirit of God. . .

CEB: Don't make the Holy Spirit of God **unhappy**. . .

GWORD: Don't give God's Holy Spirit any reason to be **upset** with you.

PHILLIPS: Never **hurt** the Holy Spirit.

TLB: Don't cause the Holy Spirit **sorrow** by the way you live.

MSG: Don't **grieve** God. Don't **break his heart.**

NCV: And do not make the Holy Spirit **sad**.

NIRV: Do not make God's Holy Spirit **mourn.**

Just *look* at those words above! By our actions, we can grieve or hurt the Holy Spirit; we can make Him unhappy, upset, sorrowful, heartbroken, sad, and mournful. Now if the Holy Spirit moved on us in an irresistible way, how could we possibly make Him sad? If the Holy Spirit moved on us in an irresistible way, we would be incapable of doing anything except exactly what He wanted us to do, and there would therefore be nothing for Him to grieve about. Except, of course, the absence of a loving relationship, which, as we saw above, must be voluntary.

Quenching the Holy Spirit

Most Christians have heard that they are not to "quench" the Holy Spirit, and that is indeed Scriptural. But what does it really mean? What would it look like? Let's investigate.

The idea comes from Paul's first epistle to the church in Thessalonica:

I Thessalonians 5:19: **Quench not** the Spirit.

> AMP: **Do not quench** [subdue, or be unresponsive to the working and guidance of] the [Holy] Spirit.
>
> CSB: **Don't stifle** the Spirit.
>
> CEB: **Don't suppress** the Spirit.
>
> CEV: **Don't turn away** God's Spirit. . .
>
> ERV: **Don't stop the work of** the Holy Spirit.
>
> EHV: **Do not extinguish** the Spirit.
>
> GNT: **Do not restrain** the Holy Spirit. . .
>
> PHILLIPS: **Never damp the fire of** the Spirit. . .
>
> TLB: **Do not smother** the Holy Spirit.
>
> NCV: **Do not hold back the work of** the Holy Spirit.
>
> NIRV: **Don't try to stop** what the Holy Spirit is doing.

This is pretty amazing. Not that we have learned more precisely what "quenching" means, but it may be momentarily surprising that *we* can quench the Holy Spirit in any way whatsoever! And then, after a moment's reflection, we realize—likely to our own embarrassment—that it is not at all difficult to quench the Holy Spirit.

Think back over your own life: how many times has God told you to do something and you were afraid, unsure, nervous, hesitant, stubborn, or simply disobedient, and ended up *not* doing what the Holy Spirit told you to do? That is quenching the Holy Spirit. Look again at the other translations above: you were "unresponsive to the working and guidance of" the Holy Spirit, you "stifled" and "suppressed" what the Holy Spirit was trying to do, and you "stopped His work." I have done the same; probably all Christians have at some point or another.

Now, of course, you didn't stop His work permanently or worldwide, but you stopped what He was trying to do in, or *through,* you at that moment. And because God is *always* good, you just "shot yourself in the foot," as the saying goes. In other words, you hurt yourself more than you hurt God, and you missed out on a chance to bless someone else by letting God work through you. *Who knows* what blessing the other person didn't get because you disobeyed?

But in the context of this book, the significant thing is that *it is possible to quench the Holy Spirit*—this is shown not only by the Scripture above, but by an honest assessment of our own lives. Which, of course, overthrows any possibility of the Reformed doctrine of Irresistible Grace being valid. (For more detail on quenching, see "The Parable of the Ten Virgins," below.)

Striving with the Holy Spirit

Ever since the Garden of Eden, and even before, God has wanted a loving relationship with humanity. Since love must be voluntary, God doesn't merely overpower us and our free wills—that would entirely miss the point of love. But He *strives* with us; trying to persuade us to do the sensible thing: turn to Him and choose to follow and obey Him.

> Genesis 6:3a (NASB): Then the LORD said, "My Spirit shall not strive with man forever. . ."

There *is* a Day of Judgment coming, and we do not have an infinite number of chances to repent. Let us *not* resist the Holy Spirit, because at some point unknown to us, He will give up striving with us to repent, and will resign us to the fate we have chosen.

God is very patient, and He does grant repentance to people:

> Acts 5:31 (AMP): **God exalted Him** to His right hand to be Prince and Leader and Savior and Deliverer and Preserver, **in order to grant repentance** to Israel and to bestow forgiveness and release from sins.

Acts 11:18 (NASB): And when they heard this, they quieted down, and glorified God, saying, "Well then, **God has granted to the Gentiles also the repentance** that leads to life."

II Timothy 2:25–26 (NIV): Those who oppose him he must gently instruct, **in the hope that God will grant them repentance** leading them to a knowledge of the truth, [26]and that they will come to their senses and escape from the trap of the devil, who has taken them captive to do his will.

God grants us the ability to repent, but as we've seen, that does not continue forever.

Here again are Scriptures that casually talk about concepts that completely overthrow several of the Reformed doctrines.

Rahab the Harlot

Do you remember Rahab? She was the prostitute in Jericho who was spiritually astute enough to realize that the God of Israel was the real thing (much like the prostitutes of Jesus' day; see Matthew 21:31–32, etc.), and humble enough to trust Him and submit herself to His plans. Therefore, she and her family survived the conquest of Jericho when everyone else in Jericho died.

Here's how the Bible describes her, and contrasts her with the rest of Jericho:

Hebrews 11:31 (AMPC): [Prompted] by faith Rahab the prostitute **was not destroyed** along with **those who refused to believe and obey**, because she had received the spies in peace [without enmity].

CEV: Rahab had been a prostitute, but **she had faith** and welcomed the spies. **So she wasn't killed with the people who disobeyed.**

EXB: It was **by faith that Rahab, the prostitute, welcomed** [welcomed with peace] the spies and was not killed [did not perish] with **those who refused to obey God** [the disobedient; or the unbelievers; Josh. 2].

TPT: **Faith provided a way of escape for Rahab** the prostitute, **avoiding the destruction of the unbelievers,** because she received the Hebrew spies in peace.

Notice that genuine faith and obedience go together (since, if you actually believe God is Who He says He is, you will gladly follow His instructions), while unbelief and disobedience—refusing to obey—also go together (if you don't obey God, it shows you don't really believe He is Who He says He is).

The inhabitants of Jericho believed that God was real—technically—but not to the point of actually trusting or obeying Him. Here's what Rahab said to the two spies:

> Joshua 2:9–11 (GWORD): She said to them, "I know the Lord will give you this land. **Your presence terrifies us. All the people in this country are deathly afraid of you.** ¹⁰**We've heard how the Lord dried up the water of the Red Sea in front of you** when you left Egypt. We've also heard what you did to Sihon and Og, the two kings of the Amorites, who ruled east of the Jordan River. We've heard how you destroyed them for the Lord. ¹¹When we heard about it, we lost heart. **There was no courage left in any of us because of you. The Lord your God is the God of heaven and earth.**"

The kind of belief that prompts obedience is the kind of belief that Jesus-followers have. This was Rahab's kind of belief. The kind of "belief" that the other Jerichoites had is often referred to nowadays as "unbelieving believers"—people who technically realize that God exists, but who do not pursue Him to develop a relationship or receive what He offers. (For more examples of such "unbelieving believers," see the section by that name in Book 3: *Extra-Biblical Truth: A Valid Concept?*.)

This latter kind of "unbelieving belief" is not particularly noteworthy, because that is the kind of belief that even demons have:

> James 2:19 (GWORD): **You believe that there is one God.** That's fine! **The demons also believe that,** and they tremble with fear.

But back to Hebrews 11:31: the fact that most of the Jerichoites *refused* to believe—as opposed to being *prevented* from believing, as Limited Atonement posits—overturns Irresistible Grace, which says it's impossible to resist the Holy Spirit. (And, by the way, the fact that Rahab repented and believed God overturns Total Depravity.)

The Pharisees

In Luke, Jesus was commending John the Baptist, whose disciples had just left to report to John all that they had seen Jesus do. Jesus was honoring

John and his ministry of calling people to repentance and warning of judgment to those who didn't repent. Jesus ended his tribute to John with this:

> Luke 7:28: For I say unto you, Among those that are born of women there is not a greater prophet than John the Baptist: but he that is least in the kingdom of God is greater than he.

All the "regular" people, even including the tax collectors, acknowledged the validity and importance of John's ministry. But the Pharisees and lawyers? Not so much. . .

> Luke 7:29–30 (AMP): And all the people who heard Him, even the tax collectors, **acknowledged the justice of God [in calling them to repentance and in pronouncing future wrath on the impenitent]**, being baptized with the baptism of John. ³⁰But **the Pharisees and the lawyers [of the Mosaic Law] annulled and rejected and brought to nothing God's purpose concerning themselves,** by [refusing and] not being baptized by him [John].

I find it intriguing that Jesus, plus all the regular people—notably *excluding* the religious leaders—all acknowledged the justice of God in calling people, through John, to repentance; something that Total Depravity says is impossible. They also acknowledged the justice of God in judging people based on their behavior, which Unconditional Election says will not happen. And finally, this verse points out that the Pharisees and lawyers rejected God's intentions toward them, which Irresistible Grace says is impossible. Fascinating.

The Parable of the Great Supper

In Luke 14, Jesus tells another parable about the Kingdom of God:

> Luke 14:16–24 (NIV): Jesus replied: "A certain man was preparing a great banquet and invited many guests. ¹⁷At the time of the banquet he sent his servant to tell those who had been invited, 'Come, for everything is now ready.'"

The Calvinist position describes those who have been invited to the banquet as the "elect," and they—and *only* they—will make it into the banquet. This is stated by the Reformed doctrine of Unconditional Election. Let's continue reading:

> ¹⁸"But they all alike began to make excuses. The first said, 'I have just bought a field, and I must go and see it. Please excuse me.' ¹⁹Another said, 'I have just bought five yoke of oxen, and I'm on my way to try

them out. Please excuse me.' ²⁰Still another said, 'I just got married, so I can't come.' ²¹The servant came back and reported this to his master. Then the owner of the house became angry and ordered his servant, 'Go out quickly into the streets and alleys of the town and bring in the poor, the crippled, the blind and the lame.' ²²'Sir,' the servant said, 'what you ordered has been done, but there is still room.' ²³Then the master told his servant, 'Go out to the roads and country lanes and make them come in, so that my house will be full. ²⁴I tell you, not one of those men who were invited will get a taste of my banquet.'"

Again, in one short parable, several of the doctrines of Calvinism are overthrown. Firstly, the One who was hosting the supper invited people, but they refused (vv. 18–20). This overthrows the Reformed doctrine of Irresistible Grace, which claims that when God invites us, the Holy Spirit operates irresistibly and we cannot refuse.

Secondly, the Lord commands His servants to go into the highways and hedges and "compel them to come in" (v. 23). This overthrows the Reformed doctrine of Unconditional Election, which claims that whether a person ultimately ends up at the supper of his Lord is decided *exclusively* by the Lord, and human beings cannot in any way influence others either to attend, or not to attend, because the decision was made in eternity past.

Thirdly, the Lord tells His servants that the ones he originally invited to the supper were no longer invited—because the invitees rejected the Lord, He therefore rejected them (v. 24). This is another case of God behaving toward us as we have behaved toward him, and this overthrows the Reformed doctrine of Limited Atonement, which says that those who end up in hell will be there because God, in eternity past, decided for them that that is where they would end up, without any input or influence from their own actions and choices.

Rather hard-hitting parable, is it not?

The Day of Pentecost

In the book of Joel, he prophesies about the coming outpouring of the Holy Spirit on the Day of Pentecost:

Joel 2:28–29 (NASB): And it will come about after this that **I will pour out My Spirit on all mankind**; And your **sons** and **daughters** will prophesy, Your **old men** will dream dreams, Your **young men** will see visions. ²⁹And **even on the male and female servants** I will pour out My Spirit in those days.

Then, on the day of Pentecost itself, the Holy Spirit is indeed poured out, the disciples begin to speak in tongues, and apparently stagger around because the Holy Spirit was on them so strongly; people accused them of being drunk. Peter quotes Joel, and says, basically, "This is that."

> Acts 2:15–18 (NASB): For these men are not drunk, as you suppose, for it is only the third hour of the day; ¹⁶but this is what was spoken of through the prophet Joel: ¹⁷'And it shall be in the last days,' God says, 'that **I will pour forth of My Spirit upon all mankind;** and your **sons** and your **daughters** shall prophesy, and your **young men** shall see visions, and your **old men** shall dream dreams; ¹⁸**even upon my bond-slaves, both men and women,** I will in those days pour forth of My Spirit and they shall prophesy.'

The relevant point here is just this: God poured out His Spirit on *all mankind*, not just a subset. This is borne out by the Old Testament prophecy, as well as its New Testament fulfillment. If the Holy Spirit moved in an irresistible way, as the Reformed doctrine of Irresistible Grace claims, then everybody, *without exception,* would ultimately be saved. After all, God's word plainly says that the Holy Spirit was poured out on *everyone,* and we can't resist, right?

The obvious problem here is that not everybody ultimately gets saved and ends up in heaven; we saw this in no uncertain terms in the Scriptures listed in the "Do All People Get Saved?" section, above. So look at the unavoidable logic:

1. Premise 1: The Holy Spirit was poured out on *all mankind* (Joel 2:28–29, Acts 2:17–18).

2. Premise 2: Not everybody gets saved (see Scriptures in "Do All People Get Saved?", above).

3. Conclusion: *It must be possible* to resist the Holy Spirit. Again, it's the height of foolishness to do so, but it must be possible nonetheless, or else some of the above Scriptures must be wrong.

Wisdom (Holy Spirit) Calling

In the first chapter of Proverbs, a personified Wisdom of God is calling out to impart understanding to whomever will listen. Many theologians consider this personification of the Wisdom of God to be none other than the Holy Spirit, but even if that is not true, this passage still says what it needs to say, because godly wisdom comes from above (James 3:17), so *some* person in the Godhead is responsible for delivering it. And the Holy Spirit seems to be the most likely candidate.

> Proverbs 1:20–33 (NIV): Wisdom calls aloud in the street, she raises her voice in the public squares; [21]at the head of the noisy streets she cries out, in the gateways of the city she makes her speech: [22]"How long will you simple ones love your simple ways? How long will mockers delight in mockery and fools hate knowledge? [23]If you had responded to my rebuke, I would have poured out my heart to you and made my thoughts known to you. [24]But since **you rejected me when I called** and **no one gave heed when I stretched out my hand,** [25]since **you ignored all my advice** and **would not accept my rebuke,** [26]I in turn will laugh at your disaster; I will mock when calamity overtakes you— [27]when calamity overtakes you like a storm, when disaster sweeps over you like a whirlwind, when distress and trouble overwhelm you. [28]Then they will call to me but I will not answer; they will look for me but will not find me. [29]Since **they hated knowledge** and **did not choose to fear the** LORD, [30]since **they would not accept my advice** and **spurned my rebuke,** [31]they will eat the fruit of their ways and be filled with the fruit of their schemes. [32]For the waywardness of the simple will kill them, and the complacency of fools will destroy them; [33]but whoever listens to me will live in safety and be at ease, without fear of harm."

This passage is just loaded with nuggets of truth:

- This whole passage is addressing the simple, the mockers, the fools. All the other people—the wise ones—are wise *because* they heeded God's wisdom already, so this passage is not directed at them.
- Wisdom (the Holy Spirit) has tried repeatedly to reach them. He called them (v. 24) and stretched out His hand to them (v. 24), offered them advice (v. 25), and rebuked them (v. 25).
- What was the fools' response to Wisdom (the Holy Spirit)? They rejected Him (v. 24), failed to give heed to Him (v. 24), ignored His advice (vv. 25, 30), and refused to accept His rebuke (vv. 23, 25, 30), and hated the knowledge He was trying to impart (v. 29), they were wayward (v. 32) and complacent (v. 32).
- The fools did not choose the fear of the Lord (v. 29), but rejected Him instead.
- As a result, the simple, the mockers, the fools will suffer severely (vv. 26–28, 21–32), which is not what God wanted for them (vv. 23, 33).

Looking at the details described in this passage, we can plainly see that, first of all, God wants *all* people to be saved. How did I arrive at this conclusion? As follows:

1. There are only two kinds of people in this world, in the context of the above passage: the ones who heed Wisdom (the Holy Spirit), and the ones who don't.
2. The ones who heeded the Holy Spirit already gained the wisdom He was imparting, which they couldn't have done unless He had offered it to them.
3. The ones who didn't heed the Holy Spirit are the ones being rebuked here for rejecting Him. Note that they had been doing this for a long time (v. 22), in spite of the fact that Spirit was trying to get through to them in many ways (vv. 24–25).
4. The people described in Item #2, plus the people described in Item #3, encompasses *all* people, as shown in Item #1.
5. The Holy Spirit reached out to both groups with the goal and intent to impart wisdom to them, and the result of heeding His wisdom is living in safety and ease, without fear of harm (v. 33). This does not *at all* describe burning in hell for eternity; therefore, God wants all people to be saved.

So we see that since God wants all people to be saved, this passage refutes the Reformed doctrines of Unconditional Election and Limited Atonement. And, since some people *did* repent and heed the Holy Spirit's wisdom, that refutes Total Depravity (we know this was a voluntary choice, and not a case of Irresistible Grace, because some people refused).

In addition to the above, we can also see that:

- Blessing (vv. 23, 33) and cursing (vv. 24–32) correlate to people's prior behavior, in the sense of reaping what you sow (Galatians 6:7–8). So we see that since this passage connects behavior and consequences in a causal relationship (and in that order), it refutes the Reformed doctrine of Unconditional Election for that reason too.
- Since the Holy Spirit reached out to *all* people, but some refused (or "rejected" or "ignored" or "would not accept" or "did not choose" or "spurned"), we see that his passage also refutes the Reformed doctrine of Irresistible Grace.

That's quite a lot we can learn from a single passage, no?

Free to Choose?

But wait—there's more! In chapter 8, Wisdom is again personified to represent the Holy Spirit, and what does He say?

Proverbs 8:1–11 (NIV): Does not wisdom **call out**? Does not understanding raise her voice? ²On the heights along the way, where the paths meet, she takes her stand; ³beside the gates leading into the city, at the entrances, she cries aloud: ⁴"**To you, O men, I call out**; I raise my voice to **all mankind**. ⁵**You who are simple,** gain prudence; **you who are foolish,** gain understanding. ⁶**Listen,** for I have worthy things to say; I open my lips to speak what is right. ⁷My mouth speaks what is true, for my lips detest wickedness. ⁸All the words of my mouth are just; none of them is crooked or perverse. ⁹To the discerning all of them are right; they are faultless to those who have knowledge. ¹⁰**Choose my instruction** instead of silver, knowledge rather than choice gold, ¹¹for wisdom is more precious than rubies, and nothing you desire can compare with her."

Again, just *loads* of momentous truths here:

- Wisdom "calls out" (v. 1); i.e., she is trying to get someone's attention. Timidly? Cautiously? Hesitantly? No, she "raises her voice" (v. 1) and "cries aloud" (v. 3), so we can see that she is *strongly* and *urgently* trying to get people's attention. Where is she doing it? Out in the boonies where no one goes? On the contrary, she cries out at main intersections, and at the city gates and entrances. But we haven't yet seen *whose* attention she is trying to get.

- As we continue reading, we see to whom Wisdom is calling out: to "men" (v. 4). Is this sexist? Is Wisdom ignoring women? Of course not; as is commonly done in the Bible, "men" refers to the *species* of man, not the *gender* of man. And just to confirm the point, the Bible clarifies by immediately saying "all mankind" (v. 4). So Wisdom (the Holy Spirit) wants *all mankind* to heed her words. This again refutes the Reformed doctrines of Unconditional Election and Limited Atonement.

- So we see that Wisdom wants all mankind to listen and heed her words. But it seems especially important that the "simple" and the "foolish" do so (v. 5); why is that? Because everyone who is no longer simple and foolish has already heeded the words of Wisdom—the Holy Spirit—that's *why* they're no longer simple and foolish. So the fact that the Holy Spirit is going specifically after everyone who hasn't

Chapter 8: Irresistible Grace

yet heeded Him again refutes Unconditional Election and Limited Atonement, which claim that God only wants to bless *some* people.

- Wisdom wants the simple and foolish to gain prudence and understanding (v. 5) and to "listen" to her (v. 6).
- The Holy Spirit rightly says that all godly Wisdom is "worthy" and "right" (v. 6), "true" (v. 7), "just" (v. 8), and "faultless" (v. 9). Why would *anybody* pass up such an offer?
- Then Wisdom says that the simple and foolish—to whom this passage is addressed (v. 5)—are to *choose* (v. 10) the instruction of Wisdom above everything else (v. 11). And this refutes the Reformed doctrine of Total Depravity, which says that ungodly people cannot choose to change their ways. That doctrine is really quite astonishing, considering the myriad places in the Bible where God tells ungodly people to change their ways. And, the fact that the simple and foolish are exhorted to choose Wisdom shows us that it *is* possible to choose it. But the Holy Spirit is talking, so the very existence of this exhortation shows that it is possible to resist the leading of the Holy Spirit. And that invalidates the Reformed doctrine of Irresistible Grace.

There are many other very cool things Wisdom says in vv. 12–31, which I am omitting for the sake of brevity. But then Wisdom says some other things in the final portion of the chapter:

> Proverbs 8:32–36 (NIV): "Now then, my sons, **listen to me**; blessed are those who keep my ways. [33]**Listen to my instruction** and be wise; **do not ignore it**. [34]Blessed is the man who listens to me, **watching** daily at my doors, **waiting** at my doorway. [35]For whoever finds me finds life and receives favor from the LORD. [36]But **whoever fails to find me harms himself; all who hate me love death**."

The following nuggets fall right out of this passage:

- Again, Wisdom reiterates to her intended audience—all mankind, but especially the simple and foolish—to listen to her instruction (vv. 32–33). As noted above, this again refutes the Reformed doctrines that claim God wants only to bless *some* of mankind (Unconditional Election and Limited Atonement).
- And again, Wisdom exhorts the hearers to *not ignore* her instruction (v. 33). As above, the very presence of this exhortation indicates that it is possible to ignore Wisdom (the Holy Spirit), which debunks the Irresistible Grace theory.

- How much are we supposed to value the Wisdom God wants to give us? If we have an ounce of sense, we'll watch and wait at her door every day (v. 34), gaining wisdom at every opportunity.
- Then are listed the consequences of heeding Wisdom's words, followed by the consequences of *not* heeding Wisdom's words. The ones who heed Wisdom find life and God's favor (v. 35), but the ones who refuse to heed Wisdom find harm and death (v. 36). And again we see that it is possible to hate and reject the Holy Spirit (v. 36). Ill-advised, yes, but possible nevertheless.

God Calling

Here's an excerpt from one of David's psalms:

Psalm 25:8 (NIV): Good and upright is the Lord; therefore **he instructs sinners in his ways.**

NET: The Lord is both kind and fair; that is why **he teaches sinners the right way to live.**

Fascinating. God teaches sinners how to live. If people are no longer sinners, they have already heeded His instruction. And the fact that God teaches sinners His ways shows yet again that He wants everyone to be saved, and He gives them the ability, and encouragement, to do so. This, too, overturns Unconditional Election and Limited Atonement.

But someone might say, "Well yes, He teaches sinners (the unelect) His ways, but since they aren't elect, they can't take advantage of it." But this idea is disallowed by the first part of the verse, which states that God is good and upright, kind and fair. Therefore, such fraudulent behavior as teaching people how to live godly, but then preventing them from doing so, and then punishing them for not obeying what He prevented them from obeying, is not a behavior that a good, upright, kind, and fair God would do—it goes against His eternal nature of Goodness.

Here's one of Asaph's psalms; does it have any bearing on the current discussion? It sure looks like it:

Psalm 81:8–16 (AMP): Hear, O My people, and I will admonish you— O Israel, **if you would listen to Me!** [9]There shall no strange god be among you, neither shall you worship any alien god. [10]I am the Lord your God, Who brought you up out of the land of Egypt. Open your mouth wide and I will fill it. [11]**But My people would not hearken to My voice, and Israel would have none of Me.** [12]So I gave them up to their own hearts' lust and **let them go after their own stubborn will,** that they might follow their own counsels. ¹³**Oh, that My people would listen to Me,** that Israel would walk in My ways! ¹⁴Speedily then I would subdue their enemies and turn My hand against their adversaries. ¹⁵[**Had Israel listened to Me in Egypt,** then] those who hated the Lord would have come cringing before Him, and their defeat would have lasted forever. ¹⁶[God] would feed [Israel now] also with the finest of the wheat; and with honey out of the rock would I satisfy you.

It's Scriptures like this (and so many others that we've seen already) that make one wonder, "Where in the world did the Reformed doctrines come from?" This one passage overturns so many of them, it's a wonder they have survived for as long as they have.

Let's get into detail:

- Verse 8: God says, "*if* you would listen to Me!" According to Irresistible Grace, it would be impossible *not* to listen to God when He speaks, so this is a fatal blow to Irresistible Grace.

- Verse 11: God bluntly says, "My people would not hearken to My voice, and Israel would have none of Me." The Jews rejected God's advances, and rejected Him as their God! Again, another fatal blow to Irresistible Grace.

- Verse 12: God "let them go after *their own stubborn will.*" If *that* isn't proof positive that people have a free will, I don't know what is. Notice that this is a fatal blow to Unconditional Election.

- Verse 13: God says, "Oh, that My people would listen to Me" and walk in His ways. He clearly *wants* people to heed His commands—because He loves them—but they don't. Yet another fatal blow to Irresistible Grace.

- Verse 14: God says, "then [if they had obeyed] I would. . ." This plainly shows that God wanted them to obey Him, but they wouldn't. It also shows God taking His cues from humans: His behavior being strongly influenced by ours. Another fatal blow to Unconditional Election.

- Verse 15: God says, "Had Israel listened to Me in Egypt, then. . ." which clearly shows God taking His cues from humans (Israelites, in that case). Yet another fatal blow to Unconditional Election.

- Verse 16: God "would" do this and He "would" do that if the condition stated in the previous verses had happened. Again, this clearly shows God taking His cues from humans. Yet another fatal blow to Unconditional Election.

One wonders how many fatal blows it will take for the Reformed doctrines to submit to Biblical evidence. . .

Now let's take a look at a passage in Zechariah, where God is talking about an interaction between Him and Israel:

Zechariah 1:2–6 (NLT): "I, the Lord, was very angry with your ancestors. ³Therefore, say to the people, 'This is what the Lord of Heaven's Armies says: **"Return to me, and I will return to you,"** says the Lord of Heaven's Armies. ⁴"Don't be like **your ancestors who would not listen or pay attention** when the earlier prophets said to them, 'This is what the Lord of Heaven's Armies says: "Turn from your evil ways, and stop all your evil practices."'" ⁵Where are your ancestors now? They and the prophets are long dead. ⁶But everything I said through my servants the prophets happened to your ancestors, just as I said. **As a result, they repented** and said, 'We have received what we deserved from the Lord of Heaven's Armies. He has done what he said he would do.'"

Did you catch all that? From this one little passage, we see the following:

- Verse 3: God is willing to return to the people *if they return to him first.* This refutes the Reformed doctrines of Total Depravity (which says we can't repent) as well as Unconditional Election (which says our response to God is not a matter of our choice). See the section "When God Takes His Cue From Us" for many other examples of this same concept.

- Verse 4: The Israelites under discussion *did not listen or pay attention to God's advances.* This refutes the Reformed doctrine of Irresistible Grace (which says when God wants to bless us, we can't refuse).

- Verses 5–6: *God's warnings through the prophets of old about the consequences of sin came true,* just as God said they would. This process of God's behavior being strongly influenced by ours refutes Unconditional Election.

- Verse 6: *The people repented.* This refutes Total Depravity.

That's quite a lot from one little passage. But let's take a look at another passage in Zechariah, where God is talking about another interaction between Him and Israel:

> Zechariah 7:8–13 (NIV): And the word of the Lord came again to Zechariah: ⁹"This is what the Lord Almighty says: 'Administer true justice; show mercy and compassion to one another. ¹⁰Do not oppress the widow or the fatherless, the alien or the poor. In your hearts do not think evil of each other.' ¹¹But **they refused** to pay attention; stubbornly **they turned their backs** and **stopped up their ears**. ¹²**They made their hearts as hard as flint** and **would not listen to the law** or **to the words that the Lord Almighty had sent by his Spirit** through the earlier prophets. So the Lord Almighty was very angry. ¹³'When I called, **they did not listen;** so when they called, I would not listen,' says the Lord Almighty."

Okay, this is interesting; this is even stronger evidence than the previous passage. On the one hand we have the Reformed doctrine of Irresistible Grace, which says that the Holy Spirit cannot be resisted; if God wants us to do something, it is impossible for us to do otherwise. On the other hand, we have this passage in the Bible which says that when God commanded Israel, by His Spirit, to behave in a godly way:

- *They* refused to pay attention;
- *They* turned their backs;
- *They* stopped up their ears;
- *They* made their hearts as hard as flint;
- *They* would not listen to the law; and
- *They* would not listen to the words that God had sent by His Spirit through the prophets.

The Reformed doctrine of Irresistible Grace and this passage say opposite, mutually exclusive things; which should we believe?

Oh, and by the way, here is another passage that shows God taking His cue on how to behave toward us, from how we have behaved toward Him. Refer back to the section "When God Takes His Cue From Us" for many more examples of this.

Here's a fascinating passage; what do you think this verse means?

> Proverbs 16:9 (WEB): A man's heart plans his course, But Yahweh directs his steps.

Free to Choose?

A person of the Reformed persuasion would read the above verse to say: "A man may choose (or may *think* he chooses) to do whatever he wants, but it won't do any good—his apparent choosing will be completely ineffectual—because God will have irresistibly caused him to do whatever God wanted him to do, and the man will be unable to refuse."

On the other hand, a person of the free-will persuasion would interpret it as, "Once a person chooses the direction he wants to go, God will arrange things so that Jesus is glorified through that person's life, even if the person's choices cause his own destruction."

These two interpretations are mutually exclusive, so they both cannot be correct (remember the Law of Non-Contradiction?). So which one is correct? From the multitude of Scriptures we've seen already, and reinforced by all those we have yet to see, the free-will interpretation certainly has the Scriptural support.

A good example of this is God choosing to glorify Himself through two different pharaohs of Egypt. The pharaoh from Joseph's day was greatly blessed because he was willing to submit himself to God's plans and heeded His word. The pharaoh from Moses' day was destroyed, along with the entire country, because he was *not* willing to submit himself to God's plans or follow His word. But in both cases, God's power and His Name were glorified. See "Pharaoh's Example" for a much more thorough treatment of this topic.

Jesus Calling

Let's look at a well-known Scripture from the apostle John's revelation of Jesus:

Revelation 3:20 (NIV): Here I am! I stand at the door and knock. **If anyone** hears my voice and **opens the door, I will come in** and eat with him, and he with me.

This is written to the *church* at Laodicea, which means that Jesus is hoping that the *church* lets Him in! Obviously, then, it must be possible for the church to *not* let Him in. And if we don't let Him in, He doesn't break the door down—as He could certainly do, if raw power were the only factor—He just continues to knock, waiting for us to choose to let Him in and fellowship with Him.

This is the same church to which Jesus says:

Revelation 3:15–16 (NIV): I know your deeds, that you are neither cold nor hot. I wish you were either one or the other! [16]So, **because you** are lukewarm—neither hot nor cold—I am about to spit you out of my mouth.

(To hear this passage set to music, listen to the song *The Lukewarm Blues* on the album *Dry Bones to Living Stones* or scan the QR code at right.)

And notice the word "because" in the verse above: Jesus spits people out of His mouth *as a result* of their being lukewarm. It is not the case that the people were lukewarm because Jesus had already spewed them out. This is yet another case of God taking His cue from us, and behaving toward us the way we have behaved toward Him.

That's rather convicting, is it not? Whatever it means for Jesus to "spit someone out of His mouth," I don't want it to happen to me. . .

So in these last three sections, we've seen God the Father, God the Son, and God the Holy Spirit all interacting with human beings, urging them to obey. And in all cases, some human beings rejected them, or spurned their advances. Note that all of the examples above overturn the idea of Irresistible Grace because humans refused to obey God.

Stretching Forth the Hands

In Romans 10, Paul says the following:

Romans 10:21: But to Israel he saith, **All day long I have stretched forth my hands unto a disobedient and gainsaying people.**

So what does it mean to "stretch forth the hands" to someone? It sounds like an invitation, as in welcoming someone "with open arms." But is it reasonable to understand it that way? Let's look at some other translations to see if that is an accurate interpretation:

ERV: But about the people of Israel God says, "All day long I stood **ready to accept** those people, but they are stubborn and refuse to obey me."

EXB: But about Israel God [or Isaiah; he] says, "All day long I stood **ready to accept** [held out my hands to] people who disobey [disbelieve] and are stubborn [defiant; rebellious; Is. 65:2]."

GNT: But concerning Israel he says, "All day long I held out my hands **to welcome** a disobedient and rebellious people."

ICB: But about Israel God says, "All day long I stood **ready to accept** people who disobey and are stubborn."

> MSG: Then he capped it with a damning indictment: "Day after day after day, I beckoned Israel **with open arms,** And got nothing for my trouble but cold shoulders and icy stares."

It sure *sounds* like God was inviting them; it *sounds* like God was ready to accept them, seeing as how God said, "All day long I stood ready to accept" them. In this passage, Paul is quoting Isaiah:

> Isaiah 65:2: **I have spread out my hands** all the day unto a rebellious people, which walketh in a way that was not good, after their own thoughts...
>
> CEV: All day long **I have reached out** to stubborn and sinful people going their own way.
>
> ERV: All day long **I stood ready to accept** those who turned against me. But they kept doing whatever they wanted to do, and all they did was wrong.
>
> EXB: All day long **I stood ready to accept** [stretched out my hands to a] people who turned [rebelled] against me, but the way they continue to live [walk] is not good; they do anything they want to do [following their own thoughts/schemes].
>
> GNT: **I have always been ready to welcome** my people, who stubbornly do what is wrong and go their own way.
>
> ICB: All day long **I stood ready to accept** people who turned against me. But the way they continue to live is not good. They do anything they want to do.
>
> TLB: But my own people—though **I have been spreading out my arms to welcome them** all day long—have rebelled; they follow their own evil paths and thoughts.
>
> MSG: I kept saying 'I'm here, I'm right here' to a nation that ignored me. **I reached out** day after day to a people who turned their backs on me...
>
> NCV: All day long **I stood ready to accept** people who turned against me, but the way they continue to live is not good; they do anything they want to do.
>
> NLT: All day long **I opened my arms** to a rebellious people. But they follow their own evil paths and their own crooked schemes.

It's pretty clear that God was inviting the people, wooing the people to follow Him. It's also pretty clear they did not. Here again, this New Testament passage, as well as the Old Testament passage it was quoting, refute the Reformed doctrine of Irresistible Grace.

And, by the way, note the numerous ways that God Himself is describing the free will that man obviously had, because he was using it to go against what God had commanded them to do: the people walked "after their own thoughts," the people were "going their own way," "they kept doing whatever they wanted to do," and "they follow their own evil paths and their own crooked schemes." Assuming God did not want them to sin (which He doesn't; see Book 2: *Is It Possible to Stop Sinning?* for great detail), these descriptions cannot be mistaken: the people were doing what they wanted to do, which, according to God Himself, was different than what He wanted them to do.

What more clear way to describe free will is there? To answer the question of whether or not free will exists, this one Scripture is all we need. But the hundreds of others listed throughout this book confirm and reinforce the fact in numerous ways, just for good measure.

The Sign of the Prophet Jonah

Remember the story of Jonah? In a nutshell: God told him to preach at Nineveh, and pronounce judgment upon the city for their sins (1:1–2). But Jonah tried to run away from the presence of God (1:3) because if they repented, Jonah figured God would be merciful and spare them (4:2). So God sent a fish to swallow Jonah (1:17) after he was thrown overboard (1:15) from the ship that was about to sink because of the storm that suddenly came up (1:4), and then while in the fish's belly, Jonah had a revelation:

> Jonah 2:8 (NIV): Those who cling to worthless idols forfeit **the grace that could be theirs.**

Note: "the grace that *could be theirs*." It wasn't theirs, but it could have been, had they not forfeited it. Grace was not being withheld from them; they forfeited it. Of course this is true in the general sense: whatever idols we cling to—whatever things we value more than we value God Himself—will keep us away from an intimate relationship with God.

But could Jonah have been also referring to a *specific* idol that he realized was in his own life? Or could God have shown him this in the general sense, so that Jonah would recognize it in his own life later? Could this idol have been perhaps a doctrine that dismisses or resents the idea of God having mercy on whomever repents of his sin? We know that Jonah was angry that God was merciful to the Ninevites and canceled the announced judgment once they had repented:

> Jonah 4:1–3 (NIV): But **Jonah was greatly displeased and became angry.** ²He prayed to the Lord, "O Lord, is this not what I said when I was still at home? That is why I was so quick to flee to Tarshish. **I knew that you are a gracious and compassionate God, slow to anger and abounding in love, a God who relents from sending calamity.** ³Now, O Lord, take away my life, for it is better for me to die than to live."

Such a Great Salvation

The writer of Hebrews gives us a very sobering warning in the discussion on the salvation that Jesus offers us:

> Hebrews 2:3 (NIV): . . .how shall we escape **if we ignore such a great salvation?** This salvation, which was first announced by the Lord, was confirmed to us by those who heard him.

> AMP: How shall we escape [appropriate retribution] **if we neglect and refuse to pay attention to such a great salvation [as is now offered to us, letting it drift past us forever]?** For it was declared at first by the Lord [Himself], and it was confirmed to us and proved to be real and genuine by those who personally heard [Him speak].

> GWORD: So how will we escape punishment **if we reject the important message,** the message that God saved us? First, the Lord told this saving message. Then those who heard him confirmed that message.

> TLB: what makes us think that we can escape **if we are indifferent to this great salvation** announced by the Lord Jesus himself and passed on to us by those who heard him speak?

Now if the Holy Spirit moved in "irresistible mode," how could we ever ignore, neglect, refuse to pay attention to, reject, or be indifferent to, salvation? The very fact that we *can* ignore, reject, and so forth, disallows the possibility of the Reformed doctrine of Irresistible Grace. In fact, this one verse tells us several things:

- First, it is possible to repent and accept salvation, because the reader is being urged to do so (which overturns Total Depravity);
- Second, salvation goes into effect in our lives only if we choose to accept it (which overturns Unconditional Election);

- Third, it is possible—though indisputably foolish—to neglect, ignore, reject, or refuse it (which overturns Irresistible Grace);
- Fourth, the consequences for ignoring or rejecting salvation are severe.

It's very enlightening to just ponder the implications of what the Bible says. . .

"Harden Not Your Heart. . ."

There are several Scriptures that present a difficult problem to those who believe that the Holy Spirit acts irresistibly:

Psalm 95:8: **Harden not your heart,** as in the provocation, and as in the day of temptation in the wilderness. . .

Hebrews 3:8: **Harden not your hearts,** as in the provocation, in the day of temptation in the wilderness. . .

Hebrews 3:15: While it is said, To day if ye will hear his voice, **harden not your hearts,** as in the provocation.

Hebrews 4:7: Again, he limiteth a certain day, saying in David, To day, after so long a time; as it is said, To day if ye will hear his voice, **harden not your hearts.**

How odd. Why would God include in the Bible even once, let alone *four times,* an exhortation for *us* not to harden our hearts if the hardness of our hearts were not something that we can influence, as the Reformed doctrines of Total Depravity and Irresistible Grace state? Our hearts would be unchangeably hard if the Holy Spirit did *not* move on us, wouldn't they? And hardening our hearts would be impossible if the Holy Spirit moved on us irresistibly, wouldn't it? Very strange indeed, why God put all these pointless commands in the Bible. . .

And here's something else that is very curious. Let's look at the same Scriptures as above, but paying attention to the conditional clause that appears in *every single one* of them:

Psalm 95:7–8: For he is our God; and we are the people of his pasture, and the sheep of his hand. To day **if ye will hear his voice,** [8]Harden not your heart, as in the provocation, and as in the day of temptation in the wilderness. . .

> Hebrews 3:7–8: Wherefore (as the Holy Ghost saith, To day **if ye will hear his voice,** ⁸Harden not your hearts, as in the provocation, in the day of temptation in the wilderness:
>
> Hebrews 3:15: While it is said, To day **if ye will hear his voice,** harden not your hearts, as in the provocation.
>
> Hebrews 4:7: Again, he limiteth a certain day, saying in David, To day, after so long a time; as it is said, To day **if ye will hear his voice,** harden not your hearts.

Intriguing. Before *every single occurrence* in the Bible of this exhortation to "harden not your hearts," there is a condition. That condition is "*if* you will hear his voice." Whose voice is it talking about? As shown in Hebrews 3:7 above, it is the Holy Ghost speaking. Now here is the question that immediately becomes apparent: if the Holy Ghost were acting in irresistible mode, there would be no "if" about it; we would necessarily have to do what the Holy Ghost wanted; i.e., to hear His voice. But the very fact that there is a condition attached to each one—the "if" clauses—shows that the Holy Ghost must *not* be acting in "irresistible mode." This, of course, overthrows the Reformed doctrine of Irresistible Grace.

Something else in Hebrews 3, between the two verses noted above, also is terribly confusing if we choose to believe the Reformed doctrine of Irresistible Grace:

> Hebrews 3:10 (GNT): And so I was angry with those people and said, 'They are always disloyal and **refuse to obey my commands.**'
>
> MSG: And I was provoked, oh, so provoked! I said, "They'll never keep their minds on God; **they refuse to walk down my road.**"
>
> NLT: So I was angry with them, and I said, 'Their hearts always turn away from me. **They refuse to do what I tell them.**'
>
> TPT: This ignited my anger with that generation and I said about them, 'They wander in their hearts just like they do with their feet, and **they refuse to learn my ways.**'

Wait, *what?* They *"refuse"* to do what Holy Spirit tells them? That would be utterly impossible if the Holy Spirit actually operated in irresistible mode. But it makes perfect sense that this would be possible if people indeed have free will.

And if we consider other commands that amount to the same thing (assuming for the moment that the Reformed doctrine of Irresistible Grace is true), but express the exhortation in different words, it becomes even more puzzling why God would put so many pointless commands in the Bible. For example:

> II Corinthians 5:20: Now then we are ambassadors for Christ, as though God did beseech you by us: **we pray you in Christ's stead, be ye reconciled to God.**

This verse, like so many we've already seen, and so many more still to come, again raises that nagging question: Why would Paul "pray" them—ask them, *beseech* them, *beg* them—to turn to God if the Holy Spirit operated in irresistible mode? If that were the case, they couldn't *help* but be reconciled to God. And, by the way, the fact that Paul is exhorting them to repent overturns Total Depravity, which claims we can't repent. And the fact that if anyone responds to Paul's exhortation (which is clearly the intent) overturns Unconditional Election, which says that people getting saved are unavoidably responding to God's edict, and therefore not responding to the evangelistic efforts of any human.

And why would Paul, when talking to the Jews about why he preaches to the Gentiles, say this?

> Acts 28:25–28 (NIV): They *[the Jews]* disagreed among themselves and began to leave after Paul had made this final statement: "The Holy Spirit spoke the truth to your forefathers when he said through Isaiah the prophet: [26]'Go to this people and say, "You will be ever hearing but never understanding; you will be ever seeing but never perceiving." [27]For this people's heart has become calloused; they hardly hear with their ears, and **they have closed their eyes.** Otherwise they might see with their eyes, hear with their ears, understand with their hearts and turn, and I would heal them.' [28]Therefore I want you to know that God's salvation has been sent to the Gentiles, and they will listen!"

Wait a minute: "they" have closed their eyes? Irresistible Grace doesn't allow that, does it? God closes their eyes by not electing them, doesn't He? Why did Paul even say that? For that matter, why did Isaiah, whom Paul was quoting, say that? Didn't they know about Irresistible Grace?

Such a list of Scriptures and the resultant troubling questions go on and on if we assume the Reformed doctrine of Irresistible Grace (or any of the other ones) are actually true.

Chapter 9:

Perseverance of the Saints

The final point of Calvinism is the Perseverance of the Saints, sometimes called "perseverance of God *with* the saints." Here, the word "saints" is used to refer to all who are set apart by God (the "elect"), and not of those who are exceptionally holy, already in heaven, or "canonized." The Perseverance of the Saints doctrine states that since God is sovereign and His will cannot be frustrated by human will or action, or indeed *anything* at all, those whom God has called into communion with himself via Unconditional Election will continue in faith until the end; it would be impossible to do otherwise.

Merely an Appearance?

The immediate and obvious response to the above doctrine is, "What about those people who were in effective ministry, but fell away? Or *walked* away?" Since, according to Perseverance of the Saints, it's impossible to *actually* fall away or walk away, those who *apparently* fall away or walk away must fall into one of two categories:

1. They never had true faith to begin with. And Scripturally, this is plausible, according to Jesus' own words:

    Matthew 7:22–23 (NIV): Many will say to me on that day, 'Lord, Lord, did we not prophesy in your name, and in your name drive out demons and perform many miracles?' ²³Then I will tell them plainly, '**I never knew you**. Away from me, you evildoers!'

2. They are actually saved but not presently walking in the Spirit, they will be disciplined by God and will ultimately repent:

> Hebrews 12:6 (NIV): . . .because **the Lord disciplines those he loves**, and he punishes everyone he accepts as a son.

Now the two scenarios above actually do happen in certain cases. The first situation can happen because God's principles and His Word are powerful, and can impart blessing—miraculous blessing, no less—even when preached by unscrupulous people:

> Philippians 1:18 (NIV): But what does it matter? The important thing is that in every way, **whether from false motives or true, Christ is preached.** And because of this I rejoice. Yes, and I will continue to rejoice. . .

The second case above is exemplified by David's response when judgment was falling upon Israel because he ordered a census—David repented when the chastisement occurred:

> I Chronicles 21:1, 7, 16–17: And Satan stood up against Israel, and provoked David to number Israel. . . . ⁷And God was displeased with this thing; therefore he smote Israel. . . . ¹⁶And David lifted up his eyes, and saw the angel of the LORD stand between the earth and the heaven, having a drawn sword in his hand stretched out over Jerusalem. Then David and the elders of Israel, who were clothed in sackcloth, fell upon their faces. ¹⁷And David said unto God, Is it not I that commanded the people to be numbered? even **I it is that have sinned and done evil indeed**; but as for these sheep, what have they done? let thine hand, I pray thee, O LORD my God, be on me, and on my father's house; but not on thy people, that they should be plagued.

Or Actuality?

So obviously, both the scenarios above are plausible and do occur on occasion. But those two scenarios, in themselves, don't really address the question of whether the doctrine of the Perseverance of the Saints (also known as "eternal security" or "once saved, always saved") is valid. In other words, just because the two scenarios above are possible, do they necessarily prevent any other conceivable scenario from being possible? And of course, for whatever answer we offer, we'd better be able to back it up with Scripture.

Breaking a Relationship

If there is a relationship between Person A and Person B, there are only three possible scenarios I can see in which such a relationship could be terminated, or broken:

1. Person A terminates the relationship.
2. Person B terminates the relationship.
3. A hostile third party, through strength or deception, breaks the relationship, though neither Party A nor Party B desired that outcome.

Putting this in the context of breaking the relationship between God and us, it would look like this:

1. God terminates the relationship.
2. We terminate the relationship.
3. Satan, through strength or deception, breaks the relationship between us and God, though neither we nor God desired that outcome.

In order for the Reformed doctrine of the Perseverance of the Saints to be valid, *all three* of these scenarios would have to be impossible. It's clear that a statement that says any particular one of them is impossible, doesn't inherently prevent the other two from being possible. Therefore, we'll have to look for Scriptures that address each one of these and *only then* can we make a categorical statement on whether the Perseverance of the Saints is a Scripturally supportable doctrine. So let's look at each of these scenarios from a Biblical perspective and see what we find.

God Breaking the Relationship

Is it conceivable that in a good relationship between God and a human, God would be the One to terminate it? Sure, it's *conceivable*—we can *imagine* it—but it's not *possible*. Why? Because of God's love, His faithfulness, His promises, the fact that He cannot lie, and so forth. God said it will never happen, and when God says it will never happen, *it will never happen.*

> Deuteronomy 7:9 (NIV): Know therefore that the LORD your God is God; **he is the faithful God, keeping his covenant of love to a thousand generations of those who love him and keep his commands.**

> Deuteronomy 31:6, 8 (NIV): Be strong and courageous. Do not be afraid or terrified because of them, for **the LORD your God goes with you; he will never leave you nor forsake you.** ⁸The LORD himself goes be-

Free to Choose?

fore you and will be with you; **he will never leave you nor forsake you. Do not be afraid; do not be discouraged.**

Joshua 1:5 (NASB): No man will be able to stand before you all the days of your life. **Just as I have been with Moses, I will be with you; I will not fail you or forsake you.**

Psalm 36:5: Thy mercy, O LORD, is in the heavens; and **thy faithfulness reacheth unto the clouds.**

Psalm 92:1–2 (NIV): **It is good to praise** the LORD and make music to your name, O Most High, ²to proclaim your love in the morning and **your faithfulness at night. . .**

I Corinthians 1:9: **God is faithful,** by whom ye were called unto the fellowship of his Son Jesus Christ our Lord.

II Thessalonians 3:3 (NIV): But **the Lord is faithful,** and he will strengthen and protect you from the evil one.

Hebrews 13:5 (TEV): Keep your lives free from the love of money, and be satisfied with what you have. **For God has said, "I will never leave you; I will never abandon you."**

Revelation 3:14 (NIV:) To the angel of the church in Laodicea write: **These are the words of the Amen, the faithful and true witness,** the ruler of God's creation.

Okay, so as we can see from the above passages that Scenario 1 (God breaking the relationship) *ain't gonna happen.* But still, that doesn't answer the questions about whether Scenario 2 or Scenario 3 might be possible. So let's keep digging.

Satan Snatching Us Away From God

Some common verses to support the idea of Perseverance of the Saints are these:

John 10:27–29: My sheep hear my voice, and I know them, and they follow me: ²⁸And I give unto them eternal life; and they shall never perish, **neither shall any man pluck them out of my hand.** ²⁹My Father, which gave them me, is greater than all; and **no man is able to pluck them out of my Father's hand.**

NIV: My sheep listen to my voice; I know them, and they follow me. ²⁸I give them eternal life, and they shall never perish; **no one can snatch them out of my hand.** ²⁹My Father, who has given them to me, is greater than all; **no one can snatch them out of my Father's hand.**

Romans 8:38–39 (NIV): For I am convinced that neither death nor life, neither angels nor demons, neither the present nor the future, nor any powers, [39]neither height nor depth, nor anything else in all creation, will be able to separate us from the love of God that is in Christ Jesus our Lord.

Adherents of Perseverance of the Saints often cite these Scriptures and say, "See? Nobody can take you away from Jesus, so you could never lose your salvation." But this situation is akin to a gradeschooler asking his teacher, "Could you show me how to divide 52 by 13?" The teacher replies, "You add the 2 and the 3 in the ones column and put the 5 there. Then you add the 5 and the 1 in the tens column and put the 6 there, and you get 65." The student looks puzzled, and says, "No, I know how to add them up. I need help on long division." So the teacher repeats her explanation.

So was the teacher's statement correct? Yes. *But that wasn't the question.* Although what she said was perfectly true, she answered a question that hadn't been asked, and she *didn't* answer the question that *was* asked. Those who cite John 10:27–29 are absolutely correct in claiming that no one can forcibly remove us from God's family or His protection. But that's only one conceivable way of losing one's salvation, and that particular one, namely Scenario 3, is not possible, as the Bible shows.

We Ourselves Terminating the Relationship

The people who quote Hebrews 13:5 are absolutely correct in saying that Jesus will never leave us or forsake us. But that verse only addresses Scenario 1.

Those who cite Romans 8:38–39 are absolutely correctly saying that none of those things can separate us from the *love of Christ*. But that doesn't address our question either (about being separated from the *salvation* of Christ), because Jesus still *loves* the people who end up in hell; His love is why it grieves Him so much when people choose to go there.

So the Scriptural statements made in the section above are completely true, but they don't address the question we're asking right here. We've only seen, so far, that Scenario 1 (God breaking the relationship) and Scenario 3 (a third party breaking the relationship) are impossible. But again, the question we're asking here is: Is it possible for a Christian to lose his salvation in *any* way? To answer this, we'll need to also address Scenario 2: Can *we* walk away?

Granted, that would be immensely stupid to do so, but *is it possible?* I think so, based on the following Scriptures. (And as we've all undoubtedly seen many times in our own lives, just because something is stupid doesn't mean no one will do it.)

The Parable of the Sower

Jesus told many parables, and below is one of the most well known:

> Mark 4:3–10, 13–20 (NIV): "Listen! A farmer went out to sow his seed. [4]As he was scattering the seed, some fell along the path, and the birds came and ate it up. [5]Some fell on rocky places, where it did not have much soil. It sprang up quickly, because the soil was shallow. [6]But when the sun came up, the plants were scorched, and they withered because they had no root. [7]Other seed fell among thorns, which grew up and choked the plants, so that they did not bear grain. [8]Still other seed fell on good soil. It came up, grew and produced a crop, multiplying thirty, sixty, or even a hundred times." [9]Then Jesus said, "He who has ears to hear, let him hear."

The above is the end of the parable that Jesus told to the crowds, but the disciples were able to get further details from Him:

> [10]When he was alone, the Twelve and the others around him asked him about the parables. [13]Then Jesus said to them, **"Don't you understand this parable? How then will you understand *any* parable?** [14]The farmer sows the word. [15]Some people are like seed along the path, where the word is sown. As soon as they hear it, **Satan comes and takes away the word** that was sown in them. [16]Others, like seed sown on rocky places, hear the word and at once **receive it with joy.** [17]But since they have no root, they last only a short time. When trouble or persecution comes because of the word, **they quickly fall away.** [18]Still others, like seed sown among thorns, hear the word; [19]but the worries of this life, the deceitfulness of wealth and the desires for other things come in and **choke the word, making it unfruitful.** [20]Others, like seed sown on good soil, hear the word, accept it, and produce a crop—thirty, sixty or even a hundred times what was sown."

I think it's very significant that Jesus said what He did in v. 13: "Don't you understand this parable? How then will you understand *any* parable?" Apparently, this concept of sowing and reaping is the most fundamental spiritual law there is, because Jesus strongly implies that if we don't understand this one—the Parable of the Sower—we won't understand *any* of the parables.

So it behooves us to really pay attention to His explanation of it to the disciples.

Here are some of the things we can understand from Jesus' explanation of the parable:

- The seed represents the Word of God (v. 14).
- The seed (the Word) going into a person represents the person accepting what Jesus offered. Since Satan doesn't like this, he will come and take away the Word if we let him (v. 15). Note that this Scripture refutes the Reformed doctrines of Unconditional Election as well as Perseverance of the Saints. We know that Satan can't take away the Word without our permission because of James 4:7: "Resist the devil, and he will flee from you." And note that Satan couldn't take the Word "away" from us unless we already had it. And indeed it had been "sown in" these people (v. 15).
- People can receive the Word and later fall away (vv. 16–17). And it is impossible to "fall away" from God without being "in" God in the first place; a person can't *leave* the United States without first having been *in* the United States. Note that this Scripture too refutes the doctrine of the Perseverance of the Saints.
- People can have the Word sown into them, and because of mis-prioritizing things in their lives, other things choke the Word, making it unfruitful (vv. 18–19). Note that the Word *had been* fruitful, but the desire for other things *made* it unfruitful (v. 19). The most fruitful thing the Word could do in a person's life is to save him and change his eternal port of call from hell to heaven. If the Word is *made* unfruitful after having been fruitful, it sounds like the heavenly destination is aborted. This is consistent with vv. 16–17 as well as Jeremiah 18:9–10 and Ezekiel 33:13, and again refutes the doctrine of Perseverance of the Saints.
- Note that the presentation of the Word required the hearer to "receive" it (v. 16) or "accept" it (v. 20). This Scripture refutes the doctrine of Total Depravity. Also note that some who receive/accept the Word are unfruitful, while others are fruitful. Bearing fruit is not a foregone conclusion; it depends on whether or not we are faithful to Him (John 15:4).

So we can clearly see that the Word can be sown into someone—i.e., he "receives" or "accepts" it—and then subsequent carelessness can derail his salvation. Satan can "take away the Word," the person can "fall away" from God, and other things can "choke the Word, making it unfruitful." In this one single parable, Jesus discredits the Reformed doctrine of the Perseverance of the Saints *three times*.

But there's more. Let's look at something that Hebrews tells us about soil and what grows in it:

> Hebrews 6:7–8 (AMP): **For the soil which** has drunk the rain that repeatedly falls upon it and **produces vegetation useful to those for whose benefit it is cultivated partakes of a blessing from God.** ⁸But if [that same soil] persistently bears thorns and thistles, it is considered worthless** and near to being cursed, whose end is to be burned.

Note again, the seed that God sows—which Jesus equates to "the Word;" that is, Himself—is not at fault (John 1:1–5, 9–14). Nor is it the fault of the rain that falls upon the soil (Joel 2:23–29), rain representing the Holy Spirit. But the ground is responsible for the crop it bears. In other words, *we are responsible for the condition of our ground,* because that determines the crop that grows.

Making Certain

Here are a couple more Scriptures that are terribly confusing if read through the lens of the Reformed doctrine of the Perseverance of the Saints:

> I Timothy 4:16 (AMP): Pay close attention to yourself [concentrate on your personal development] and to your teaching; persevere in these things [hold to them], for as you do this **you will ensure salvation both for yourself and for those who hear you.**
>
> NASB: Pay close attention to yourself and to your teaching; persevere in these things, for as you do this **you will ensure salvation both for yourself and for those who hear you.**
>
> WEYMTH: Be on your guard as to yourself and your teaching. Persevere in these things; for by doing this **you will make certain your own salvation and that of your hearers.**

Isn't that odd? Paul is telling Timothy that he (Timothy) has to do something to "ensure" or "make certain" of his salvation? Apparently Paul didn't realize the Reformed doctrine of Perseverance of this Saints would already have made it certain.

Not only that, Paul is telling Timothy that if he (Timothy) continues in these things, he (Timothy) will make certain of the salvation of *his hearers* as well. Didn't Paul realize that the Reformed doctrine of Unconditional Election prevents this from being true? Again, apparently he didn't.

Other translations say something to the effect of "do this and you will *save* yourself and your hearers." But if you think about it, that means the same thing, unless you conclude that Timothy and the church he was leading in Ephesus were not yet Christians when Paul wrote to him. (But we know Timothy was saved long before this—Acts 16:1–2.)

Here's the other passage that is confusing if read with the assumption of the validity of the Perseverance of the Saints:

> I Thessalonians 3:5 (AMP): For this reason, when I could no longer endure the suspense, I sent someone to find out about your faith [how you were holding up under pressure], for fear that somehow the tempter had tempted you and **our work [among you] would prove to be ineffective.**
>
> CSB: For this reason, when I could no longer stand it, I also sent him to find out about your faith, fearing that the tempter had tempted you and that **our labor might be for nothing.**
>
> CEB: That's why I sent Timothy to find out about your faithfulness when I couldn't stand it anymore. I was worried that the tempter might have tempted you so that **our work would have been a waste of time.**
>
> DARBY: For this reason I also, no longer able to refrain myself, sent to know your faith, lest perhaps the tempter had tempted you and **our labour should be come to nothing.**
>
> ESV: For this reason, when I could bear it no longer, I sent to learn about your faith, for fear that somehow the tempter had tempted you and **our labor would be in vain.**

The people in the Thessalonian church were saved, as we can tell from much of what Paul writes elsewhere in his epistles to them. But here he mentions the possibility that his labor could—*retroactively*—have been rendered "ineffective," "for nothing," "a waste of time," or "in vain." If his evangelistic efforts resulted in the Thessalonian people getting to heaven when they died, Paul's labor would not have been—*could* not have been—lost. The Thessalonians' final destination being heaven is a *huge* gain compared to where they started, not a loss in any sense. Which means, then, that the possibility of Paul's labor being ineffective or in vain must mean the potential loss of salvation of people in the Thessalonian church.

Which, of course, overturns the Reformed doctrine of the Perseverance of the Saints once again.

For It Is Impossible. . .

Hebrews 6 describes the process of someone abandoning his faith, and the dire consequences of the choice:

> Hebrews 6:4–6: For it is impossible for those who **were once enlightened**, and **have tasted** of the heavenly gift, and **were made partakers** of the Holy Ghost, ⁵And **have tasted** the good word of God, and the powers of the world to come, ⁶**If they shall fall away**, to renew them **again** unto repentance; seeing they crucify to themselves the Son of God afresh, and put him to an open shame.

> AMP: For it is impossible [to **restore** and bring **again** to repentance] those who **have been** once for all enlightened, who **have consciously tasted** the heavenly gift and **have become sharers** of the Holy Spirit, ⁵And **have felt** how good the Word of God is and the mighty powers of the age and world to come, ⁶If they **then** deviate from the faith and **turn away from their allegiance**—[it is impossible] to bring them **back** to repentance, for (because, while, as long as) they nail upon the cross the Son of God afresh [as far as they are concerned] and are holding [Him] up to contempt and shame and public disgrace.

> BBE: As for those who **at one time saw the light, tasting the good things from heaven, and having their part in the Holy Spirit,** ⁵**With knowledge of the good word of God, and of the powers of the coming time,** ⁶And then **let themselves be turned away, it is not possible for their hearts to be made new a second time**; because they themselves put the Son of God on the cross again, openly shaming him.

> TEV: For how can **those who abandon their faith** be brought back to repent again? **They were once** in God's light; **they tasted** heaven's gift and **received their share of the Holy Spirit;** ⁵they **knew from experience** that God's word is good, and **they had felt the powers** of the coming age. ⁶And **then they abandoned their faith!** It is impossible to **bring them back** to repent again, because they are again crucifying the Son of God and exposing him to public shame.

Note that this is not just a flippant or casual decision from someone who didn't know better. Like in the discussion of Romans 1 above, such people have no excuse *because they know better*.

This passage contains quite an impressive list of "requirements" a person would have to have experienced in order for his falling away/turning away/ abandonment of the faith to be irretrievable. Look at the list:

- The person was "once enlightened." This mean that he wasn't "in the dark" about spiritual things; he *knew* what was going on.
- The person has "tasted of the heavenly Gift." Let's try to determine what is being referred to here, since there are several things that this gift could refer to:
  - Jesus Himself as in John 4:10;
  - The baptism of the Holy Spirit, as in Acts 2:38, 8:20, and 10:45;
  - Salvation through Jesus' atoning death on the cross, as in Acts 11:17, Romans 5:15–18, 6:23, II Corinthians 9:15, Ephesians 2:8, 4:7, and I Peter 4:10; or
  - A supernatural enablement to perform miracles, as in Romans 11:29, I Corinthians 1:7, 12:1, 4, 9, 30, 13:2, 14:1, 12, I Timothy 4:14, II Timothy 1:6, and Hebrews 2:4.

  . . .but regardless of which one Hebrews 6 is referring to, it implies an intimate knowledge of God; not just a casual, superficial, shallow knowledge.

- The person was made a "partaker of the Holy Ghost." Because the Holy Ghost is specifically mentioned here by name, that implies that the reference to the "heavenly gift" above refers to salvation by Jesus' atoning death. Otherwise, it would be mentioning the identical item twice in the same list.
- The person has "tasted the good word of God." This too indicates more than a passing knowledge. Jesus said "the words that I speak unto you, they are spirit, and they are life."
- The person has "tasted. . . the powers of the world to come." This person is intimately enough involved with the spiritual realm that he is experientially familiar with moving in the miraculous.

So again, such a person has no excuse for walking away. He was enlightened, saved, baptized in the Spirit, knew the power of God's word, and moved in the miraculous. Because He was so knowledgeable and experienced with the things of the Kingdom, when such a person walks away, there is no possibility of return.

Sinning Willfully

Four chapters later, the writer of Hebrews again addresses the prospect of losing one's salvation:

> Hebrews 10:26–29: For if we sin wilfully **after that we have received** the knowledge of the truth, there **remaineth** no more sacrifice for sins, ²⁷But a certain fearful looking for of judgment and fiery indignation, which shall devour the adversaries. ²⁸He that despised Moses' law died without mercy under two or three witnesses: ²⁹Of how much sorer punishment, suppose ye, shall he be thought worthy, who hath trodden under foot the Son of God, and hath counted the blood of the covenant, wherewith **he was sanctified,** an unholy thing, and hath done despite unto the Spirit of grace?

Again, this is not just a case of, "Well, I guess he was never saved in the first place;" no, there is no question that such a person was actually saved and subsequently *loses* his salvation. Look at the wording:

- Such a person *has received the knowledge of the truth* (v. 26). Not just pretended, but actually received it.

- There *remains* no more sacrifice for his sins (v. 26). The sacrifice for his sins was there and in effect before the person sinned willfully, *but it no longer remains.* You can't "remain" in any situation or condition without having first entered that situation or condition.

- The person *was sanctified by the blood of the covenant* (v. 29), but then willfully sins, walking on the Son of God, considering the blood unholy, and insulting the Holy Spirit. At this point there is nothing to look forward to but judgment and fiery indignation, and that is certain (v. 27).

So this person has received the knowledge of the truth, had accepted the sacrifice for his sins, and had been sanctified by Jesus' blood. He was definitely saved. Then he throws it all away by sinning willfully.

Escaping Corruption... Temporarily

Peter reinforces what Hebrews talks about:

> II Peter 2:20–21: For **if after they have escaped** the pollutions of the world **through the knowledge of the Lord and Saviour Jesus Christ,** they are **again entangled** therein, and **overcome, the latter end is worse with them than the beginning.** ²¹For **it had been better for them not to**

have known the way of righteousness, **than, after they have known it, to turn from the holy commandment** delivered unto them.

NIV: If **they have escaped** the corruption of the world **by knowing our Lord and Savior** Jesus Christ and are **again entangled in it and overcome,** they are **worse off at the end than they were at the beginning.** [21]It would have been **better for them not to have known** the way of righteousness, **than to have known it and then to turn their backs on the sacred command** that was passed on to them.

This is definitely a sobering verse. Look at who Peter is talking about: the kind of people he is referring to is the kind who "have escaped the corruption of the world" (v. 20). How did they escape it? By "knowing our Lord and Savior Jesus Christ" (v. 20). This is remarkably unambiguous: they *knew Jesus,* and thereby, escaped the corruption of the world. What better way to describe salvation?

Then notice what Peter says next: If any member of this group of people (who escaped the corruption of the world by knowing Jesus) is "again entangled in it"—here, the word "it" refers to the corruption of the world—*and overcome,* they are worse off than if they'd never been saved. But before you get saved, you're on your way to hell anyway, so what could be worse than that? Simply because of what Jesus said:

Matthew 16:27: For the Son of man shall come in the glory of his Father with his angels; and then **he shall reward every man according to his works.**

If our works are great, we'll receive a great reward, and it goes the other way too: if our works are born of rebellion and disobedience, our reward will be in kind. (Note that this is not talking about a works-based salvation, but simply works-based rewards.) And because the person Peter is talking about knew good and well the salvation he was abandoning when he got entangled and overcome by the corruption in the world, since he knew more, his punishment was greater.

But wait a minute: is that even a Scriptural concept? Is it a Biblically based idea that if you know more, you're punished more severely if you walk away? Actually, yes. Read this:

Luke 12:47 (GNT): The servant who **knows** what his master wants him to do, but does not get himself ready and do it, will be punished with a **heavy whipping.** [48]But the servant who **does not know** what his master wants, and yet does something for which he deserves a whipping, will be punished with a **light whipping**. **Much is required from the person to whom much is given; much more is required from the person to whom much more is given.**

John 9:41 (NIV): Jesus said, "If you were blind, you would not be guilty of sin; but **now that you claim you can see, your guilt remains.**"

John 15:22: **If I had not come and spoken unto them, they had not had sin:** but now they have no cloke for their sin.

CEV: **If I had not come and spoken to them, they would not be guilty of sin.** But now they have no excuse for their sin.

Romans 2:12 (MSG): If you sin without knowing what you're doing, God takes that into account. **But if you sin knowing full well what you're doing, that's a different story entirely.**

Jesus reiterates this concept after He had performed many mighty signs and wonders—actually, the *majority* of them—in three particular cities: Chorazin, Bethsaida, and Capernaum:

Matthew 11:20–24 (NASB): Then He began to reproach the cities in which **most of His miracles** were done, because they did not repent. [21]"Woe to you, Chorazin! Woe to you, Bethsaida! For if the miracles had occurred in Tyre and Sidon which occurred in you, they would have repented long ago in sackcloth and ashes. [22]Nevertheless I say to you, **it shall be more tolerable for Tyre and Sidon** in the day of judgment, than for you. [23]And you, Capernaum, will not be exalted to heaven, will you? You shall descend to Hades; for if the miracles had occurred in Sodom which occurred in you, it would have remained to this day. [24]Nevertheless I say to you that **it shall be more tolerable for the land of Sodom** in the day of judgment, than for you."

The people Jesus was addressing *knew* good and well that God was real; Jesus had shown them proof beyond any doubt, by the presence, the number, and the sheer magnitude of miraculous deeds He did in those cities. And in spite of the infallible proofs He did, they still remained hard-hearted and stiff-necked; they refused to repent and turn to God.

And because of their refusal to repent—in spite of the overwhelming proofs God offered—their punishment would be greater than even that of three notoriously sinful cities of the Old Testament: Tyre and Sidon (Isaiah 23) and Sodom (Genesis 18–19), upon which judgment had already been pronounced. So again, *why* were Chorazin, Bethsaida, and Capernaum going to be judged more harshly than even Tyre, Sidon, and Sodom? *Because they knew more.*

The people of Chorazin, Bethsaida, and Capernaum in Jesus' time were even more hard-hearted and stiff-necked than the people of antiquity in Tyre, Sidon, and Sodom. How do we know that? Because the people of Tyre, Sidon, and Sodom *would have repented* had those same miracles been done in them (vv. 21, 23).

Miracles are much more effective at convincing people of the power of God than mere words are, which is why doing signs and wonders was Jesus' approach to evangelism. Jesus states here that if those miracles had been performed in Tyre, Sidon, and Sodom, their inhabitants would have been convinced of the power and goodness of God, they would have repented of their sin, and the cities would have been spared. But even with the miraculous power of God being manifest, it is still possible to maintain a hard heart: Chorazin, Bethsaida, and Capernaum all did.

And this is not the first time this had happened: in a long prayer by priests who were repenting on behalf of the entire Hebrew nation, they first list many of the miracles God did to protect, provide for, and exalt Israel. But then they continue:

> Nehemiah 9:16–17 (NIV): But they, our forefathers, became arrogant and stiff-necked, and did not obey your commands. ¹⁷**They refused to listen and failed to remember the miracles you performed among them.** They became stiff-necked and in their rebellion appointed a leader in order to return to their slavery. But you are a forgiving God, gracious and compassionate, slow to anger and abounding in love. Therefore you did not desert them. . .

The priests expressed astonishment that the people still rejected God: after seeing His undeniably miraculous power, *they knew better.* And, this same principle is evident in Jesus' warning about the hypocrisy of the Pharisees: because they knew the Law of Moses, they ought to have known better than to be so prideful, selfish, and uncaring of others:

> Luke 20:46–47 (AMP): Beware of the scribes, who like to walk about in long robes and love to be saluted [with honor] in places where people congregate and love the front and best seats in the synagogues and places of distinction at feasts, ⁴⁷Who make away with and devour widows' houses, and [to cover it up] with pretense make long prayers. **They will receive the greater condemnation (the heavier sentence, the severer punishment).**

Note the cause and effect here: *Because* they knew better, but still were ungodly in their behavior, the *effect* of this combination was that they received "the greater condemnation, the heavier sentence, the severer punishment."

So getting back to Peter's statement about the people who "escaped the corruption of this world" only to let themselves again get entangled in it: yes, it would have been better if they had never known the way of righteousness.

Being On Guard

Peter again reinforces his earlier words, as well as those warnings in Hebrews, when he says this:

> II Peter 3:16b (CEB): Some of his *[Paul's]* remarks are hard to understand, and **people** who are ignorant and **whose faith is weak twist them to their own destruction**, just as they do the other scriptures.

That's pretty significant already. Even though Peter describes people whose faith is weak, *they still have faith.* The implication is that they are already believers, but not yet strong in the faith. And when they twist and distort Paul's epistles for whatever reason, they do so *to their own destruction.*

In other words, Peter is restating something He had heard from Jesus earlier. In the parable of the sower, Jesus said:

> Matthew 13:20–21 (ERV): And what about the seed that fell on rocky ground? That is like the people who hear the teaching and **quickly and gladly accept it.** [21]But they do not let the teaching go deep into their lives. **They keep it only a short time. As soon as trouble or persecution comes because of the teaching they accepted, they give up.**

Now think about this: If Peter was describing people who were not believers at all, it wouldn't be the distortion of Paul's writings that would have led them to destruction, but the fact that they rejected Jesus in the first place. As Jesus said:

> John 3:18 (NASB): He who believes in Him is not judged; **he who does not believe has been judged already, because he has not believed in the name of the only begotten Son of God.**

But Peter's next statement is even more clear. Based on what he says to his readers in the verse quoted above, Peter goes on to give them a warning:

> II Peter 3:17: Ye therefore, beloved, seeing ye know these things before, **beware lest ye** also, being led away with the error of the wicked, **fall from your own stedfastness.**

ERV: Dear friends, you already know about this. So be careful. Don't let these evil people lead you away by the wrong they do. **Be careful that you do not fall from your strong faith.**

NIV: Therefore, dear friends, since you already know this, **be on your guard so that you may not** be carried away by the error of lawless men and **fall from your secure position.**

WE: My dear brothers, you know about these things before they happen. Take care that you do not do the same things that bad people do. **Take care that you do not stop believing the right way.**

This certainly makes it sound like it is possible—the Perseverance of the Saints doctrine notwithstanding—to fall from your secure position, to fall from your strong faith, and stop believing the right way, doesn't it?

Forsaking

Here's an interesting set of Scriptures:

Deuteronomy 28:20 (NIV): The LORD will send on you curses, confusion and rebuke in everything you put your hand to, until you are destroyed and come to sudden ruin **because of the evil you have done in forsaking him.**

I Kings 11:30–33 (NIV): . . .and Ahijah took hold of the new cloak he was wearing and tore it into twelve pieces. [31]Then he said to Jeroboam, "Take ten pieces for yourself, for this is what the LORD, the God of Israel, says: 'See, I am going to tear the kingdom out of Solomon's hand and give you ten tribes. [32]But for the sake of my servant David and the city of Jerusalem, which I have chosen out of all the tribes of Israel, he will have one tribe. [33]I will do this because **they have forsaken me** and worshiped Ashtoreth the goddess of the Sidonians, Chemosh the god of the Moabites, and Molech the god of the Ammonites, and have not walked in my ways, nor done what is right in my eyes, nor kept my statutes and laws as David, Solomon's father, did.'"

I Kings 18:18: Elijah replied, I have not troubled Israel, but you *[Ahab]* have, and your father's house, **by forsaking the commandments of the Lord** and by following the Baals.

I Kings 19:10 (NASB): And he *[Elijah]* said, "I have been very zealous for the LORD, the God of hosts; for **the sons of Israel have forsaken Thy covenant,** torn down Thine altars and killed Thy prophets with the sword. And I alone am left; and they seek my life, to take it away."

Free to Choose?

> I Chronicles 28:9 (NASB): "As for you, my son Solomon, know the God of your father, and serve Him with a whole heart and **a willing mind; for the LORD searches all hearts, and understands every intent of the thoughts. If you seek Him, He will let you find Him; but if you forsake Him, He will reject you forever.**"

The verse above is King David speaking; the man after God's own heart (Acts 13:22). Doesn't it make sense that he would know how God behaves? Notice that David is saying that God acts toward us as we have acted toward Him. Not a hint of Calvinism in the one described by God Himself as "after my own heart." But what does it mean to be "after" God's heart? Does it mean to simply be *pursuing* His heart, as in a businessman saying, "I'm after a promotion and a raise this year."? No; as the following translations indicate, it means he thought about things the same way God does (as much as a human can think like God, given Isaiah 55:8–9).

The word "after," as it is translated in numerous versions of the Bible, is translated "who shares my desires" (CEV), "loyal to me" (HCSB), "whose heart beats to my heart" (MSG), "the kind of man I like" (TEV), and "according to my heart" (YLT). So David, who thought about things very much like God does, says that if we seek God, we will find Him, but if we reject Him, He will reject us. A far cry from the Reformed doctrine of Unconditional Election, which claims that our ultimate salvation or damnation has nothing to do with our behavior or choices. Now, back to the list of Scriptures that reinforce this idea:

> II Chronicles 12:5 (AMP): Then Shemaiah the prophet came to Rehoboam and the princes of Judah who had gathered at Jerusalem because of Shishak, and said to them, **Thus says the Lord: You have forsaken Me, so I have abandoned you** into the hands of Shishak.

> II Chronicles 15:1–2 (NASB): Now the Spirit of God came on Azariah the son of Oded, ²and he went out to meet Asa and said to him, "Listen to me, Asa, and all Judah and Benjamin: **the LORD is with you when you are with Him.** And if you seek Him, He will let you find Him; but **if you forsake Him, He will forsake you.**"

> II Chronicles 21:10 (AMP): So Edom revolted from the rule of Judah to this day. Then Libnah also revolted from Jehoram's rule, because **he had forsaken the Lord,** the God of his fathers.

> II Chronicles 24:20 (NIV): Then the Spirit of God came upon Zechariah son of Jehoiada the priest. He stood before the people and said, "This is what God says: 'Why do you disobey the LORD's commands? You

will not prosper. **Because you have forsaken the LORD, he has forsaken you.'"**

II Chronicles 24:24 (NIV): Although the Aramean army had come with only a few men, the LORD delivered into their hands a much larger army. Because **Judah had forsaken the LORD,** the God of their fathers, judgment was executed on Joash.

II Chronicles 28:6 (NASB): For Pekah the son of Remaliah slew in Judah 120,000 in one day, all valiant men, because **they had forsaken the LORD God** of their fathers.

Ezra 8:22 (NIV): I was ashamed to ask the king for soldiers and horsemen to protect us from enemies on the road, because we had told the king, "The gracious hand of our God is on everyone who looks to him, but **his great anger is against all who forsake him."**

Isaiah 1:4 (NIV): Ah, sinful nation, a people loaded with guilt, a brood of evildoers, children given to corruption! **They have forsaken the LORD; they have spurned the Holy One of Israel and turned their backs on him.**

Isaiah 1:28: And the destruction of the transgressors and of the sinners shall be together, and **they that forsake the LORD shall be consumed.**

Isaiah 65:11–12 (NIV): "But as for **you who forsake the LORD** and forget my holy mountain, who spread a table for Fortune and fill bowls of mixed wine for Destiny, ¹²I will destine you for the sword, and you will all bend down for the slaughter; for **I called but you did not answer, I spoke but you did not listen. You did evil in my sight and chose what displeases me."**

Jeremiah 2:17 (NIV): Have you not brought this on yourselves **by forsaking the LORD your God** when he led you in the way?

TEV: Israel, you brought this on yourself! **You deserted me, the LORD your God,** while I was leading you along the way.

Jeremiah 9:13–15 (AMP): And the Lord says, Because **they have forsaken My law,** which I set before them, and have not listened to and obeyed My voice or walked in accordance with it ¹⁴But have walked stubbornly after their own hearts and after the Baals, as their fathers taught them, ¹⁵Therefore thus says the Lord of hosts, the God of Israel: Behold, I will feed them, even this people, with wormwood and give them bitter and poisonous water to drink.

> Jeremiah 16:11–13 (AMP): Then you shall say to them, [It is] **because your fathers have forsaken Me**, says the Lord, and have walked after other gods and have served and worshiped them and have forsaken Me and have not kept My law, ¹²And **because you have done worse than your fathers.** For behold, every one of you walks after the stubbornness of his own evil heart, so that you do not listen to and obey Me. ¹³**Therefore I will cast you out of this land** [of Judah] into the land [of the Babylonians] neither you nor your fathers have known, and there you will serve other gods day and night, for I will show you no favor there.
>
> Jeremiah 15:6 (AMP): **You have rejected and forsaken Me, says the Lord.** You keep going in reverse. Therefore I will stretch out My hand against you and destroy you; I am weary of relenting [concerning your punishment].
>
> Jeremiah 22:8–9 (NIV): People from many nations will pass by this city and will ask one another, '**Why has the LORD done such a thing to this great city?**' ⁹And the answer will be: '**Because they have forsaken the covenant of the LORD their God** and have worshiped and served other gods.'

And yet again, there are many more that could reconfirm the multitude of Scriptures above. But what is the point of these verses? To show that it is possible to forsake the Lord, which the Reformed doctrine of Perseverance of the Saints denies. (Foolish, of course. But possible nonetheless.) Many of the passages above have God Himself saying that the people had forsaken Him.

We must realize when reading verses such as those above, that it is impossible to *forsake* someone if you never had a relationship with him in the first place. To "forsake" means to "leave," "desert," or "abandon." You can't abandon your spouse if you've never been married; you can't desert a friend you never had; you can't leave your kids if you've never become a parent. "Forsake" means to terminate a relationship, and *you can't terminate a relationship if it was not there in the first place.*

Said another way, *you can't forsake a nonexistent relationship*. You could *avoid* it, so as to prevent a relationship from ever starting, but that's not what these verses say. So the very fact that these people forsook God proves that they had a relationship with Him prior to the forsaking. Again, this shows the Reformed doctrine of Perseverance of the Saints to be false.

God's Promise vs. the People's Behavior

God promised to not forsake Israel, and Moses relates that promise to the people *three times:*

Deuteronomy 4:31 (For **the Lord thy God** is a merciful God;) he **will not forsake thee,** neither destroy thee, nor forget the covenant of thy fathers which he sware unto them.

Deuteronomy 31:6: Be strong and of a good courage, fear not, nor be afraid of them: for **the Lord thy God,** he it is that doth go with thee; **he will not** fail thee, nor **forsake thee.**

Deuteronomy 31:8: And **the Lord,** he it is that doth go before thee; he will be with thee, he **will not** fail thee, neither **forsake thee:** fear not, neither be dismayed.

But of course, two-party covenants, like this one between God and Israel, require both parties to adhere to it, and if one party abandons the covenant, the other party is not obligated to continue abiding by it. Thus, immediately after Moses reiterated God's promises to not forsake Israel, God speaks:

Deuteronomy 31:16–17: And the Lord said unto Moses, Behold, thou shalt sleep with thy fathers; and **this people** will rise up, and go a whoring after the gods of the strangers of the land, whither they go to be among them, and **will forsake me,** and break my covenant which I have made with them. [17]**Then** my anger shall be kindled against them in that day, and **I will forsake them,** and I will hide my face from them, and they shall be devoured, and many evils and troubles shall befall them; so that they will say in that day, Are not these evils come upon us, because our God is not among us?

So again we see that God behaves toward us as we behave toward Him, even in the area of forsaking. His promises not to forsake us are contingent on our not forsaking Him. God says very plainly, "This people will forsake me, then I will forsake them." Difficult to misunderstand, isn't it?

"All That He Has Given Me. . ."

In the Gospel of John, Jesus makes the following statement:

John 6:39 (AMP): And **this is the will of Him Who sent Me, that I should not lose any of all that He has given Me,** but that I should give new life and raise [them all] up at the last day.

Many who support Perseverance of the Saints quote this Scripture as proof that no one who has ever been saved could ever have become unsaved; i.e., lost his salvation, or walked away from God. And it could indeed be taken that way *if* two underlying assumptions are actually valid. These are the two assumptions:

- The "will of Him Who sent Me" refers to the sovereign will of the Father, which cannot be hindered or frustrated in any way by the actions or choices of humans.
- "All that He has given to Me" refers to "all the [people] that He has given Me [to elect for eternal salvation]."

Are these two assumptions reasonable? We've already seen that God's will is *not* always done (refer to the abundance of Scriptures in God's Sovereignty for confirmation). But because God *is* infinite in power, there must be some other factor involved—if God's raw power were the only factor, it's certainly true that no one would be able to withstand it for a microsecond.

And take note of these verses:

I Thessalonians 4:3 (NIV): **It is God's will** that you should be sanctified: **that you should avoid sexual immorality. . .**

I Thessalonians 5:18 (NIV): **Give thanks in all circumstances, for this is God's will for you** in Christ Jesus.

I Peter 2:13–15: **Submit yourselves to every ordinance of man** for the Lord's sake: whether it be to the king, as supreme; [14]Or unto governors, as unto them that are sent by him for the punishment of evildoers, and for the praise of them that do well. [15]**For so is the will of God,** that with well doing ye may put to silence the ignorance of foolish men. . .

Does anyone seriously claim that *everyone in the world* avoids sexual immorality? And gives thanks in all circumstances? And obeys *all* governmental laws? Or even that all the *Christians* in the world do? So it's clear that just because something is God's will doesn't mean it always gets done. And therefore it's equally clear that His power is not the only factor involved with whether or not His will is accomplished.

So now let's go back to Jesus' statement about all that God had given Him. Later on, Jesus again uses this phrase:

John 17:12 (AMP): While I was with them, I kept and preserved them in Your Name [in the knowledge and worship of You]. **Those You have given Me I guarded and protected, and not one of them has perished or is lost except the son of perdition** [Judas Iscariot—the one who is now doomed to destruction, destined to be lost], that the Scripture might be fulfilled.

A very important point here: None that was given to Jesus was lost *except for Judas Iscariot.* But the fact that even *one* person was lost invalidates the theory of the Perseverance of the Saints.

I once heard an audio teaching of one of the foremost Reformed theologians of our day, using this verse to prove Perseverance of the Saints, and I was astonished to hear him stop quoting the verse *right before the word "except,"* where it refers to Judas.

That seemed *so* disingenuous for such a reputable man to quote only the half of the verse that seemed to support his viewpoint, and omit the rest of the sentence that refuted his viewpoint. I was very surprised that he would do such a thing, but not at all surprised as to *why* he would be tempted to do so: it completely invalidated the point he was trying to support.

And here's another very important point we can glean from the verse above. Was Judas predestined/fated/bound to betray Jesus and end up in hell? No; read the verse again: it refers to "Judas Iscariot—the one who is *now* doomed to destruction, destined to be lost." Judas wasn't doomed or destined to be lost from eternity past, but "now" he is. Why "now?" Because Judas chose to sin, and then (unlike Peter), ran away from God, lost sight of God's forgiveness, and therefore did not repent. Judas could have been forgiven, just like Peter was. But when Judas died, *not* having repented for his sin, and *not* having cried out to God for mercy, at that moment, he was indeed "doomed to destruction, destined to be lost."

One more thing: When Jesus used the phrase "all that He has given Me" (where "He" means the Father), who was Jesus referring to? All of mankind, as Reformed theology states? If we take it that way, that means that of all the billions of human beings who have ever lived, *only Judas was lost.* Are we really prepared to state that claim? No, it is clear from the context, that "all that He has given Me" refers to the twelve disciples, and Judas was the only one *of the twelve* who was lost. But Judas certainly was not the only person in history to ever be lost.

And notice that Jesus "kept" and "guarded" those whom God the Father had given Him. But still, Judas was lost. So the question is: was Judas lost because of some failure on the Jesus' part? Clearly not. And if not, Judas' free will must have been a factor in the situation, because if his free will was *not* a factor, then Jesus must have failed to "keep" and "guard" him adequately.

Here's another thought: In John 6 (which we saw above), Jesus expresses the same concept in two different ways, and from this we can gain some understanding on what it means for God to "give" someone to Jesus. Let's add one verse to what we saw earlier:

> John 6:39–40 (NIV): And this is the will of him who sent me, that I shall lose none of **all that he has given me**, but raise them up at the last day. ⁴⁰For my Father's will is that **everyone who looks to the Son and believes in him** shall have eternal life, and I will raise him up at the last day.

That's very enlightening: we can see that those people whom God "gives" to Jesus refers to everyone who has "looked to the Son and believes in Him." If we look to Jesus and believe in Him, we are thereby included in those that the Father "gives" to Jesus. So again we see that the decision of whether we are saved or damned is not one made for us in eternity past, but is our choice to make during our lives on earth. Let us choose wisely.

Falling From Grace

It is not uncommon for people to talk about someone "falling from grace," implying that that person's previously existing approval or acceptance has disappeared. But is that an actual thing, in the context of God? Just because people use it as a figure of speech doesn't mean it is a concept worthy (or capable) of supporting someone's doctrine.

It so happens that "falling from grace" *is* an actual thing. Let's read from Paul's epistle to the church in Galatia:

> Galatians 5:4: **Christ is become of no effect unto you**, whosoever of you are justified by the law; **ye are fallen from grace.**
>
> GWORD: Those of you who try to earn God's approval by obeying his laws **have been cut off from Christ. You have fallen out of God's favor.**
>
> NIV: You who are trying to be justified by law **have been alienated from Christ; you have fallen away from grace.**

Wow. So falling from grace *is* an actual possibility, and it comes about by us trying to *stay* in God's favor by obeying rules, after having already *received* God's favor through choosing to accept by faith His offer of salvation (5:1).

And notice how this verse casually dismantles the Reformed doctrine of the Perseverance of the Saints: it shows how "Christ *becomes* of no effect" to us (although Christ had earlier been of great effect in our lives), we are "cut off from Christ" (which wouldn't be possible had we not been connected to

Him in the first place), and we are "alienated from Christ" (after having begun in the Spirit, see 3:3). Then, just in case the previous verbiage was unclear, Paul reinforces his statement: if we do such things, we fall "from grace," "out of God's favor," and "away from grace." Is it even possible to misunderstand such clear statements?

And then there's Paul's warning to Timothy, in his first epistle to him:

> I Timothy 4:1–2: Now the Spirit speaketh expressly, that in the latter times **some shall depart from the faith**, giving heed to seducing spirits, and doctrines of devils; ²Speaking lies in hypocrisy; having their conscience seared with a hot iron. . .
>
> v. 1a, CEV: God's Spirit clearly says that in the last days **many people will turn from their faith.**
>
> GWORD: The Spirit says clearly that in later times **some believers will desert the Christian faith.**
>
> TLB: But the Holy Spirit tells us clearly that in the last times **some in the church will turn away from Christ. . .**
>
> NASB: But the Spirit explicitly says that in later times **some will fall away from the faith. . .**
>
> NIV: The Spirit clearly says that in later times **some will abandon the faith. . .**

Notice the verbs here: you can't "depart" from a place you've never been; you can't "turn from" your faith if you've never had it; you can't "desert" the Christian faith if you've never believed it; you can't "fall away" from a faith you've never experienced; you can't "abandon" a faith you've never embraced.

This passage Paul wrote to Timothy would be completely pointless and highly misleading if the Reformed doctrine of Perseverance of the Saints were true. Since they are mutually contradictory, which one should we believe?

Closely related to "falling from grace" is a concept the apostle John talks about in one of his epistles:

> II John 8 (NIV): **Watch out that you do not lose what you have worked for,** but that you may be rewarded fully.

What is John referring to here, in the phrase "what you have worked for"? In the verse immediately before this one, John warns the people about being deceived by a spirit of antichrist, and right after the above verse, he warns the reader about not adding anything to the doctrines of Christ. So it sounds like

v. 8, nestled between vv. 7 and 9, must be talking about losing the truth of Jesus being the Messiah and the power and freedom that His gospel brings.

One more thing. We just mentioned v. 9; let's actually take a look at it:

> II John 9 (CSB): Anyone who does not remain in Christ's teaching but **goes beyond it** does not have God. The one who remains in that teaching, this one has both the Father and the Son.
>
> EXB: Anyone who goes beyond [runs ahead of] Christ's teaching and **does not continue to follow only his teaching [abide/remain in it]** does not have God. But whoever continues to follow [abides/remains in] the teaching of Christ [the teaching] has both the Father and the Son.
>
> PHILLIPS: The man who is so "advanced" that he is **not content with what Christ taught** has in fact no God. The man who bases his life on Christ's teaching, however, has both the Father and the Son as his God.
>
> NABRE: Anyone who is so "progressive" as **not to remain in the teaching of the Christ** does not have God; whoever remains in the teaching has the Father and the Son.

What do you think it means to "go beyond" the teachings of Christ? Or to "not be content with" what Christ taught, or "not remain in" it? Could the Reformed doctrines fall into this category? They do seem to be unsubstantiated extensions to the Gospel Jesus taught. With all due respect, let's look at how they compare to Christ's teachings.

CHAPTER 9: PERSEVERANCE OF THE SAINTS

Total Depravity: "It is impossible to repent."	Matthew 4:17 (NIV): From that time on Jesus began to preach, "**Repent,** for the kingdom of heaven is near."
Unconditional Election: "God chooses whether we are saved or not."	Matthew 11:28 (ESV): Come to me, **all** who labor and are heavy laden, and I will give you rest.
Limited Atonement: "God wants only some people saved."	Matthew 18:14 (NLT): In the same way, it is not my heavenly Father's will that **even one** of these little ones should perish.
Irresistible Grace: "It's impossible to refuse God's invitation."	Matthew 23:37b (AMP): How often would I have gathered your children together as a mother fowl gathers her brood under her wings, and **you refused!**
Perseverance of the Saints: "Once saved, always saved."	Luke 8:13 (NIV): Those on the rock are the ones who receive the word with joy when they hear it, but they have no root. They believe for a while, but in the time of testing **they fall away.**

That's rather sobering, is it not?

Paul realized the possibility of falling from grace, and actively took steps to avoid such an eventuality:

> I Corinthians 9:27 (AMP): But [like a boxer] I buffet my body [handle it roughly, discipline it by hardships] and subdue it, **for fear that** after proclaiming to others the Gospel and things pertaining to it, **I myself should become unfit** [not stand the test, be unapproved and rejected as a counterfeit].

> BRG: But I keep under my body, and bring it into subjection: **lest** that by any means, when I have preached to others, **I myself should be a castaway.**

> CSB: Instead, I discipline my body and bring it under strict control, **so that** after preaching to others, **I myself will not be disqualified.**

> CEV: I keep my body under control and make it my slave, **so I won't lose out** after telling the good news to others.

> DLNT: But I bruise my body and make it my slave, **that** having proclaimed to others, **I myself should not somehow become disapproved.**

> TLB: Like an athlete I punish my body, treating it roughly, training it to do what it should, not what it wants to. Otherwise **I fear that after enlisting others for the race, I myself might be declared unfit and ordered to stand aside.**

And to anyone who might read the above Scriptures and think, "Well, he's not talking about missing out on *salvation*," let's read the context. What was Paul just talking about? He was talking about preaching the gospel to get people saved (vv. 18–19), winning people to faith in Jesus Christ (v. 22), sharing in the blessings of the gospel (v. 23). So yes, Paul was talking about salvation.

The Lamb's Book of Life, Take 2

This topic was discussed at some length in the section "The Lamb's Book of Life" above, so I won't duplicate that discussion here, but I just want to draw your attention to a few Scriptures from that discussion that are very relevant here. As mentioned, the Reformed doctrine of the Perseverance of the Saints says that since God made the decision as to our salvation in eternity past, and since He doesn't make mistakes, once a person is saved, that status can *never* change.

But look again at the Scriptures that talk about people's names being *removed* from the Book of Life:

> Exodus 32:32–33 (AMP): Yet now, if You will forgive their sin—and if not, **blot me, I pray You, out of Your book** which You have written! ³³But the Lord said to Moses, **Whoever has sinned against Me, I will blot him [not you] out of My book.**

> Psalm 69:28: **Let them be blotted out of the book of the living**; and with the just let them not be written.

> Revelation 3:3–5: Remember therefore how thou hast received and heard, and **hold fast, and repent.** If therefore thou shalt not watch, I will come on thee as a thief, and thou shalt not know what hour I will come upon thee. ⁴Thou hast a few names even in Sardis which have not defiled their garments; and they shall walk with me in white: for they are worthy. ⁵He that overcometh, the same shall be clothed in white raiment; and **I will not blot out his name out of the book of life**, but I will confess his name before my Father, and before his angels.

It's interesting to note in the above Scripture that *the person who overcomes* will be clothed in white raiment, and Jesus will not blot his name out of the

Book of Life. The obvious implication is that the person who does *not* overcome will *not* be clothed in white raiment, and Jesus *will* blot his name out of the Book of Life. Sobering, that.

> Revelation 22:19: And if any man shall take away from the words of the book of this prophecy, **God shall take away his part out of the book of life,** and out of the holy city, and from the things which are written in this book.

This Scripture, like the one before it, gives an example where God's actions toward us mirror our actions toward Him. In Revelation 3:5, our white raiment and our name remaining in the Book of Life are dependent on whether we overcame or not. In Revelation 22:19, our name remaining in the Book of Life is dependent on whether we take away from the words of the Revelation prophecy. Note that in both cases, our actions are *our choice.*

Here's the point: If, as the Reformed doctrines of Unconditional Election and the Perseverance of the Saints claim, God had unalterably chosen every person's eternal destiny in eternity past and that status couldn't ever be changed, *why are some people removed from the Lamb's Book of Life?* Again, they couldn't be removed unless they were in there to begin with.

And, by the way, the whole concept of people being blotted out of the Book of Life supports the notion of limited omniscience, because it would be pointless, and therefore extremely unlikely for God to put someone's name *into* the Book of Life, while in full, omniscient awareness that He would subsequently *remove* that person's name, with no regard for that person's actions, attitudes, or choices. Why bother putting a name in, if there is an unchangeable intention of taking it back out?

Ezekiel 33

In Ezekiel 33, briefly mentioned above in the section "Does God Want Everyone to be Saved?", God says something that pertains to the Perseverance of the Saints:

> Ezekiel 33:12–13 (NIV): Therefore, son of man, say to your countrymen, **'The righteousness of the righteous man will not save him when he disobeys,** and the wickedness of the wicked man will not cause him to fall when he turns from it. The righteous man, if he sins, will not be allowed to live because of his former righteousness.' [13]**If I tell the righteous man that he will surely live, but then he trusts in his righteousness and does evil, none of the righteous things he has done will be remembered; he will die for the evil he has done.**

This very clearly and bluntly says it is possible for a righteous man (who could only get that way through God's gift of righteousness; see Romans 5:17) to disobey God, turn to evil, and die as a result. Again, just this one, tiny passage completely discredits the Reformed doctrine of the Perseverance of the Saints.

But just in case there's any doubt, God reiterates it in v. 18:

> Ezekiel 33:18 (NIV): **If a righteous man turns** from his righteousness and does evil, **he will die** for it.

Note that this is talking about *spiritual* life and death here, not physical life and death. Clearly, if it were talking about *physical* life and death, this Scripture would mean that Christians never physically die. Obviously, this is silly.

Actual Perseverance of the Saints

Now, lest someone think that the above Scriptures indicate that our salvation is on shaky ground, let me be quick to point out that it doesn't have to be. Just because we *can* walk away from Christ and the salvation He offers—even after accepting it—doesn't mean that our eternal destination is in a precarious position. So what does it depend on?

Again, like in so many of the Scriptures quoted earlier in this book, *God acts toward us like we act toward Him;* i.e., we reap what we sow. Which means that if we want our salvation to be secure, we must remain faithful to Him. Our final landing-place is not a matter of an unchangeable decision made for us by God in eternity past, but rather our ongoing faithfulness to Him.

And as before, if I make such a blunt statement, I'd better be able to back it up Scripturally. So please consider the following passages, each of which either *commands* us to be faithful to God, or describes the *results* of being faithful to God, or is an *example* of someone doing so. Then ask yourself in each case, "Would this statement or command make any sense at all if Perseverance of the Saints were true?"

> Psalm 31:23 (NASB): O love the LORD, all you His godly ones! **The LORD preserves the faithful,** and fully recompenses the proud doer.

> Psalm 101:6 (NASB): **My eyes shall be upon the faithful of the land, that they may dwell with me;** He who walks in a blameless way is the one who will minister to me.

> Matthew 10:22 (NIV): All men will hate you because of me, but **he who stands firm to the end will be saved.**

Matthew 25:21 (NIV): His master replied, **'Well done, good and faithful servant! You have been faithful** with a few things; I will put you in charge of many things. **Come and share your master's happiness!'**

Acts 11:23 (NIV): When he *[Barnabas]* arrived and saw the evidence of the grace of God, he was glad and **encouraged them all to remain true to the Lord** with all their hearts.

Acts 13:43 (NIV): When the congregation was dismissed, many of the Jews and devout converts to Judaism followed Paul and Barnabas, who talked with them and **urged them to continue in the grace of God.**

Acts 14:21–22 (NASB): And after they had preached the gospel to that city and had made many disciples, they *[Paul and Barnabas]* returned to Lystra and to Iconium and to Antioch, ²²strengthening the souls of the disciples, **encouraging them to continue in the faith,** and saying, "Through many tribulations we must enter the kingdom of God."

I Corinthians 4:1–2: Let a man so account of us, as of the ministers of Christ, and stewards of the mysteries of God. ²Moreover **it is required in stewards, that a man be found faithful.**

I Corinthians 15:1–2 (NASB): Now I make known to you, brethren, the gospel which I preached to you, which also you received, in which also you stand, ²by which also **you are saved, if you hold fast the word** which I preached to you, unless you believed in vain.

II Corinthians 6:1 (TEV): In our work together with God, then, we beg you who have received God's grace **not to let it be wasted.**

Galatians 2:2 (NIV): I went in response to a revelation and set before them the gospel that I preach among the Gentiles. But I did this privately to those who seemed to be leaders, **for fear that I was running or had run my race in vain.**

Philippians 2:12 (TEV): So then, dear friends, as you always obeyed me when I was with you, it is even more important that you obey me now while I am away from you. **Keep on working with fear and trembling to complete your salvation. . .**

Colossians 1:22–23a (NIV): But now he has reconciled you by Christ's physical body through death to present you holy in his sight, without blemish and free from accusation— ²³**if you continue in your faith, established and firm, not moved** from the hope held out in the gospel.

II Timothy 2:11–12 (NIV): Here is a trustworthy saying: If we died with him, we will also live with him; ¹²**if we endure, we will also reign with him.** If we disown him, he will also disown us. . .

Hebrews 2:1–3a (NASB): For this reason we must pay much closer attention to what we have heard, **lest we drift away from it.** ²For if the word spoken through angels proved unalterable, and every transgression and disobedience received a just recompense, ³**how shall we escape if we neglect so great a salvation?** *(Keep in mind that Hebrews was written to believers.)*

Hebrews 3:6 (NIV): But Christ is faithful as a son over God's house. And we are his house, **if we hold on to our courage and the hope of which we boast.**

Hebrews 3:12–14 (CEB): Watch out, brothers and sisters, **so that none of you** have an evil, unfaithful heart that **abandons the living God.** ¹³Instead, encourage each other every day, as long as it's called "today," so that none of you **become insensitive to God** because of sin's deception.

Hebrews 10:23: **Let us hold fast the profession of our faith** without wavering; (for he is faithful that promised;). . .

Hebrews 10:35–36 (NIV): So **do not throw away your confidence**; it will be richly rewarded. ³⁶**You need to persevere** so that when you have done the will of God, **you will receive what he has promised.**

II Peter 1:10–11 (NIV): Therefore, my brothers, be all the more eager to **make your calling and election sure.** For **if you do these things, you will never fall,** ¹¹and **you will receive a rich welcome into the eternal kingdom** of our Lord and Savior Jesus Christ.

II Peter 3:17 (NIV): Therefore, dear friends, since you already know this, **be on your guard so that you may not** be carried away by the error of lawless men and **fall from your secure position.**

Jude 21 (AMP): **Guard and keep yourselves** in the love of God; expect and patiently wait for the mercy of our Lord Jesus Christ (the Messiah)—[which will bring you] unto life eternal.

Revelation 2:7, 11, 17, 25–26, 3:5, 11, 12a, 21, 21:7 (NIV): He who has an ear, let him hear what the Spirit says to the churches. **To him who overcomes, I will give the right to eat from the tree of life, which is in the paradise of God.** ¹¹He who has an ear, let him hear what the Spirit says to the churches. **He who overcomes** will not be hurt at all by the second death. ¹⁷He who has an ear, let him hear what the Spirit says to the churches. **To him who overcomes,** I will give some of the hidden manna. I will also give him a white stone with a new name written on it, known only to him who receives it. ²⁵Only **hold on to what you have** until I come. ²⁶**To him who overcomes and does my will to the end,** I will give authority over the nations. . . ³:⁵**He that overcometh,** the same shall be clothed in white raiment; and **I will not blot out his name out of the book of life,** but I will confess his name before my Father, and before his angels. ¹¹I am coming soon. **Hold on to what you have,** so that no one will take your crown. ¹²ᵃ**Him who overcomes** I will make a pillar in the temple of my God. ²¹**To him who overcomes,** I will give the right to sit with me on my throne, just as I overcame and sat down with my Father on his throne. ²¹:⁷**He who overcomes** will inherit all this, and I will be his God and he will be my son.

The inescapable conclusion from reading the above Scriptures is that our salvation is totally, ultimately, and eternally secure *if and only if we remain faithful to God*. Of course, we can believe otherwise, but only at the cost of disregarding the Scriptures above (and *so* many more) that make the facts plain to see. And there will be consequences for our faithfulness, or lack thereof—we can be sure of that. Remember Galatians 6:7–8?

The Parable of the Wedding Feast

In Matthew 22, Jesus tells the parable of the wedding feast. There are several very sobering concepts He elucidates in this parable, especially as they pertain to the Reformed doctrines:

> Matthew 22:1–14 (NIV): Jesus spoke to them again in parables, saying: ²"The kingdom of heaven is like a king who prepared a wedding banquet for his son. ³He sent his servants to those who had been invited to the banquet to tell them to come, but they refused to come. ⁴Then he sent some more servants and said, 'Tell those who have been invited that I have prepared my dinner: My oxen and fattened cattle have been butchered, and everything is ready. Come to the wedding banquet.' ⁵But they paid no attention and went off—one to his field, another to his business. ⁶The rest seized his servants, mistreated them and killed them."

In this parable, the king represents God, his son represents Jesus, his servants represent the prophets and anyone else who would point people toward God, and the ones invited to the banquet represent Israel. Indeed, throughout the historical and prophetic books of the Old Testament, we see that God sent His servants the prophets to Israel repeatedly to urge them to repent of their

FREE TO CHOOSE?

sins and turn back to Him, because He had great blessings awaiting them. And so often, they ignored His invitations, and they ignored, mistreated, and even killed His servants.

It's interesting to note that the king *invited* the people to come; he didn't *force* them to come. The king obviously wanted them to come to his banquet; otherwise, he would not have invited them in the first place. But he gave them the choice of whether or not to respond positively to his invitation, and he *allowed them to refuse,* even though it was foolish to do so. This clearly conflicts with the Reformed doctrines of Unconditional Election and Irresistible Grace.

So what happened when the invitees refused the king's invitation, and even killed the king's servants? Let's continue:

> [7]"The king was enraged. He sent his army and destroyed those murderers and burned their city."

And sure enough, we find in the Old Testament that God incited enemy nations to come and chastise His people—to conquer them and carry them away into bondage for a time—for rebelling against Him. But once that was done, what happened next?

> [8]"Then he said to his servants, 'The wedding banquet is ready, but those I invited did not deserve to come. [9]Go to the street corners and invite to the banquet anyone you find.'"

So once His own people rejected His invitation to the wedding banquet, the king invited everyone else: He sent His servants out to invite those who were *not* His people. The symbolism here is God allowing and welcoming Gentiles into the Kingdom—not just Jews—and we see this played out repeatedly in the book of Acts, the epistles, and Revelation.

And notice what the king said about those who refused to accept his invitation to the banquet: they "did not deserve to come." When he initially sent the invitation, he obviously had thought them deserving, or at least *potentially* so—after all, he did invite them—but the fact that they refused his invitation showed that ultimately they did not deserve to come. On the other hand, those who accept his invitation *do* deserve to be there, by virtue of their having accepted the invitation.

How does this pertain to the Reformed doctrines? Again, we see the king *inviting* people, not *forcing* them, to come to his banquet. As noted above, this conflicts with Irresistible Grace. Not only that, but because the king told

402

his servants to invite "anyone you find," that conflicts with Limited Atonement.

Let's keep reading:

> [10]"So the servants went out into the streets and gathered all the people they could find, both good and bad, and the wedding hall was filled with guests. [11]But when the king came in to see the guests, he noticed a man there who was not wearing wedding clothes. [12]'Friend,' he asked, 'how did you get in here without wedding clothes?' The man was speechless. [13]Then the king told the attendants, 'Tie him hand and foot, and throw him outside, into the darkness, where there will be weeping and gnashing of teeth.'"

Now this is odd. This guy was thrown out of the wedding banquet because he wasn't wearing "wedding clothes" (or "wedding garments," as other translations render it). What are "wedding clothes" or "wedding garments?" And how did this man get into the wedding banquet in the first place without wearing them?

These are good questions; are there other Scriptures that might shed some light on what the wedding garments are? Yes; Revelation 19 describes the marriage supper of the Lamb:

> Revelation 19:7–9 (NASB): "Let us rejoice and be glad and give the glory to Him, for the marriage of the Lamb has come and **His bride has made herself ready.**" [8]And it was given to her to **clothe herself in fine linen,** bright and clean; for the **fine linen is the righteous acts** of the saints. [9]And he said to me, "Write, 'Blessed are those who are invited to the marriage supper of the Lamb.'" And he *[the angel]* said to me, "These are true words of God."

So what we are to wear to the wedding banquet is, in the words of the Apostle John, "fine linen." And just to make sure we don't misunderstand what "fine linen" represents, He immediately tells us, in the second half of v. 8: our "righteous acts." That is, our wedding garments are our acts of obedience to God in doing the good works that He has ordained for us to do (Ephesians 2:10, Revelation 3:1–6).

So, going back to Matthew 22, we see that the man got into the wedding banquet, but was not allowed to stay because he didn't have the proper wedding garments on—he did not have the works that proved his repentance was real (Matthew 3:8, Acts 26:20, Revelation 2:5). We know that self-deception is the result of hearing the word but not actually doing it (James 1:22), and here is a classic example of "faith without works is dead" (James 2:20).

Free to Choose?

So what are characteristics of "dead faith?" These renditions, from other translations of the Bible, give us a pretty good idea:
- ASV: It "is barren"
- AMP: It "is useless"
- AMPC: It "is inactive and ineffective and worthless"
- CEB: It "has no value at all"
- ERV: It "is worth nothing"
- TLB: It "is not real faith"
- NLV: It "is of no use"
- WE: It "does not do anything good"
- WYC: It "is idle"

So the man got into the wedding feast without having any good works to his name, as Matthew 22:10 confirms when it says that the king's servants gathered "both good and bad" into the wedding hall. This reaffirms the idea of salvation by grace through faith: if works were required for entry, that would indeed be salvation by works. However, even though works are not required to be invited to—and to *go* to—the wedding banquet, they *are* required in order to *remain* there.

Jesus reiterates this thought—that clothes represent good works—and He also indicates that the good works must *continue*. It's not good enough, after being saved by grace, to do a few good works and then quit. We must *keep* doing good works—not as a legalistic requirement of the law, but as a natural outflow of service that indicates our continued healthy relationship with God:

Revelation 16:15 (NIV): "Behold, I come like a thief! **Blessed is he who stays awake and *keeps his clothes with him,* so that he may not go naked and be shamefully exposed.**"

Paul describes this as follows:

Galatians 6:9: **And let us not be weary in well doing: for in due season we shall reap, if we faint not.**

So this idea of getting into the wedding banquet but not being allowed to stay on account of the absence of wedding garments, of course, refutes the Reformed doctrine of the Perseverance of the Saints.

Rounding out Jesus' parable of the Wedding Feast, He makes one final statement:

14"For many are invited, but few are chosen."

This one short statement tells us several profound things.

- First, *many* are invited, not just few. So this refutes the Reformed doctrine of Limited Atonement.
- Second, God *invites* us to the wedding feast, He doesn't coerce us. So this refutes the Reformed doctrine of Unconditional Election.
- Third, the fact that *many* are invited but only *few* are chosen shows us that the Holy Spirit does not work in "irresistible mode." So this refutes the Reformed doctrine of Irresistible Grace.
- Fourth, it shows us that whether or not we are chosen is a matter of *how we respond* to God's invitation (II Timothy 2:20, Revelation 17:14), not an unchangeable decision God made for us in eternity past. So this refutes the Reformed doctrine of Unconditional Election.
- And fifth, because this statement was made immediately after the description of a man being ejected from the wedding feast, it shows that it's possible to *get* in but not *stay* in. So this refutes the Reformed doctrine of the Perseverance of the Saints.

A lot of meat there, no?

The Parable of the Good and Wicked Servants

A couple chapters later, Jesus tells another parable. Notice in this parable that there are two different servants being discussed:

> Matthew 24:45–51 (NIV): Who then is the **faithful and wise servant,** whom the master has put in charge of the servants in his household to give them their food at the proper time? ⁴⁶**It will be good for that servant whose master finds him doing so** when he returns. ⁴⁷I tell you the truth, he will put him in charge of all his possessions. ⁴⁸But suppose that servant is wicked and says to himself, 'My master is staying away a long time' ⁴⁹and he then begins to beat his fellow servants and to eat and drink with drunkards. ⁵⁰The master of that servant will come on a day when he does not expect him and at an hour he is not aware of. ⁵¹**He will cut him to pieces and assign him a place with the hypocrites, where there will be weeping and gnashing of teeth.**

It is very significant that *both* servants—the good one and the wicked one—*were indeed servants of the Master.* It's not comparing or contrasting one servant of the Master, and one foreigner. Both were His servants. So what made one of them "good" and the other one "wicked?" Reading the story again makes it clear that the difference was in whether or not they *remained* faithful to the Master. Both were faithful initially, but after "a long time"

FREE TO CHOOSE?

(v. 48), one gets lazy, complacent, and careless, then cruel to his fellow servants, and finally dissolute.

What was the result of the two servants' long-term faithfulness (or lack thereof)? The good servant was greatly rewarded. The wicked servant—the one whose faithfulness was short-lived—was severely, *and terminally,* punished. Refer back to v. 51: how much destruction, hypocrisy, weeping, and gnashing of teeth do you think there will be in heaven? If you (correctly) say there will be none, then this servant, who became wicked through his unfaithfulness, *didn't end up there.* And this, yet again, invalidates the Reformed doctrine of the Perseverance of the Saints.

The Parable of the Ten Virgins

Immediately after Jesus told the parable discussed above, He told another one: the Parable of the Ten Virgins. Let's read it and see what it says:

> Matthew 25:1–13 (NIV): At that time the kingdom of heaven will be like ten virgins who took their lamps and went out to meet the bridegroom. ²Five of them were foolish and five were wise. ³The foolish ones took their lamps but did not take any oil with them. ⁴The wise, however, took oil in jars along with their lamps. ⁵The bridegroom was a long time in coming, and they all became drowsy and fell asleep. ⁶At midnight the cry rang out: 'Here's the bridegroom! Come out to meet him!' ⁷Then all the virgins woke up and trimmed their lamps. ⁸The foolish ones said to the wise, 'Give us some of your oil; our lamps are going out.' ⁹'No,' they replied, 'there may not be enough for both us and you. Instead, go to those who sell oil and buy some for yourselves.' ¹⁰But while they were on their way to buy the oil, the bridegroom arrived. The virgins who were ready went in with him to the wedding banquet. And the door was shut. ¹¹Later the others also came. 'Sir! Sir!' they said. 'Open the door for us!' ¹²But he replied, 'I tell you the truth, I don't know you.' ¹³Therefore keep watch, because you do not know the day or the hour.

There are some very significant points in this parable, but before we examine them, it will be very helpful to understand that oil is a symbol of the Holy Spirit. This is widely accepted in Christendom, but as always, if we want to rely on it as a valid doctrine, we need to have some Scriptural support for it. In this Scripture:

> Exodus 29:7: Then shalt thou take the **anointing oil**, and pour it upon his head, and **anoint** him.

The word "anoint" in this verse, and dozens more, is translated from the Hebrew word מָשַׁח (*mashach*, H4886), which means "to rub with oil," and by implication, "to consecrate," where "consecrate" means to set apart, to declare sacred, to dedicate for a divine purpose, or to ordain. (The word "anointing" in the above verse comes from another form of the same Hebrew word.)

So oil and anointing are tightly linked, as shown by the following verses:

> I Samuel 16:13 (TEV): Samuel took the **olive oil and anointed** David in front of his brothers. Immediately the **spirit of the LORD took control of David** and was with him from that day on. Then Samuel returned to Ramah.

> Isaiah 61:1: The **Spirit of the LORD God** is upon me; **because the LORD hath anointed me** to preach good tidings unto the meek; he hath sent me to bind up the brokenhearted, to proclaim liberty to the captives, and the opening of the prison to them that are bound. . .

> (To hear this passage set to music, listen to the song *The Spirit of the Lord* on the album *Songs of the Tribe of Judah* or scan the QR code at right.)

> Luke 4:18 (NIV): "The **Spirit of the Lord is on me, because he has anointed me** to preach good news to the poor. He has sent me to proclaim freedom for the prisoners and recovery of sight for the blind, to release the oppressed, ¹⁹to proclaim the year of the Lord's favor."

> Acts 10:38 (NASB): You know of Jesus of Nazareth, how **God anointed Him with the Holy Spirit and with power,** and how He went about doing good, and healing all who were oppressed by the devil; for God was with Him.

The New Testament usages of "anoint" shown above come from the Greek word χρίω (*chrio*, G5548), which means "to smear or rub with oil, i.e. (by implication) to consecrate to an office or religious service: — anoint." So as we can see, the Old Testament and the New Testament agree on the definition of anoint, and that oil symbolizes the Holy Spirit.

And two more, rather conclusive observations: the Hebrew word translated into the English word "Messiah," as it appears in Daniel 9:25–26, is מָשִׁיחַ (*mashiyach*, H4899), whose root is מָשַׁח (*mashach*, H4886), which we saw above. And, interestingly enough, the corresponding Greek word translated into the English word "Christ," as it appears in Matthew 1:1, is Χριστός (*Christos*, G5547), whose root word is χρίω (*chrio*, G5548), also seen above. So both Messiah and Christ literally mean "the anointed One."

FREE TO CHOOSE?

Now, back to the important points of the parable:
- *All ten virgins* were intending on meeting the Bridegroom (v. 1).
- *All ten virgins* had oil in their lamps; they all had the Holy Spirit. This means they were saved, as Romans 8:9 shows: ". . .if any man have not the Spirit of Christ, he is none of his."
- The foolish virgins had only their current supply of oil (Holy Spirit), but the wise virgins were not satisfied with the amount they had received earlier; they knew they would need a fresh supply beyond what their lamps could currently carry (vv. 3–4). Compare to the concept of "yesterday's manna" (Exodus 16:15–20).
- Like the Parable of the Good and Wicked Servants discussed earlier, "a long time" passed (v. 5).
- When the Bridegroom showed up, they all realized (v. 7) they would need more oil (Holy Spirit) than what they currently had in their lamps. The wise ones had planned ahead and already had what they needed; the foolish ones did not.
- When the foolish ones asked the wise ones for some of their oil, the wise ones could not (vv. 8–9)—we cannot supply the Holy Spirit to each other; we all need to go directly to the Source.
- When the Bridegroom arrived, the foolish ones were belatedly trying to accomplish what should already have been done, but the wise ones were ready for Him (v. 10).
- When the foolish virgins were finally ready, it was too late to accept the invitation to the wedding banquet, and they were refused entry (vv. 11–12).

Significant in the context of this book are these points: First, the lamps of the foolish virgins were "going out." Note that they *were* lit—they had had the Holy Spirit in their lives—but they said "our lamps are *going* out." Lamps can't "go" out if they had never been lit, and they couldn't have been lit without having had at least some oil.

And secondly, note what the Bridegroom says to the foolish virgins: "I don't know you." Although Jesus will tell some people, "I *never* knew you" (Matthew 7:23), He doesn't say that here. Rather, He says, "I *don't* know you" (v. 12). The strong implication, solidified by the fact that the foolish virgins *had* had oil (Holy Spirit) at some point, is that they had lost it/Him through laziness, complacency, and carelessness, like the wicked servant in the previous parable.

And yet again, here is another passage that refutes the Reformed doctrine of the Perseverance of the Saints.

But before we leave this topic, rest assured that the above parable does not endanger people who simply *didn't know* something. In this parable, five of the virgins were "foolish," but what does that mean? Does it mean they were merely mentally deficient? Or untrained in some fashion? Unlikely. In the Bible, foolishness—also known as "folly"—in an adult is usually associated with sin:

> Genesis 34:7: And the sons of Jacob came out of the field when they heard it: and the men were grieved, and they were very wroth, because he had wrought **folly** in Israel in lying with Jacob's daughter; which thing **ought not to be done.**
>
> Numbers 12:11: And Aaron said unto Moses, Alas, my lord, I beseech thee, lay not the sin upon us, wherein **we have done foolishly, and wherein we have sinned.**
>
> Joshua 7:15: And it shall be, that he that is taken with the accursed thing shall be burnt with fire, he and all that he hath: because he hath **transgressed the covenant** of the Lord, and because he hath **wrought folly** in Israel.
>
> I Samuel 13:13: And Samuel said to Saul, **Thou hast done foolishly: thou hast not kept the commandment** of the Lord thy God, which he commanded thee: for now would the Lord have established thy kingdom upon Israel for ever.
>
> I Samuel 25:25 (NIV): May my lord pay no attention to that **wicked man Nabal**. He is just like his name—**his name is Fool, and folly goes with him.** But as for me, your servant, I did not see the men my master sent.
>
> I Samuel 26:21: Then said Saul, **I have sinned**: return, my son David: for I will no more do thee harm, because my soul was precious in thine eyes this day: behold, **I have played the fool,** and have erred exceedingly.
>
> II Samuel 24:10: And David's heart smote him after that he had numbered the people. And David said unto the Lord, **I have sinned** greatly in that I have done: and now, I beseech thee, O Lord, take away the **iniquity** of thy servant; for **I have done very foolishly.**
>
> Job 1:22: In all this **Job sinned not, nor charged God foolishly.**
>
> Psalm 107:17: Fools **because of their transgression, and because of their iniquities,** are afflicted.

Isaiah 32:6 (CEV): **Fools talk foolishness. They always make plans to do sinful things,** to lie about the LORD, to let the hungry starve, and to keep water from those who are thirsty.

And there are many more, but you get the point. If someone is "foolish" in the sense of not having a mental capacity to make wise decisions, it is against God's character to punish him for things such as that. For example, a child before the age of accountability, or an adult with a severe developmental handicap, or a senior citizen with Alzheimer's or some other kind of dementia. God's love is far too great to shut someone out of the marriage feast for such a reason.

No, since foolishness in this context implies sin, it seems to me that the foolishness in the five foolish virgins was some kind of sin; perhaps complacency or pride, or even disobedience. As we saw in the section "What's Your Excuse?," God holds people accountable for what they know and deliberately reject.

There is another reason that also points to the five foolish virgins' shortage of oil being a result of sin, and not simply mental incapacity or lack of knowledge. Let's look again at v. 8:

Matthew 25:8: And the foolish said unto the wise, Give us of your oil; for our lamps are **gone out.**

NIV: The foolish ones said to the wise, 'Give us some of your oil; our lamps are **going out.**'

The Greek word translated "gone out" or "going out" in the verse above is σβέννυμι (*sbennumi*, G4570), and its definitions are to "extinguish, quench, suppress, and thwart." The definition of this word seems a lot more active and deliberate than simply "Oops, I guess I wasn't paying attention."

Even more disturbing is when you look at where else this word is used:

Matthew 12:20 (ESV): . . .a bruised reed he will not break, and a smoldering wick he will not **quench,** until he brings justice to victory. . .

Mark 9:44 || 9:46 || 9:48: Where their worm dieth not, and the fire is not **quenched.**

Ephesians 6:16 (AMP): Lift up over all the [covering] shield of saving faith, upon which you can **quench** all the flaming missiles of the wicked [one].

I Thessalonians 5:19 (NASB): Do not **quench** the Spirit;

Hebrews 11:34 (NIV): *[Other heroes of faith]* **quenched** the fury of the flames, and escaped the edge of the sword; whose weakness was turned to strength; and who became powerful in battle and routed foreign armies.

In *every other case* of the Greek word *sbennumi* being used in the New Testament, it implies an active suppression or extinguishing, not merely inattention. The parable of the ten virgins might be more serious that we had previously realized. (And remember what we discovered about "quenching" in "Quenching the Holy Spirit," earlier.)

And just in case it's not clear who the virgins represent, they represent believers:

II Corinthians 11:2: For I am jealous over you with godly jealousy: for I have espoused you to one husband, that I may present **you as a chaste virgin** to Christ.

Paul Chimes In

In Romans 11, Paul explains actual Perseverance of the Saints (which, as we've seen, is *not* the same as the Reformed idea of Perseverance of the Saints). He clearly shows that those people who are ultimately saved are not saved simply because of an eternal decision made by God in eternity past, but because *they remain faithful to Him*. This is yet another case of God behaving toward us as we have behaved toward Him:

Romans 11:20–24 (CEB): Fine. They *[the Jews]* were broken off because they weren't faithful, but **you stand only by your faithfulness.** So don't think in a proud way; instead be afraid.

Wow. Talking to believers, Paul explains how Perseverance of the Saints *actually* works: we need to be faithful to Him. It's not a done deal that is unrelated to our behavior. Saying the Sinner's Prayer once, and then continuing to live like the devil won't cut it. No, it is required of a steward that he be found *faithful* (I Corinthians 4:2). We need to *abide* in Jesus, like He said in John 15:4: "Abide in Me, and I in you. As the branch cannot bear fruit of itself, unless it abides in the vine, so neither can you, unless you abide in Me."

But getting back to Paul:

[21]If God didn't spare the natural branches, **he won't spare you either.**

Paul doesn't pull any punches, does he? He had just said that the original branches were cut off because they weren't faithful, and here he says that God imposes the same requirement on the Christians in the church in Rome. Isn't that rather harsh? Yes, but only if you turn your back on God:

> [22]So look at God's kindness and harshness. It's harshness toward those who fell, but it's God's kindness for you, **provided you continue in his kindness; otherwise, you could be cut off too.**

So if we ever blow it, are we doomed? No, because we can repent (Total Depravity notwithstanding). Specifically, we can repent of our faithlessness, and become faithful again, just like the Jews:

> [23]And even **those who were cut off will be grafted back in if they don't continue to be unfaithful,** because God is able to graft them in again. [24]If you were naturally part of a wild olive tree and you were cut off from it, and then, contrary to nature, you were grafted into the cultivated olive tree, won't these natural branches stand an even better chance of being grafted back onto their own olive tree?

So even in the area of Perseverance of the Saints, God takes His cue from us, and will give us as much of Himself as we want.

Chapter 10:

Miscellaneous Topics

This chapter contains various topics that either didn't fit precisely into any single one of the previous six chapters, or they fit into *so many* of the previous chapters that it would have been almost misleading to put them in any one particular place. It seemed better to put such topics in this chapter, and then have pointers back to other sections as necessary, for more complete treatment of a topic being mentioned here.

Hungering for God

Many places in the Bible is there a command or the promise of a blessing for those who hunger after God enough to seek after Him. Verses like the following come to mind:

Deuteronomy 4:29 (TEV): There you will look for the LORD your God, and **if you search for him with all your heart, you will find him.**

I Chronicles 28:9 (NIV): . . .the LORD searches every heart and understands every motive behind the thoughts. **If you seek him, he will be found by you. . .**

Hebrews 11:6: But without faith it is impossible to please him: for he that cometh to God must believe that he is, and that **he is a rewarder of them that diligently seek him.**

So, seeking God is a result of wanting Him, or, to put it in a more poetic form, seeking God is a result of *hungering and thirsting* after Him (to hear a song based on this concept, listen to *Getting Hungry* on the album *Go Into All the World*). The Bible has many things to say on our hungering and thirsting after God; let's check out some of them. Some are commands to hunger and/or thirst after God; some are descriptions of blessing to those who do, and some are simply examples of godly people doing so.

But notice that some of the entreaties—the commands or exhortations—are not addressed to the people who *already* hunger for Him; they're already aware of its importance. Such exhortations are addressed to the people who *need to* hear it and heed it; i.e., they're not doing it yet.

So let's look at a few of these passages.

Psalm 42:2 (TEV): **I thirst for you, the living God.** When can I go and worship in your presence?

Psalm 63:1 (TEV): O God, you are my God, and **I long for you.** My whole being desires you; like a dry, worn-out, and waterless land, **my soul is thirsty for you.**

Psalm 63:8 (AMP): **My whole being follows hard after You** and clings closely to You; Your right hand upholds me.

Psalm 107:9 (NASB): For He has satisfied **the thirsty soul**, and **the hungry soul** He has filled with what is good.

Psalm 143:6 (AMP): I spread forth my hands to You; **my soul thirsts after You like a thirsty land [for water].** Selah [pause, and calmly think of that]!

Psalm 147:11 (AMP): The **Lord takes pleasure in those who reverently and worshipfully fear Him,** in those who hope in His mercy and loving-kindness.

Isaiah 44:3 (AMP): For **I will pour water upon him who is thirsty,** and floods upon the dry ground. I will pour My Spirit upon your offspring, and My blessing upon your descendants.

Isaiah 55:1 (TEV): The LORD says, "Come, **everyone who is thirsty**—here is water! Come, **you that have no money**— buy grain and eat! Come! Buy wine and milk— it will cost you nothing!"

Matthew 5:6 (NIV): Blessed are those who **hunger and thirst for righteousness,** for they will be filled.

The Scripture immediately above is particularly hard-hitting because of the intensity of meaning in the Greek, which doesn't come across in the translation. "Hunger" in the above verse comes from the Greek word πεινάω (*peinao*, G3983), whose definition includes the concepts of "hungering," "craving," "pining," and "starving." So this is not just a half-hearted or occasional interest in going after God.

Similarly, the word "filled" in the above verse comes from the Greek word χορτάζω (*chortazo*, G5526), whose definition incudes the concepts of "fed," "filled," "satisfied," "food in abundance," and "gorged." So the result of an intense hunger for God is not just a "spiritual hors d'oeuvre," so to speak, but a massive feast.

That's the kind of hunger that we need to have for God, and His response to that kind of hunger.

> John 7:37–39 (NIV): On the last and greatest day of the Feast, Jesus stood and said in a loud voice, **"If anyone is thirsty, let him come to me and drink.** ³⁸Whoever believes in me, as the Scripture has said, streams of living water will flow from within him." ³⁹By this he meant the Spirit, whom those who believed in him were later to receive. Up to that time the Spirit had not been given, since Jesus had not yet been glorified.

Note that Jesus addressed this invitation to "anyone"—so here is yet another verse that confutes the Reformed doctrine of Total Depravity. And just in case anyone was thinking that the thirst we've been talking about is for physical, liquid water to put into our bodies, the above should dispel that notion. We need to hunger and thirst after the things of God.

Available, But Not to be Taken for Granted

Many, perhaps even most, of God's blessings fall into the category of "available, but not to be taken for granted." What do I mean by that? Simply that if we want some blessing from God, we can't just sit around thinking, "Well, God knows my address. If He wants to bless me, He'll just do it." Is this idea Biblical?

The first example that comes to mind will be covered in more detail in "Two-Ditch" Problems below, so I'll just mention it in passing here. Remember when Jacob was wrestling with God? Do we really think Jacob was overpowering God and holding God hostage when he said, "I won't let you go until you bless me!"? Of course not; God was just seeing if Jacob was serious about pursuing Him.

Another example is when the children of Israel were delivered from Egypt. God brought them *to the very border* of the Promised Land—they were looking into it—and then the fearful reports of ten of the twelve spies caused everyone except Joshua and Caleb to succumb to doubt. Listen to what Moses said to the tribes of Gad and Reuben when they requested to *not* go into the Promised Land:

> Numbers 32:6–13 (NASB): But Moses said to the sons of Gad and to the sons of Reuben, "Shall your brothers go to war while you yourselves sit here? [7]Now why are you discouraging the sons of Israel from crossing over into the land which the Lord has given them? [8]This is what your fathers did when I sent them from Kadesh-barnea to see the land. [9]**For when they went up to the valley of Eshcol and saw the land, they discouraged the sons of Israel so that they did not go into the land which the Lord had given them.** [10]So the Lord's anger burned in that day, and He swore, saying, [11]'None of the men who came up from Egypt, from twenty years old and upward, shall see the land which I swore to Abraham, to Isaac and to Jacob; for they did not follow Me fully, [12]except Caleb the son of Jephunneh the Kenizzite and Joshua the son of Nun, for they have followed the Lord fully.' [13]**So the Lord's anger burned against Israel, and He made them wander in the wilderness forty years, until the entire generation of those who had done evil in the sight of the Lord was destroyed.**"

Another example is when the disciples were in a bad storm on the Sea of Galilee, and Jesus was walking on the water:

> Mark 6:48–51 (NASB): And seeing them straining at the oars, for the wind was against them, at about the fourth watch of the night, He came to them, walking on the sea; and **He intended to pass by them.** [49]But when they saw Him walking on the sea, they supposed that it was a ghost, and cried out; [50]for they all saw Him and were frightened. But immediately He spoke with them and said to them, "Take courage; it is I, do not be afraid." [51]And He got into the boat with them, and the wind stopped; and they were greatly astonished, [52]for they had not gained any insight from the incident of the loaves, but their heart was hardened.

Why was Jesus planning on passing them by? He had already told them to "go to the other side" (v. 45), so they knew what God's will was. And they had already seen the miracle of the feeding of the 5,000, so they should have known better than to approach a problem with what they *didn't* have or *couldn't* do (v. 44). So Jesus was just checking to see if they had gotten the message. They hadn't (v. 52).

Or this one: Just before Jesus fed the five thousand, He asked Philip where they could get food. Why did He do that?

> John 6:5–6 (NIV): When Jesus looked up and saw a great crowd coming toward him, he said to Philip, "Where shall we buy bread for these people to eat?" **⁶He asked this only to test him, for he already had in mind what he was going to do.**

Here's another one. When Jesus met Cleopas and his friend on the road to Emmaus, they didn't recognize Him, so he taught them out of the law and the prophets how it was necessary for the Messiah to have suffered and died for the sins of the world. Then. . .

> Luke 24:28–29 (NIV): As they approached the village to which they were going, **Jesus acted as if he were going farther.** ²⁹**But they urged him strongly,** "Stay with us, for it is nearly evening; the day is almost over." **So he went in to stay with them.**

It's the same with us today: God wants to bless us more than we can imagine, but if we're no more than casually interested, we're not mature enough to be trusted with His power, His anointing, His favor. Apparently, the writer of Hebrews was on to something:

> Hebrews 11:6: But without faith it is impossible to please him: for he that cometh to God must believe that he is, and that he is a rewarder of them that **diligently** seek him.
>
> ICB: . . .he rewards those who **truly** want to find him.
>
> NIV: . . .he rewards those who **earnestly** seek him.
>
> NLT: . . .he rewards those who **sincerely** seek him.
>
> NLV: . . .to the one who **keeps on** looking for Him.

Steve Thompson (founder of NU World Ministries and author of *You May All Prophesy*) expresses it very aptly: "Generally, God will meet us at our level of hunger. If we feel like we can live without something, we probably will."

When God Does "Bad" Things

One of the ideas that is commonly used to support the Reformed view of the Sovereignty of God—that view that is implicit and required by the Five Points of Calvinism—comes from the many places in the Bible where God does things that are seemingly bad, painful, destructive.

Such things might be a nation being conquered by someone else, someone heeding bad advice, someone doing an ungodly or foolish behavior, and so forth. The sovereignty idea comes into play when the Bible specifically says that God *caused* these things to happen. And indeed it does, in quite a few places. The problem with reports like this is that, in most, if not all cases, an essential part of the story has been omitted, and because of that, the resulting inferences and interpretation—the messages being portrayed—are badly skewed.

For example, I read a book recently that is from the Reformed viewpoint, and there is a large section that talks primarily about the "bad" things that God does. The point the author makes was (usually) not that God is the source of bad things, but that He does everything sovereignly and unrelated to our wills, and because He did these things, they couldn't *really* be bad things after all, even though they appear that way to us.

In reading this book, it is obvious that the author loves God with all his heart, and is serving Him to the best of his ability, as all sincere Christians do. So I am in no wise accusing him of being malicious or deceptive when he left out those essential parts of the Bible stories to which I referred above. Much more likely is that he has grown up in the Reformed-theology environment, and has seen these passages quoted many times, but simply didn't look around them for other relevant content.

In all the subsequent subsections of this "When God Does 'Bad' Things" section, the structure will be similar, since the error in the original presentation I read was similar in every case. Each of the following subsections will have four parts: "The Scripture Quoted," "The Message Communicated," "The Content Omitted," and "The More Complete Message." *Every one* of these examples came from the book I referred to above.

"I, the Lord, Create Evil"

The Scripture Quoted

> Isaiah 45:7: I form the light, and **create darkness:** I make peace, and **create evil:** I the LORD do all these things.
>
> NIV: I form the light and **create darkness,** I bring prosperity and **create disaster;** I, the LORD, do all these things.

The Message Communicated

Even when God does things we consider to be evil or unpleasant, He is always right. God works in mysterious ways, and we may never understand (this side of heaven) why He does some stuff.

The Content Omitted
Isaiah 45 is addressed to Cyrus (v. 1), the heathen king of Babylon. Through Isaiah, God is "introducing" Himself to Cyrus, and telling him that, even though Cyrus was unaware of the fact, it was God who raised him up to be a king, to do His bidding, and He would continue to do so (vv. 2–3). Cyrus's power and success did not come from himself, but he was being directed to accomplish God's purposes to bless Israel (v. 4). God states in no uncertain terms that He is The Boss (vv. 5–8). He also adds that Cyrus would be much better off if he actually *deliberately* started to serve God (vv. 9–12). God finishes by saying that He will use Cyrus to rebuild Jerusalem (v. 13).

The More Complete Message
God gets His will accomplished, the free will of man notwithstanding, and it is much better for us if we willingly serve Him rather than resist Him.

"He Turns Rivers Into a Wilderness"

The Scripture Quoted
Psalm 107:33: He turneth rivers into a wilderness, and the watersprings into dry ground. . .

The Message Communicated
God causes death and disaster on occasion, and that's just the way it is. He has His reasons.

The Content Omitted
Much was omitted from this quote: All the context that describes God in a good light: His goodness (v. 1), His mercy (v. 1), His redeeming us (v. 2), His delivering us (v. 6), His guidance (v. 7), His goodness again and His wonderful works toward mankind (v. 8), and the fulfillment that comes from hungering after Him (v. 9).

Also omitted was the description of those who receive "bad" things from God: they sit in darkness, they sit in the shadow of death, they are bound with affliction and iron (v. 10). And why are they in that situation? Because they *rebelled* against the Lord, *spurned* God's counsel (v. 11), and therefore, they crashed and burned (a paraphrase of v. 12). But even this hardship was an act of God's mercy, because the result of the hardships was that the rebels repented, cried out to God, and He rescued them (v. 13). If God *hadn't* cared about them, He would have left them in their sin until they died, after which there would have been no hope.

To avoid making this too long, I'll omit some of the smaller details, but only those whose omission doesn't change the tenor of the passage. Throughout, there is a recurring theme of God's goodness and His wonderful works to the children of men, and it goes on to say that fools suffer *because of* their rebellion, but the suffering again motivates them to repent, and so they cry out to God and He saves them (vv. 17–20).

Right here is where the aforementioned author quoted the verses that sounded negative (vv. 33–34), and then stopped quoting right at the point where it changes back to positive (v. 35).

The summary of the Psalm is in v. 43, which says, "Who is wise? Let him give heed to these things; and consider the lovingkindnesses of the LORD." The phrase "these things" in this verse refers to the things previously mentioned in the Psalm, and the vast majority of them are about God's goodness and mercy. It is very misleading and intellectually dishonest to extract two negative-sounding verses from their much larger positive context and infer a gloomy picture about God's mysterious ways. The context shows a loving God doing everything He can to persuade people to repent of their sin before it's too late.

The More Complete Message

This passage, taken in context, shows God to be the source of every good thing (James 1:17), and He goes to great lengths to persuade us to submit ourselves to Him, but we must be diligent to faithfully obey Him in order to be fruitful (see "The Parable of the Sower" above), and we will surely reap what we sow (Galatians 6:7–8).

"God Did Vex Them. . ."

The Scripture Quoted

II Chronicles 15:6: And nation was destroyed of nation, and city of city: for God did vex them with all adversity.

The Message Communicated

God destroys things and people sometimes, and we have no right to question His actions.

The Content Omitted

This is the prophet Azariah talking to Asa, the king of Judah. Asa was the first godly king for quite a while, and God blessed him. This passage starts with three very plain and blunt statements that say God will behave toward us like we behave toward Him, all from 15:2 (NIV):

- "The LORD is with you when you are with him."
- "If you seek him, he will be found by you."
- "If you forsake him, he will forsake you."

That's pretty difficult to misinterpret. Azariah then goes on to give a little history lesson, and he's talking about the period of apostasy that Asa brought to an end; he describes it as Israel being "without the true God, without a priest to teach and without the law," so of course they were clueless about how to conduct themselves. Those were the days, when no one was serving God, that "God did vex them." Why did He vex them? Again, was it because He was just itching to push the "Smite" button and teach those lousy no-good sinners a thing or two? No, because He was being merciful, as we can see by the results of the trouble:

> II Chronicles 15:4 (NIV): But **in their distress they turned to the LORD, the God of Israel, and sought him, and he was found by them.**

The More Complete Message
We reap what we sow (Galatians 6:7–8), and God will go to great lengths, even causing severe problems in the flesh in order to bring people to repentance while there's still time, so the spirit might be saved.

"I Send Pestilence Among My People. . ."

The Scripture Quoted
> II Chronicles 7:13: If I shut up heaven that there be no rain, or if I command the locusts to devour the land, or if I send pestilence among my people. . .

The Message Communicated
God sometimes causes drought and famine and sickness. No one knows why.

The Content Omitted
This is a particularly egregious omission, because if we simply read the rest of the sentence, the whole sense of the passage is reversed from the gloomy feeling that comes across when the rest of the sentence is omitted. In fact, many Christians will recognize the next verse (which contains the rest of the sentence started above), as it is very comforting and reassuring:

> II Chronicles 7:14: **If my people,** which are called by my name, shall humble themselves, and pray, and seek my face, and **turn from their wicked ways; then will I hear from heaven, and will forgive their sin, and will heal their land.**

Simply finishing the sentence by including v. 14 shows just how biased the author was in his understanding of God—although, again, I'm sure he was not deliberately and maliciously being deceptive. But just to make sure about the intent of God's message here, let's look at the whole context, and not just the rest of this one sentence.

II Chronicles 5–7 is about the dedication of Solomon's Temple. Construction had just been completed (5:1), and the Levites brought the tabernacle's holy vessels to the temple (5:5). Solomon offered sacrifices (5:6), and the Levites brought in the Ark of the Covenant (5:7–10), worshipped the Lord with instruments and voices, singing "for He is good and His mercy endures forever" (5:13), and the glory of the Lord filled the temple so intensely that the priests couldn't even stand up anymore (5:13–14).

Solomon then addressed the people (6:1–11), prayed a prayer of dedication of the temple (6:14–42) and the fire of God came down and consumed the sacrifices (7:1), and the glory of the Lord *again* filled the temple so intensely that the priests couldn't even go in (7:1–2). Then *all* the children of Israel bowed before the Lord in worship and praise, saying "for He is good and His mercy endures forever" (7:3). They offered more sacrifices (7:4), and the Levites, with musical instruments, praised the Lord God with all Israel listening to them (7:6).

Then Solomon threw a seven-day feast for the whole nation (7:8), and on the eighth day he made a solemn assembly (7:9). After the assembly, Solomon sent them all home rejoicing (7:10). Then the Lord appeared to Solomon by night and spoke to him (7:12–22). In this address to Solomon, God promised that His ears would be attentive to the prayers made in the temple and, as usual, God included two specific things, basically saying: "If you obey Me, things will go well" (vv. 17–18), and "if you don't, things will not" (vv. 19–22), almost implying that God behaves toward us as we do toward Him.

So again, even if we leave out all the wonderful happenings in chapters 5 and 6, the lion's share of II Chronicles 7 is filled with miracles (v. 1), glory (vv. 1–2), worship (v. 3), praise (v. 3), God's goodness and mercy (v. 3), sacrifices of joy (v. 4–5), music (v. 6), feasting (v. 8), gladness (v. 10), and a visitation from the Lord (v. 12). Oh yes, and a warning from God saying, "If things go badly for you, repent, and I'll bless you again." But that is a far cry from the oppressive emphasis of the Reformed author I was reading.

But in all fairness, I can see why he left out v. 14 (the second half of the sentence started in II Chronicles 7:13): it shows God urging people to repent, which the Reformed doctrine of Total Depravity says is impossible. So in order to preserve that doctrine, this is one of many Scriptures one would be motivated to ignore.

The More Complete Message

God is amazingly good and loving, and wants to bless people. And He will do so, as long as we follow His direction in our lives. But if we reject Him—the *only* source of good things in our lives—the sole alternative is bad things in our lives.

"Evil Came Down from the LORD. . ."

The Scripture Quoted

> Micah 1:12: For the inhabitant of Maroth waited carefully for good: but evil came down from the LORD unto the gate of Jerusalem.

The Message Communicated

Sometimes God does evil things, but He is sovereign, and there must be a reason, even if we don't know what it is.

The Content Omitted

God says very clearly, a few verses earlier, *why* the disasters, calamity, and excessive hardships came:

> Micah 1:5 (NIV): **All this is because of Jacob's transgression, because of the sins of the house of Israel.** What is Jacob's transgression? Is it not Samaria? What is Judah's high place? Is it not Jerusalem?

In v. 7, God says that all Samaria's idols would be destroyed. Is that a good thing? In the spiritual realm, and from the eternal perspective, it most certainly *is* a good thing to have our idols destroyed (although it may be temporarily upsetting to the idolaters). Why would God do this? Because He loves us and doesn't want us to end up burning in hell forever.

And just in case we missed the message in v. 5, God reiterates why things are going badly for the people, as He addresses the instigators and promoters of the idolatry in which all of Israel was eventually caught up:

> Micah 1:13 (NIV): You who live in Lachish, harness the team to the chariot. **You were the beginning of sin to the Daughter of Zion, for the transgressions of Israel were found in you.**

Again, we reap what we sow (Galatians 6:7–8); this is not rocket science. If we don't want disasters, calamity, and excessive hardships in our lives, we shouldn't forsake God, reject God, and rebel against His Word.

This reminds me of people in my town who were all upset with automated speed traps, because they got speeding tickets more often. They complained vociferously with cries of "Unfair!" and "Entrapment!" But as I pointed out in a Letter to the Editor of our local newspaper, "If you don't want to get a speeding ticket, *don't speed.*" This is not that hard to figure out.

The More Complete Message

It grieves God when we reject Him, and there is no question that our rejection of Him will result in disaster.

The disaster that is sure to come will come by way of one of these three mechanisms:

- The disaster might be from Satan, whom we empower and authorize to steal from, kill, and destroy us when we rebel against God; or
- The disaster might be from God Who, in His mercy, makes it difficult enough for us that it gets our attention, so we'll repent while we still have the chance; or
- The disaster might be simply a natural result of the most fundamental spiritual law there is (see "The Parable of the Sower" above): that we reap what we sow.

A few relevant verses bear repeating; these relate to the three mechanisms described above:

John 10:10 (NIV): **The thief comes only to steal and kill and destroy**; I have come that they may have life, and have it to the full.

Hebrews 12:10–11 (TEV): Our human fathers punished us for a short time, as it seemed right to them; but **God does it for our own good, so that we may share his holiness.** ¹¹When we are punished, it seems to us at the time something to make us sad, not glad. Later, however, **those who have been disciplined by such punishment reap the peaceful reward of a righteous life.**

Galatians 6:8 (NIV): **The one who sows to please his sinful nature, from that nature will reap destruction;** the one who sows to please the Spirit, from the Spirit will reap eternal life.

"The Evil That I Have Brought. . ."

The Scripture Quoted

Jeremiah 44:2: Thus saith the LORD of hosts, the God of Israel; Ye have seen all the evil that I have brought upon Jerusalem, and upon all the cities of Judah; and, behold, this day they are a desolation, and no man dwelleth therein. . .

The Message Communicated
God does bad things and brings evil upon people sometimes, but God works in mysterious ways, and we may never know why He does the things He does.

The Content Omitted
Here is another example of a Scripture fragment being presented in a terribly misleading way, simply because it was truncated—the end of the sentence, which explains *why* the LORD brought evil upon Jerusalem, was inexplicably excluded. Let's read the rest of the sentence and see if that sheds any light on the subject (it does):

> Jeremiah 44:3: **Because of their wickedness** which they have committed to provoke me to anger, in that **they went to burn incense, and to serve other gods,** whom they knew not, neither they, ye, nor your fathers.

That's a pretty important "detail" to leave out. But wait; there's more. If we keep reading (again, context is a wonderful thing), we see that God had repeatedly sent prophets to them to call them to repentance, but they refused to listen:

> Jeremiah 44:4–6 (NIV): **Again and again I sent my servants the prophets,** who said, 'Do not do this detestable thing that I hate!' ⁵But **they did not listen** or pay attention; **they did not turn from their wickedness** or stop burning incense to other gods. ⁶**Therefore,** my fierce anger was poured out; it raged against the towns of Judah and the streets of Jerusalem and made them the desolate ruins they are today.

That's pretty unambiguous, isn't it? It wasn't God's "mysterious ways" that caused Him to send disaster, *it was their sin.* He wanted to bless them, but they refused to obey.

And as we continue reading, He reiterates His reasoning:

> Jeremiah 44:7–8 (NASB): Now then thus says the LORD God of hosts, the God of Israel, "**Why are you doing great harm to yourselves,** so as to cut off from you man and woman, child and infant, from among Judah, leaving yourselves without remnant, ⁸**provoking Me to anger with the works of your hands, burning sacrifices to other gods** in the land of Egypt, where you are entering to reside, so that you might be

cut off and become a curse and a reproach among all the nations of the earth?"

God then references (in vv. 9–10) the sins of their forefathers, points out that they are continuing in those same sins, and then states the result of their actions:

> Jeremiah 44:11 (NIV): **Therefore,** this is what the LORD Almighty, the God of Israel, says: "I am determined to bring disaster on you and to destroy all Judah."

Here is another situation where I can understand why the Reformed author I was reading omitted the explanatory text from his quotation. It is another case of those Scriptures refuting one or more of the Reformed doctrines, the Five Points of Calvinism. Specifically, we have God wanting to, and attempting to, have a good relationship with people, but they refused (v. 5). The fact that they refused invalidates the Reformed doctrine of Irresistible Grace, which says that it is impossible to refuse or resist the moving of the Holy Spirit when God wants to save someone.

And, the fact that God's behavior was a direct result of the people's behavior also refutes the Reformed doctrine of Unconditional Election, which says that whether people respond to God or not is God's decision alone, made in eternity past, completely apart from our attitudes, actions, or decisions, before He even created the heavens and the earth.

And the fact that God repeatedly sent prophets to urge them to repent, refutes the Reformed doctrine of Total Depravity, which claims that people *cannot* choose to repent, and that they're inherently unable to until *after* God saves them.

The More Complete Message

God loves everyone, wants to bless everyone, and will go to great lengths to persuade us to make a sensible decision on whether or not to love Him and obey Him. However, if we insist on choosing foolishly, He won't stop us, but there will be consequences for rejecting the only Source of all good things: all *bad* things.

"I Will Tear and Go Away"

The Scripture Quoted

> Hosea 5:14: For I will be unto Ephraim as a lion, and as a young lion to the house of Judah: I, even I, will tear and go away; I will take away, and none shall rescue him.

The Message Communicated
Disasters often come from God; that's just the way it is.

The Content Omitted
As usual, the content omitted was that which shows the mercy and goodness of God. It starts with vv. 1–2:

> Hosea 5:1–2 (NASB): Hear this, O priests! Give heed, O house of Israel! Listen, O house of the king! For the judgment applies to you, For you have been a snare at Mizpah, and a net spread out on Tabor. ²And the revolters have gone deep in depravity, but **I will chastise** all of them.

So right away (assuming we read it in context), we see that the people have revolted against God and adopted depraved behavior. What is God's response? He said He would chastise them. And what is the purpose of chastisement? Any of you parents whose toddler has run out into the street probably gave him a spanking and scolding for doing so. Why? Because you wanted to inflict pain on him? Of course not; it was to *avoid* much more serious, and possible fatal, pain later on.

Hebrews 12 gives more detail on God's motivation for His chastising us:

> Hebrews 12:5–11 (NIV): And you have forgotten that word of encouragement that addresses you as sons: "My son, do not make light of the Lord's discipline, and do not lose heart when he rebukes you, ⁶because **the Lord disciplines those he loves,** and he punishes everyone he accepts as a son." ⁷Endure hardship as discipline; God is treating you as sons. For what son is not disciplined by his father? ⁸If you are not disciplined (and everyone undergoes discipline), then you are illegitimate children and not true sons. ⁹Moreover, we have all had human fathers who disciplined us and we respected them for it. How much more should we submit to the Father of our spirits and live! ¹⁰Our fathers disciplined us for a little while as they thought best; but **God disciplines us for our good, that we may share in his holiness.** ¹¹**No discipline seems pleasant at the time, but painful.** Later on, however, **it produces a harvest of righteousness and peace** for those who have been trained by it.

Now back to Hosea 5: in vv. 3–7, God shows *why* the disasters were coming: the unrepentant sins of the people. And finally, at the end of chapter 5 and the beginning of chapter 6, God describes how it will turn out: When the hardship gets severe enough, they will repent and turn back to God. His mercy prevails and the people are saved:

> Hosea 5:15–6:2 (AMP): I will return to My place [on high] **until they acknowledge their offense and feel their guilt and seek My face;** in their affliction and distress **they will seek, inquire for, and require Me** earnestly, saying, [6:1]Come and **let us return to the Lord, for He has torn so that He may heal us; He has stricken so that He may bind us up.** [2]After two days He will revive us (quicken us, give us life); on the third day **He will raise us up that we may live before Him.**

The first verse of chapter 6 is pivotal, and again, was left out of the Reformed author's book: that God "has torn *so that He may heal us;* He has stricken *so that He may bind us up."* God's purposes are redemptive, not vindictive. We saw this in Jeremiah 31:18, mentioned in "A Woman Shall Compass a Man," and we see it again in the passages below:

> Psalm 107:10–14, 17–20 (CEB): Some of the redeemed had been sitting in darkness and deep gloom; they were prisoners suffering in chains [11]because they had disobeyed God's instructions and rejected the Most High's plans. [12] So God humbled them with hard work. They stumbled, and there was no one to help them. [13]So they cried out to the Lord in their distress, and **God saved them from their desperate circumstances.** [14]**God brought them out from the darkness and deep gloom; he shattered their chains.** . . . [17]Some of the redeemed were fools because of their sinful ways. They suffered because of their wickedness. [18]They had absolutely no appetite for food; they had arrived at death's gates. [19]So they cried out to the Lord in their distress, and **God saved them from their desperate circumstances.** [20]**God gave the order and healed them; he rescued them from their pit.**

. . .and it is confirmed yet again in the New Testament:

> I Corinthians 11:32 (NASB): But when we are judged, we are disciplined by the Lord **in order that we may not be condemned** along with the world.

> Hebrews 12:10b–11 (NIV): God disciplines us **for our good, that we may share in his holiness.** [11]No discipline seems pleasant at the time, but painful. Later on, however, **it produces a harvest of righteousness and peace** for those who have been trained by it.

Again, it's understandable that the merciful emphasis of these Scriptures would be left out by the author I read, because this passage shows God's behavior toward us being based on our prior behavior toward Him, which flies in the face of the Reformed doctrine of Unconditional Election, where God unchangeably chose in eternity past who would be able to respond to Him, in a way that is completely independent of our actions and attitudes toward Him. Also, once the people's pain gets severe enough, they are motivated to repent and turn to God, which the Reformed doctrine of Total Depravity says is not possible.

The More Complete Message

We see that God's discipline and chastisement shows that He loves us. And it's for our ultimate good: it is intended to cause our holiness, righteousness and peace, and it will gloriously do so if we repent of our sin.

"Desolation Shall Come Upon You Suddenly. . ."

The Scripture Quoted

> Isaiah 47:11: Therefore shall evil come upon thee; thou shalt not know from whence it riseth: and mischief shall fall upon thee; thou shalt not be able to put it off: and desolation shall come upon thee suddenly, which thou shalt not know.

The Message Communicated

Evil happens sometimes, and the Lord is probably behind it. Just suffer through it and perhaps you'll understand someday.

The Content Omitted

This prophecy is addressed to the Chaldeans in Babylon. Right there, it should tell us something, because Babylon was not known for its holiness. Let's read further and see if ungodliness had anything to do with their pronouncement of judgment:

> Isaiah 47:12–15 (NIV): Keep on, then, with your **magic spells** and with your many **sorceries,** which you have labored at since childhood. Perhaps you will succeed, perhaps you will cause terror. [13]All the counsel you have received has only worn you out! Let your **astrologers** come forward, those **stargazers who make predictions** month by month, let them save you from what is coming upon you. [14]Surely they are like stubble; the fire will burn them up. They cannot even save themselves from the power of the flame. Here are no coals to warm anyone; here is no fire to sit by. [15]That is all they can do for you—these you have labored with and trafficked with since childhood. Each of them goes on in his error; there is not one that can save you.

Hmm. They were involved in magic, sorcery, astrology, and had been doing it since childhood. So yes, their sin sounds pretty severe. And notice that God had given them ample opportunity to repent, but they still didn't, just like described in Peter's second epistle:

> II Peter 3:9 (AMP): The Lord does not delay and is not tardy or slow about what He promises, according to some people's conception of slowness, but **He is long-suffering (extraordinarily patient)** toward you, not desiring that any should perish, but that all should turn to repentance.

God is indeed longsuffering, but He is also just, and sooner or later, unrepentant sin results in reaping what one has sown.

The More Complete Message

God loves us right where we are, but he loves us too much to leave us there. Remember Galatians 6:8? "The one who sows to please his sinful nature, from that nature will reap destruction; the one who sows to please the Spirit, from the Spirit will reap eternal life" (NIV). So He chastises us when necessary, in an effort to steer us away from a rejection of Him that would have eternally destructive consequences. God follows our lead in the relationship between Him and us.

"Hath Not the LORD Done This Evil?"

The Scripture Quoted

> Amos 3:6: Shall a trumpet be blown in the city, and the people not be afraid? Shall there be evil in a city, and the LORD hath not done it?

The Message Communicated

Evil comes from God.

The Content Omitted

Judging from the pattern we've seen in the past several sections, perhaps we should see if this judgment from the LORD might be related to. . . oh, I don't know, maybe. . . *sin?*

> Amos 3:1–2 (NIV): Hear this word the LORD has spoken against you, O people of Israel—against the whole family I brought up out of Egypt: ²"You only have I chosen of all the families of the earth; therefore I will punish you **for all your sins.**"

A few verses later we see another important point that God is making:

> Amos 3:7–8 (NIV): Surely the Sovereign Lord does nothing without revealing his plan to **his servants the prophets.** ⁸The lion has roared—who will not fear? The Sovereign Lord has spoken—who can but prophesy?

Why do you think God brought up the subject of "His servants the prophets" in this pronouncement of judgment? Because long before the judgment comes, exhortations, warnings, and heartfelt pleas come from the heart of God. He wants us to repent and live instead of rebel and die. Remember Ezekiel's message to Israel?

> Ezekiel 33:11–20 (NIV): "Say to them, 'As surely as I live, declares the Sovereign Lord, I take no pleasure in the death of the wicked, but **rather that they turn from their ways and live. Turn! Turn from your evil ways!** Why will you die, O house of Israel?'"

And remember what God said, through Jeremiah, to the Israelites?

> Jeremiah 44:4-7 (NIV): **Again and again I sent my servants the prophets,** who said, 'Do not do this detestable thing that I hate!'

Because He loves us, God warns us repeatedly to stop doing those things that kill us. And sin kills us (Romans 6:23).

The More Complete Message

God says, "Please turn away from sin! Repent! I have so much blessing for you if you will only obey My voice!"

Calamities from the Most High

The Scripture Quoted

> Lamentations 3:38 (NIV): Is it not from the mouth of the Most High that both calamities and good things come?

The Message Communicated

God might bless you, but He might send disaster instead.

The Content Omitted

Here again is an egregious omission: *every one* of the *five* verses following the one quoted show that the calamity was because of Israel's sin, not God's capriciousness:

> Lamentations 3:39–44 (TEV): Why should we ever complain when **we are punished for our sin?** ⁴⁰Let us examine our ways and **turn back to the Lord.** ⁴¹**Let us open our hearts to God** in heaven and pray, ⁴²"**We**

have sinned and rebelled, and you, O LORD, have not forgiven us. ⁴³You pursued us and killed us; your mercy was hidden by your anger, ⁴⁴By a cloud of fury too thick for our prayers to get through."

So let's look at these verses one by one and see what they reveal:

- Verse 39: Jeremiah plainly acknowledges that they were being punished for their sin, and that it was silly to be surprised at the punishment, or to resent it.
- Verse 40: In encouraging Israel to "turn *back* to the LORD," he indicates that they had been with God earlier, but then *had turned away* from Him. Hence, the punishment.
- Verse 41: In encouraging Israel to open their hearts to God, he admits that their hearts had been closed to God before that.
- Verse 42: Self-evident: "We have sinned and rebelled." It might be momentarily startling to see that God had *not* forgiven them. Why didn't He? *Because they had not yet repented.* We know that God does forgive us when we repent (II Chronicles 7:14).
- Verse 43: Here Jeremiah shows that the punishment was actually an act of God's mercy. How can that be so? Because God chastens those He loves (see "I Will Tear and Go Away", above, for a more complete treatment).

The More Complete Message

God loves us so much, He is willing to go to great lengths to convince us to turn to Him, or turn *back* to Him, before it's too late.

The Lord of the Holocaust

The Scripture Quoted

II Chronicles 36:17 (NIV): He *[God]* brought up against them *[Israel]* the king of the Babylonians, who killed their young men with the sword in the sanctuary, and spared neither young man nor young woman, old man or aged. God handed all of them over to Nebuchadnezzar.

The Message Communicated

God sends a holocaust sometimes. That's harsh, we know, but He's God.

The Content Omitted

This passage begins when Jehoiakim became king of Israel. In the *very first verse* (as well as the second verse) that describes his reign, Scripture indicates his evil ways.

The description says:

II Chronicles 36:5, 8 (NIV): **Jehoiakim** was twenty-five years old when he became king, and he reigned in Jerusalem eleven years. He **did evil in the eyes of the LORD** his God. ⁸The other events of Jehoiakim's reign, **the detestable things he did and all that was found against him,** are written in the book of the kings of Israel and Judah.

Sounds like Jehoiakim was not just an "amateur" sinner; sounds like he was a professional. And not surprisingly, his influence as the king gave everyone else in the country tacit "permission" to sin also.

Here are some quotes from Jeremiah where he describes Jehoiakim's reign:

Jeremiah 25:2–7 (NIV): So Jeremiah the prophet said to **all the people of** Judah and to **all** those living in Jerusalem:

(By the way, the fact that God is addressing *all* the people refutes Limited Atonement.)

³**For twenty-three years**—from the thirteenth year of Josiah son of Amon king of Judah until this very day—the word of the LORD has come to me and **I have spoken to you again and again, but you have not listened.**

(By the way, the fact that the people didn't listen refutes Irresistible Grace.)

⁴And though **the LORD has sent all his servants the prophets to you again and again, you have not listened or paid any attention.** ⁵They said, "**Turn now, each of you, from your evil ways and your evil practices.** . .

(By the way, the fact that God sent prophets to urge them to repent refutes Total Depravity.)

. . .and you can stay in the land the LORD gave to you and your fathers for ever and ever. ⁶**Do not follow other gods** to serve and worship them; do not provoke me to anger with what your hands have made. Then I will not harm you."

(By the way, the fact that God's actions toward the people reflected the people's prior actions toward Him refutes Unconditional Election.)

⁷"**But you did not listen to me,**" declares the LORD, "and you have provoked me with what your hands have made, and **you have brought harm to yourselves.**"

(By the way, the fact that the people didn't listen again refutes Irresistible Grace.)

So, yeah, this is a problem. Israel had been worshipping idols for *decades* (it started before Jehoiakim's reign, but he did nothing to oppose it), and God sent not only Jeremiah, but *many* other prophets as well, warning them of impending disaster if they didn't repent. Finally, the other shoe drops:

> Jeremiah 25:8–9a (NIV): Therefore the LORD Almighty says this: "**Because you have not listened to my words,** I will summon all the peoples of the north and my servant Nebuchadnezzar king of Babylon," declares the LORD, "and I will bring them against this land and its inhabitants. . ."

The More Complete Message

Fighting against God is not a good plan; someone is going to lose, and it won't be Him. And again, the calamity is a direct result of their sin, which they could have stopped at any time (for more detail, see Book 2: *Is It Possible to Stop Sinning?*). Plus, this calamity on earth was an act of mercy, because while on earth, people can still repent. Once we're dead, there's no more opportunity to get right with God.

And So Forth

There were quite a few more examples that the Reformed author quoted in this section of his book, but in *every case*, he included only the verbiage that cast God in a negative light; i.e., the source of bad stuff as well as good stuff. *In every case* he omitted what is included above; those other "details" that showed that the judgment came because they had forsaken God, turned away from His Word, ignored His warnings, chosen to do evil (against God's advice, warnings, and pleadings), and reveled in sin. And *in every case* he omitted pointing out that even God's judgment is an act of mercy, steering us toward repentance and forgiveness, if we'll only listen.

But also, in every case, I can see why one would be tempted to omit such "details"—each one clearly refuted one or more of the Five Points of Calvinism.

But just in case the above examples were insufficient, there are more Scriptures that show God's punishment and chastisement are remedial, not punitive. That is, they are acts of mercy even though they are temporarily unpleasant and painful.

For example, look at this one from the Psalms:

Psalm 78:32–35 (AMP): In spite of all this, **they sinned still more,** for they believed not in (relied not on and adhered not to Him for) His wondrous works. ³³**Therefore their days He consumed** like a breath [in emptiness, falsity, and futility] and their years in terror and sudden haste. ³⁴**When He slew [some of] them, [the remainder] inquired after Him diligently, and they repented and sincerely sought God** [for a time]. ³⁵And they [earnestly] remembered that God was their Rock, and the Most High God their Redeemer.

Here's another one; look at this one from Isaiah:

Isaiah 26:9 (NIV): My soul yearns for you in the night; in the morning my spirit longs for you. **When your judgments come upon the earth, the people of the world learn righteousness.**

And then this one, just a few chapters later:

Isaiah 30:15–17 (AMP): For thus said the Lord God, the Holy One of Israel: **In returning [to Me] and resting [in Me] you shall be saved;** in quietness and in [trusting] confidence shall be your strength. **But you would not,** ¹⁶And **you said, No!** We will speed [our own course] on horses! Therefore you will speed [in flight from your enemies]! You said, We will ride upon swift steeds [doing our own way]! **Therefore will they who pursue you be swift, [so swift that]** ¹⁷**One thousand of you will flee at the threat of one of them;** at the threat of five you will flee till you are left like a beacon or a flagpole on the top of a mountain, and like a signal on a hill.

So God says, "Return to me and you will be saved and strengthened," and Israel says, "No, thanks." So judgment comes, but not because God enjoys hurting people; on the contrary, He is making it uncomfortable for them while there is still time to repent. And God promises good things to those who do:

Isaiah 30:26 (AMP): Moreover, the light of the moon will be like the light of the sun, and the light of the sun will be sevenfold, like the light of seven days [concentrated in one], in the day that **the Lord binds up the hurt of His people, and heals their wound [inflicted by Him because of their sins].**

Note what God says to Jeremiah the prophet:

Jeremiah 26:3 (NASB): Perhaps they will listen and everyone will turn from his evil way, **that I may repent of the calamity which I am planning to do to them because of the evil of their deeds.**

Jeremiah 26:13 (AMP): Therefore now **amend your ways and your doings** and obey the voice of the Lord your God; **then the Lord will relent and reverse the decision concerning the evil which He has pronounced against you.**

Or how about this one:

Jeremiah 29:11–14 (NIV): "For I know the plans I have for you," declares the Lord, "plans to prosper you and not to harm you, plans to give you hope and a future. [12]Then you will call upon me and come and pray to me, and I will listen to you. [13]You will seek me and find me when you seek me with all your heart. [14]I will be found by you," declares the Lord, "and **will bring you back from captivity.** I will gather you from all the nations and places where **I have banished you**," declares the Lord, "and will bring you back to the place from which **I carried you into exile.**"

The unpleasant part was that God "banished" Israel, carried them into "captivity," and into "exile." Why? Because of their sin. But the unpleasantness of the exile gave them motivation to repent and return to God, which was God's intent and desire all along. Note God's plans were to "prosper and not to harm," and to give Israel "hope and a future." God's discipline is *always* remedial, not punitive.

Or this one:

Jeremiah 30:11–19 (NIV): "I am with you and will save you," declares the Lord. "Though I completely destroy all the nations among which I scatter you, I will not completely destroy you. I will discipline you but only with justice; I will not let you go entirely unpunished." [12]This is what the Lord says: "Your wound is incurable, your injury beyond healing. [13]There is no one to plead your cause, no remedy for your sore, no healing for you. [14]All your allies have forgotten you; they care nothing for you. **I have struck you as an enemy would and punished you as would the cruel, because your guilt is so great and your sins so many.** [15]Why do you cry out over your wound, your pain that has no cure? **Because of your great guilt and many sins I have done these things to you.** [16]But all who devour you will be devoured; all your enemies will go into exile. Those who plunder you will be plundered; all who make spoil of you I will despoil. ¹⁷**But I will restore you to health and heal your wounds,**" declares the Lord, "because you are called an outcast, Zion for whom no one cares." ¹⁸This is what the Lord says: "I will **restore the fortunes** of Jacob's tents and **have compassion** on his dwellings; the city will be **rebuilt** on her ruins, and the palace will **stand** in its proper place. ¹⁹From them will come songs of **thanksgiving** and the sound of **rejoicing.** I will **add** to their numbers, and they will not be decreased; I will bring them **honor,** and they will **not be disdained."**

When God, through the prophet Jeremiah, confronts Jehoiakim's evil, he says:

Jeremiah 26:1–3 (NLT): This message came to Jeremiah from the Lord early in the reign of Jehoiakim son of Josiah, king of Judah. ²"This is what the Lord says: Stand in the courtyard in front of the Temple of the Lord, and make an announcement to the people who have come there to worship from all over Judah. Give them my entire message; include every word. ³**Perhaps they will listen and turn from their evil ways. Then I will change my mind about the disaster I am ready to pour out on them because of their sins."**

The religious leaders are incensed at Jeremiah's gall to accuse them of sin, so they threatened Jeremiah with death. He reiterates God's heart to bless if they would only repent of their sin:

Jeremiah 26:12–14 (NLT): Then Jeremiah spoke to the officials and the people in his own defense. "The Lord sent me to prophesy against this Temple and this city," he said. "The Lord gave me every word that I have spoken. ¹³But **if you stop your sinning and begin to obey the Lord your God, he will change his mind about this disaster that he has announced against you.** ¹⁴As for me, I am in your hands—do with me as you think best."

At this point, some older and wiser men came to Jeremiah's defense by reminding them of Hezekiah's wise response to a similar prophecy from Micah in earlier years:

Jeremiah's 26:19 (NLT): But did King Hezekiah and the people kill him for saying this? No, **they turned from their sins and worshiped the Lord. They begged him for mercy. Then the Lord changed his mind about the terrible disaster he had pronounced against them.** So we are about to do ourselves great harm.

This shows God's heart yet again: He would rather see us repent on our own than have to suffer disaster for our sins.

Of course, there are many more. But the common thread to them all is that God wants us to repent and change our ways to something that is not fatal, while we still have the option of choosing.

"Two-Ditch" Problems

One of the main reasons I've heard from Reformed teachers why they can't accept the idea of free will is that, in their understanding, the idea of free will is necessarily mutually exclusive with the idea of the sovereignty of God.

The situation is like the driver of a car wanting so much to avoid going into the ditch on the right side of the road (the mistaken idea that humans are autonomous agents) that he happily goes into the ditch on the left side of the road (another mistaken idea that God irresistibly controls absolutely everything), thinking that one ditch is infinitely preferable to the other. But there might be a third option: *staying on the road.*

The first idea is mistaken because humans are *not* autonomous: we are utterly dependent upon God for every breath we take, and much more. So that is not the extremity to which most free-will adherents go. But neither is God controlling everything with a velvet-covered iron fist, so that nothing happens that He didn't directly, deliberately cause.

"Staying on the road," in this context, is the idea that God is *so* sovereign that He gets His must-do items accomplished, even though He created humans with the *actual* ability to freely choose Him or not (see the sections "The Definition of Sovereignty" and "Sovereignty: Infinite Power and Authority" above for details). This is in stark contrast to the Reformed idea of free will, where the Holy Spirit "irresistibly causes" us to "freely" choose Him. This self-contradictory idea, at best, has us only *thinking* we're making free-will choices, when all along, the Holy Spirit irresistibly caused us to choose those choices. That kind of will is obviously not free.

Another manifestation of a "two-ditch problem" is what the Reformed author I referred to above scornfully referred to as the "Gentleman God." In his view, a Gentleman God, in allowing people to make free choices, would necessarily have to be completely detached from the universe—aloof, separate, withdrawn. This is the ditch on the right side of the road, and this idea was so repugnant to him, and so unscriptural (and it is), that he concluded that the only alternative must be a God that directly, deliberately causes every single event in the universe throughout all time (the ditch on the left side of the road).

But again, there might be a third option: staying on the road. In this context, that would be a God who is involved in the universe He created, loves all the people He created, and endeavors to interact with them as any loving father would want to do with his children. Adherents to free will generally do not claim that God is separate, aloof, and uninvolved with His universe, since such a viewpoint is impossible to support Scripturally, as the passages above clearly show.

Reformed theologians seem to think that God would have to be so puny and powerless as to not deserve the title of "God" if we humans could say No to Him. And if that were the *only* factor—if we were talking simply about raw power—that would certainly be the case. But we're *not* simply talking about raw power. We're talking about love, which, if you remember, *must be voluntary,* or it is meaningless (see the section "What Is Love?" for a fuller discussion of this). The fact that the Lord does not override our wills does not make Him unworthy of the title "God;" it simply shows Him to be a God Who is not a dictator.

Remember the parable of the Prodigal Son? This story, found in Luke 15:11–32, shows the father *letting his son go* when he wanted to go. He didn't stop his son, although he surely could have; rather, he chose to have a son who was absent than a prisoner who was present.

But is that even reasonable? To think that God would abide by *our* decisions? Or ask for *our* permission to do something? Or ask what *we* want Him to do? Or allow us to steal anything from Him? Or allow us to "beat" Him at anything? He certainly doesn't need to, and He certainly has the power to prevent it, so would God ever do such a thing?

Actually, yes. Before Solomon built the Temple, God appeared to him in a dream, as we saw earlier:

> I Kings 3:5 (TEV): That night the LORD appeared to him in a dream and asked him, **"What would you like me to give you?"**

If God were in the habit of controlling absolutely everything, and our choice either didn't exist or didn't matter, why would God ask a person what he wanted? And then in the following Scripture, when Jesus healed Bartimaeus:

> Luke 18:40–41 (NIV): Jesus stopped and ordered the man to be brought to him. When he came near, Jesus asked him, [41]**"What do you want me to do for you?"** "Lord, I want to see," he replied.

I seriously doubt that Jesus was unaware that this guy was blind, but He still asked him what he wanted. And then at the Pool of Bethesda, Jesus talks to. . .

> John 5:5–6 (NIV): . . .one who was there had been an invalid for thirty-eight years. ⁶When Jesus saw him lying there and learned that he had been in this condition for a long time, he asked him, "**Do you want to get well?**"

I think it's significant that Jesus *asked* him first whether He wanted to be healed. It wasn't just a matter of God's sovereignty deciding for him, *God asked*. It's almost as if the following Scripture were true:

> James 4:2 (NIV): You want something but don't get it. You kill and covet, but you cannot have what you want. You quarrel and fight. **You do not have, because you do not ask God.**

And notice what God says in Malachi 3:

> Malachi 3:8 (NIV): Will a man rob God? **Yet you rob me.** But you ask, 'How do we rob you?' In tithes and offerings.

Again, did some human sneak into the treasuries of heaven without God's knowledge and surreptitiously abscond with some valuables? Of course not. God's power is not the only factor involved in how He interacts with us.

Now think back to when Jacob wrestled with God:

> Genesis 32:24–26, 30 (AMP): And Jacob was left alone, and a Man wrestled with him until daybreak. ²⁵And when [**the Man**] **saw that He did not prevail against** [**Jacob**], He touched the hollow of his thigh; and Jacob's thigh was put out of joint as he wrestled with Him. ²⁶Then He said, Let Me go, for day is breaking. But [Jacob] **said, I will not let You go** unless You declare a blessing upon me. ³⁰And Jacob called the name of the place Peniel [the face of God], saying, For **I have seen God face to face**, and my life is spared and not snatched away.

> TEV: So Jacob was left alone. Then a man wrestled with him until daybreak. ²⁵When **the man saw that he could not defeat Jacob,** he struck the socket of his hip so the socket of Jacob's hip was dislocated while he wrestled with him. ²⁶Then the man said, "Let me go, for the dawn is breaking." "**I will not let you go,**" **Jacob replied,** "unless you bless me." ³⁰So Jacob named the place Peniel, explaining, "Certainly **I have seen God face to face** and have survived."

Now seriously: Does anyone really think that Jacob, a mere human, could defeat God Himself—the Creator of heaven and earth, the One who maintains every atomic particle in the universe—in a wrestling match, if the only contest was in raw power? That's absurd, of course. Raw power was obviously not the only factor here; God was bringing Jacob to the end of himself so he would realize he needed to change his ways. God changes his name here from Jacob (supplanter, schemer, trickster, swindler) to Israel (contender with God).

But if one completely ignores the fact that God is desiring a *loving* relationship with us (which, as we've seen, must be voluntary), and instead focuses on God's power as the *only* attribute that pertains to His relationship with us, of course a "Gentleman God" would be distasteful, because any ability on our part to refuse God's overtures would necessarily imply weakness in Him.

It's interesting that the concept of a "Gentleman God" is so despised in Reformed theology, especially in light of these Scriptures, and others like them:

II Samuel 22:36 (ASV): Thou hast also given me the shield of thy salvation; and **thy gentleness** hath made me great.

Psalm 18:35 (NASB): You have also given me the shield of Your salvation, and Your right hand upholds me; and **Your gentleness** makes me great.

Zechariah 9:9 > Matthew 21:5 (NIV): Rejoice greatly, O Daughter of Zion! Shout, Daughter of Jerusalem! See, **your king** comes to you, righteous and having salvation, **gentle** and riding on a donkey, on a colt, the foal of a donkey. > "Say to the Daughter of Zion, 'See, **your king** comes to you, **gentle** and riding on a donkey, on a colt, the foal of a donkey.'"

Matthew 11:28–30 (NIV): "Come to me, all you who are weary and burdened, and I will give you rest. ²⁹Take my yoke upon you and learn from me, for **I am gentle** and humble in heart, and you will find rest for your souls. ³⁰For my yoke is easy and my burden is light."

II Corinthians 10:1 (NIV): By the meekness and **gentleness of Christ**, I appeal to you—I, Paul, who am "timid" when face to face with you, but "bold" when away!

Galatians 5:22–23 (NIV): But **the fruit of the Spirit is** love, joy, peace, patience, kindness, goodness, faithfulness, ²³**gentleness** and self-control. Against such things there is no law.

I Timothy 6:11b (GWORD): But you, man of God, must avoid these things. **Pursue what God approves of:** a godly life, faith, love, endurance, and **gentleness**.

James 3:17 (NASB): But **the wisdom from above is** first pure, then peaceable, **gentle**, reasonable, full of mercy and good fruits, unwavering, without hypocrisy.

So what, exactly, would be the objection to God being a gentleman?

The Problem of Judas Iscariot

Above, I made the statement that God's sovereignty is big enough that He could get His must-do items complete, while still allowing people to choose whether or not they would serve Him. In other words, God does indeed have some plans that are unchangeable, but *who participates* in those plans, and *how* they participate, is a matter of their own free will. Is there Scriptural support for such a concept?

This is inextricably linked to how predestination is defined: is it an unchangeable "fatedness," with our choices being nonexistent or irrelevant? Or is it God's original intended destination for everybody to be blessed in heaven with Him, although we can choose otherwise if we insist upon it?

Specifically, in the case of Judas, was he unavoidably fated to betray Jesus and inevitably doomed to burn in hell forever because of it? As in, "After all, *somebody* had to do it. . ." (But think of the violence that fact would do to the God's claims of not being a respecter of persons!) Or could Judas have repented, even of *that* sin, had he chosen to?

There are some who believe that Judas Iscariot could *not* have repented, that he was unavoidably destined—fated—to betray Jesus, and then to suffer eternally in hell for his dastardly deed. Of course Judas *deserves* to burn in hell forever for his sins, but so does every one of us. Except Jesus Himself, Who never sinned (Hebrews 4:15), every human being in the history of this planet deserves to burn in hell for his sins. But that doesn't answer the question. The question was, "Was Judas unchangeably fated to betray Jesus, and then inevitably doomed to hell because of it?" Let's look at the Scriptures.

Firstly, it is important to note that in many places, the Bible states that God is not a respecter of persons; that is, He is utterly fair and impartial, and does not play favorites. Refer back to the section "God is Not a Respecter of Persons" for Scriptural support of this statement. Clearly, if Judas was fated from eternity past to betray Jesus and suffer for it, without any choice in the matter, it would contradict God's claims of fairness and impartiality. So already, the theory of Judas' "doomed-ness" starts to look suspicious.

Secondly, Judas had been granted an equal share of the ministry Jesus gave to the disciples. Here is a quote from Peter when he was addressing the disciples in the upper room shortly before Pentecost:

> Acts 1:17: For he *[Judas]* was numbered with us, and **had obtained part of this ministry.**
>
> > AMP: For he was counted among us and **received his share [by divine allotment] in this ministry.**
> >
> > CJB: . . .he was one of us and **had been assigned a part in our work.**
> >
> > ERV: Judas **served together with us.**
> >
> > ISV: . . .because he was one of our number and **was appointed to share in this ministry.**
> >
> > TLB: Judas was one of us, **chosen to be an apostle just as we were.**
> >
> > NOG: He had been one of us and **had been given an active role in this ministry.**
> >
> > NIRV: But Judas was one of us. **He shared with us in our work for God.**

So since Judas was given a share of the ministry of the Gospel like to that of the other disciples, we cannot conclude that Judas was inevitably predestined for hell without concluding the same about the other disciples.

Thirdly, Jesus had already offered them—the disciples—rulership in heaven. Note that there is no hint that Judas was not present when Jesus made this offer:

> Matthew 19:28: And Jesus said unto them *[the disciples]*, Verily I say unto you, That **ye which have followed me,** in the regeneration when the Son of man shall sit in the throne of his glory, **ye also shall sit upon twelve thrones, judging the twelve tribes of Israel.**
>
> > AMP: Jesus said to them, "I assure you and most solemnly say to you, in the renewal [that is, the Messianic restoration and regeneration of all things] when the Son of Man sits on His glorious throne, **you [who have followed Me, becoming My disciples] will also sit on twelve thrones, judging the twelve tribes of Israel.**"

Notice the numbers here: twelve disciples, twelve thrones, twelve tribes. Coincidence? Jesus makes the same offer again during the Last Supper, as we'll see below.

Luke 22:29–30: And **I appoint unto you a kingdom,** as my Father hath appointed unto me; ³⁰**That ye may eat and drink at my table in my kingdom, and sit on thrones judging the twelve tribes of Israel.**

v. 30, CEV: **You will eat and drink with me in my kingdom, and you will each sit on a throne to judge the twelve tribes of Israel.**

The point of this section is merely to direct your attention to the fact that if Judas had already been predestined to burn in hell forever, Jesus' offer to him to eat and drink at His table in heaven, and to sit on one of the thrones and reign over one of the tribes of Israel would have been fraudulent.

As you have undoubtedly perceived, I think God's sovereignty is big enough that He could get His must-do items complete, while still allowing people to choose how, or whether, they participate. Let's dig into the Word a little farther and see what it says on that topic.

First, let's confirm that Judas was indeed present at the Last Supper:

Matthew 26:19–20: And the disciples did as Jesus had appointed them; and they made ready the passover. ²⁰Now when the even was come, he sat down with the **twelve.**

Matthew 26:21: And as they did eat, he said, Verily I say unto you, that **one of you** shall betray me.

Matthew 26:25 (NIV): Then Judas, the one who would betray him, said, "Surely not I, Rabbi?" Jesus answered, "Yes, **it is you.**"

Mark 14:16–18: And his disciples went forth, and came into the city, and found as he had said unto them: and they made ready the passover. ¹⁷And in the evening he cometh with the **twelve.** ¹⁸And as they sat and did eat, Jesus said, Verily I say unto you, **one of you** which eateth with me shall betray me.

Luke 22:13–14: And they went, and found as he had said unto them: and they made ready the passover. ¹⁴And when the hour was come, he sat down, and the **twelve** apostles with him.

Luke 22:21: But, behold, **the hand of him that betrayeth me is with me on the table.**

John 13:10–11: Jesus saith to him, He that is washed needeth not save to wash his feet, but is clean every whit: and **ye are clean, but not all.** ¹¹For he knew who should betray him; therefore said he, **Ye are not all clean.**

John 13:21: When Jesus had thus said, he was troubled in spirit, and testified, and said, Verily, verily, I say unto you, that **one of you** shall betray me.

John 13:25–27: He then lying on Jesus' breast saith unto him, Lord, who is it? ²⁶Jesus answered, **He it is, to whom I shall give a sop, when I have dipped it.** And **when he had dipped the sop, he gave it to Judas Iscariot, the son of Simon.** ²⁷And after the sop Satan entered into him. Then said Jesus unto him, That thou doest, do quickly.

So there is no question that Judas Iscariot was indeed present at the Last Supper:

- Matthew, Mark, and Luke all say that the "twelve" disciples were with Jesus, and the Greek word for twelve—*dodeka,* which literally means "two and ten"—is present in the original text; it was not added by the translators.
- Jesus said that the betrayer's hand was with His on the table.
- Jesus said *"You* are not all clean," clearly referring to the sin of Judas.
- Jesus said, "One *of you* will betray me."
- Jesus talked to Judas face to face, multiple times.

So unquestionably, Judas most definitely *was* present at the Last Supper. And here is where that fact becomes very significant. Notice what Jesus said to all His disciples, *Judas included:*

Matthew 26:27–28 (AMP): And He took a cup, and when He had given thanks, He gave it to them, saying, Drink of it, **all of you;** ²⁸For this is My blood of the new covenant, which [ratifies the agreement and] is being poured out for many for the forgiveness of sins.

Matthew 26:28: **Take of it, all of you,** for this is my blood of the testament, which is given for men **for the forgiveness of sins.**

Mark 14:23: And he took the cup, and when he had given thanks, **he gave it to them: and they** *all* **drank of it.**

Now of course, drinking the communion wine is only a *symbol* of the forgiveness Jesus was offering, just like baptism in water is a symbol of being buried and resurrected with Christ (Romans 6:4–5). And clearly, simply "going through the motions" with the appropriate physical symbols does not cause the spiritual transaction to have taken place. In this context, just because Judas drank the wine, it doesn't mean that he had actually repented and re-

FREE TO CHOOSE?

ceived forgiveness for his sins. And as we'll see below, he did not. But he *could* have.

So Jesus gave the wine, which represented His redeeming blood, to *all* of the disciples, including Judas. This clearly shows that forgiveness was available to Judas, even after he had decided to betray Jesus. We know that Judas had already decided to betray Jesus because of the following:

> John 13:1–2 (NIV): **It was just before the Passover Feast.** Jesus knew that the time had come for him to leave this world and go to the Father. Having loved his own who were in the world, he now showed them the full extent of his love. ²The evening meal was being served, and **the devil had already prompted Judas Iscariot, son of Simon, to betray Jesus.**

Then Jesus goes on to say:

> Matthew 26:29 (AMP): **I say to you,** I shall not drink again of this fruit of the vine until that day when **I drink it with you** new and of superior quality **in My Father's kingdom.**

Here we have Jesus saying to all the disciples, *including Judas,* that He wouldn't drink wine again until He could drink it *with His disciples in His Father's kingdom.* Clearly, Judas was being invited into the Kingdom along with all the rest of them. Continuing on:

> Luke 22:19–20 (NASB): And when He had taken some bread and given thanks, He broke it and gave it to them, saying, "**This is My body which is given for you;** do this in remembrance of Me." ²⁰And in the same way He took the cup after they had eaten, saying, "This cup which is **poured out for you** is the new covenant in My blood."

And here is Jesus saying that His body was given for His disciples, *including Judas,* and His blood was poured out for His disciples, *including Judas.* So, forgiveness was unquestionably being offered to Judas, even for his sin of betraying Jesus!

But perhaps the most amazing thing that Jesus said, pertaining to whether or not Judas was irretrievably predestined to hell for unavoidably betraying Jesus, was this one, which was alluded to above:

> Luke 22:29–30 (NASB): . . .and just as My Father has granted Me a kingdom, **I grant you** ³⁰**that you may eat and drink at My table in My kingdom, and you will sit on thrones judging the twelve tribes of Israel.**

Did you see that? Jesus again granted His disciples, including Judas, the privilege of eating and drinking with Him, *at His table,* and *in His Kingdom!* And then He goes farther yet by saying that He granted them—the *twelve* disciples—the authority to sit on thrones and judge the *twelve* tribes of Israel! So he reiterates the promise He gave more than a week earlier, and shown above in Matthew 19:28.

John's Gospel also tells us that during the Last Supper, Jesus washed the feet of the disciples. Again, there is no indication that Jesus did not wash Judas' feet:

> John 13:5, 12 After that he poureth water into a bason, and began to **wash the disciples' feet,** and to wipe them with the towel wherewith he was girded. [12]So **after he had washed their feet,** and had taken his garments, and was set down again, **he said unto them,** Know ye what I have done to you?

We know that the cleansing by Jesus, which is symbolized by His washing their feet, was necessary for salvation, as indicated by Jesus' statement to Peter:

> John 13:8b: Jesus answered him, If I wash thee not, thou hast no part with me.

This verse reinforces yet again that Jesus did indeed offer forgiveness—cleansing, acceptance, salvation—to *all* the disciples, including Judas.

Now it is definitely true that Jesus knew Judas would betray him:

> John 6:63–64: It is the spirit that quickeneth; the flesh profiteth nothing: the words that I speak unto you, they are spirit, and they are life. [64]But there are some of you that believe not. For **Jesus knew from the beginning who they were that believed not, and who should betray him.**

However, the knowledge that Judas *would* betray Jesus did not *cause* Judas to betray Him—if it had, all of Jesus' aforementioned statements to Judas would have been fraudulent and deceptive, as mentioned above.

But there is still more: Both Judas *and Peter* committed treasonous acts against Jesus. But Jesus knew that Peter would repent:

> Luke 22:31–32: And the Lord said, Simon, Simon, behold, Satan hath desired to have you, that he may sift you as wheat: [32]But I have prayed for thee, that thy faith fail not: and **when thou art converted, strengthen thy brethren.**

Likewise, Jesus knew that Judas would *not* repent:

> Mark 14:21: The Son of man indeed goeth, as it is written of him: but **woe to that man by whom the Son of man is betrayed! good were it for that man if he had never been born.**

This situation is similar to a statement I once heard, describing the two thieves being crucified with Jesus: "One was saved, that none may despair, but *only* one, that none may presume." What was the difference between the two thieves, that determined their eternal destination? What was the difference between Peter and Judas? One repented; the other did not.

> **Peter (repentant):** [75]And Peter remembered the saying of Jesus, "Before the cock crows, you will deny me three times." And **he went out and wept bitterly.** (Matthew 26:75)

> **Thief (repentant):** [42]And he said, "**Jesus, remember me when you come into your kingdom.**" [43]And he said to him, "Truly, I say to you, today you will be with me in Paradise." (Luke 23:42–43)

Note that repentant thief didn't *start out* with humility and repentance; he initially reviled Jesus right along with the other thief (Mark 15:32). But later, he chose to humble himself in the sight of the Lord (James 4:10) and sure enough, the Lord lifted him up.

Now contrast the above with this:

> **Judas (unrepentant):** And he cast down the pieces of silver in the temple, and departed, and **went and hanged himself.** (Matthew 27:5)

> **Thief (unrepentant):** And **one of the malefactors** which were hanged **railed on him,** saying, If thou be Christ, save thyself and us. (Luke 23:39)

All of the Scriptures above show that although Jesus' betrayal and death were predestined, *Judas' role in these events was not.* If Judas had repented of his sin (like Peter did), Judas would have been forgiven (like Peter was). And, if Judas had not chosen to betray Jesus at all, there were plenty of other people who would have been willing to perform that role:

> Luke 23:13, 20–21: And Pilate . . . called together **the chief priests and the rulers and the people.** . . . [20]Pilate therefore, willing to release Jesus, spake again to them. [21]But **they cried, saying, Crucify him, crucify him.**

And there is still more Scriptural insight into how and why Judas turned against Jesus. Here is an excerpt from Peter's post-Ascension and pre-Pentecost exhortation on selecting someone to replace Judas:

Acts 1:25: That he *[the replacement apostle they were about to select]* may take part of this ministry and apostleship, from which **Judas by transgression fell,** that he might go to his own place.

ASV: . . .to take the place in this ministry and apostleship from which **Judas fell away,** that he might go to his own place.

BRG: That he may take part of this ministry and apostleship, from which **Judas by transgression fell,** that he might go to his own place.

GWORD: Show us who is to take the place of Judas as an apostle, since **Judas abandoned his position** to go to the place where he belongs.

JUB: . . .that he may take the lot or inheritance of this ministry and apostleship, from which **Judas rebelled** that he might go to his own place.

NIRV: Show us who should take the place of Judas as an apostle. **He gave up being an apostle** to go where he belongs.

NLV: He is to take the place of Judas in this work and be a missionary. **Judas lost his place** and went where he belonged **because of sin.**

NOG: Show us who is to take the place of Judas as an apostle, since **Judas abandoned his position** to go to the place where he belongs.

As the Scriptures above clearly show, Judas "fell away," he "rebelled," he "abandoned," and he "gave up" his ministry and position of being an apostle. And how did he do that?

Reading the above translations again, we see that he lost his place through transgression and sin. Since God commands us not to sin (Psalm 4:4, 37:27, Isaiah 1:16, Jeremiah 18:6, Ezekiel 33:11, 19, John 5:14, 8:11, I Corinthians 15:34a, etc., etc.; see Book 2: *Is It Possible to Stop Sinning?* for great detail), we can safely conclude that Judas sinned of his own free will. And that, plainly, is incompatible with the theory of an unchangeable decision made by God in eternity past, that resulted in Judas' eternal damnation, regardless of any free choice Judas may have attempted.

That's pretty amazing! So *all* the disciples, including Judas, were included in the Atonement, and were offered the same promises and privileges. But at the same time, we realize that Judas did *not* end up in heaven, will *not* be eating and drinking at Jesus' table in His kingdom, and will *not* be judging one of the twelve tribes of Israel. But why not, if it was offered to him?

Simply because he did not repent. Remember, both Judas *and* Peter engaged in treasonable offenses. Judas betrayed Jesus, and Peter denied Him: he disowned Jesus vociferously, multiple times, and even swearing oaths to that effect:

> Matthew 26:69–74 (AMP): Now Peter was sitting outside in the courtyard, and one maid came up to him and said, You were also with Jesus the Galilean! ⁷⁰But **he denied it falsely before them all, saying, I do not know what you mean.** ⁷¹And when he had gone out to the porch, another maid saw him, and she said to the bystanders, This fellow was with Jesus the Nazarene! ⁷²**And again he denied it and disowned Him with an oath, saying, I do not know the Man!** ⁷³After a little while, the bystanders came up and said to Peter, You certainly are one of them too, for even your accent betrays you. ⁷⁴Then **Peter began to invoke a curse on himself and to swear, I do not even know the Man!** And at that moment a rooster crowed.

Now remember, when Jesus first sent the disciples out to heal the sick, cleanse the lepers, raise the dead, and cast out demons, in that *very same address to the disciples,* Peter had heard Jesus say:

> Matthew 10:32–33 (AMP): Therefore, everyone who acknowledges Me before men and confesses Me [out of a state of oneness with Me], I will also acknowledge him before My Father Who is in heaven and confess [that I am abiding in] him. ³³But **whoever denies and disowns Me before men, I also will deny and disown him before My Father** Who is in heaven.

So it looks like Peter sealed his own fate here. Of course, *any* sin is enough to justly condemn us to hell (James 2:10), but Peter's disowning of Christ seems especially bad, don't you think?

So what caused the difference between Peter's outcome and Judas' outcome? The simple fact that Peter repented of his sin, and Judas did not. Again, here's how Peter responded when he realized his sin:

> Matthew 26:75 (NIV): Then Peter remembered the word Jesus had spoken: "Before the rooster crows, you will disown me three times." And **he went outside and wept bitterly.**

Peter felt soul-wrenching remorse, regret, and contrition for his actions; he certainly wished he could undo them. Continuing Peter's story, we see that he continued to fellowship with the disciples (John 20:19–31), responded to Jesus' invitation to eat with Him (John 21:8–13), and submitted to and received a commissioning from Jesus to spread the Gospel (John 21:14–19).

Now contrast that story with Judas' response when he realized his sin:

> Matthew 27:3–5 (GWORD): Then Judas, who had betrayed Jesus, regretted what had happened when he saw that Jesus was condemned. He brought the 30 silver coins back to the chief priests and leaders. ⁴He said, "I've sinned by betraying an innocent man." They replied, "What do we care? That's your problem." ⁵So **he threw the money into the temple, went away, and hanged himself.**

Did Judas ask forgiveness from the only One Who could have forgiven him? No. Did he continue in fellowship with the rest of the disciples, humbling himself after his failure? No. He simply ran away and "ended it all," so he was no longer around for the resurrection of Christ, for restoration and reconciliation with Him, and for the forgiveness that Jesus had already offered. If Jesus hadn't *really* offered these things to Judas as well as the other disciples, many of His statements during the Last Supper would have been lies. So we can only conclude that they truly must have been available also to Judas.

So the fact that Jesus offered the benefit of His broken body and His shed blood to the disciples, *including Judas,* and the fact that He granted all the disciples, *including Judas,* the privilege of eating and drinking with Him, at His table, in His kingdom, and to sit on thrones and judge the twelve tribes of Israel, shows that Judas had the opportunity to be restored in his fellowship with Jesus. But he didn't seek the Lord; he didn't repent.

This is an important point: It wasn't Judas' *sin* that doomed him to hell; it was the absence of subsequent *repentance* of that sin that doomed him to hell. Think about it: if it were sin that doomed us to hell, we would all end up there, because all have sinned (Romans 3:23). But since repentance is an option, some people do that, and those people don't end up in hell (Luke 15:7).

So Jesus offered Judas a position in the kingdom of God, and He had to do so with integrity. Which means that Judas *could* have accepted it. However, Jesus still knew that Judas would betray him. This is shown very clearly in the Gospels:

> Matthew 26:21 (NLT): While they were eating, he said, "I tell you the truth, **one of you will betray me."**

> Matthew 26:25 (NIV): Then Judas, the one who would betray him, said, "Surely not I, Rabbi?" Jesus answered, **"Yes, it is you."**

> Mark 14:42 (AMP): Get up, let us be going! See, **My betrayer is at hand!**
>
> John 6:64 (GWORD): "But some of you don't believe." **Jesus knew from the beginning** those who wouldn't believe and the one **who would betray him.**
>
> John 6:70–71 (NASB): Jesus answered them, "Did I Myself not choose you, the twelve, and yet **one of you is a devil?**" ⁷¹Now **He meant Judas** the son of Simon Iscariot, for he, one of the twelve, **was going to betray Him.**

Since it would have been disingenuous, even deceptive, for Jesus to offer those things to Judas if he were actually being prevented from receiving them, or was unable to receive them, that shows that Judas *could* have received them, had he chosen to repent. (This overturns the Reformed doctrines of Total Depravity and Unconditional Election.) But Judas refused to accept what Jesus was offering. (This overturns the doctrine of Irresistible Grace.)

Also note that Jesus *knew* Judas would not repent, but nevertheless He did not *prevent* Judas from repenting—He couldn't truthfully offer Judas the benefits of His broken body and shed blood, plus the opportunity of ruling one of the tribes of Israel, while still preventing him from accepting it without being fraudulent. This indicates that the simple fact that God may *know* what someone will choose, but that knowledge doesn't *cause* him to make that choice.

So the atoning, vicarious death of Jesus was something that was on God's must-do list. Several Scriptures indicate the existence of things that God was determined to get accomplished, and nothing could stand in the way—and the Atonement was one of them:

> Isaiah 46:10 (GWORD): From the beginning I revealed the end. From long ago I told you things that had not yet happened, saying, "**My plan will stand, and I'll do everything I intended to do.**"
>
> Acts 2:23 (AMP): This Jesus, when delivered up according to **the definite and fixed purpose and settled plan and foreknowledge of God,** you crucified and put out of the way [killing Him] by the hands of lawless and wicked men.
>
> Ephesians 3:10–11 (AMP): . . .the manifold wisdom of God might now be made known through the church to the rulers and the authorities in the heavenly places. ¹¹This was in accordance with **the eternal purpose which He carried out in Christ Jesus our Lord. . .**

Chapter 10: Miscellaneous Topics

Notice in Acts 2:23 above that Jesus' crucifixion was "fixed" and "settled" in eternity. However, *who* actually performed the betrayal was not hard-wired into the equation—the fact of Judas Iscariot doing the actual betrayal was *not* fixed and settled in eternity. If Judas had not betrayed Jesus, there were plenty of other people who would have happily done the job. Remember, the whole crowd was crying, "Crucify Him! Crucify Him!" (Mark 15:13–14)

If Judas' participation *had* been determined in eternity past, without regard to his free will, Jesus' offers to Judas (about His body being broken for him, His blood being shed for him, the invitation to eat and drink with Him, at His table, in His kingdom, and to sit on a throne judging one of the twelve tribes of Israel) would have been dishonest and fraudulent. And I think you will agree that Jesus is *not* dishonest or fraudulent.

So Jesus did, in all honesty and sincerity, offer Judas the same privileges and invitations He offered all the rest of the disciples. However, Judas did not repent of his sin, and therefore he doomed himself to an eternity without God. This is what Jesus described in the following passage:

> Mark 14:21 (NIV): The Son of Man will go just as it is written about him. But **woe to that man who betrays the Son of Man! It would be better for him if he had not been born.**

Jesus' first statement in the verse above refers to an item on God's must-do list: the Son of Man redeeming humankind. The second statement Jesus makes refers to Judas, of course, although He wouldn't have made that statement, had Judas chosen to repent. And the third statement above shows the result of Judas' failure to repent: The *only* way it could be better for a person if he had never been born to compare it to that person suffering in hell for the rest of eternity. Since Judas did not repent, he sealed his fate to do just that.

So even though Judas did not repent in the Scriptural sense of turning himself back toward God, he was sorry for his actions, as we can see in the following Scriptures:

> Matthew 27:3–5 (NIV): When Judas, who had betrayed him, saw that Jesus was condemned, **he was seized with remorse and returned the thirty silver coins to the chief priests and the elders.** ⁴"I have sinned," he said, "for I have betrayed innocent blood." "What is that to us?" they replied. "That's your responsibility." ⁵So **Judas threw the money into the temple and left.** Then he went away and hanged himself.

But Peter was also sorry for his actions of denying Jesus multiple times:

Matthew 26:75 (NIV): Then Peter remembered the word Jesus had spoken: "Before the rooster crows, you will disown me three times." And **he went outside and wept bitterly.**

So what's the difference? Since both Peter and Judas were sorry for their actions, why was the outcome so different? Peter repented in the Scriptural sense, and Judas did not. Paul describes the situation as follows:

II Corinthians 7:10 (NIV): Godly sorrow brings repentance that leads to salvation and leaves no regret, but worldly sorrow brings death.

So we can see that while Jesus' betrayal and death (and, of course, His resurrection) were unalterably predestined, *Judas' role in the whole process was a matter of his own choice.* Hence, God is completely fair and just to reward him, and all people, according to their deeds.

None Righteous; No, Not One

On the topic of Total Depravity—which, again, is based on Augustine's Gnostic-inspired idea of Original Sin—one of the most oft-quoted passages is from Paul's epistle to the Romans:

Romans 3:10–11: As it is written, **There is none righteous, no, not one:** [11]There is none that understandeth, there is none that seeketh after God.

Verse 10 and verse 11 say related, but not identical things, so I'll address them individually.

Verse 10: None Righteous

Adherents to Reformed theology point to v. 10 and say, "How could you possibly misunderstand that? Paul says very bluntly that *no one* is righteous. And, just in case you didn't hear it the first time, he repeats himself: 'No, *not one.*'" That does sound rather open-and-shut, doesn't it? It sounds like it applies to all people, everywhere, under all circumstances, throughout history.

Perhaps. But let's take a look at some other relevant Scriptures and see what we find. Now a word of caution: there is a rather lengthy list of passages here, and the commentary after each Scripture states the logical conclusion to which we are compelled *if* we assume that Romans 3:10 actually does apply to all people, everywhere, under all circumstances, throughout history, as Reformed theology states. These logical conclusions are *so* absurd (remember *reductio ad absurdum?*) that the commentary may sound a bit sarcastic. That is not my intent. My goal is to show that while Romans 3:10 is absolutely true, some of our assumptions about when it applies are not.

> Genesis 7:1: And the LORD said unto **Noah**, Come thou and all thy house into the ark; for **thee have I seen righteous** before me in this generation.

God Himself must have been mistaken when He said Noah was righteous, because "there is none righteous; no, not one."

> Ezekiel 14:14 (AMP): Even if these three men, **Noah, Daniel, and Job** were in it, they would save but their own lives by **their righteousness (their uprightness and right standing with Me),** says the Lord God.

God must have been mistaken here when He said that Noah, Daniel, and Job were righteous, because "there is none righteous; no, not one."

> Luke 1:5–6 (NASB): In the days of Herod, king of Judea, there was a certain priest named **Zacharias,** of the division of Abijah; and he had a wife from the daughters of Aaron, and her name was **Elizabeth.** ⁶And **they were both righteous in the sight of God,** walking blamelessly in all the commandments and requirements of the Lord.

Luke must have been mistaken when he said Zacharias and Elisabeth were righteous, because "there is none righteous; no, not one." (By the way, this passage shows *why* they were righteous in the sight of God: they walked blamelessly in *all* the commandments and requirements of the Lord.)

> Hebrews 11:4: By faith **Abel** offered unto God a more excellent sacrifice than Cain, by which he **obtained witness that he was righteous**, God testifying of his gifts: and by it he being dead yet speaketh.

The writer of Hebrews must have been mistaken when he said Abel was righteous, because "there is none righteous; no, not one."

> Matthew 23:35 (NIV): And so upon you will come all **the righteous blood** that has been shed on earth, from the blood of righteous Abel **to the blood of Zechariah son of Berekiah,** whom you murdered between the temple and the altar.

Jesus must have been mistaken when He said the prophet Zechariah was righteous, because "there is none righteous; no, not one."

> II Peter 2:7–8: And delivered just **Lot**, vexed with the filthy conversation of the wicked: (For **that righteous man** dwelling among them, in seeing

and hearing, vexed **his righteous soul** from day to day with their unlawful deeds;)

Peter must have been mistaken when he said Lot was righteous, because "there is none righteous; no, not one."

Exodus 23:8: Do not accept a bribe, for **a bribe** blinds those who see and **twists the words of the righteous.**

Bribes apparently don't twist the words of anyone, because "there is none righteous; no, not one."

Deuteronomy 25:1: If there be a controversy between men, and they come unto judgment, that the judges may judge them; then **they shall justify the righteous,** and condemn the wicked.

Apparently nobody will be justified in this situation, because "there is none righteous; no, not one."

I Samuel 26:23: The LORD render to **every man his righteousness** and his faithfulness: for the LORD delivered thee into my hand to day, but I would not stretch forth mine hand against the LORD's anointed.

GNT: The LORD rewards **those who are** faithful and **righteous.** Today he put you in my power, but I did not harm you, whom the LORD made king.

Apparently the LORD doesn't reward anyone, because "there is none righteous; no, not one."

Psalm 5:12: For **thou, LORD, wilt bless the righteous;** with favour wilt thou compass him as with a shield.

The Lord is not going to be blessing anyone here, because "there is none righteous; no, not one."

Psalm 7:11: **God judgeth the righteous,** and God is angry with the wicked every day.

Apparently God won't judge anyone either, because "there is none righteous; no, not one."

Psalm 31:18: Let the lying lips be put to silence; which speak grievous things proudly and contemptuously **against the righteous.**

Apparently no lying lips will be put to silence, because "there is none righteous; no, not one."

Psalm 34:15: **The eyes of the** LORD **are upon the righteous,** and his ears are open unto their cry.

Apparently the Lord's eyes and ears are not open to anyone, because "there is none righteous; no, not one."

Psalm 34:19: Many are the afflictions of **the righteous:** but the LORD delivereth him out of them all.

Apparently the Lord doesn't deliver anybody, because "there is none righteous; no, not one."

Psalm 37:17: For the arms of the wicked shall be broken: but **the** LORD **upholdeth the righteous.**

Apparently the Lord won't uphold anyone, because "there is none righteous; no, not one."

Psalm 37:21: The wicked borroweth, and payeth not again: but **the righteous sheweth mercy, and giveth.**

Apparently no one shows mercy and gives, because "there is none righteous; no, not one."

In Isaiah 58:5–7, God tells Israel the kind of fast that He prefers: basically, doing justly and loving mercy (which He later reinforces in Micah 6:8). Then, God states the *results* of obeying Him in this way:

Isaiah 58:8 (BBE): Then will light be shining on you like the morning, and your wounds will quickly be well: and *your righteousness* **will go before you,** and the glory of the Lord will come after you.

(To hear this passage set to music, listen to the song *This Is the Fast* on the album *Worship the King* or scan the QR code at right.)

What? *Our* righteousness? Yes.

At this point, I will skip many, many more Scriptures addressed to the righteous, because it is obvious that the Old Testament acknowledges the existence of righteous people. But what about the New Testament?

Matthew 5:6 (NIV): Blessed are those who hunger and thirst for righteousness, for **they will be filled.**

Either nobody ever hungered and thirsted this way, or Jesus must have been mistaken, because "there is none righteous; no, not one."

Free to Choose?

> Matthew 10:41b (NIV): . . .anyone who receives a righteous man **because he is a righteous man** will receive a righteous man's reward.

Nobody should expect this kind of reward, because "there is none righteous; no, not one."

> Matthew 13:17: For verily I say unto you, That **many prophets and righteous men** have desired to see those things which ye see, and have not seen them; and to hear those things which ye hear, and have not heard them.

Well, at least the *prophets* desired to see those things, because "there is none righteous; no, not one."

> Matthew 13:43 (NIV): Then **the righteous will shine like the sun** in the kingdom of their Father. He who has ears, let him hear.

Nobody will be shining like the sun, because "there is none righteous; no, not one."

> Matthew 25:37 (NIV): Then **the righteous will answer him,** 'Lord, when did we see you hungry and feed you, or thirsty and give you something to drink?'

Nobody will ever say this, because "there is none righteous; no, not one."

> Matthew 25:46: And these shall go away into everlasting punishment: but **the righteous into life eternal.**

Hmm. I guess no one will go into life eternal, because "there is none righteous; no, not one."

> Acts 10:35: But in every nation he that feareth him, and **worketh righteousness,** is accepted with him.

It looks like no one will be accepted by Jesus, because "there is none righteous; no, not one."

> Romans 5:19: For as by one man's disobedience many were made sinners, so by the obedience of one shall **many be made righteous.**

This must not have worked, because "there is none righteous; no, not one."

> I Peter 3:12: For **the eyes of the Lord are over the righteous,** and his ears are open unto their prayers: but the face of the Lord is against them that do evil.

Of course, such a conclusion is silly. But *why* is it silly? "All" means "all," doesn't it? The reason the conclusion is silly, even though it seems to be correct on some level, is because of a misplaced Universe of Discourse. This high-falutin' phrase simply means everything ("universe") that ("of") we're talking about ("discourse").

The silliness in the scenario above comes from the fact that my wife's Universe of Discourse—what she was talking about—was buying eggs at Safeway, and not cosmology. *Every time* she had been at Safeway and needed eggs, they had them available. That's 100% of the sample size; i.e., *all* the time. Her statement was correct, in the context of what she was talking about. But if I take her statement and apply it to a different Universe of Discourse—say, cosmology—I might come to a ridiculous conclusion. And that is exactly what happened.

So, in short, the Universe of Discourse could also be called the "context." And as you surely remember, we've seen time and time again in this book how very important the context is when reading Scripture.

Back to Romans 3:10

Okay, so how does the parable above apply to the Bible verse we're studying? Simply that Paul's statement in Romans 3:10 is entirely true *unless we change the Universe of Discourse.* In that case, all bets are off. So it behooves us to find out exactly what Paul was talking about, what his Universe of Discourse was, what his context was. Because if we don't, as we've seen, we can arrive at ludicrous conclusions.

So rather than extracting this single snippet from its environment, let's read the whole passage in context:

> Romans 3:1–18 (NIV): What advantage, then, is there in being a Jew, or what value is there in circumcision? [2]Much in every way! First of all, they have been entrusted with the very words of God. [3]What if some did not have faith? Will their lack of faith nullify God's faithfulness? [4]Not at all! Let God be true, and every man a liar. As it is written: "So that you may be proved right when you speak and prevail when you judge." [5]But if our unrighteousness brings out God's righteousness more clearly, what shall we say? That God is unjust in bringing his wrath on us? (I am using a human argument.) [6]Certainly not! If that were so, how could God judge the world? [7]Someone might argue, "If my falsehood enhances God's truthfulness and so increases his glory, why am I still condemned as a sinner?" [8]Why not say—as we are being slanderously reported as saying and as some claim that we say—"Let

I think I've made my point. And again, my apologies if I sounded sarcastic in the commentary above; my intent was to point out that if we assume that Romans 3:10 applies to *all* people, *every*where, under *all* circumstances, *throughout* history, we arrive at absurd conclusions.

But Romans 3:10 *is* correct in what it states. Therefore, at least one of the universal inclusives, or **universal affirmatives,** which many people have *assumed*, shouldn't be universal. In other words, at least one, and maybe more, of the four universal affirmatives above should be changed to **particular affirmatives,** as shown below:

1. It applies to some, *but not all,* people.
2. It applies to people in some, *but not all,* locations.
3. It applies under some, *but not all,* circumstances.
4. It applies to some, *but not all,* of history.

Looking at the above list with at least a modicum of Scriptural knowledge would lead most Christians to conclude that Item #2 (application varies by location) is unlikely to be true. Item #1 might be true, because there is a distinctly different spiritual state between believers and non-believers (II Corinthians 5:17). Item #3 might also be true, because the attitude of the heart is very important, and in *many* cases, God modifies his behavior based on our attitudes (e.g., II Samuel 22:26–27). And finally, Item #4 might be true, because a person's spiritual situation is very different *before* he gets saved than it is *after* he gets saved.

The rest of this section will attempt to determine which of the four *universal* affirmatives above are unwarranted, and should be replaced by *particular* affirmatives. But first, a parable.

The Parable of Grocery Shopping

Suppose I'm getting ready to go to the grocery store, and my wife calls out, "Could you pick up a dozen eggs while you're there?" I reply that I will, and proceed to the grocery store. When I get home, she looks through the grocery sacks, finds no eggs, and asks, "Did you forget the eggs?" To which I reply, "No, Safeway doesn't sell eggs." She looks at me incredulously, and says, "Of course they do. I buy eggs there all the time."

Now what, precisely, did she say? She said, "I buy eggs there all the time." Note that she said: "*all the time.*" *All* the time. That means, does it not, that not even a moment has elapsed where she has not been buying eggs at Safeway? *Every single nanosecond* since the creation of the universe, she has been buying eggs at Safeway. That's what "all" the time would mean, right?

Here is another fascinating tidbit that pertains to the topic at hand. Let's look at something Paul wrote to Timothy:

> I Timothy 1:8–11 (NIV): We know that the law is good if one uses it properly. [9]We also know that **law is made not for the righteous but for lawbreakers** and rebels, the ungodly and sinful, the unholy and irreligious; for those who kill their fathers or mothers, for murderers, [10]for adulterers and perverts, for slave traders and liars and perjurers— and for whatever else is contrary to the sound doctrine [11]that conforms to the glorious gospel of the blessed God, which he entrusted to me.

Isn't that interesting? The Law of Moses was not made for the righteous, but for lawbreakers. First, this tells us that there have been righteous people all along, even in the Old Testament, which, as we just saw, is indeed the case. In addition—and this is important—*they were not under the Law.* Not everybody, even in the old-covenant wandering-in-the-wilderness days, was under the Law. Why not? Because some people were righteous, and the Law wasn't even made for them.

Well, who, then, were the righteous? Those who accepted redemption by faith, as we saw above. These were those people who, as Jesus put it, "had ears to hear." These were the people who received salvation by faith. Even in the Old Testament? Yes. Even *before* the Old Testament? Yes. Like Abraham did, whose faith is our prototype to copy (Romans 4:11–12). For much more detail, see the "Old vs. New" sections in Book 7: *Be Filled with the Spirit.*

It's obvious that even *Paul* didn't intend for his statement in Romans 3:10–11 to refer to all people, throughout history, everywhere, under all circumstances. How do we know this? Because *Paul himself* talks in many places about how people become righteous:

> Romans 3:21–22 (AMP): But now the righteousness of God has been revealed independently and altogether apart from the Law, although actually it is attested by the Law and the Prophets, [22]Namely, **the righteousness of God which comes by believing with personal trust and confident reliance on Jesus Christ (the Messiah). [And it is meant] for all who believe.** For there is no distinction. . .

> Romans 4:3 (BBE): But what does it say in the holy Writings? And **Abraham had faith in God, and it was put to his account as righteousness.**

And yes, there are many more, including Romans 3:24, 26, 28, 30, 4:5, 6, 9, 11, 13, 21-22, 25, etc.

CHAPTER 10: MISCELLANEOUS TOPICS

Apparently the eyes of the Lord are not over anyone, nor are His ears open to anyone's prayers, because "there is none righteous; no, not one."

Titus 3:7 (CEB): So, **since we have been made righteous** by his grace, we can inherit the hope for eternal life.

Apparently, we cannot inherit the hope for eternal life, because "there is none righteous; no, not one."

I John 3:7: Little children, let no man deceive you: **he that doeth righteousness is righteous**, even as he is righteous.

John must not be talking about anyone here, because "there is none righteous; no, not one."

Then, upon a little bit more study, we realize to our chagrin that the Greek word translated "righteous" is δίκαιος (*dikaios*, G1342) is also translated "just." Which means that these Scriptures also come into play:

Matthew 1:19: Then Joseph her husband, being a **just** *[=righteous]* man, and not willing to make her a publick example, was minded to put her away privily.

Mark 6:20: For Herod feared John, knowing that he was a **just** *[=righteous]* man and an holy, and observed him; and when he heard him, he did many things, and heard him gladly.

Luke 2:25: And, behold, there was a man in Jerusalem, whose name was Simeon; and the same man was **just** *[=righteous]* and devout, waiting for the consolation of Israel: and the Holy Ghost was upon him.

Luke 23:50–51: And, behold, there was a man named Joseph, a counsellor; and he was a good man, and a **just** *[=righteous]*: [51](The same had not consented to the counsel and deed of them;) he was of Arimathaea, a city of the Jews: who also himself waited for the kingdom of God.

Acts 10:22: And they said, Cornelius the centurion, a **just** *[=righteous]* man, and one that feareth God, and of good report among all the nation of the Jews, was warned from God by an holy angel to send for thee into his house, and to hear words of thee.

Oh, dear. Now we have Joseph, John the Baptist, Simeon, Joseph of Arimathaea, and Cornelius as five other righteous people God forgot about when He mistakenly stated "there is none righteous; no, not one."

CHAPTER 10: MISCELLANEOUS TOPICS

us do evil that good may result"? Their condemnation is deserved. ⁹What shall we conclude then? Are we any better? Not at all! We have already made the charge that Jews and Gentiles alike are all under sin. ¹⁰As it is written: "There is no one righteous, not even one; ¹¹there is no one who understands, no one who seeks God. ¹²All have turned away, they have together become worthless; there is no one who does good, not even one." ¹³"Their throats are open graves; their tongues practice deceit." "The poison of vipers is on their lips." ¹⁴"Their mouths are full of cursing and bitterness." ¹⁵"Their feet are swift to shed blood; ¹⁶ruin and misery mark their ways, ¹⁷and the way of peace they do not know." ¹⁸"There is no fear of God before their eyes."

As we start reading this passage as a unit, without strategically extracting little bits and pieces from it, we immediately see in v. 1 that it's talking about the advantages of being a Jew. As opposed to what? Being a non-Jew, of course—a Gentile. It sounds like the passage analyzes whether there is, in some manner not yet specified, an advantage that Jews have over Gentiles.

So as we continue reading this passage, we must ask ourselves two questions. First, is there a confirmation later in the passage that Paul is indeed comparing Jews to Gentiles? And second, what is the way, or manner, in which Jews and Gentiles are being compared? In other words, compared, as it pertains to what?

When we get to v. 9, we see the answer to both of these questions. First, yes, it is indeed talking about comparing Jews to Gentiles to see if Jews have an advantage. And second, the *way* they are being compared—the purpose and topic and gist of the discussion—is whether Jews, because they're God's chosen people, are any less sinful than Gentiles and therefore might not need a Redeemer like the Gentiles do. Paul's summary question and his answer are: "Are we any better? Not at all! We have already made the charge that Jews and Gentiles alike are all under sin."

Thus we see that, *when read in context,* the topic under discussion is whether Jews are any less "under sin" than Gentiles. And it is in *that* context that Paul states, "There is no one righteous, not even one." A paraphrasing of Paul's statement, keeping the context in mind, might be: "Are we any better? No! Both Jews and Gentiles are sinful. *Nobody* is righteous enough to not need the Redeemer."

Remember the four universal affirmatives we saw earlier? Reading this passage in context shows that Universal Affirmative #1 must be changed to a Particular Affirmative ("It applies to some, but not all, people."), and Universal

FREE TO CHOOSE?

Affirmative #3 must be changed to a Particular Affirmative ("It applies under some, but not all, circumstances"), and Universal Affirmative #4 must be changed to a Particular Affirmative ("It applies to some, but not all, of history").

So "there is no one righteous, not even one" doesn't apply in all circumstances—it *couldn't*—because of the other Scriptures that declare various people to be righteous. (The same God wrote all these passages.) So how did they become righteous? The same way Abraham did:

> Romans 4:3–5 (NIV): What does the Scripture say? **"Abraham believed God, and it was credited to him as righteousness."** ⁴Now when a man works, his wages are not credited to him as a gift, but as an obligation. ⁵However, to the man who does not work but trusts God who justifies the wicked, **his faith is credited as righteousness.**

So Abraham became righteous by believing in God, which shows that Particular Affirmative #1 ("It applies to some, but not all, people") is true: After God counted Abraham's belief in Him as righteousness, he was no longer unrighteous, so Romans 3:10 no longer applied to him.

Particular Affirmative #3 ("It applies under some, but not all, circumstances") is also true, the difference being one specific circumstance—believing in God for your redemption—is an enormous game-changer, so Romans 3:10 doesn't apply to those who have experienced the redemption brought about by that belief.

And finally, Particular Affirmative #4 ("It applies to some, but not all, of history") is also true because at whatever point you believe in God and are therefore saved, there is a huge difference between your state *before* that moment versus *after* that moment, so Romans 3:10 doesn't apply to people after they've made Jesus Lord of their lives.

And just for good measure, let's see how, if we insist that Paul's statement "there is none righteous, no, not one" applies to everyone, everywhere, under all circumstances, throughout history, Paul would have contradicted *himself* in all those places where he says believers are righteous:

> Romans 3:22: Even **the righteousness of God which is by faith of Jesus Christ unto all and upon all them that believe:** for there is no difference. . .

> Romans 5:17 (NIV): For if, by the trespass of the one man, death reigned through that one man, how much more will **those who receive** God's abundant provision of grace and of **the gift of righteousness** reign in life through the one man, Jesus Christ.

Romans 8:10 (NIV): But **if Christ is in you,** your body is dead because of sin, yet **your spirit is alive because of righteousness.**

Romans 10:4 (NIV): Christ is the end of the law so that there may be **righteousness for everyone who believes.**

Romans 10:6 (AMP): But the **righteousness based on faith** [imputed by God and bringing right relationship with Him] says, Do not say in your heart, Who will ascend into Heaven? that is, to bring Christ down. . .

I Corinthians 1:30 (NASB): But by His doing you are in Christ Jesus, who became to us wisdom from God, and **righteousness** and sanctification, and redemption. . .

> NIV: It is because of him that you are in Christ Jesus, who has become for us wisdom from God—that is, **our righteousness,** holiness and redemption.

Philippians 1:11 (NIV): . . .**filled with the fruit of righteousness** that comes through Jesus Christ—to the glory and praise of God.

Philippians 3:9: And be found in him, not having mine own righteousness, which is of the law, but **that which is through the faith of Christ, the righteousness which is of God by faith.** . .

And not only that, but look at the verb tenses in this passage:

Romans 5:8–10 (AMP): But God shows and clearly proves His [own] love for us by the fact that **while we were still sinners,** Christ (the Messiah, the Anointed One) died for us. ⁹Therefore, since **we are now justified (acquitted, made righteous, and brought into right relationship with God)** by Christ's blood, how much more [certain is it that] **we shall be saved by Him from the indignation and wrath of God.** ¹⁰For if while we **were** enemies we were reconciled to God through the death of His Son, it is much more [certain], **now** that we are reconciled, that we **shall be** saved (daily delivered from sin's dominion) through His [resurrection] life.

This is profound! Notice the verb tenses in the three statements in vv. 8–9:

- ". . .while we were yet sinners. . ." (past tense): Note that v. 8 shows that the state of our being sinners is in the past: we *were* sinners, but we aren't anymore. Back when we *were* still sinners, Christ died for us.

465

- "...we are now justified..." (present tense): The reason we are not still sinners like we used to be is that, as v. 9 states, we are *now* justified. How did that happen? In v. 8, we are told that Christ died for us, and since we accepted that free gift by faith, we were acquitted, *made righteous,* and brought into right relationship with God.
- "...we shall be saved" from the wrath of God (future tense): When Judgment Day happens and Jesus separates the sheep from the goats, we will not experience any of God's wrath that will fall upon sinners. Why? Because of the two-party covenant between Jesus and us: He offered salvation, and we accepted it, so now we are righteous.

Then Paul reiterates the significance of those three verb tenses in v. 10:

- "...we *were* enemies..."
- "...*now*... we are reconciled..."
- "...we *shall be* saved (daily delivered from sin's dominion)..."

And just for fun, let's see if Paul really meant that when he wrote it to the Romans. Does he say a comparable thing anywhere else? Oh, look; he does:

> Ephesians 2:1–3 (NASB): And you **were dead** in your trespasses and sins, ²in which you **formerly walked** according to the course of this world, according to the prince of the power of the air, of the spirit that is now working in the sons of disobedience. ³Among them we too all **formerly lived** in the lusts of our flesh, indulging the desires of the flesh and of the mind, and **were** by nature children of wrath, even as the rest.

Think about it: if "none righteous, no, not one" applied to believers, we *wouldn't* have been justified (acquitted, made righteous, and brought into right relationship with God), we *couldn't* avoid the wrath and indignation of God at Judgment, we *wouldn't* have been reconciled to God, and we *wouldn't* be daily delivered from sin's dominion.

So again, if we assume that Paul's statement "there is none righteous, no, not one" applies universally, we will have to throw out *so many* other things that Paul also said. Remember the "Preponderance of Scripture" discussion?

Whom was Paul Quoting?

It's understandable that many people don't realize the context of Paul's statement in Romans 3:10 (if they haven't read it in its own context, and haven't questioned their assumptions, based on the many seemingly contradictory statements Paul makes elsewhere), because they usually don't realize the context of the Old Testament passage he was quoting.

CHAPTER *10*: MISCELLANEOUS TOPICS

When Paul wrote Romans 3:10, he was quoting King David, from two places in the Psalms:

Psalm 14:1–4: The fool hath said in his heart, There is no God. They are corrupt, they have done abominable works, there is none that doeth good. ²The LORD looked down from heaven upon the children of men, to see if there were any that did understand, and seek God. ³They are all gone aside, they are all together become filthy: **there is none that doeth good, no, not one.** ⁴Have all the workers of iniquity no knowledge? who eat up my people as they eat bread, and call not upon the LORD.

Psalm 53:1–4: The fool hath said in his heart, There is no God. Corrupt are they, and have done abominable iniquity: **there is none that doeth good.** ²God looked down from heaven upon the children of men, to see if there were any that did understand, that did seek God. ³Every one of them is gone back: they are altogether become filthy; **there is none that doeth good, no, not one.** ⁴Have the workers of iniquity no knowledge? who eat up my people as they eat bread: they have not called upon God.

These two passages are virtually identical in content and the verse numbers in which statements are made, so I'll just comment on Psalm 14, but these comments will also apply to Psalm 53.

- 14:1a: *The fool hath said in his heart, There is no God.* Right here in the very first sentence, the psalm establishes its Universe of Discourse—the context, what's it's talking about. It's talking about fools; i.e., those who deny the existence of God.

- 14:1b: *They are corrupt, they have done abominable works, there is none that doeth good.* Well, of course people who deny the existence of God are "corrupt" and will do "abominable works." Not one of them "does good" because they have no moral compass, having denied the existence of God. Do you see who the second half of this verse is describing? Not everybody, anywhere in the world, throughout history, under all circumstances, but *those who deny the existence of God.*

- 14:2a: *The LORD looked down from heaven upon the children of men. . .* God looked down here to where every living person resides; i.e., He looked down to the earth.

- 14:2b: *. . .to see if there were any that did understand, and seek God.* To see if there were any *what* that did understand? Any children of men? No, that's *where* He was looking—among the children of men—but *what* was He looking to see if there were any of, and who would understand and seek Him? The same thing He was talking about in the previous verse: Fools. Those who deny God's existence. God looked down upon the children of men (down here where everybody lives) to see if there were any of those who denied Him but who still had understanding.

- 14:3: *They are all gone aside, they are all together become filthy: there is none that doeth good, no, not one.* Who does "they" refer to? All people, everywhere, throughout history, under all circumstances? No; remember the context set up in v. 1: David is talking about fools; those who deny God. Everyone *of them* has gone aside; every one *of them* is altogether filthy, and not one *of them* does good; no, not one. (It certainly changes the tenor of the verse when you leave it in its original context, doesn't it?)

- 14:4a: *Have all the workers of iniquity no knowledge?* The workers of iniquity, remember, are those described in v. 1: the ones who do "abominable works;" those who deny God.

- 14:4b: *. . .who eat up my people as they eat bread, and call not upon the* LORD. Here is yet another confirmation that we're still talking about the fools: David contrasts them to "my people," because they (those who deny God) "*eat up* my people," David said. Obviously, "my people" refers to a different group of humanity than those who "*eat up* my people." And then just for good measure, David confirms one more time who he's talking about: the ones who "call not upon the LORD."

This becomes even more clear when reading these translations of the statements being made about fools:

Psalm 14:1 (CEB): Fools say in their hearts, There is no God. **They** are corrupt and do evil things; not one **of them** does anything good.

CEV: *(A psalm by David for the music leader.)* Only a fool would say, "There is no God!" **People like that** are worthless; **they** are heartless and cruel and never do right.

ERV: *To the director: A song of David.* Only fools think there is no God. **People like that** are evil and do terrible things. **They** never do what is right.

ICB: *For the director of music. Of David.* A wicked fool says to himself, "There is no God." **Fools** are evil. **They** do terrible things. None **of them** does anything good.

ISV: *To the Director: A Davidic Psalm.* Fools say to themselves, "There is no God." **They** are corrupt and commit evil deeds; not one **of them** practices what is good.

TLB: That man is a fool who says to himself, "There is no God!" **Anyone who talks like that** is warped and evil and cannot really be a good person at all.

NET: *For the music director, by David.* Fools say to themselves, "There is no God." **They** sin and commit evil deeds; none **of them** does what is right.

NLT: *For the choir director: A psalm of David.* Only fools say in their hearts, "There is no God." **They** are corrupt, and **their** actions are evil; not one **of them** does good!

VOICE: *For the worship leader. A song of David.* A wicked and foolish man truly believes there is no God. **They** are vile, **their** sinfulness nauseating to their Creator; **their** actions are soiled and repulsive; every deed is depraved; not one **of them** does good.

The above translations state explicitly what the context already made clear: the translations that say "there is no one who does good" must be understood in the context of what the psalm is talking about. That is, fools—those who deny the existence of God. In other words, it is obviously not saying "there is no one *in the world* who does good," because of the Scriptures that mention people doing good, or are commands to do good (II Chronicles 24:16, Psalm 34:14, 37:3, 27, Proverbs 11:17, Jeremiah 18:11, Matthew 5:44, Luke 6:9–10, 27, 35, John 5:29, Galatians 6:10, I Timothy 6:17–18, Hebrews 13:16, James 4:17, I Peter 3:11, III John 11, etc.). If "there is no one who does good" applied to everyone in the world, all such Scriptures that describe people as doing good would be wrong, and all such Scriptures that command us to do good would be impossible to obey, which would make God unjust in giving us the command. Therefore, the context demands that we understand "there is no one who does good," to mean "there is no one *of the fools we are currently talking about* who does good."

So the Universe of Discourse for Paul's "there is none righteous, no, not one" is the same as David's: those who deny God. This Psalm was written by a Jew, for Jewish priests to use during Jewish worship, and it is talking about those who deny God and deny the need for a Redeemer. Paul uses this Psalm to get across the point that *anyone* who denies God, Jew or Gentile, needs a Redeemer. Those who have already put their faith in God already *have* the Redeemer.

Context is a wonderful thing.

Verse 11: None Understands

Verse 11 is similar to v. 10 in the sense that it is absolutely true when applied to the Universe of Discourse Paul was using, but if we transplant it to a different and unwarranted Universe of Discourse, we can come to ridiculous conclusions. We already saw that Paul was quoting from the Psalms, and we looked at the context there. But let's pretend for a moment that we haven't yet seen that, and we're still looking at Paul's statement in Romans 3, analyzing the validity of the assumption that it applies to all people, everywhere, throughout history, under all circumstances. So here again is v. 11:

[11]**there is no one who understands,** no one who seeks God.

What? There is no one who understands? There is no one who understands what? Or should I say, there is no one who understands *whom?* If this verse is talking about understanding *things,* either physical or spiritual, are there other Scriptures that address this concept?

> Exodus 31:2–5 (NASB): See, I have called by name Bezalel, the son of Uri, the son of Hur, of the tribe of Judah. [3]I have **filled him with the Spirit of God in wisdom, in understanding,** in knowledge, and in all kinds of craftsmanship, [4]to make artistic designs for work in gold, in silver, and in bronze, [5]and in the cutting of stones for settings, and in the carving of wood, that he may work in all kinds of craftsmanship.

Hmm. With the Holy Spirit, God filled Bezalel with understanding. God must have forgotten that when He said, "There is no one who understands."

> Exodus 36:1 (NASB): Now **Bezalel and Oholiab, and every skillful person in whom the Lord has put skill and understanding** to know how to perform all the work in the construction of the sanctuary, shall perform in accordance with all that the Lord has commanded.

Wow! Now it's not just Bezalel who has understanding, but Oholiab, and a whole bunch more people too. God must've forgotten all these people also, when He said, "There is no one who understands."

> Deuteronomy 1:13: **Choose some wise, understanding and respected men** from each of your tribes, and I will set them over you.

Uh-oh. This must not have worked out very well, since "there is no one who understands."

> Deuteronomy 4:5–6 (NIV): See, I have taught you decrees and laws as the Lord my God commanded me, so that you may follow them in the land you are entering to take possession of it. [6]**Observe them carefully,**

> for this will show your wisdom and understanding to the nations, who will hear about all these decrees and say, "**Surely this great nation is a wise and understanding people.**"

So either Moses (and therefore God) was asking for the impossible, or the Israelites didn't show anything to the nations, because "there is no one who understands."

> I Kings 3:9–10 (NASB): "So **give Your servant an understanding heart** to judge Your people to discern between good and evil. For who is able to judge this great people of Yours?" ¹⁰It was pleasing in the sight of the Lord that Solomon had asked this thing.

The Lord may have been pleased with what Solomon asked for, but apparently He didn't give it to him, because "there is no one who understands."

> I Kings 4:29: **God gave Solomon** wisdom and very great insight, and **a breadth of understanding** as measureless as the sand on the seashore.

Oops, maybe God *did* give Solomon understanding. But He must've just forgotten that He had done so, because He also said "there is no one who understands."

Okay, I think I've made my point. If you assume that the phrase in Romans 3:11—"there is no one who understands"—to apply to *all* people, in *all* circumstances, in *all* locations, throughout *all* time, you come up with ridiculous conclusions that contradict countless other Scriptures. But let's plow on for just a little longer. . .

Verse 11: None Seek God

Verse 11 is similar to v. 10 in the sense that it is absolutely true when applied to the Universe of Discourse Paul was using, but if we transplant it to a different and unwarranted Universe of Discourse, we can come to ridiculous conclusions. We already saw that Paul was quoting from the Psalms, and we looked at the context there. But let's pretend for a moment that we haven't yet seen that, and we're still looking at Paul's statement in Romans 3, analyzing the validity of the assumption that it applies to all people, everywhere, throughout history, under all circumstances. So here again is v. 11:

> ¹¹there is no one who understands, **no one who seeks God.**

Let's look at the second part of that verse, and assume for the moment that it applies with those same Universal Affirmatives we saw above, as Reformed theology teaches. What is the logical fallout of that assumption?

> Exodus 33:7 (NET): Moses took the tent and pitched it outside the camp, at a good distance from the camp, and he called it the tent of meeting. **Anyone seeking the LORD would go out to the tent of meeting** that was outside the camp.

Apparently, nobody went out to the tent of meeting, because there is "no one who seeks God."

> Deuteronomy 4:29 (NIV): But **if from there you seek the LORD your God, you will find him** if you look for him with all your heart and with all your soul.

Apparently, nobody found God, because there is "no one who seeks God."

> I Chronicles 16:10–11 (NASB): Glory in His holy name; **Let the heart of those who seek the LORD be glad.** ¹¹Seek the LORD and His strength; Seek His face continually.

Apparently, nobody's hearts were glad, and nobody ever obeyed this Scripture, because there is "no one who seeks God."

> I Chronicles 28:9 (ASV): And thou, Solomon my son, know thou the God of thy father, and serve him with a perfect heart and with a willing mind; for Jehovah searcheth all hearts, and understandeth all the imaginations of the thoughts: **If thou seek him, he will be found of thee;** but if thou forsake him, he will cast thee off for ever.

Apparently, Solomon never found God, because there is "no one who seeks God."

> II Chronicles 7:14 (ESV): . . .**if my people** who are called by my name humble themselves, and pray and **seek my face** and turn from their wicked ways, then I will hear from heaven and will forgive their sin and heal their land.

Apparently, this Scripture is just so much "filler," and not even God's people can seek Him, because there is "no one who seeks God."

> II Chronicles 11:16 (GWORD): **People from every tribe of Israel who were determined to seek the LORD God of Israel** followed the Levitical priests to Jerusalem to sacrifice to the LORD God of their ancestors.

Apparently, the total number of people following the priests to Jerusalem was zero, because there is "no one who seeks God."

> II Chronicles 14:7 (HCSB): So he [Asa] said to the people of Judah, "Let's build these cities and surround them with walls and towers, with doors and bars. **The land is still ours because we sought the LORD our God.**

We sought Him and He gave us rest on every side." So they built and succeeded.

Apparently, Asa only *thought* they had sought the Lord, and he only *thought* God gave them rest on every side, because there is "no one who seeks God."

II Chronicles 15:2, 4 (NLT): . . .and he [Azariah the prophet] went out to meet King Asa as he was returning from the battle. "Listen to me, Asa!" he shouted. "Listen, all you people of Judah and Benjamin! The LORD will stay with you as long as you stay with him! **Whenever you seek him, you will find him.** But if you abandon him, he will abandon you. . ." ⁴But **whenever they were in trouble and turned to the LORD, the God of Israel, and sought him out, they found him.**

Apparently, nobody in Judah or Benjamin ever found the Lord, because there is "no one who seeks God."

II Chronicles 15:12–15 (AMP): And they [the people of Benjamin and Judah] **entered into a covenant to seek the Lord,** the God of their fathers, and to yearn for Him with all their heart's desire and with all their soul; ¹³And that **whoever would not seek the Lord, the God of Israel, should be put to death,** whether young or old, man or woman. ¹⁴They took an oath to the Lord with a loud voice, with shouting, with trumpets, and with cornets. ¹⁵And **all Judah** rejoiced at the oath, for they had sworn with all their heart and **sought Him** [yearning for Him] with their whole desire, and **He was found by them.** And the Lord gave them rest and peace round about.

Apparently, everybody in Benjamin and Judah broke the covenant, and everyone in both tribes was put to death, nobody sought the Lord, and He wasn't found by them, because there is "no one who seeks God."

II Chronicles 17:3–4 (DARBY): And Jehovah was with Jehoshaphat, for he walked in the first ways of his father David, and sought not unto the Baals; ⁴but **he sought the God of his father,** and walked in his commandments, and not after the doings of Israel.

Apparently, the Bible is mistaken here, because there is "no one who seeks God."

II Chronicles 20:3–4 (RSV): Then **Jehoshaphat feared, and set himself to seek the LORD,** and proclaimed a fast throughout all Judah. ⁴And

Judah assembled to seek help from the LORD; from all the cities of Judah they came to seek the LORD.

Apparently, the Bible is mistaken here too, and Jehoshaphat didn't really seek the Lord, and neither did all of Judah, because there is "no one who seeks God."

II Chronicles 26:5 (WEB): He *[Uzziah]* **set himself to seek God** in the days of Zechariah, who had understanding in the vision of God: and **as long as he sought Yahweh, God made him to prosper.**

Apparently, Uzziah never did seek God, and God never did make him prosper, because there is "no one who seeks God."

Matthew 6:33: But **seek ye first the kingdom of God,** and his righteousness; and all these things shall be added unto you.

Apparently, "all these things" won't be added unto anybody, because there is "no one who seeks God."

Acts 15:15–17 (WEBSTR): And to this agree the words of the prophets; as it is written, [16]After this I will return, and will build again the tabernacle of David which is fallen down; and I will build again the ruins of it; and I will set it up: [17]**That the residue of men may seek after the Lord,** and all the Gentiles, upon whom my name is called, saith the Lord, who doeth all these things.

Apparently, the reestablishment of the Tabernacle of David will fail in its intended purpose, because there is "no one who seeks God."

Acts 17:26–27 (NIV): From one man he made every nation of men, that they should inhabit the whole earth; and he determined the times set for them and the exact places where they should live. [27]**God did this so that men would seek him** and perhaps reach out for him and find him, though he is not far from each one of us.

Apparently, God's plan didn't work out so well, because there is "no one who seeks God."

Hebrews 11:6 (NASB): And without faith it is impossible to please Him, for he who comes to God must believe that He is, and that **He is a rewarder of those who seek Him.**

Apparently, God doesn't reward anybody, because there is "no one who seeks God."

And so forth. Again, my apologies if my commentary above sounded sarcastic. My intent was not to sound sarcastic, but to point out that when you take a statement from its intended Universe of Discourse (context) and transplant it to another Universe of Discourse (context), you can come up with ridiculous conclusions. Which we did, in spades.

It is also clear that King David *himself* did not take Psalms 14 and 53 to be referring to all people throughout history when he said in vv. 2–3 that God looked down from heaven to see if there were any who did "seek God," and then answered in the negative. In fact, David did not even include himself in these statements. We can conclude this with much certainty, because if David did include all people, he would have contradicted himself many times over, or would have been describing hypothetical but impossible situations, or (inspired by the Holy Spirit) he would have been making promises to fictional and nonexistent people groups, in all of the Scriptures below:

Psalm 9:10: And they that know thy name will put their trust in thee: for **thou, Lord, hast not forsaken them that seek thee.**

Psalm 22:26: The meek shall eat and be satisfied: **they shall praise the Lord that seek him:** your heart shall live for ever.

Psalm 24:6: This is **the generation of them that seek him, that seek thy face, O Jacob.** Selah.

Psalm 27:4 One thing have I desired of the LORD, **that will I seek after; that I may dwell in the house of the LORD all the days of my life, to behold the beauty of the LORD, and to enquire in his temple.**

(To hear this passage set to music, listen to the song *That Will I Seek After* on the album *I Have Not Forgotten You* or scan the QR code at right.)

Psalm 27:8: When thou saidst, Seek ye my face; **my heart said unto thee, Thy face, Lord, will I seek.**

Psalm 34:10: The young lions do lack, and suffer hunger: but **they that seek the Lord shall not want any good thing.**

Psalm 40:16: **Let all those that seek thee rejoice and be glad in thee:** let such as love thy salvation say continually, The Lord be magnified.

Psalm 63:1: O God, thou art my God; **early will I seek thee:** my soul thirsteth for thee, my flesh longeth for thee in a dry and thirsty land, where no water is. . .

> Psalm 69:32 (NASB): The humble have seen it and are glad; **you who seek God, let your heart revive.**
>
> Psalm 70:4: **Let all those that seek thee rejoice and be glad** in thee: and let such as love thy salvation say continually, Let God be magnified.
>
> Psalm 105:3–4: Glory ye in his holy name: **let the heart of them rejoice that seek the Lord.** [4]Seek the Lord, and his strength: seek his face evermore. *[Anonymous]*
>
> Psalm 119:2, 45: **Blessed are they** that keep his testimonies, and **that seek him with the whole heart.** [45]And I will walk at liberty: for **I seek thy precepts.** *[Anonymous]*

In all of the Scriptures above, David (and the unknown author of Psalms 105 and 119) casually refer to themselves seeking God, or refer to others seeking God, or exhort the reader to seek God. If indeed Psalm 14 and Psalm 53 are referring to *all* people *everywhere* in *all* situations *throughout* history, then all these commands would be impossible to obey, and these statements would reference a nonexistent people group—those who seek God.

And the Scriptures above did not even include other psalms by Asaph and others, or other statements, promises, or commands by other Biblical writers. So it is *absolutely conclusive* that Psalms 14 and 53 do not apply to all people, in all cases, everywhere, throughout history.

And even though the list above may have seemed long, I left out for the sake of brevity *scores* of other passages that either command us to seek God, or describe people who did seek God. And all of those Scriptures would have to be considered either wrong or impossible to obey *if* we read Romans 3:10–11 with the Universe of Discourse that Reformed theology assumes.

Watchman on the Wall

In Ezekiel 3, God tells him that He has made him a "watchman" to Israel and it was Ezekiel's responsibility to warn those who were in sin and to point them back to God. In reading the passage below, examine each statement and command that God says, and decide for yourself whether it would make any sense at all in the context of the Five Points of Calvinism:

> Ezekiel 3:16–21 (NIV): At the end of seven days the word of the Lord came to me: [17]"Son of man, I have made you a watchman for the house of Israel; so hear the word I speak and give them warning from me."

Already, this is suspicious: what good would it do to make a *human* a "watchman" over other people if their serving God had already been decided

CHAPTER *10*: MISCELLANEOUS TOPICS

in eternity past, and nothing could change that fact? What good would it do to give them warning if—assuming they had been selected as part of the "*un*-elect"—it would be impossible for them to respond to it? What good would it do to give them warning if—assuming they had been selected as part of the "elect"—it would be impossible for them *not* to respond to it?

Curious that God would say that, if the Reformed doctrines were valid. But let's continue:

> [18]"When I say to a wicked man, 'You will surely die,' and you do not warn him or speak out to dissuade him from his evil ways in order to save his life, that wicked man will die for his sin, and I will hold you accountable for his blood. [19]But if you do warn the wicked man and he does not turn from his wickedness or from his evil ways, he will die for his sin; but you will have saved yourself."

What? God will hold the *watchman* accountable if he doesn't warn the sinner? How could that be an example of justice or impartiality if God was the One—and the *only* one—involved in determining whether or not people turned from their evil ways? That would be like a father punishing his child because one nation invaded another: How could the *kid* prevent that from happening? Since this passage talks about a *human* dissuading a sinner from his ways "in order to save his life" (which is the whole point of evangelism):

- It flies in the face of Total Depravity, because the sinner is called upon to repent;
- It also flies in the face of Unconditional Election, because the sinner himself is being given the responsibility to choose his destiny;
- It also flies in the face of Unconditional Election because the sinner will die *for his sin,* instead of merely having been put in the category of "the unelect" by an all-powerful third party;
- It also flies in the face of Unconditional Election and Irresistible Grace because the watchman is being held accountable to obey God, for the simple reason that the watchman can influence another person's eternal destiny;
- It also flies in the face of Limited Atonement, because God is going after the unelect.

Very sobering observations here. Let's go on:

> [20]"Again, when a righteous man turns from his righteousness and does evil, and I put a stumbling block before him, he will die. Since you

did not warn him, he will die for his sin. The righteous things he did will not be remembered, and I will hold you accountable for his blood. ²¹But if you do warn the righteous man not to sin and he does not sin, he will surely live because he took warning, and you will have saved yourself."

Amazing! Here's the watchman being held accountable for not encouraging godly people to *remain* godly. This short, two-verse passage brings up even more observations that are very disturbing for adherents to Reformed theology:

- Because it refers to a righteous man *turning from righteousness* and doing evil, this flies in the face of Irresistible Grace and Perseverance of the Saints;
- Because it shows God putting a stumblingblock before the man *as a result of* his turning from righteousness, it shows God following our lead, which flies in the face of Unconditional Election;
- Because it says that the man will die "for his sin" and not "for his being unelect," this also flies in the face of Unconditional Election;
- Because it says the watchman will be held accountable for *someone else* dying in his sin, this implies that evangelism is actually beneficial, and not merely an exercise in futility, which flies in the face of Total Depravity and Unconditional Election.

Any one of these passages we've seen is, by itself, enough to put the Reformed doctrines on the teetering edge of collapse, simply because they are mutually exclusive with what God states and what He commands. But there's even more. . .

Ezekiel 18

In Ezekiel 18 (a few scattered verses of which we have already seen), God talks to Ezekiel and clarifies some misunderstandings that were common in Israel at that point. God's exhortation here is quite enlightening, especially in light of the question about free will versus Calvinistic predestination.

We've seen a few snippets of Ezekiel 18 earlier in this book, and profound they were, but there are many more riches to be gleaned when we read the entire chapter in context:

Ezekiel 18:1–3 (NIV): The word of the Lord came to me: ²"What do you people mean by quoting this proverb about the land of Israel: 'The fathers eat sour grapes, and the children's teeth are set on edge'? ³As

CHAPTER 10: MISCELLANEOUS TOPICS

surely as I live, declares the Sovereign Lord, **you will no longer quote this proverb in Israel.**"

At this point in Israel's history, there was a commonly accepted proverb—a "wise saying," if you will—which happened to be wrong, and God wanted to set the story straight. As we can tell from the passage above, this commonly held belief was that when the fathers engage an ungodly activity, the children are somehow held responsible and are punished for it.

Note that God says "you will *no longer* quote this proverb"—there is no ending point to God's prohibition here. In other words, God is not saying "you will cease quoting this proverb *until such-and-such happens. . .*" The prohibition was permanent. Other translations render it "You shall *not have occasion anymore* to use this proverb" (KJV), "you will *no longer have this saying*" (BBE), "*You will not repeat* this proverb" (TEV), and so forth.

So basically, God is saying, "Never again." Why? What's the big deal? If we continue to read, we will find out why God was so adamant that the above proverb not be said anymore. In short, we discover that the above proverb was wrong, and dramatically so:

Ezekiel 18:4 (NIV): For every living soul belongs to me, the father as well as the son—both alike belong to me. **The soul who sins is the one who will die.**

So here we see why God objected to the "wise saying" that had been so popular: it did not reflect spiritual realities. Rather, as God points out, each person is responsible for, and will answer to God for, *his own choices.* This idea is encapsulated in v. 4 above, and then God goes into more detail in subsequent verses, elaborating on the concept.

First, a description of a godly man:

Ezekiel 18:5–9 (NIV): "Suppose there is **a righteous man who does what is just and right.** ⁶He does not eat at the mountain shrines or look to the idols of the house of Israel. He does not defile his neighbor's wife or lie with a woman during her period. ⁷He does not oppress anyone, but returns what he took in pledge for a loan. He does not commit robbery but gives his food to the hungry and provides clothing for the naked. ⁸He does not lend at usury or take excessive interest. He withholds his hand from doing wrong and judges fairly between man and man. ⁹**He follows my decrees and faithfully keeps my laws. That man is righteous; he will surely live,** declares the Sovereign Lord."

God goes on with His scenario, and talks about this godly man's son, who does not follow in his father's righteous footsteps:

> Ezekiel 18:10–13 (NIV): "Suppose he has a violent son, who sheds blood or does any of these other things ¹¹(though the father has done none of them): He eats at the mountain shrines. He defiles his neighbor's wife. ¹²He oppresses the poor and needy. He commits robbery. He does not return what he took in pledge. He looks to the idols. He does detestable things. ¹³He lends at usury and takes excessive interest. **Will such a man live? He will not!** *Because* **he has done all these detestable things, he will surely be put to death and his blood will be on his own head.**"

Note that this man will die. And also note that the reason this man will die is "*because* he has done all these detestable things," which applies to the topic of this book: he will not die on account of a decision made by God in eternity past, but *because he sinned.* Therefore it is entirely just that his blood be on his own head.

Let's continue reading God's discourse:

> Ezekiel 18:14–18 (NIV): "But **suppose this son has a son** who sees all the sins his father commits, **and though he sees them, he does not do such things:** ¹⁵He does not eat at the mountain shrines or look to the idols of the house of Israel. He does not defile his neighbor's wife. ¹⁶He does not oppress anyone or require a pledge for a loan. He does not commit robbery but gives his food to the hungry and provides clothing for the naked. ¹⁷He withholds his hand from sin and takes no usury or excessive interest. **He keeps my laws and follows my decrees. He will not die for his father's sin; he will surely live.** ¹⁸**But his father will die for his own sin,** because he practiced extortion, robbed his brother and did what was wrong among his people."

This is so clear, it's difficult to misunderstand. The evildoer dies because of his sin; the righteous man lives because of his righteousness. In other words, people don't go to heaven on their parents' apron strings, nor do they go to hell on their parents' apron strings: each person chooses for himself how he responds to God, and is rewarded accordingly.

But because God knows that some people will object to the way He does things, He addresses that question before it even arises:

> Ezekiel 18:19–20 (NIV): "Yet you ask, 'Why does the son not share the guilt of his father?' **Since the son has done what is just and right and has been careful to keep all my decrees, he will surely live.** ²⁰The soul

who sins is the one who will die. The son will not share the guilt of the father, nor will the father share the guilt of the son. **The righteousness of the righteous man will be credited to him, and the wickedness of the wicked will be charged against him."**

But someone might say, "In the scenarios above, it looks like one man was righteous his whole life, while another man was wicked his whole life. Is it possible to change, partway through?" The answer is yes, and God addresses that next:

> Ezekiel 18:21–23 (NIV): "But **if a wicked man turns away from all the sins he has committed and keeps all my decrees and does what is just and right, he will surely live; he will not die.** ²²None of the offenses he has committed will be remembered against him. Because of the righteous things he has done, he will live. ²³Do I take any pleasure in the death of the wicked? declares the Sovereign Lord. **Rather, am I not pleased when they turn from their ways and live?"**

So what God is describing here is simply repenting from sin, which includes a change of heart, and a corresponding change in behavior. And notice that what God prefers is that people *repent* of their sin, rather than *die* in their sin, even though they would deserve it. And why is that His preference? Because He loves us.

A perfect example of this is Jonah preaching to Nineveh. Nineveh was exceedingly sinful, so God pronounced judgment upon them (Jonah 1:2). After Jonah's well known attempt to run away from God (1:3–2:10), he ultimately arrives at Nineveh, and announces God's judgment (3:3–4). When they heard about the impending judgment, they believed Jonah and repented (3:5–10), God saw that they had stopped sinning, and canceled the announced judgment (3:10). A textbook example of repentance averting disaster.

But God is not done talking to Ezekiel. Let's continue reading what He had to say:

> Ezekiel 18:24 (NIV): "But **if a righteous man turns from his righteousness and commits sin** and does the same detestable things the wicked man does, will he live? None of the righteous things he has done will be remembered. **Because of the unfaithfulness he is guilty of and because of the sins he has committed, he will die."**

So it is also possible to repent of doing good, and turn to evil. Of course, this is the epitome of foolishness, *but it is possible.* And notice the results: All of the righteousness that he had done before is ignored, and his current state of sin is what is taken into account. Because of his sin, he will die.

A textbook example of this is Judas Iscariot. He was one of the twelve original apostles (Matthew 10:2–4); he preached the Gospel, healed the sick, cleansed lepers, cast out demons, and raised the dead as much as the other apostles (Matthew 10:5–8, Mark 6:7–13, Luke 9:1–6); and he participated in—he didn't merely watch—the feeding of the 5000 (Luke 9:16). Yet after he betrayed Jesus, he did not cry out to God for mercy, as Peter did after his three denials, but instead hanged himself (Matthew 27:5).

Again, God knows that some people will complain about how He judges people according to their actions, and again He answers the question before it even arises:

> Ezekiel 18:25–29 (NIV): "Yet you say, 'The way of the Lord is not just.' Hear, O house of Israel: Is my way unjust? Is it not your ways that are unjust? ²⁶**If a righteous man turns from his righteousness and commits sin, he will die for it; because of the sin he has committed he will die.** ²⁷**But if a wicked man turns away from the wickedness he has committed and does what is just and right, he will save his life.** ²⁸Because he considers all the offenses he has committed and turns away from them, he will surely live; he will not die. ²⁹Yet the house of Israel says, 'The way of the Lord is not just.' Are my ways unjust, O house of Israel? Is it not your ways that are unjust?"

To the people saying to God that He is wrong to judge people according to their actions, He replies, "No, *you* are wrong." So after reiterating the fact that God will judge each person according to his actions, He brings it from the theoretical and hypothetical into the very practical, rubber-meets-the-road reality of everyday living:

> Ezekiel 18:30–32 (NIV): "Therefore, O house of Israel, **I will judge you, each one according to his ways,** declares the Sovereign Lord. **Repent! Turn away from all your offenses; then sin will not be your downfall.** ³¹Rid yourselves of all the offenses you have committed, and get a new heart and a new spirit. Why will you die, O house of Israel? ³²**For I take no pleasure in the death of anyone, declares the Sovereign Lord. Repent and live!"**

Notice God's heart here. He will judge everyone according to his ways; that is a given. And because sin kills people, He tells people to stop. He doesn't want us to die in our sins, so He urges us to repent and obey Him. And if we do, we will live.

So here is yet another passage which, all by itself, does the following:

- It overturns the Reformed doctrine of Total Depravity, because we can repent and turn to God (we must be able to repent, or else God would be unjust in commanding us to do so);
- It overturns the Reformed doctrine of Unconditional Election, because God is leaving the decision of whether or not to serve Him up to us (it would be misleading and completely pointless for Him to tell us to change our behavior if He was the only one who decided whether our behavior changed);
- It overturns the Reformed doctrine of Limited Atonement, because God is calling *all* people to Himself (the righteous He already has, and He is calling the unrighteous: those two groups together constitute all people);
- It overturns the Reformed doctrine of Irresistible Grace because God is pleading with people not to resist His overtures (He wouldn't plead with us to repent if our choosing were impossible or irrelevant);
- It overturns the Reformed doctrine of the Perseverance of the Saints because He gives an example of someone who was obedient, and therefore righteous, subsequently turning away from Him (this would be impossible if Perseverance of the Saints were true).

Basically, Ezekiel 18 offers a great deal of elaboration on the concepts God puts forth in Micah:

Micah 6:8 (NIV): He has showed you, O man, what is good. And **what does the Lord require of you? To act justly and to love mercy and to walk humbly with your God.**

Hmm. Not bad for one passage.

Romans 9–11

Chapters 9 through 11 of Paul's epistle to the Romans contains several verses that are often used to support the Five Points of Calvinism in general, and, in particular, the Reformed understanding of predestination and God's sovereignty. So let's look at this section of Romans and see if those Scriptures are being used, well, *Scripturally.*

The first thing to do when analyzing a passage is to see what the plain, surface meaning is. As mentioned in the beginning of the book, this is the meaning that any unbiased, literate person would come to upon reading the text. When I read it for its plain, surface meaning, it sounds to me that Paul is talking about the nation and people of Israel—the Jews—and their calling to spread the gospel to the Gentiles.

Here is why I think that:

- Paul refers to "my brothers, those of my own race" (9:3, NIV). Since we know Paul himself was a Jew (11:1 and II Corinthians 11:22) this seems like it's talking about Jews.
- Continuing Paul's thought, we see that he is indeed talking about the Jews: he says, ". . .the people of Israel" (v. 4).
- Paul mentions Israel again in v. 6; the seed of Abraham and the seed of Isaac (from whom the Jews are descended) in v. 7; the "children of the promise" (given to Abraham) in v. 8; Abraham's wife Sarah in v. 9; Abraham's son Isaac and his wife Rebekah in v. 10; Rebekah's twins, Jacob and Esau (all progenitors of the Jews), in vv. 11; 12, and 13; Moses (who led Israel out of Egyptian bondage) in v. 15; the Egyptian Pharaoh (from whom the Israelites were delivered) in v. 17; Jews and Gentiles (for the sake of contrast and comparison) in v. 24; Israel again in v. 27 and 31; and Zion (a nickname of Israel) in v. 33. And that's just in Chapter 9!
- In Chapter 10, Paul again mentioned the Israelites (10:1); Moses and the Law (v. 5); Jews and Gentiles (v. 12); Israelites again in v. 16; Israel and Moses in v. 19; Israel again in v. 21.
- In Chapter 11, Paul mentions "God's people," Israelites, and being a descendent of Abraham and Benjamin, Israel in v. 2; then again in v. 7; King David in v. 9; salvation having come to the Gentiles because of Israel's sin in v. 11; more blessings to the Gentiles when Israel repents in vv. 12 and 13; Paul mentions "his own people" in v. 14; Israel and Gentiles again in v. 25; Israel, Zion, and Jacob in v. 26.

Clearly, unmistakeably, undeniably, the topic—the context—of this passage is the nation and people of Israel, and how God has not forsaken them, but used them to bring salvation to the Gentiles. So with this context in mind, let's re-examine the Scriptures taken from this passage and used in an effort to support Reformed theology.

...The Purpose of God According to Election...

The following passage, from Romans 9:11, is often quoted (I have heard this from the one whom many would consider to be the preeminent Reformed theologian in the country today) as:

> Romans 9:11: . . .the purpose of God **according to election** might stand, **not of works, but of him that calleth**. . .

This fragment is usually quoted along with commentary to the effect of: "See? The purposes of God in calling the elect *will* stand; no question about it. And notice that it is *not* of works, but only of Him—God—who calls us to be the elect."

Is that a valid interpretation of that portion of the verse? Let's look at the context and see.

> Romans 9:6–13 (NIV): It is not as though God's word had failed. For not all who are descended from Israel are Israel. ⁷Nor because they are his descendants are they all Abraham's children. On the contrary, "**It is through Isaac that your offspring will be reckoned.**" ⁸In other words, it is not the natural children who are God's children, but it is the children of the promise who are regarded as Abraham's offspring. ⁹For this was how the promise was stated: "At the appointed time I will return, and Sarah will have a son." ¹⁰Not only that, but Rebekah's children had one and the same father, our father Isaac. ¹¹Yet, before the twins were born or had done anything good or bad—in order that God's purpose in election might stand: ¹²not by works but by him who calls—she was told, "**The older will serve the younger.**" ¹³Just as it is written: "Jacob I loved, but Esau I hated."

So we can see that this passage is talking about how God chose Isaac, not Ishmael, to be one of the patriarchs of His chosen people (see Genesis 21), and also how God chose Jacob, not Esau, to be one of the patriarchs and the namesake of His chosen people (see Genesis 25). But doesn't v. 13 above fly in the face of the idea that God is not a respecter of persons, which I've made such a big deal about? Actually no, if you read the story Paul is referring to:

> Genesis 25:29–34 (NIV): Once when Jacob was cooking some stew, Esau came in from the open country, famished. ³⁰He said to Jacob, "Quick, let me have some of that red stew! I'm famished!" (That is why he was also called Edom.) ³¹Jacob replied, "First sell me your birthright." ³²"Look, I am about to die," Esau said. "What good is the birthright to me?" ³³But Jacob said, "Swear to me first." So he swore an oath to

him, selling his birthright to Jacob. ³⁴Then Jacob gave Esau some bread and some lentil stew. He ate and drank, and then got up and left. So Esau despised his birthright.

Why is it significant that Esau despised his birthright? The birthright was not only a double portion of the inheritance passed on from the earthly father, but it symbolized what the heavenly Father would give to his children. As shown above in Romans 9:8, it is the children of the promise (not the natural lineage) who are God's children; i.e., those who choose to receive God's promises as if each promise God makes is offered specifically to them. *Which they are.*

So now it makes a bit more sense why God said, "Jacob I loved, but Esau I hated." It wasn't that He loved the *person* of Jacob more than the *person* of Esau; on the contrary, the point is that He loved the *attitude* of Jacob more than the *attitude* of Esau. As we can see from the story above, Jacob was hungry for the things of God—he valued them, he craved them, and was willing to go to great lengths to obtain them. In contrast, Esau, who rightfully owned the birthright, considered it of little or no value and was willing to give it up for the momentary pleasure of a good meal.

And that attitude—considering the blessings of God to be of little value, and loving earthly things more—God indeed hates. Why? Because we are choosing to destroy ourselves, and that grieves His heart terribly. We are *all* created in God's image, and He designed us to fulfill unimaginably great potential, but we can't do it if we refuse to follow Him.

We can now reliably conclude that Romans 9:11 is not talking about individuals being elected to be saved, while others are elected to suffer damnation and torment forever. The context reveals that God's election of Abraham, Isaac, and Jacob was to be the progenitors of the nation that was called to bring the Gospel of God's free gift of salvation to *everyone* in the world willing to receive it. See "What Does Paul Say About Mercy?", above for further confirmation.

Pharaoh's Example

Another of the most-used Scriptures to support Reformed theology comes from Paul's epistle to the Romans:

> Romans 9:15–18 (AMP): For He says to Moses, I will have mercy on whom I will have mercy and I will have compassion (pity) on whom I will have compassion. ¹⁶So then [God's gift] is not a question of human will and human effort, but of God's mercy. [It depends not on one's

own willingness nor on his strenuous exertion as in running a race, but on God's having mercy on him.] ¹⁷For the Scripture says to Pharaoh, I have raised you up for this very purpose of displaying My power in [dealing with] you, so that My name may be proclaimed the whole world over. ¹⁸So then He has mercy on whomever He wills (chooses) and He hardens (makes stubborn and unyielding the heart of) whomever He wills.

Reformed thinkers read that and say, "See? God hardens some people's hearts and is merciful to other people. And that's *His* choice, not ours." And on the surface, and without the context, it does indeed sound that way. But let's look at Pharaoh and the Exodus story to see if there is anything else in it that is not immediately obvious from Paul's short quote here.

> Exodus 1:8-14 (NIV): Then a new king, who did not know about Joseph, came to power in Egypt. ⁹"Look," he said to his people, "the Israelites have become much too numerous for us. ¹⁰Come, we must deal shrewdly with them or they will become even more numerous and, if war breaks out, will join our enemies, fight against us and leave the country." ¹¹So **they put slave masters over them to oppress them with forced labor,** and they built Pithom and Rameses as store cities for Pharaoh. ¹²But the more they were oppressed, the more they multiplied and spread; so the Egyptians came to dread the Israelites ¹³and **worked them ruthlessly.** ¹⁴**They made their lives bitter with hard labor** in brick and mortar and with **all kinds of work in the fields;** in all their hard labor **the Egyptians used them ruthlessly.** . . .

Verse 8 in the NIV (shown above) seems to have an unfortunate translation when describing the new Pharaoh's awareness of Joseph. NIV translates it "know about," where KJV and many others translate it "know." This word comes from the Hebrew word יָדַע (*yada*, H3045), which means much more than a casual intellectual awareness; it is the same word used in Genesis 4:1, where "Adam *knew* Eve his wife, and she conceived and bore Cain." In the context of Exodus 1, the CEV probably says it best: "Many years later a new king came to power. He did not know what Joseph had done for Egypt. . ." In my estimation, it's very unlikely that the new Pharaoh had never *heard* of Joseph—being a historical figure and all—but he didn't know the *details* of the story of Joseph, and therefore didn't realize that Egypt was the superpower of the world *because* of the God of the Hebrews.

In any case, this Pharaoh saw that the Hebrews were very prolific, and he feared (at least) these three things: 1) the Hebrews would get even more numerous, 2) if Egypt got in a war with someone, the Hebrews would join forces with Egypt's enemy, and Egypt would end up the losing side, and 3) the Hebrews would flee the country, leaving Egypt without a workforce.

So here is what Pharaoh (and of course, everyone under his command) did:

- He put slave masters over the Hebrews.
- He oppressed them with hard labor.
- He worked them ruthlessly.
- He made their lives bitter with hard labor.
- He made them do all kinds of work in the fields.
- He used them ruthlessly.

So we can already see that this Pharaoh did *not* exhibit the fruit of the Spirit. Then, as if the ruthless slavery of hard labor weren't enough, he told the Hebrew midwives to kill all the boy babies that the Hebrew women bore. They didn't. (Interesting aside here: God blessed the Hebrew midwives for engaging in civil disobedience when the government was demanding ungodly actions.) And then, since many of the Hebrew families apparently lived with their Egyptian masters, Pharaoh told the Egyptian households to do it:

Exodus 1:22: Then Pharaoh gave this order to all **his people:** "Every boy that is born you must throw into the Nile, but let every girl live."

So here we have a Pharaoh who is cruel, arrogant, hard-hearted, willing to order the murder of tens (or hundreds) of thousands of babies, and totally unconcerned with the needs or feelings of others. Then the story continues with Moses' birth, adoption, early adulthood, and his time in Midian. While he was there, that Pharaoh died (2:23), and his son, just as bad as his old man, took the throne of Egypt, while the Israelites were still being oppressed. Then in Exodus 3, Moses talked to God in the burning bush, and in Exodus 4, Moses is given the miraculous signs with which to persuade the Israelites that he was indeed called by God.

One of the things that God instructs Moses to tell Pharaoh was this:

Exodus 4:22–23 (AMP): And you shall say to Pharaoh, Thus says the Lord, Israel is My son, even My firstborn. [23]And I say to you, Let My son go, that he may serve Me; and **if you refuse** to let him go, behold, I will slay your son, your firstborn.

As you know, this will play out in a horrific fashion in the final plague. And notice that God said "*if* you refuse. . ." Almost as if it was up to Pharaoh

CHAPTER 10: MISCELLANEOUS TOPICS

to choose his response to God. But back to the story: Moses goes to talk to Pharaoh, and basically says, "Let my people go." Let's take up the story again at that point:

> Exodus 5:1–19 (NIV): Afterward Moses and Aaron went to Pharaoh and said, "This is what the LORD, the God of Israel, says: 'Let my people go, so that they may hold a festival to me in the desert.'" ²Pharaoh said, **"Who is the LORD, that I should obey him and let Israel go? I do not know the LORD and I will not let Israel go."**

Wow. Right off the bat, Pharaoh is acting terminally foolish.

> ³Then they said, "The God of the Hebrews has met with us. Now let us take a three-day journey into the desert to offer sacrifices to the LORD our God, or he may strike us with plagues or with the sword." ⁴But the king of Egypt said, "Moses and Aaron, why are you taking the people away from their labor? Get back to your work!" ⁵Then Pharaoh said, "Look, the people of the land are now numerous, and you are stopping them from working." ⁶That same day Pharaoh gave this order to the slave drivers and foremen in charge of the people: ⁷**"You are no longer to supply the people with straw** for making bricks; let them go and gather their own straw. ⁸**But require them to make the same number of bricks as before; don't reduce the quota.** They are lazy; that is why they are crying out, 'Let us go and sacrifice to our God.' ⁹**Make the work harder** for the men so that they keep working and pay no attention to lies." ¹⁰Then the slave drivers and the foremen went out and said to the people, "This is what Pharaoh says: 'I will not give you any more straw. ¹¹Go and get your own straw wherever you can find it, but your work will not be reduced at all.'" ¹²So the people scattered all over Egypt to gather stubble to use for straw. ¹³**The slave drivers kept pressing them,** saying, "Complete the work required of you for each day, just as when you had straw." ¹⁴The **Israelite foremen appointed by Pharaoh's slave drivers were beaten** and were asked, "Why didn't you meet your quota of bricks yesterday or today, as before?" ¹⁵Then the Israelite foremen went and appealed to Pharaoh: "Why have you treated your servants this way? ¹⁶Your servants are given no straw, yet we are told, 'Make bricks!' Your servants are being beaten, but the fault is with your own people." ¹⁷Pharaoh said, "Lazy, that's what you are—lazy! That is why you keep saying, 'Let us go and sacrifice to the LORD.' ¹⁸Now get to work. You will not be given any straw, yet you must produce your full quota of bricks." ¹⁹The Israelite foremen realized they

were in trouble when they were told, "You are not to reduce the number of bricks required of you for each day."

So the Israelites were already subject to slavery, oppression, forced labor, ruthless treatment, being worked to exhaustion and even death. Then Pharaoh says, "You keep making the same number of bricks, but now we won't give you raw material to make them." The Hebrews already had such a heavy workload they couldn't do any more, and then Pharaoh doubles it with no more time to accomplish the work. Is this a godly man? Obviously not. He had already rejected God in no uncertain terms; look at his statement in v. 2 above: "Who is the Lord, that I should obey him and let Israel go? *I do not know the* LORD and I will *not* let Israel go." To put it colloquially, Pharaoh is "cruisin' for a bruisin'."

So now Moses is in the hot seat, because the people blame him for their workload having been increased. So he prays, and God replies:

> Exodus 6:2–5: And God spake unto Moses, and said unto him, I am the LORD: ³And I appeared unto Abraham, unto Isaac, and unto Jacob, by the name of God Almighty, but by my name JEHOVAH was I not known to them. ⁴And I have also established my **covenant** with them, to give them the land of Canaan, the land of their pilgrimage, wherein they were strangers. ⁵And I have also heard the groaning of the children of Israel, whom the Egyptians keep in bondage; and I have remembered my **covenant.**

. . .and shortly after that, God sends the plagues, resulting in the Hebrews being delivered from their bondage and leaving Egypt. But notice in the passage above, God mentions Abraham, Isaac, and Jacob, and also talks about His covenant with them. What was His covenant with Abraham and his descendents?

> Genesis 12:1–3: Now the LORD had said unto Abram, Get thee out of thy country, and from thy kindred, and from thy father's house, unto a land that I will shew thee: ²And I will make of thee a great nation, and I will bless thee, and make thy name great; and thou shalt be a blessing: ³And **I will bless them that bless thee, and curse him that curseth thee:** and in thee shall all families of the earth be blessed.

As we see, Pharaoh was just reaping what he had sown. He had cursed the children of Abraham, so God cursed him. As I've said several times already, "When you reject the Right Answer, it doesn't really matter which wrong answer you choose." In Pharaoh's case, it could be phrased, "When you reject the Truth, it doesn't really matter which lie you believe."

Since Pharaoh had already rejected God (i.e., the Truth), God was just arranging circumstances so His Name would be exalted. God caused Pharaoh to believe whatever lies He wanted him to believe, so the deliverance His people would be all the more glorious. And God does indeed do this to people who disobey and reject Him; it is described in Isaiah:

> Isaiah 66:4: **I also will choose their delusions, and will bring their fears upon them;** because when I called, none did answer; when I spake, they did not hear: but **they did evil before mine eyes, and chose that in which I delighted not.**
>
> AMP: So **I also will choose their delusions** and mockings, their calamities and afflictions, and **I will bring their fears upon them**—because when I called, no one answered; when I spoke, they did not listen or obey. But **they did what was evil in My sight and chose that in which I did not delight.**
>
> GNV: Therefore **will I choose out their delusions, and I will bring their fear upon them,** because I called and none would answer: I speak, and they would not hear: but **they did evil in my sight, and chose the things which I would not.**

As an aside, it is interesting that God describes the wicked people as having chosen their *own* paths, not Him choosing for them. This, of course, refutes the Reformed doctrine of Total Depravity: if they actually *chose* to do evil, it must have been possible to choose good. Why? Because if doing evil was inevitable, they couldn't have *chosen* it; it would have been forced upon them because there was no alternative option. And this passage also refutes Unconditional Election, where God supposedly chooses for us whether or not we serve Him.

But back to the subject at hand: I find the phrase "I will choose their delusions" fascinating. What is a delusion? A belief that something is true when it is not. Pharaoh had already chosen to reject the most important truth of all: "God is *God*," so God caused him to believe whatever fit in with His plans. How did he do that? Also from the verse above: "I will bring their fears upon them."

Remember what Pharaoh feared?

> Exodus 1:10 (NIV): Come, we must deal shrewdly with them or **they will become even more numerous** and, if war breaks out, **will join our enemies,** fight against us and **leave the country.**

Free to Choose?

And what happened?

- The Israelites became even more numerous:

  Exodus 1:12 (NIV): But the more they were oppressed, the more they multiplied and spread; so the Egyptians came to dread the Israelites. . .

- War did indeed break out, although it wasn't anything so piddly as a human army. Pharaoh declared war on *God*. [Author's note: This is not a good idea.] And sure enough, the Israelites sided with Pharaoh's enemy.

  Exodus 14:14 (NIV): The LORD will fight for you; you need only to be still.

- The Israelites did, in fact, leave the country of Egypt, so the Egyptians' workforce was gone.

  Exodus 12:51 (NIV): And it came to pass the selfsame day, that the LORD did bring the children of Israel out of the land of Egypt by their armies.

God certainly did bring Pharaoh's fears upon him.

So now that the context has been shown, let's consider Paul's statement in Romans, where He is quoting God:

Romans 9:18 (NIV): Therefore God has mercy on whom he wants to have mercy, and he hardens whom he wants to harden.

Although that Scripture is entirely true as it stands in its own context, it becomes glaringly false when we add the underlying assumption that there is nothing we can do about it, and there's no way we can influence the outcome. We are shown in multiple ways that that is simply not true. If we repent, He will have mercy. If we harden our own hearts once too many times, He will harden us terminally.

Now we've already seen that Pharaoh's heart was hardened already; Pharaoh and the Egyptians had chosen to harden their hearts, and even Israel's enemies knew that, centuries later, as shown in the following passage. The background of the story here is that the Philistines had stolen the Ark of the Covenant, and had been struck with a plague of hemorrhoids. (To quote Psalm 78:66, God "smote his enemies in the hinder parts. . .") The Philistines asked their priests what to do:

I Samuel 6:3–6 (DARBY): And they said, If ye send away the ark of the God of Israel, send it not empty; ye must at any rate return him a trespass-offering: then ye shall be healed, and it shall be known to you why his hand is not removed from you. ⁴Then they said, What is the trespass-offering which we shall return to him? And they said, Five golden hemorrhoids, and five golden mice, the number of the lords of the Philistines; for one plague is upon them all, and upon your lords. ⁵And ye shall make images of your hemorrhoids, and images of your mice that destroy the land, and give glory to the God of Israel: perhaps he will lighten his hand from off you, and from off your gods, and from off your land. ⁶And **why will ye harden your heart, as the Egyptians and Pharaoh hardened their heart?** When he had wrought mightily among them, did they not let them go, and they departed?

So again, it was common knowledge *even to the enemies of Israel,* hundreds of years later, that Pharaoh and his nation had hardened their own hearts. From Pharaoh's childhood, he no doubt heard his father, the previous Pharaoh, express hatred and cruelty toward the Hebrews, and he no doubt was instructed by his father on how to run the kingdom, before his father died.

So Pharaoh was reaping what he had sown from his hardness of heart, and when God saw that Pharaoh had rejected God's way, He chose Pharaoh's delusions (remember, if you reject the Right Answer, which *wrong* answer you end up with doesn't really matter), and then God hardened Pharaoh's heart more:

Exodus 7:13: And **he hardened Pharaoh's heart,** that he hearkened not unto them; as the LORD had said.

And here's the scary part: Even *after* God hardened Pharaoh's heart, Pharaoh chose to harden his *own* heart yet more!

Exodus 8:15: But **when Pharaoh saw that there was respite, *he* hardened his heart,** and hearkened not unto them; as the LORD had said.

Exodus 8:32: And *Pharaoh* **hardened his heart** at this time also, neither would he let the people go.

Exodus 9:34: And when Pharaoh saw that the rain and the hail and the thunders were ceased, *he* **sinned yet more, and** *hardened his heart,* **he and his servants.**

Exodus 10:3 (AMP): So Moses and Aaron went to Pharaoh, and said to him, Thus says the Lord, the God of the Hebrews, **How long will *you* refuse to humble yourself before Me?** Let My people go, that they may serve Me.

FREE TO CHOOSE?

This context is what doesn't come across from Paul's quote, but which the Christians in Rome would have known about (the Old Testament is all the Bible they had at the time). If you're unfamiliar with the story of the Exodus, reading Romans 9:15–18 does indeed portray God in a way that could seem arbitrary, capricious, and uncaring about all those people that "He" sends to hell. It's clear that God hardened Pharaoh's heart, but Pharaoh was not somebody that God just picked at random to harden. Pharaoh had already made his choice, very plainly and vociferously, and God used even Pharaoh's rebellion to serve His purposes. But God didn't *cause* him to rebel in the first place. If He had, so many other Scriptures would have to be ignored.

One more thing. Look at this verse, from the passage above:

Romans 9:17 (NIV): For the Scripture says to Pharaoh: "**I raised you up for this very purpose, that I might display my power in you** and that my name might be proclaimed in all the earth."

When reading this verse, as well as Exodus 9:16, which it is quoting, many people read it as if it says "I raised you up for this very purpose, that *by your destruction* I might display my power in you and that my name might be proclaimed in all the earth." I know I read it that way for years. *But that's not what it says.* Read it again; there's nothing about *how* God would display His power in Pharaoh; that was determined by Pharaoh's response to Him.

God did not intrinsically hate Pharaoh or the Egyptians. He raised Pharaoh up in order to show Himself strong through him, but the destruction of Egypt wasn't necessarily, and didn't *have* to be, the mechanism. The Lord certainly *knew* Pharaoh was going to harden his heart, but He didn't predestine him to do so; remember, Pharaoh had already rejected God and hardened his own heart long before God hardened it further.

Think back to the days of Jacob's son Joseph: same country, same culture, same governmental structure, and God displayed His power and showed Himself strong through that Pharaoh too. However, since the Pharaoh of Joseph's day was willing to heed God's warning and follow His instructions, God made Egypt the preeminent superpower of the world, not to mention the wealthiest.

That could have happened to the Pharaoh of Moses' day as well. But, since Moses' Pharaoh chose to harden his heart, Egypt was destroyed, and it has not—even today—recovered. A far cry from the dominant superpower of the world it used to be.

But even now, there is hope. At some point, Egypt will turn back to the Lord, and He, true to His loving ways, will save them:

> Isaiah 19:19–25 (NIV): In that day **there will be an altar to the Lord in the heart of Egypt,** and a monument to the Lord at its border. [20]It will be a sign and witness to the Lord Almighty in the land of Egypt. **When they cry out to the Lord** because of their oppressors, **he will send them a savior and defender, and he will rescue them.** [21]So the Lord will make himself known to the Egyptians, and in that day they will acknowledge the Lord. They will worship with sacrifices and grain offerings; they will make vows to the Lord and keep them.

That's already amazing, but there's more, and it shows the redemptive nature of God's discipline:

> [22]The Lord will strike Egypt with a plague; **he will strike them and heal them. They will turn to the Lord, and he will respond to their pleas and heal them.** [23]In that day there will be a highway from Egypt to Assyria. The Assyrians will go to Egypt and the Egyptians to Assyria. The Egyptians and Assyrians will worship together. [24]In that day Israel will be the third, along with Egypt and Assyria, a blessing on the earth. [25]**The Lord Almighty will bless them, saying, "Blessed be Egypt my people, Assyria my handiwork, and Israel my inheritance."**

God *will* display His power, one way or another. But whether we are blessed by it or destroyed by it is up to us. Let us resolve to *not* harden our hearts when God speaks to us.

So as Exodus 9:16 says, God was going to get glory through the Pharaoh of Egypt one way or another. But it was *Pharaoh* who chose to rebel against God, therefore destroying Egypt in the process. Read the very next two verses:

> Exodus 9:17–18 (NIV): **You still set yourself against my people** and will not let them go. [18]**Therefore,** at this time tomorrow I will send the worst hailstorm that has ever fallen on Egypt, from the day it was founded till now.

So we can see from these two verses that *Pharaoh* determined the kind of mechanism through which God would get the glory. We can see at the beginning of v. 18 above, that the word "therefore" is very revealing: it was *because* of Pharaoh's obstinacy that the plagues happened and Egypt was destroyed.

God was not bent on destroying the people of Egypt, although He was making a very clear statement that He was far and away more powerful than the so-called "gods" of Egypt. In fact, He plainly stated that He was going to show Himself superior to all of the idols and false gods the Egyptians worshiped:

> Exodus 12:12b: . . .**against all the gods of Egypt I will execute judgment**: I am the LORD.

So although God was destroying the credibility of the false gods of Egypt, He had no desire to destroy the *people* of Egypt. Those people, like all other people, were created in God's image and His likeness, and He loves them. It's not that God lacked the ability to destroy them, had He wanted to, as this passage shows:

> Exodus 9:15–16 (NLT): **By now I could have lifted my hand and struck you and your people with a plague to wipe you off the face of the earth.** ¹⁶But I have spared you for a purpose—to show you my power and to spread my fame throughout the earth.

Again, the people of Egypt who were destroyed were not destroyed because God was acting spiteful or petty, but because of a natural fallout of their Pharaoh obstinately trying to pit his own strength against that of God.

And indeed, God's fame quickly spread:

> Exodus 15:14 (NLT): **The peoples hear and tremble;** anguish grips those who live in Philistia.

> Exodus 18:10–11 (NLT): "Praise the LORD," Jethro said, "for he has rescued you from the Egyptians and from Pharaoh. Yes, he has rescued Israel from the powerful hand of Egypt! ¹¹**I know now that the LORD is greater than all other gods, because he rescued his people from the oppression of the proud Egyptians.**"

Note that these two Pharaohs—the one in Joseph's day and the one in Moses' day—correspond to the two thieves being crucified alongside Jesus, the main difference being that the decisions made by these two Pharaohs had consequences that were on a national scale. The Pharaoh in Joseph's day corresponds to the thief who repented, and soon joined Jesus in paradise. The Pharaoh of Moses' day corresponds to the thief who did not repent, and was destroyed in a most severe way.

Again, God's discipline (punishments, judgments) are redemptive in nature; they are intended to make our rebellion against Him so uncomfortable that we come to Him (or *back* to Him) before it's too late. But if we insist, we can reject His invitations, just like Moses' Pharaoh did.

We can see this very clearly in this passage:

Amos 4:6–11 (NKJV): "Also I gave you cleanness of teeth *[famine]* in all your cities. And lack of bread in all your places; **yet you have not returned to Me," says the Lord.** ⁷"I also withheld rain from you, when there were still three months to the harvest. I made it rain on one city, I withheld rain from another city. One part was rained upon, and where it did not rain the part withered. ⁸So two or three cities wandered to another city to drink water, but they were not satisfied; **yet you have not returned to Me," says the Lord.** ⁹"I blasted you with blight and mildew. When your gardens increased, your vineyards, your fig trees, and your olive trees, the locust devoured them; **yet you have not returned to Me," says the Lord.** ¹⁰"I sent among you a plague after the manner of Egypt; your young men I killed with a sword, along with your captive horses; I made the stench of your camps come up into your nostrils; **yet you have not returned to Me," says the Lord.** ¹¹"I overthrew some of you, as God overthrew Sodom and Gomorrah, and you were like a firebrand plucked from the burning; **yet you have not returned to Me," says the Lord.**

It's clear from the above passage, that God's judgments got ever more severe, so that the people would repent and come back to God. *Five times* in the above passage, God marvels at the utter self-destructive foolishness of the people, that they were so rebellious, stubborn, hard-hearted, and stiff-necked, that they refused to return to God, even though it meant continually increasing hardship. It truly is astonishing that people can be so dead set against repentance, and thus so dead set on self-destruction. But regardless, whether rebellion or repentance, it is a matter of a person's freewill choice, not an inevitable fatedness.

And there's even more Scriptural support for the idea that Pharaoh was not unavoidably fated to disobey God, because then God would be in the position of ordering someone to obey a command ("Let my people go!") while simultaneously preventing that person from obeying the command. This would not only result in God being unjust, but would also be an example of a kingdom divided against itself, which, according to Jesus Himself, "cannot stand" (Mark 3:24–25).

It's almost as if (he said with more than a little irony) Jesus was right when He said, in reference to His being the Cornerstone:

Luke 20:18: Whosoever shall fall upon that stone shall be broken; but on whomsoever it shall fall, it will grind him to powder.

> AMP: Everyone who falls on that Stone will be broken [in pieces]; but upon whomever It falls, It will crush him [winnow him and scatter him as dust].
>
> CEV: Anyone who stumbles over this stone will get hurt, and anyone it falls on will be smashed to pieces.

It's up to us whether we fall on Him, or He falls on us; one of the two *will* happen. But back to Exodus: remember when I said that God did not intrinsically hate Pharaoh or the Egyptians? Note in the following Scripture that God was willing to bless any Egyptians who believed in Him and followed Him. Look at this verse, describing the exodus of the people of Israel from Egypt:

> Exodus 12:37–38: And the children of Israel journeyed from Rameses to Succoth, about six hundred thousand on foot that were men, beside children. ³⁸And a **mixed multitude** went up also with them; and flocks, and herds, even very much cattle.
>
> 38, ERV: **A great number of people who were not Israelites** went with them, along with many sheep, cattle, and other livestock.
>
> EXB: **Many other people who were not Israelites** [a mixed multitude] went with them, as well as a large number of sheep, goats, and cattle.
>
> HCSB: **An ethnically diverse crowd** also went up with them, along with a huge number of livestock, both flocks and herds.
>
> NABRE: **A crowd of mixed ancestry** also went up with them, with livestock in great abundance, both flocks and herds.
>
> NIV: **Many other people** went up with them, and also large droves of livestock, both flocks and herds.
>
> VOICE: **Another crowd, made up of various and sundry peoples,** accompanied them, as well as herds, flocks, and a great number of livestock.

So who were these "other people who were not Israelites," this "ethnically diverse crowd," this "mixed multitude?" It doesn't take too much thought to realize that they were—primarily, at least—Egyptians who had *not* hardened their hearts, and chose to acknowledge that the LORD was indeed God, and to obey Him.

It may have even included some of the magicians who initially challenged God, but later realized that the God of the Hebrews was much more powerful than they:

Exodus 8:19 (GWORD): *[during the plague of lice]* So **the magicians said to Pharaoh, "This is the hand of God!"** Yet, Pharaoh continued to be stubborn and would not listen to Moses and Aaron, as the LORD had predicted.

Exodus 9:20 (AMP): *[after Moses announced the plague of hail]* Then **he who feared the word of the Lord among the servants of Pharaoh** made his servants and his livestock flee into the houses and shelters.

Exodus 10:7 (NIV): *[after Moses announced the plague of locusts]* **Pharaoh's officials said to him**, "How long will this man be a snare to us? **Let the people go,** so that they may worship the LORD their God. Do you not yet realize that Egypt is ruined?"

Exodus 11:3 (NASB): *[just before Moses announced the plague of the death of the firstborn]* And the LORD gave the people favor in the sight of the Egyptians. Furthermore, the man **Moses himself was greatly esteemed in the land of Egypt, both in the sight of Pharaoh's servants** and in the sight of the people.

So when Paul said that God raised up Pharaoh in order to display His power in him, let's realize from now on that the outcome could have been very different, had Pharaoh chosen to obey God in the first place. Pharaoh had the same choice the Pharisees would have millennia later in the book of Acts, when Gamaliel spoke to them with admirable wisdom about these pesky Christians who were running around doing miracles and generally causing people to become moral. Gamaliel ends his speech with this:

Acts 5:38–39 (NIV): Therefore, in the present case I advise you: Leave these men alone! Let them go! For if their purpose or activity is of human origin, it will fail. ³⁹But **if it is from God, you will not be able to stop these men; you will only find yourselves fighting against God.**

In Pharaoh's case, the same idea could have been phrased: "Let them leave! If this is just Moses' idea and God *doesn't* help them, they'll be right back here after a few days with no food or water. But if this is God's idea, you *don't* want to get in the way. . ."

And of course, we have the same choice in our own lives: God *will* derive glory from our lives, one way or another.

> Hebrews 3:14–4:7: For we are made partakers of Christ, if we hold the beginning of our confidence stedfast unto the end; ¹⁵While it is said, To day if ye will hear his voice, **harden not your hearts**, as in the provocation.

Note that it is a warning to *us* not to harden our hearts. Then, the writer of Hebrews elaborates:

> ¹⁶For some, when they had heard, did provoke: howbeit not all that came out of Egypt by Moses. ¹⁷But with whom was he grieved forty years? was it not with them that had sinned, whose carcases fell in the wilderness? ¹⁸And to whom sware he that they should not enter into his rest, but to them that believed not? ¹⁹So we see that they could not enter in because of unbelief. ⁴:¹Let us therefore fear, lest, a promise being left us of entering into his rest, any of you should seem to come short of it. ²For **unto us was the gospel preached**, *as well as unto them:* **but the word preached did not profit them, not being mixed with faith in them that heard it.**

So the Israelites heard the gospel just like we have. It's always been by faith.

> ³For we which have believed do enter into rest, as he said, As I have sworn in my wrath, if they shall enter into my rest: although the works were finished from the foundation of the world. ⁴For he spake in a certain place of the seventh day on this wise, And God did rest the seventh day from all his works. ⁵And in this place again, If they shall enter into my rest. ⁶Seeing therefore it remaineth that some must enter therein, and they to whom it was first preached entered not in because of unbelief: ⁷Again, he limiteth a certain day, saying in David, To day, after so long a time; as it is said, To day if ye will hear his voice, **harden not your hearts**.

Again, the writer of Hebrews urges us not to harden our hearts. It behooves us to think long and hard about how we choose to fit into His plan: as a sheep or a goat; as wheat or chaff; as a co-laborer or a rebel.

The Potter and the Clay

Another classic support from Romans 9–11 for the Reformed theology—specifically, the idea of an unchangeable God-chosen predestination for a nation or an individual—is that of Paul's use of the concept of Potter and Clay, taken from Romans 9:

> Romans 9:15, 21: For he saith to Moses, **I will have mercy on whom I will have mercy,** and I will have compassion on whom I will have compassion. [21]**Hath not the potter power over the clay,** of the same lump to make one vessel unto honour, and another unto dishonour?

These verses are used in support of the Reformed doctrine by saying something to the effect of, "See? *God* chooses who gets mercy and who doesn't! He'll have mercy and compassion on whomever He chooses, and if we don't like it, that doesn't matter, because He's the Potter, and we're just the clay! We have nothing to say in the matter."

The passage that Paul is quoting here comes from Jeremiah the prophet:

> Jeremiah 18:1–6 (NIV): This is the word that came to Jeremiah from the LORD: [2]"Go down to the potter's house, and there I will give you my message." [3]So I went down to the potter's house, and I saw him working at the wheel. [4]But the pot he was shaping from the clay was marred in his hands; so the potter formed it into another pot, shaping it as seemed best to him. [5]Then the word of the LORD came to me: [6]"O house of Israel, can I not do with you as this potter does?" declares the LORD. "Like clay in the hand of the potter, so are you in my hand, O house of Israel."

At this point, some will say, "Ha! See there? The potter can do whatever He wants with the clay!" And of course that is true. But a very important question to answer is, "What does He *want* to do with the clay?" Let's continue reading with the very next verse and see if the context provides any answers.

> Jeremiah 18:7–12 (NIV): "If at any time I announce that a nation or kingdom is to be uprooted, torn down and destroyed, [8]and **if that nation I warned repents of its evil, then I will relent and not inflict on it the disaster I had planned.** [9]And if at another time I announce that a nation or kingdom is to be built up and planted, [10]and **if it does evil in my sight and does not obey me, then I will reconsider the good I had intended to do** for it. [11]Now therefore say to the people of Judah and those living in Jerusalem, 'This is what the LORD says: Look! **I am preparing a disaster for you and devising a plan against you. So turn from your evil ways,** each one of you, and reform your ways and your actions.' [12]But they will reply, 'It's no use. We will continue with our own plans; each of us will follow the stubbornness of his evil heart.'"

So we see that, included with the "potter has power over the clay" concept, God also hastens to point out that His intentions and actions can be strongly influenced, and even reversed, *by our attitudes and behavior*. Look at vv. 7–10 above again: If God pronounces destruction on us but we repent, He will *change His mind* about our destruction. And if God pronounces blessing, but we rebel against Him, again *He will change His mind* about our blessing. It's right there in the Bible.

And He tells that story to Jeremiah (and thus to us) as a preface to what He says in v. 11: Disaster is coming, so repent! He *wants* to bless us, save us, redeem us, and more, but He doesn't *force* us to choose wisely; He only exhorts us to do so. Why? Again, because He wants us to actually *love* Him, which, as we've seen, must be voluntary.

So if God is the Potter and we're "just" the clay, why would He change His mind, based on our actions? Because He's not only our Creator, the Almighty, and the King of Kings—He's our Father (Luke 15:11–24); our Friend (John 15:14–15), and our Lover (Song of Solomon). The Lord is good, and His mercy endures forever (Psalm 118:1–4). He is Love (I John 4:8). And on and on.

But are we sure that's what that passage in Jeremiah means? I mean, sure, it *says* God will change His mind based on our attitudes and actions, but can that possibly be? Does God really *mean* it? If God really meant to say that, He would confirm it somewhere else in the Bible, wouldn't He? Just to make sure we didn't misunderstand?

Glad you asked.

Read the following passage from Ezekiel, where God says basically the same thing to him as He did to Jeremiah: that God's actions toward us depend on our actions toward Him.

> Ezekiel 33:11–20 (NIV): "Say to them, 'As surely as I live, declares the Sovereign LORD, I take no pleasure in the death of the wicked, but rather that they turn from their ways and live. Turn! **Turn from your evil ways! Why will you die,** O house of Israel?' ¹²Therefore, son of man, say to your countrymen, 'The righteousness of the righteous man will not save him when he disobeys, and the wickedness of the wicked man will not cause him to fall when he turns from it. **The righteous man, if he sins, will not be allowed to live because of his former righteousness.**' ¹³If I tell the righteous man that he will surely live, but then he trusts in his righteousness and does evil, none of the righteous things he has done will be remembered; he will die for the evil he has done.

¹⁴And **if I say to the wicked man, 'You will surely die,' but he then turns away from his sin and does what is just and right—** ¹⁵if he gives back what he took in pledge for a loan, returns what he has stolen, follows the decrees that give life, and does no evil, **he will surely live; he will not die.** ¹⁶None of the sins he has committed will be remembered against him. He has done what is just and right; he will surely live. ¹⁷Yet your countrymen say, 'The way of the Lord is not just.' But it is their way that is not just. ¹⁸If a righteous man turns from his righteousness and does evil, he will die for it. ¹⁹And **if a wicked man turns away from his wickedness and does what is just and right, he will live by doing so.** ²⁰Yet, O house of Israel, you say, 'The way of the Lord is not just.' But I will judge each of you according to his own ways."

By reading the above passage, you might almost get the impression that we reap what we sow.

But does God actually do that? Are there any cases where that happened? Where God pronounced judgment, but because the intended recipient(s) of the judgment repented, God changed His mind and cancelled the judgment? As a matter of fact, yes. This works on a person-by-person basis, as shown in the story of Hezekiah, which we briefly mentioned in the "Limited Omniscience" section above:

> II Kings 20:1–6: In those days was Hezekiah sick unto death. And the prophet Isaiah the son of Amoz came to him, and said unto him, Thus saith the LORD, Set thine house in order; for **thou shalt die, and not live.** ²Then he turned his face to the wall, and prayed unto the LORD, saying, ³I beseech thee, O LORD, remember now how I have walked before thee in truth and with a perfect heart, and have done that which is good in thy sight. And Hezekiah wept sore. ⁴And it came to pass, afore Isaiah was gone out into the middle court, that the word of the LORD came to him, saying, ⁵Turn again, and tell Hezekiah the captain of my people, Thus saith the LORD, the God of David thy father, I have heard thy prayer, I have seen thy tears: behold, **I will heal thee:** on the third day thou shalt go up unto the house of the LORD. ⁶And I will add unto thy days fifteen years; and I will deliver thee and this city out of the hand of the king of Assyria; and I will defend this city for mine own sake, and for my servant David's sake.

So here, for this one person, God's pronouncement of "thou shalt die, and not live" was changed to "I have heard thy prayer, I have seen thy tears: behold, I will heal thee." Here is a perfect example of how Jeremiah 18 and Ezekiel

33 work in the life of a single person. We see that God is indeed the Potter and He can do anything He wants to with the clay. *But He's also a Lover,* and He wants to cancel His pronounced judgments, if we'll only repent.

Look again at Ezekiel 33:11, shown above, and hear His heart: "I take no pleasure in the death of the wicked, but rather that they turn from their ways and live. Turn! Turn from your evil ways! Why will you die, O house of Israel?"

But how about a large group of people? How about a whole city or nation? Will God do the same thing on a much larger scale than just a single person? Yes, according to the Scripture just mentioned. But *has* God actually done it? Again, yes, and one example comes from the story of Jonah. After he (unsuccessfully) tried to run away from God, was swallowed by the fish, and vomited up onto dry land, he finally went to Nineveh and did what God had told him to do:

> Jonah 3:1–10 (NASB): Now the word of the LORD came to Jonah the second time, saying, ²"Arise, go to Nineveh the great city and proclaim to it the proclamation which I am going to tell you." ³So Jonah arose and went to Nineveh according to the word of the LORD. Now Nineveh was an exceedingly great city, a three days' walk. ⁴Then Jonah began to go through the city one day's walk; and he cried out and said, "Yet **forty days and Nineveh will be overthrown.**" ⁵Then the people of Nineveh believed in God; and they called a fast and put on sackcloth from the greatest to the least of them. ⁶When the word reached the king of Nineveh, he arose from his throne, laid aside his robe from him, covered himself with sackcloth, and sat on the ashes. ⁷And he issued a proclamation and it said, "In Nineveh by the decree of the king and his nobles: Do not let man, beast, herd, or flock taste a thing. Do not let them eat or drink water. ⁸But both man and beast must be covered with sackcloth; and let men call on God earnestly that each may turn from his wicked way and from the violence which is in his hands. ⁹Who knows, God may turn and relent, and withdraw His burning anger so that we shall not perish?" ¹⁰**When God saw their deeds, that they turned from their wicked way, then God relented concerning the calamity which He had declared He would bring upon them. And He did not do it.**

So here again, we see that God is indeed the Potter and He can do anything He wants to with the clay. But since He's also a Lover, He wants to cancel any justified, intended, and even *announced,* judgments. But judgment comes only from rebelling against Him, so we must repent, and then God will be merciful. Paul's primary point in Romans 9, then, is that God can call Israel to a particular calling, and that's His decision alone. By obvious extension, we as individuals are also called to various ministries and callings. But of course, people can choose to obey Him and be blessed, or rebel against Him and be destroyed.

Vessels Unto Honor

Romans 9, quoted above, talked about the potter and the clay, but it also talked about vessels of honor and vessel unto dishonor. It is commonly stated by adherents to Reformed theology that God will make some vessels unto honor and others unto dishonor.

That is completely true. *However,* the unspoken assumption that usually goes along with a Reformed-theology quoting of the Scripture is that God arbitrarily, and from eternity past, decided who would be a vessel unto honor, and who would be a vessel unto dishonor, and they are unchangeably predetermined by God to be so. Such a decision, having been made in eternity past would of course be made without regard to our actions, desires, or choices (since we didn't exist at that point). Is this unspoken assumption supported by Scripture?

To find out the answer, let's look at another passage also written by Paul (under the inspiration of the Holy Spirit):

> II Timothy 2:19–21: Nevertheless the foundation of God standeth sure, having this seal, The Lord knoweth them that are his. And, Let every one that nameth the name of Christ **depart from iniquity.** ²⁰But in a great house there are not only **vessels** of gold and of silver, but also of wood and of earth; and **some to honour, and some to dishonour.** ²¹**If a man therefore purge himself** from these, **he shall be a vessel unto honour,** sanctified, and meet for the master's use, and prepared unto every good work.

> AMP: But the firm foundation of (laid by) God stands, sure and unshaken, bearing this seal (inscription): The Lord knows those who are His, and, Let everyone who names [himself by] the name of the Lord **give up all iniquity** and stand aloof from it. ²⁰But in a great house there are not only **vessels** of gold and silver, but also [utensils] of wood and earthenware, and **some for honorable and noble [use] and some for menial and ignoble [use].** ²¹So **whoever cleanses himself** [from what is ignoble and unclean, who separates himself from contact with contaminating and corrupting influences] **will [then himself] be a vessel set apart and useful for honorable and noble**

purposes, consecrated and profitable to the Master, fit and ready for any good work.

Wow, that's certainly enlightening. The context is Paul telling Timothy that every Christian should stop sinning (for much more detail, see Book 2: *Is It Possible to Stop Sinning?*). Paul then acknowledges that there exist both vessels to honor and other vessels to dishonor. *But he doesn't leave it at that.*

Paul doesn't leave the reader hanging, with the impression of "If you're a vessel unto dishonor, too bad for you. There's nothing you can do about it." On the contrary, Paul goes on to point out that if a man "cleanses himself" or "purges himself" of sin, he will be a vessel unto honor. This concept is very important; note how other translations render v. 21:

CEB: So if anyone **washes filth off** themselves. . .

CJB: If a person **keeps himself free of defilement.** . .

CEV: The ones who **stop doing evil** and **make themselves pure.** . .

ERV: . . .**make yourself clean from all evil.**

ESV: Therefore, if anyone **cleanses himself from what is dishonorable.** . .

HCSB: So if anyone **purifies himself** from anything dishonorable. . .

PHILLIPS: If a man **keeps himself clean** from the contaminations of evil. . .

TLB: If you **stay away from sin.** . .

NCV: All who **make themselves clean from evil.** . .

NLT: If you **keep yourself pure.** . .

RSV: If any one **purifies himself** from what is ignoble. . .

VOICE: So tell them, if they will **clean up their lives.** . .

Fascinating. We can see from the Scripture above that it is *our* choice whether we are a vessel of honor or a vessel of dishonor. Note again that v. 21 says, "if a man cleanse *himself.* . ."

But we *can't* clean ourselves up; we need the forgiveness made available by Jesus' death on the cross, right? Of course. But since He made forgiveness and salvation available to everybody (refer back to the sections "Does God Want Everyone to be Saved?" and "God Is Not a Respecter of Persons" for relevant Scriptures), once we accept/receive Him, He forgives our past sins. And, since He told us to repent in the first place, we know that He has given us the power to obey Him (otherwise He would be unjust, as described in the section

"Is God Just?"). So it is up to us to actually employ in our lives what He has made available. Will we love Him and be faithful to obey Him? Even in this Scripture where it says we are to cleanse ourselves?

And just in case there is still any question whether we actually can do such a thing as clean ourselves up (using the power God has given us, of course), Paul's letter to the church at Ephesus confirms the same idea:

> Ephesians 4:22–24 (AMP): **Strip yourselves of your former nature** [put off and discard your old unrenewed self] which characterized your previous manner of life and becomes corrupt through lusts and desires that spring from delusion; [23]And **be constantly renewed** in the spirit of your mind [having a fresh mental and spiritual attitude], [24]And **put on the new nature (the regenerate self) created in God's image,** [Godlike] in true righteousness and holiness.
>
> NIV: You were taught, with regard to your former way of life, to **put off your old self,** which is being corrupted by its deceitful desires; [23]to be made new in the attitude of your minds; [24]and to **put on the new self,** created to be like God in true righteousness and holiness.

So if we clean up our lives by obeying Him, we will be set apart, useful, and suitable for God to use us. That is, we will be vessels unto honor. And if we do clean ourselves up in the way II Timothy 2:19–21 and Ephesians 4:22–24 command us, He *will* choose us for His use, as He did King David:

> I Kings 11:34: Howbeit I will not take the whole kingdom out of his [Solomon's] hand: but I will make him prince all the days of his life for David my servant's sake, whom **I chose, because he kept my commandments and my statutes...**

It's kinda hard to argue with when God Himself says He chose David "*because* he kept my commandments and my statutes..."

...Vessels of Wrath Fitted to Destruction...

At the end of Paul's discussion of vessels unto honor or dishonor, there is a verse that says:

> Romans 9:22–23: What if God, willing to shew his wrath, and to make his power known, endured with much longsuffering the vessels of wrath fitted to destruction: [23]And that he might make known the riches of his glory on the vessels of mercy, which he had afore prepared unto glory...

Teachings and books supporting Reformed theology claim that the above verses prove that God chooses some people to be vessels of wrath, "fitted" (predestined) to destruction, and other people to be vessels of mercy, "prepared" (predestined) for glory. Is that a supportable interpretation?

As we saw at the beginning of this whole section on Romans 9–11, the plain, surface meaning and context of this passage is God's dealings with Israel as the people through which the Gospel would come to the Gentiles. And throughout the Old Testament, we see that God severely punished people for rebelling against Him, and blessed and had mercy on those who obeyed Him. So the fact that vv. 22–23 refers to Israel is confirmed basically *everywhere* in the Old Testament. But how about the extended meaning, applying to individuals? Does the Reformed interpretation hold water?

Here is a classic case of strategically picking verses from strategically picked Bible version(s) that seem to support a theory, while ignoring large bodies of Scripture that say otherwise. Let's look at some other translations to see what other translators consider this passage to say, and see if it still supports the Reformed theology as well as some think it does. Let's cover v. 22 first:

> Romans 9:22 (CJB): Now what if God, even though he was quite willing to demonstrate his anger and make known his power, **patiently put up with people who deserved punishment and were ripe for destruction?**
>
> CEV: God wanted to show his anger and reveal his power against **everyone who deserved to be destroyed.** But instead, he patiently put up with them.
>
> GWORD: If God wants to demonstrate his anger and reveal his power, he can do it. But can't he be extremely patient with people who are objects of his anger because **they are headed for destruction?**
>
> PHILLIPS: May it not be that God, though he must sooner or later expose his wrath against sin and show his controlling hand, has yet most patiently endured **the presence in his world of things that cry out to be destroyed?**
>
> TLB: Does not God have a perfect right to show his fury and power against **those who are fit only for destruction,** those he has been patient with for all this time?

So we can see that phrases like "fitted to destruction," "prepared for destruction," and "made for destruction," while they *can* be interpreted in isolation as meaning "God's perfect and unchangeable will is that they burn forever," can also be interpreted as meaning the natural result of "you reap what you sow." And this latter interpretation fits *so* much better with the mountains of relevant Scriptures in the Bible, many of which have been already mentioned in this book. Such as those in "Does God Want Everyone to be Saved?" and "God is Not a Respecter of Persons," above.

In other words, "fitted to destruction" and similar phrases do not mean "I have unchangeably predestined some people for the sole purpose of burning in hell." We can see, both from the other translations above, as well as the quantities of Scriptures already mentioned, that it would have to mean, "I have predestined that everyone who chooses to rebel against Me will be destroyed." That is, we reap what we sow. And we have seen very clearly that the decision of whether or not we rebel against God *is ours alone*.

Now let's look at v. 23:

Romans 9:23: And that he might make known the riches of his glory on the vessels of mercy, which **he had afore prepared unto glory**. . .

EXB: He waited with patience so that **he could make known his rich glory** [the riches of his glory] **to the people who receive his** [vessels/objects of] **mercy**. He has prepared these people to have his glory [to experience his glory; for glory]. . .

ICB: God waited with patience so that he could make known his rich glory. **He wanted to give that glory to the people who receive his mercy**. He has prepared these people to have his glory. . .

PHILLIPS: Can we not see, in this, his purpose in demonstrating the boundless resources of his glory **upon those whom he considers fit** to receive his mercy, and whom he long ago planned to raise to glorious life?

NCV: He waited with patience so that he could make known his rich glory **to the people who receive his mercy.** He has prepared these people to have his glory. . .

And so forth. Note in the above translations, it refers to God giving His glory to those who *receive his mercy*. We know because of the Scriptures in "Does God Want Everyone to be Saved?" and "God is Not a Respecter of Persons," that it is not God's way to play favorites, and we know from the Scriptures in "A Gift is Something You Receive" that God's offer of salvation must be *received* in order for it to be of any benefit to us.

In reading the Phillips translation above, we must keep in mind that *no one* is "fit" to receive God's mercy in himself, but everyone who accepts Jesus' offer of salvation by faith *is* fit to receive God's mercy. And remember Romans 11:32, which states the number of people upon whom God has mercy:

> Romans 11:32: For God hath concluded them all in unbelief, **that he might have mercy upon** ***all***.

The Founders of Reformed Theology

There are many people who have contributed to creating and shaping Reformed theology, but the two most prominent were Martin Luther (1483–1546) and of course, John Calvin (1509–1564), after whom the Five Points of Calvinism were named. Both of these gentlemen were very heavily influenced by the teachings of Augustine.

With Romans 9–11 being quoted so often in support of Reformed theology, with apparently little or no regard for the plain, surface meaning of the passage—that God was not done with Israel and had not rejected them or broken His covenant with them—it is amazing to me that both Calvin and Luther were openly and vocally anti-semitic.

Calvin bluntly stated that the Jews are a rejected people.[5] He once wrote, "I have had much conversation with many Jews: I have never seen either a drop of piety or a grain of truth or ingenuousness—nay, I have never found common sense in any Jew."[6]

Luther was even more hostile and vituperative toward the Jews, and wrote a 65,000-word treatise entitled *On the Jews and Their Lies,* the cover of which is shown at right. Some quotes from this treatise—an abbreviated list—is shown below:

- "Therefore the blind Jews are truly stupid fools. . ."
- "Now just behold these miserable, blind, and senseless people. . . their blindness and arrogance are as solid as an iron mountain."

---

[5] Pak, G. Sojin. *John Calvin and the Jews: His Exegetical Legacy.* Reformed Institute of Metropolitan Washington, 2009, p. 25.

[6] Calvin's commentary of Daniel 2:44–45, translated by Myers, Thomas. *Calvin's Commentaries.* Grand Rapids, Michigan: Eerdmans, 1948, quoted in Lange van Ravenswaay 2009, p. 146.

- "I had made up my mind to write no more either about the Jews or against them. But since I learned that these miserable and accursed people do not cease to lure to themselves even us, that is, the Christians, I have published this little book, so that I might be found among those who opposed such poisonous activities of the Jews who warned the Christians to be on their guard against them. I would not have believed that a Christian could be duped by the Jews into taking their exile and wretchedness upon himself. However, the devil is the god of the world, and wherever God's word is absent he has an easy task, not only with the weak but also with the strong. May God help us. Amen."

- "Learn from this, dear Christian, what you are doing if you permit the blind Jews to mislead you. Then the saying will truly apply, 'When a blind man leads a blind man, both will fall into the pit' [cf. Luke 6:39]. You cannot learn anything from them except how to misunderstand the divine commandments. . ."

- "Therefore be on your guard against the Jews, knowing that wherever they have their synagogues, nothing is found but a den of devils in which sheer self-glory, conceit, lies, blasphemy, and defaming of God and men are practiced most maliciously and veheming his eyes on them."

- "Moreover, they are nothing but thieves and robbers who daily eat no morsel and wear no thread of clothing which they have not stolen and pilfered from us by means of their accursed usury. Thus they live from day to day, together with wife and child, by theft and robbery, as archthieves and robbers, in the most impenitent security."

- "If I had to refute all the other articles of the Jewish faith, I should be obliged to write against them as much and for as long a time as they have used for inventing their lies—that is, longer than two thousand years."

- "Did I not tell you earlier that a Jew is such a noble, precious jewel that God and all the angels dance when he farts?"

- "Alas, it cannot be anything but the terrible wrath of God which permits anyone to sink into such abysmal, devilish, hellish, insane baseness, envy, and arrogance. If I were to avenge myself on the devil himself I should be unable to wish him such evil and misfortune as God's wrath inflicts on the Jews, compelling them to lie and to blaspheme so monstrously, in violation of their own conscience. Anyway, they have their reward for constantly giving God the lie."

- ". . .but then eject them forever from this country. For, as we have heard, God's anger with them is so intense that gentle mercy will only tend to make them worse and worse, while sharp mercy will reform them but little. Therefore, in any case, away with them!"

- "Over and above that we let them get rich on our sweat and blood, while we remain poor and they suck the marrow from our bones."

- "I brief, dear princes and lords, those of you who have Jews under your rule—if my counsel does not please you, find better advice, so that you and we all can be rid of the unbearable, devilish burden of the Jews, lest we become guilty sharers before God in the lies, blasphemy, the defamation, and the curses which the mad Jews indulge in so freely and wantonly against the person of our Lord Jesus Christ, this dear mother, all Christians, all authority, and ourselves. Do not grant them protection, safeconduct, or communion with us. . . . With this faithful counsel and warning I wish to cleanse and exonerate my conscience."

- "However, we must avoid confirming them in their wanton lying, slandering, cursing, and defaming. Nor dare we make ourselves partners in their devilish ranting and raving by shielding and protecting them, by giving them food, drink, and shelter. . ."

- "What shall we Christians do with this rejected and condemned people, the Jews? Since they live among us, we dare not tolerate their conduct, now that we are aware of their lying and reviling and blaspheming. If we do, we become sharers in their lies, cursing and blasphemy. Thus we cannot extinguish the unquenchable fire of divine wrath, of which the prophets speak, nor can we convert the Jews. With prayer and the fear of God we must practice a sharp mercy to see whether we might save at least a few from the glowing flames. We dare not avenge ourselves. Vengeance a thousand times worse than we could wish them already has them by the throat. I shall give you my sincere advice:"

    1. "First to set fire to their synagogues or schools and to bury and cover with dirt whatever will not burn, so that no man will ever again see a stone or cinder of them. This is to be done in honor of our Lord and of Christendom, so that God might see that we are Christians, and do not condone or knowingly tolerate such

CHAPTER 10: MISCELLANEOUS TOPICS

public lying, cursing, and blaspheming of his Son and of his Christians. For whatever we tolerated in the past unknowingly—and I myself was unaware of it—will be pardoned by God. But if we, now that we are informed, were to protect and shield such a house for the Jews, existing right before our very nose, in which they lie about, blaspheme, curse, vilify, and defame Christ and us (as was heard above), it would be the same as if we were doing all this and even worse ourselves, as we very well know."

2. "Second, I advise that their houses also be razed and destroyed. For they pursue in them the same aims as in their synagogues. Instead they might be lodged under a roof or in a barn, like the gypsies. This will bring home to them that they are not masters in our country, as they boast, but that they are living in exile and in captivity, as they incessantly wail and lament about us before God."

3. "Third, I advise that all their prayer books and Talmudic writings, in which such idolatry, lies, cursing and blasphemy are taught, be taken from them. . ."

4. "Fourth, I advise that their rabbis be forbidden to teach henceforth on pain of loss of life and limb. For they have justly forfeited the right to such an office by holding the poor Jews captive with the saying of Moses (Deuteronomy 17 [:10 ff.]) in which he commands them to obey their teachers on penalty of death, although Moses clearly adds: 'what they teach you in accord with the law of the Lord.' Those villains ignore that. They wantonly employ the poor people's obedience contrary to the law of the Lord and infuse them with this poison, cursing, and blasphemy. In the same way the pope also held us captive with the declaration in Matthew 16 [:18], 'You are Peter,' etc., inducing us to believe all the lies and deceptions that issued from his devilish mind. He did not teach in accord with the word of God, and therefore he forfeited the right to teach."

5. "Fifth, I advise that safe-conduct on the highways be abolished completely for the Jews. For they have no business in the countryside, since they are not lords, officials, tradesmen, or the like. Let them stay at home. . ."

6. "Sixth, I advise that usury be prohibited to them, and that all cash and treasure of silver and gold be taken from them and put aside for safekeeping. The reason for such a measure is that, as

513

said above, they have no other means of earning a livelihood than usury, and by it they have stolen and robbed from us all they possess. Such money should now be used in no other way than the following: Whenever a Jew is sincerely converted, he should be handed one hundred, two hundred, or three hundred florins, as personal circumstances may suggest. With this he could set himself up in some occupation for the support of his poor wife and children, and the maintenance of the old or feeble. For such evil gains are cursed if they are not put to use with God's blessing in a good and worthy cause."

7. "Seventh, I commend putting a flail, an ax, a hoe, a spade, a distaff, or a spindle into the hands of young, strong Jews and Jewesses and letting them earn their bread in the sweat of their brow, as was imposed on the children of Adam (Gen 3[:19]). For it is not fitting that they should let us accursed Goyim toil in the sweat of our faces while they, the holy people, idle away their time behind the stove, feasting and farting, and on top of all, boasting blasphemously of their lordship over the Christians by means of our sweat. No, one should toss out these lazy rogues by the seat of their pants."

- "Accordingly, it must and dare not be considered a trifling matter but a most serious one to seek counsel against this and to save our souls from the Jews, that is, from the devil and from eternal death. My advice, as I said earlier, is: First, that their synagogues be burned down, and that all who are able toss in sulphur and pitch; it would be good if someone could also throw in some hellfire. That would demonstrate to God our serious resolve and be evidence to all the world that it was in ignorance that we tolerated such houses, in which the Jews have reviled God, our dear Creator and Father, and his Son most shamefully up till now but that we have now given them their due reward."

- "I wish and I ask that our rulers who have Jewish subjects exercise a sharp mercy toward these wretched people, as suggested above, to see whether this might not help (though it is doubtful). They must act like a good physician who, when gangrene has set in, proceeds without mercy to cut, saw, and burn flesh, veins, bone, and marrow. Such a procedure must also be followed in this instance. Burn down their synagogues, forbid all that I enumerated earlier, force them to work, and deal harshly with them, as Moses did in the wilderness, slaying three thousand lest the whole people perish. They surely do not know

CHAPTER 10: MISCELLANEOUS TOPICS

what they are doing; moreover, as people possessed, they do not wish to know it, hear it, or learn it. There it would be wrong to be merciful and confirm them in their conduct. If this does not help we must drive them out like mad dogs, so that we do not become partakers of their abominable blasphemy and all their other vices and thus merit God's wrath and be damned with them. I have done my duty. Now let everyone see to his. I am exonerated."

- "My essay, I hope, will furnish a Christian (who in any case has no desire to become a Jew) with enough material not only to defend himself against the blind, venomous Jews, but also to become the foe of the Jews' malice, lying, and cursing, and to understand not only that their belief is false but that they are surely possessed by all devils. May Christ, our dear Lord, convert them mercifully and preserve us steadfastly and immovably in the knowledge of him, which is eternal life. Amen."

And there are many more, but the above excerpts are more than sufficient to get the gist of his meaning. I leave as an exercise to the reader to analyze Luther's tirades above and simply count how many places they violate Scriptural principles, God's character, or Biblical commands. They are numerous.

It's interesting to note that Luther was not always this hostile toward the people of Israel, nor was he originally a proponent of the version of Christianity that later became known as Calvinism. He had an understanding of Christianity that, based on all the Scriptures we've seen in this book, it certainly appears to have all the Biblical support. Let's look at some of the documentation on Luther's early years.

Luther wasn't always a Calvinist; early on, he believed staunchly in free will, as this quote shows:

> Either sin is with you, lying on your shoulders, or it is lying on Christ, the Lamb of God. Now if it is lying on your back, you are lost; but if it is resting on Christ, you are free, and you will be saved. **Now choose what you want.**

Later, Luther wanted to increase his education. His father wanted him to study law, but Martin became a monk instead. And notice *where:*

> "In spite of his father's fury with his decision to become a monk, Martin chose the strictest monastery, the Order of the Augustinian Hermits in Erfurt, Germany."[7]

---

[7] Roberts Liardon, *God's Generals: The Roaring Reformers*, (Whitaker House, New Kensington, PA, 2003), Chapter 3: "Martin Luther", Kindle edition: Location 1258 of 4495.

Free to Choose?

Because he attended a strict Augustinian monastery, Luther was exposed to Augustine's Gnostic influences, and that is likely where his "conversion" toward what would become Calvinism began. At first, Luther himself acknowledged the incongruity of God's choosing for people where they would spend eternity, regardless of those people's actions or choices:

> "Later on, he *[Luther's mentor Johann von Staupitz]* spoke of the despair Luther felt at the time, saying, '**Is it not against all natural reason that God out of his mere whim deserts men, hardens them, damns them, as if He delighted in sins and in such torments of the wretched for eternity,** He who is said to be of such mercy and goodness? **This appears iniquitous, cruel, and intolerable in God, by which very many have been offended in all ages. And who would not be?** I was myself more than once driven to the very abyss of despair so that I wished I had never been created. Love God? I hated Him!'."[8]

Luther "couldn't shake the image of a righteous God **judging unrighteous men when it was impossible for them to be anything else.**"[9]

So reading the above quotes, we can see that Luther was originally solidly in the free-will camp, and understood that in order for God to be just and impartial, He had to judge people according to their own deeds. It was only later, after attending the Augustinian monastery and interacting with John Calvin that things changed. The more his and Calvin's doctrines developed and the Five Points became formalized, the more venomous he became toward the Jews. Is there a correlation? I don't know.

But the fact remains, that *so* rancorous and acrimonious was Luther's treatise against the Jews, that the Nazis displayed *On the Jews and Their Lies* during their Nuremberg rallies. The city of Nuremberg presented a first edition to Julius Streicher, Roman Catholic editor of the Nazi newspaper *Der Stürmer*, and when Streicher first read the treatise in 1937, he, in his newspaper, described it as the most radically anti-semitic tract ever published.[10]

---

[8] Heinrich Boehmer, *Martin Luther: Road to Reformation* (London, England: Meridian Books, Muhlenberg Press, 1957): p. 44, emphasis added.

[9] Roberts Liardon, *God's Generals: The Roaring Reformers*, (Whitaker House, New Kensington, PA, 2003), Chapter 3: "Martin Luther", Kindle edition: Location 1395 of 4495. Emphasis added.

[10] Ellis, Marc H. *Hitler and the Holocaust, Christian Anti-Semitism*, Baylor University Center for American and Jewish Studies, Spring 2004, slide 14. Also see Nuremberg Trial Proceedings, Vol. 12, p. 318, Avalon Project, Yale Law School, April 19, 1946.

Understandably, modern Lutheranism has, since the 1980s, renounced and disassociated themselves with Luther's anti-semitic polemics. In November 1998, on the 60th anniversary of Kristallnacht (a coordinated series of attacks on Jews in Germany in November 1938), the Lutheran Church of Bavaria issued a statement: "It is imperative for the Lutheran Church, which knows itself to be indebted to the work and tradition of Martin Luther, to take seriously also his anti-Jewish utterances, to acknowledge their theological function, and to reflect on their consequences. It has to distance itself from every [expression of] anti-Judaism in Lutheran theology."[11]

As I mentioned, the above is a very abbreviated collection of quotes from Luther's book *On the Jews and Their Lies*. When I first discovered this material, while doing research for this book, I was astonished to see his vitriolic hatred and crude invective against the Jews. And both Calvin and Luther bluntly stated that God had rejected the Jews. With all the verses from Romans—especially the ninth, tenth, and eleventh chapters—being used to support Reformed theology, it is amazing that they would have missed the first two verses of chapter 11:

> Romans 11:1–2: I say then, **Hath God cast away his people? God forbid.** For I also am an Israelite, of the seed of Abraham, of the tribe of Benjamin. ²**God hath not cast away his people** which he foreknew. . .
>
> AMP: I ask then: **Has God totally rejected and disowned His people? Of course not!** Why, I myself am an Israelite, a descendant of Abraham, a member of the tribe of Benjamin! ²**No, God has not rejected and disowned His people** [whose destiny] He had marked out and appointed and foreknown from the beginning. . .
>
> CEB: So I ask you, **has God rejected his people? Absolutely not!** I'm an Israelite, a descendant of Abraham, from the tribe of Benjamin. ²**God hasn't rejected his people,** whom he knew in advance. . .
>
> EXB: So I ask: **Did God throw out [cast away; reject] his people? No [Absolutely not; May it never be]!** I myself am an Israelite from the family [descendants; seed] of Abraham, from the tribe of Benjamin. ²**God has not thrown out [cast away; rejected] his people,** whom he chose [or knew] long ago [from the beginning; beforehand]. . .

Are we really supposed to consider "God has rejected the Jews" to be within the range of valid interpretations of "God has *not* rejected the Jews"? Unlikely. Of course, the fact that Calvin and Luther were so wildly wrong

---

[11] *Christians and Jews: A Declaration of the Lutheran Church of Bavaria,* November 24, 1998, also printed in Freiburger Rundbrief, 6:3 (1999), pp. 191–197.

about the Jews, does not mean that they were wrong about everything else. *However,* the fact that they were so wildly wrong about such blunt and clear Scriptural statements, and from a passage on which they base much doctrine, should motivate us to take their doctrinal statements and compare them to the whole body of Scripture to see if they are supported—or contradicted—elsewhere in the Bible. And as we've seen by the multitudes of Scriptures above, it's not looking good for the Reformed doctrines.

As I read the above quotes from Luther, several Scriptures kept coming back to my mind, over and over, one of which was:

> James 3:8–10 (NIV): . . .no man can tame the tongue. **It is a restless evil, full of deadly poison.** [9]With the tongue we praise our Lord and Father, and **with it we curse men**, who have been made in God's likeness. [10]Out of the same mouth come praise and cursing. **My brothers, this should not be.**

Other Scriptures that sprang to mind were James 2:9, I John 2:9–11, 3:15, and 4:20. What makes the ideas put forth in Luther's book so insidious is that they're wrapped up in Christian-sounding rhetoric, references to Jesus and the Bible and all. This gives Christianity a serious black eye, especially since the world intuitively knows that we ought to reflect Jesus' description of His followers:

> Matthew 22:35–39 (NIV): One of them, an expert in the law, tested him with this question: [36]"Teacher, which is the greatest commandment in the Law?" [37]Jesus replied: "'Love the Lord your God with all your heart and with all your soul and with all your mind.' [38]This is the first and greatest commandment. [39]And the second is like it: '**Love your neighbor as yourself.**'"

> John 13:34–35: A new commandment I give unto you, That ye **love one another**; as I have loved you, that ye also love one another. [35]**By this shall all men know that ye are my disciples, if ye have love one to another.**

In spite of their anti-semitism and the creation of a collection of doctrines that have very little Scriptural support, I do not mean to imply that everything these two men did was bad. Martin Luther, especially in his earlier years, did many things that were enormously helpful to the body of Christ in his day: He vociferously (and rightly) disputed the Roman Catholic Church's doctrine that forgiveness could be purchased with money; he taught that salvation is by faith in Jesus; he taught that the Bible is the only valid source of doctrine and practice about God; he translated the Bible into the common language so everyone could read it; he wrote hymns; and more.

Likewise, John Calvin accomplished many things that were of great value to the church of his day, as well as today: He wrote commentaries on most of the books of the Bible; assisted in a popular grassroots rejection of the doctrinal abuses of the Roman Catholic Church, which were common occurrences in that day; he wrote his *Institutes of the Christian Religion*, which contained many good teachings that were more Scripturally supportable than the Five Points were; promoted the idea of justification by faith; and more.

However, in the last 500 years, we have been able to step back and analyze their work in light of centuries more of Biblical study. Like the Bereans, who "searched the scriptures daily, whether those things were so" (Acts 17:10–11), Paul's injunction commands us to do the same:

I Thessalonians 5:21 (NIV): **Test everything.** Hold on to the good.

In more modern terminology, this simply says, "Eat the hay, and spit out the sticks." Good advice.

No teacher in the history of this planet, with the exception of Jesus Himself, has been 100% correct in all his statements. So it is with no malice or sense of superiority that I have analyzed the Reformed doctrines in light of many, many Scriptures. And neither should you uncritically accept *my* teaching without doing a similar analysis. If you still are undecided on the question of the validity of Reformed theology, reread the Scriptures I've covered in this book, and see if each one supports, is unrelated to, or refutes one or more of Reformed theology's principal doctrines.

"Draw" = "Compel?"

One of Jesus' statements about coming to God is as follows:

John 6:44 (TEV): People cannot come to me unless the Father who sent me **draws them to me;** and I will raise them to life on the last day.

The image communicated by this verse is that the Father woos us, romances us, courts us, as does the bridegroom in the Song of Solomon. But some adherents to Reformed theology disagree and, in support of Irresistible Grace, claim that the Greek word ἑλκύω (*helkuo*, G1670) translated "draw" in this verse, is much more forceful than "wooing" suggests.

FREE TO CHOOSE?

To support that idea, verses like these are quoted:

Acts 16:19: And when her masters saw that the hope of their gains was gone, they caught Paul and Silas, and **drew** them into the marketplace unto the rulers. . .

Acts 21:30: And all the city was moved, and the people ran together: and they took Paul, and **drew** him out of the temple: and forthwith the doors were shut.

In the Scriptures above, "draw" or "drew" comes from the same Greek root: *helkuo*, and the conclusion is reached, "See? They didn't 'woo' Paul and Silas to the marketplace; they didn't 'woo' Paul out of the temple. They *compelled* them; they *dragged* them. That's what God does for us in Unconditional Election and Irresistible Grace, since we can't respond to Him because of Total Depravity."

Granted, that Greek word *can* mean "compel" or "drag," but is it reasonable to assume that it *always* means that? Or that it *must* mean that? I don't think so, and here's why. That same Greek word *helkuo* is used when Jesus said:

John 12:32–33: And I, if I be lifted up from the earth, will **draw** all men unto me. ³³This he said, signifying what death he should die.

If *helkuo* meant "drag" or "compel" *in every case*, we would have to conclude that Jesus was saying everybody in the history of the planet would get saved and end up in heaven. Such universalism, where *everybody* is ultimately saved, is completely refuted by Scripture, as shown in the section "Do All People Get Saved?" above. So here is another example of *reductio ad absurdum*: if we assume that *helkuo* means "compel" or "drag" *in every case*, we are driven to absurd conclusions.

But are there any other Scriptures that talk about God "drawing" us in a way that implies a loving, wooing, courting way? Or is it the irresistible, dragging, compulsive way? Read these next verses and decide for yourself.

Song of Solomon 1:2–4 (AMP): Let him kiss me with the kisses of his mouth! [she cries. Then, realizing that Solomon has arrived and has heard her speech, she turns to him and adds] For your love is better than wine! ³[And she continues] The odor of your ointments is fragrant; your name is like perfume poured out. Therefore do the maidens love you. ⁴**Draw me! We will run after you!** The king brings me into his apartments! We will be glad and rejoice in you! We will recall [when we were favored with] your love, more fragrant than wine. The upright [are not offended at your choice, but sincerely] love you.

Here in v. 4, the Shulammite woman (Solomon's wife and lover, who symbolizes the Bride of Christ) calls out to Solomon (the King, who symbolizes Christ), "Draw me!" In a passionate love relationship, does this sound like the under-compulsion, dragging usage? Or the courting, wooing usage? Also note that she says, "We will run after you!"—clearly indicating the use of her own free will in pursuing the King.

Then in chapter 8, we find this:

Song 8:5a: Who is this that cometh up from the wilderness, **leaning upon her beloved?**

> CEB: Who is this coming up from the wilderness **leaning against her lover?**
>
> CJB: Who is this, coming up from the desert, **leaning on her darling?**
>
> CEV: Who is this young woman coming in from the desert and **leaning on the shoulder of the one she loves?**
>
> GWORD: Who is this young woman coming from the wilderness **with her arm around her beloved?**
>
> GNT: Who is this coming from the desert, **arm in arm with her lover?**
>
> NIRV: Who is this woman coming up from the desert? **She's leaning on the one who loves her.**

Does this sound to you like she was coming with him because she was being required to or "compelled" to? Or was "irresistibly caused" to come with him? Or could it possibly be that she is with him because. . . oh, I don't know, maybe. . . she *loves* him?

And compare this passage too:

Jeremiah 31:3 (NASB): The LORD appeared to him *[Israel]* from afar, saying, "I have loved you with an everlasting love; therefore I have **drawn you with lovingkindness.**"

That sounds to me more like the loving, wooing, courting way. And look at this one, talking about how God will bring His people back to Him:

Hosea 2:14: Therefore, behold, **I will allure her,** and bring her into the wilderness, and **speak comfortably unto her.**

> CEB: Therefore, **I will charm her,** and bring her into the desert, and **speak tenderly to her heart.**

ERV: So **I, the Lord, will speak romantic words to her.** I will lead her into the desert and **speak tender words.**

EXB: So **I am going to attract [allure; woo] her;** I will lead her into the desert [wilderness; as in the Exodus, when God rescued Israel from slavery and cared for her; Ex. 12–17] and **speak tenderly to her.**

HCSB: Therefore, **I am going to persuade her,** lead her to the wilderness, and **speak tenderly to her.**

ICB: So **I am going to attract her.** I will lead her into the desert and **speak tenderly to her.**

JUB: Therefore, behold, **I will induce her** and bring her into the wilderness and **speak unto her heart.**

TLB: But **I will court her again** and bring her into the wilderness, and I will **speak to her tenderly there.**

MSG: And now, here's what I'm going to do: I'm going to start all over again. I'm taking her back out into the wilderness where we had our first date, and **I'll court her.**

VOICE: . . . **I'll entice her** and lead her out into the wilderness where we can be alone, and **I'll speak right to her heart and try to win her back.**

This too sounds to me more like the wooing, courting way. Especially since the Bible uses words like "woo" and "court." Now seriously: with verbs like "allure," "charm," "attract," "woo," "persuade," "induce," "court," and "entice," can anyone really interpret God as "compelling" her or "irresistibly causing" her to be with Him? With words and phrases like "romantic," "comfortably," "tenderly," speaking "to her heart," and "winning her back," can anyone really interpret God as treating her in a forceful manner without regard to her will?

Later in Hosea, God says the following:

Hosea 11:3–5 (TEV): Yet **I was the one who taught Israel to walk. I took my people up in my arms,** but they did not acknowledge that I took care of them. ⁴**I drew them to me with affection and love. I picked them up and held them to my cheek; I bent down to them and fed them.** ⁵They refuse to return to me, and so they must return to Egypt, and Assyria will rule them.

Again, does this sound like coercion? Or alluring?

It has been said—and I think it's true—that a lot of Biblical misinterpretations could be avoided by simply realizing that God is madly, passionately in love with humanity. And here is one of those cases.

I Have Chosen You. . .

Another verse often quoted by adherents to Reformed theology is this one:

John 15:16a: Ye have not chosen me, but I have chosen you. . .

"See?" some will say, "*We* don't 'choose' to come to Christ, *He* chooses *us!*" Let's look into it a little deeper and see if that's a reasonable interpretation of this verse.

The "Efficiency" of a Theory

In science, theology, mathematics, nutrition, economics—indeed, in *any* field of study, as we investigate, we tend to develop theories to explain how we think things work. Then, if we are reputable researchers, we test our theories to see if they accurately predict what they are supposed to predict, or they accurately explain what we actually observe. And this approach is good; it helps us learn.

But as we all know, some theories are better than others. And that brings up a good question: How do we *measure* theories to see which ones are better and which ones are worse? Or, which ones are more accurate and which ones are less accurate?

One way is to measure the "efficiency" of the theories and compare the results. One way to test the efficiency of a theory would be to count the number of assumptions you have to make, and also count the number of real-world observations that your theory explains (or accurately predicts). Divide the number of things explained (or accurately predicted) by the number of assumptions made, and that will give you a rough estimate of the efficiency of the theory.

For example, if your theory explains only three real-world observations, but it required fifteen assumptions to be made, its efficiency is only 0.2—not very good. But if your theory explains 25 real-world observations, and it required only two assumptions, its efficiency is 12.5—a *much* better score, and a much better theory.

Keep in mind that just because something is an assumption, that doesn't mean it's not true. It *could* be true, but we don't know. Still, our theory depends on it, so we have to take it into account. So before even addressing how many things our theory explains/predicts, it would be a good idea to examine our assumptions and see if they are valid.

Back to Choosing. . .

So let's get back to the Scripture we're analyzing:

John 15:16a: Ye have not chosen me, but I have chosen you. . .

Are there any assumptions made in the Reformed interpretation of this verse? Actually, there are. For this verse to be helpful in supporting the Reformed doctrines of Unconditional Election and/or Limited Atonement, there are some assumptions that must be made:

1. The kind of "choosing" Jesus was referring to was the unchangeable eternity-past decision of God to save some (the "elect") and damn others (the "unelect"). After all, there are many things people could be chosen for; which one was Jesus talking about?

2. Any "choosing" on the part of the disciples is either impossible or irrelevant, since the decision of election was made for them in eternity past.

Let's look at Assumption #1 and see if it's reasonable. First, as we've seen, we can avoid many grievous errors if we simply read the passage in context. So, does the context give us any light on the subject? Yes. We see that Jesus is talking to the disciples about Him being the Vine and we are the branches, and close to the beginning of this passage, He tells the disciples:

John 15:4a: Abide in me. . .
   AMP: Dwell in Me. . .
   CEB: Remain in me. . .
   CJB: Stay united with me. . .
   CEV: Stay joined to me. . .
   GNT: Remain united to me. . .
   TLB: Take care to live in me. . .
   NIRV: Remain joined to me. . .

Hmm. This is already curious, perhaps even to the point of raising the proverbial "red flag" in our minds. If the Reformed doctrines of Unconditional Election and the Perseverance of the Saints were valid, why would Jesus enjoin the disciples to "abide" or "remain" or "stay" with Him? If Unconditional Election and Perseverance of the Saints were valid, it would be impossible for them to do otherwise, so what's the point of His command? Curious.

But let's put that question on the back burner for a moment and continue reading.

A few verses later, in v. 7, Jesus says:

John 15:7: **If** ye abide in me, and my words abide in you, ye shall ask what ye will, and it shall be done unto you.

Here's another curiosity: Why in the world would Jesus say, "*If* you abide in Me. . ." since the Reformed doctrine of Perseverance of the Saints claims that it is impossible to do otherwise? Now it's definitely a red flag.

Then in v. 10:

John 15:10: **If** ye keep my commandments, ye shall abide in my love; even as I have kept my Father's commandments, and abide in his love.

Again, why would Jesus say "If" here, since the Reformed idea of God's sovereignty has Him controlling absolutely everything? It's a pointless command, if God makes all the decisions. Then in v. 14:

John 15:14: Ye are my friends, **if** ye do whatsoever I command you.

This verse is a double whammy, because it brings up yet again the question brought up by vv. 4, 7, and 10 above. But not only that, it gives a condition for being a friend of Jesus, and that condition *indicates the direction of causality.* It says, in a nutshell, "If you obey Me, you are My friends." In other words, obedience to Christ causes us to become His friends; *not* the other way around. Note that it does *not* say, "If I make you My friends, you will be able to obey Me." This latter rendition (that v. 14 does *not* indicate) is in accordance with, and *essential* to, the Reformed doctrines of Total Depravity and Unconditional Election. But it's interesting to observe that the Bible says the causality goes the opposite direction.

Finally, in v. 16, we get to the point where Jesus says to the disciples, "Ye have not chosen me, but I have chosen you." At this point, it's already difficult to believe that Jesus is talking about "choosing" in the Calvinistic sense, because four different statements Jesus just made would have to be ignored, or judged to be pointless, if the Five Points of Calvinism were valid. But let's look at the whole verse from which the above snippet is taken:

John 15:16 (NIV): You did not choose me, but I chose you and appointed you to go and bear fruit—fruit that will last. Then the Father will give you whatever you ask in my name.

Wow. When we read the whole verse, it's surprising that there was any question in the first place about what kind of "choosing" Jesus was doing.

FREE TO CHOOSE?

Even without taking into account all the statements above that make no sense or have no point when applied within the Reformed context, just reading the rest of the verse shows that He's clearly not saying He chose them as part of "the elect." Jesus says right there what He chose the disciples for: "to go and bear fruit." And because of Scriptures like Matthew 13:23 and Luke 13:9, we know that what Jesus means by "bearing fruit," in the spiritual sense, is reproducing other Christians; i.e., evangelizing, leading people to Christ, bringing them into the Kingdom. And that in itself is yet another problem for Total Depravity, which claims that "leading" people to Christ or "persuading" them to accept Jesus is impossible, because allegedly we can't respond to God until *after* we're saved.

It sounds like Jesus was saying He chose them to go preach the Good News of the Kingdom, which, if received, results in salvation. But do we have other Scriptures that support this interpretation? It just so happens that we do:

> Matthew 10:1, 5–8: And when he had called unto him his twelve disciples, he gave them power against unclean spirits, to cast them out, and to heal all manner of sickness and all manner of disease. ⁵**These twelve Jesus sent forth,** and commanded them, saying, Go not into the way of the Gentiles, and into any city of the Samaritans enter ye not: ⁶But **go** rather to the lost sheep of the house of Israel. ⁷**And as ye go, preach,** saying, The kingdom of heaven is at hand. ⁸Heal the sick, cleanse the lepers, raise the dead, cast out devils: freely ye have received, freely give.

> Luke 9:1–2: Then he called his twelve disciples together, and gave them power and authority over all devils, and to cure diseases. ²And **he sent them to preach** the kingdom of God, and to heal the sick.

How odd. Why did Jesus send the disciples out to preach when, according to Unconditional Election, preaching couldn't possibly make any difference? But let's look at some other places where Jesus talks about people being chosen:

> Matthew 22:14: For many are called, but few are chosen.
>> AMP: For many are called (invited and summoned), but few are chosen.
>> CEV: Many are invited, but only a few are chosen.
>> MSG: That's what I mean when I say, 'Many get invited; only a few make it.'
>> WE: Many people are asked to come, but only a few are chosen.

This passage is the final verse—the punchline, if you will—of the Parable of the Wedding Feast (Matthew 22:1–14). Jesus said that the Kingdom of heaven is like a king who prepared a wedding banquet for his son, and invited many people, but they refused to come. So the king told his servants to go find as many people as they could find, both good and bad, and invite them to the banquet.

Just in passing, it's interesting to note that Jesus' parable shows that people who are invited *can refuse to come.* This discredits the Reformed doctrine of Irresistible Grace, which says that if and when God calls you, it is impossible to refuse.

But in addition to that, why would only a "few" be chosen, after they were invited? Did God change His mind? Did they get "disinvited" to the banquet? No. Remember what Paul said about the vessels unto honor and vessels unto dishonor? Those who "cleanse themselves" from sin and evil, will be set aside for honorable use, "fit and ready for any good work" (II Timothy 2:21, AMP). God will not choose us for good works if we're not fit for it, and whether we're fit for it or not depends on whether we are diligent enough to cleanse ourselves. Refer back to Vessels Unto Honor for a more complete treatment of this passage.

Another place where Jesus chooses is described in Luke's gospel. It refers to Jesus shortly after His earthly ministry started. Already, He had many disciples, but it was too large a group to pour Himself into on a personal basis. So out of this large number, He chose twelve:

> Luke 6:12–13 (NIV): One of those days Jesus went out to a mountainside to pray, and spent the night praying to God. ¹³When morning came, he called his disciples to him and **chose twelve of them**, whom he also designated apostles. . .

So yes, Jesus "chose" these men, but it is obvious from the context that he was not referring to the sense of election, but only picking the twelve to be His immediate ministry team to teach how the Kingdom of God works. Later on, he again refers to how He called His disciples:

> John 6:70: Jesus answered them, **Have not I chosen you** twelve, and one of you is a devil?

Well, *that's* interesting. If, every time Jesus is described as "choosing" someone, we assume it means election in the Unconditional Election sense, we would have to conclude that Judas Iscariot was ultimately saved, simply because he was chosen. But if Judas were saved, why did Jesus say in Mark 14:21 that it would have been better for Judas if he had never been born?

Clearly, if Judas ended up in heaven, Jesus' statement here would have been completely wrong. So we must conclude that Jesus was not "choosing" the disciples in an Unconditional Election sense.

Still later, right after washing the disciples' feet, Jesus says:

John 13:18: I speak not of you all: **I know whom I have chosen:** but that the scripture may be fulfilled, He that eateth bread with me hath lifted up his heel against me.

Then, shortly after the "I have chosen you" Scripture often used to support Reformed theology, Jesus says:

John 15:19: If ye were of the world, the world would love his own: but because ye are not of the world, but **I have chosen you** out of the world, therefore the world hateth you.

So we can see that it was pretty common for Jesus to talk about how He had chosen the disciples for a variety of reasons. Therefore, if we are to pick one out of the bunch and claim that it supports the Reformed doctrine of Unconditional Election, we'd better have some solid Scriptural backing to support that claim. But as we've seen, solid Scriptural backing is not only very slim, but that Reformed interpretation flies in the face of, or renders pointless, *scores*, perhaps *hundreds*, of Jesus' other statements. And four of them—those shown earlier in this section—were from the very passage from which the alleged "support" was taken!

"Altogether Conceived in Sin"

The doctrine of Original Sin, as we saw above, was a Gnostic doctrine that goes *way* beyond the Biblical teaching that "all have sinned," into the idea that "since we are physical people, and since everything physical is evil, we can't turn to God." Augustine heavily promoted this doctrine—apparently leftover baggage from his Gnostic days—after He got saved out of Gnosticism, and Augustine is one of the main reasons, if not *the* main reason this doctrine really got a foothold in Christianity.

A verse that is often used to support the idea of Original Sin comes from Psalm 51, which David wrote after he repented from his sin with Bathsheba:

Psalm 51:5: Behold, I was shapen in iniquity; and **in sin did my mother conceive me.**

Adherents to Reformed theology say, "See? As soon as you're *conceived,* you're sinful!" Well, let's look a little deeper. If we look carefully at the verse above, it does not support the doctrine of Original Sin and its logical result,

CHAPTER *10*: MISCELLANEOUS TOPICS

Total Depravity, in the sense that "we are so corrupted that we cannot choose God." Read it again; all David is saying is that he was a sinner from way back, and/or that his mother was a sinner when he was conceived. Paul confirms this:

> Romans 5:12 (AMP): Therefore, as **sin came into the world** through one man, and death as the result of sin, so death spread to all men, [no one being able to stop it or to escape its power] because **all men sinned.**

So the fact that all humanity tends to be sinful is nothing new. (For much detail on whether we are bound to *continue* in sin even after we turn to the Lord, see Book 2: *Is It Possible to Stop Sinning?*) And it might be dangerous to Reformed theology to have people read Psalm 51 too much, because v. 11 quotes David praying that God would not do something which, if Reformed theology is correct, could not occur anyway:

> Psalm 51:11 (AMP): **Cast me not away from Your presence** and take not Your Holy Spirit from me.

If Perseverance of the Saints is true, being cast away from God's presence would be impossible, so why would David have prayed this? Then in v. 13:

> Psalm 51:13 (NASB): Then **I will teach transgressors Thy ways, and sinners will be converted** to Thee.

This is describing evangelism, where people influence others to turn to God. Which, of course, refutes Unconditional Election. These verses I found simply by reading the context of a verse that supposedly supports Reformed theology. It really is difficult to read the Bible for more than a few minutes without finding Scriptures that militate against one or more of the Reformed doctrines.

But back to the subject: "conceived in sin." There's something else that is troublesome, and that is the phrase "in sin." What does that mean? Nowadays, if two people are living "in sin," it means they are living together and being sexually active with each other while not being married to each other. Could that be what David was referring to?

Some theologians think David was an illegitimate son of Jesse; that Jesse had had a "fling" with a woman who was not his wife, and the result of that illicit affair was David. Is there any Biblical evidence to support this? Let's pick up the story at the point right after Saul had disobeyed the Lord one too many times...

> I Samuel 16:1 (AMP): The LORD said to Samuel, How long will you mourn for Saul, seeing I have rejected him from reigning over Israel?

Fill your horn with oil; **I will send you to Jesse the Bethlehemite. For I have provided for Myself a king among his sons.**

So Samuel knows that one of Jesse's sons will be the next king, and that he is supposed to go to Bethlehem and anoint him as such. So he does:

> I Samuel 16:4–5 (AMP): And Samuel did what the Lord said, and came to Bethlehem. And the elders of the town trembled at his coming and said, Have you come peaceably? ⁵And he said, Peaceably; I have come to sacrifice to the Lord. Consecrate yourselves and come with me to the sacrifice. And **he consecrated Jesse and his sons and called them to the sacrifice.**

Note what happened here: Samuel consecrated Jesse and his sons, and called them to the sacrifice. But something is fishy: *why was David excluded?* David was not included with the rest of Jesse's sons when they were consecrated, and then when they were called to go to the location where the sacrifice was being made, again, *David was not included.* Why not? Why was he being treated like a second-class citizen?

> I Samuel 16:6–10 (AMP): When they had come, he looked on **Eliab** [the eldest son] and said, Surely the Lord's anointed is before Him. ⁷But the Lord said to Samuel, Look not on his appearance or at the height of his stature, for I have rejected him. For the Lord sees not as man sees; for man looks on the outward appearance, but the Lord looks on the heart. ⁸Then Jesse called **Abinadab** and made him pass before Samuel. But Samuel said, Neither has the Lord chosen this one. ⁹Then Jesse made **Shammah** pass by. Samuel said, Nor has the Lord chosen him. ¹⁰Jesse made **seven of his sons** pass before Samuel. And Samuel said to Jesse, **The Lord has not chosen any of these.**

Now this is weird. Samuel had consecrated Jesse and his sons, and then called them all to the sacrifice. One by one, they pass before Samuel, and in each case, God says, "Nope. Not this one." Pretty soon, they have *all* passed by, and God had rejected every one. It looks like there's a contradiction going on: God said that the new king of Israel would be one of Jesse's sons, but *every one* of Jesse's sons that just walked by was rejected for the job.

Again, why was David being snubbed? It's not likely that Jesse and all his other sons just suddenly "forgot" that there was another son in the family. But if David was born out of an ungodly relationship between Jesse and some other woman that was not his wife, that would have been a point of embarrassment and shame, and could easily have been reason enough for them to exclude him from "honorable" events such as this.

So Samuel reasons, "Jesse must have another son that he's not showing me for some reason."

> I Samuel 16:11 (NASB): And Samuel said to Jesse, "Are these all the children?" And he said, "There remains yet the youngest, and behold, he is tending the sheep." Then Samuel said to Jesse, "Send and bring him; for we will not sit down until he comes here."

Jesse is busted. His youngest son, David, whom he was apparently trying to keep secret, was now known. "But he was busy keeping the sheep," someone might say. As if David was the only one of Jesse's sons who had a job to do? As if all Jesse's other sons were just sitting around all day eating chocolates and watching soap operas, waiting for Samuel to show up? No, surely all of Jesse's sons were hard at work when word came that Samuel had arrived.

And it was quite an honor to have the Prophet of the Lord show up in your town; remember how the elders of the town "trembled" at his appearing? And then it's even more of an honor to have your family selected to worship with such a prophet and then eat supper with him. You would make every effort to make as good an impression as possible to such an important visitor. And Jesse and his sons simply "forgot" that David was part of the family? That sounds very suspicious. Why would they do such a thing? Was David the proverbial "skeleton in the closet?"

And look at what Samuel said: "Send and bring him; for we will not sit down until he comes here." So David must not have been *that* far away; they weren't even going to sit down until David arrived. It's sounding like they hadn't wanted Samuel to know about him for some reason.

> I Samuel 16:12–13 (NASB): So he sent and brought him in. Now he was ruddy, with beautiful eyes and a handsome appearance. And the LORD said, "Arise, anoint him; for this is he." [13]Then Samuel took the horn of oil and anointed him in the midst of his brothers; and the Spirit of the LORD came mightily upon David from that day forward. And Samuel arose and went to Ramah.

So David was chosen to be King of Israel. God apparently cares less about our parentage than our hearts; remember why God chose David to be king of Israel? I've mentioned this Scripture a couple times already, but it bears repeating:

> I Kings 11:34: Howbeit I will not take the whole kingdom out of his *[Solomon's]* hand: but I will make him prince all the days of his life for **David my servant's sake, whom I chose, because he kept my commandments and my statutes. . .**

We don't know for sure, of course, whether David was actually an illegitimate son of Jesse; I haven't found enough Scriptural evidence to make a firm statement either way. But it would explain the behavior of Jesse and his other sons when Samuel came to town. And it would also explain David's statement in Psalm 51:

> Psalm 51:5: Behold, I was shapen in iniquity; and **in sin did my mother conceive me.**

And here's another interesting thought. Take a look at these two psalms, in which David describes himself as "the son of your handmaid" (or "female servant" or "maidservant"):

> Psalm 86:16: O turn unto me, and have mercy upon me; give thy strength unto thy servant, and save **the son of thine handmaid.**

> Psalm 116:16: O Lord, truly I am thy servant; I am thy servant, and **the son of thine handmaid:** thou hast loosed my bonds.

David's authorship of Psalm 86 is in the text itself. And, although it's not in the text itself of Psalm 116, David's authorship of it is generally acknowledged by Bible scholars.[12] According to the marginal notes of the NET Bible, the phrase "the son of your female servant" is used to describe the son born to a "secondary wife or concubine," and is exemplified in Exodus 23:12. So here in Psalms are two more places where we have evidence that is suggestive (though admittedly not conclusive) that David may not have been the son of Jesse's wife, but was born as a result of a different kind of relationship than the normal marital one.

Here's another oddity:

> Psalm 27:10 (AMP): Although **my father and my mother have forsaken me,** yet the LORD will take me up [adopt me as His child].

> CJB: Even though **my father and mother have left me,** ADONAI will care for me.

> ISV: Though **my father and my mother abandoned me,** the LORD gathers me up.

> VOICE: **My father and mother have deserted me,** yet the ETERNAL will take me in.

With the importance that the Hebrew culture placed on family, it is amazing that David's parents forsook, left him, abandoned, and deserted him! Why would they do such a thing? Could it be that his presence was a constant re-

---

[12] Marilyn Hickey, *Psalms: Classic Library Edition*, 1997, p. 226.

minder of Jesse's fling with another woman? Granted, many other translations render this as merely a potentiality: "*If* my father and mother forsake me. . ." But there is a large number of Bible translations—and hence translation teams—that render this as a historical fact, and not just a hypothetical scenario. The number of translations that do present it as a fact makes it seem like it's a distinct possibility.

An important point is that the sin here is not simply the fact that David's parents were having sex. We know that sexual relations within the context of a man and woman who are married to each other is perfectly acceptable to God. But is it not merely "tolerated" as a necessary evil to bear children; it is *commanded*:

> Genesis 1:27–28a (NIV): So God created man in his own image, in the image of God he created him; male and female he created them. ²⁸God blessed them and said to them, **"Be fruitful and increase in number; fill the earth and subdue it."**

> I Corinthians 7:5 (AMP): **Do not refuse and deprive and defraud each other [of your due marital rights]**, except perhaps by mutual consent for a time, so that you may devote yourselves unhindered to prayer. But **afterwards resume marital relations,** lest Satan tempt you [to sin] through your lack of restraint of sexual desire.

So a man having sex with his wife, and her conceiving, is *not* a sin. When David said what he said in Psalm 51:5, it may indeed have been him stating that his mother was not Jesse's wife, and that's *why* he was conceived in sin. *But even if it doesn't,* this verse, when read for what it actually says, and not reading anything into it, does not support Original Sin.

At this point, some may object to the possibility of David's having been an illegitimate son of Jesse, on the grounds that God would surely not allow such a stain in the genealogy of Jesus. But even without that, Solomon is in the genealogy of Jesus (Matthew 1:6), and we must remember that Solomon was born of Bathsheba, Uriah's wife—the woman David got pregnant and then had her husband killed in an attempt to cover it up (II Samuel 11). Not only that, but Rahab the prostitute (Joshua 2:1–21) is in the genealogy of Jesus as well (Matthew 1:5).

Again, God cares less about our parentage than our hearts. As has been so aptly pointed out by so many, "You can't choose your parents." Much more important to God than *where we've been* is *where we're going.*

"The Just Shall Live by Faith"

As mentioned earlier, Martin Luther and John Calvin were the two most influential architects of the Reformed doctrines. Perhaps the two most far-reaching and profound things that Luther did were, first, translating the Bible into the language of the common people and, second, to raise awareness of the Biblical truth that "the just shall live by faith." This idea was a revelation to many Christians back in the 16th century, for two reasons. First, most people didn't know much of anything about the Bible because the Roman Catholic church kept it "hidden," as it were, by having it only in Latin until Martin Luther translated it into German, the common language of the people. And second, it revealed the error in the Roman Catholic doctrine of "indulgences," which were basically "forgiveness fees" paid to the priests.

As we can see below, this concept must be very important because God put it in the Bible in no less than four different places:

Habakkuk 2:4: Behold, his soul which is lifted up is not upright in him: but the **just shall live by his faith.**

Romans 1:17: For therein is the righteousness of God revealed from faith to faith: as it is written, **The just shall live by faith.**

Galatians 3:11: But that no man is justified by the law in the sight of God, it is evident: for, **The just shall live by faith.**

Hebrews 10:38 Now **the just shall live by faith:** but if any man draw back, my soul shall have no pleasure in him.

I could bring up the idea mentioned earlier about how the word "just" comes from the Greek word *dikaios*, which means "righteous." Thus, these passages are saying that "the righteous live by faith," but then that might bring to mind the Scripture, "There is none righteous; no, not one." But I won't bring that up here. . . (Refer to the section "None Righteous; No, Not One" to see in gory detail how that passage is often taken out of context by adherents of Calvinism.)

So we can see that this idea of "the just shall live by faith" must be important. But the above verses, from the KJV, use archaic words, grammar, and usage, so the full impact and importance of these verses is often missed by people today. Let's look at these verses in translations that use more modern language, so we can more clearly see what God is saying. Specifically, what does "by" mean, in this verse?

AMP: Look at the proud; his soul is not straight or right within him, but **the [rigidly] just and the [uncompromisingly] righteous man shall live *by* his faith and in his faithfulness.**

CJB: Look at the proud: he is inwardly not upright; but **the righteous will attain life *through* trusting faithfulness.**

CEV: "I, the Lord, refuse to accept anyone who is proud. **Only those who live *by* faith are acceptable to me.**"

ERV: This message cannot help those who refuse to listen to it, but **those who are good will live *because* they believe it.**

EXB: [Look; Behold] The evil nation [He] is very proud of itself [puffed up]; it [his soul] is not living as it should [upright]. But **those who are right with God [the righteous] will live *by* faith [or *because* of their faithfulness**; Rom. 1:17; Gal. 3:11; Heb. 10:38].

GWORD: "Look at the proud person. He is not right in himself. But **the righteous person will live *because* of his faithfulness.**"

GNT: And this is the message: 'Those who are evil will not survive, but **those who are righteous will live *because* they are faithful to God.**'

ICB: See, the nation that is evil and trusts in itself will fail. But **those who do right *because* they trust in God will live.**

TLB: Look at that man, bloated by self-importance— full of himself but soul-empty. But **the person in right standing before God *through* loyal and steady believing is fully alive, really alive.**

NOG: Look at the proud person. He is not right in himself. But **the righteous person will live *because of* his faithfulness.**

NABRE: See, the rash have no integrity; but **the just one who is righteous *because of* faith shall live.**

NET: Look, the one whose desires are not upright will faint from exhaustion, but **the person of integrity will live *because of* his faithfulness.**

Now, isn't that interesting! This is Martin Luther's trademark verse; the one about which he received a revelation from God, the one he popularized more than any other, and the one for which he is most famous. But notice the direction of causality shown in the various translations above. We can clearly see that "by" means "because of." As in, "the just (or righteous) shall live *because of* their faith in God and/or faithfulness to God."

535

This is particularly fascinating because this one verse overturns the Reformed doctrine of Unconditional Election, which states that people live because of an immutable choice God made in eternity past, rather than because of their own faithfulness to, or faith in, God's offer of salvation, as this verse states.

Said another way: This Bible verse says that people live *because* they had faith (believed) in God, whereas Reformed theology claims that regeneration precedes faith; that is, "you can believe in God because *you have been already given life.*" This is clearly backwards. (For much more detail, refer back to the section "Regeneration Precedes Faith? Or Vice Versa?")

So Martin Luther's trademark verse contradicts the very doctrines he and John Calvin later developed and promoted. Fascinating.

Speaking of Faith. . .

I have said much in this book about how having faith results in salvation, but faith in what or whom? Jesus, of course. Most Christians would say that with their words, but all too often, a very subtle error creeps in: we *try* to have faith.

But what is wrong with trying to have faith? Aren't we supposed to have faith? Of course we are supposed to have faith, but when we "try" to have faith, we end up "working it up" ourselves, turning faith itself into a work. That is, we start putting *faith in our faith.*

A good way to detect whether we are having faith in Jesus (which is desirable) or faith in our faith (which is not desirable) is to notice if, and how often, we ask ourselves questions such as these: "Do I have enough faith?" "What do I need to do to increase my faith?" "Have I done something recently to damage my faith?" If you often find yourself asking yourself questions such as these, you may have fallen into the very subtle form of idolatry of having faith in your faith, instead of having faith in Jesus.

Faith in Jesus is the effortless realization that *He* did the work of salvation and filling us with the Holy Spirit and empowering us to live a supernatural lifestyle and more, and we merely have to take His word for it. It is the simple acknowledgment that we have nothing to contribute to making our salvation and the other blessings possible: he did it *all*, so we might as well participate. *Can* we refuse to participate? Of course, foolish though it is, but that doesn't change the fact that He has already made it available to all people everywhere, and indeed, He *commands* us to take advantage of it (Acts 17:30).

Ponder these Scriptures and their profound and deep meaning:

Luke 23:34a: Then said Jesus, **Father, forgive them;** for they know not what they do.

Romans 5:18 (NIV): Consequently, just as the result of one trespass was condemnation for all men, so also **the result of one act of righteousness was justification that brings life for** *all men.*

I Corinthians 15:22 (NASB): For as in Adam all die, so also **in Christ** *all* **shall be made alive.**

II Corinthians 5:14–15 (GWORD): Clearly, Christ's love guides us. We are convinced of the fact that **one man has died for** *all* **people.** Therefore, all people have died. ¹⁵He died for all people so that those who live should no longer live for themselves but for the man who died and was brought back to life for them.

II Corinthians 5:19 (NLT): For God was in Christ, **reconciling** *the world* **to himself, no longer counting people's sins against them.** And he gave us this wonderful message of reconciliation.

Colossians 1:21–22 (TEV): At one time you were far away from God and were his enemies because of the evil things you did and thought. ²²But now, by means of the physical death of his Son, **God has made you his friends,** in order to bring you, holy, pure, and faultless, into his presence.

I John 2:2 (WEB): And he is the atoning sacrifice for our sins, and **not for ours only, but also for the** *whole world.*

When we realize that we can't "help" Jesus save us, we can thank Him that *He* did all the heavy lifting and, regardless of our current spiritual state, freely submit ourselves to Him. When we simply follow His direction—when we humble ourselves in the sight of the Lord, when we choose to be doers of the Word and not hearers only, when we choose life over death—life is *so* exciting, and once we see the amazing things He can do, and how much He *likes* to do them, our faith grows more than we would have imagined, *effortlessly,* as an automatic by-product of our obedience. God is so good!

Chapter 11:

What Shall We Say, Then?

So now, after seeing the mountains of Scriptures above, and considering them within their own contexts, what can we conclude?

The Definition of Sovereignty, Take 2

In the section "The Definition of Sovereignty," much earlier in this book, I made this statement: "But there may be an even better idea of sovereignty, and one that squares with Scripture much more compatibly than does the Reformed version." Recall that the first definition of sovereignty we looked at was the one put forth by Reformed theology; basically, "God makes everything happen."

The second one we looked at was what I called a "better idea of sovereignty;" this is the one wherein God is *so* sovereign that He can create beings that truly have free will and not just *think* they have a free will when they were actually "irresistibly caused" by the Holy Spirit to do things.

Now that we've seen all the Scriptures I presented above, did my statement turn out to be true? If you remember, we discovered quite a few problems reconciling the Reformed definition of sovereignty (and hence all of the Five Points of Calvinism as well) with the Bible. Let's look into those problems we discovered along the way, and see if they go away when we use the second definition of sovereignty.

- **God's Justice:** The problem of God's being unjust to command us to do things we had no way of doing, no ability to obey (see "Is God

Just?"). And especially so, if He then punishes us for disobedience when it is impossible for us to do otherwise. This problem goes away with the second definition of sovereignty.

- **God's Wasting of Words:** The problem of God's numerous exhortations for us to behave in a certain way, when our alleged lack of free will would guarantee evil behavior for all the unelect (see "Does God Waste Words?"). Why waste time and space filling the Bible with exhortations if it's not within our ability to obey them? This problem goes away with the second definition of sovereignty.

- **God's Acknowledgement of Free Will:** The problem of reconciling a no-free-will doctrine and the many Scriptures that talk about people using free will is difficult to resolve (see "Free Will Isn't Even Mentioned in the Bible!"). Why does the Bible, in *numerous* cases, casually refer to using our free will if it doesn't exist? This problem goes away with the second definition of sovereignty.

- **God's Love:** The problem of God being the personification of love, while creating people who have no chance of escaping an eternity of torment in hell (see "What Is Love?"). How is that loving? This problem goes away with the second definition of sovereignty.

- **God's Heartcry:** The problem of reconciling God's heartcry for us to repent with His alleged decision to prevent it from ever happening (see "The Cry of God's Heart"). Why would He lament over our lack of repentance if He is preventing it? This problem goes away with the second definition of sovereignty.

- **God's Desire:** The problem of realizing God's desire clearly being that everyone be saved (see "Does God Want Everyone to be Saved?"), but the reality being that not everyone *will* be saved (see "Do All People Get Saved?"), that someone must be *overriding* God if our will is not a factor (see "The Upshot"). This problem goes away with the second definition of sovereignty.

- **The World:** The problem of the Greek word κόσμος (*kosmos*, G2889) meaning "all mankind" along with the numerous Scriptures saying God came to save "the world" (see "The World"). Why would God say that if He intended for only *some* of mankind to be saved? This problem goes away with the second definition of sovereignty.

- **God's Rationality:** The problem of punishing people for sinning when He prevented them from doing otherwise—as rational and sensible as imprisoning a baseball that was used as a murder weapon (see

CHAPTER 11: WHAT SHALL WE SAY, THEN?

"Crime and Punishment"). This problem goes away with the second definition of sovereignty.

- **God's Responding to Us:** The problem of a profusion of Scriptures distinctly showing God responding to people, whether good or bad, when He supposedly is making all choices for everyone (see "When God Takes His Cue From Us"). This problem goes away with the second definition of sovereignty.

- **God's Conditionals:** The problem of God saying in so many places that His blessings on us are conditional—"*If* you do this, I will do that"—which is meaningless if we have no say in the matter of our behavior (see "Conditional Blessing"). This problem goes away with the second definition of sovereignty.

- **Faith Being a Work:** The problem of faith being considered a "work," which is why adherents to Reformed theology reject the idea of "accepting" Christ. But the Bible says that faith is not a work (see "Faith vs. Works"). This problem goes away with the second definition of sovereignty.

- **Faith Preceding Justification:** The problem of justification being required *before* faith (according to Reformed thought), in spite of the immense number of Scriptures clearly saying it's the other way around (see "Regeneration Precedes Faith? Or Vice Versa?"). This problem goes away with the second definition of sovereignty.

- **God's Gifts:** The problem of salvation being called a "gift" if there's no way we can accept the gift (see "Is Salvation a Gift?"). This problem goes away with the second definition of sovereignty.

- **"Receiving" Christ:** The problem of our alleged inability to accept *or* reject Christ, being reconciled with the abundance of Scriptures that give examples of people doing both (see "A Gift is Something You Receive"). This problem goes away with the second definition of sovereignty.

- **God's Respect of Persons:** The problem of God's intrinsic respect of persons (if indeed He decides who gets saved and who doesn't), in spite of the fact that He calls respect of persons a sin (see "God Is Not a Respecter of Persons"). This problem goes away with the second definition of sovereignty.

- **Being "Elect:"** The problem with the Reformed definition of the word "elect," since the Bible also says that angels, Jesus, and even

541

whole nations are "elect" (see "Election"). This problem goes away with the second definition of sovereignty.

- **Predestination:** The problem of "predestination" being defined as "unchangeable, inevitable, set in stone, fated, certain, doomed," and so forth, as required by Reformed theology, but inconsistent with so many pleas from God and His servants calling people to repent (see "Predestination"). This problem goes away with the second definition of sovereignty.

- **The Lamb's Book of Life:** The problem of people's names being removed from the Lamb's Book of Life, when allegedly, that would be impossible (see "The Lamb's Book of Life"). This problem goes away with the second definition of sovereignty.

- **"Limited" Omniscience:** The problem of God, in *many* places, saying things like "maybe," "possibly," "perhaps," "I thought," "they might," and so forth (see "Limited Omniscience"). This problem goes away with the second definition of sovereignty.

- **Evangelism:** The problem of the utter futility of evangelism if, as Reformed theology states, the heaven-or-hell decision has already been made for you (see "Limited Atonement"). This problem goes away with the second definition of sovereignty.

- **Excuses, Excuses:** The problem of Paul saying that people, since God had shown Himself to them, had "no excuse" for rejecting Him, but if Reformed theology is true, the unelect have an *ironclad* excuse: they rejected God because it was impossible for them to do otherwise (see "What's *Your* Excuse?"). This problem goes away with the second definition of sovereignty.

- **Resisting the Holy Spirit:** The problem of Stephen stating that the Jews resisted the Holy Spirit, *many* times, when Reformed doctrine claims it's impossible to do so (see "Resisting the Holy Spirit"). This problem goes away with the second definition of sovereignty.

- **Forsaking God:** The problem of the Bible stating in numerous places that individuals or groups had forsaken Him when Reformed theology claims this is impossible (see "Forsaking"). This problem goes away with the second definition of sovereignty.

- **"I Will Harden Whom I Will. . ."** The problem of Paul's reference to God hardening Pharaoh's heart, when the context shows that Pharaoh hardened his own heart first (see "Pharaoh's Example"). This problem goes away with the second definition of sovereignty.

- **None Righteous:** The problem of using Romans 3:10–11 to support Reformed theology, when the context of both the New Testament argument and the Old Testament passage show that the people-group under discussion was those who reject God (see "None Righteous; No, Not One"). This problem goes away with the second definition of sovereignty.
- **Potter and Clay:** The problem of Paul's reference to the Potter and the Clay being used to support the Reformed doctrine of Unconditional Election, when the context plainly shows that God will change His mind if we do first (see "The Potter and the Clay"). This problem goes away with the second definition of sovereignty.
- **Vessels of Honor:** The problem of using the "vessels of honor" passage to support Reformed theology, when Paul states that when we cleanse ourselves from evil, we will be vessels of honor, so it's *our* decision, not God's, whether we are fit for His use (see "Vessels Unto Honor"). This problem goes away with the second definition of sovereignty.

And there are more. Wow. That is a pretty amazing list of problems that just evaporate when we adopt a definition of "sovereignty" that allows God to be big enough that He could create beings who *actually*, not just *seemingly*, have free will. After looking at the list above, the Reformed view of sovereignty—where God simply "makes everything happen"—seems rather pallid and anemic, and it seems entirely appropriate to expand our idea of God's power, magnificence, and grandeur to something that is much more compatible with the whole of Scripture.

My Surprising Discovery

When I began this book, I was planning on having two parallel chapters close to the front, where one of the chapters would list the Scriptures supporting the free-will viewpoint, and the other chapter giving the Scriptures supporting the Calvinistic viewpoint. After these two chapters that presented the respective viewpoints and their supporting Scriptures, subsequent chapters would compare their claims and analyze them Scripturally.

Once I got into the actual creation of the chapters, I was astonished to realize that, after reading the passages in context and disallowing unsupported presuppositions, I could not find *any* Scriptures that supported the Calvinist viewpoint. I honestly was intending to have the chapter containing Calvinism's supporting Scriptures, but *I actually couldn't find any* when I read them in context and removed assumptions that couldn't be confirmed Scripturally.

This in itself was quite a revelation. I realized that the Scriptures that are used to support Calvinism—specifically, the Five Points of Calvinism—must necessarily be taken only as tiny snippets, removed from their contexts, or presuppositions had to be assumed, which were themselves unsupportable in Scripture, or both, in order to make them supportive of the Calvinistic viewpoint.

Or, as I realized upon more study, to make them *appear* to be supportive of the Calvinistic viewpoint. When the context around the "supporting" passages was read, it became clear that the Scriptures being used to support Calvinism actually didn't. This was demonstrated a great number of times in previous chapters, and the realization was quite startling, but highly revealing.

Both of the situations above occurred repeatedly. In many cases, simply reading a whole passage, instead of the tiny snippet that was initially proffered, revealed a meaning that was completely opposite of what the snippet was being used to "prove." In many other cases, a passage could be construed as supporting Calvinism only if you assumed, going into it, that the passage supported Calvinism. In other words, classic circular reasoning: you could prove something was true only by first assuming it's true.

Only after discovering that all the Scriptural "support" for Calvinism evaporated under scrutiny did this book take on its current structure.

So, with the huge quantities of Scriptures above pointing to the inescapable conclusion that we do, in fact, have free will in the area of whether or not we serve God, we should then use it to our full advantage, as God commands us in Deuteronomy 30:19:

I call heaven and earth as witnesses today against you, that **I have set before you life and death, blessing and cursing;** *therefore choose life*, that both you and your descendants may live. . .

Appendix A:

Bible-Study Strategies

As you have already seen, if you have read any of the books in the THOUGHTS ON series, I place a very high value on the Bible and its authority as the normative standard for Christian doctrine, teaching, and behavior. As I study the Bible, I employ quite a few different study techniques that I have found, over the decades, to be quite useful and reliable. Great wisdom can be gained from reading the Bible, and using these practices will significantly reduce misinterpretations caused by lack of awareness of Jewish culture, language, laws, and so forth.

To that end, please allow me to describe these Bible-study techniques I use when researching pretty much anything related to spiritual subjects. After that, we'll get into the main subject matter of this book. I describe these techniques below for two reasons: First, so you can see how and why I arrived at the conclusions I did, and second, so you can incorporate these practices into your own Bible study, should you choose to do so.

Multiple Translations

As you may have seen in other books in the THOUGHTS ON series, I often include relevant verses from several different translations of the Bible. This seems prudent, and more reliable, because I have seen Bible teachings that were based entirely on a single translation of the Bible, and if the "wrong" translation was used, it failed to support, and sometimes even contradicted, the whole point of the teaching.

In those cases where a passage of Scripture is quoted out of several translations, you may be tempted to read just the first one, and skip the rest. But, I encourage you to thoughtfully read each translation's rendering of the verses, and note the different shades of meaning. You will be pretty amazed at what the Bible says. . .

Multiple References

Also, you'll notice that when I make a doctrinal statement, I often support my statement with a series of Scriptures. Sometimes I use the same Scripture out of different translations as described above, but also I will often give a list of *different* Scriptures, all of which support the point I am trying to make. This also seems prudent, because it lessens the likelihood of misinterpretation. For example, if I make a statement and back it up with only a single Scripture, that's good, but someone could respond with "That's not what that says! You misinterpreted that verse!" And that is certainly possible.

But an even better approach is this: if I offer a list of *ten* different Scriptures, *all* of which support my point, it becomes more and more likely that I am understanding Scripture correctly, and less and less likely that I happened to misinterpret *all* of them in an identical manner. As a result, my assertions that are backed up with a larger number of Scriptures are probably more reliable than those backed up by only one or two.

Since my goal is to understand as accurately as possible what God is saying through His Word, and to communicate that as accurately as possible to the reader, please bear with me when I support a statement with a list of Scriptures that you may feel is excessively long. I, for one, am comforted when my doctrinal beliefs are supported by a plethora of Scriptures instead of just one or two.

The Preponderance of Scripture

This concept is similar, but not identical, to the one above, so I mention it separately.

The "preponderance of Scripture" is another good Bible-study tool. Basically, it looks at *how many* Scriptures can reasonably be interpreted one particular way, as opposed to how many can be interpreted in some alternate way. For example, if I have a verse that seems to say one thing, or at least it *could be interpreted* one particular way, but a dozen verses that say the opposite, and *couldn't* be interpreted in such a way as to support the other verse, it's not rocket science to conclude that the interpretation supported by the dozen

Scriptures is more likely to be reliable than the interpretation supported by only the one.

For this reason, too, when I present a statement or doctrine that I believe to be true, I usually give quite a bit of supporting Scriptural evidence that upholds that statement or doctrine. It's all part of I Peter 3:15 (NIV): "Always be prepared to give an answer to everyone who asks you to give the reason for the hope that you have." And in doing so, I'd better have my doctrinal "ducks in a row," so to speak, because I, as a teacher, will be judged with a stricter judgment (James 3:1).

The Plain, Surface Meaning

While it is often valuable to refer back to Hebrew and Greek, the original languages in which the Bible was written, for clarification and/or subtle nuances of meaning in the text, it shouldn't be necessary to resort to the original languages for major doctrines. The Bible is for the purpose of God communicating with us, so reading it in our own language should give us plenty of understanding on the essential doctrines of Christianity.

As a result, you'll notice in this book that I refer to English translations of the Bible for most of my content, with only occasional excursions into the Hebrew or Greek, where such an excursion would be useful to clarify or reveal a nuance of meaning. In other words, I go in most cases by the *plain, surface meaning* of the text: the meaning that any unbiased, literate speaker of English would derive from the text.

If I am *required* to go to the original languages for some concept because there is insufficient evidence from plain, surface meaning at least *somewhere* in the Bible, it seems to me that that concept is either questionable or, if it is undisputable, it is relatively unimportant.

Basing major doctrines on things that can *only* be supported by a knowledge of Greek or Hebrew, sounds dangerously close to what the organized church in the Middle Ages did: keeping the Bible obscure, only in Latin, so the "common folk" were dependent upon approved religious leaders to interpret it for them. Wouldn't want them to get all confused by reading God's Word for themselves. . .

The Bible Itself Defining Its Terms

As you may have seen in other books in the Thoughts On series, one good way of finding out what the Bible means by a particular word or phrase in some verse is to see if the Bible uses, or even *defines,* that same word or phrase elsewhere. If it does, then you're more likely to have learned something the Bible actually intended, as opposed to some commentator's or theologian's opinion on what the Bible meant.

There are many verses that refer to various Scriptural concepts. Of course, that's not a problem—they are obviously Scriptural words—but the problem arises when we apply a different *meaning* to the word than that which the Biblical authors (read: "God") intended. This is very easy to do; we, as modern-day Americans, don't typically know a lot about ancient Hebrew or Greek laws, customs, feasts, traditions, vocabulary, grammar, idioms, and so forth. Usually the resulting misinterpretation is not malicious; it's just a result of insufficient study. The problem that arises here is simply: How do we know what the correct meanings of Biblical words are?

Here's an illustration: Suppose I send you a letter, and after you receive it, you redefine the words that I used in the letter. If you do that—deliberately *or* accidentally—you can "cause" me to have said any number of things I didn't intend. This is what happens all too often when people read the Bible: they use the words that appear in the Bible, but (usually unwittingly) understand different, Scripturally unsupportable meanings for those words. The result is that they can "prove" all sorts of unscriptural things. This kind of mistake can be drastically reduced by seeing how the Bible itself uses its terms.

In some cases, we need to go back to the original languages, and that's fine when necessary, but often it's possible to learn what Biblical words mean because the Bible itself defines them. In such cases, the definition is usually in a different verse, because if it were in the *same* verse, there wouldn't have been a question in the first place.

You may have seen that this approach was used to determine the Biblical meaning of the word "repent" in the section "Jonah Preaching in Nineveh," and the word "grace" in the section "Being Under Grace," both in Book 2: *Is It Possible to Stop Sinning?*, the word "healed" in the section "Wounded For Our Transgressions" in Book 5, *If It be Thy Will,* and the word "faith" in Book 8: *Going Beyond Christianity 101*. This approach will not work in every case, because not all controversial Biblical words are clearly defined elsewhere in Scripture. But when it does, it is very enlightening, and *very* reliable.

Another thing that Biblical usage of words can often tell us is what a word does *not* mean. For example, I've heard it said, in an attempt to support the idea that *all* consumption of alcohol is sinful, that the "wine" back in Bible days was not actually alcoholic, but was only a kind of grape juice. But one immediately has to ask, "Why, then, does the Bible show examples of people getting drunk on it, and warn us not to do the same?" (Genesis 9:21, Isaiah 28:1, Joel 1:5, Proverbs 23:20–21, Ephesians 5:18, etc.).

It doesn't take too much deep thought to realize that the existence of Biblical stories describing people getting drunk on wine, plus the presence of Biblical warnings *not* to get drunk on wine, clearly shows that it must be possible to do it. Therefore, the wine in the Bible was not just grape juice; it must have contained alcohol. And therefore, since Jesus provided wine for others (John 2:1–11) and drank wine himself (Matthew 11:18f ‖ Luke 7:33f) but remained sinless (Hebrews 4:15), we are forced to conclude that drinking alcohol, as long as it is not to the point of drunkenness, is not sinful.

Reading in Context

Perhaps the most neglected aspect of common-sense study of the Bible is that of reading passages in their contexts. That is, reading the passages such that they make sense in the larger environment in which they reside, so that when taken individually, the message communicated by the snippets won't contradict the message communicated by the larger passage from which they were taken.

It's astonishing how many common Christian beliefs are based on snippets of Scripture taken dramatically out of context. Some of these beliefs are admittedly minor details, but others are major doctrines. One of the largest areas in which context errors are prevalent is in studying the topic of Free Will vs. Predestination (in the TULIP sense). I was astonished when researching the topic for this book just how common it was.

When doing the research, I read and listened to many teachings that supported Calvinistic predestination, and many short fragments of Scriptures were quoted. The messages communicated by these Scripture snippets did indeed seem to support the concept of Calvinistic predestination. But when I read those fragments in their own contexts, an entirely different message became apparent.

One of the most amazing things I realized was that so many of the messages communicated by the fragments *were completely reversed* when the entire passage was read, instead of only the strategically selected snippets that supposedly supported the doctrine. And in several cases, I found tiny passages offered where, *if one simply reads the rest of the sentence,* the tenor of the perceived message is completely reversed. For massive amounts of documentation on this topic, and numerous examples showing the critical importance of context, keep reading.

Of course, the above topic is certainly not the *only* topic you could find where out-of-context Scripture fragments put forth a message that the enclosing context completely reverses. But the above topic is a textbook example, and it makes the importance of context especially obvious.

Now, Onward...

Hopefully, the above practices will be useful to you in your own study of the Bible. I encourage you to resolve in your heart to learn God's Word more deeply and listen to God's Spirit more intently than you ever have before. And be prepared for the Lord to absolutely astonish you with His goodness!

About the Author

David Arns was raised in church, but didn't start actually serving the Lord until his sophomore year of high school, in 1972. Being of a rather analytical turn of mind, he was delighted to see that there is a Biblical mandate for all Christians to be analytical: I Thessalonians 5:21 (NIV) says "Test everything. Hold on to the good." That, coupled with Paul's exhortation to teach what "the Holy Ghost teaches," not depending on man's wisdom (I Corinthians 2:11–14), and with the commendation of the Bereans, who "searched the Scriptures daily, whether those things were so" (Acts 17:11), pretty much define Dave's life, in the spiritual realm, as well as the natural realm. In the mid-1970s, Dave heard a sermon in which he was exhorted to "know *what* you believe and *why* you believe it," and he has been trying to put that into practice ever since. He has been known to abandon long-held beliefs when someone showed him that they were incompatible with Scripture; that attitude seems to be necessary if we want to continue to grow in the Lord.

Books in the "THOUGHTS ON" Series

This book is a member of the "THOUGHTS ON" series of books. The phrase "Thoughts On" is deliberately ambiguous, because it is meaningful and accurate either way you interpret it. First, it indicates where the seeds of the whole series came from: they were from a large list of informal Bible studies Dave had put together for his own interest and edification as a result of his "thoughts on" various topics that occurred to him during his quiet times with the Lord. And second, it indicates one of Dave's goals as a teacher: to persuade people to turn their "thoughts on" and consider logically what God has said in His word, and how it is very much to our benefit to take heed to what He says.

When reading *The Chronicles of Narnia* to his son Matthew when he was little, Dave came across the Professor's exasperated musing: "'Logic!' said the Professor half to himself. 'Why don't they teach logic at these schools?'" Oh, did that ring true with him! Many are the times Dave has heard a preacher or Bible teacher make a statement from the pulpit, and the crowd responds with a hearty "Amen!" Dave looks around astonished, thinking, "That statement's not true! I can think of three Scriptures off the top of my head that refute it!" And he just grieves for the complacency evident in most Christians; there is *so* much God wants to bless them with, and they miss out because they don't check the Bible to verify statements they hear.

So, Dear Reader, please turn your Thoughts On. . .

To see the names and descriptions of the other books in the "THOUGHTS ON" series, see the list below. To see the sources from which they are available, or to contact the author, see the website BibleAuthor.DaveArns.com. Books are available both in electronic form and in paperback. Note that the numbers of these books within the THOUGHTS ON series are merely the order in which they were written; they do not need to be read in sequential order. All of them are stand-alone books, so Book 1, for example, does not need to be read before Book 2, and so on.

BOOK 1: *Prophets vs. Seers: Is There a Difference?* This book looks at that question from a Biblical viewpoint. There are Bible teachers teaching that prophets and seers are fundamentally different, and they offer some supporting evidence, while others say they are merely variations in the manifestation of fundamentally the same gift and calling. Is there enough Scriptural evidence to conclude that they are the same kind of person, or the same kind of calling, or are they indeed different? An in-depth analysis of related Scriptures leads the author to a solid conclusion.

BOOK 2: *Is It Possible to Stop Sinning?* There are a couple common beliefs in Christianity today: one holds that Christians living on earth will inevitably continue to sin until they graduate to heaven, and the other holds that it is possible for Christians to be without sin even while living on earth. Of course, the major factor in this discussion is what the Bible says. For example, What is sin? What does God say about it? What does God tell us to do about it? What did Jesus provide in the atonement? This book delves into great detail on the subject and includes Biblical support from many relevant Scriptures, showing God's heart on the matter, in a way that is both theologically relevant and practical in everyday life.

BOOK 3: *Extra-Biblical Truth: A Valid Concept?* There is a theory that says that God will not do nor say anything for which there is not a Biblical precedent, nor would He reveal a doctrine that was hitherto unheard of. Is this theory reasonable? Does the Bible itself address the question of God doing or saying things that are not already exemplified in the Bible itself? Actually, the Bible does address this question very clearly, and in several different ways. This book illustrates how to analyze and discern, from a Scriptural

point of view, events and practices for which the Bible doesn't have specific examples.

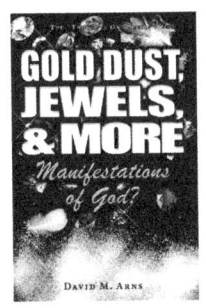

Book 4: Gold Dust, Jewels, and More: Manifestations of God? For the last couple of decades, there have been more and more reports of "unusual" occurrences taking place at meetings in which the Holy Spirit is allowed to move freely. These occurrences include gold dust appearing on people and things, jewels suddenly popping into existence, people "falling under the power" (a.k.a., being "slain in the Spirit"), glory clouds hovering or swirling, oil coming from people's hands, and more. Are these real manifestations of God, or just the result of overzealous but unethical leaders? Is there a Biblical basis for any of these? This book delves into the Scriptures and analyzes passages that are often overlooked, to give a thoughtful and Biblically sound response to these reports of unusual manifestations.

BOOK 5: *If It Be Thy Will* Many people in the Body of Christ, when they pray for physical healing, end their prayers with ". . .if it be Thy will." That brings up a very important point: *Is it* God's will to heal us? Never, sometimes, or always? How do we know? What does the Bible say? So often, Jesus said to the people He just healed, "Your faith has made you well." Where did they get that faith, and can we learn from them? This book goes into great detail about what the Bible says—and does *not* say—about physical healing, and whether praying for it is something we are forbidden, discouraged, permitted, encouraged, or commanded to do. The Bible has much to say on this subject, and we can learn a great deal by just looking at what it says, and noting the obvious implications.

BOOK 6: *Free to Choose?* One of the most hotly debated concepts in the last 500 years or so has been that of whether or not people actually have a free will to choose their eternal destiny. People debate each other with—shall we say, *religious* fervor—and people on both sides of the debate offer Scriptures to support their viewpoints. On the one hand, we have people who believe that God offers us a choice to voluntarily repent and turn to Him. On the other hand, we have people who believe that God is sovereign, and that sovereignty necessarily means that God determines the eternal destination of everyone, with no regard to our choices. These two viewpoints can't both be

correct, because they say mutually exclusive things. But fortunately, the Bible is remarkably unambiguous in its teachings: reading Scriptures in context and thinking about how various passages relate to each other make it abundantly clear which one of these viewpoints is actually the Biblical position.

BOOK 7: ***Be Filled With the Spirit*** In the last fifty years or so, there has been a tremendous resurgence of interest in the baptism of the Holy Spirit and the accompanying gifts of the Spirit. In some, the interest is entirely academic; in others, it is a passionate hunger to experience it firsthand. But there are people who claim that such things faded away around the end of the first century, and are therefore no longer available. Did they really fade away? We need to know because other people claim to have been baptized in the Holy Spirit and use the gifts of the Spirit every day, as a normal part of Christian life. As always, the Bible is the normative standard for living the Christian life, so what does the Bible say on this topic? Quite a lot, and if we follow what the Bible says, our Christian lives will become much more exciting and fruitful in the things of the Kingdom.

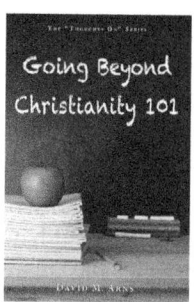

BOOK 8: ***Going Beyond Christianity 101*** What would be the content of a "Christianity 101" class? In other words, what is "elementary" Christianity? To avoid pet doctrines and the inevitable differences of opinion, we should see what the Bible itself describes as the "elementary doctrines" or the "foundational principles" of the faith. These are enumerated in Hebrews 6:1–2 as: repentance from sin, faith toward God, baptisms (plural), the laying on of hands, the resurrection of the dead, and eternal judgment. Listening to the amount of heated discussion in the body of Christ on these topics, we soon realize that as a whole, the body of Christ doesn't even have a good handle on the *elementary* doctrines yet. The Bible says much on these doctrines that is often overlooked by those doing only a casual study. This book looks at the Scriptures pertaining to these six topics in great detail, and then speculates on what it might mean to "go beyond" these foundational teachings, as Hebrews 6:1 encourages us to do.

BOOK 9: *Searching the Word: Bible Word-Search Puzzles on Steroids* What do you get when you cross a word-lover with a Word-lover? In other words, what do you get when you cross a person who enjoys word games with a student of the Bible? And then, for good measure, throw in a teacher and a writer. What do you get? This book. Much more than just a book of word-search puzzles, and much more than just a book of Bible lists, this book combines the fun of solving word problems with a fascinating way to study the Bible. Words or phrases from the Bible, and which fit into the same category, are used as the word lists for the puzzles. While you're looking for words, sooner or later you're bound to think, "What does *that* mean?" and when you check the info section for that puzzle, you'll learn something and realize you've discovered a delightful new way to study the Bible!

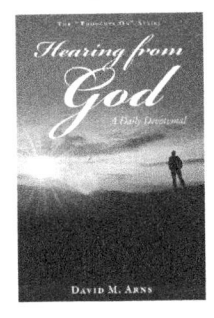

BOOK 10: *Hearing from God: A Daily Devotional* Many daily devotionals are in very small, bite-sized installments that you can read in three minutes or less. This may be very appropriate for people who are always on the go, and are doing so at God's leading. But such tiny tidbits, while they may be very good and very true, are still pretty small, and as such, have insufficient room to get very deep. As such, they are barely spiritual *hors d'oeuvres*, let alone a hearty spiritual meal of "strong meat." If you have a bit more time, this devotional is a good alternative. It goes into greater depth and breadth in the Scriptural support and elaboration. You may notice that the list of Scripture references at the bottom of each day's entry is longer than you have seen in other daily devotionals. This is deliberate: You'll be blessed if you read all the Scriptures for each day's devotional, even if two or three passages seem to say the same thing—when the Bible makes similar statements but expresses them slightly differently, the various nuances of meaning are significant and enlightening; they are not merely accidental. There is amazing depth in the Scriptures. . .

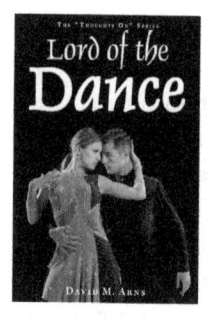

BOOK 11: ***Lord of the Dance*** The Bible talks about dancing in many places, both as an act of worship, and as a normal expression of joy. The church, after a lengthy period of thunder-fisted condemnation of all dance, as if it could not possibly occur without wallowing in sin, is recognizing their previous overreaction and seeing dance in many positive aspects: as an expression of worship, an enjoyable social activity, and a way to improve bodily fitness and mental acuity, to name but a few. Having been a dance instructor since 1999, and a student of the Word for even longer, the author could not help noticing that there are a great many correlations between a man and a woman dancing, and a husband and wife in a marriage. These correlations were vividly brought into focus while teaching engaged couples how to dance for their upcoming weddings—it's remarkable how often dance lessons included, almost unavoidably, significant premarital counseling. And those same correlations apply with even more eternal import in our relationship with Christ our Redeemer. This book explores many of those correlations and similarities in a way that presents concepts of dance almost as parables whose meanings, for those who have ears to hear, are nothing less than profound in the marital and spiritual realms.

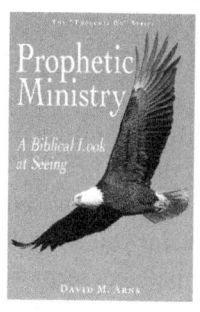

BOOK 12: ***Prophetic Ministry: A Biblical Look at Seeing*** Scripture tells us to "eagerly desire spiritual gifts, especially the gift of prophecy" (I Corinthians 14:1, NIV). Why "especially" the gift of prophecy? The Bible seems to emphasize prophecy as the highest gift, so there must be a good reason. And indeed, there is; in fact, there are many. This book examines Scriptures that tell us about how prophecy works: Who is authorized to pursue this gift, how people can perceive messages from God, what forms they can take, how to deliver them to the intended recipients, the necessary attitude and demeanor when doing so, common pitfalls, and more. If you have been hungering to hear the voice of God, rest assured that you can, because Jesus said, "My sheep hear my voice" (John 10:27). You *do* hear His voice. That is wonderful in itself. But when you have the privilege of speaking into someone else's life God's own words *for that specific person and moment and situation,* that is even more wonderful. Yes, eagerly desire spiritual gifts, *especially* the gift of prophecy. You'll be glad you did.

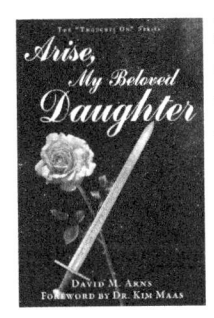

BOOK 13: *Arise, My Beloved Daughter* Recently, an increasing number of prophetic words from established, world-class prophets—of both genders—are calling for women to arise and fulfill the callings and destinies that God ordained for them before the world began. And women are rising to the call: thoughtful, godly, competent women, with compassion for the lost, deep intimacy with God, and a passion to see the mercy and blessings of Jesus poured out onto a seriously damaged world. Also, there is a dawning awareness on the part of males in church leadership that they have been missing out on much of what God wants to pour out because highly gifted women have been disregarded, ignored, passed over, and even actively suppressed in their attempts at ministry. God is opening up revelation about things that have been in the Word all along, but about which we have long had a flawed understanding. Why is God revealing it now? Because with the glory that God is intending to pour out in the Third Great Awakening, the Church no longer has the "luxury" of limping along with half of its soldiers in the brig because the other half thinks they're incapable.

BOOK 14: *Oh, Evolve! (Good Luck With That. . .)* When the question of Creation vs. Evolution comes up, many people immediately assume it is a question of science vs. religion. But is it really? There are many scientists with impressive credentials in a variety of fields—many of them clearly *not* creationists—who are becoming more vocal all the time about the problems with the whole Darwinian idea of how everything came to be. And it's true: there are more discoveries every year that militate against the ideas of the Big Bang, deep time, the Nebular Hypothesis of how the solar system was formed, uniformitarianism, life "arising" by random and undirected processes, and more. This book examines the problems with a variety of evolutionary assumptions, many of which are expressed by evolutionists themselves, and shows, in laymen's terms, why the theory of evolution is collapsing under the weight of its own presuppositions. Evidence from cosmology, geology, chemistry, genetics, biology, and more, is becoming increasingly hostile to evolutionary notions. Because of this, more and more "rescue devices" (supplementary theories intended to explain why observations don't match evolutionary predictions) are needed each year, to prop up the teetering theory. Not only will you see that evolution is no less a religion than Christianity, but you'll see that the Creation vs. Evolution debate is science vs. science. Check out the evidence, and see which model is more supported by real-world observations!

BOOK 15: *One Nation Under God . . .Again!* One of the recent discussions that has been generating more heat than light lately pertains to the spiritual underpinnings of the Founding Fathers of these United States: whether or not they intended to include Biblical/Christian principles in the founding documents, and therefore the entire fabric of our American society. There are some modern scholars who say the Founders were godless and secular, and other modern scholars who say they were solid Biblical Christians. Who is right? Rather than simply quoting recent writings concerning what the Founders "must have" meant, it is much more reliable to look at the writings of the Founders themselves, in context, compare their content to the Bible, and see how well they match. Unlike some modern scholars who "omit the scholarly practice" of including citations, expecting their readers to simply trust their conclusions, this book includes hundreds of footnotes containing citations, so you can go to the original documents themselves and verify the statements herein. When you do, you will see that our Declaration of Independence, Constitution, and Bill of Rights are not at all "godless" documents written from a secular mindset, but are filled with Biblical references, concepts, and wisdom. Armed with that knowledge and understanding, you will be able to confidently promote, as did the Founders, the strength of character and solid societal foundations that originally formed the basis of this country. If the Body of Christ rises to the challenge, we will indeed be one nation under God . . .*again!*

Music in the "Worship On" Series

Dave's current music project is the "Worship On" series of albums. The phrase "Worship On" not only parallels Dave's "Thoughts On" series of books, but it also points out a very significant truth about the destiny of those who choose to make Jesus Christ the Lord of their lives: Though many other aspects of normal Christian life on earth—evangelism, healing the sick, casting out demons, raising the dead, suffering persecution, and so forth—will go away once we're in heaven, worship will not. Throughout all eternity, we will worship Jesus, the King of Kings. Far from being an arduous chore we will be required to do, we will spontaneously burst out into joyous praise and worship every time we see another aspect of God's goodness and love and holiness. As we discover more of God's marvelousness moment by moment, it will be more clear than ever that He is the only One worthy of our worship—no one and nothing else even comes close. Indeed, the word "worship" comes from the Old English phrase "worth-ship," and He is certainly worth all of our worship.

So, Dear Listener, when listening to this music, feel free to Worship On. And on and on. . . . :)

The music below is available both in downloadable electronic form and as CDs, and is available from the sources mentioned on the website Music.DaveArns.com.

CD 1: *Songs of the Tribe of Judah* In the early 1980s, Dave was a member of the worship team at the church he attended. In addition to that, a subset of that worship team formed a band that sang on other occasions and in other, more public venues. This smaller group called themselves the Tribe of Judah, after the name referring to Jesus in Revelation 5:5. Dave and one other member of the group wrote most of the songs they performed, and in this album are the songs that Dave wrote, along with improved orchestration. The reason for the name of this album is twofold: first, these songs were written when Dave was writing songs to be performed by the band called the Tribe of Judah, and second, because Judah means "praise and worship," which is what Dave prays this music will inspire in you.

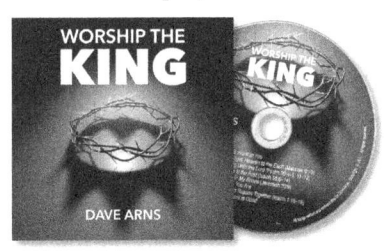

CD 2: *Worship the King* The second album in the "Worship On" series, *Worship the King* is intended to draw the listener from a passive "listening" mode and into a more active "worshiping" mode. As you listen to the words of these songs, you'll notice than many of them are taken straight from the Bible, and as such, are excellent tools with which to learn Scripture. Even the ones that are not taken directly from the Bible are laden with Scriptural concepts, whether their context is worshiping Him in the beauty of holiness, the story of an Appalachian moonshiner who encounters the living God, a description of every believer's job on earth, a joyous proclamation of God's glorious traits, or a simple acknowledgement of the most basic understanding of every believer: that the Lord is good.

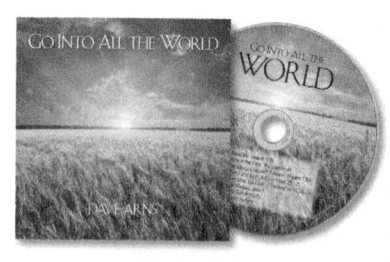

CD 3: *Go Into All the World* This album, the third in the "Worship On" series, acknowledges the importance of Jesus' exhortation to "Go into all the world" and preach the gospel to everyone (Mark 16:15–20). The wheat field image recalls Jesus' commands to pray that laborers will go into the fields, because the harvest is plentiful (Matthew 9:37–38). Because of that emphasis, this album contains songs echoing Isaiah's cry "Send me!", marveling at God's mercy, showing how a Caribbean man sees Jesus gloriously working among his people, expressing the hunger that God's children feel to get into His presence, recalling a portion of one of David's psalms that he gave to Asaph and the other worshippers to sing, and more. My hope is that your heart will be touched with compassion for those who don't yet know the inexpressible joy of being a child of God.

CD 4: *I Have Not Forgotten You* This album, the fourth in the "Worship On" series, endeavors to respond to those in the body of Christ who have heard God's promises, both those in the Bible and those He has spoken to them personally, who remember His prophetic words, and who feel like it is taking for*ever* for those promises to come to pass. To such people, as well as to those who have experienced great hardship in their lives, God's unchanging faithfulness comes through in *I Have Not Forgotten You*, and His love in a conversation between the heavenly Father and one of His beloved children in *That Will I Seek After*. In *Hear and Do*, a believer discovers the simple but profound secret to living in God's presence, and in *Truckin'*, a truck driver has a divine appointment with a couple of the Lord's servants. Other songs include the word of the Lord coming to a cattle driver crossing Death Valley, a believer echoing Moses' heartfelt cry to see God's glory, and an expression of intense spiritual hunger when such a large outpouring of that glory—a "glory storm"—is seen building on the horizon.

CD 5: *Dry Bones to Living Stones*

This album, the fifth in the "Worship On" series, describes several different aspects of God's process of building His people—His "living stones—into a holy and glorious temple He can inhabit. One song tells of the Father's desire to give us the Kingdom; another tells about a surfer hearing the voice of God promising a wave of the Holy Spirit; another portrays the hunger to drink deeply of God's Spirit—a hunger we should all have. Yet another describes the realization that the long-awaited revival of societal transformation into wholeness and health has finally arrived; another tells the story of a bored and lukewarm Christian discovering that there is more! Another relates the little-known key to Jesus' success in ministry, and another tells in a new way the story of Shadrach, Meshach, and Abednego being thrown into the fiery furnace. And finally, a song that expresses the passion of a believer who doesn't want to miss out on what God is doing in these days.

*Books: **BibleAuthor.DaveArns.com***
*Music: **Music.DaveArns.com***

Free to Choose?

Made in the USA
Middletown, DE
07 November 2023